S0-AXV-208

CHRYSLER | CARAVAN/VOYAGER/TOWN & COUNTRY
2003-06 REPAIR MANUAL

Covers U.S. and Canadian models of
**Dodge Caravan, Chrysler Voyager
and Town & Country**

*Does not include information specific to all-wheel drive
or diesel engine models*

by **John Wegmann**

CHILTON *Automotive Books*

PUBLISHED BY **HAYNES NORTH AMERICA. Inc.**

Manufactured in USA
©2006 Haynes North America, Inc.
ISBN-13: 978-1-56392-621-1
ISBN-10: 1-56392-621-0
Library of Congress Control Number 2006927868

Haynes Publishing Group
Sparkford Nr Yeovil
Somerset BA22 7JJ England

Haynes North America, Inc
861 Lawrence Drive
Newbury Park
California 91320 USA

ABCDE
FGHIJ
KLMNO
PQR

4L1

Chilton is a registered trademark of W.G. Nichols, Inc., and has been licensed to Haynes North America, Inc.

Contents

Mechanic and photographer with a 2005 Dodge Grand Caravan

ACKNOWLEDGEMENTS

Technical writers who contributed to this project include Mike Stubblefield, Rob Maddox and Joe L. Hamilton. Wiring diagrams provided exclusively for the publisher by Valley Forge Technical Information Services.

All rights reserved. No part of this book may be reproduced or transmitted in any form or by any means, electronic or mechanical, including photocopying, recording or by any information storage or retrieval system, without permission in writing from the copyright holder.

While every attempt is made to ensure that the information in this manual is correct, no liability can be accepted by the authors or publishers for loss, damage or injury caused by any errors in, or omissions from, the information given.

About this manual

ITS PURPOSE

The purpose of this manual is to help you get the best value from your vehicle. It can do so in several ways. It can help you decide what work must be done, even if you choose to have it done by a dealer service department or a repair shop; it provides information and procedures for routine maintenance and servicing; and it offers diagnostic and repair procedures to follow when trouble occurs.

We hope you use the manual to tackle the work yourself. For many simpler jobs, doing it yourself may be quicker than arranging an appointment to get the vehicle into a shop and making the trips to leave it and pick it up. More importantly, a lot of money can be saved by avoiding the expense the shop must pass on to you to cover its labor and overhead costs. An added benefit is the sense of satisfaction and accomplishment that you feel after doing the job yourself.

USING THE MANUAL

The manual is divided into Chapters. Each Chapter is divided into numbered Sections. Each Section consists of consecutively numbered paragraphs.

At the beginning of each numbered Section you will be referred to any illustrations which apply to the procedures in that Section. The reference numbers used in illustration captions pinpoint the pertinent Section and the Step within that Section. That is, illustration 3.2 means the illustration refers to Section 3 and Step (or paragraph) 2 within that Section.

Procedures, once described in the text, are not normally repeated. When it's necessary to refer to another Chapter, the reference will be given as Chapter and Section number. Cross references given without use of the word "Chapter" apply to Sections and/or paragraphs in the same Chapter. For example, "see Section 8" means in the same Chapter.

References to the left or right side of the vehicle assume you are sitting in the driver's seat, facing forward.

Even though we have prepared this manual with extreme care, neither the publisher nor the author can accept responsibility for any errors in, or omissions from, the information given.

➡ **NOTE**

A *Note* provides information necessary to properly complete a procedure or information which will make the procedure easier to understand.

❊❊ **CAUTION**

A *Caution* provides a special procedure or special steps which must be taken while completing the procedure where the Caution is found. Not heeding a Caution can result in damage to the assembly being worked on.

❊❊ **WARNING**

A *Warning* provides a special procedure or special steps which must be taken while completing the procedure where the Warning is found. Not heeding a Warning can result in personal injury.

Introduction to the Dodge Caravan, Chrysler Voyager and Town & Country

The Dodge Caravan, Chrysler Voyager and Town & Country are front engine, front wheel drive mini-van models. These models are available in either standard length and long length bodies, are equipped with a standard rear liftgate door and sliding side doors on both sides of the vehicle. They feature transversely mounted four-cylinder or V6 engines, equipped with electronic multi-port fuel injection. The engine drives the front wheels through a four-speed automatic transaxle via independent driveaxles.

The fully-independent front suspension consists of coil spring/strut units, lower control arms with stabilizer bar links connecting the stabilizer bar. The rear suspension uses a beam axle and spindle/hub units supported by leaf springs. A lateral bar called a panhard rod locates the beam axle, and is connected between the beam axle unit and the vehicle body. A rear stabilizer bar is installed on some models.

The power-assisted rack-and-pinion steering unit is mounted behind the engine.

Front brakes are discs; the rear brakes are either drum or optional disc-type. Power brake assist is standard with an Antilock Brake System (ABS) optional.

Vehicle Identification Numbers

Modifications are a continuing and unpublicized process in vehicle manufacturing. Since spare parts manuals and lists are compiled on a numerical basis, the individual vehicle numbers are essential to correctly identify the component required.

VEHICLE IDENTIFICATION NUMBER (VIN)

This very important identification number is stamped on a plate attached to the left side of the dashboard just inside the windshield on the driver's side of the vehicle (see illustration). The VIN also appears on the Vehicle Certificate of Title and Registration. It contains information such as where and when the vehicle was manufactured, the model year and the body style.

VIN YEAR AND ENGINE CODES

Two particularly important pieces of information located in the VIN are the model year and engine codes. Counting from the left, the engine code is the eighth digit and the model year code is the 10th digit.

On the models covered by this manual the engine codes are:

B	2.4L 4-cylinder
R	3.3L V6
L	3.8L V6

On the models covered by this manual the model year codes are:

3	2003
4	2004
5	2005
6	2006

EQUIPMENT IDENTIFICATION PLATE

This plate is located on the inside of the hood. It contains valuable information concerning the production of the vehicle as well as information on all production or special equipment.

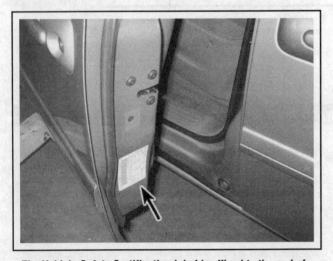

The Vehicle Safety Certification label is affixed to the end of the driver's door

SAFETY CERTIFICATION LABEL

The Safety Certification label is affixed to the left front door (see illustration). The plate contains the name of the manufacturer, the month and year of production, the Gross Vehicle Weight Rating (GVWR) and the safety certification statement. This label also contains the paint code. It is especially useful for matching the color and type of paint during repair work.

ENGINE IDENTIFICATION NUMBER

The engine identification number on all engines is stamped into the rear of the engine block, below the cylinder head.

TRANSAXLE IDENTIFICATION NUMBER

The ID number on the automatic transaxle is a bar code label that is affixed to the top of the transaxle (see illustration).

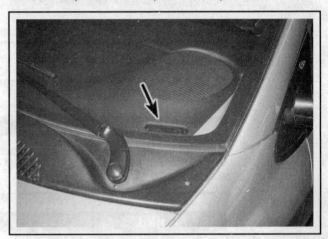

The VIN plate is visible from outside of the vehicle, through the driver's side of the windshield

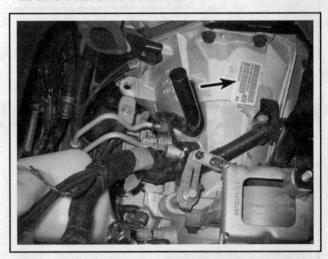

Typical automatic transaxle identification number location

Recall information

Vehicle recalls are carried out by the manufacturer in the rare event of a possible safety-related defect. The vehicle's registered owner is contacted at the address on file at the Department of Motor Vehicles and given the details of the recall. Remedial work is carried out free of charge at a dealer service department.

If you are the new owner of a used vehicle which was subject to a recall and you want to be sure that the work has been carried out, it's best to contact a dealer service department and ask about your individual vehicle - you'll need to furnish them your Vehicle Identification Number (VIN).

The table below is based on information provided by the National Highway Traffic Safety Administration (NHTSA), the body which oversees vehicle recalls in the United States. The recall database is updated constantly. For the latest information on vehicle recalls, check the NHTSA website at www.nhtsa.gov, or call the NHTSA hotline at 1-888-327-4236.

Recall date	Recall campaign number	Model(s) affected	Concern
3/7/2003	03V094000	2003 Grand Caravan	Certain running boards that contain a courtesy light or lights may overheat when the wire harness is exposed to excessive moisture and road salt
9/23/2003	03E045000	2003 Town & Country 2004 Caravan/Town & Country	Some aftermarket fuel filters manufactured between September 17, 2002, and January 20, 2003. The filter may experience malfunction of the quick connector, either blocking fuel flow or causing a fuel leak
10/2/2003	03E053000	2003 Grand Caravan/Town & Country/Voyager 2004 Caravan/Town & Country	Some aftermarket fuel filters can cause the fuel lines to leak
8/3/2004	04V386000	2003 Grand Caravan/Town & Country 2004 Caravan/Town & Country/Voyager	Certain models equipped with 3.3 or 3.8L engines, the upper power steering cooler hose may split and cause a fluid leak
10/7/2005	04V047000	2005 Caravan/Grand Caravan/Town & Country	Certain models equipped without the available Stow-N-Go seating option, the right front seat belt retractor assembly may have been improperly assembled
4/5/2005	05V134000	2003 Caravan/Town & Country	On certain models, the power liftgate latch may not engage the striker, allowing the liftgate to open while driving

Buying parts

Replacement parts are available from many sources, which generally fall into one of two categories - authorized dealer parts departments and independent retail auto parts stores. Our advice concerning these parts is as follows:

Retail auto parts stores: Good auto parts stores will stock frequently needed components which wear out relatively fast, such as clutch components, exhaust systems, brake parts, tune-up parts, etc. These stores often supply new or reconditioned parts on an exchange basis, which can save a considerable amount of money. Discount auto parts stores are often very good places to buy materials and parts needed for general vehicle maintenance such as oil, grease, filters, spark plugs, belts, touch-up paint, bulbs, etc. They also usually sell tools and general accessories, have convenient hours, charge lower prices and can often be found not far from home.

Authorized dealer parts department: This is the best source for parts which are unique to the vehicle and not generally available elsewhere (such as major engine parts, transmission parts, trim pieces, etc.).

Warranty information: If the vehicle is still covered under warranty, be sure that any replacement parts purchased - regardless of the source - do not invalidate the warranty!

To be sure of obtaining the correct parts, have engine and chassis numbers available and, if possible, take the old parts along for positive identification.

Maintenance techniques, tools and working facilities

MAINTENANCE TECHNIQUES

There are a number of techniques involved in maintenance and repair that will be referred to throughout this manual. Application of these techniques will enable the home mechanic to be more efficient, better organized and capable of performing the various tasks properly, which will ensure that the repair job is thorough and complete.

Fasteners

Fasteners are nuts, bolts, studs and screws used to hold two or more parts together. There are a few things to keep in mind when working with fasteners. Almost all of them use a locking device of some type, either a lockwasher, locknut, locking tab or thread adhesive. All threaded fasteners should be clean and straight, with undamaged threads and undamaged corners on the hex head where the wrench fits. Develop the habit of replacing all damaged nuts and bolts with new ones. Special locknuts with nylon or fiber inserts can only be used once. If they are removed, they lose their locking ability and must be replaced with new ones.

Rusted nuts and bolts should be treated with a penetrating fluid to ease removal and prevent breakage. Some mechanics use turpentine in a spout-type oil can, which works quite well. After applying the rust penetrant, let it work for a few minutes before trying to loosen the nut or bolt. Badly rusted fasteners may have to be chiseled or sawed off or removed with a special nut breaker, available at tool stores.

If a bolt or stud breaks off in an assembly, it can be drilled and removed with a special tool commonly available for this purpose. Most automotive machine shops can perform this task, as well as other repair procedures, such as the repair of threaded holes that have been stripped out.

Flat washers and lockwashers, when removed from an assembly, should always be replaced exactly as removed. Replace any damaged washers with new ones. Never use a lockwasher on any soft metal surface (such as aluminum), thin sheet metal or plastic.

Fastener sizes

For a number of reasons, automobile manufacturers are making wider and wider use of metric fasteners. Therefore, it is important to be able to tell the difference between standard (sometimes called U.S.

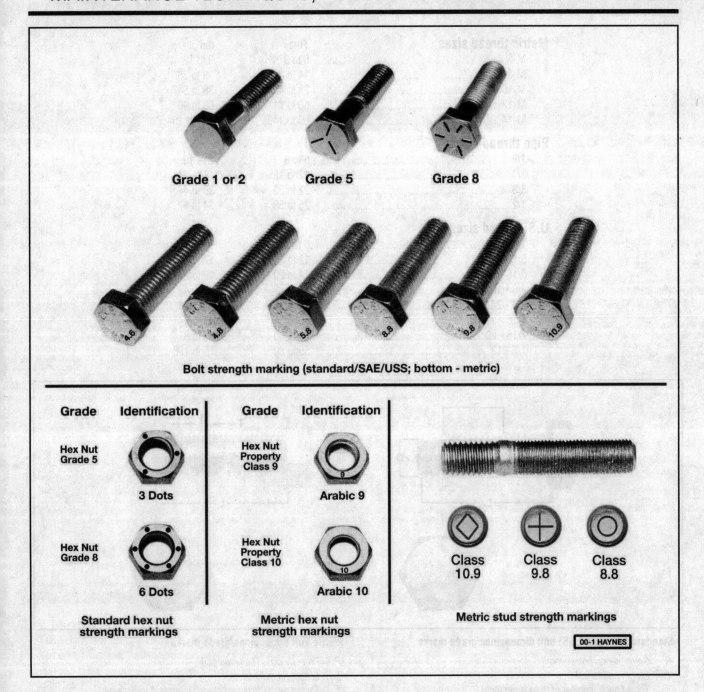

Grade 1 or 2   Grade 5   Grade 8

Bolt strength marking (standard/SAE/USS; bottom - metric)

Grade	Identification	Grade	Identification
Hex Nut Grade 5	3 Dots	Hex Nut Property Class 9	Arabic 9
Hex Nut Grade 8	6 Dots	Hex Nut Property Class 10	Arabic 10

Standard hex nut strength markings

Metric hex nut strength markings

Class 10.9   Class 9.8   Class 8.8

Metric stud strength markings

00-1 HAYNES

or SAE) and metric hardware, since they cannot be interchanged.

All bolts, whether standard or metric, are sized according to diameter, thread pitch and length. For example, a standard 1/2 - 13 x 1 bolt is 1/2 inch in diameter, has 13 threads per inch and is 1 inch long. An M12 - 1.75 x 25 metric bolt is 12 mm in diameter, has a thread pitch of 1.75 mm (the distance between threads) and is 25 mm long. The two bolts are nearly identical, and easily confused, but they are not interchangeable.

In addition to the differences in diameter, thread pitch and length, metric and standard bolts can also be distinguished by examining the bolt heads. To begin with, the distance across the flats on a standard bolt head is measured in inches, while the same dimension on a metric bolt is sized in millimeters (the same is true for nuts). As a result, a standard wrench should not be used on a metric bolt and a metric wrench should not be used on a standard bolt. Also, most standard bolts have

slashes radiating out from the center of the head to denote the grade or strength of the bolt, which is an indication of the amount of torque that can be applied to it. The greater the number of slashes, the greater the strength of the bolt. Grades 0 through 5 are commonly used on automobiles. Metric bolts have a property class (grade) number, rather than a slash, molded into their heads to indicate bolt strength. In this case, the higher the number, the stronger the bolt. Property class numbers 8.8, 9.8 and 10.9 are commonly used on automobiles.

Strength markings can also be used to distinguish standard hex nuts from metric hex nuts. Many standard nuts have dots stamped into one side, while metric nuts are marked with a number. The greater the number of dots, or the higher the number, the greater the strength of the nut.

Metric studs are also marked on their ends according to property class (grade). Larger studs are numbered (the same as metric bolts), while smaller studs carry a geometric code to denote grade.

Metric thread sizes	Ft-lbs	Nm
M-6	6 to 9	9 to 12
M-8	14 to 21	19 to 28
M-10	28 to 40	38 to 54
M-12	50 to 71	68 to 96
M-14	80 to 140	109 to 154

Pipe thread sizes		
1/8	5 to 8	7 to 10
1/4	12 to 18	17 to 24
3/8	22 to 33	30 to 44
1/2	25 to 35	34 to 47

U.S. thread sizes		
1/4 - 20	6 to 9	9 to 12
5/16 - 18	12 to 18	17 to 24
5/16 - 24	14 to 20	19 to 27
3/8 - 16	22 to 32	30 to 43
3/8 - 24	27 to 38	37 to 51
7/16 - 14	40 to 55	55 to 74
7/16 - 20	40 to 60	55 to 81
1/2 - 13	55 to 80	75 to 108

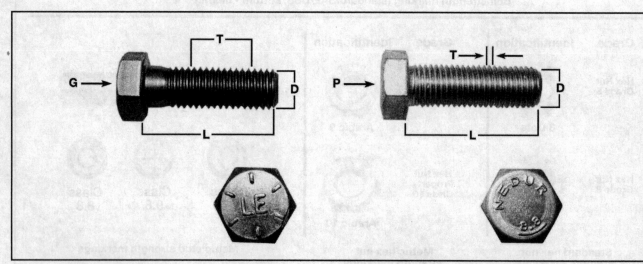

Standard (SAE and USS) bolt dimensions/grade marks

G Grade marks (bolt strength)
L Length (in inches)
T Thread pitch (number of threads per inch)
D Nominal diameter (in inches)

Metric bolt dimensions/grade marks

P Property class (bolt strength)
L Length (in millimeters)
T Thread pitch (distance between threads in millimeters)
D Diameter

It should be noted that many fasteners, especially Grades 0 through 2, have no distinguishing marks on them. When such is the case, the only way to determine whether it is standard or metric is to measure the thread pitch or compare it to a known fastener of the same size.

Standard fasteners are often referred to as SAE, as opposed to metric. However, it should be noted that SAE technically refers to a non-metric fine thread fastener only. Coarse thread non-metric fasteners are referred to as USS sizes.

Since fasteners of the same size (both standard and metric) may have different strength ratings, be sure to reinstall any bolts, studs or nuts removed from your vehicle in their original locations. Also, when replacing a fastener with a new one, make sure that the new one has a strength rating equal to or greater than the original.

Tightening sequences and procedures

Most threaded fasteners should be tightened to a specific torque value (torque is the twisting force applied to a threaded component such as a nut or bolt). Overtightening the fastener can weaken it and cause it to break, while undertightening can cause it to eventually come loose. Bolts, screws and studs, depending on the material they are made of and their thread diameters, have specific torque values, many of which are noted in the Specifications at the end of each Chapter. Be sure to follow the torque recommendations closely. For fasteners not assigned a specific torque, a general torque value chart is presented here as a guide. These torque values are for dry (unlubricated) fasteners threaded into steel or cast iron (not aluminum). As was previously mentioned, the size and grade of a fastener determine the amount of torque that can

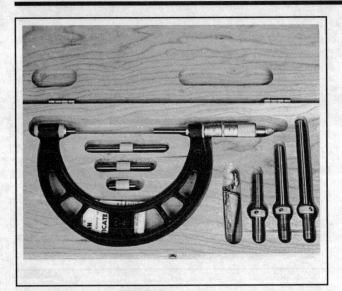

Micrometer set

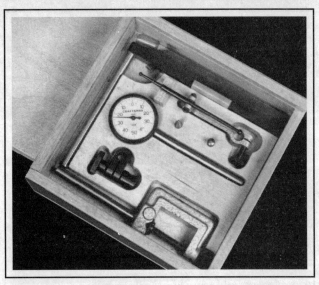

Dial indicator set

safely be applied to it. The figures listed here are approximate for Grade 2 and Grade 3 fasteners. Higher grades can tolerate higher torque values.

Fasteners laid out in a pattern, such as cylinder head bolts, oil pan bolts, differential cover bolts, etc., must be loosened or tightened in sequence to avoid warping the component. This sequence will normally be shown in the appropriate Chapter. If a specific pattern is not given, the following procedures can be used to prevent warping.

Initially, the bolts or nuts should be assembled finger-tight only. Next, they should be tightened one full turn each, in a criss-cross or diagonal pattern. After each one has been tightened one full turn, return to the first one and tighten them all one-half turn, following the same pattern. Finally, tighten each of them one-quarter turn at a time until each fastener has been tightened to the proper torque. To loosen and remove the fasteners, the procedure would be reversed.

Component disassembly

Component disassembly should be done with care and purpose to help ensure that the parts go back together properly. Always keep track of the sequence in which parts are removed. Make note of special characteristics or marks on parts that can be installed more than one way, such as a grooved thrust washer on a shaft. It is a good idea to lay the disassembled parts out on a clean surface in the order that they were removed. It may also be helpful to make sketches or take instant photos of components before removal.

When removing fasteners from a component, keep track of their locations. Sometimes threading a bolt back in a part, or putting the washers and nut back on a stud, can prevent mix-ups later. If nuts and bolts cannot be returned to their original locations, they should be kept in a compartmented box or a series of small boxes. A cupcake or muffin tin is ideal for this purpose, since each cavity can hold the bolts and nuts from a particular area (i.e. oil pan bolts, valve cover bolts, engine mount bolts, etc.). A pan of this type is especially helpful when working on assemblies with very small parts, such as the carburetor, alternator, valve train or interior dash and trim pieces. The cavities can be marked with paint or tape to identify the contents.

Whenever wiring looms, harnesses or connectors are separated, it is a good idea to identify the two halves with numbered pieces of masking tape so they can be easily reconnected.

Gasket sealing surfaces

Throughout any vehicle, gaskets are used to seal the mating surfaces between two parts and keep lubricants, fluids, vacuum or pressure contained in an assembly.

Many times these gaskets are coated with a liquid or paste-type gasket sealing compound before assembly. Age, heat and pressure can sometimes cause the two parts to stick together so tightly that they are very difficult to separate. Often, the assembly can be loosened by striking it with a soft-face hammer near the mating surfaces. A regular hammer can be used if a block of wood is placed between the hammer and the part. Do not hammer on cast parts or parts that could be easily damaged. With any particularly stubborn part, always recheck to make sure that every fastener has been removed.

Avoid using a screwdriver or bar to pry apart an assembly, as they can easily mar the gasket sealing surfaces of the parts, which must remain smooth. If prying is absolutely necessary, use an old broom handle, but keep in mind that extra clean up will be necessary if the wood splinters.

After the parts are separated, the old gasket must be carefully scraped off and the gasket surfaces cleaned. Stubborn gasket material can be soaked with rust penetrant or treated with a special chemical to soften it so it can be easily scraped off.

✸✸ CAUTION:

Never use gasket removal solutions or caustic chemicals on plastic or other composite components.

A scraper can be fashioned from a piece of copper tubing by flattening and sharpening one end. Copper is recommended because it is usually softer than the surfaces to be scraped, which reduces the chance of gouging the part. Some gaskets can be removed with a wire brush, but regardless of the method used, the mating surfaces must be left clean and smooth. If for some reason the gasket surface is gouged, then a gasket sealer thick enough to fill scratches will have to be used during reassembly of the components. For most applications, a non-drying (or semi-drying) gasket sealer should be used.

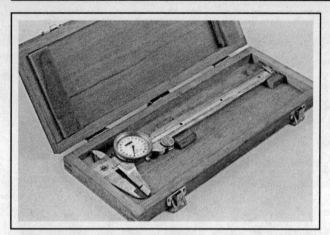

Dial caliper

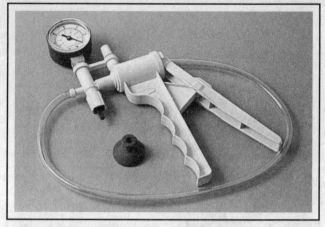

Hand-operated vacuum pump

Timing light

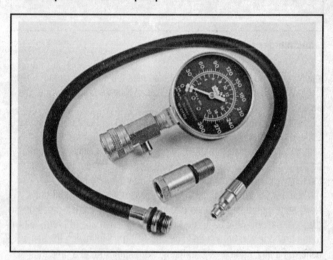

Compression gauge with spark plug hole adapter

Hose removal tips

✸✸ WARNING:

If the vehicle is equipped with air conditioning, do not disconnect any of the A/C hoses without first having the system depressurized by a dealer service department or a service station.

Hose removal precautions closely parallel gasket removal precautions. Avoid scratching or gouging the surface that the hose mates against or the connection may leak. This is especially true for radiator hoses. Because of various chemical reactions, the rubber in hoses can bond itself to the metal spigot that the hose fits over. To remove a hose, first loosen the hose clamps that secure it to the spigot. Then, with slip-joint pliers, grab the hose at the clamp and rotate it around the spigot. Work it back and forth until it is completely free, then pull it off. Silicone or other lubricants will ease removal if they can be applied between the hose and the outside of the spigot. Apply the same lubricant to the inside of the hose and the outside of the spigot to simplify installation.

As a last resort (and if the hose is to be replaced with a new one anyway), the rubber can be slit with a knife and the hose peeled from the spigot. If this must be done, be careful that the metal connection is not damaged.

If a hose clamp is broken or damaged, do not reuse it. Wire-type clamps usually weaken with age, so it is a good idea to replace them with screw-type clamps whenever a hose is removed.

TOOLS

A selection of good tools is a basic requirement for anyone who plans to maintain and repair his or her own vehicle. For the owner who has few tools, the initial investment might seem high, but when compared to the spiraling costs of professional auto maintenance and repair, it is a wise one.

To help the owner decide which tools are needed to perform the tasks detailed in this manual, the following tool lists are offered: *Maintenance and minor repair, Repair/overhaul and Special.*

The newcomer to practical mechanics should start off with the *maintenance and minor repair* tool kit, which is adequate for the simpler jobs performed on a vehicle. Then, as confidence and experience grow, the owner can tackle more difficult tasks, buying additional tools as they are needed. Eventually the basic kit will be expanded into the *repair and overhaul* tool set. Over a period of time, the experienced do-it-yourselfer will assemble a tool set complete enough for most repair and overhaul procedures and will add tools from the special category when it is felt that the expense is justified by the frequency of use.

Damper/steering wheel puller

General purpose puller

Hydraulic lifter removal tool

Valve spring compressor

Valve spring compressor

Ridge reamer

Maintenance and minor repair tool kit

The tools in this list should be considered the minimum required for performance of routine maintenance, servicing and minor repair work. We recommend the purchase of combination wrenches (box-end and open-end combined in one wrench). While more expensive than open end wrenches, they offer the advantages of both types of wrench.

Combination wrench set (1/4-inch to 1 inch or 6 mm to 19 mm)
Adjustable wrench, 8 inch
Spark plug wrench with rubber insert
Spark plug gap adjusting tool
Feeler gauge set
Brake bleeder wrench
Standard screwdriver (5/16-inch x 6 inch)
Phillips screwdriver (No. 2 x 6 inch)
Combination pliers - 6 inch
Hacksaw and assortment of blades
Tire pressure gauge
Grease gun
Oil can
Fine emery cloth
Wire brush
Battery post and cable cleaning tool
Oil filter wrench
Funnel (medium size)
Safety goggles
Jackstands (2)
Drain pan

➡**Note: If basic tune-ups are going to be part of routine maintenance, it will be necessary to purchase a good quality stroboscopic timing light and combination tachometer/dwell meter. Although they are included in the list of special tools, it is mentioned here because they are absolutely necessary for tuning most vehicles properly.**

Repair and overhaul tool set

These tools are essential for anyone who plans to perform major repairs and are in addition to those in the maintenance and minor repair tool kit. Included is a comprehensive set of sockets which, though expensive, are invaluable because of their versatility, especially when various extensions and drives are available. We recommend the 1/2-inch drive over the 3/8-inch drive. Although the larger drive is bulky and more expensive, it has the capacity of accepting a very wide range of large sockets. Ideally, however, the mechanic should have a 3/8-inch drive set and a 1/2-inch drive set.

Socket set(s)
Reversible ratchet
Extension - 10 inch
Universal joint
Torque wrench (same size drive as sockets)
Ball peen hammer - 8 ounce
Soft-face hammer (plastic/rubber)
Standard screwdriver (1/4-inch x 6 inch)
Standard screwdriver (stubby - 5/16-inch)
Phillips screwdriver (No. 3 x 8 inch)
Phillips screwdriver (stubby - No. 2)
Pliers - vise grip

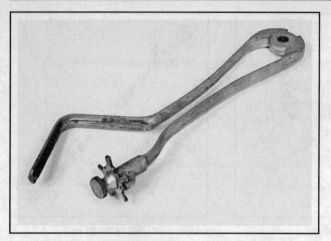

Piston ring groove cleaning tool

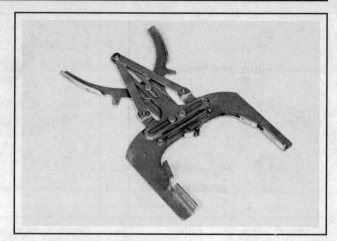

Ring removal/installation tool

Ring compressor

Cylinder hone

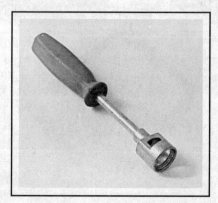

Brake hold-down spring tool

Pliers - lineman's
Pliers - needle nose
Pliers - snap-ring (internal and external)
Cold chisel - 1/2-inch
Scribe
Scraper (made from flattened copper tubing)
Centerpunch
Pin punches (1/16, 1/8, 3/16-inch)
Steel rule/straightedge - 12 inch
Allen wrench set (1/8 to 3/8-inch or 4 mm to 10 mm)
A selection of files
Wire brush (large)
Jackstands (second set)
Jack (scissor or hydraulic type)

➡**Note: Another tool which is often useful is an electric drill with a chuck capacity of 3/8-inch and a set of good quality drill bits.**

Special tools

The tools in this list include those which are not used regularly, are expensive to buy, or which need to be used in accordance with their manufacturer's instructions. Unless these tools will be used frequently, it is not very economical to purchase many of them. A consideration would be to split the cost and use between yourself and a friend or friends. In addition, most of these tools can be obtained from a tool rental shop on a temporary basis.

This list primarily contains only those tools and instruments widely available to the public, and not those special tools produced by the vehicle manufacturer for distribution to dealer service departments. Occasionally, references to the manufacturer's special tools are included in the text of this manual. Generally, an alternative method of doing the job without the special tool is offered. However, sometimes there is no alternative to their use. Where this is the case, and the tool cannot be purchased or borrowed, the work should be turned over to the dealer service department or an automotive repair shop.

Valve spring compressor
Piston ring groove cleaning tool
Piston ring compressor
Piston ring installation tool
Cylinder compression gauge
Cylinder ridge reamer
Cylinder surfacing hone
Cylinder bore gauge
Micrometers and/or dial calipers
Hydraulic lifter removal tool
Balljoint separator
Universal-type puller
Impact screwdriver
Dial indicator set
Stroboscopic timing light (inductive pick-up)
Hand operated vacuum/pressure pump
Tachometer/dwell meter
Universal electrical multimeter
Cable hoist
Brake spring removal and installation tools
Floor jack

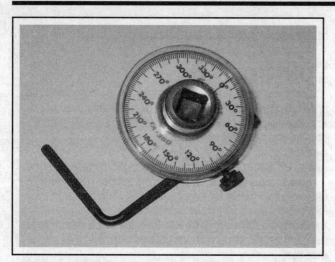

Torque angle gauge

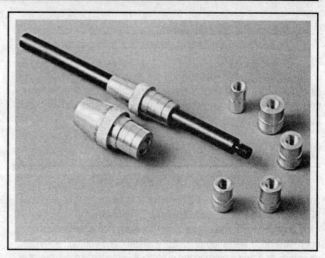

Clutch plate alignment tool

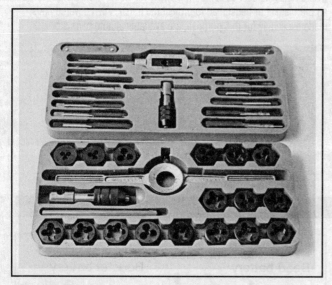

Tap and die set

Buying tools

For the do-it-yourselfer who is just starting to get involved in vehicle maintenance and repair, there are a number of options available when purchasing tools. If maintenance and minor repair is the extent of the work to be done, the purchase of individual tools is satisfactory. If, on the other hand, extensive work is planned, it would be a good idea to purchase a modest tool set from one of the large retail chain stores. A set can usually be bought at a substantial savings over the individual tool prices, and they often come with a tool box. As additional tools are needed, add-on sets, individual tools and a larger tool box can be purchased to expand the tool selection. Building a tool set gradually allows the cost of the tools to be spread over a longer period of time and gives the mechanic the freedom to choose only those tools that will actually be used.

Tool stores will often be the only source of some of the special tools that are needed, but regardless of where tools are bought, try to avoid cheap ones, especially when buying screwdrivers and sockets, because they won't last very long. The expense involved in replacing cheap tools will eventually be greater than the initial cost of quality tools.

Care and maintenance of tools

Good tools are expensive, so it makes sense to treat them with respect. Keep them clean and in usable condition and store them properly when not in use. Always wipe off any dirt, grease or metal chips before putting them away. Never leave tools lying around in the work area. Upon completion of a job, always check closely under the hood for tools that may have been left there so they won't get lost during a test drive.

Some tools, such as screwdrivers, pliers, wrenches and sockets, can be hung on a panel mounted on the garage or workshop wall, while others should be kept in a tool box or tray. Measuring instruments, gauges, meters, etc. must be carefully stored where they cannot be damaged by weather or impact from other tools.

When tools are used with care and stored properly, they will last a very long time. Even with the best of care, though, tools will wear out if used frequently. When a tool is damaged or worn out, replace it. Subsequent jobs will be safer and more enjoyable if you do.

HOW TO REPAIR DAMAGED THREADS

Sometimes, the internal threads of a nut or bolt hole can become stripped, usually from overtightening. Stripping threads is an all-too-common occurrence, especially when working with aluminum parts, because aluminum is so soft that it easily strips out.

Usually, external or internal threads are only partially stripped. After they've been cleaned up with a tap or die, they'll still work. Sometimes, however, threads are badly damaged. When this happens, you've got three choices:

1) *Drill and tap the hole to the next suitable oversize and install a larger diameter bolt, screw or stud.*

2) *Drill and tap the hole to accept a threaded plug, then drill and tap the plug to the original screw size. You can also buy a plug already threaded to the original size. Then you simply drill a hole to the specified size, then run the threaded plug into the hole with a bolt and jam nut. Once the plug is fully seated, remove the jam nut and bolt.*

3) *The third method uses a patented thread repair kit like Heli-Coil or Slimsert. These easy-to-use kits are designed to repair damaged threads in straight-through holes and blind holes. Both are available as kits which can handle a variety of sizes and thread*

patterns. Drill the hole, then tap it with the special included tap. Install the Heli-Coil and the hole is back to its original diameter and thread pitch.

Regardless of which method you use, be sure to proceed calmly and carefully. A little impatience or carelessness during one of these relatively simple procedures can ruin your whole day's work and cost you a bundle if you wreck an expensive part.

WORKING FACILITIES

Not to be overlooked when discussing tools is the workshop. If anything more than routine maintenance is to be carried out, some sort of suitable work area is essential.

It is understood, and appreciated, that many home mechanics do not have a good workshop or garage available, and end up removing an engine or doing major repairs outside. It is recommended, however, that the overhaul or repair be completed under the cover of a roof.

A clean, flat workbench or table of comfortable working height is an absolute necessity. The workbench should be equipped with a vise that

has a jaw opening of at least four inches.

As mentioned previously, some clean, dry storage space is also required for tools, as well as the lubricants, fluids, cleaning solvents, etc. which soon become necessary.

Sometimes waste oil and fluids, drained from the engine or cooling system during normal maintenance or repairs, present a disposal problem. To avoid pouring them on the ground or into a sewage system, pour the used fluids into large containers, seal them with caps and take them to an authorized disposal site or recycling center. Plastic jugs, such as old antifreeze containers, are ideal for this purpose.

Always keep a supply of old newspapers and clean rags available. Old towels are excellent for mopping up spills. Many mechanics use rolls of paper towels for most work because they are readily available and disposable. To help keep the area under the vehicle clean, a large cardboard box can be cut open and flattened to protect the garage or shop floor.

Whenever working over a painted surface, such as when leaning over a fender to service something under the hood, always cover it with an old blanket or bedspread to protect the finish. Vinyl covered pads, made especially for this purpose, are available at auto parts stores.

Booster battery (jump) starting

Observe these precautions when using a booster battery to start a vehicle:

a) *Before connecting the booster battery, make sure the ignition switch is in the Off position.*

b) *Turn off the lights, heater and other electrical loads.*

c) *Your eyes should be shielded. Safety goggles are a good idea.*

d) *Make sure the booster battery is the same voltage as the dead one in the vehicle.*

e) *The two vehicles MUST NOT TOUCH each other!*

f) *Make sure the transaxle is in Neutral (manual) or Park (automatic).*

g) *If the booster battery is not a maintenance-free type, remove the vent caps and lay a cloth over the vent holes.*

Connect the red jumper cable to the positive (+) terminals of each battery (see illustration).

Connect one end of the black jumper cable to the negative (-) terminal of the booster battery. The other end of this cable should be connected to a good ground on the vehicle to be started, such as a bolt or bracket on the body.

Start the engine using the booster battery, then, with the engine running at idle speed, disconnect the jumper cables in the reverse order of connection.

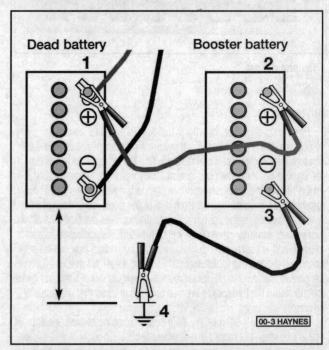

Make the booster battery cable connections in the numerical order shown (note that the negative cable of the booster battery is NOT attached to the negative terminal of the dead battery)

Jacking and towing

JACKING

The jack supplied with the vehicle should only be used for raising the vehicle for changing a tire or placing jackstands under the frame.

❊❊ WARNING:

Never crawl under the vehicle or start the engine when the jack is being used as the only means of support.

All vehicles are supplied with a scissors-type jack. When jacking the vehicle, it should be engaged with the rocker panel flange, between the two cutouts (see illustration).

The vehicle should be on level ground with the wheels blocked and the transmission in Park. Pry off the hub cap (if equipped) using the tapered end of the lug wrench. Loosen the lug nuts one-half turn and leave them in place until the wheel is raised off the ground.

Place the jack under the side of the vehicle in the indicated position. Use the supplied wrench to turn the jackscrew clockwise until the wheel is raised off the ground. Remove the lug nuts, pull off the wheel and install the spare.

With the beveled side in, install the lug nuts and tighten them until snug. Lower the vehicle by turning the jackscrew counterclockwise. Remove the jack and tighten the nuts in a diagonal pattern to the torque listed in the Chapter 1 Specifications. If a torque wrench is not available, have the torque checked by a service station as soon as possible. Install the hubcap by placing it in position and using the heel of your hand or a rubber mallet to seat it.

TOWING

As a general rule, the vehicle should be towed with the front (drive) wheels off the ground or, preferably, on a flat bed car carrier. If the front wheels can't be raised or a carrier isn't available, place them on a dolly. The ignition key must be in the ACC position, since the steering lock mechanism isn't strong enough to hold the front wheels straight while towing.

The jack fits over the rocker panel flange (there are two jacking points on each side of the vehicle)

In emergency situations the vehicle can be towed from the front with all four wheels on the ground, provided that speeds don't exceed 40 mph and the distance is not over 100 miles. Before towing, check the transaxle fluid level (see Chapter 1). If the level is below the HOT mark on the dipstick, add fluid.

Towing equipment specifically designed for this purpose should be used and should be attached to the main structural members of the vehicle, not the bumper or brackets.

Safety is a major consideration when towing and all applicable state and local laws must be obeyed. A safety chain system must be used for all towing.

While towing, the parking brake must be released and the transmission must be in Neutral. The steering must be unlocked (ignition switch in the Off position). Remember that power steering and power brakes will not work with the engine off.

Automotive chemicals and lubricants

A number of automotive chemicals and lubricants are available for use during vehicle maintenance and repair. They include a wide variety of products ranging from cleaning solvents and degreasers to lubricants and protective sprays for rubber, plastic and vinyl.

CLEANERS

Carburetor cleaner and choke cleaner is a strong solvent for gum, varnish and carbon. Most carburetor cleaners leave a dry-type lubricant film which will not harden or gum up. Because of this film it is not recommended for use on electrical components.

Brake system cleaner is used to remove brake dust, grease and brake fluid from the brake system, where clean surfaces are absolutely necessary. It leaves no residue and often eliminates brake squeal caused by contaminants.

Electrical cleaner removes oxidation, corrosion and carbon deposits from electrical contacts, restoring full current flow. It can also be used to clean spark plugs, carburetor jets, voltage regulators and other parts where an oil-free surface is desired.

Demoisturants remove water and moisture from electrical components such as alternators, voltage regulators, electrical connectors and fuse blocks. They are non-conductive and non-corrosive.

Degreasers are heavy-duty solvents used to remove grease from the outside of the engine and from chassis components. They can be sprayed or brushed on and, depending on the type, are rinsed off either with water or solvent.

LUBRICANTS

Motor oil is the lubricant formulated for use in engines. It normally contains a wide variety of additives to prevent corrosion and reduce foaming and wear. Motor oil comes in various weights (viscosity ratings) from 0 to 50. The recommended weight of the oil depends on the season, temperature and the demands on the engine. Light oil is used in cold climates and under light load conditions. Heavy oil is used in hot climates and where high loads are encountered. Multi-viscosity oils are designed to have characteristics of both light and heavy oils and are available in a number of weights from 5W-20 to 20W-50.

Gear oil is designed to be used in differentials, manual transmissions and other areas where high-temperature lubrication is required.

Chassis and wheel bearing grease is a heavy grease used where increased loads and friction are encountered, such as for wheel bearings, balljoints, tie-rod ends and universal joints.

High-temperature wheel bearing grease is designed to withstand the extreme temperatures encountered by wheel bearings in disc brake equipped vehicles. It usually contains molybdenum disulfide (moly), which is a dry-type lubricant.

White grease is a heavy grease for metal-to-metal applications where water is a problem. White grease stays soft under both low and high temperatures (usually from -100 to +190-degrees F), and will not wash off or dilute in the presence of water.

Assembly lube is a special extreme pressure lubricant, usually containing moly, used to lubricate high-load parts (such as main and rod bearings and cam lobes) for initial start-up of a new engine. The assembly lube lubricates the parts without being squeezed out or washed away until the engine oiling system begins to function.

Silicone lubricants are used to protect rubber, plastic, vinyl and nylon parts.

Graphite lubricants are used where oils cannot be used due to contamination problems, such as in locks. The dry graphite will lubricate metal parts while remaining uncontaminated by dirt, water, oil or acids. It is electrically conductive and will not foul electrical contacts in locks such as the ignition switch.

Moly penetrants loosen and lubricate frozen, rusted and corroded fasteners and prevent future rusting or freezing.

Heat-sink grease is a special electrically non-conductive grease that is used for mounting electronic ignition modules where it is essential that heat is transferred away from the module.

SEALANTS

RTV sealant is one of the most widely used gasket compounds. Made from silicone, RTV is air curing, it seals, bonds, waterproofs, fills surface irregularities, remains flexible, doesn't shrink, is relatively easy to remove, and is used as a supplementary sealer with almost all low and medium temperature gaskets.

Anaerobic sealant is much like RTV in that it can be used either to seal gaskets or to form gaskets by itself. It remains flexible, is solvent resistant and fills surface imperfections. The difference between an anaerobic sealant and an RTV-type sealant is in the curing. RTV cures when exposed to air, while an anaerobic sealant cures only in the absence of air. This means that an anaerobic sealant cures only after the assembly of parts, sealing them together.

Thread and pipe sealant is used for sealing hydraulic and pneumatic fittings and vacuum lines. It is usually made from a Teflon compound, and comes in a spray, a paint-on liquid and as a wrap-around tape.

CHEMICALS

Anti-seize compound prevents seizing, galling, cold welding, rust and corrosion in fasteners. High-temperature anti-seize, usually made with copper and graphite lubricants, is used for exhaust system and exhaust manifold bolts.

Anaerobic locking compounds are used to keep fasteners from vibrating or working loose and cure only after installation, in the absence of air. Medium strength locking compound is used for small nuts, bolts and screws that may be removed later. High-strength locking compound is for large nuts, bolts and studs which aren't removed on a regular basis.

Oil additives range from viscosity index improvers to chemical treatments that claim to reduce internal engine friction. It should be noted that most oil manufacturers caution against using additives with their oils.

Gas additives perform several functions, depending on their chemical makeup. They usually contain solvents that help dissolve gum and varnish that build up on carburetor, fuel injection and intake parts. They also serve to break down carbon deposits that form on the inside surfaces of the combustion chambers. Some additives contain upper cylinder lubricants for valves and piston rings, and others contain chemicals to remove condensation from the gas tank.

MISCELLANEOUS

Brake fluid is specially formulated hydraulic fluid that can withstand the heat and pressure encountered in brake systems. Care must be taken so this fluid does not come in contact with painted surfaces or plastics. An opened container should always be resealed to prevent contamination by water or dirt.

Weatherstrip adhesive is used to bond weatherstripping around doors, windows and trunk lids. It is sometimes used to attach trim pieces.

Undercoating is a petroleum-based, tar-like substance that is designed to protect metal surfaces on the underside of the vehicle from corrosion. It also acts as a sound-deadening agent by insulating the bottom of the vehicle.

Waxes and polishes are used to help protect painted and plated surfaces from the weather. Different types of paint may require the use of different types of wax and polish. Some polishes utilize a chemical or abrasive cleaner to help remove the top layer of oxidized (dull) paint on older vehicles. In recent years many non-wax polishes that contain a wide variety of chemicals such as polymers and silicones have been introduced. These non-wax polishes are usually easier to apply and last longer than conventional waxes and polishes.

CONVERSION FACTORS

LENGTH (distance)

Inches (in)	X	25.4	= Millimeters (mm)	X 0.0394	= Inches (in)
Feet (ft)	X	0.305	= Meters (m)	X 3.281	= Feet (ft)
Miles	X	1.609	= Kilometers (km)	X 0.621	= Miles

VOLUME (capacity)

Cubic inches (cu in; in^3)	X	16.387	= Cubic centimeters (cc; cm^3)	X 0.061	= Cubic inches (cu in; in^3)
Imperial pints (Imp pt)	X	0.568	= Liters (l)	X 1.76	= Imperial pints (Imp pt)
Imperial quarts (Imp qt)	X	1.137	= Liters (l)	X 0.88	= Imperial quarts (Imp qt)
Imperial quarts (Imp qt)	X	1.201	= US quarts (US qt)	X 0.833	= Imperial quarts (Imp qt)
US quarts (US qt)	X	0.946	= Liters (l)	X 1.057	= US quarts (US qt)
Imperial gallons (Imp gal)	X	4.546	= Liters (l)	X 0.22	= Imperial gallons (Imp gal)
Imperial gallons (Imp gal)	X	1.201	= US gallons (US gal)	X 0.833	= Imperial gallons (Imp gal)
US gallons (US gal)	X	3.785	= Liters (l)	X 0.264	= US gallons (US gal)

MASS (weight)

Ounces (oz)	X	28.35	= Grams (g)	X 0.035	= Ounces (oz)
Pounds (lb)	X	0.454	= Kilograms (kg)	X 2.205	= Pounds (lb)

FORCE

Ounces-force (ozf; oz)	X	0.278	= Newtons (N)	X 3.6	= Ounces-force (ozf; oz)
Pounds-force (lbf; lb)	X	4.448	= Newtons (N)	X 0.225	= Pounds-force (lbf; lb)
Newtons (N)	X	0.1	= Kilograms-force (kgf; kg)	X 9.81	= Newtons (N)

PRESSURE

Pounds-force per square inch (psi; lbf/in^2; lb/in^2)	X	0.070	= Kilograms-force per square centimeter (kgf/cm^2; kg/cm^2)	X 14.223	= Pounds-force per square inch (psi; lbf/in^2; lb/in^2)
Pounds-force per square inch (psi; lbf/in^2; lb/in^2)	X	0.068	= Atmospheres (atm)	X 14.696	= Pounds-force per square inch (psi; lbf/in^2; lb/in^2)
Pounds-force per square inch (psi; lbf/in^2; lb/in^2)	X	0.069	= Bars	X 14.5	= Pounds-force per square inch (psi; lbf/in^2; lb/in^2)
Pounds-force per square inch (psi; lbf/in^2; lb/in^2)	X	6.895	= Kilopascals (kPa)	X 0.145	= Pounds-force per square inch (psi; lbf/in^2; lb/in^2)
Kilopascals (kPa)	X	0.01	= Kilograms-force per square centimeter (kgf/cm^2; kg/cm^2)	X 98.1	= Kilopascals (kPa)

TORQUE (moment of force)

Pounds-force inches (lbf in; lb in)	X	1.152	= Kilograms-force centimeter (kgf cm; kg cm)	X 0.868	= Pounds-force inches (lbf in; lb in)
Pounds-force inches (lbf in; lb in)	X	0.113	= Newton meters (Nm)	X 8.85	= Pounds-force inches (lbf in; lb in)
Pounds-force inches (lbf in; lb in)	X	0.083	= Pounds-force feet (lbf ft; lb ft)	X 12	= Pounds-force inches (lbf in; lb in)
Pounds-force feet (lbf ft; lb ft)	X	0.138	= Kilograms-force meters (kgf m; kg m)	X 7.233	= Pounds-force feet (lbf ft; lb ft)
Pounds-force feet (lbf ft; lb ft)	X	1.356	= Newton meters (Nm)	X 0.738	= Pounds-force feet (lbf ft; lb ft)
Newton meters (Nm)	X	0.102	= Kilograms-force meters (kgf m; kg m)	X 9.804	= Newton meters (Nm)

VACUUM

Inches mercury (in. Hg)	X	3.377	= Kilopascals (kPa)	X 0.2961	= Inches mercury
Inches mercury (in. Hg)	X	25.4	= Millimeters mercury (mm Hg)	X 0.0394	= Inches mercury

POWER

Horsepower (hp)	X	745.7	= Watts (W)	X 0.0013	= Horsepower (hp)

VELOCITY (speed)

Miles per hour (miles/hr; mph)	X	1.609	= Kilometers per hour (km/hr; kph)	X 0.621	= Miles per hour (miles/hr; mph)

FUEL CONSUMPTION *

Miles per gallon, Imperial (mpg)	X	0.354	= Kilometers per liter (km/l)	X 2.825	= Miles per gallon, Imperial (mpg)
Miles per gallon, US (mpg)	X	0.425	= Kilometers per liter (km/l)	X 2.352	= Miles per gallon, US (mpg)

TEMPERATURE

Degrees Fahrenheit = (°C x 1.8) + 32   Degrees Celsius (Degrees Centigrade; °C) = (°F - 32) x 0.56

It is common practice to convert from miles per gallon (mpg) to liters/100 kilometers (l/100km), where mpg (Imperial) x l/100 km = 282 and mpg (US) x l/100 km = 235

FRACTION/DECIMAL/MILLIMETER EQUIVALENTS

DECIMALS to MILLIMETERS

Decimal	mm	Decimal	mm
0.001	0.0254	0.500	12.7000
0.002	0.0508	0.510	12.9540
0.003	0.0762	0.520	13.2080
0.004	0.1016	0.530	13.4620
0.005	0.1270	0.540	13.7160
0.006	0.1524	0.550	13.9700
0.007	0.1778	0.560	14.2240
0.008	0.2032	0.570	14.4780
0.009	0.2286	0.580	14.7320
		0.590	14.9860
0.010	0.2540		
0.020	0.5080		
0.030	0.7620		
0.040	1.0160	0.600	15.2400
0.050	1.2700	0.610	15.4940
0.060	1.5240	0.620	15.7480
0.070	1.7780	0.630	16.0020
0.080	2.0320	0.640	16.2560
0.090	2.2860	0.650	16.5100
		0.660	16.7640
0.100	2.5400	0.670	17.0180
0.110	2.7940	0.680	17.2720
0.120	3.0480	0.690	17.5260
0.130	3.3020		
0.140	3.5560		
0.150	3.8100		
0.160	4.0640	0.700	17.7800
0.170	4.3180	0.710	18.0340
0.180	4.5720	0.720	18.2880
0.190	4.8260	0.730	18.5420
		0.740	18.7960
0.200	5.0800	0.750	19.0500
0.210	5.3340	0.760	19.3040
0.220	5.5880	0.770	19.5580
0.230	5.8420	0.780	19.8120
0.240	6.0960	0.790	20.0660
0.250	6.3500		
0.260	6.6040		
0.270	6.8580	0.800	20.3200
0.280	7.1120	0.810	20.5740
0.290	7.3660	0.820	21.8280
		0.830	21.0820
0.300	7.6200	0.840	21.3360
0.310	7.8740	0.850	21.5900
0.320	8.1280	0.860	21.8440
0.330	8.3820	0.870	22.0980
0.340	8.6360	0.880	22.3520
0.350	8.8900	0.890	22.6060
0.360	9.1440		
0.370	9.3980		
0.380	9.6520		
0.390	9.9060		
		0.900	22.8600
0.400	10.1600	0.910	23.1140
0.410	10.4140	0.920	23.3680
0.420	10.6680	0.930	23.6220
0.430	10.9220	0.940	23.8760
0.440	11.1760	0.950	24.1300
0.450	11.4300	0.960	24.3840
0.460	11.6840	0.970	24.6380
0.470	11.9380	0.980	24.8920
0.480	12.1920	0.990	25.1460
0.490	12.4460	1.000	25.4000

FRACTIONS to DECIMALS to MILLIMETERS

Fraction	Decimal	mm	Fraction	Decimal	mm
1/64	0.0156	0.3969	33/64	0.5156	13.0969
1/32	0.0312	0.7938	17/32	0.5312	13.4938
3/64	0.0469	1.1906	35/64	0.5469	13.8906
1/16	0.0625	1.5875	9/16	0.5625	14.2875
5/64	0.0781	1.9844	37/64	0.5781	14.6844
3/32	0.0938	2.3812	19/32	0.5938	15.0812
7/64	0.1094	2.7781	39/64	0.6094	15.4781
1/8	0.1250	3.1750	5/8	0.6250	15.8750
9/64	0.1406	3.5719	41/64	0.6406	16.2719
5/32	0.1562	3.9688	21/32	0.6562	16.6688
11/64	0.1719	4.3656	43/64	0.6719	17.0656
3/16	0.1875	4.7625	11/16	0.6875	17.4625
13/64	0.2031	5.1594	45/64	0.7031	17.8594
7/32	0.2188	5.5562	23/32	0.7188	18.2562
15/64	0.2344	5.9531	47/64	0.7344	18.6531
1/4	0.2500	6.3500	3/4	0.7500	19.0500
17/64	0.2656	6.7469	49/64	0.7656	19.4469
9/32	0.2812	7.1438	25/32	0.7812	19.8438
19/64	0.2969	7.5406	51/64	0.7969	20.2406
5/16	0.3125	7.9375	13/16	0.8125	20.6375
21/64	0.3281	8.3344	53/64	0.8281	21.0344
11/32	0.3438	8.7312	27/32	0.8438	21.4312
23/64	0.3594	9.1281	55/64	0.8594	21.8281
3/8	0.3750	9.5250	7/8	0.8750	22.2250
25/64	0.3906	9.9219	57/64	0.8906	22.6219
13/32	0.4062	10.3188	29/32	0.9062	23.0188
27/64	0.4219	10.7156	59/64	0.9219	23.4156
7/16	0.4375	11.1125	15/16	0.9375	23.8125
29/64	0.4531	11.5094	61/64	0.9531	24.2094
15/32	0.4688	11.9062	31/32	0.9688	24.6062
31/64	0.4844	12.3031	63/64	0.9844	25.0031
1/2	0.5000	12.7000	1	1.0000	25.4000

Regardless of how enthusiastic you may be about getting on with the job at hand, take the time to ensure that your safety is not jeopardized. A moment's lack of attention can result in an accident, as can failure to observe certain simple safety precautions. The possibility of an accident will always exist, and the following points should not be considered a comprehensive list of all dangers. Rather, they are intended to make you aware of the risks and to encourage a safety conscious approach to all work you carry out on your vehicle.

ESSENTIAL DOS AND DON'TS

DON'T rely on a jack when working under the vehicle. Always use approved jackstands to support the weight of the vehicle and place them under the recommended lift or support points.

DON'T attempt to loosen extremely tight fasteners (i.e. wheel lug nuts) while the vehicle is on a jack - it may fall.

DON'T start the engine without first making sure that the transmission is in Neutral (or Park where applicable) and the parking brake is set.

DON'T remove the radiator cap from a hot cooling system - let it cool or cover it with a cloth and release the pressure gradually.

DON'T attempt to drain the engine oil until you are sure it has cooled to the point that it will not burn you.

DON'T touch any part of the engine or exhaust system until it has cooled sufficiently to avoid burns.

DON'T siphon toxic liquids such as gasoline, antifreeze and brake fluid by mouth, or allow them to remain on your skin.

DON'T inhale brake lining dust - it is potentially hazardous (see *Asbestos* below).

DON'T allow spilled oil or grease to remain on the floor - wipe it up before someone slips on it.

DON'T use loose fitting wrenches or other tools which may slip and cause injury.

DON'T push on wrenches when loosening or tightening nuts or bolts. Always try to pull the wrench toward you. If the situation calls for pushing the wrench away, push with an open hand to avoid scraped knuckles if the wrench should slip.

DON'T attempt to lift a heavy component alone - get someone to help you.

DON'T rush or take unsafe shortcuts to finish a job.

DON'T allow children or animals in or around the vehicle while you are working on it.

DO wear eye protection when using power tools such as a drill, sander, bench grinder, etc. and when working under a vehicle.

DO keep loose clothing and long hair well out of the way of moving parts.

DO make sure that any hoist used has a safe working load rating adequate for the job.

DO get someone to check on you periodically when working alone on a vehicle.

DO carry out work in a logical sequence and make sure that everything is correctly assembled and tightened.

DO keep chemicals and fluids tightly capped and out of the reach of children and pets.

DO remember that your vehicle's safety affects that of yourself and others. If in doubt on any point, get professional advice.

ASBESTOS

Certain friction, insulating, sealing, and other products - such as brake linings, brake bands, clutch linings, torque converters, gaskets, etc. - may contain asbestos. Extreme care must be taken to avoid inhalation of dust from such products, since it is hazardous to health. If in doubt, assume that they do contain asbestos.

FIRE

Remember at all times that gasoline is highly flammable. Never smoke or have any kind of open flame around when working on a vehicle. But the risk does not end there. A spark caused by an electrical short circuit, by two metal surfaces contacting each other, or even by static electricity built up in your body under certain conditions, can ignite gasoline vapors, which in a confined space are highly explosive. Do not, under any circumstances, use gasoline for cleaning parts. Use an approved safety solvent.

Always disconnect the battery ground (-) cable at the battery before working on any part of the fuel system or electrical system. Never risk spilling fuel on a hot engine or exhaust component. It is strongly recommended that a fire extinguisher suitable for use on fuel and electrical fires be kept handy in the garage or workshop at all times. Never try to extinguish a fuel or electrical fire with water.

FUMES

Certain fumes are highly toxic and can quickly cause unconsciousness and even death if inhaled to any extent. Gasoline vapor falls into this category, as do the vapors from some cleaning solvents. Any draining or pouring of such volatile fluids should be done in a well ventilated area.

When using cleaning fluids and solvents, read the instructions on the container carefully. Never use materials from unmarked containers.

Never run the engine in an enclosed space, such as a garage. Exhaust fumes contain carbon monoxide, which is extremely poisonous. If you need to run the engine, always do so in the open air, or at least have the rear of the vehicle outside the work area.

If you are fortunate enough to have the use of an inspection pit, never drain or pour gasoline and never run the engine while the vehicle is over the pit. The fumes, being heavier than air, will concentrate in the pit with possibly lethal results.

THE BATTERY

Never create a spark or allow a bare light bulb near a battery. They normally give off a certain amount of hydrogen gas, which is highly explosive.

Always disconnect the battery ground (-) cable at the battery before working on the fuel or electrical systems.

If possible, loosen the filler caps or cover when charging the battery from an external source (this does not apply to sealed or maintenance-free batteries). Do not charge at an excessive rate or the battery may burst.

Take care when adding water to a non maintenance-free battery and when carrying a battery. The electrolyte, even when diluted, is very corrosive and should not be allowed to contact clothing or skin.

Always wear eye protection when cleaning the battery to prevent the caustic deposits from entering your eyes.

HOUSEHOLD CURRENT

When using an electric power tool, inspection light, etc., which operates on household current, always make sure that the tool is correctly connected to its plug and that, where necessary, it is properly grounded. Do not use such items in damp conditions and, again, do not create a spark or apply excessive heat in the vicinity of fuel or fuel vapor.

SECONDARY IGNITION SYSTEM VOLTAGE

A severe electric shock can result from touching certain parts of the ignition system (such as the spark plug wires) when the engine is running or being cranked, particularly if components are damp or the insulation is defective. In the case of an electronic ignition system, the secondary system voltage is much higher and could prove fatal.

Troubleshooting

CONTENTS

This section provides an easy reference guide to the more common problems which may occur during the operation of your vehicle. Various symptoms and their possible causes are grouped under headings denoting components or systems, such as Engine, Cooling system, etc. They also refer to the Chapter and/or Section that deals with the problem.

Remember that successful troubleshooting isn't a mysterious art practiced only by professional mechanics. It's simply the result of knowledge combined with an intelligent, systematic approach to a problem. Always use a process of elimination, starting with the simplest solution and working through to the most complex - and never over-

look the obvious. Anyone can run the gas tank dry or leave the lights on overnight, so don't assume that you're exempt from such oversights.

Finally, always establish a clear idea why a problem has occurred and take steps to ensure that it doesn't happen again. If the electrical system fails because of a poor connection, check all other connections in the system to make sure they don't fail as well. If a particular fuse continues to blow, find out why - don't just go on replacing fuses. Remember, failure of a small component can often be indicative of potential failure or incorrect functioning of a more important component or system.

ENGINE AND PERFORMANCE

1 Engine will not rotate when attempting to start

1 Battery terminal connections loose or corroded (Chapter 1).
2 Battery discharged or faulty (Chapter 1).
3 Automatic transaxle not completely engaged in Park (Chapter 7).
4 Broken, loose or disconnected wiring in the starting circuit (Chapters 5 and 12).
5 Starter motor pinion jammed in flywheel ring gear (Chapter 5).
6 Starter solenoid faulty (Chapter 5).
7 Starter motor faulty (Chapter 5).
8 Ignition switch faulty (Chapter 12).
9 Transmission Range (TR) sensor faulty (Chapter 7).
10 Starter pinion or driveplate teeth worn or broken (Chapter 5).

2 Engine rotates but will not start

1 Fuel tank empty.
2 Battery discharged (engine rotates slowly) (Chapter 5).
3 Battery terminal connections loose or corroded (Chapter 1).
4 Leaking fuel injector(s), fuel pump, pressure regulator, etc. (Chapter 4).
5 Fuel not reaching fuel injection system (Chapter 4).
6 Ignition components damp or damaged (Chapter 5).
7 Worn, faulty or incorrectly gapped spark plugs (Chapter 1).
8 Broken, loose or disconnected wiring in the starting circuit (Chapter 5).
9 Broken, loose or disconnected wires at the ignition coil(s) or faulty coil(s) (Chapter 5).

3 Engine hard to start when cold

1 Battery discharged or low (Chapter 1).
2 Fuel system malfunctioning (Chapter 4).
3 Emissions or engine control system malfunctioning (Chapter 6).

4 Engine hard to start when hot

1 Air filter clogged (Chapter 1).
2 Fuel not reaching the fuel injection system (Chapter 4).
3 Corroded battery connections, especially ground (Chapter 1).
4 Emissions or engine control system malfunctioning (Chapter 6).

5 Starter motor noisy or excessively rough in engagement

1 Pinion or driveplate gear teeth worn or broken (Chapter 5).
2 Starter motor mounting bolts loose or missing (Chapter 5).

6 Engine starts but stops immediately

1 Loose or faulty electrical connections at coil pack or alternator (Chapter 5).
2 Insufficient fuel reaching the fuel injectors (Chapter 4).
3 Vacuum leak at the gasket between the intake manifold/plenum and throttle body (Chapters 1 and 4).
4 Restricted exhaust system (most likely the catalytic converter) (Chapters 4 and 6).

7 Oil puddle under engine

1 Oil pan gasket and/or oil pan drain bolt seal leaking (Chapters 1 and 2).
2 Oil pressure sending unit leaking (Chapter 2).
3 Rocker arm cover gaskets leaking (Chapter 2).
4 Engine oil seals leaking (Chapter 2).

8 Engine lopes while idling or idles erratically

1 Vacuum leakage (Chapter 4).
2 Leaking EGR valve or plugged PCV valve (Chapter 6).
3 Air filter clogged (Chapter 1).
4 Fuel pump not delivering sufficient fuel to the fuel injection system (Chapter 4).
5 Leaking head gasket (Chapter 2).
6 Camshaft lobes worn (Chapter 2).

9 Engine misses at idle speed

1 Spark plugs worn or not gapped properly (Chapter 1).
2 Faulty spark plug wires (Chapter 1).
3 Vacuum leaks (Chapters 1 and 4).
4 Uneven or low compression (Chapter 2C).

10 Engine misses throughout driving speed range

1 Fuel filter clogged and/or impurities in the fuel system (Chapters 1 and 4).
2 Low fuel output at the injector(s) (Chapter 4).
3 Faulty or incorrectly gapped spark plugs (Chapter 1).
4 Leaking spark plug wires (Chapter 1).
5 Faulty emission system components (Chapter 6).
6 Low or uneven cylinder compression pressures (Chapter 2).
7 Weak or faulty ignition system (Chapter 5).
8 Vacuum leak in fuel injection system, intake manifold or vacuum hoses (Chapter 4).

11 Engine stumbles on acceleration

1 Spark plugs fouled (Chapter 1).
2 Fuel injection system problem (Chapter 4).
3 Fuel filter clogged (Chapter 1).
4 Intake manifold air leak (Chapter 4).

12 Engine surges while holding accelerator steady

1 Intake air leak (Chapter 4).
2 Fuel pump faulty (Chapter 4).
3 Loose fuel injector harness connections (Chapter 4).
4 Defective PCM (Chapter 6).

13 Engine stalls

1 Idle speed incorrect (Chapters 1 and 4).
2 Fuel filter clogged and/or water and impurities in the fuel system (Chapters 1 and 4).
3 Ignition components damp or damaged (Chapter 5).

4 Faulty emissions system components (Chapter 6).
5 Faulty or incorrectly gapped spark plugs (Chapter 1).
6 Faulty spark plug wires (Chapter 1).
7 Vacuum leak in the intake manifold or vacuum hoses (Chapter 4).

14 Engine lacks power

1 Faulty or incorrectly gapped spark plugs (Chapter 1).
2 Restricted exhaust system (most likely the catalytic converter (Chapters 4 and 6).
3 Fuel injection system malfunctioning (Chapter 4).
4 Faulty coil(s) (Chapter 5).
5 Brakes binding (Chapter 1).
6 Automatic transaxle fluid level incorrect (Chapter 1).
7 Fuel filter clogged and/or impurities in the fuel system (Chapter 1).
8 Emission control system not functioning properly (Chapter 6).
9 Low or uneven cylinder compression pressures (Chapter 2).

15 Engine backfires

1 Emissions system not functioning properly (Chapter 6).
2 Fuel injection system malfunctioning (Chapter 4).
3 Vacuum leak at fuel injectors, intake manifold or vacuum hoses (Chapter 4).
4 Valves sticking (Chapter 2).

16 Pinging or knocking engine sounds during acceleration or uphill

1 Incorrect grade of fuel.
2 Fuel injection system malfunctioning Chapter 4).
3 Improper or damaged spark plugs or wires (Chapter 1).
4 Worn or damaged ignition components (Chapter 5).
5 Faulty emissions system (Chapter 6).
6 Vacuum leak (Chapter 4).

17 Engine runs with oil pressure light on

1 Low oil level (Chapter 1).
2 Short in wiring circuit (Chapter 12).
3 Faulty oil pressure sender (Chapter 2).
4 Oil viscosity too low or oil diluted.
5 Worn engine bearings and/or oil pump (Chapter 2).

18 Engine diesels (continues to run) after switching off

1 Excessive engine operating temperature (Chapter 3).
2 Excessive carbon deposits on valves and pistons.

ENGINE ELECTRICAL SYSTEM

19 Battery will not hold a charge

1 Alternator drivebelt defective or not adjusted properly (Chapter 1).
2 Battery terminals loose or corroded (Chapter 1).
3 Alternator not charging properly (Chapter 5).

4 Loose, broken or faulty wiring in the charging circuit (Chapter 5).
5 Short in vehicle wiring (Chapters 5 and 12).
6 Internally defective battery (Chapters 1 and 5).

20 Voltage warning light fails to go out

1 Faulty alternator or charging circuit (Chapter 5).
2 Alternator drivebelt defective or out of adjustment (Chapter 1).
3 Alternator voltage regulator inoperative (Chapter 5).

21 Voltage warning light fails to come on when key is turned on

1 Warning light bulb defective (Chapter 12).
2 Fault in the printed circuit, dash wiring or bulb holder (Chapter 12).

FUEL SYSTEM

22 Excessive fuel consumption

1 Dirty or clogged air filter element (Chapter 1).
2 Emissions system not functioning properly (Chapter 6).
3 Fuel injection system malfunctioning (Chapter 4).
4 Low tire pressure or incorrect tire size (Chapter 1).

23 Fuel leakage and/or fuel odor

1 Leak in a fuel feed or vent line (Chapter 4).
2 Tank overfilled.
3 Evaporative emissions control canister defective (Chapter 6).
4 Fuel injector seals faulty (Chapter 4).

COOLING SYSTEM

24 Overheating

1 Insufficient coolant in system (Chapter 1).
2 Water pump drivebelt defective or out of adjustment (Chapter 1).
3 Radiator core blocked or grille restricted (Chapter 3).
4 Thermostat faulty (Chapter 3).
5 Electric cooling fan blades broken or cracked (Chapter 3).
6 Radiator cap not maintaining proper pressure (Chapter 3).

25 Overcooling

Incorrect (opening temperature too low) or faulty thermostat (Chapter 3).

26 External coolant leakage

1 Deteriorated/damaged hoses or loose clamps (Chapters 1 and 3).
2 Water pump seal defective (Chapters 1 and 3).
3 Leakage from radiator core (Chapter 3).
4 Engine drain or water jacket core plugs leaking (Chapter 2).

27 Internal coolant leakage

1 Leaking cylinder head gasket (Chapter 2).
2 Cracked cylinder bore or cylinder head (Chapter 2).

28 Coolant loss

1 Too much coolant in system (Chapter 1).
2 Coolant boiling away because of overheating (Chapter 3).
3 Internal or external leakage (Chapter 3).
4 Faulty radiator cap (Chapter 3).

29 Poor coolant circulation

1 Inoperative water pump (Chapter 3).
2 Restriction in cooling system (Chapters 1 and 3).
3 Water pump drivebelt defective or out of adjustment (Chapter 1).
4 Thermostat sticking (Chapter 3).

AUTOMATIC TRANSAXLE

➡**Note: Due to the complexity of the automatic transaxle, it's difficult for the home mechanic to properly diagnose and service this component. For problems other than the following, the vehicle should be taken to a dealer service department or a transmission shop.**

30 Fluid leakage

1 Automatic transmission fluid is a deep red color. Fluid leaks should not be confused with engine oil, which can easily be blown by airflow to the transaxle.
2 To pinpoint a leak, first remove all built-up dirt and grime from the transaxle housing with degreasing agents and/or steam cleaning. Drive the vehicle at low speeds so air flow will not blow the leak far from its source. Raise the vehicle and determine where the leak is coming from. Common areas of leakage are:

   a) Fluid pan
   b) Fluid cooler lines (Chapter 7)
   c) Vehicle Speed Sensor (Chapter 6)

31 Transaxle fluid brown or has a burned smell

Transaxle overheated. Change fluid (Chapter 1).

32 General shift mechanism problems

1 Chapter 7 deals with checking and adjusting the shift linkage on automatic transaxles. Common problems which may be attributed to a poorly adjusted linkage are:

   a) Engine starting in gears other than Park or Neutral.
   b) Indicator on shifter pointing to a gear other than the one actually being used.
   c) Vehicle moves when in Park.

2 Refer to Chapter 7 for the shift linkage adjustment procedure.

33 Engine will start in gears other than Park or Neutral

Transmission Range (TR) sensor malfunctioning (Chapter 6).

34 Transaxle slips, shifts roughly, is noisy or has no drive in forward or reverse gears

There are many probable causes for the above problems, but the home mechanic should be concerned with only one possibility - fluid level. Before taking the vehicle to a repair shop, check the level and condition of the fluid as described in Chapter 1.

Correct the fluid level as necessary or change the fluid and filter if needed. If the problem persists, have a professional diagnose the probable cause.

DRIVEAXLES

35 Clicking noise in turns

Worn or damaged outer CV joint. Check for cut or damaged boots (Chapter 1). Repair as necessary (Chapter 8).

36 Knock or clunk when accelerating after coasting

Worn or damaged CV joint. Check for cut or damaged boots (Chapter 1). Repair as necessary (Chapter 8).

37 Shudder or vibration during acceleration

1 Worn or damaged CV joints. Repair or replace as necessary (Chapter 8).
2 Sticking inner joint assembly. Correct or replace as necessary (Chapter 8).

BRAKES

➡**Note: Before assuming that a brake problem exists, make sure . . .**

   a) The tires are in good condition and properly inflated (Chapter 1).
   b) The front end alignment is correct (Chapter 10).
   c) The vehicle isn't loaded with weight in an unequal manner.

38 Vehicle pulls to one side during braking

1 Incorrect tire pressures (Chapter 1).
2 Front end out of alignment (have the front end aligned).
3 Unmatched tires on same axle.
4 Restricted brake lines or hoses (Chapter 9).
5 Sticking caliper or wheel cylinder piston (Chapter 9).
6 Loose suspension parts (Chapter 10).
7 Contaminated brake pad or shoe material (Chapter 9).

39 Noise (grinding or high-pitched squeal) when the brakes are applied

1 Disc brake pads worn out. Replace pads with new ones immediately (Chapter 9).
2 Drum brake shoes worn out. Replace the shoes immediately (Chapter 9).

40   Brake roughness or chatter (pedal pulsates)

1   Excessive brake disc lateral runout or brake drum out-of-round (Chapter 9).
2   Parallelism of disc not within specifications (Chapter 9).
3   Uneven pad wear caused by caliper not sliding due to improper clearance or dirt (Chapter 9).
4   Defective brake disc (Chapter 9).

41   Excessive pedal effort required to stop vehicle

1   Malfunctioning power brake booster (Chapter 9).
2   Partial system failure (Chapter 9).
3   Excessively worn pads (Chapter 9).
4   One or more caliper or wheel cylinder pistons seized or sticking (Chapter 9).
5   Brake pads contaminated with oil or grease (Chapter 9).
6   New pads or shoes installed and not yet seated. It will take a while for the new material to seat.

42   Excessive brake pedal travel

1   Partial brake system failure (Chapter 9).
2   Insufficient fluid in master cylinder (Chapters 1 and 9).
3   Air trapped in system (Chapter 9).
4   Faulty master cylinder (Chapter 9).

43   Dragging brakes

1   Master cylinder pistons not returning correctly (Chapter 9).
2   Restricted brake lines or hoses (Chapters 1 and 9).
3   Incorrect parking brake adjustment (Chapter 9).
4   Defective brake calipers (Chapter 9).

44   Grabbing or uneven braking action

1   Malfunction of proportioning valve (Chapter 9).
2   Malfunction of power brake booster unit (Chapter 9).
3   Binding brake pedal mechanism (Chapter 9).
4   Contaminated brake linings (Chapter 9).

45   Brake pedal feels spongy when depressed

1   Air in hydraulic lines (Chapter 9).
2   Master cylinder mounting bolts loose (Chapter 9).
3   Master cylinder defective (Chapter 9).

46   Brake pedal travels to the floor with little resistance

Little or no fluid in the master cylinder reservoir caused by leaking caliper, or loose, damaged or disconnected brake lines (Chapter 9).

47   Parking brake does not hold

Parking brake cables improperly adjusted (Chapter 9).

SUSPENSION AND STEERING SYSTEMS

➡Note: Before attempting to diagnose the suspension and steering systems, perform the following preliminary checks:

a)   *Check the tire pressures and look for uneven wear.*
b)   *Check the steering universal joints or coupling from the column to the steering gear for loose fasteners and wear.*
c)   *Check the front and rear suspension and the steering gear assembly for loose and damaged parts.*
d)   *Look for out-of-round or out-of-balance tires, bent rims and loose and/or rough wheel bearings.*

48   Vehicle pulls to one side

1   Mismatched or uneven tires (Chapter 10).
2   Broken or sagging springs (Chapter 10).
3   Wheel alignment incorrect (Chapter 10).
4   Front brakes dragging (Chapter 9).

49   Abnormal or excessive tire wear

1   Front wheel alignment incorrect (Chapter 10).
2   Sagging or broken springs (Chapter 10).
3   Tire out-of-balance (Chapter 10).
4   Worn strut or shock absorber (Chapter 10).
5   Overloaded vehicle.
6   Tires not rotated regularly.

50   Wheel makes a "thumping" noise

1   Blister or bump on tire (Chapter 1).
2   Improper strut or shock absorber action (Chapter 10).

51   Shimmy, shake or vibration

1   Tire or wheel out-of-balance or out-of-round (Chapter 10).
2   Loose or worn wheel bearings (Chapter 10).
3   Worn tie-rod ends (Chapter 10).
4   Worn balljoints (Chapter 10).
5   Excessive wheel runout (Chapter 10).
6   Blister or bump on tire (Chapter 1).

52   Hard steering

1   Balljoints, tie-rod ends or steering gear worn (Chapter 10).
2   Front wheel alignment incorrect (Chapter 10).
3   Low tire pressure (Chapter 1).

53   Steering wheel does not return to center position correctly

1   Balljoints or tie-rod ends worn (Chapters 1 and 10).
2   Binding in steering column (Chapter 10).
3   Defective rack-and-pinion assembly (Chapter 10).
4   Front wheel alignment problem (Chapter 10).

54 Abnormal noise at the front end

1 Balljoints or tie-rod ends worn (Chapter 1).
2 Loose upper strut mount (Chapter 10).
3 Worn tie-rod ends (Chapter 10).
4 Loose stabilizer bar (Chapter 10).
5 Loose wheel lug nuts (Chapter 1).
6 Loose suspension bolts (Chapter 10).

55 Wander or poor steering stability

1 Mismatched or uneven tires (Chapter 10).
2 Balljoints or tie-rod ends worn (Chapters 1 and 10).
3 Worn struts or shock absorbers (Chapter 10).
4 Loose stabilizer bar (Chapter 10).
5 Broken or sagging springs (Chapter 10).
6 Front wheel alignment incorrect.
7 Worn steering gear clamp bushing (Chapter 10).

56 Erratic steering when braking

1 Wheel bearings worn (Chapter 10).
2 Broken or sagging springs (Chapter 10).
3 Leaking caliper (Chapter 9).
4 Warped brake discs (Chapter 9).
5 Worn steering gear clamp bushing (Chapter 10).
6 Wheel alignment incorrect.

57 Excessive pitching and/or rolling around corners or during braking

1 Loose stabilizer bar (Chapter 10).
2 Worn struts/shock absorbers or mounts (Chapter 10).
3 Broken or sagging springs (Chapter 10).
4 Overloaded vehicle.

58 Suspension bottoms

1 Overloaded vehicle.
2 Worn struts or shock absorbers (Chapter 10).
3 Incorrect, broken or sagging springs (Chapter 10).

59 Cupped tires

1 Front wheel alignment incorrect (Chapter 10).
2 Worn struts or shock absorbers (Chapter 10).
3 Wheel bearings worn (Chapter 10).
4 Excessive tire or wheel runout (Chapter 10).
5 Worn balljoints (Chapter 10).

60 Excessive tire wear on outside edge

1 Inflation pressures incorrect (Chapter 1).
2 Excessive speed in turns.
3 Wheel alignment incorrect (excessive toe-in or positive camber). Have professionally aligned.
4 Suspension arm bent or twisted (Chapter 10).

61 Excessive tire wear on inside edge

1 Inflation pressures incorrect (Chapter 1).
2 Wheel alignment incorrect (toe-out or excessive negative camber). Have professionally aligned.
3 Loose or damaged steering components (Chapter 10).

62 Tire tread worn in one place

1 Tires out-of-balance.
2 Damaged or buckled wheel. Inspect and replace if necessary.
3 Defective tire (Chapter 1).

63 Excessive play or looseness in steering system

1 Wheel bearings worn (Chapter 10).
2 Tie-rod end loose or worn (Chapter 10).
3 Steering gear loose (Chapter 10).

64 Rattling or clicking noise in steering gear

1 Steering gear mounting bolts loose (Chapter 10).
2 Steering gear defective (Chapter 10).

Notes

Section

1

TUNE-UP AND ROUTINE MAINTENANCE

Typical engine compartment layout

1	Air filter housing	5	Underhood fuse/relay block	9	Upper radiator hose
2	Power steering fluid reservoir	6	Coolant reservoir	10	Engine oil dipstick
3	Brake fluid reservoir	7	Transaxle fluid dipstick	11	Windshield washer fluid reservoir
4	Battery	8	Engine oil filler cap	12	Radiator cap

Typical engine compartment underside components

1	Lower radiator hose	3	Automatic transaxle pan	5	Driveaxle boots
2	Engine oil filter	4	Engine oil drain plug	6	Brake calipers

1   Dodge Caravan/Chrysler Town & Country Maintenance schedule

The following maintenance intervals are based on the assumption that the vehicle owner will be doing the maintenance or service work, as opposed to having a dealer service department do the work. Although the time/mileage intervals are loosely based on factory recommendations, most have been shortened to ensure, for example, that such items as lubricants and fluids are checked/changed at intervals that promote maximum engine/driveline service life. Also, subject to the preference of the individual owner interested in keeping his or her vehicle in peak condition at all times, and with the vehicle's ultimate resale in mind, many of the maintenance procedures may be performed more often than recommended in the following schedule. We encourage such owner initiative.

When the vehicle is new it should be serviced initially by a factory authorized dealer service department to protect the factory warranty. In many cases the initial maintenance check is done at no cost to the owner (check with your dealer service department for more information).

EVERY 250 MILES OR WEEKLY, WHICHEVER COMES FIRST

Check the engine oil level (Section 4)
Check the engine coolant level (Section 4)
Check the windshield washer fluid level (Section 4)
Check the brake fluid level (Section 4)
Check the power steering fluid level (Section 4)
Check the automatic transaxle fluid level (Section 4)
Check the tires and tire pressures (Section 5)
Check the operation of all lights
Check the horn operation

EVERY 3,000 MILES OR 3 MONTHS, WHICHEVER COMES FIRST

All items listed above, plus:

Change the engine oil and filter (Section 6)

EVERY 6,000 MILES OR 6 MONTHS, WHICHEVER COMES FIRST

All items listed above, plus:

Check the wiper blade condition (Section 7)
Check and clean the battery and terminals (Section 8)
Rotate the tires (Section 9)
Check the seatbelts (Section 10)
Check the condition of all underhood hoses and connections (Section 11)
Check the cooling system hoses and connections for leaks and damage (Section 12)
Check and replace, if necessary, the air filter element (Section 13)

EVERY 12,000 MILES OR 12 MONTHS, WHICHEVER COMES FIRST

All items listed above, plus:

Check the brake system (Section 14)
Check the suspension components and driveaxle boots (Section 15)

Check the exhaust pipes and hangers (Section 16)
Check the fuel system hoses and connections for leaks and damage (Section 17)
Replace the interior ventilation filter, if equipped (Section 18)

EVERY 30,000 MILES OR 30 MONTHS, WHICHEVER COMES FIRST

All items listed above, plus:

Check the drivebelts and adjust if necessary (Section 19)
Replace the air filter element (Section 13)*
Replace the brake fluid (Section 20)

EVERY 60,000 MILES OR 60 MONTHS, WHICHEVER COMES FIRST

All items listed above, plus:

Replace the spark plugs (four-cylinder engine) (Section 21)*
Replace the spark plug wires (four-cylinder engine) (Section 22)
Check and replace, if necessary, the PCV valve (Section 23)*

EVERY 60 MONTHS (REGARDLESS OF MILEAGE)

Service the cooling system (drain, flush and refill) (Section 24)

EVERY 100,000 MILES

Replace the spark plugs (V6 engines) (Section 21)
Replace the spark plug wires (V6 engines) (Section 22)
Change the automatic transaxle fluid and filter (Section 25)*

EVERY 120,000 MILES OR 120 MONTHS, WHICHEVER COMES FIRST

Replace the timing belt (four-cylinder engine only) (Chapter 2A)

*This item is affected by "severe" operating conditions as described below. If the vehicle in question is operated under "severe" conditions, perform all maintenance procedures marked with an asterisk (*) at the intervals specified by the mileage headings below.

Consider the conditions "severe" if most driving is done . . .
In dusty areas
Towing a trailer
Idling for extended periods and/or low-speed operation
When outside temperatures remain below freezing and most trips are less than four miles
In heavy city traffic where outside temperatures regularly reach 90-degrees F or higher

EVERY 3,000 MILES

Check and replace, if necessary, the air filter element (Section 13)

EVERY 60,000 MILES

Check and replace, if necessary, the PCV valve (Section 23)
Change the automatic transaxle fluid and filter (Section 25)

2 Introduction

This Chapter is designed to help the home mechanic maintain the Dodge Caravan/Chrysler Town & Country with the goals of maximum performance, economy, safety and reliability in mind.

Included is a master maintenance schedule, followed by procedures dealing specifically with each item on the schedule. Visual checks, adjustments, component replacement and other helpful items are included. Refer to the accompanying illustrations of the engine compartment and the underside of the vehicle for the locations of various components.

Adhering to the mileage/time maintenance schedule and following the step-by-step procedures, which is simply a preventive maintenance program, will result in maximum reliability and vehicle service life. Keep in mind that it's not possible for this comprehensive program to produce the same results if you maintain some items at the specified intervals but not others.

As you service the vehicle, you'll discover that many of the procedures can - and should - be grouped together because of the nature of the particular procedure you're performing or because of the close proximity of two otherwise unrelated components to one another.

For example, if the vehicle is raised, you should inspect the exhaust, suspension, steering and fuel systems while you're under the vehicle. When you're rotating the tires, it makes good sense to check the brakes, since the wheels are already removed. Finally, let's suppose you have to borrow or rent a torque wrench. Even if you only need it to tighten the spark plugs, you might as well check the torque of as many critical fasteners as time allows.

The first step in this maintenance program is to prepare before the actual work begins. Read through all the procedures you're planning, then gather together all the parts and tools needed. If it looks like you might run into problems during a particular job, seek advice from a mechanic or an experienced do-it-yourselfer.

OWNER'S MANUAL AND VECI LABEL INFORMATION

Your vehicle owner's manual was written for your year and model and contains very specific information on component locations, specifications, fuse ratings, part numbers, etc. The Owner's Manual is an important resource for the do-it-yourselfer to have; if one was not supplied with your vehicle, it can generally be ordered from a dealer parts department.

Among other important information, the Vehicle Emissions Control Information (VECI) label contains specifications and procedures for applicable tune-up adjustments and, in some instances, spark plugs (see Chapter 6 for more information on the VECI label). The information on this label is the exact maintenance data recommended by the manufacturer. This data often varies by intended operating altitude, local emissions regulations, month of manufacture, etc.

This Chapter contains procedural details, safety information and more ambitious maintenance intervals than you might find in manufacturer's literature. However, you may also find procedures or specifications in your Owner's Manual or VECI label that differ with what's printed here. In these cases, the Owner's Manual or VECI label can be considered correct, since it is specific to your particular vehicle.

3 Tune-up general information

The term "tune-up" is used in this manual to represent a combination of individual operations rather than one specific procedure.

The engine will be kept in relatively good running condition and the need for additional work will be minimized if the routine maintenance schedule is followed closely and frequent checks are made of fluid levels and high wear items, as suggested throughout this manual from the time the vehicle is new.

More likely than not, however, there will be times when the engine is running poorly due to lack of regular maintenance. This is even more likely if a used vehicle, which hasn't received regular and frequent maintenance checks, is purchased. In such cases, an engine tune-up will be needed outside of the regular routine maintenance intervals.

The first step in any tune-up or diagnostic procedure to help correct a poor running engine is a cylinder compression check. A compression check (see Chapter 2, Part C) will help determine the condition of internal engine components and should be used as a guide for tune-up and repair procedures. For instance, if a compression check indicates serious internal engine wear, a conventional tune-up will not improve the performance of the engine and would be a waste of time and money. Because of its importance, someone with the right equipment and the knowledge to use it properly should do the compression check.

The following procedures are those most often needed to bring a generally poor running engine back into a proper state of tune:

MINOR TUNE-UP

Check all engine related fluids (see Section 4)
Clean and inspect the battery (see Section 8)
Check all underhood hoses (see Section 11)
Check and adjust the drivebelts (see Section 19)
Check the air filter (see Section 13)
Service the cooling system (see Section 24)
Replace the spark plugs (see Section 21)
Check the PCV valve (see Section 23)

MAJOR TUNE-UP

All items listed under Minor tune-up plus . . .

Check the fuel system (see Section 17)
Replace the air filter (see Section 13)
Replace the spark plug wires (see Section 22)
Check the charging system (see Chapter 5)

4 Fluid level checks (every 250 miles or weekly)

➡Note: The following are fluid level checks to be done on a 250 mile or weekly basis. Additional fluid level checks can be found in specific maintenance procedures that follow. Regardless of the intervals, develop the habit of checking under the vehicle periodically for evidence of fluid leaks.

1 Fluids are an essential part of the lubrication, cooling, brake and window washer systems. Because the fluids gradually become depleted and/or contaminated during normal operation of the vehicle, they must be replenished periodically. See *Recommended lubricants and fluids* at the end of this Chapter before adding fluid to any of the following components.

➡Note: The vehicle must be on level ground when fluid levels are checked.

ENGINE OIL

▶ Refer to illustrations 4.2, 4.4 and 4.5

2 Engine oil level is checked with a dipstick that is located on the side of the engine facing the front of the vehicle (see illustration). The

4.2 The engine oil dipstick is located at the front of the engine and is clearly marked

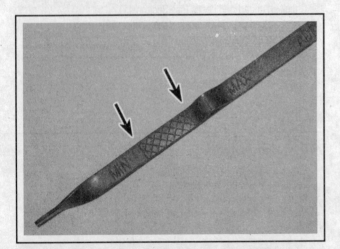

4.4 The oil level should be between the MIN and MAX marks, near the top of the cross-hatched area on the dipstick - if it isn't, add enough oil to bring the level up to or near the upper mark (do not overfill)

dipstick extends through a tube and into the oil pan at the bottom of the engine.

3 The oil level should be checked before the vehicle has been driven, or about 5 minutes after the engine has been shut off. If the oil is checked immediately after driving the vehicle, some of the oil will remain in the upper engine components, resulting in an inaccurate reading on the dipstick.

4 Pull the dipstick out of the tube and wipe all the oil off the end with a clean rag or paper towel. Insert the clean dipstick all the way back into the tube, then pull it out again. Note the oil level at the end of the dipstick. Add oil as necessary to bring the oil level to the top of the cross-hatched area, or MAX mark (see illustration).

5 Oil is added to the engine after removing a cap located on the valve cover (see illustration). Use a funnel to prevent spills as the oil is added.

6 Don't allow the level to drop below the MIN mark on the dipstick or engine damage may occur. On the other hand, don't overfill the engine by adding too much oil - it may result in oil aeration and loss of oil pressure and also could result in oil fouled spark plugs, oil leaks or seal failures.

7 Checking the oil level is an important preventive maintenance step. A consistently low oil level indicates oil leakage through damaged seals, defective gaskets or past worn rings or valve guides. If the oil looks milky in color or has water droplets in it, the block or head may be cracked and leaking coolant is entering the crankcase. The engine should be checked immediately. The condition of the oil should also be checked. Each time you check the oil level, slide your thumb and index finger up the dipstick before wiping off the oil. If you see small dirt or metal particles clinging to the dipstick, the oil should be changed (see Section 6).

ENGINE COOLANT

▶ Refer to illustration 4.9

✳✳ WARNING:

Do not allow antifreeze to come in contact with your skin or painted surfaces of the vehicle. Flush contaminated areas immediately with plenty of water. Don't store new coolant or leave old coolant lying around where it's accessible to children or pets – they're attracted by its sweet smell. Ingestion of even a small amount of coolant can be fatal! Wipe up garage floor and drip pan spills immediately. Keep antifreeze containers covered and repair cooling system leaks as soon as they're noticed.

8 All vehicles covered by this manual are equipped with a coolant recovery system. A white plastic coolant reservoir is located at the front of the engine compartment and is connected by a hose to the radiator filler neck. If the coolant heats up sufficiently during operation, in excess of the radiator cap pressure rating, it can escape past the filler cap and in to the reservoir. As the engine cools, the coolant is drawn back into the cooling system to maintain the correct level.

9 The coolant level in the reservoir should be checked regularly.

✳✳ WARNING:

Do not remove the radiator cap to check the coolant level when the engine is warm!

4.5 Turn the oil filler cap counterclockwise to remove it

4.9 Maintain the coolant level between the MIN and MAX marks on the reservoir

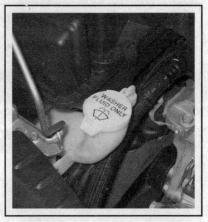

4.14 The windshield washer fluid reservoir is located in the right (passenger's) side of the engine compartment

The level in the reservoir varies with the temperature of the engine. When the engine is cold, the coolant level should be slightly above the ADD mark on the reservoir. Once the engine has warmed up, the level should be at or near the FULL HOT mark. If it isn't, allow the engine to cool, then remove the cap from the tank and add a 50/50 mixture of ethylene glycol based antifreeze and water (see illustration).

10 Drive the vehicle and recheck the coolant level. If only a small amount of coolant is required to bring the system up to the proper level, water can be used. However, repeated additions of water will dilute the antifreeze and water solution. In order to maintain the proper ratio of antifreeze and water, always top up the coolant level with the correct mixture. Don't use rust inhibitors or additives. An empty plastic milk jug or bleach bottle makes an excellent container for mixing coolant.

11 If the coolant level drops consistently, there may be a leak in the system. Inspect the radiator, hoses, filler cap, drain plugs and water pump (see Section 12). If no leaks are noted, have the pressure cap pressure tested by a service station.

12 If you have to remove the radiator cap, wait until the engine has cooled completely, then wrap a thick cloth around the cap and turn it to the first stop. If coolant or steam escapes, or if you hear a hissing noise, let the engine cool down longer, then remove the cap.

13 Check the condition of the coolant as well. It should be relatively clear. If it's brown or rust colored, the system should be drained, flushed and refilled. Even if the coolant appears to be normal, the corrosion inhibitors wear out, so it must be replaced at the specified intervals.

WINDSHIELD AND REAR WINDOW WASHER FLUID

▶ **Refer to illustration 4.14**

14 The fluid for the windshield and rear window washer system is stored in a plastic reservoir which is located at the right front corner of the engine compartment (see illustration). The reservoir level should be maintained about one inch (25 mm) below the filler cap.

15 In milder climates, plain water can be used in the reservoir, but it should be kept no more than two-thirds full to allow for expansion if the water freezes. In colder climates, use windshield washer system antifreeze, available at any auto parts store, to lower the freezing point of the fluid. Mix the antifreeze with water in accordance with the manufacturer's directions on the container.

4.17 Brake fluid level, indicated on the translucent white plastic brake fluid reservoir, should be kept at the upper (FULL) mark

※※ **CAUTION:**

DO NOT use cooling system antifreeze - it will damage the vehicle's paint.

To help prevent icing in cold weather, warm the windshield with the defroster before using the washer.

BRAKE FLUID

▶ **Refer to illustration 4.17**

16 The brake fluid reservoir is located on top of the brake master cylinder on the driver's side of the engine compartment near the firewall.

17 The fluid level should be maintained at the upper (FULL or MAX) mark on reservoir (see illustration).

18 If additional fluid is necessary to bring the level up, use a rag to clean all dirt off the top of the reservoir to prevent contamination of the system. Also, make sure all painted surfaces around the reservoir are covered, since brake fluid will ruin paint. Carefully pour new, clean brake fluid obtained from a sealed container into the reservoir. Be sure the specified fluid is used; mixing different types of brake fluid can cause damage to the system. See *Recommended lubricants and fluids* at the end of this Chapter or your owner's manual.

4.24 Location of the power steering fluid reservoir

19 At this time the fluid and the master cylinder should be inspected for contamination. Normally the brake hydraulic system won't need periodic draining and refilling, but if rust deposits, dirt particles or water droplets are observed in the fluid, the system should be dismantled, cleaned and refilled with fresh fluid. Over time brake fluid will absorb moisture from the air. Moisture in the fluid lowers the fluid boiling point; if the fluid boils, the brakes will become ineffective. Normal brake fluid is clear in color. If the brake fluid is dark brown in color, it's a good idea to replace it (see Chapter 9).

20 Reinstall the fluid reservoir cap.

21 The brake fluid in the master cylinder will drop slightly as the brake lining material at each wheel wears down during normal operation. If the master cylinder requires repeated replenishing to maintain the correct level, there is a leak in the brake system that should be corrected immediately. Check all brake lines and connections, along with the calipers (disc brakes), wheel cylinders (drum brakes) and power brake booster (see Section 14 and Chapter 9 for more information).

22 If you discover that the reservoir is empty or nearly empty, the system should be thoroughly inspected, refilled and then bled (see Chapter 9 for brake system bleeding).

POWER STEERING FLUID

♦ **Refer to illustrations 4.24 and 4.26**

23 Check the power steering fluid level periodically to avoid steering system problems, such as damage to the pump.

✳✳ CAUTION:

DO NOT hold the steering wheel against either stop (extreme left or right turn) for more than five seconds. If you do, the power steering pump could be damaged.

24 The power steering reservoir, located on top of the left end of the engine (see illustration).

25 For the check, the front wheels should be pointed straight ahead and the engine should be off.

26 The reservoir has ADD and FILL RANGE fluid level marks on the side. The fluid level can be seen without removing the reservoir cap (see illustration).

4.26 At normal operating temperature, the power steering fluid level should be between the FILL RANGE marks

27 If additional fluid is required, pour the specified type directly into the reservoir, using a funnel to prevent spills.

28 If the reservoir requires frequent fluid additions, all power steering hoses, hose connections, steering gear and the power steering pump should be carefully checked for leaks.

AUTOMATIC TRANSAXLE

♦ **Refer to illustrations 4.31 and 4.34**

29 The automatic transaxle fluid level should be carefully maintained. Low fluid level can lead to slipping or loss of drive, while overfilling can cause foaming and loss of fluid.

30 With the parking brake set, start the engine, then move the shift lever through all the gear ranges, ending in Neutral. The fluid level must be checked with the vehicle level and the engine running at idle.

➡**Note: Incorrect fluid level readings will result if the vehicle has just been driven at high speeds for an extended period, in hot weather in city traffic, or if it has been pulling a trailer. If any of these conditions apply, wait until the fluid has cooled (about 30 minutes).**

31 With the transaxle at normal operating temperature, remove the dipstick from the filler tube. The dipstick is located on the left side of the engine compartment (see illustration).

➡**Note: Normal operating temperature is after a few miles of driving.**

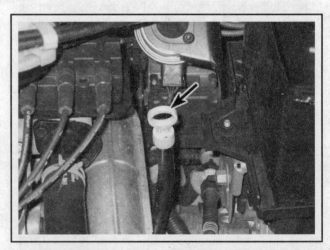

4.31 The automatic transaxle dipstick is located at the left end of the engine

32 Wipe the fluid from the dipstick with a clean rag and push it back into the filler tube until the cap seats.

33 Pull the dipstick out again and note the fluid level.

34 At normal operating temperature, the fluid level should be between the two upper reference holes (HOT) (see illustration). If additional fluid is required, add it directly into the tube using a funnel. Add the fluid a little at a time and keep checking the level until it's correct.

➡Note: **Wait at least two minutes before rechecking the fluid level allowing the fluid to fully drain into the transaxle.**

35 The condition of the fluid should also be checked along with the level. If the fluid at the end of the dipstick is a dark reddish-brown color, or if it smells burned, it should be changed. If you are in doubt about the condition of the fluid, purchase some new fluid and compare the two for color and smell.

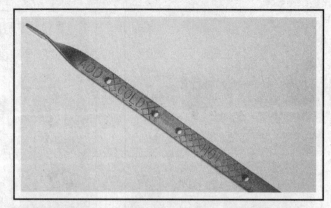

4.34 Check the fluid with the transaxle at normal operating temperature - the level should be kept in the HOT range

5   Tire and tire pressure checks (every 250 miles or weekly)

▶ **Refer to illustrations 5.2, 5.3, 5.4a, 5.4b and 5.8**

1 Periodic inspection of the tires may spare you the inconvenience of being stranded with a flat tire. It can also provide you with vital information regarding possible problems in the steering and suspension systems before major damage occurs.

2 The original tires on this vehicle are equipped with 1/2-inch wide bands that will appear when tread depth reaches 1/16-inch, at which point they can be considered worn out. Tread wear can be monitored with a simple, inexpensive device known as a tread depth indicator (see illustration).

3 Note any abnormal tread wear (see illustration). Tread pattern irregularities such as cupping, flat spots and more wear on one side than the other are indications of front end alignment and/or balance problems. If any of these conditions are noted, take the vehicle to a tire shop or service station to correct the problem.

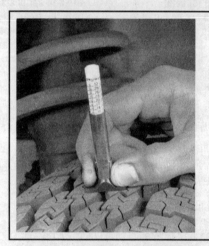

5.2 A tire tread depth indicator should be used to monitor tire wear - they are available at auto parts stores and service stations and cost very little

UNDERINFLATION

CUPPING

Cupping may be caused by:
- Underinflation and/or mechanical irregularities such as out-of-balance condition of wheel and/or tire, and bent or damaged wheel.
- Loose or worn steering tie-rod or steering idler arm.
- Loose, damaged or worn front suspension parts.

OVERINFLATION

5.3 This chart will help you determine the condition of your tires, the probable cause(s) of abnormal wear and the corrective action necessary

INCORRECT TOE-IN OR EXTREME CAMBER

FEATHERING DUE TO MISALIGNMENT

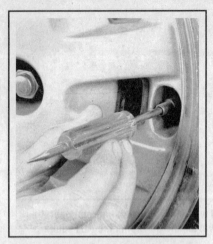

5.4a If a tire loses air on a steady basis, check the valve core first to make sure it's snug (special inexpensive wrenches are commonly available at auto parts stores)

5.4b If the valve core is tight, raise the corner of the vehicle with the low tire and spray a soapy water solution onto the tread as the tire is turned slowly - slow leaks will cause small bubbles to appear

5.8 To extend the life of your tires, check the air pressure at least once a week with an accurate gauge (don't forget the spare!)

4   Look closely for cuts, punctures and embedded nails or tacks. Sometimes a tire will hold air pressure for a short time or leak down very slowly after a nail has embedded itself in the tread. If a slow leak persists, check the valve stem core to make sure it is tight (see illustration). Examine the tread for an object that may have embedded itself in the tire or for a plug that may have begun to leak (radial tire punctures are repaired with a plug that is installed in a puncture). If a puncture is suspected, it can be easily verified by spraying a solution of soapy water onto the puncture area (see illustration). The soapy solution will bubble if there is a leak. Unless the puncture is unusually large, a tire shop or service station can usually repair the tire.

5   Carefully inspect the inner sidewall of each tire for evidence of brake fluid leakage. If you see any, inspect the brakes immediately.

6   Correct air pressure adds miles to the life span of the tires, improves mileage and enhances overall ride quality. Tire pressure cannot be accurately estimated by looking at a tire, especially if it's a radial.

A tire pressure gauge is essential. Keep an accurate gauge in the glove compartment. The pressure gauges attached to the nozzles of air hoses at gas stations are often inaccurate.

7   Always check tire pressure when the tires are cold. Cold, in this case, means the vehicle has not been driven over a mile in the three hours preceding a tire pressure check. A pressure rise of four to eight pounds is not uncommon once the tires are warm.

8   Unscrew the valve cap protruding from the wheel or hubcap and push the gauge firmly onto the valve stem (see illustration). Note the reading on the gauge and compare the figure to the recommended tire pressure shown on the tire placard on the driver's side door. Be sure to reinstall the valve cap to keep dirt and moisture out of the valve stem mechanism. Check all four tires and, if necessary, add enough air to bring them up to the recommended pressure.

9   Don't forget to keep the spare tire inflated to the specified pressure (refer to the pressure molded into the tire sidewall).

6   Engine oil and filter change (every 3000 miles or 3 months)

▶ Refer to illustrations 6.2, 6.7, 6.12 and 6.14

1   Frequent oil changes are the best preventive maintenance the home mechanic can give the engine, because aging oil becomes diluted and contaminated, which leads to premature engine wear.

2   Make sure you have all the necessary tools before you begin this procedure (see illustration). You should also have plenty of rags or newspapers handy for mopping up any spills.

3   Access to the underside of the vehicle is greatly improved if the vehicle can be lifted on a hoist, driven onto ramps or supported by jackstands.

❋❋ WARNING:

Do not work under a vehicle which is supported only by a bumper, hydraulic or scissors-type jack.

4   If this is your first oil change, get under the vehicle and familiar-

ize yourself with the locations of the oil drain plug and the oil filter. The engine and exhaust components will be warm during the actual work, so try to anticipate any potential problems before the engine and accessories are hot.

5   Park the vehicle on a level spot. Start the engine and allow it to reach its normal operating temperature. Warm oil and sludge will flow out more easily. Turn off the engine when it's warmed up. Remove the filler cap from the valve cover.

6   Raise the vehicle and support it securely on jackstands.

❋❋ WARNING:

Never get beneath the vehicle when it is supported only by a jack. The jack provided with your vehicle is designed solely for raising the vehicle to remove and replace the wheels. Always use jackstands to support the vehicle when it becomes necessary to place your body underneath the vehicle.

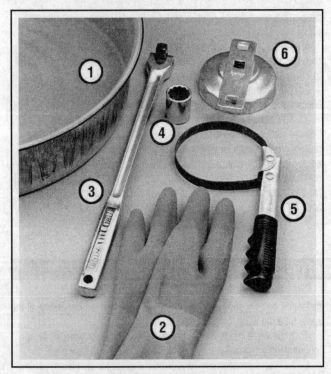

6.2 These tools are required when changing the engine oil and filter

1   **Drain pan** - It should be fairly shallow in depth, but wide in order to prevent spills
2   **Rubber gloves** - When removing the drain plug and filter, it is inevitable that you will get oil on your hands (the gloves will prevent burns)
3   **Breaker bar** - Sometimes the oil drain plug is pretty tight and a long breaker bar is needed to loosen it
4   **Socket** - To be used with the breaker bar or a ratchet (must be the correct size to fit the drain plug)
5   **Filter wrench** - This is a metal band-type wrench, which requires clearance around the filter to be effective
6   **Filter wrench** - This type fits on the bottom of the filter and can be turned with a ratchet or beaker bar (different size wrenches are available for different types of filters)

7   Being careful not to touch the hot exhaust components, place the drain pan under the drain plug in the bottom of the pan and remove the plug (see illustration). You may want to wear gloves while unscrewing the plug the final few turns if the engine is hot.

8   Allow the old oil to drain into the pan. It may be necessary to move the pan farther under the engine as the oil flow slows to a trickle. Inspect the old oil for the presence of metal shavings and chips.

9   After all the oil has drained, wipe off the drain plug with a clean rag. Even minute metal particles clinging to the plug would immediately contaminate the new oil.

10   Clean the area around the drain plug opening, reinstall the plug and tighten it securely, but do not strip the threads.

11   Move the drain pan into position under the oil filter.

12   Loosen the oil filter (see illustration) by turning it counterclockwise with an oil filter wrench. Once the filter is loose, use your hands to unscrew it from the block. Keep the open end pointing up to prevent the oil inside the filter from spilling out.

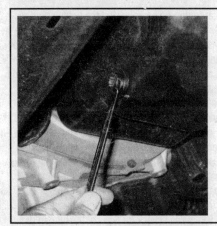

6.7 Use a proper size box-end wrench or socket to remove the oil drain plug and avoid rounding it off

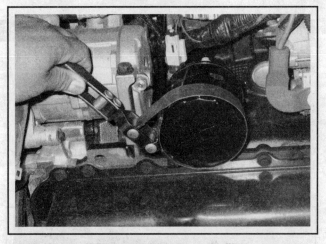

6.12 Use an oil filter wrench to remove the filter

❋❋ **WARNING:**

The exhaust system may still be hot, so be careful.

13   With a clean rag, wipe off the mounting surface on the block. If a residue of old oil is allowed to remain, it will smoke when the block is heated up. Also make sure that none of the old gasket remains stuck to the mounting surface. It can be removed with a scraper if necessary.

14   Compare the old filter with the new one to make sure they are the same type. Smear some clean engine oil on the rubber gasket of the new filter (see illustration).

6.14 Lubricate the oil filter gasket with clean engine oil before installing the filter on the engine

15 Attach the new filter to the engine, following the tightening directions printed on the filter canister or packing box. Most filter manufacturers recommend against using a filter wrench due to the possibility of overtightening and damaging the seal.

16 Remove all tools, rags, etc. from under the vehicle, being careful not to spill the oil in the drain pan, then lower the vehicle.

17 Add new oil to the engine through the oil filler cap in the valve cover. Use a funnel, if necessary, to prevent oil from spilling onto the top of the engine. Pour three quarts of fresh oil into the engine. Wait a few minutes to allow the oil to drain into the pan, then check the level on the oil dipstick (see Section 4). If the oil level is at or near the FULL mark on the dipstick, install the filler cap hand tight, start the engine and allow the new oil to circulate.

18 Allow the engine to run for about a minute. While the engine is running, look under the vehicle and check for leaks at the oil pan drain plug and around the oil filter. If either is leaking, stop the engine and tighten the plug or filter.

19 Wait a few minutes to allow the oil to trickle down into the pan, then recheck the level on the dipstick and, if necessary, add enough oil to bring the level to the FULL mark.

20 During the first few trips after an oil change, make it a point to check frequently for leaks and proper oil level.

21 The old oil drained from the engine cannot be reused in its present state and should be disposed of. Check with your local auto parts store, disposal facility or environmental agency to see if they will accept the oil for recycling. After the oil has cooled it can be drained into a container (capped plastic jugs, topped bottles, milk cartons, etc.) for transport to one of these disposal sites. Don't dispose of the oil by pouring it on the ground or down a drain!

7 Windshield wiper blade inspection and replacement (every 6,000 miles or 6 months)

▶ **Refer to illustrations 7.5a and 7.5b**

1 The windshield wiper and blade assembly should be inspected periodically for damage, loose components and cracked or worn blade elements.

2 Road film can build up on the wiper blades and affect their efficiency, so they should be washed regularly with a mild detergent solution.

3 The action of the wiping mechanism can loosen bolts, nuts and fasteners, so they should be checked and tightened, as necessary, at the same time the wiper blades are checked.

4 If the wiper blade elements are cracked, worn or warped, or no longer clean adequately, they should be replaced with new ones.

5 Lift the arm assembly away from the glass for clearance, press the release lever, then slide the wiper blade assembly out of the hook at the end of the arm (see illustrations).

6 Attach the new wiper to the arm. Connection can be confirmed by an audible click.

7.5a To release the blade holder, push the release lever . . .

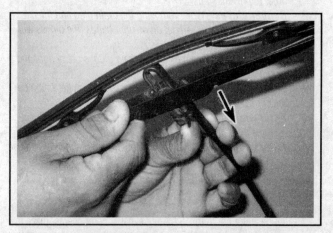

7.5b . . . and pull the wiper blade in the direction of the arrow to separate it from the arm

8 Battery check, maintenance and charging (every 6,000 miles or 6 months)

▶ **Refer to illustrations 8.1, 8.6a, 8.6b, 8.7a and 8.7b**

✳✳ **WARNING:**

Certain precautions must be followed when checking and servicing the battery. Hydrogen gas, which is highly flammable, is always present in the battery cells, so keep lighted tobacco and all other open flames and sparks away from the battery. The electrolyte inside the battery is actually diluted sulfuric acid, which will cause injury if splashed on your skin or in your eyes.

It will also ruin clothes and painted surfaces. When removing the battery cables, always detach the negative cable first and hook it up last!

1 A routine preventive maintenance program for the battery in your vehicle is the only way to ensure quick and reliable starts. But before performing any battery maintenance, make sure that you have the proper equipment necessary to work safely around the battery (see illustration).

8.1 Tools and materials required for battery maintenance

1   **Face shield/safety goggles** - *When removing corrosion with a brush, the acidic particles can easily fly up into your eyes*
2   **Baking soda** - *A solution of baking soda and water can be used to neutralize corrosion*
3   **Petroleum jelly** - *A layer of this on the battery posts will help prevent corrosion*
4   **Battery post/cable cleaner** - *This wire brush cleaning tool will remove all traces of corrosion from the battery posts and cable clamps*
5   **Treated felt washers** - *Placing one of these on each post, directly under the cable clamps, will help prevent corrosion*
6   **Puller** - *Sometimes the cable clamps are very difficult to pull off the posts, even after the nut/bolt has been completely loosened. This tool pulls the clamp straight up and off the post without damage*
7   **Battery post/cable cleaner** - *Here is another cleaning tool which is a slightly different version of number 4 above, but it does the same thing*
8   **Rubber gloves** - *Another safety item to consider when servicing the battery; remember that's acid inside the battery*

2   There are also several precautions that should be taken whenever battery maintenance is performed. Before servicing the battery, always turn the engine and all accessories off and disconnect the cable from the negative terminal of the battery (see Chapter 5, Section 1).

3   The battery produces hydrogen gas, which is both flammable and explosive. Never create a spark, smoke or light a match around the battery. Always charge the battery in a ventilated area.

4   Electrolyte contains poisonous and corrosive sulfuric acid. Do not allow it to get in your eyes, on your skin on your clothes. Never ingest it. Wear protective safety glasses when working near the battery. Keep children away from the battery.

5   Note the external condition of the battery. If the positive terminal and cable clamp on your vehicle's battery is equipped with a rubber protector, make sure that it's not torn or damaged. It should completely

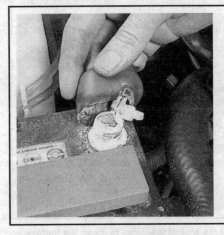

8.6a Battery terminal corrosion usually appears as light, fluffy powder

8.6b Removing a cable from the battery post with a wrench - sometimes a pair of special battery pliers are required for this procedure if corrosion has caused deterioration of the nut hex (always remove the ground (-) cable first and hook it up last!)

cover the terminal. Look for any corroded or loose connections, cracks in the case or cover or loose hold-down clamps. Also check the entire length of each cable for cracks and frayed conductors.

6   If corrosion, which looks like white, fluffy deposits (see illustration) is evident, particularly around the terminals, the battery should be removed for cleaning. Loosen the cable clamp bolts with a wrench, being careful to remove the ground cable first, and slide them off the terminals (see illustration). Then disconnect the hold-down clamp bolt and nut, remove the clamp and lift the battery from the engine compartment.

7   Clean the cable clamps thoroughly with a battery brush or a terminal cleaner and a solution of warm water and baking soda (see

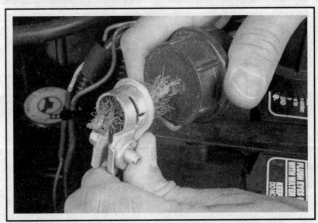

8.7a When cleaning the cable clamps, all corrosion must be removed (the inside of the clamp is tapered to match the taper on the post, so don't remove too much material)

8.7b Regardless of the type of tool used to clean the battery posts, a clean, shiny surface should be the result

illustration). Wash the terminals and the top of the battery case with the same solution but make sure that the solution doesn't get into the battery. When cleaning the cables, terminals and battery top, wear safety goggles and rubber gloves to prevent any solution from coming in contact with your eyes or hands. Wear old clothes too - even diluted, sulfuric acid splashed onto clothes will burn holes in them. If the terminals have been extensively corroded, clean them up with a terminal cleaner (see illustration). Thoroughly wash all cleaned areas with plain water.

8 Make sure that the battery tray is in good condition and the hold-down clamp fasteners are tight. If the battery is removed from the tray, make sure no parts remain in the bottom of the tray when the battery is reinstalled. When reinstalling the hold-down clamp bolts, do not over-tighten them.

9 Information on removing and installing the battery can be found in Chapter 5. If you disconnected the cable(s) from the negative and/or positive battery terminals, see Chapter 5, Section 1. Information on jump starting can be found at the front of this manual.

CLEANING

10 Corrosion on the hold-down components, battery case and surrounding areas can be removed with a solution of water and baking soda. Thoroughly rinse all cleaned areas with plain water.

11 Any metal parts of the vehicle damaged by corrosion should be covered with a zinc-based primer, then painted.

CHARGING

※ WARNING:

When batteries are being charged, hydrogen gas, which is very explosive and flammable, is produced. Do not smoke or allow open flames near a charging or a recently charged battery. Wear eye protection when near the battery during charging. Also, make sure the charger is unplugged before connecting or disconnecting the battery from the charger.

12 Slow-rate charging is the best way to restore a battery that's discharged to the point where it will not start the engine. It's also a good way to maintain the battery charge in a vehicle that's only driven a few miles between starts. Maintaining the battery charge is particularly important in the winter when the battery must work harder to start the engine and electrical accessories that drain the battery are in greater use.

13 It's best to use a one or two-amp battery charger (sometimes called a "trickle" charger). They are the safest and put the least strain on the battery. They are also the least expensive. For a faster charge, you can use a higher amperage charger, but don't use one rated more than 1/10th the amp/hour rating of the battery. Rapid boost charges that claim to restore the power of the battery in one to two hours are hardest on the battery and can damage batteries not in good condition. This type of charging should only be used in emergency situations.

14 The average time necessary to charge a battery should be listed in the instructions that come with the charger. As a general rule, a trickle charger will charge a battery in 12 to 16 hours.

9 Tire rotation (every 6,000 miles or 6 months)

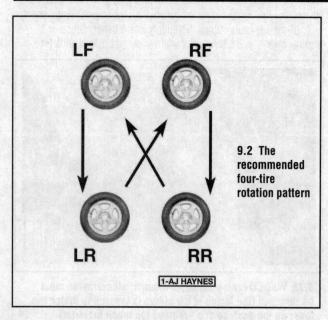

9.2 The recommended four-tire rotation pattern

1-AJ HAYNES

▶ **Refer to illustration 9.2**

1 The tires should be rotated at the specified intervals and whenever uneven wear is noticed.

2 Refer to the accompanying illustration for the preferred tire rotation pattern.

3 Refer to the information in *Jacking and towing* at the front of this manual for the proper procedures to follow when raising the vehicle and changing a tire. If the brakes are to be checked, don't apply the parking brake as stated. Make sure the tires are blocked to prevent the vehicle from rolling as it's raised.

4 Preferably, the entire vehicle should be raised at the same time. This can be done on a hoist or by jacking up each corner and then lowering the vehicle onto jackstands placed under the frame rails. Always use four jackstands and make sure the vehicle is safely supported.

5 After rotation, check and adjust the tire pressures as necessary. Tighten the lug nuts to the torque listed in this Chapter's Specifications.

10 Seat belt check (every 6,000 miles or 6 months)

1   Check seat belts, buckles, latch plates and guide loops for obvious damage and signs of wear.

2   Where the seat belt receptacle bolts to the floor of the vehicle, check that the bolts are secure.

3   See if the seat belt reminder light comes on when the key is turned to the Run or Start position.

11 Underhood hose check and replacement (every 6,000 miles or 6 months)

GENERAL

✷✷ CAUTION:

Replacement of air conditioning hoses must be left to a dealer service department or air conditioning shop that has the equipment to depressurize the system safely and recover the refrigerant. Never remove air conditioning components or hoses until the system has been depressurized.

1   High temperatures in the engine compartment can cause the deterioration of the rubber and plastic hoses used for engine, accessory and emission systems operation. Periodic inspection should be made for cracks, loose clamps, material hardening and leaks. Information specific to the cooling system hoses can be found in Section 12.

2   Some, but not all, hoses are secured to their fittings with clamps. Where clamps are used, check to be sure they haven't lost their tension, allowing the hose to leak. If clamps aren't used, make sure the hose has not expanded and/or hardened where it slips over the fitting, allowing it to leak.

VACUUM HOSES

3   It's quite common for vacuum hoses, especially those in the emissions system, to be color-coded or identified by colored stripes molded into them. Various systems require hoses with different wall thickness, collapse resistance and temperature resistance. When replacing hoses, be sure the new ones are made of the same material.

4   Often the only effective way to check a hose is to remove it completely from the vehicle. If more than one hose is removed, be sure to label the hoses and fittings to ensure correct installation.

5   When checking vacuum hoses, be sure to include any plastic T-fittings in the check. Inspect the fittings for cracks and the hose where it fits over the fitting for distortion, which could cause leakage.

6   A small piece of vacuum hose (1/4-inch inside diameter) can be used as a stethoscope to detect vacuum leaks. Hold one end of the hose to your ear and probe around vacuum hoses and fittings, listening for the "hissing" sound characteristic of a vacuum leak.

✷✷ WARNING:

When probing with the vacuum hose stethoscope, be very careful not to come into contact with moving engine components such as the drivebelt, cooling fan, etc.

FUEL HOSE

✷✷ WARNING:

There are certain precautions that must be taken when inspecting or servicing fuel system components. Work in a well-ventilated area and do not allow open flames (cigarettes, appliances, etc.) or bare light bulbs near the work area. Mop up any spills immediately and do not store fuel soaked rags where they could ignite. The fuel system is under high pressure, so if any fuel lines are to be disconnected, the pressure in the system must be relieved first (see Chapter 4 for more information).

7   Check all rubber fuel lines for deterioration and chafing. Check especially for cracks in areas where the hose bends and just before fittings, such as where a hose attaches to the fuel filter.

8   High quality fuel line, made specifically for high-pressure fuel injection systems, must be used for fuel line replacement. Never, under any circumstances, use unreinforced vacuum line, clear plastic tubing or water hose for fuel lines.

9   Spring-type clamps are commonly used on fuel lines. These clamps often lose their tension over a period of time, and can be "sprung" during removal. Replace all spring-type clamps with screw clamps whenever a hose is replaced.

METAL LINES

10 Sections of metal line are routed along the frame, between the fuel tank and the engine. Check carefully to be sure the line has not been bent or crimped and that cracks have not started in the line.

11 If a section of metal fuel line must be replaced, only seamless steel tubing should be used, since copper and aluminum tubing don't have the strength necessary to withstand normal engine vibration.

12 Check the metal brake lines where they enter the master cylinder and brake proportioning unit for cracks in the lines or loose fittings. Any sign of brake fluid leakage calls for an immediate and thorough inspection of the brake system.

12 Cooling system check (every 6,000 miles or 6 months)

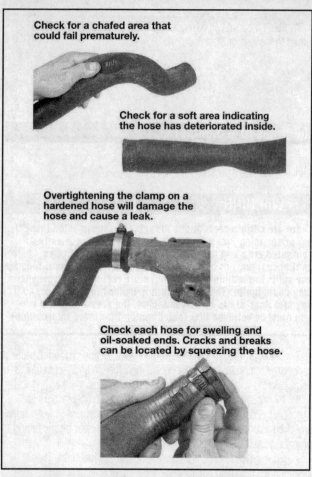

Check for a chafed area that could fail prematurely.

Check for a soft area indicating the hose has deteriorated inside.

Overtightening the clamp on a hardened hose will damage the hose and cause a leak.

Check each hose for swelling and oil-soaked ends. Cracks and breaks can be located by squeezing the hose.

12.4 Hoses, like drivebelts, have a habit of failing at the worst possible time - to prevent the inconvenience of a blown radiator or heater hose, inspect them carefully as shown here

▶ **Refer to illustration 12.4**

1   Many major engine failures can be attributed to a faulty cooling system. Since the vehicle is equipped with an automatic transaxle, the cooling system also cools the transaxle fluid and thus plays an important role in prolonging transaxle life.

2   The cooling system should be checked with the engine cold. Do this before the vehicle is driven for the day or after it has been shut off for at least three hours.

3   Remove the radiator pressure cap and thoroughly clean the cap, inside and out, with clean water. Also clean the filler neck on the radiator. All traces of corrosion should be removed. The coolant inside the radiator should be relatively transparent. If it is rust-colored, the system should be drained, flushed and refilled (see Section 24). If the coolant level is not up to the top, add additional anti freeze/coolant mixture (see Section 4).

4   Carefully check the large upper and lower radiator hoses along with the smaller diameter heater hoses that run from the engine to the firewall. Inspect each hose along its entire length, replacing any hose that is cracked, swollen or shows signs of deterioration. Cracks may become more apparent if the hose is squeezed (see illustration). Regardless of condition, it's a good idea to replace hoses with new ones every two years.

5   Make sure all hose connections are tight. A leak in the cooling system will usually show up as white or rust-colored deposits on the areas adjoining the leak. If wire-type clamps are used at the ends of the hoses, it may be a good idea to replace them with more secure screw-type clamps.

6   Use compressed air or a soft brush to remove bugs, leaves, etc. from the front of the radiator or air conditioning condenser. Be careful not to damage the delicate cooling fins or cut yourself on them.

7   Every other inspection, or at the first indication of cooling system problems, have the cap and system pressure tested. If you don't have a pressure tester, most repair shops will do this for a minimal charge.

13 Air filter check and replacement (every 6,000 miles 6 months)

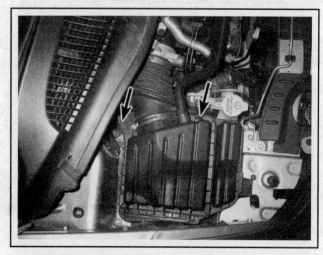

13.1a Loosen the clamp (A) and detach the intake duct, release the spring clips (B) . . .

▶ **Refer to illustrations 13.1a and 13.1b**

1   The air filter is located inside a housing at the right (passenger's) side of the engine compartment. To remove the air filter, loosen the clamp securing the inlet tube to the air filter cover, release the clamps that secure the two halves of the air cleaner housing together, then separate the cover halves and remove the air filter element (see illustrations).

2   Inspect the outer surface of the filter element. If it is dirty, replace it. If it is only moderately dusty, it can be reused by blowing it clean from the back to the front surface with compressed air. Because it is a pleated paper type filter, it cannot be washed or oiled. If it cannot be cleaned satisfactorily with compressed air, discard and replace it. While the cover is off, be careful not to drop anything down into the housing.

3   Wipe out the inside of the air cleaner housing.

4   Place the new filter into the air cleaner housing, making sure it seats properly.

5   Installation of the housing is the reverse of removal.

13.1b . . . then lift the air filter housing cover and remove the air filter element

14 Brake system check (every 12,000 miles or 12 months)

> ※※ **WARNING:**
>
> The dust created by the brake system is harmful to your health. Never blow it out with compressed air and don't inhale any of it. An approved filtering mask should be worn when working on the brakes. Do not, under any circumstances, use petroleum-based solvents to clean brake parts. Use brake system cleaner only!

➡Note: For detailed photographs of the brake system, refer to Chapter 9.

1   In addition to the specified intervals, the brakes should be inspected every time the wheels are removed or whenever a defect is suspected.

2   Any of the following symptoms could indicate a potential brake system defect: The vehicle pulls to one side when the brake pedal is depressed; the brakes make squealing or dragging noises when applied; brake pedal travel is excessive; the pedal pulsates; or brake fluid leaks, usually onto the inside of the tire or wheel.

DISC BRAKES

◆ Refer to illustrations 14.6a and 14.6b

3   Disc brakes can be visually checked without removing any parts except the wheels. Remove the hub caps (if applicable) and loosen the wheel lug nuts a quarter turn each.

4   Raise the vehicle and place it securely on jackstands.

> ※※ **WARNING:**
>
> Never work under a vehicle that is supported only by a jack!

5   Remove the wheels. Now visible is the disc brake caliper which contains the pads. There is an outer brake pad and an inner pad. Both must be checked for wear.

6   Measure the thickness of the outer pad at each end of the caliper and the inner pad through the inspection hole in the caliper body (see illustrations). Compare the measurement with the limit given in this Chapter's Specifications; if any brake pad thickness is less than speci-

14.6a With the wheel off, check the thickness of the inner pad through the inspection hole

14.6b The outer pad is more easily checked at the edge of the caliper

fied, then all brake pads must be replaced (see Chapter 9).

7   If you're in doubt as to the exact pad thickness or quality, remove them for measurement and further inspection (see Chapter 9).

8   Check the disc for score marks, wear and burned spots. If any of these conditions exist, the disc should be removed for servicing or

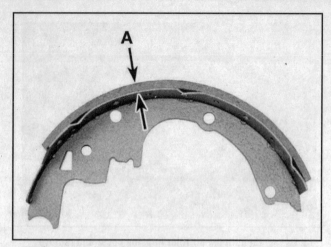

14.14 If the lining is bonded to the brake shoe, measure the lining thickness (A) from the outer surface to the metal shoe; if the lining is riveted to the shoe, measure from the lining outer surface to the rivet head

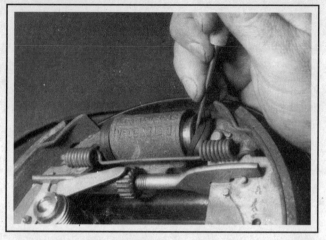

14.16 Use a small screwdriver to carefully pry the boot away from the cylinder and check for fluid leakage

replacement (see Chapter 9).

9 Before installing the wheels, check all the brake lines and hoses for damage, wear, deformation, cracks, corrosion, leakage, bends and twists, particularly in the vicinity of the rubber hoses and calipers.

10 Install the wheels, lower the vehicle and tighten the wheel lug nuts to the torque given in this Chapter's Specifications.

DRUM BRAKES

▶ **Refer to illustrations 14.14 and 14.16**

11 On models with rear drum brakes, make sure the parking brake is released, then tap on the outside of the drum with a rubber mallet to loosen it.

12 Remove the brake drums. If the drum still won't come off, refer to Chapter 9 and retract the brake shoes.

13 With the drums removed, carefully clean the brake assembly with brake system cleaner.

✳✳ WARNING:

Don't blow the dust out with compressed air and don't inhale any of it (it is harmful to your health).

14 Note the thickness of the lining material on both front and rear brake shoes (see illustration). Compare the measurement with the limit given in this Chapter's Specifications; if any lining thickness is less than specified, then all of the brake shoes must be replaced (see Chapter 9). The shoes should also be replaced if they're cracked, glazed (shiny areas), or covered with brake fluid.

15 Make sure all the brake assembly springs are connected and in

good condition.

16 Check the brake components for signs of fluid leakage. With your finger or a small screwdriver, carefully pry back the rubber cups on the wheel cylinder located at the top of the brake shoes (see illustration). Any leakage here is an indication that the wheel cylinders should be replaced immediately (see Chapter 9). Also, check all hoses and connections for signs of leakage.

17 Wipe the inside of the drum with a clean rag and denatured alcohol or brake cleaner. Again, be careful not to breathe the dust.

18 Check the inside of the drum for cracks, score marks, deep scratches and "hard spots" which will appear as small discolored areas. If imperfections cannot be removed with fine emery cloth, the drum must be taken to an automotive machine shop for resurfacing.

19 Repeat the procedure for the remaining wheel. If the inspection reveals that all parts are in good condition, reinstall the brake drums, install the wheels and lower the vehicle to the ground.

BRAKE BOOSTER CHECK

20 Sit in the driver's seat and perform the following sequence of tests.

21 With the brake fully depressed, start the engine - the pedal should move down a little when the engine starts.

22 With the engine running, depress the brake pedal several times - the travel distance should not change.

23 Depress the brake, stop the engine and hold the pedal in for about 30 seconds - the pedal should neither sink nor rise.

24 Restart the engine, run it for about a minute and turn it off. Then firmly depress the brake several times - the pedal travel should decrease with each application.

25 If your brakes do not operate as described, the brake booster has failed. Refer to Chapter 9 for the replacement procedure.

15 Steering, suspension and driveaxle boot check (every 12,000 miles or 12 months)

▶ Refer to illustrations 15.4, 15.10, 15.11 and 15.14

➡Note: For detailed illustrations of the steering and suspension components, refer to Chapter 10.

WITH THE WHEELS ON THE GROUND

1   With the vehicle stopped and the front wheels pointed straight ahead, rock the steering wheel gently back and forth. If freeplay is excessive, a front wheel bearing, steering shaft universal joint or lower arm balljoint is worn or the steering gear is out of adjustment or broken. Refer to Chapter 10 for the appropriate repair procedure.

2   Other symptoms, such as excessive vehicle body movement over rough roads, swaying (leaning) around corners and binding as the steering wheel is turned, may indicate faulty steering and/or suspension components.

3   Check the shock absorbers by pushing down and releasing the vehicle several times at each corner. If the vehicle does not come back to a level position within one or two bounces, the shocks/struts are worn and must be replaced. When bouncing the vehicle up and down, listen for squeaks and noises from the suspension components.

4   Check the struts and shock absorbers for evidence of fluid leakage (see illustration). A light film of fluid is no cause for concern. Make sure that any fluid noted is from the struts/shocks and not from some other source. If leakage is noted, replace the struts/shocks as a set.

5   Check the struts and shocks to be sure they are securely mounted and undamaged. Check the upper mounts for damage and wear. If damage or wear is noted, replace the shocks as a set (front and rear).

6   If the struts or shocks must be replaced, refer to Chapter 10 for the procedure.

UNDER THE VEHICLE

7   Raise the vehicle and support it securely on jackstands.

8   Check the tires for irregular wear patterns and proper inflation. See Section 5 in this Chapter for information regarding tire wear and Chapter 10 for information on wheel bearing replacement.

9   Inspect the universal joint between the steering shaft and the steering gear housing. Check the steering gear housing for lubricant leakage. Make sure that the dust seals and boots are not damaged and that the boot clamps are not loose. Check the steering linkage for looseness or damage. Check the tie-rod ends for excessive play. Look for loose bolts, broken or disconnected parts and deteriorated rubber bushings on all suspension and steering components. While an assistant turns the steering wheel from side to side, check the steering components for free movement, chafing and binding. If the steering components do not seem to be reacting with the movement of the steering wheel, try to determine where the slack is located.

10 Check the balljoints for wear by trying to move each control arm up and down with a prybar (see illustration) to ensure that its balljoint has no play. If any balljoint does have play, replace it. Try to turn the balljoint grease fitting with your fingers. If you can move the grease fitting, the balljoint is worn out. See Chapter 10 for the balljoint replacement procedure.

11 Inspect the balljoint boots for damage and leaking grease (see illustration). Replace the balljoints with new ones if they are damaged (see Chapter 10).

15.4 Check the struts and shocks for leakage at the indicated area

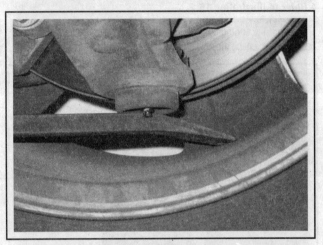

15.10 To check the balljoint for wear, try to pry the control arm up and down to make sure there is no play in the balljoint (if there is, replace it)

12 At the rear of the vehicle, inspect the suspension arm bushings for deterioration. Additional information on suspension components can be found in Chapter 10.

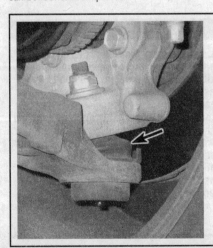

15.11 Check the balljoint boot for damage

15.14 Flex the driveaxle boots by hand to check for cracks and leaking grease

DRIVEAXLE BOOT CHECK

→Note: For detailed illustrations of the driveaxles, refer to Chapter 8.

13 The driveaxle boots are very important because they prevent dirt, water and foreign material from entering and damaging the constant velocity (CV) joints. Oil and grease can cause the boot material to deteriorate prematurely, so it's a good idea to wash the boots with soap and water. Because it constantly pivots back and forth following the steering action of the front hub, the outer CV boot wears out sooner and should be inspected regularly.

14 Inspect the boots for tears and cracks as well as loose clamps (see illustration). If there is any evidence of cracks or leaking lubricant, they must be replaced as described in Chapter 8.

16 Exhaust system check (every 12,000 miles or 12 months)

▶ Refer to illustration 16.2

1 With the engine cold (at least three hours after the vehicle has been driven), check the complete exhaust system from the engine to

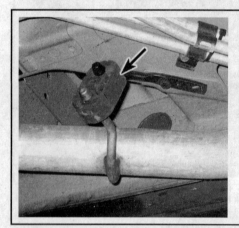

16.2 Check the exhaust system for rust, damage, or broken rubber hangers

the end of the tailpipe. Ideally, the inspection should be done with the vehicle on a hoist to permit unrestricted access. If a hoist isn't available, raise the vehicle and support it securely on jackstands.

2 Check the exhaust pipes and connections for evidence of leaks, severe corrosion and damage. Make sure that all brackets and hangers are in good condition and tight (see illustration).

3 At the same time, inspect the underside of the body for holes, corrosion, open seams, etc. which may allow exhaust gases to enter the passenger compartment. Seal all body openings with silicone or body putty.

4 Rattles and other noises can often be traced to the exhaust system, especially the mounts and hangers. Try to move the pipes, muffler and catalytic converter. If the components can come in contact with the body or suspension parts, secure the exhaust system with new mounts.

5 Check the running condition of the engine by inspecting inside the end of the tailpipe. The exhaust deposits here are an indication of engine state-of-tune. If the pipe is black and sooty or coated with white deposits, the engine may need a tune-up, including a thorough fuel system inspection and adjustment.

17 Fuel system check (every 12,000 miles or 12 months)

▶ Refer to illustration 17.6

❋❋ **WARNING:**

Gasoline is flammable, so take extra precautions when you work on any part of the fuel system. Don't smoke or allow open flames or bare light bulbs near the work area, and don't work in a garage where a gas-type appliance (such as a water heater or clothes dryer) is present. Since fuel is carcinogenic, wear fuel-resistant gloves when there's a possibility of being exposed to fuel, and, if you spill any fuel on your skin, rinse it off immediately with soap and water. Mop up any spills immediately and do not store fuel-soaked rags where they could ignite. When you perform any kind of work on the fuel system, wear safety glasses and have a Class B type fire extinguisher on hand. The fuel system is under constant pressure, so, before any lines are disconnected, the fuel system pressure must be relieved (see Chapter 4).

1 If you smell gasoline while driving or after the vehicle has been sitting in the sun, inspect the fuel system immediately.

2 Remove the fuel filler cap and inspect if for damage and corrosion. The gasket should have an unbroken sealing imprint. If the gasket is damaged or corroded, install a new cap.

3 Inspect the fuel feed line for cracks. Make sure that the connections between the fuel lines and the fuel injection system.

❋❋ **WARNING:**

Your vehicle is fuel injected, so you must relieve the fuel system pressure before servicing fuel system components. The fuel system pressure relief procedure is outlined in Chapter 4.

4 Since some components of the fuel system - the fuel tank and the fuel lines, for example - are underneath the vehicle, they can be inspected more easily with the vehicle raised on a hoist. If that's not

possible, raise the vehicle and support it on jackstands.

5   With the vehicle raised and safely supported, inspect the gas tank and filler neck for punctures, cracks and other damage. The connection between the filler neck and the tank is particularly critical. Sometimes a rubber filler neck will leak because of loose clamps or deteriorated rubber. Inspect all fuel tank mounting brackets and straps to be sure that the tank is securely attached to the vehicle.

✳✳ WARNING:

Do not, under any circumstances, try to repair a fuel tank (except rubber components). A welding torch or any open flame can easily cause fuel vapors inside the tank to explode.

6   Carefully check all hoses and lines leading away from the fuel tank. Check for loose connections, deteriorated hoses, crimped lines and other damage (see illustration). Repair or replace damaged sections as necessary (see Chapter 4).

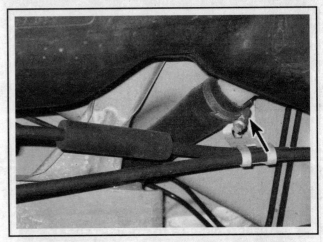

17.6 Check the fuel system hoses and clamps for damage and deterioration

18   Interior ventilation filter replacement (every 12,000 miles or 12 months)

✳✳ WARNING:

The models covered by this manual are equipped with a Supplemental Restraint System (SRS), more commonly known as airbags. Always disable the airbag system before working in the vicinity of any airbag system component to avoid the possibility of accidental deployment of the airbag, which could cause personal injury (see Chapter 12).

1   Some models are equipped with an air filtering element in the air conditioning system, located in a housing next to the evaporator, under the right side of the instrument panel.
2   Locate the air filter door latch and slide it toward the rear of the vehicle
3   Remove the filter from the air evaporator housing.
4   Installation is the reverse of the removal procedure.

19   Drivebelt check, adjustment and replacement (every 30,000 miles or 30 months)

✳✳ WARNING:

The electric cooling fan(s) on these models can activate at any time the ignition switch is in the ON position. Make sure the ignition is OFF when working in the vicinity of the fan(s).

1   The drivebelt(s) are located at the front of the engine and play an important role in the operation of the vehicle and its components. Due to their function and material makeup, the belts are prone to failure after a period of time and should be inspected and adjusted periodically to prevent major damage.

2   Four-cylinder engine models are equipped with two belts. One belt transmits power from the crankshaft to the alternator and air conditioning compressor. The power steering pump is driven by its own belt. The V6 engines use a single serpentine belt to drive all the components.

CHECK

▸ **Refer to illustrations 19.3 and 19.4**

3   With the engine off, open the hood and use your fingers (and a flashlight, if necessary), to move along the belt checking for cracks and separation of the belt plies. Also check for fraying and glazing, which gives the belt a shiny appearance. Also check the ribs on the underside of the belt. They should all be the same depth, with none of the surface uneven (see illustration).

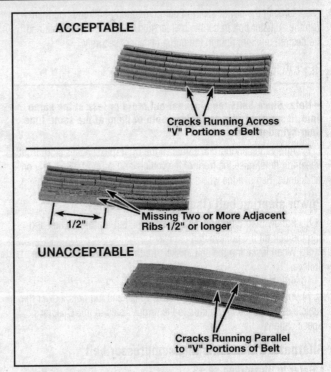

19.3 Here are some of the more common problems associated with drivebelts (check the belts very carefully to prevent an untimely breakdown)

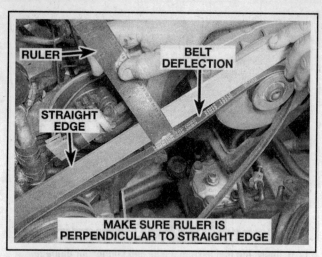

MAKE SURE RULER IS
PERPENDICULAR TO STRAIGHT EDGE

19.4 Measure the drivebelt deflection with a straightedge and ruler - make sure the ruler is perpendicular to the straightedge

4   The power steering belt tension on four-cylinder models is checked by pushing on it at a distance halfway between the pulleys. Apply about 20 pounds of force with your thumb and see how much the belt moves down (deflects). Measure the deflection with a ruler (see illustration). The belt should deflect about 1/4-inch if the distance between pulleys is between 7 and 11 inches and around 1/2-inch if the distance is between 12 and 16 inches.

5   The alternator/air conditioning compressor belt tension is adjusted by an automatic tensioner.

ADJUSTMENT (FOUR-CYLINDER ENGINE POWER STEERING BELT)

6   Loosen the power steering pump mounting bolt and nut, then turn the adjuster bolt to set the belt tension. When you have obtained the desired tension, tighten the pump fasteners securely.

REPLACEMENT

➡ **Note: Since belts tend to wear out more or less at the same time, it's a good idea to replace both of them at the same time (four-cylinder models).**

7   Apply the parking brake, loosen the right (passenger's side) front wheel lug nuts, raise the front of the vehicle and support it securely on jackstands. Remove the wheel, then remove the drivebelt splash shield.

Power steering belt (four-cylinder models)

8   Follow Step 6 for drivebelt adjustment, but loosen the belt and slip the belt off the pulleys and remove it.

9   When installing the belt, make sure the belt is centered on the pulleys.

10   Adjust the belt as described in Step 6.

11   Install the drivebelt splash shield, wheel and lug nuts. Lower the vehicle and tighten the lug nuts to the torque listed in this Chapter's Specifications.

Alternator/air conditioning compressor belt

♦ **Refer to illustration 19.13**

12   If you're working on a four-cylinder engine, remove the power steering belt (see Step 8).

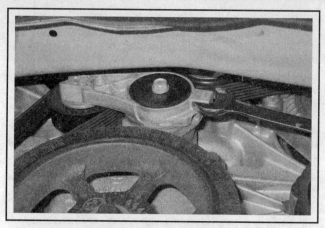

19.13 Place a wrench on the tensioner pulley lug and rotate it to relieve the belt tension (V6 engine shown)

13   The automatic tensioner must be released to allow drivebelt replacement. Place a wrench on the tensioner pulley lug and rotate it clockwise on four-cylinder engines or counterclockwise on V6 engines until the belt can be removed (see illustration). Remove the belt and slowly release the tensioner.

14   Installation is the reverse of removal. When installing the belt, make sure the belt is centered on the pulleys.

15   If you're working on a four-cylinder engine, install and adjust the power steering belt.

16   Install the drivebelt splash shield, wheel and lug nuts. Lower the vehicle and tighten the lug nuts to the torque listed in this Chapter's Specifications.

AUTOMATIC TENSIONER REPLACEMENT

♦ **Refer to illustration 19.18**

17   Remove the alternator/air conditioning compressor drivebelt (see Steps 12 and 13).

18   Unscrew the tensioner mounting bolt and remove the tensioner (see illustration).

19   Install the new tensioner assembly by reversing the removal procedure. Tighten the mounting bolt to the torque listed in this Chapter's Specifications.

20   Install the drivebelt as described previously in this Section.

21   Install the drivebelt splash shield, wheel and lug nuts. Lower the vehicle and tighten the lug nuts to the torque listed in this Chapter's Specifications.

19.18 The drivebelt tensioner is secured by a single bolt

20 Brake fluid change (every 30,000 miles or 30 months)

✳✳ WARNING:

Brake fluid can harm your eyes and damage painted surfaces, so use extreme caution when handling or pouring it. Do not use brake fluid that has been standing open or is more than one year old. Brake fluid absorbs moisture from the air. Excess moisture can cause a dangerous loss of braking effectiveness.

1   At the specified intervals, the brake fluid should be drained and replaced. Since the brake fluid may drip or splash when pouring it, place plenty of rags around the master cylinder to protect any surrounding painted surfaces.

2   Before beginning work, purchase the specified brake fluid (see *Recommended lubricants and fluids* at the end of this Chapter).

3   Remove the cap from the master cylinder reservoir.

4   Using a hand suction pump or similar device, withdraw the fluid from the master cylinder reservoir.

5   Add new fluid to the master cylinder until it rises to the base of the filler neck.

6   Bleed the brake system as described in Chapter 9 at all four brakes until new and uncontaminated fluid is expelled from the bleeder screw. Be sure to maintain the fluid level in the master cylinder as you perform the bleeding process. If you allow the master cylinder to run dry, air will enter the system.

7   Refill the master cylinder with fluid and check the operation of the brakes. The pedal should feel solid when depressed, with no sponginess.

✳✳ WARNING:

Do not operate the vehicle if you are in doubt about the effectiveness of the brake system.

21 Spark plug check and replacement (see Maintenance schedule for intervals)

▶ **Refer to illustrations 21.2, 21.5, 21.7, 21.9, 21.10, 21.11 and 21.12**

1   The spark plugs are located in the cylinder head(s).

2   In most cases the tools necessary for spark plug replacement include a spark plug socket which fits onto a ratchet (this special socket is padded inside to protect the porcelain insulators on the new plugs and hold them in place), various extensions and a feeler gauge to check and adjust the spark plug gap (see illustration). Since these engines are equipped with an aluminum cylinder head, a torque wrench should be used when tightening the spark plugs.

3   The best approach when replacing the spark plugs is to purchase the new spark plugs beforehand, adjust them to the proper gap and then replace each plug one at a time. When buying the new spark plugs, be sure to obtain the correct plug for your specific engine. This information can be found in the Specification Section at the front of this Chapter, in your owner's manual or on the Vehicle Emissions Control Information (VECI) label located under the hood. If differences exist between the sources, purchase the spark plug type specified on the VECI label as it was printed for your specific engine.

4   Allow the engine to cool completely before attempting to remove any of the plugs. During this cooling off time, each of the new spark plugs can be inspected for defects and the gaps can be checked.

5   The gap is checked by inserting the proper thickness gauge between the electrodes at the tip of the plug (see illustration). The gap between the electrodes should be as listed in this Chapter's Specifications or in your owner's manual. The wire should touch each of the electrodes.

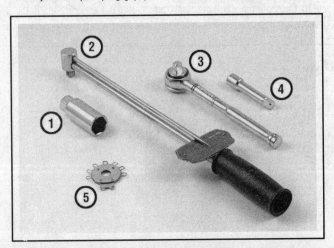

21.2 Tools required for changing spark plugs

1   Spark plug socket - This will have special padding inside to protect the spark plug porcelain insulator

2   Torque wrench - Although not mandatory, use of this tool is the best way to ensure that the plugs are tightened properly

3   Ratchet - Standard hand tool to fit the plug socket

4   Extension - Depending on model and accessories, you may need special extensions and universal joints to reach one or more of the plugs

5   Spark plug gap gauge - This gauge for checking the gap comes in a variety of styles. Make sure the gap for your engine is included

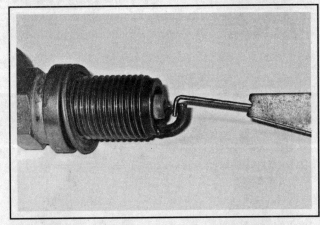

21.5 Spark plug manufacturers recommend using a wire-type gauge when checking the gap - the wire should slide between the electrodes with a slight drag

21.7 Use a spark plug boot pulling tool to remove each end of a spark plug wire - never pull on the wire itself

21.9 Use a ratchet and extension to remove the spark plugs

❊❊ CAUTION:

The manufacturer recommends against checking the gap on platinum-tipped spark plugs; the platinum coating could be scraped off.

Also, at this time check for cracks in the spark plug body (if any are found, the plug must not be used).

6 Cover the fender to prevent damage to the paint. Fender covers are available from auto parts stores but an old blanket will work just fine.

7 Using a twisting motion, detach one of the spark plug wires from the spark plug. Pull only on the boot at the end of the wire - do not pull on the wire (see illustration).

8 If compressed air is available, use it to blow any dirt or foreign material away from the spark plug area.

❊❊ WARNING:

Wear eye protection!

The idea here is to eliminate the possibility of material falling into the cylinder through the spark plug hole as the spark plug is removed.

9 Place the spark plug socket over the plug and remove it from the engine by turning it in a counterclockwise direction (see illustration).

10 Compare the spark plug with this chart to get an indication of the overall running condition of the engine (see illustration).

A normally worn spark plug should have light tan or gray deposits on the firing tip.

A carbon fouled plug, identified by soft, sooty, black deposits, may indicate an improperly tuned vehicle. Check the air cleaner, ignition components and engine control system.

An oil fouled spark plug indicates an engine with worn piston rings and/or bad valve seals allowing excessive oil to enter the chamber.

This spark plug has been left in the engine too long, as evidenced by the extreme gap- Plugs with such an extreme gap can cause misfiring and stumbling accompanied by a noticeable lack of power.

A physically damaged spark plug may be evidence of severe detonation in that cylinder. Watch that cylinder carefully between services, as a continued detonation will not only damage the plug, but could also damage the engine.

A bridged or almost bridged spark plug, identified by a build-up between the electrodes caused by excessive carbon or oil build-up on the plug.

21.10 Inspect the spark plug to determone engine running conditions

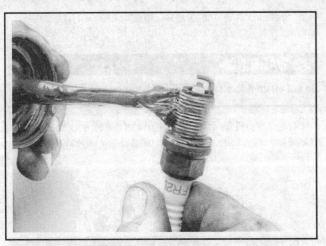

21.11 Apply a thin coat of anti-seize compound to the spark plug threads

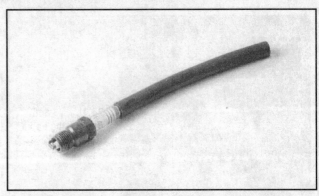

21.12 A length of snug-fitting rubber hose will save time and prevent damaged threads when installing the spark plugs

11 It's a good idea to lightly coat the threads of the spark plugs with an anti-seize compound (see illustration) to insure that the spark plugs do not seize in the aluminum cylinder head.

12 It's often difficult to insert spark plugs into their holes without cross-threading them. To avoid this possibility, fit a piece of rubber hose over the end of the spark plug (see illustration). The flexible hose acts as a universal joint to help align the plug with the plug hole. Should the plug begin to cross-thread, the hose will slip on the spark plug, preventing thread damage. Install the spark plug and tighten it to the torque listed in this Chapter's Specifications.

13 Attach the plug wire to the new spark plug, again using a twisting motion on the boot until it is firmly seated on the end of the spark plug.

14 Follow the above procedure for the remaining spark plugs, replacing them one at a time to prevent mixing up the spark plug wires.

22 Spark plug wire check and replacement (see Maintenance schedule for intervals)

1 The spark plug wires should be replaced at the recommended intervals and/or checked when new spark plugs are installed.

2 Disconnect the spark plug wire from the ignition coil pack. Pull only on the boot at the end of the wire; don't pull on the wire itself. Use a twisting motion to free the boot/wire from the coil. Disconnect the same spark plug wire from the spark plug, using the same twisting method while pulling on the boot.

3 Check inside the boot for corrosion, which will look like a white, crusty powder (don't mistake the white dielectric grease used on some plug wire boots for corrosion protection).

4 Now push the wire and boot back onto the end of the spark plug. It should be a tight fit on the plug end. If not, remove the wire and use a pair of pliers to carefully crimp the metal connector inside the wire boot until the fit is snug.

5 Now push the wire and boot back into the end of the ignition coil terminal. It should be a tight fit in the terminal. If not, remove the wire and use a pair of pliers to carefully crimp the metal connector inside the wire boot until the fit is snug.

6 Now, using a cloth, clean each wire along its entire length. Remove all built-up dirt and grease. As this is done, inspect for burned areas, cracks and any other form of damage. Bend the wires in several places to ensure that the conductive material inside hasn't hardened. Repeat the procedure for the remaining wires.

7 If you are replacing the spark plug wires, purchase a complete set for your particular engine. The terminals and rubber boots should already be installed on the wires. Replace the wires one at a time to avoid mixing up the firing order and make sure the terminals are securely seated on the coil pack and the spark plugs.

8 Attach the plug wire to the new spark plug and to the ignition coil pack using a twisting motion on the boot until it is firmly seated.

23 Positive Crankcase Ventilation (PCV) valve check and replacement (every 60,000 miles or 60 months)

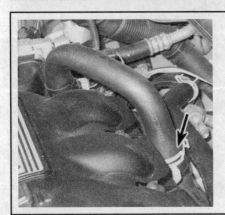

23.1a Disconnect the PCV valve hose . . .

♦ Refer to illustrations 23.1a and 23.1b

1 The PCV valve is located on the valve cover. Detach the PCV hose and remove the valve (see illustration).

23.1b . . . and remove the valve

2   Shake the valve. The valve should rattle freely - if it doesn't, replace it.

✳✳ WARNING:

Do not attempt to clean the PCV valve.

3   Replace the PCV valve with the correct one for your specific vehicle and engine size. Compare the old and new valves to make sure they're identical.

24 Cooling system servicing (draining, flushing and refilling) (every 60 months)

✳✳ WARNING 1:

Do not allow coolant (antifreeze) to come in contact with your skin or painted surfaces of the vehicle. Flush contaminated areas immediately with plenty of water. Do not store new coolant or leave old coolant lying around where it's accessible to children or pets - they're attracted by its sweet smell. Ingestion of even a small amount of coolant can be fatal! Wipe up garage floor and drip pan spills immediately. Keep antifreeze containers covered and repair cooling system leaks as soon as they're noticed. Check with local authorities about the disposal of used antifreeze. Many communities have collection centers which will see that antifreeze is disposed of properly.

✳✳ WARNING 2:

The electric cooling fan(s) on these models can activate at any time the ignition switch is in the ON position. Make sure the ignition is OFF when working in the vicinity of the fan(s).

➡Note: These vehicles are originally filled with Mopar 5 year/100,000 mile coolant that shouldn't be mixed with other coolants. Check the coolant reservoir under the hood to determine what type coolant you have. Always refill with the correct coolant.

1   Periodically, the cooling system should be drained, flushed and refilled to replenish the coolant (antifreeze) mixture and prevent formation of rust and corrosion, which can impair the performance of the cooling system and cause engine damage.

2   At the same time the cooling system is serviced, all hoses and the radiator (pressure) cap should be inspected, tested and replaced if faulty (see Section 12).

DRAINING

▶ Refer to illustrations 24.5 and 24.6

✳✳ WARNING:

Wait until the engine is completely cool before beginning this procedure.

3   With the engine cold, remove the radiator cap and set the heater control to maximum heat.

4   Move a large container capable of holding at least 12 quarts under the radiator drain fitting to catch the coolant mixture as it's drained.

5   Open the drain fitting located at the bottom of the radiator (see illustration). Allow the coolant to completely drain out.

6   After the coolant stops flowing out of the radiator, move the container under the engine block drain plugs and allow the coolant in the block to drain (see illustration).

24.5 The drain fitting is located at the bottom of the radiator

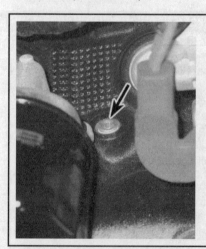

24.6 The block drain plugs are generally located about one to two inches above the oil pan - there is one on each side of the engine block

7   While the coolant is draining, check the condition of the radiator hoses, heater hoses and clamps. Replace any damaged clamps or hoses (see Section 12).

8   Reinstall the block drain plugs and tighten them securely.

FLUSHING

♦ **Refer to illustration 24.10**

9   Once the system is completely drained, remove the thermostat from the engine (see Chapter 3). Then reinstall the thermostat housing without the thermostat. This will allow the system to be thoroughly flushed.

10 Disconnect the upper radiator hose from the radiator, then place a garden hose in the upper radiator inlet and flush the system until the water runs clear at the upper radiator hose (see illustration).

11 Severe cases of radiator contamination or clogging will require removing the radiator (see Chapter 3) and reverse flushing it. This involves inserting the hose in the bottom radiator outlet to allow the clean water to run against the normal flow, draining out through the top. A radiator repair shop should be consulted if further cleaning or repair is necessary.

12 When the coolant is regularly drained and the system refilled with the correct coolant mixture there should be no need to employ chemical cleaners or descalers.

13 Disconnect the coolant reservoir hose, remove the reservoir from the vehicle and flush it with clean water (see Chapter 3). Inspect it for damage and replace if necessary.

REFILLING

14 Install the thermostat, the thermostat housing and reconnect the radiator hose (see Chapter 3).

15 Install the coolant reservoir, reconnect the hose and close the radiator drain fitting.

16 Remove the radiator cap. Add the correct mixture of the proper type of antifreeze/coolant and water in the ratio specified on the anti-

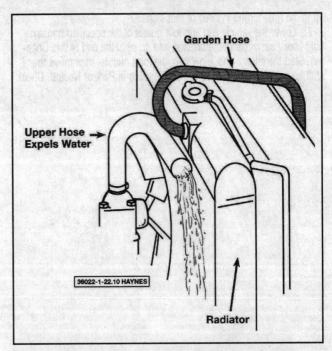

24.10 With the thermostat removed, disconnect the upper radiator hose and flush the radiator and engine block with a garden hose

freeze container or in this Chapter's Specifications through the filler neck until it reaches the radiator cap seat.

17 Add the same coolant mixture to the reservoir until the level is between the FULL HOT and ADD marks. Install the radiator cap.

18 Run the engine until normal operating temperature is reached (the fans will cycle on, then off), then allow the engine to cool. With the engine cold, add coolant as necessary to bring it up to the correct level.

19 Keep a close watch on the coolant level and the various cooling system hoses during the first few miles of driving and check for any coolant leaks. Tighten the hose clamps and add more coolant mixture as necessary.

25 Automatic transaxle fluid and filter change (every 100,000 miles)

♦ **Refer to illustration 25.3**

1   The automatic transaxle fluid and filter should be changed and the magnet cleaned at the recommended intervals.

2   Raise the front of the vehicle, support it securely on jackstands, and apply the parking brake.

3   Place a container under the transaxle pan and loosen the pan bolts (see illustration). Completely remove the bolts along the rear of the pan. Tap the corner of the pan to break the seal and allow the fluid to drain into the container (the remaining bolts will prevent the pan from separating from the transaxle). Remove the remaining bolts and detach the pan.

4   Install a new filter and O-ring, clean the magnet(s).

5   Remove the old sealant from the pan and transaxle body (don't nick or gouge the sealing surfaces) and clean the pan magnet with a clean, lint-free cloth.

6   Apply a 1/8-inch bead of RTV to the pan sealing surface and position it on the transaxle. Install the bolts and tighten them to the torque in this Chapter's Specifications using a criss-cross pattern. Work

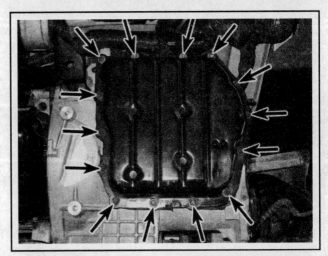

25.3 Use a socket and extension to remove the transaxle pan bolts

up to the final torque in three or four steps.

7   Lower the vehicle and add four quarts of the specified transaxle fluid (see *Recommended lubricants and fluids* at the end of this Chapter). Start the engine and allow it to idle for a minute, then move the shift lever through each gear position, ending in Park or Neutral. Check

for fluid leaks around the pan.

8   If necessary, add more fluid (a little at a time) until the level is between the Add and Full marks (be careful not to overfill it).

9   Make sure the dipstick is completely seated or dirt could get into the transaxle.

Specifications

Recommended lubricants and fluids

Engine oil
    Type   API "Certified for gasoline engines"
    Viscosity
        Four-cylinder engine   SAE 5W-30
        V6 engines   SAE 5W-20

Automatic transaxle fluid	Mopar® ATF +4 automatic transmission fluid or equivalent
Power steering fluid	Mopar® ATF +4 automatic transmission fluid or equivalent
Brake fluid	DOT type 3 brake fluid
Engine coolant	50/50 mixture of Mopar® 5 year/100,000 mile Formula (MS-9769) antifreeze/coolant with HOAT (Hybrid Organic Additive Technology) and water*
Door and liftgate latch	Multi-purpose grease
Fuel filler door remote control latch mechanism	Multi-purpose grease
Hood, door and liftgate hinge lubricant	Engine oil
Key lock cylinder lubricant	Graphite spray
Parking brake mechanism grease	Mopar Spray White Lube or equivalent

*These vehicles are filled with a 50/50 mixture of Mopar 5 year/100,000 mile coolant that shouldn't be mixed with other coolants. Refer to the coolant reservoir label under the hood to determine what type coolant you have. Always refill with the correct coolant.

Capacities*

Engine oil (including filter)
    Four-cylinder engine   5.0 quarts
    V6 engines   5.0 quarts
Automatic transaxle (drain and refill)**   4.0 quarts
Cooling system***
    Four-cylinder engine   11.4 quarts
    V6 engines   13.4 quarts

  * All capacities approximate. Add as necessary to bring to appropriate level.

  ** The best way to determine the amount of fluid to add during a routine fluid change is to measure the amount drained. It's important to not overfill the transaxle.

  *** Includes heater and coolant reservoir.

Brakes

Disc brake pad wear limit	1/8 inch (3 mm)
Drum brake shoe wear limit	1/16 inch (1.5 mm)

Ignition system

Spark plug type and gap*
    Type
        Four-cylinder engine   RE14MCC5
        V6 engines   RE14PLP5
    Gap
        Four-cylinder engine   0.048 to 0.053
        V6 engines   0.048 to 0.053

Ignition system (continued)

Firing order

Four-cylinder engine	1-3-4-2
V6 engines	1-2-3-4-5-6

Refer to the Vehicle Emission Control Information label in the engine compartment and follow the information on the label if it differs from that shown here.

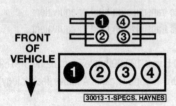

Cylinder and coil terminal location diagram -
2.4L four-cylinder engine

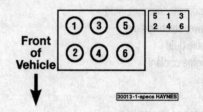

Cylinder and coil terminal location diagram -
3.3 and 3.8L V6 engines

Torque specifications Ft-lbs (unless otherwise indicated)

Automatic transaxle oil pan mounting bolts	165 in-lbs
Drivebelt tensioner mounting bolt	
Four-cylinder engine	40
V6 engines	20
Engine oil drain plug	20
Spark plugs	13
Wheel lug nuts	100

Section

Reference to other Chapters

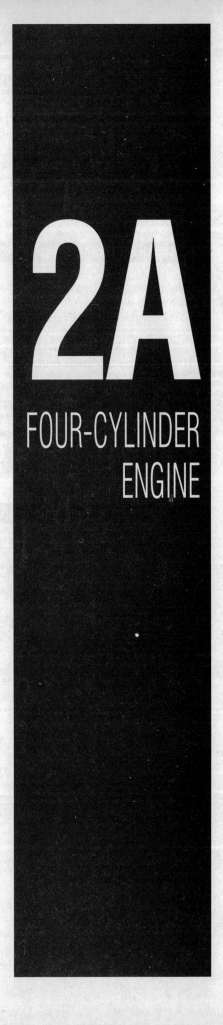

2A
FOUR-CYLINDER ENGINE

1 General information

Chapter 2A covers in-vehicle engine repair procedures on the 2.4 liter four-cylinder engine. Information concerning engine removal and installation can be found in Chapter 2C.

The following repair procedures are based on the assumption that the engine is installed in the vehicle. If the engine has been removed from the vehicle and mounted on a stand, many of the steps outlined in Chapter 2A will not apply.

The four-cylinder 2.4L Double Overhead Camshaft (DOHC) engine covered in this Chapter features four valves per cylinder arranged in two inline banks. The cylinder block is the closed deck design used for cooling and weight reduction and has the water pump molded into the block. The 2.4L engine has two balance shafts mounted in a carrier at the bottom of the engine. For more information on the balance shafts refer to Chapter 2C.

2 Repair operations possible with the engine in the vehicle

Many repair operations can be accomplished without removing the engine from the vehicle.

Clean the engine compartment and the exterior of the engine with degreaser before any work is done. It will make the job easier and help keep dirt out of the internal parts of the engine.

It may be helpful to remove the hood to improve access to the engine when repairs are performed (see Chapter 11). Cover the fenders to prevent damage to the paint. Special pads are available, but an old bedspread or blanket will also work.

If vacuum, exhaust, oil, or coolant leaks develop, indicating a need for gasket or seal replacement, the repairs can generally be made with the engine in the vehicle. The intake and exhaust manifold gaskets, oil pan gasket, camshaft, and crankshaft oil seals and cylinder head gasket are all accessible with the engine in place.

Exterior engine components, such as the intake and exhaust manifolds, the oil pan, the oil pump, the water pump, the starter motor, the alternator, the distributor, and fuel system components can be removed for repair with the engine in place.

The camshafts and the cylinder head can be removed without pulling the engine and valve component servicing can also be accomplished with the engine in the vehicle. Timing belt and sprockets replacement is also possible with the engine in the vehicle.

Repair or replacement of piston rings, pistons, connecting rods, and rod bearings is possible with the engine in the vehicle. However, this practice is not recommended because of the cleaning and preparation work that must be done to the components involved.

3 Top Dead Center (TDC) for number one piston - locating

1   Top Dead Center (TDC) is the highest point in the cylinder that each piston reaches as it travels up the cylinder bore. Each piston reaches TDC on the compression stroke and again on the exhaust stroke, but TDC generally refers to piston position on the compression stroke.

2   Positioning the piston(s) at TDC is an essential part of many procedures such as camshaft and timing belt/sprocket removal.

3   Before beginning this procedure, be sure to place the transmission in Neutral and apply the parking brake or block the rear wheels. Disable the ignition system by disconnecting the primary electrical connectors at the ignition coil packs and remove the spark plugs (see Chapter 1). Also, disable the fuel pump by removing the fuel pump relay (see Chapter 4, Section 2).

4   In order to bring any piston to TDC, the crankshaft must be turned using one of the methods outlined below. When looking at the front of the engine, normal crankshaft rotation is clockwise.

a) *The preferred method is to turn the crankshaft with a socket and ratchet attached to the bolt threaded into the front of the crankshaft. Turn the bolt in a clockwise direction only. Never turn the bolt counterclockwise.*

b) *A remote starter switch, which may save some time, can also be used. Follow the instructions included with the switch. Once the piston is close to TDC, use a socket and ratchet as described in the previous paragraph.*

c) *If an assistant is available to turn the ignition switch to the Start position in short bursts, you can get the piston close to TDC without a remote starter switch. Make sure your assistant is out of the vehicle, away from the ignition switch, then use a socket and ratchet as described in Paragraph (a) to complete the procedure.*

5   Install a compression pressure gauge in the number one spark plug hole (refer to Chapter 2C). It should be a gauge with a screw-in fitting and a hose at least six inches long.

6   Rotate the crankshaft using one of the methods described above while observing for pressure on the compression gauge. The moment the gauge shows pressure, indicates that the number one cylinder has begun the compression stroke.

7   Once the compression stroke has begun, TDC for the compression stroke is reached by bringing the piston to the top of the cylinder.

➡**Note: If a compression gauge is not available, you can simply place a blunt object over the spark plug hole and listen for compression as the engine is rotated. Once compression at the No.1 spark plug hole is noted, the remainder of the Step is the same.**

8   These engines are not equipped with external components (vibration damper, flywheel, timing hole, etc.) that are marked to identify the position of number 1 TDC. Therefore the only method to precisely set the position of TDC number 1 is to remove the timing belt cover to access the timing belt sprockets and alignment marks (see Section 7) or with the use of a degree wheel and a positive stop timing device threaded into the spark plug hole for cylinder number 1.

9   After the number one piston has been positioned at TDC on the compression stroke, TDC for any of the remaining cylinders can be located by turning the crankshaft 180 degrees and following the firing order (refer to the Specifications). For example, rotating the engine 180 degrees past TDC #1 will put the engine at TDC compression for cylinder #3.

4   Valve cover - removal and installation

REMOVAL

1 Disconnect the cable from the negative terminal of the battery (see Chapter 5, Section 1).

2 Remove the spark plug wires (see Chapter 1) and the ignition coil pack (see Chapter 5).

3 Remove the upper intake manifold (see Section 5).

4 Label and disconnect the PCV hoses and electrical cables which connect to or cross over the valve cover.

5 Remove the upper intake manifold support brackets from the cylinder head cover studs.

6 Remove the valve cover bolts and lift the cover off. If the cover

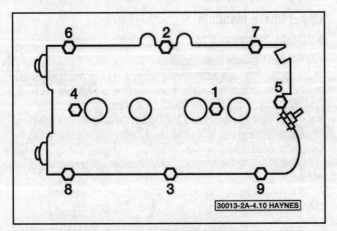

4.10 Valve cover bolt tightening sequence

sticks to the cylinder head, tap on it with a soft-faced hammer or place a wood block against the cover and tap on the wood with a hammer.

❋❋ CAUTION:

If you pry between the valve cover and the cylinder head, be careful not to gouge or nick the gasket surfaces of either part. A leak could develop after reassembly.

7 Remove the valve cover gasket spark plug round seals. Thoroughly clean the valve cover and remove all traces of old gasket material. Gasket removal solvents are available from auto parts stores and may prove helpful. After cleaning the surfaces, degrease them with a rag soaked in lacquer thinner or acetone.

INSTALLATION

▶ **Refer to illustration 4.10**

8 Install new valve cover gaskets and spark plug seals.

9 Install the 1/2 round seal and apply anaerobic RTV sealant to the camshaft cap corners and at the top edges of the 1/2 round seal.

10 Place the valve cover on the engine and install the cover bolts. Tighten the valve cover bolts in 3 steps to the torque listed in this Chapter's Specifications using the correct sequence (see illustration).

11 Installation of the remaining components is the reverse of removal.

12 When installation is complete, start the engine and check for oil leaks.

5   Intake manifold - removal, inspection and installation

❋❋ WARNING:

Allow the engine to cool completely before beginning this procedure.

1 Relieve the fuel system pressure (see Chapter 4).

2 Disconnect the cable from the negative terminal of the battery (see Chapter 5, Section 1).

REMOVAL

Upper intake manifold

3 Disconnect the electrical connector from the inlet air temperature sensor (see Chapter 4).

4 Disconnect the air intake tube from the throttle body and remove the air filter housing (see Chapter 4).

5 Disconnect the electrical connector from the throttle position sensor (TPS) (see Chapter 6).

6 Disconnect the electrical connector from the MAP sensor (see Chapter 6).

7 Disconnect the vacuum lines for the purge solenoid and PCV valve from the intake manifold.

8 Label and disconnect the vacuum lines for the power brake

booster, the Leak Detection Pump (LDP) or Natural Vacuum Leak Detection (NVLD) system (see Chapter 6), the EGR transducer and cruise control vacuum reservoir, if equipped, from the fittings on the intake manifold.

9 Disconnect the accelerator cable, the cruise control cable, if equipped, from the throttle lever and bracket (see Chapter 4).

10 Disconnect the EGR pipe from the EGR valve (see Chapter 6).

11 Remove the upper manifold support bracket bolts.

12 Remove the dipstick from the tube.

13 Remove the upper intake manifold bolts (see illustration 5.28). Lift the upper intake manifold from the lower intake manifold.

Lower intake manifold

14 Remove the upper intake manifold (see Steps 1 through 13).

15 Disconnect the fuel lines at the fuel rail (see Chapter 4).

16 Drain the cooling system (see Chapter 1). Remove the heater supply and radiator upper hoses at the intake manifold.

17 Disconnect the coolant temperature sensor (ECT) and the fuel injector wire harness connector.

18 Remove the lower intake manifold support bracket upper bolts.

19 Disconnect the fuel injector electrical harness connector.

20 Remove the power steering reservoir bolts and set the reservoir aside. Do not disconnect the fluid line from the reservoir.

21 Remove the lower intake manifold support bracket bolts and

manifold bolts (see illustration 5.24) and remove the intake manifold assembly. If it sticks, lightly tap the manifold with a soft-face hammer or carefully pry it from the cylinder head.

❊❊ CAUTION:

Do not pry between the gasket sealing surfaces.

INSPECTION

22 Carefully scrape all traces of gasket material from both the cylinder head and the intake manifold surfaces.

❊❊ CAUTION:

The cylinder head and intake manifold are made of aluminum and are easily nicked or gouged. Don't damage the gasket surfaces or a leak may result after the work is complete. Gasket removal solvents are available from auto parts stores and may prove helpful.

23 Use a straightedge and feeler gauge to check the intake manifold mating surface for warpage. Check the intake manifold surface on the cylinder head also. If warpage on any surface exceeds the limits listed

in this Chapter's Specifications, the intake manifold and/or cylinder head must be replaced or resurfaced by an automotive machine shop.

INSTALLATION

Lower intake manifold

▶ **Refer to illustration 5.24**

24 Install the intake manifold, using a new gasket. Tighten the bolts following the recommended sequence (see illustration), to the torque listed in this Chapter's Specifications.
25 Install the lower intake manifold support bracket and tighten the bolts to the torque listed in this Chapter's Specifications.
26 Installation of the remaining components is the reverse of removal.

Upper intake manifold

▶ **Refer to illustration 5.28**

27 Install the lower intake manifold.
28 On 2003 through 2005 models, apply a 1/16-inch diameter bead of RTV sealant around the intake openings of the lower intake manifold. On 2006 models, install a new gasket on the lower intake manifold. Install the upper intake manifold and tighten the bolts following the recommended sequence (see illustration), to the torque listed in this Chapter's Specifications.
29 Installation of the remaining components is the reverse of removal.
30 Refill the cooling system (see Chapter 1). Run the engine and check for leaks.

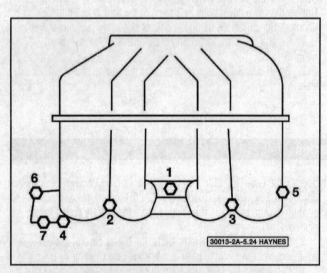

5.24 Lower intake manifold bolt tightening sequence

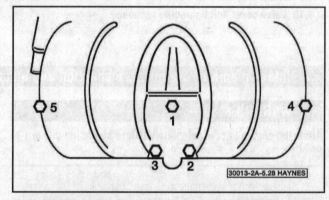

5.28 Upper intake manifold bolt tightening sequence

6   Exhaust manifold - removal, inspection and installation

❊❊ WARNING:

Allow the engine to cool completely before beginning this procedure.

REMOVAL

1 Disconnect the cable from the negative terminal of the battery (see Chapter 5, Section 1).
2 Set the parking brake and block the rear wheels.

3 Raise the front of the vehicle and support it securely on jackstands.
4 Working under the vehicle, apply penetrating oil to the exhaust pipe-to-manifold fasteners to make removal easier. Remove the exhaust pipe from the exhaust manifold at the flex-joint.
5 Disconnect the wiring harness from the upstream oxygen sensor (see Chapter 6).
6 Remove the exhaust manifold bolts, and the exhaust manifold.

➡**Note: The exhaust pipe may have to be removed from the vehicle to ease manifold removal (see Chapter 4).**

INSPECTION

7   Use a wire brush to clean the exhaust manifold bolts. Replace any that have thread damage.

8   Use a scraper to remove all traces of gasket material from the exhaust flange mating surfaces and inspect them for wear and cracks.

❊❊ CAUTION:

When removing gasket material, be very careful not to scratch or gouge the sealing surface. Any damage to the surface may cause a leak after reassembly. Gasket removal solvents are available from auto parts stores and may prove helpful.

9   Use a straightedge and feeler gauge to check the exhaust manifold-to-cylinder head mating surface for warpage. Check the surface on the cylinder head also. If warpage exceeds the limits listed in this Chapter's Specifications, the exhaust manifold and/or cylinder head must be replaced, or resurfaced by an automotive machine shop.

INSTALLATION

10   Apply Loctite No. 271 to the mounting bolt threads prior to installation.

11   Install the new gasket (dry - use no sealant), manifold, and bolts. Tighten the bolts in several stages, starting with the center bolts and following a circular pattern to the outer bolts, to the torque listed in this Chapter's Specifications.

12   Installation of the remaining components is the reverse of removal.

➡Note: **Install a new gasket between the exhaust manifold and exhaust pipe.**

13   Run the engine and check for exhaust leaks.

7   Timing belt and covers - removal, inspection and installation

➡Note: **If the timing belt failed with the engine operating, damage to the valves has most likely occurred. Perform an engine compression check after belt replacement to determine if any valve damage is present.**

REMOVAL

◆ **Refer to illustrations 7.5, 7.6 and 7.11**

❊❊ CAUTION:

Do not turn the crankshaft or camshafts after the timing belt has been removed. This will damage the valves from contact with the pistons. Do not try to turn the crankshaft with the camshaft sprocket bolts and do not rotate the crankshaft counterclockwise.

1   Disconnect the cable from the negative terminal of the battery (see Chapter 5, Section 1).

2   Raise the vehicle and support it securely on jackstands.

3   Remove the right inner splash shield (see Chapter 11).

4   Remove the accessory drivebelts (see Chapter 1).

5   Loosen the center bolt in the crankshaft pulley. If it is tight, break it loose by inserting a large screwdriver or bar through the opening in the pulley, to hold the pulley stationary. Loosen the bolt with a socket and breaker bar (see illustration).

6   Install a three-jaw puller on center hub of the pulley and remove the pulley from the crankshaft (see illustration). Use the proper insert to keep the puller from damaging the threads in the end of the crankshaft. If the pulley is difficult to remove, tap the center bolt of the puller with a brass mallet to break it loose.

❊❊ CAUTION:

Do not use a puller that has jaws which grip the outer diameter of the pulley. The pulley damper and hub may separate. Use only the type shown in the illustration.

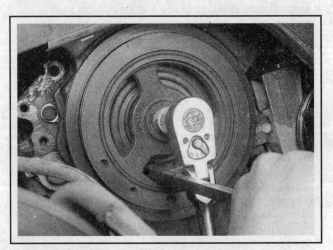

7.5 Insert a large screwdriver or bar through the opening in the crankshaft pulley and wedge it against the engine block, then loosen the bolt with a socket and breaker bar

7.6 Install a three-jaw puller onto the pulley, position the center post of the puller on the crankshaft end (use the proper insert to keep from damaging the crankshaft threads), and remove the pulley from the crankshaft

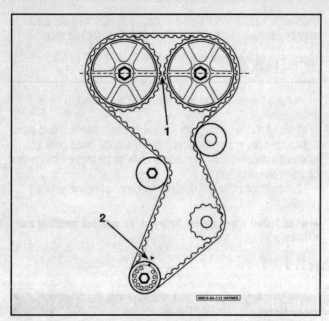

7.11 Before removing the timing belt, make sure the camshaft sprockets (1) and crankshaft (2) timing marks align with their respective marks - rotate the engine (clockwise only as viewed from the crankshaft end) as required to align both sets of timing marks. The crankshaft sprocket timing mark is aligned on the trailing edge of the sprocket tooth

7 Remove the lower timing belt cover fasteners and the cover.

8 Lower the vehicle and remove the upper timing belt fasteners and the cover.

9 Reinstall the crankshaft bolt using an appropriate spacer (this will enable you to turn the crankshaft later).

10 Remove the right (passenger side) engine mount (see Section 17) and mounting bracket. Make sure the engine is supported with a floor jack placed under the oil pan. Place a wood block on the jack head to prevent it from denting or damaging the oil pan.

11 Align the camshaft sprocket(s) and crankshaft timing marks before removing the timing belt (see illustration). If necessary, align the timing marks by rotating the crankshaft - clockwise only! If you plan to re-use the timing belt, paint an arrow on it to indicate the direction of rotation (clockwise).

12 Insert a 6 mm Allen wrench in the hexagon fitting in the tensioner pulley. First loosen the tensioner lock bolt and apply light pressure to the Allen wrench and rotate the tensioner pulley CLOCKWISE until there is sufficient slack on the timing belt (see illustration 7.23).

13 Slip the timing belt off the sprockets and set it aside. If you plan to reuse the timing belt, store it in a plastic bag - do not allow the belt to come in contact with oil or coolant; this will greatly shorten belt life.

14 If it's necessary to remove the camshaft sprocket(s), and/or timing belt rear cover (for camshaft seal replacement) see Section 9.

INSPECTION

▶ **Refer to illustration 7.18**

15 Inspect the crankshaft front oil seal for leaks. Replace it, if necessary (see Section 7).

16 Inspect the water pump for evidence of leakage (usually indicated by a trail of wet or dried coolant). Check the pulley for excessive play and bearing roughness. Replace it, if necessary (see Chapter 3).

17 Rotate the tensioner pulley and idler pulley and move them

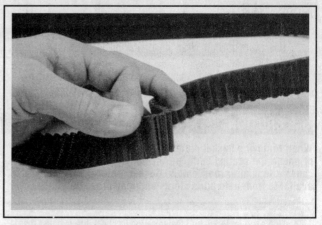

7.18 Carefully inspect the timing belt - bending it backwards will often make wear or damage more apparent

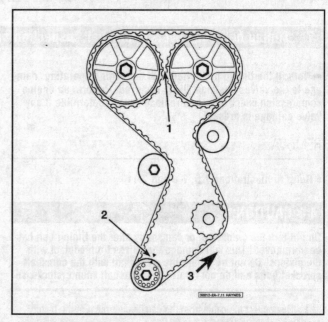

7.20 When installing the timing belt, the intake camshaft sprocket mark should be in line with the cylinder head surface, and the exhaust camshaft sprocket mark should be 1/2 tooth advanced

1   *Exhaust camshaft timing mark at "1/2 notch location"*
2   *Crankshaft mark at TDC*
3   *Install belt in this direction*

side-to-side to check for bearing roughness and excess play. Visually inspect timing belt sprockets for signs of damage or wear. Replace parts as necessary.

18 Inspect the timing belt for cracks, separation, wear missing teeth, and oil contamination (see illustration). Replace the belt if it's in questionable condition or the engine mileage is close to that referenced in the *Maintenance schedule* (see Chapter 1).

INSTALLATION

▶ **Refer to illustrations 7.20 and 7.23**

19 Confirm that the timing marks on the camshaft sprockets are aligned.

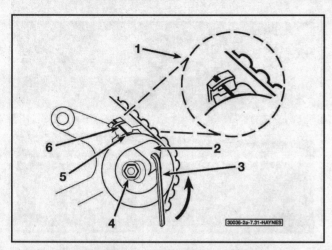

7.23 To apply tension to the timing belt, place the appropriate size Allen wrench into the hexagon opening and rotate the Allen wrench in a counterclockwise direction until the setting notch is aligned with the spring tang

1	Setting notch and spring tang alignment details	4	Lock nut
2	Top plate	5	Setting notch
3	6 mm Allen wrench	6	Spring tang

20 Rotate the exhaust camshaft sprocket clockwise so the timing mark is 1/2 notch below the intake camshaft timing mark (see illustration).

21 Align the crankshaft sprocket timing mark with the arrow mark on the oil pump housing (see illustration 7.11).

22 Install the timing belt as follows: Place the belt on the crankshaft sprocket; maintaining tension on the belt, wrap it around the water pump sprocket, idler pulley, camshaft sprockets, and the tensioner pulley. To take up belt slack, rotate the exhaust camshaft counterclockwise until the timing marks on both sprockets align.

23 Insert a 6 mm Allen wrench into the hex opening on the tensioner pulley (see illustration). Then, using the 6 mm Allen wrench as a lever, rotate the belt tensioner COUNTERCLOCKWISE until there is tension on the timing belt. Continue to rotate the tension until the setting notch is aligned with the spring tang. Grip the Allen wrench to prevent the tensioner from rotating, and torque the tensioner lock bolt to 19 ft-lbs. Recheck the alignment marks. If they are incorrect, loosen the bolt and repeat the procedure.

24 Use the bolt in the center of the crankshaft sprocket to turn the crankshaft clockwise two complete revolutions.

❋❋ CAUTION:

If you feel resistance while turning the crankshaft, STOP - the valves may be hitting the pistons due to incorrect valve timing. Re-check the valve timing.

➡**Note: The camshaft and crankshaft sprocket marks will align every two revolutions of the crankshaft.**

25 Recheck the alignment of the timing marks (see illustrations 7.11). If the marks do not align properly, loosen the tensioner, slip the belt off the camshaft sprocket, realign the marks, reinstall the belt, and recheck the alignment.

26 Installation of the remaining components is the reverse of removal. Tighten the crankshaft pulley bolt to the torque listed in this Chapter's Specifications.

27 Start the engine and road test the vehicle.

8 Crankshaft front oil seal - replacement

▶ **Refer to illustrations 8.2, 8.3, 8.5 and 8.6**

❋❋ CAUTION:

Do not rotate the camshaft(s) or crankshaft when the timing belt is removed or damage to the engine may occur.

1 Remove the timing belt (see Section 7).

2 Remove the crankshaft timing belt sprocket from the crankshaft with a bolt-type gear puller (see illustration). Remove the Woodruff key from the crankshaft keyway.

3 Working from below the right inner fender, carefully pry the seal out of its bore (see illustration). Take care to prevent damaging the oil pump assembly, the crankshaft, and the seal bore.

4 Clean and inspect the seal bore and sealing surface on the crank-

8.2 Attach a bolt-type gear puller to the crankshaft sprocket and remove the sprocket from the crankshaft

8.3 Carefully pry the seal from its bore (typical)

8.5 Lubricate the new crankshaft front seal with engine oil and, using a hammer and socket, drive the seal into the bore until it's flush with the oil pump housing

8.6 Position the crankshaft sprocket with the word FRONT facing out and install it onto the crankshaft

shaft. Minor imperfections can be removed with emery cloth. If there is a groove worn in the crankshaft sealing surface (from contact with the seal), installing a new seal will probably not stop the leak.

5   Lubricate the new seal with engine oil and use a hammer and the appropriate size socket, to drive the seal into the bore until it's flush with the oil pump housing (see illustration).

6   Install the Woodruff key and the crankshaft timing belt sprocket with the word FRONT facing out on the crankshaft (see illustration).

> ❊❊ **CAUTION:**
>
> The crankshaft timing sprocket must be installed with special tool 6792. This tool pre-sets the depth of the sprocket for correct timing belt tracking. If the sprocket is installed incorrectly, timing belt damage may develop.

7   Installation of the remaining components is the reverse of removal. Tighten the crankshaft pulley bolt to the torque listed in this Chapter's Specifications.

8   Start the engine and check for oil leaks.

9   Camshaft oil seal - replacement

▶ Refer to illustrations 9.5, 9.8a, 9.8b and 9.10

> ❊❊ **CAUTION:**
>
> Do not rotate the camshaft(s) or crankshaft when the timing belt is removed or damage to the engine may occur.

1   Remove the timing belt (see Section 6).

2   Rotate the crankshaft counterclockwise until the crankshaft sprocket is three notches BTDC (see illustration 7.11). This will prevent engine damage if the camshaft sprocket rotates during sprocket bolt removal.

3   Hold the camshaft sprocket and remove the camshaft sprocket bolt.

➡**Note: To hold the camshaft/sprocket while loosening the bolt, a strap-type pulley holder tool is recommended and is available at most auto parts stores.**

Use two large screwdrivers to pry the sprocket off the camshaft. If the strap wrench is unavailable, remove the valve cover and access the camshaft wrenching flats.

4   Remove the idler pulley.

5   Remove the bolts holding the rear cover to the engine block and cylinder head. Remove the rear cover (see illustration).

6   Pry out the camshaft oil seal (see illustration 8.3). Don't scratch the bore or damage the camshaft in the process (if the camshaft is damaged, the new seal will leak).

7   Clean the bore and coat the outer edge of the new seal with engine oil or multi-purpose grease. Lubricate the seal lip.

8   Use a socket (with an outside diameter slightly smaller than the outside diameter of the seal) and a hammer (see illustration). Carefully

9.5 Remove the rear timing belt cover

9.8a Using a hammer and socket, gently tap the new seal into place with the spring side facing inward

9.8b If space is limited and you can't use a hammer and socket to install the seal, a seal installer can be made from a section of pipe (of appropriate diameter), a bolt and washer. Place the pipe over the seal and press it into place by tightening the bolt

drive the new seal into the cylinder head until it's flush with the face of the cylinder head. If a socket isn't available, a short section of pipe will work.

➡Note: If engine location makes it difficult to use a hammer to install the camshaft seal, fabricate a seal installation tool from a piece of pipe cut to the appropriate length, a bolt, and a large washer (see illustration). Place the pipe over the seal and thread the bolt into the camshaft. The seal can now be pressed into the bore by tightening the bolt.

9 Install the rear timing belt cover and idler pulley.
10 Install the camshaft sprocket, aligning the pin in the camshaft with the hole in the sprocket (see illustration). Hold the camshaft sprocket (see Step 2) and tighten the sprocket bolt to the torque listed in this Chapter's Specifications.
11 Reinstall the timing belt (see Section 7).
12 Run the engine and check for oil leaks at the camshaft seal.

9.10 When installing a camshaft sprocket, make sure the pin in the camshaft is aligned with the hole in the sprocket

10 Rocker arm and hydraulic valve lash adjuster - removal, inspection and installation

REMOVAL

1 Remove the camshafts (see Section 11).
2 After the camshafts have been removed, the rocker arms can be lifted off.

✳✳ CAUTION:

Each rocker arm and valve lash adjuster must be returned to it's original location, so mark them or place them in a marked container (such as an egg carton or cupcake tray) so they won't get mixed up.

3 Remove the rocker arms and hydraulic valve lash adjusters from the cylinder head.

INSPECTION

4 Visually check the rocker arm tip, roller, and lash adjuster pocket for wear. Replace them if wear or damage is found.
5 Inspect each adjuster carefully for signs of wear and damage particularly on the ball tip that contacts the rocker arm. Lash adjusters frequently become clogged, we recommend replacing them if you're concerned about their condition or if the engine is exhibiting valve "tapping" noises.

INSTALLATION

6 Prior to installation, the lash adjusters must be partially full of engine oil - indicated by little or no plunger action when the adjuster is depressed. If there is excessive plunger travel, place the rocker arm assembly in clean engine oil and pump the plunger until the plunger travel is eliminated.

➡Note: If the plunger still travels within the rocker arm when full of oil, it's defective and the rocker arm assembly must be replaced.

7 Install the hydraulic lash adjusters and rocker arms in their original locations on the cylinder head.
8 Install the camshafts (see Section 11).
9 When re-starting the engine after replacing the rocker arm/lash adjusters, the adjusters will normally make "tapping" noises. After warming-up the engine, slowly increase the engine speed from idle to 3,000 rpm and back to idle over one minute period. If the adjuster(s) do not become quiet, they should be replaced.

11 Camshaft(s) - removal, inspection and installation

REMOVAL

1   Remove the valve cover (see Section 4).
2   Remove the timing belt (see Section 7).
3   Remove the camshaft sprockets and the rear timing belt cover (see Section 9).
4   The camshaft bearing caps are identified with their numbered location in the cylinder head.
5   Remove the outside bearing caps at each end of the camshafts, Remove the remaining camshaft bearing caps. Loosen the bolts a little at a time to prevent distorting the camshafts, starting with the center cap bolts and working toward the outer cap bolts in a circular pattern. When the bearing caps have all been loosened enough for removal, they may still be difficult to remove. Use the bearing cap bolts for leverage and move the cap back and forth to loosen the cap from the cylinder head. If they are still difficult to remove you can tap them gently with a soft face mallet until they can be lifted off.

✳✳ CAUTION:

Store them in order so they can be returned to their original locations, with the same side facing forward.

6   Carefully lift the camshafts out of the cylinder head. Mark the camshafts INTAKE and EXHAUST. They cannot be mixed-up.
7   Remove the front seal from each camshaft.

➡**Note: It would be prudent to inspect the rocker arms and lash adjusters at this time (see Section 10).**

INSPECTION

▶ **Refer to illustration 11.9**

8   Clean the camshaft(s) and the gasket surface. Inspect the camshaft for wear and/or damage to the lobe surfaces, bearing journals, and seal contact surfaces. Inspect the camshaft bearing surfaces in the cylinder head and bearing caps for scoring and other damage.
9   Measure the camshaft bearing journal diameters (see illustra-

tion). Measure the inside diameter of the camshaft bearing surfaces in the cylinder head, using a telescoping gauge (temporarily install the bearing caps). Subtract the journal measurement from the bearing measurement to obtain the camshaft bearing oil clearance. Compare this clearance with the value listed in this Chapter's Specifications. Replace worn components as required.
10   Replace the camshaft if it fails any of the above inspections.

➡**Note: If the lobes are worn, replace the rocker arms and lash adjusters along with the camshaft.**

The cylinder head may need to be replaced, if the camshaft bearing surfaces in the head are damaged or excessively worn.

11   Clean and inspect the cylinder head. Have this work performed by a qualified automotive machine shop.

Camshaft end play measurement

12   Lubricate the camshaft(s) and cylinder head bearing journals with clean engine oil.
13   Place the camshaft in its original location in the cylinder head.

➡**Note: Do not install the rocker arms for this check.**

Install the rear bearing cap and tighten the bolts to the torque listed in this Chapter's Specifications.
14   Install a dial indicator on the cylinder head and place the indicator tip on the camshaft at the sprocket end.
15   Use a screwdriver to carefully pry the camshaft fully to the rear (toward the camshaft position sensor) until it stops. Zero the dial indicator and pry the camshaft fully to the front (toward the dial indicator end). The amount of indicator travel is the camshaft endplay. Compare the endplay with the tolerance given in this Chapter's Specifications. If the endplay is excessive, check the camshaft and cylinder head bearing journals for wear. Replace as necessary.

INSTALLATION

▶ **Refer to illustrations 11.17 and 11.19**

16   Install the valve lash adjusters and rocker arms (see Section 9).
17   Clean the camshaft and bearing journals and caps. Liberally coat the journals, lobes, and thrust portions of the camshaft with assembly lube or engine oil (see illustration).
18   Carefully install the camshafts in the cylinder head in their origi-

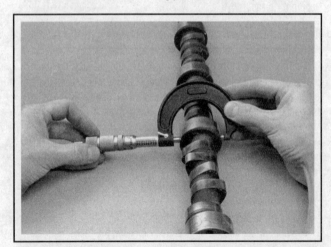

11.9 Measure the camshaft bearing journal diameters with a micrometer and compare the measurements to the dimensions given in this Chapter's Specifications

11.17 Prior to installing the camshaft, lubricate the bearing journals, thrust surfaces and lobes with assembly lube or clean engine oil

nal location. Temporarily install the camshaft sprockets and rotate the camshafts so their timing marks align (see illustration 7.11). Make sure the crankshaft is positioned with the crankshaft sprocket timing mark at three notches BTDC.

✳✳ CAUTION:

If the pistons are at TDC when tightening the camshaft bearing caps, damage to the engine may occur.

19 Install the bearing caps, except for the No. 1 and No. 6 (left side) end caps. Tighten the bolts in several steps, in the sequence shown to the torque listed in this Chapter's Specifications (see illustration).

20 Apply a 1/8-inch bead of anaerobic sealant to the sealing surfaces of the No. 1 and No. 6 bearing caps. Install the bearing caps and tighten the bolts to the torque listed in this Chapter's Specifications.

21 Install new camshaft oil seals (see Section 8).

22 Install the timing belt, covers, and related components (see Section 6).

23 Run the engine and check for oil leaks.

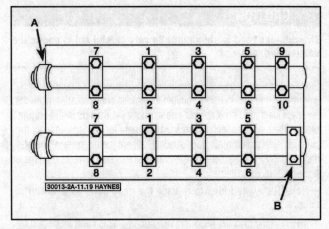

11.19 Tighten the camshaft bearing caps progressing in three equal steps in the sequence shown to the torque value given in this Chapter's Specifications

A   *Number 1 end cap assembly*
B   *Number 6 end cap on the left camshaft*

12 Cylinder head - removal and installation

✳✳ WARNING:

Allow the engine to cool completely before beginning this procedure.

REMOVAL

♦ **Refer to illustration 12.14**

1   Position the number one piston at Top Dead Center (see Section 3).

2   Relieve the fuel system pressure (see Chapter 4), then disconnect the cable from the negative terminal of the battery (see Chapter 5, Section 1).

3   Drain the cooling system (see Chapter 1).

4   Remove the coil packs, spark plug wires and spark plugs (see Chapters 1 and 5).

5   Remove the intake manifold (see Section 4). Cover the intake ports on the manifold and cylinder head with duct tape to keep out debris and contamination.

6   Remove the power steering reservoir and hoses and place them out of the way (see Chapter 10).

7   Remove the exhaust manifold (see Section 6).

➡Note: The exhaust manifold is easier to remove after the cylinder head is removed. If possible, leave it attached.

8   Disconnect the upper radiator hose from the thermostat housing (see Chapter 3).

9   Disconnect the electrical connector from the camshaft position sensor (see Chapter 5). Disconnect the electrical connectors from the fuel injectors and lay the harness aside (see Chapter 4).

10 Remove the timing belt (see Section 7).

11 Remove the camshaft sprockets, idler pulley and rear timing belt cover (see Section 8).

12 Remove the camshafts, rocker arms and valve lash adjusters (see Sections 9 and 10).

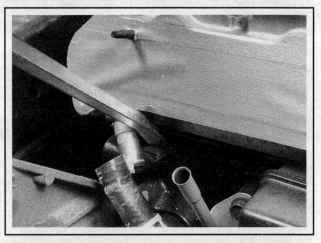

12.14 If the head is stuck to the engine block, dislodge it by placing a wood block against the head casting and tapping the wood with a hammer or by prying the head with a prybar placed carefully on a casting protrusion

13 Loosen the cylinder head bolts, 1/4-turn at a time, in the reverse order of the tightening sequence (see illustration 12.19) until they can be removed by hand.

➡Note: Write down the location of the different length bolts so they can be reinstalled in their original locations.

14 Carefully lift the cylinder head straight up and place it on wood blocks to prevent damage to the sealing surfaces. If the head sticks to the engine block, dislodge it by placing a wood block against the head casting and tapping the wood with a hammer or by prying the head with a prybar placed carefully on a casting protrusion (see illustration).

➡Note: It's also a good idea to have the head checked for warpage, even if you're just replacing the cylinder head gasket.

15 Remove all traces of old gasket material from the block and head. Special gasket removal solvents that soften gaskets and make removal much easier are available at auto parts stores.

✳✳ CAUTION:

The cylinder head is aluminum. Be very careful not to gouge the sealing surfaces.

Place clean shop rags into the cylinders to help keep out debris when working on the block. Use a vacuum to remove contamination from the engine. Use a tap of the correct size to chase the threads in the engine block. Clean and inspect all threaded fasteners for damage. Inspect the cylinder head bolt threads for "necking," where the diameter of threads narrow due to bolt stretching. If a cylinder head bolt exhibits damage or necking, it must be replaced.

➡Note: It's a good idea to replace the head bolts as a matter of course.

16 Have the cylinder head and head bolts cleaned and inspected by a qualified automotive machine shop.

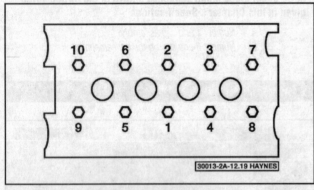

12.19 Cylinder head bolt TIGHTENING sequence

INSTALLATION

◗ **Refer to illustration 12.19**

17 Place a new gasket and the cylinder head in position on the engine block.

18 Apply clean engine oil to the cylinder head bolt threads and install them in their original locations.

19 Tighten the cylinder head bolts in the sequence shown, (see illustration) progressing in three stages to the torque listed in this Chapter's Specifications. After the third pass, tighten the bolts an additional 90-degrees (1/4 turn).

➡Note: A torque wrench is not required for the final step. Mark the bolts in relation to the cylinder head and place another mark 90-degrees clockwise from the starting mark. Using a socket and breaker bar, tighten the bolts in sequence an additional 90-degrees.

20 Install the rocker arms and hydraulic valve lash adjusters (see Section 10).

21 Install the rear timing belt cover, camshafts, and camshaft sprockets (see Section 11).

22 Install the timing belt (see Section 7). After installation, slowly rotate the crankshaft manually, clockwise through two complete revolutions. Recheck the camshaft timing marks.

23 Installation of the remaining components is the reverse of removal.

24 Refill the cooling system and check fluid levels (see Chapter 1).

25 Start the engine and run it until normal operating temperature is reached. Check for leaks and proper operation.

13 Oil pan - removal and installation

REMOVAL

◗ **Refer to illustrations 13.8a, 13.8b and 13.9**

1 Disconnect the cable from the negative terminal of the battery (see Chapter 5, Section 1).

2 Raise the vehicle and support it securely on jackstands.

3 Remove the accessory drivebelt splash shield (see Chapter 11).

4 Drain the engine oil (see Chapter 1).

13.8a If the oil pan is stuck to the block, tap it with a soft faced mallet to break it loose

5 Remove the front engine mount bracket (see Section 17).

6 Remove the bolts attaching the structural collar to the engine, the oil pan, and the transaxle.

7 On air conditioned models, remove the compressor bracket to oil pan bolt.

8 Use a criss-cross pattern to loosen and remove the mounting bolts, then lower the oil pan from the vehicle. If the pan is stuck, tap

13.8b Remove the oil pan from the block - be careful not to spill any residual oil that may be inside

13.9 Unscrew the bolt and remove the oil pump pick-up tube assembly - clean both the tube and screen thoroughly and inspect for damage or foreign debris

it with a soft-faced hammer (see illustrations) or place a wood block against the pan and tap the wood block with a hammer.

> **※※ CAUTION:**
>
> **If you're wedging something between the oil pan and the engine block to separate the two, be extremely careful not to gouge or nick the gasket surface of either part; an oil leak could result.**

9   Remove the oil pump pick-up tube and screen assembly (see illustration). Remove the O-ring seal from the oil pick-up tube and discard it. Thoroughly clean the tube and screen.

10   Clean the sealing surfaces on the oil pan and block. Use a scraper to remove all traces of old gasket material. Gasket removal solvents are available at auto parts stores and may prove helpful. Check the oil pan sealing surface for distortion. Straighten or replace as nec-

essary. After cleaning and straightening (if necessary), wipe the gasket surfaces of the pan and block clean with a rag soaked in lacquer thinner or acetone.

INSTALLATION

11   Place a new O-ring on the oil pick-up tube and install it on the oil pump housing. Tighten the bolt to the torque listed in this Chapter's Specifications.

12   Apply a 1/8-inch bead of RTV sealant at the cylinder block-to-oil pump assembly joint at the oil pan flange. Install a new oil pan gasket.

13   Place the oil pan in position and install the bolts finger tight. Working side-to-side from the center out, tighten the bolts to the torque listed in this Chapter's Specifications.

14   On air-conditioned models, install the compressor bracket bolt.

15   Install the structural collar using the following procedure:

> **※※ CAUTION:**
>
> **The structural collar must be installed as described or damage to the collar or oil pan could occur.**

a)   Place the collar into position and install the structural collar to transaxle bolts, hand-tight only.

b)   Install the structural collar to oil pan bolts, hand-tight only.

c)   Tighten the structural collar to transaxle bolts to the torque listed in this Chapter's Specifications.

d)   Tighten structural collar to oil pan bolts to the torque listed in this Chapter's Specifications.

16   Install the front engine mount bracket.

17   The remaining installation steps are the reverse of removal.

18   Refill the crankcase with the proper quantity and grade of oil (see *Recommended lubricants and fluids* Section in Chapter 1).

19   Run the engine and check for leaks.

20   Road test the vehicle and recheck for leaks.

14   Oil pump - removal, inspection and installation

➡**Note: The oil pump pressure relief valve can be serviced without removing the oil pan and oil pick-up tube.**

REMOVAL

▶ **Refer to illustrations 14.5, 14.6a, 14.6b, 14.6c, 14.8 and 14.9**

1   Disconnect the cable from the negative terminal of the battery (see Chapter 5, Section 1).

2   Remove the timing belt (see Section 7).

3   Remove the oil pan and pick-up tube assembly (see Section 13).

4   Remove the crankshaft sprocket (see Section 8).

5   Remove the bolts and detach the oil pump assembly from the engine.

14.5 If the pump will not come off by hand, tap it gently with a soft-faced hammer or pry gently on a casting protrusion

14.6a Remove the rotor cover mounting screws . . .

14.6b . . . and lift off the rotor cover

14.6c Exploded view of the oil pump assembly

A	Rotor cover	C	Inner rotor
B	Outer rotor	D	Oil pump body

✳✳ CAUTION:

If the pump doesn't come off by hand, tap it gently with a soft-faced hammer or pry on a casting boss (see illustration).

6   Remove the mounting screws and the rotor assembly cover from the oil pump housing. Pull the inner and outer rotors from the body (see illustrations).

✳✳ CAUTION:

Be very careful with these components. Close tolerances are critical in creating the correct oil pressure. Nicks or other damage will require replacement of the complete pump assembly.

7   Use a hammer and brass drift to remove the crankshaft front seal from the oil pump housing, then discard it.
8   Remove the O-ring seal from the oil pump housing discharge port and discard it (see illustration).
9   Disassemble the relief valve assembly; take note of the way the relief valve piston is installed. Remove the cap bolt, and the bolt, washer, spring, and relief valve (see illustration).

14.8 Remove the discharge port O-ring seal from the oil pump body - apply clean engine oil to the new seal at installation

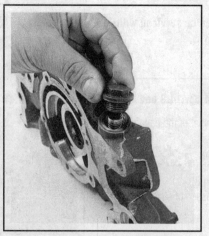

14.9 Remove the oil pressure relief valve cap bolt from the oil pump body and withdraw the spring and the relief valve piston

14.12a Measure the outer rotor thickness at four locations equally spaced and calculate the average

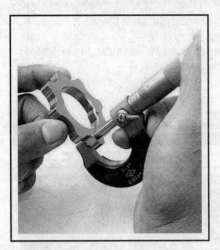

14.12b Measure the inner rotor thickness with a micrometer or caliper

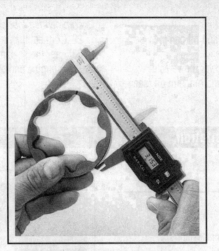

14.12c Measure the outer rotor's diameter with a micrometer or caliper

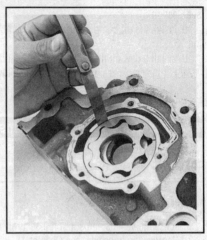

14.12d Use a flat feeler gauge to measure the outer rotor-to-oil pump body clearance

INSPECTION

▶ **Refer to illustrations 14.12a, 14.12b, 14.12c, 14.12d and 14.12e**

10 Clean all components, including the block surfaces and oil pan, with solvent. Inspect all surfaces for excessive wear and/or damage.

11 Inspect the oil pressure relief valve piston sliding surface and valve spring for damage. If either the spring or the valve is damaged, they must be replaced as a set.

12 Check the oil pump rotor dimensions and clearances with a micrometer or vernier calipers and a feeler gauge (see illustrations) and compare the results to the values listed in this Chapter's Specifications. Replace both rotors if any dimension is out of tolerance.

INSTALLATION

▶ **Refer to illustration 14.16**

13 Lubricate the relief valve piston, piston bore, and spring with

clean engine oil. Install the relief valve piston in the bore with the grooved end going in first, followed by the spring and cap bolt. Tighten the cap bolt to the torque listed in this Chapter's Specifications.

➡**Note: If the relief valve piston is installed incorrectly, serious engine damage could occur.**

14 Lubricate the oil pump rotor recess in the housing and the inner and outer rotors with clean engine oil and install both rotors in the body. If the inner rotor has a chamfer, install it with the chamfer facing the rotor cover. Fill the rotor cavity with clean engine oil and install the cover. Tighten the cover screws to the torque listed in this Chapter's Specifications.

15 Install a new O-ring in the oil discharge passage.

16 Apply anaerobic sealant to the oil pump body sealing surface (see illustration) and position the pump assembly on the block, aligning the inner rotor and crankshaft drive flats. Tighten the oil pump bolts to the torque listed in this Chapter's Specifications.

17 Install the new crankshaft front seal in the oil pump housing (see Section 7).

18 Install the crankshaft sprocket (see Section 7) and timing belt

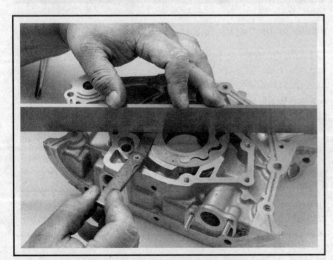

14.12e With the rotors installed, place a precision straightedge across the rotor cover surface and measure the clearance between the rotors and the rotor cover surface

14.16 Apply a bead of anaerobic sealant to the oil pump housing sealing surface as shown

(see Section 6).

19 Install the oil pump pick-up tube assembly and oil pan (see Section 13).

20 Install a new oil filter (see Chapter 1) and lower the vehicle.

21 Fill the crankcase with the proper quantity and grade of oil (see

Recommended lubricants and fluids Section in Chapter 1).

22 Connect the negative battery cable.

23 After the sealant has cured, per the manufacturer's directions, start the engine and check for leaks.

15 Driveplate - removal and installation

REMOVAL

▶ **Refer to illustration 15.4**

1 Raise the vehicle and support it securely on jackstands.

2 Remove the transaxle (see Chapter 7).

3 To ensure correct alignment during reinstallation, match-mark the driveplate and backing plate to the crankshaft so they can be reassembled in the same position.

4 Remove the bolts that hold the driveplate to the crankshaft (see illustration). A special tool is available at most auto parts stores to hold the driveplate while loosening the bolts. If the tool is not available, wedge a screwdriver in the starter ring gear teeth to jam the driveplate.

5 Remove the driveplate from the crankshaft. The driveplate is fairly heavy, be sure to support it while removing the last bolt.

6 Clean the driveplate to remove grease and oil. Inspect the driveplate for damage or other defects (see Chapter 2A).

7 Clean and inspect the mating surfaces of the driveplate and the crankshaft.

8 If the crankshaft rear main seal is leaking, replace it before reinstalling the driveplate (see Section 16).

INSTALLATION

9 Position the driveplate and backing plate against the crankshaft. Align the previously applied match marks. Before installing the bolts,

15.4 Match-mark the position of the driveplate and backing plate to the crankshaft and, using an appropriate tool to hold the driveplate, remove the bolts

apply thread-locking compound to the threads.

10 Hold the driveplate with the holding tool, or wedge a screwdriver in the starter ring gear teeth to keep the driveplate from turning. Tighten the bolts to the torque listed in this Chapter's Specifications.

11 The remaining installation steps are the reverse of removal.

16 Rear main oil seal - replacement

16.3 Using a flat blade screwdriver, very carefully pry the crankshaft rear main seal out of it's bore - DO NOT nick or scratch the sealing surfaces on the crankshaft or seal bore

▶ **Refer to illustrations 16.3 and 16.5**

1 The rear main oil seal is pressed into a bore machined into the rear main bearing cap and engine block.

2 Remove the driveplate (see Section 15).

➡**Note: Verify that the oil seal is installed flush with the outer surface of the block.**

3 Pry out the old seal with a flat blade screwdriver (see illustration).

✳✳ CAUTION:

To prevent an oil leak, be careful not to scratch or damage the crankshaft sealing surface or the seal bore in the engine block.

4   Clean the crankshaft and seal bore in the block thoroughly and de-grease them by wiping them with a rag soaked in lacquer thinner or acetone. DO NOT lubricate the lip or outer diameter of the new seal - it must be installed like it comes from the manufacturer - DRY.

5   Position the new seal on the crankshaft.

➡Note: When installing the new seal, the words THIS SIDE OUT on the seal must face out.

Use an appropriate size driver and pilot tool to drive the seal into the cylinder block until it is flush with the outer surface of the block. If the seal is driven in past flush, there will be an oil leak. Make sure that the seal is flush (see illustration).

6   Installation of the remaining components is the reverse of removal.

16.5 Position the new seal with the words THIS SIDE OUT facing out. Install this seal DRY! DO NOT lubricate! Gently and evenly drive the seal into the cylinder block until it is FLUSH with the outer surface of the block. DO NOT drive it past flush or there will be an oil leak - the seal must be FLUSH!

17 Engine mounts - check and replacement

1   The engine mounting system on these models consists of four mounts. The right and left mounts support the engine/transaxle assembly while the front and rear mounts control powertrain torque. The right side engine mount is fluid-filled while the other three mounts are molded rubber.

2   Engine mounts seldom require attention, but broken or deteriorated mounts should be replaced immediately or the added strain placed on driveline components may cause damage or accelerated wear.

CHECK

3   During the check, the engine must be raised slightly to remove the weight from the mounts.

4   Raise the vehicle and support it securely on jackstands, then position a jack under the engine oil pan. Place a large wood block between the jack head and the oil pan to prevent oil pan damage, then carefully raise the engine just enough to take the weight off the mounts

❈ WARNING:

DO NOT place any part of your body under the engine when it's supported only by a jack!

5   Check the mounts to see if the rubber is cracked, hardened or separated from the metal backing. Sometimes the rubber will split right down the center.

6   Check for relative movement between the mount plates and the engine or frame (use a large screwdriver or pry bar to attempt to move the mounts). If movement is noted, lower the engine and tighten the mount fasteners.

7   Rubber preservative may be applied to the mounts to slow deterioration.

REPLACEMENT

Front mount

8   Raise the front of the vehicle and support it securely on jackstands.

9   Place a floor jack under the engine (with a wood block between the jack head and oil pan) and raise the engine slightly to relieve the weight from the mounts.

10 Remove the front engine mount through-bolt from the insulator and front crossmember-mounting bracket.

11 Remove the front engine mount bolts, the mounting bracket bolts and remove the insulator assembly.

12 Install the new mount and tighten the bolts securely.

Left mount

13 Raise the front of the vehicle and support it securely on jackstands.

14 Remove the left, front wheel.

15 Place a floor jack under the engine (with a wood block between the jack head and oil pan) and raise the engine slightly to relieve the weight from the mounts.

16 Remove the insulator cover and the insulator through-bolt from the mount.

17 Remove the transmission mount fasteners and remove the mount.

18 Install the new mount and tighten the bolts securely.

Right mount

19 Raise the front of the vehicle and support it securely on

jackstands. Remove the air filter housing and the air intake duct from the throttle body (see Chapter 4).

20 Disconnect the PCV ventilation hose from the valve cover.

21 Place a floor jack under the engine (with a wood block between the jack head and oil pan) and raise the engine slightly to relieve the weight from the mounts.

22 Remove the two, right engine mount insulator vertical fasteners from the frame rail and loosen the one horizontal fastener.

23 Remove the vertical and horizontal fasteners from the engine side bracket. Remove the mount assembly.

24 Install the new mount and tighten the bolts securely.

Rear mount

25 Raise the front of the vehicle and support it securely on jackstands. Remove the left front wheel.

26 Place a floor jack under the engine (with a wood block between the jack head and oil pan) and raise the engine slightly to relieve the weight from the mounts.

27 Remove the rear mount heat shield.

28 Remove the insulator through-bolt from the mount and rear mount bracket.

29 Remove the four mount fasteners and remove the mount.

30 Install the new mount and tighten the bolts securely.

Specifications

General

Displacement	148 cubic inches
Bore	3.445 inches
Stroke	3.976 inches
Compression ratio	
2003	9.4:1
2004 and later	9.5:1
Compression pressure	170 to 225 psi
Firing order	1-3-4-2
Oil pressure	
At idle speed	4 psi (minimum)
At 3,000 rpm	25 to 80 psi

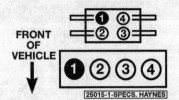

Cylinder and coil terminal locations

Camshaft

Bearing journal diameter	
2003 and 2004	1.021 to 1.022 inches
2005 and later	1.022 to 1.023 inches
Bearing bore diameter	1.024 to 1.025 inches
Bearing clearance	
2003 and 2004	0.0027 to 0.0030 inch
2005 and later	0.0009 to 0.0025 inch
End play	0.0019 to 0.0066 inch
Lobe lift	
Intake	0.324 inch
Exhaust	0.259 inch

Cylinder head warpage

Head gasket surface	0.004 inch maximum
Exhaust manifold mounting surfaces	0.006 inch maximum (per foot)

Intake and exhaust manifolds

Warpage limit	0.006 inch maximum (per foot)

Oil pump

Cover warpage limit	0.001 inch
Inner rotor thickness	0.370 inch (minimum)
Outer rotor thickness	0.370 inch (minimum)
Outer rotor diameter	3.148 inches (minimum)
Rotor-to-pump cover clearance	0.004 inch
Outer rotor-to-housing clearance	0.015 inch (maximum)
Inner rotor-to-outer rotor lobe clearance	0.008 inch (maximum)

Torque specifications*	Ft-lbs (unless otherwise indicated)
Camshaft bearing cap bolts	
M6 bolts	105 in-lbs
M8 bolts	21
Camshaft position sensor bolts	20
Camshaft sprocket bolt	
2003 through 2005	75
2006	85
Crankshaft pulley bolt	100
Cylinder head bolts (in sequence - see illustration 12.19)	
2003 through 2005	
Step 1	25
Step 2	50
Step 3	50
Step 4	Tighten an additional 90-degrees (1/4 turn)
2006	
Step 1	25
Step 2	60
Step 3	60
Step 4	Tighten an additional 90-degrees (1/4 turn)
Driveplate-to-crankshaft bolts	70
Engine mount bracket bolts	45
Exhaust manifold-to-cylinder head bolts	170 in-lbs
Exhaust manifold-to-exhaust pipe bolts	27
Intake manifold (lower)-to-cylinder head bolts	250 in-lbs
Intake manifold (upper)-to-lower intake manifold	250 in-lbs
Intake manifold lower support bracket bolts	
Bracket-to-engine bolts	40
Bracket-to-manifold bolts	250 in-lbs
Oil pan bolts	105 in-lbs
Oil pump	
Attaching bolts	20
Cover screws	105 in-lbs
Pick-up tube bolt	20
Relief valve cap bolt	30
Structural collar bolts	
Collar-to-transaxle bolts	75
Collar-to-oil pan bolts	40
Thermostat housing bolts	17
Timing belt	
Cover bolts	
M6 bolts	105 in-lbs
M8 bolts	250 in-lbs
Tensioner bolt	45
Tensioner pulley lock bolt	19
Timing belt idler pulley bolt	45
Valve cover bolts	
Step 1	40 in-lbs
Step 2	80 in-lbs
Step 3	105 in-lbs

*Refer to Part C for additional torque Specifications

Section

Reference to other Chapters

2B

3.3L AND 3.8L V6
ENGINES

1 General information

Chapter 2B is devoted to in-vehicle repair procedures for the 3.3L and 3.8L V6 engines. These engines utilize a cast-iron engine block with six cylinders arranged in a "V" shape with a 60-degree angle between the two banks. The overhead valve aluminum cylinder heads are equipped with replaceable valve guides and seats. An in-block camshaft, chain driven from the crankshaft, and hydraulic roller lifters actuate the valves through tubular pushrods.

Information concerning engine removal and installation and camshaft removal and installation can be found in Chapter 2C. The following repair procedures are based on the assumption that the engine is installed in the vehicle. If the engine has been removed from the vehicle and mounted on a stand, many of the steps outlined in Chapter 2B do not apply.

2 Repair operations possible with the engine in the vehicle

Many major repair operations can be done without removing the engine from the vehicle.

Clean the engine compartment and the exterior of the engine with degreaser before any work is done. It'll make the job easier and help keep dirt out of internal parts of the engine.

It may be helpful to remove the hood to improve engine access when repairs are performed (see Chapter 11). Cover the fenders to prevent damage to the paint. Special pads are available, but an old bedspread or blanket will also work.

If vacuum, exhaust, oil, or coolant leaks develop, indicating a need for gasket or seal replacement, the repairs can generally be done with the engine in the vehicle. The intake and exhaust manifold gaskets, timing chain cover gasket, oil pan gasket, crankshaft oil seals, and cylinder head gaskets are all accessible with the engine in the vehicle.

Exterior engine components, such as the intake and exhaust manifolds, the oil pan, the oil pump, the timing chain cover, the water pump, the starter motor, the alternator, and fuel system components can be removed for repair with the engine in the vehicle.

Cylinder heads can be removed without pulling the engine. Valve component servicing can also be done with the engine in the vehicle. Replacement of the timing chain and sprockets is also possible with the engine in the vehicle, but the camshaft cannot be removed with the engine in the vehicle. Refer to Chapter 2C for camshaft removal and installation.

Repair or replacement of piston rings, pistons, connecting rods, and rod bearings is possible with the engine in the vehicle, however, this practice is not recommended because of the cleaning and preparation work that must be done to the components.

3 Top Dead Center (TDC) for number one piston - locating

1 Top Dead Center (TDC) is the highest point in the cylinder that each piston reaches as it travels up the cylinder bore. Each piston reaches TDC on the compression stroke and again on the exhaust stroke, but TDC generally refers to piston position on the compression stroke.

2 Positioning the piston(s) at TDC is an essential part of certain procedures such as camshaft and timing chain/sprocket removal.

3 Before beginning this procedure, be sure to place the transmission in Neutral and apply the parking brake or block the rear wheels. Disable the ignition system by disconnecting the primary electrical connector at the ignition coil pack and remove the spark plugs (see Chapter 1). Also disable the fuel pump (see Chapter 4, Section 2).

4 In order to bring any piston to TDC, the crankshaft must be turned using one of the methods outlined below. When looking at the front of the engine, normal crankshaft rotation is clockwise.

   a) *The preferred method is to turn the crankshaft with a socket and ratchet attached to the bolt threaded into the front of the crankshaft. Turn the bolt in a clockwise direction only. Never turn the bolt counterclockwise.*

   b) *A remote starter switch, which may save some time, can also be used. Follow the instructions included with the switch. Once the piston is close to TDC, use a socket and ratchet as described in the previous paragraph.*

   c) *If an assistant is available to turn the ignition switch to the Start position in short bursts, you can get the piston close to TDC without a remote starter switch. Make sure your assistant is out of the vehicle, away from the ignition switch, then use a socket and ratchet as described in Paragraph (a) to complete the procedure.*

5 Install a compression pressure gauge in the number one spark plug hole (refer to Chapter 2C). It should be a gauge with a screw-in fitting and a hose at least six inches long.

6 Rotate the crankshaft using one of the methods described above while observing for pressure on the compression gauge. The moment the gauge shows pressure, indicates that the number one cylinder has begun the compression stroke.

7 Once the compression stroke has begun, TDC for the compression stroke is reached by bringing the piston to the top of the cylinder.

8 If there was no compression, the piston was on the exhaust stroke. Continue rotating the crankshaft 360-degrees (1-turn).

➡ **Note: If a compression gauge is not available, you can simply place a blunt object over the spark plug hole and listen for compression as the engine is rotated. Once compression at the No.1 spark plug hole is noted, the remainder of the Step is the same.**

9 These engines are not equipped with external components (crankshaft pulley, flywheel, timing hole, etc.) that are marked to identify the position of number 1 TDC. Therefore, the only method to double-check the location of TDC number 1 is to remove the timing chain cover to access the timing gears and alignment marks (see Section 10) or with the use of a degree wheel and a positive stop timing device threaded into the spark plug hole for cylinder number 1.

10 After the number one piston has been positioned at TDC on the compression stroke, TDC for any of the remaining cylinders can be located by turning the crankshaft 120-degrees and following the firing order (refer to the Specifications). For example on V6 engines, rotating the engine 120-degrees past TDC number 1 will put the engine at TDC compression for cylinder number 2.

4   Valve covers - removal and installation

REMOVAL

1   Disconnect the cable from the negative terminal of the battery (see Chapter 5, Section 1).

Front valve cover

♦ **Refer to illustration 4.4**

2   Remove the spark plug wires from the spark plugs (see Chapter 1). Label each wire before removal to ensure correct reinstallation.
3   Remove the crankcase vent hose from the valve cover.
4   Remove the valve cover bolts (see illustration).
5   Remove the valve cover.

➡**Note: If the valve cover sticks to the cylinder head, slide a putty knife under the edge dislodge it.**

Rear valve cover

♦ **Refer to illustration 4.12**

6   Remove the spark plug wires from the spark plugs (see Chapter 1). Label each wire before removal to ensure correct reinstallation.
7   Remove the cowl cover and the wiper assembly (see Chapter 12).
8   Label and detach the vacuum lines from the throttle body.
9   Remove the ignition coil pack (see Chapter 5).

10   Remove the upper intake manifold (see Section 6).
11   Remove the breather hose from the PCV valve.
12   Remove the valve cover bolts (see illustration).
13   Detach the valve cover.

➡**Note: If the valve cover sticks to the cylinder head, slide a putty knife under the edge dislodge it.**

INSTALLATION

14   The mating surfaces of the cylinder heads and valve covers must be perfectly clean when the valve covers are installed. If there's sealant or oil on the mating surfaces when the valve cover is installed, oil leaks may develop. Be extra careful not to nick or gouge the mating surfaces while cleaning.
15   Clean the mounting bolt threads with a die, if necessary, to remove corrosion and restore damaged threads. Use a tap to clean the threaded holes in the cylinder heads.
16   Place the valve cover and new gasket in position, then install the bolts. Tighten the bolts in several steps to the torque listed in this Chapter's Specifications.
17   Installation of the remaining components is the reverse of removal.
18   Start the engine and check carefully for oil leaks.

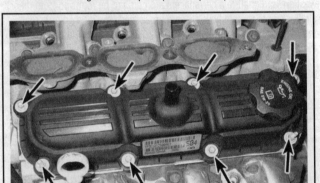

4.4 **Front valve cover mounting bolts**

4.12 **Rear valve cover mounting bolts (two bolts hidden from view)**

5   Rocker arms and pushrods - removal, inspection and installation

REMOVAL

♦ **Refer to illustrations 5.2, 5.3 and 5.4**

1   Remove the valve covers (see Section 3).
2   Loosen each rocker arm shaft bolt a little at a time, until they are all loose enough to be removed by hand (see illustration).

5.2 **Remove the rocker arm shaft bolts from the cylinder head - be sure to start with the outer ones first**

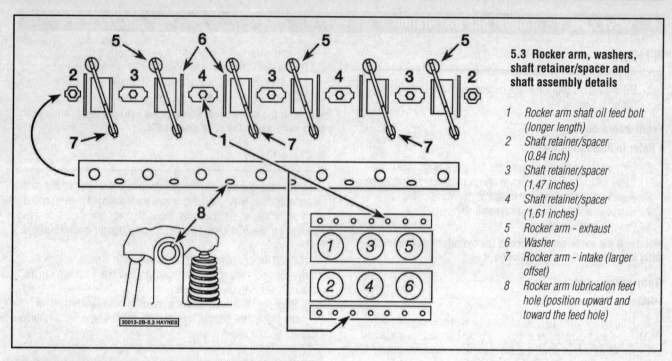

5.3 Rocker arm, washers, shaft retainer/spacer and shaft assembly details

1 Rocker arm shaft oil feed bolt (longer length)
2 Shaft retainer/spacer (0.84 inch)
3 Shaft retainer/spacer (1.47 inches)
4 Shaft retainer/spacer (1.61 inches)
5 Rocker arm - exhaust
6 Washer
7 Rocker arm - intake (larger offset)
8 Rocker arm lubrication feed hole (position upward and toward the feed hole)

5.4 Be sure to store the pushrods in an organized manner to make sure they're reinstalled in their original locations

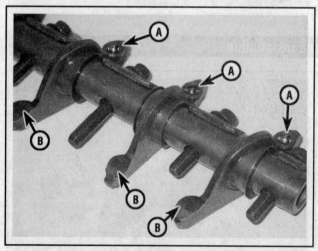

5.5 Check each rocker arm at the ball socket pivots (A) for chipping and wear and at the tips (B) for scuffing, wear and other damage

3 Remove the rocker arm and shaft assembly. If the rocker arms, washers and shaft retainer/spacers are going to be removed from the shaft, be sure to note how they are positioned (see illustration). To remove the bolts and retainer/spacers, use pliers and grip the edges of the retainer/spacers and pull them straight up off the shaft.

4 Remove the pushrods and store them in order to make sure they don't get mixed up during installation (see illustration).

INSPECTION

▶ **Refer to illustration 5.5**

5 Check each rocker arm for wear, cracks and other damage (see illustration), especially where the pushrods and valve stems contact the rocker arm.

6 Check the pivot seat in each rocker arm and the pivot faces. Look for galling, stress cracks and unusual wear patterns. If the rocker arms are worn or damaged, replace them with new ones and install new pivots or shafts as well.

➡**Note: Keep in mind that there is no valve adjustment on these engines, so excessive wear or damage in the valve train can easily result in excessive valve clearance, which in turn will cause valve noise when the engine is running.**

7 On shaft mounted rocker arms, inspect the shafts for galling and excessive wear. Inspect the oil holes for plugging.

8 Inspect the pushrods for cracks and excessive wear at the ends. Roll each pushrod across a piece of plate glass to see if it's bent (if it wobbles, it's bent).

INSTALLATION

✳✳ **CAUTION 1:**

Be sure that the one rocker shaft bolt that is longer than the other bolts is installed into the correct position (see illustration 5.3).

✳✳ **CAUTION 2:**

The rocker shafts should be tightened down slowly starting with the center bolts and working toward the outer bolts. Allow at least 20 minutes bleed-down time after installing both rocker arm shafts before operating the engine.

9 Lubricate the lower end of each pushrod with clean engine oil or moly-base grease and install them in their original locations. Make sure each pushrod seats completely in the lifter socket.

10 Apply moly-base grease to the ends of the valve stems and the upper ends of the pushrods.

11 Apply moly-base grease to the rocker arm shaft. If removed, install the rocker arms, washers, shaft retainer/spacers and bolts in the correct order. Install the rocker arm assembly onto the cylinder head. Tighten the bolts, a little at a time (working from the center out), to the torque listed in this Chapter's Specifications. As the bolts are tightened, make sure the pushrods engage properly in the rocker arms.

✳✳ **CAUTION:**

Allow the engine to set for 20 minutes before starting.

12 Install the valve covers.

6   Intake manifold - removal and installation

✳✳ **WARNING:**

Wait until the engine is completely cool before beginning this procedure.

REMOVAL

1 Relieve the fuel system pressure (see Chapter 4).

2 Disconnect the cable from the negative terminal of the battery (see Chapter 5, Section 1).

3 Drain the cooling system (see Chapter 3).

Upper intake manifold

♦ **Refer to illustration 6.12**

4 Remove the air filter housing and the air intake duct (see Chapter 4).

5 Disconnect the throttle cable and the cruise control cable, if equipped (see Chapter 4).

6 Disconnect the Automatic Idle Speed (AIS) motor, the Throttle Position Sensor (TPS) and Manifold Absolute Pressure (MAP) sensor connectors (see Chapter 6).

7 Disconnect the vapor purge vacuum hose (see Chapter 6).

8 Disconnect the Positive Crankcase Ventilation (PCV) hose (see Chapter 6).

9 Remove the power steering reservoir mounting bolts and loosen the side nut and remove the power steering reservoir from the bracket. Position the assembly off to the side without disconnecting the fluid lines.

10 Disconnect the power brake booster (see Chapter 9) and Leak Detection Pump (LDP) or Natural Vacuum Leak Detection (NVLD) system vacuum hoses from the manifold (see Chapter 6).

11 Remove the EGR pipe from the manifold (see Chapter 6).

12 Remove the upper intake manifold bolts (see illustration 6.29). Separate the assembly from the lower intake manifold.

➡ **Note: Be sure to cover the intake manifold runners to prevent any objects from falling into the lower intake manifold while the upper manifold is off (see illustration).**

Lower intake manifold

♦ **Refer to illustrations 6.19 and 6.20**

13 Remove the upper intake manifold (see Steps 1 through 12).

14 Disconnect the fuel hose fitting. Remove the fuel line (see Chapter 4).

15 Remove the ignition coil pack and bracket (see Chapter 5).

16 Disconnect the heater supply hose (see Chapter 3) and the engine coolant temperature sensor (ECT) (see Chapter 6).

17 Remove the fuel rail and injector assembly (see Chapter 4).

18 Disconnect the upper radiator hose (see Chapter 3).

19 Remove the bolts and the lower intake manifold and separate the lower intake manifold from the engine (see illustration 6.26). If the lower intake manifold is stuck, carefully pry on a casting protrusion

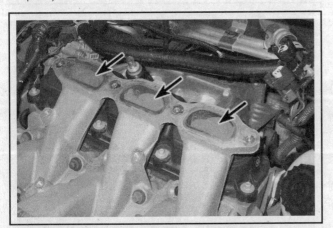

6.12 Here, shop towels have been installed in the manifold runners to prevent any objects falling into the lower intake manifold

6.19 Pry on the intake manifold only in the areas where the gasket mating surface will not get damaged

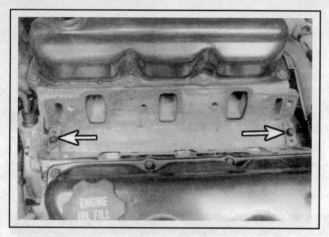

6.20 Remove the intake manifold gasket retainer screws

6.23 Apply RTV sealant to the corners of the cylinder head and engine block

(see illustration) - don't pry between the lower intake manifold, and the cylinder heads, as damage to the gasket sealing surfaces may result. If you're installing a new lower intake manifold, transfer all fittings and sensors to the new lower intake manifold.

20 Remove the lower intake manifold gasket retaining screws and remove the gasket from the cylinder block (see illustration).

INSTALLATION

Lower intake manifold

▶ **Refer to illustrations 6.23 and 6.26**

➥**Note: The mating surfaces of the cylinder heads, cylinder block, and the intake manifold must be perfectly clean when the lower intake manifold is installed. Gasket removal solvents are available at most auto parts stores and may be helpful when removing old gasket material that's stuck to the cylinder heads, cylinder block and lower intake manifold (the lower intake manifold is made of aluminum - aggressive scrapping can cause damage). Be sure to follow the instructions printed on the solvent container.**

21 Use a gasket scraper to remove all traces of sealant and old gasket material, then clean the mating surfaces with lacquer thinner or acetone. If there's old sealant or oil on the mating surfaces when the

lower intake manifold is installed, oil or vacuum leaks may develop. Use a vacuum cleaner to remove gasket material that falls into the intake ports or the lifter valley.

22 Use a tap of the correct size to chase the threads in the bolt holes, then use compressed air (if available) to remove debris from the holes.

✳✳ WARNING:

Wear safety glasses or a face shield to protect your eyes when using compressed air!

23 Apply a 1/4-inch bead of RTV sealant or equivalent to the cylinder heads-to-engine block junctions (see illustration).

24 Install the lower intake gasket and tighten the retainer screws.

25 Carefully lower the lower intake manifold into place and install the mounting bolts finger-tight.

26 Tighten the mounting bolts in three steps, following the recommended tightening sequence (see illustration), to the torque listed in this Chapter's Specifications.

Upper intake manifold

▶ **Refer to illustrations 6.27 and 6.29**

27 Check the condition of the rubber seals that are installed into

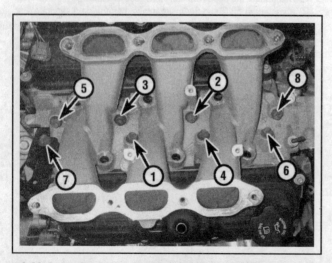

6.26 Lower intake manifold bolt tightening sequence

6.27 Be sure to replace the upper intake manifold seals with new ones if they are damaged

each intake runner on the upper intake manifold (see illustration). If they are damaged, replace the seals in the upper intake manifold.

28 Install the upper intake manifold onto the lower intake manifold. Install the special screws into the composite material and turn slowly to prevent damage to the upper intake manifold,

29 Tighten the mounting screws following the correct sequence (see illustration) to the torque listed in this Chapter's Specifications.

30 Installation of the remaining components is the reverse of removal.

31 Refill the cooling system (see Chapter 1), start the engine and check for leaks and proper operation.

6.29 Upper intake manifold bolt tightening sequence

7 Exhaust manifolds - removal and installation

1 Disconnect the cable from the negative terminal of the battery (see Chapter 5, Section 1).

REMOVAL

Rear exhaust manifold

▶ **Refer to illustrations 7.4a, 7.4b, 7.6 and 7.7**

2 Remove the cowl cover (see Chapter 11) and the wiper unit (see Chapter 12).

3 Disconnect the rear bank of spark plug wires.

4 Unbolt the crossover pipe where it joins the rear exhaust manifold (see illustrations).

5 Disconnect and remove the upstream oxygen sensor connector. Remove the upstream oxygen sensor (see Chapter 6).

6 Remove the bolts and the upper heat shield (see illustration).

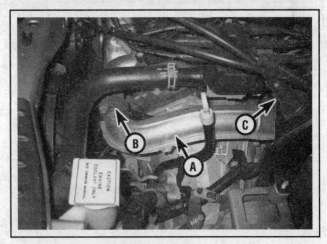

7.4a Exhaust crossover pipe details

A *Exhaust crossover pipe*
B *Front (left bank) exhaust manifold-to-crossover pipe flange*
C *Rear (right bank) exhaust manifold-to-crossover pipe flange (behind cruise control actuator)*

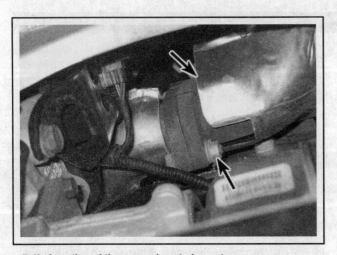

7.4b Location of the rear exhaust pipe nuts

7.6 Location of the exhaust manifold heat shield mounting bolts

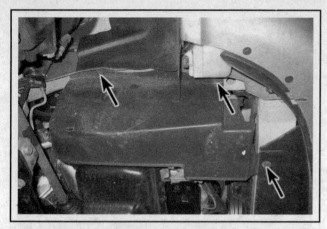

7.7 Right side splash shield retainers

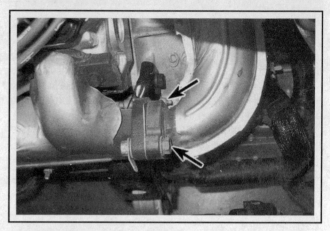

7.13 Location of the front exhaust pipe nuts

7   Raise the vehicle, support it securely on jackstands, and remove the engine splash shield from the passenger's side (see illustration).

8   Loosen the power steering pump support strut lower bolt.

9   Disconnect the downstream oxygen sensor connector.

10 Remove the bolts and disconnect the catalytic converter from the exhaust manifold (see Chapter 6).

11 Lower the vehicle and remove the power steering pump support strut upper bolt.

12 Remove the bolts attaching the rear exhaust manifold to the cylinder head, and remove the rear exhaust manifold.

Front exhaust manifold

♦ **Refer to illustration 7.13**

13 Unbolt the crossover pipe where it joins the front exhaust manifold (see illustration).

14 Disconnect the front bank of spark plug wires (see Chapter 1).

15 Remove the bolts and the upper heat shield.

16 Remove the bolts attaching the front exhaust manifold to the cylinder head, and remove the front exhaust manifold.

INSTALLATION

17 Clean the mating surfaces to remove all traces of old gasket material, then inspect the exhaust manifolds for distortion and cracks. Check for warpage with a precision straight edge held against the mating surface. If a feeler gauge thicker than 0.030-inch can be inserted between the straightedge and the mating surface, take the exhaust manifold(s) to an automotive machine shop for resurfacing.

18 Place the exhaust manifold in position with a new gasket and install the mounting bolts finger tight.

➡**Note: Be sure to identify the exhaust manifold gasket by the correct cylinder designation and the position of the exhaust ports on the gasket.**

19 Starting in the middle and working out toward the ends, tighten the bolts to the torque listed in this Chapter's Specifications.

20 Installation of the remaining components is the reverse of removal.

21 Start the engine and check for exhaust leaks between the exhaust manifolds and the cylinder heads and between the exhaust manifolds, crossover pipe and catalytic converter.

8   Crankshaft pulley - removal and installation

8.6a Carefully wedge a flat-bladed screwdriver between the driveplate teeth and the engine block at the transaxle bellhousing to lock the crankshaft in place

REMOVAL

♦ **Refer to illustrations 8.6a, 8.6b and 8.7**

1   Disconnect the cable from the negative terminal of the battery (see Chapter 5, Section 1).

2   Loosen the lug nuts on the right front wheel, raise the vehicle, and support it securely on jackstands.

3   Remove the right front wheel.

4   Remove the passenger side inner fender splash shield (see Section 7).

5   Remove the serpentine drivebelt (see Chapter 1).

6   Remove the driveplate cover and position a large screwdriver in the ring gear teeth to keep the crankshaft from turning (see illustration) while a helper removes the crankshaft pulley-to-crankshaft bolt (see illustration).

8.6b Remove the crankshaft pulley bolt with a breaker bar and a socket

7   Pull the crankshaft pulley off the crankshaft with a two-jaw puller attached to the inner hub (see illustration).

❋❋ CAUTION 1:

Do not attach the puller to the outer edge of the pulley or damage to the pulley may result.

❋❋ CAUTION 2:

Because the pulley is recessed, an adapter may be needed between the puller bolt and the crankshaft (to prevent damage to the bore and threads in the end of the crankshaft).

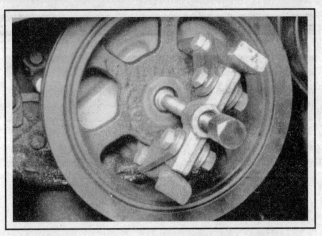

8.7 Remove the crankshaft pulley with a two-jaw puller attached to the inner hub - DO NOT pull on the outer edge of the pulley or damage may result!

INSTALLATION

8   Install the crankshaft pulley with a special installation tool that threads to the crankshaft in place of the crankshaft pulley bolt (available at most automotive parts stores). Be sure to apply clean engine oil or multi-purpose grease to the seal contact surface of the damper hub (if it isn't lubricated, the seal lip could be damaged and oil leakage would result). If the tool isn't available, the crankshaft pulley bolt and several washers used as spacers, may be used as long as the crankshaft pulley bolt torque is not exceeded.

9   Remove the tool and install the crankshaft pulley bolt and tighten it to the torque listed in this Chapter's Specifications.

10 Installation of the remaining components is the reverse of removal.

9   Crankshaft front oil seal - replacement

▶ **Refer to illustrations 9.2 and 9.3**

1   Remove the crankshaft pulley (see Section 8).

2   Note how the seal is installed - the new one must be installed to the same depth and face the same way. Carefully pry the oil seal out of the cover with a seal puller or a large screwdriver (see illustration). Be very careful not to distort the cover or scratch the crankshaft! Wrap tape

around the tip of the screwdriver to avoid damage to the crankshaft.

3   Apply clean engine oil or multi-purpose grease to the outer edge of the new seal, then install it in the cover with the lip (spring side) facing IN. Drive the seal into place (see illustration) with a seal driver or a large socket and a hammer. Make sure the seal enters the bore squarely. Stop when the front face is at the proper depth.

4   Reinstall the crankshaft pulley.

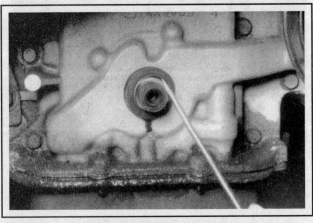

9.2 Be very careful not to damage the crankshaft surface when removing the front seal

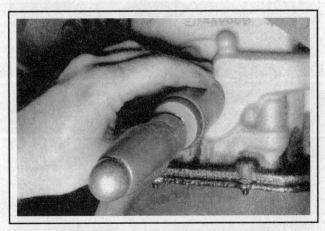

9.3 Use a seal driver or a large deep socket and gently tap the seal into place

10 Timing chain and sprockets - removal, inspection and installation

✳ WARNING:

Wait until the engine is completely cool before beginning this procedure.

REMOVAL

♦ **Refer to illustrations 10.11, 10.15 and 10.16**

1 Disconnect the cable from the negative terminal of the battery (see Chapter 5, Section 1).

2 Drain the coolant (see Chapter 1).

3 Loosen the right-front wheel lug nuts. Raise the vehicle and support it securely on jackstands. Drain the engine oil (see Chapter 1).

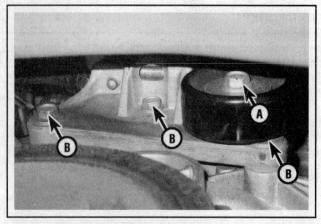

10.11 Engine mount bracket details

A *Idler pulley mounting bolt*
B *Engine bracket bolts (one bolt behind idler pulley and another bolt on top of bracket not visible)*

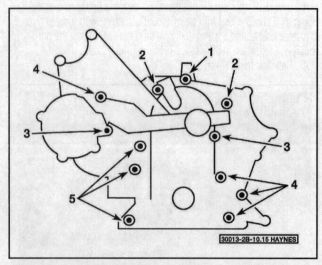

10.15 Timing chain cover bolt locations

1	M8 1.25 X 95	4	M8 1.25 X 80
2	M10 1.5 X 100	5	M8 1.25 X 45
3	M10 1.5 X 85		

4 Remove the right-front wheel and inner splash shield (see Section 7).

5 Remove the oil pan (see Section 13) and the oil pump pick-up tube.

6 Remove the drivebelt (see Chapter 1).

7 Unbolt the air conditioning compressor from its bracket and set it off to one side. Use mechanics wire to tie the assembly to the fender to keep it away from the work area (see Chapter 3).

✳ WARNING:

The refrigerant hoses are under pressure - don't disconnect them.

8 Remove the crankshaft pulley (see Section 8).

9 Remove the radiator lower hose (see Chapter 3). Remove the heater hose from the timing chain cover housing, or water pump inlet (oil cooler equipped models).

10 Remove the right side engine mount (see Section 18).

11 Unbolt and remove the idler pulley from the engine mount bracket (see illustration).

12 Remove the bolts and remove the engine mount bracket. Remove the camshaft sensor from the timing chain cover (see Chapter 6).

13 Remove the water pump (see Chapter 3).

14 Remove the bolt and remove the power steering pump support strut to the front cover.

15 Remove the timing chain cover-to engine block bolts (see illustration).

16 Temporarily install the crankshaft pulley bolt and turn the crankshaft with the bolt to align the timing marks on the crankshaft and camshaft sprockets. The crankshaft arrow should be at the top (12 o'clock position) and the camshaft sprocket arrow should be in the 6 o'clock position (see illustration).

17 Remove the camshaft sprocket bolt. Do not turn the camshaft in

10.16 Timing chain and sprocket alignment details

A *Crankshaft sprocket alignment mark*
B *Camshaft sprocket alignment mark*
C *Camshaft sprocket bolt*

the process (if you do, realign the timing marks before the sprocket is removed).

18 Use two large screwdrivers to carefully pry the camshaft sprocket off the camshaft dowel pin.

19 Timing chains and sprockets should be replaced in sets. If you intend to install a new timing chain, remove the crankshaft sprocket with a puller and install a new one. Be sure to align the key in the crankshaft with the keyway in the sprocket during installation.

INSPECTION

20 Inspect the timing chain dampener (guide) for cracks and wear and replace it, if necessary.

21 Clean the timing chain and sprockets with solvent and dry them with compressed air (if available).

☀ WARNING:

Wear eye protection when using compressed air.

22 Inspect the components for wear and damage. Look for teeth that are deformed, chipped, pitted, and cracked.

23 The timing chain and sprockets should be replaced with a new one if the engine has high mileage, the chain has visible damage, or total freeplay midway between the sprockets exceeds one inch. Failure to replace a worn timing chain and sprockets may result in erratic engine performance, loss of power, and decreased fuel mileage. Loose chains can "jump" timing. In the worst case, chain "jumping" or break-age will result in severe engine damage.

INSTALLATION

▶ **Refer to illustration 10.25**

24 Use a gasket scraper to remove all traces of old gasket material and sealant from the cover and engine block. The cover is made of alu-minum, so be careful not to nick or gouge it. Clean the gasket sealing surfaces with lacquer thinner or acetone.

25 Turn the camshaft to position the dowel pin at 6 o'clock (see illustration 10.16). Mesh the timing chain with the camshaft sprocket, then engage it with the crankshaft sprocket. The timing marks should be aligned (see illustration 10.16).

10.25 Be sure the timing chain colored reference links align with marks on the sprockets

➡Note: If the crankshaft has moved, turn it until the arrow stamped on the crankshaft sprocket is exactly at the top. If the camshaft was turned, install the sprocket temporarily and turn the camshaft until the sprocket timing mark is at the bottom, opposite the mark on the crankshaft sprocket. The arrows should point to each other. The timing chain colored reference links should align with the camshaft and crankshaft timing marks that are in the 3 o'clock position (see illustration). If you are using replacement parts, check this alignment.

26 Install the camshaft sprocket bolt and tighten it to the torque listed in this Chapter's Specifications.

27 Lubricate the chain and sprocket with clean engine oil.

28 Stick the new gasket to the cover, making sure the bottom edge of the gasket is flush with the bottom of the cover. Attach the cover to the engine block, making sure the flats of the oil pump gear are aligned with the flats on the crankshaft. Install the bolts and tighten them in a criss-cross pattern, in three steps, to the torque listed in this Chapter's Specifications.

29 Installation of the remaining components is the reverse of removal.

30 Add oil and coolant (see Chapter 1), start the engine and check for leaks.

11 Hydraulic roller lifters - removal, inspection and installation

1 A noisy valve lifter can be isolated when the engine is idling. Hold a mechanic's stethoscope or a length of hose near each valve while listening at the other end. Another method is to remove the valve cover and, with the engine idling, touch each of the valve spring retain-ers, one at a time. If a valve lifter is defective, it'll be evident from the shock felt at the retainer each time the valve seats.

2 The most likely causes of noisy valve lifters are dirt trapped inside the lifter and lack of oil flow, viscosity, or pressure. Before con-demning the lifters, check the oil for fuel contamination, correct level, cleanliness, and correct viscosity.

REMOVAL

▶ **Refer to illustrations 11.6, 11.7, 11.8 and 11.9**

3 Remove the intake manifold (see Section 6) and valve covers (see Section 4).

4 Remove the rocker arms and pushrods (see Section 5).

5 Remove the cylinder heads from the engine block (see Sec-tion 12).

11.6 Remove the bolts that attach the lifter retaining plate

11.7 Lift off the alignment yokes

6   Remove the retaining plate bolts (see illustration) and lift the plate to gain access to the hydraulic roller lifters.

7   Each pair of lifters is retained with an alignment yoke. Lift the yoke from the lifters (see illustration).

8   There are several ways to extract the lifters from the bores. A special tool designed to grip and remove lifters is manufactured by many tool companies and is available at most automotive parts stores, but it may not be required in every case. On newer engines without a lot of

varnish buildup, the lifters can often be removed with a small magnet or even with your fingers (see illustration). A machinist's scribe with a bent end can be used to pull the lifters out by positioning the point under the retainer ring in the top of each lifter.

11.8 On engines with low mileage, the roller lifters can be removed by hand - if the lifters are coated with varnish, a special lifter removal tool may be required

⁂ CAUTION:

Don't use pliers to remove the lifters unless you intend to replace them with new ones. The pliers may damage the precision machined and hardened lifters, rendering them useless.

9   Store the lifters in a box clearly labeled to ensure they're reinstalled in their original locations (see illustration).

INSPECTION

▸ Refer to illustration 11.11

10 Clean the lifters with solvent and dry them thoroughly. Do not mix them up.

11 Check each lifter wall and pushrod seat for scuffing, score marks, and uneven wear. If the lifter walls are damaged or worn inspect the lifter bores in the engine block (see illustration).

12 Check the roller of each lifter for freedom of movement, excessive looseness, flat spots, or pitting. The camshaft must also be inspected for signs of abnormal wear.

11.9 Store the lifters in a box so each one will be reinstalled in its original bore

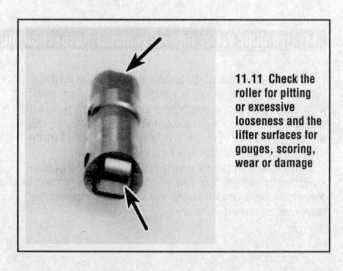

11.11 Check the roller for pitting or excessive looseness and the lifter surfaces for gouges, scoring, wear or damage

➡**Note: Used roller lifters can be reinstalled with a new camshaft or the original camshaft can be used if new roller lifters are installed, provided the used components are in good condition.**

INSTALLATION

13 When installing used lifters, make sure they're replaced in their original bores. Position the valve lifter with the lubrication hole facing upward toward the middle of the engine block. Soak the lifters in oil to remove trapped air. Coat the lifters with moly-based grease or engine assembly lube prior to installation.

14 Installation of the remaining components is the reverse of removal.

15 Tighten the retaining plate bolts to the torque listed in this Chapter's Specifications.

16 Run the engine and check for oil leaks.

12 Cylinder heads - removal and installation

✳✳ CAUTION:

Allow the engine to cool completely before loosening the cylinder head bolts.

REMOVAL

▶ **Refer to illustration 12.9**

1 Disconnect the cable from the negative terminal of the battery (see Chapter 5, Section 1).

2 Remove the intake manifold (see Section 4).

3 Disconnect all wires and vacuum hoses from the cylinder heads. Label them to simplify reinstallation.

4 Disconnect the ignition wires and remove the spark plugs (see Chapter 1). Label the ignition wires to simplify reinstallation.

5 Remove the exhaust manifold (see Section 5).

6 Remove the valve covers (see Section 3).

7 Remove the rocker arms and pushrods (see Section 10).

8 Using the new cylinder head gasket, outline the cylinders and bolt pattern on a piece of cardboard. Be sure to indicate the front (timing chain end) of the engine for reference. Punch holes at the bolt locations. Loosen each of the cylinder head mounting bolts, 1/4-turn at a time, until they can be removed by hand - work from bolt-to-bolt in a pattern that's the reverse of the tightening sequence (see illustration 12.18). Store the bolts in the cardboard holder as they're removed - this will ensure they are reinstalled in their original locations, which is absolutely essential.

9 Lift the cylinder heads from the engine. If resistance is felt, don't pry between the cylinder head and engine block, damage to the mating surfaces will result. Recheck for cylinder head bolts that may have been overlooked, then use a hammer and wood block to tap up on the cylinder head and break the gasket seal (see illustration). Be careful because there are locating dowels in the engine block to position each cylinder head. As a last resort, pry each cylinder head up at the rear corner only and be careful not to damage anything. After removal, place the cylinder head on wood blocks to prevent damage to the gasket surfaces.

10 Have the cylinder head inspected and serviced by a qualified automotive machine shop.

INSTALLATION

▶ **Refer to illustrations 12.12, 12.15 and 12.18**

11 The mating surfaces of each cylinder head and the engine block must be perfectly clean when the cylinder head is installed.

12 Use a gasket scraper to remove all traces of carbon and old gasket material (see illustration), then clean the mating surfaces with lacquer thinner or acetone. If there's oil on the mating surfaces when the cylinder head is installed, the gasket may not seal correctly and leaks may develop. When working on the engine block, it's a good idea to cover the lifter valley with shop rags to keep debris out of the engine. Use a shop rag or vacuum cleaner to remove any debris that falls into the cylinders.

13 Check the engine block and cylinder head mating surfaces for

12.9 Do not pry on the cylinder head near the gasket mating surface - use the corners under the casting protrusions

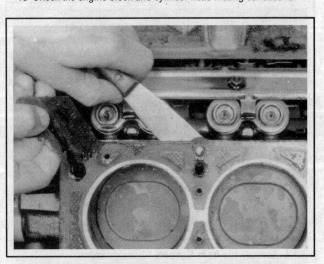

12.12 Use a putty knife or gasket scraper to remove the gasket from the cylinder head

12.15 Be sure the stamped designations are facing up and forward

12.18 Cylinder head bolt TIGHTENING sequence

nicks, deep scratches, and other damage. If damage is slight, it can be removed with a file; if it's excessive, machining may be the only alternative.

14 Use a tap of the correct size to chase the threads in the cylinder head bolt holes. Dirt, corrosion, sealant, and damaged threads will affect torque readings.

15 Position the new gasket over the dowel pins in the engine block. Some gaskets are marked TOP or FRONT to ensure correct installation (see illustration).

16 Carefully position the cylinder head on the engine block without disturbing the gasket.

17 With a straight-edge, check each cylinder head bolt for necking-down or stretching. If all of the threads do not contact the straight-edge, replace the bolt.

18 Install the head bolts and tighten them in the recommended sequence to the torque listed in this Chapter's Specifications (Step 1) (see illustration). Next, tighten them following the recommended sequence to the Step 2 torque listed in this Chapter's Specifications. Tighten the bolts again to the same torque as a double check (Step 3). Finally, tighten each bolt an additional 90-degrees (1/4-turn) following the recommended sequence (Step 4). Do not use a torque wrench for this step; apply a paint mark to the bolt head or use a torque-angle gauge (available at most automotive parts stores) and a socket and breaker bar.

19 Installation of the remaining components is the reverse of removal.

20 Change the oil and filter (see Chapter 1).

21 Refill the cooling system (see Chapter 1). Start the engine and check for leaks and proper operation.

13 Oil pan - removal and installation

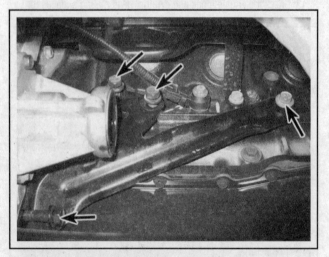

13.4 Remove the bolts from the transaxle brace

REMOVAL

▶ **Refer to illustrations 13.4, 13.7a and 13.7b**

1 Disconnect the cable from the negative terminal of the battery (see Chapter 5, Section 1).

2 Raise the front of the vehicle and support it securely on jackstands. Apply the parking brake and block the rear wheels to keep it from rolling off the stands.

3 Drain the engine oil (see Chapter 1).

4 Remove the engine/transaxle brace (see illustration).

5 Remove the lower driveplate cover.

6 Remove the starter (see Chapter 5).

7 Remove the bolts and nuts, then carefully separate the oil pan from the engine block (see illustration). Don't pry between the engine

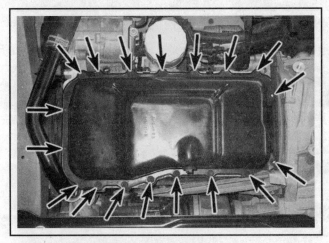

13.7a Remove the bolts from the oil pan

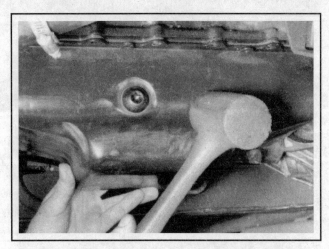

13.7b Use a soft faced hammer to loosen the oil pan - be careful not to dent the pan

block and the pan or damage to the sealing surfaces could occur and oil leaks may develop. Tap the pan with a soft-face hammer to break the gasket seal (see illustration). If it still sticks, slip a putty knife between the engine block and oil pan to break the bond (but be careful not to scratch the surfaces).

INSTALLATION

8   Clean the pan with solvent and remove all old sealant and gasket material from the engine block and pan mating surfaces. Clean the mating surfaces with lacquer thinner or acetone and make sure the bolt holes in the engine block are clear. Check the oil pan flange for distortion, particularly around the bolt holes. If necessary, place the pan on a

wood block and use a hammer to flatten and restore the gasket surface.
9   Apply a bead of RTV sealant to the bottom surface of the timing chain cover and to the bottom of the rear main oil seal retainer. Install a new gasket on the oil pan flange.
10 Place the oil pan in position on the engine block and install the nuts/bolts.
11 Tighten the bolts to the torque listed in this Chapter's Specifications. Starting at the center, follow a criss-cross pattern and work up to the final torque in three steps.
12 Installation of the remaining components is the reverse of removal.
13 Refill the engine with oil (see Chapter 1), run it until normal operating temperature is reached, and check for leaks.

14 Oil pump - removal, inspection and installation

REMOVAL

▶ Refer to illustration 14.2

1   Remove the oil pan (see Section 13).
2   Remove the timing chain cover (see Section 10). Remove the oil pump cover (plate) from the timing chain cover (see illustration).

14.2 Remove the oil pump cover screws

INSPECTION

▶ Refer to illustrations 14.4, 14.5, 14.7, 14.8 and 14.9

3   Clean all parts thoroughly in solvent and carefully inspect the rotors, pump cover, and timing chain cover for nicks, scratches, or burrs. Replace the assembly if it is damaged.
4   Use a straightedge and a feeler gauge to measure the oil pump

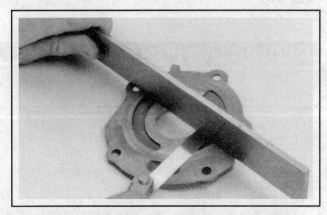

14.4 Place a straightedge across the oil pump cover and check it for warpage with a feeler gauge

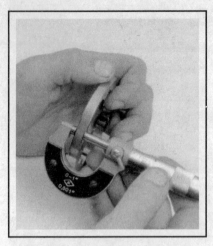

14.5 Use a micrometer to measure the thickness of the outer rotor

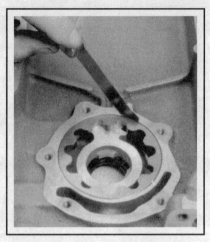

14.7 Check the outer rotor-to-housing clearance with a feeler gauge

14.8 Check the clearance between the lobes of the inner and outer rotors

cover for warpage (see illustration). If it's warped more than the limit listed in this Chapter's Specifications, the pump should be replaced.

5   Measure the thickness of the outer rotor (see illustration). If the thickness is less than the value listed in this Chapter's Specifications, the pump should be replaced.

6   Measure the thickness of the inner rotor. If the thickness is less than the value listed in this Chapter's Specifications, the pump should

14.9 Using a straightedge and feeler gauge, check the clearance between the surface of the oil pump cover and the rotors

be replaced.

7   Insert the outer rotor into the timing chain cover/oil pump housing and measure the clearance between the rotor and housing (see illustration). If the measurement is more than the maximum allowable clearance listed in this Chapter's Specifications, the pump should be replaced.

8   Install the inner rotor in the oil pump assembly and measure the clearance between the lobes on the inner and outer rotors (see illustration). If the clearance is more than the value listed in this Chapter's Specifications, the pump should be replaced.

➠Note: Install the inner rotor with the mark facing up.

9   Place a straightedge across the face of the oil pump assembly (see illustration). If the clearance between the pump surface and the rotors is greater than the limit listed in this Chapter's Specifications, the pump should be replaced.

INSTALLATION

10   Install the pump cover and tighten the bolts to the torque listed in this Chapter's Specifications.

11   Install the timing chain cover (see Section 10) and tighten the bolts to the torque listed in this Chapter's Specifications.

12   Installation of the remaining components is the reverse of removal.

13   Refill the engine with oil and change the oil filter (see Chapter 1).

15   Oil cooler - removal and installation

REMOVAL

1   Disconnect the cable from the negative terminal of the battery (see Chapter 5, Section 1).

2   Drain the coolant (see Chapter 1).

3   Raise the vehicle and support it securely on jackstands. Drain the engine oil and remove the oil filter (see Chapter 1).

4   Disconnect the coolant hoses from the inlet and outlet ports.

5   Unscrew and remove the oil cooler fitting and remove the oil cooler.

INSTALLATION

6   Lubricate the oil cooler connector on the oil filter adapter with clean engine oil.

7   Position the flat side of the oil cooler parallel to the oil pan rail and install the oil cooler onto the adapter. Install the fitting and tighten to the torque listed in this Chapter's Specifications.

8   Install the oil filter and refill the engine with oil (see Chapter 1). Also install a new oil filter.

9   Refill the cooling system (see Chapter 1). Run the engine until normal operating temperature is reached, and check for leaks.

16 Driveplate - removal and installation

This procedure is essentially the same for all engines. Refer to Chapter 2A, Section 15, and follow the procedure outlined there, but use the torque listed in this Chapter's Specifications.

17 Rear main oil seal - replacement

This procedure is essentially the same for all engines. Refer to Chapter 2A, Section 16, and follow the procedure outlined there.

18 Engine mounts - check and replacement

◆ **Refer to illustrations 18.1a, 18.1b, 18.1c and 18.1d**

This procedure is essentially the same for all engines. Refer to Chapter 2A, Section 17, and follow the procedure outlined there, but refer to the illustrations listed here.

18.1b Access the left side transaxle mount through bolt using the hole in the inner fenderwell

18.1a Location of the front engine mount through bolt

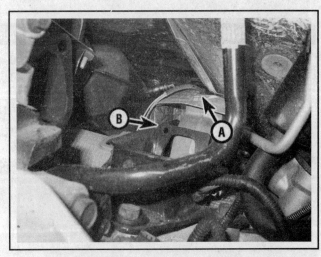

18.1d Remove the heat shield mounting bolt (A) and the heat shield to access the rear engine mount through bolt (B)

18.1c Remove the right side engine mount bracket and brace mounting bolts and separate the assembly from the engine mount bracket and engine compartment

Specifications

General

Displacement

3.3L	201 cubic inches
3.8L	231 cubic inches

Bore

3.3L	3.660 inches
3.8L	3.779 inches

Stroke

3.3L	3.188 inches
3.8L	3.425 inches

Compression ratio

3.3L	9.35:1
3.8L	9.6:1

Cylinder numbers (drivebelt end-to-transmission end)

Rear bank	1-3-5
Front bank (radiator side)	2-4-6

Firing order   1-2-3-4-5-6

Oil pressure

At idle speed	5 psi (minimum)
At 3,000 rpm	30 to 80 psi

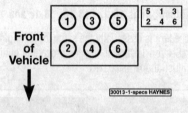

Cylinder and coil terminal locations

Oil pump

Cover warpage limit	0.001 inch
Outer rotor thickness (minimum)	0.301 inch
Inner rotor thickness (minimum)	0.301 inch
Rotor-to-pump cover clearance	0.004 inch
Outer rotor-to-housing clearance	0.015 inch
Inner rotor-to-outer rotor lobe clearance	0.008 inch

Torque specifications   Ft-lbs (unless otherwise indicated)

Camshaft sprocket bolt	40
Crankshaft pulley bolt	40
Cylinder head bolts (in sequence - see illustration 12.18)	
Step 1	45
Step 2	65
Step 3	65
Step 4	Tighten an additional 90-degrees (1/4 turn)
Drivebelt idler sprocket bolt	24
Driveplate-to-crankshaft bolts	70
Engine mount bracket bolts	
M8	21
M10	40
Exhaust manifold-to-cylinder head bolts	17
Exhaust manifold heat shield nut	105 in-lbs
Exhaust crossover bolts	30

Torque specifications   Ft-lbs (unless otherwise indicated)

Hydraulic lifter retaining bolts	105 in-lbs
Intake manifold (upper) retaining bolts*	105 in-lbs
Intake manifold (lower)-to-block bolts	17
Oil cooler fitting	20
Oil pan drain plug	20
Oil pan bolts	105 in-lbs
Oil pump pick-up tube mounting bolts	21
Oil pump cover (plate) screws	105 in-lbs
Rear main oil seal retainer bolts	105 in-lbs
Rocker arm shaft bolts	17
Timing chain cover bolts	
M8	20
M10	40
Timing chain sprocket-to-camshaft bolt	40
Valve cover-to-cylinder head bolts	105 in-lbs
Water pump bolts	See Chapter 3

*Apply a non-hardening thread-locking compound to the bolt threads before installation

Notes

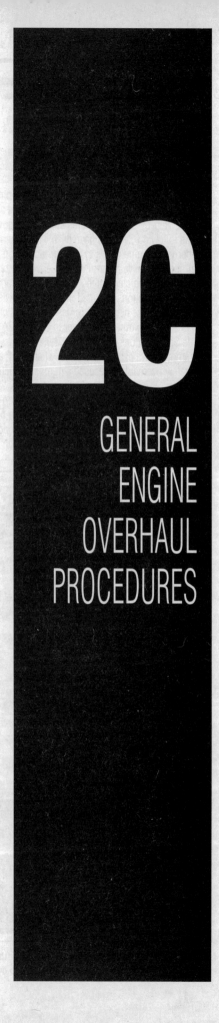

2C

GENERAL ENGINE OVERHAUL PROCEDURES

Section

Reference to other Chapters

1   General information - engine overhaul

▶ **Refer to illustrations 1.1, 1.2, 1.3, 1.4, 1.5 and 1.6**

Included in this portion of Chapter 2 are general information and diagnostic testing procedures for determining the overall mechanical condition of your engine.

The information ranges from advice concerning preparation for an overhaul and the purchase of replacement parts and/or components to detailed, step-by-step procedures covering removal and installation.

The following Sections have been written to help you determine whether your engine needs to be overhauled and how to remove and install it once you've determined it needs to be rebuilt. For information concerning in-vehicle engine repair, see Chapter 2A or 2B.

The Specifications included in this Part are general in nature and include only those necessary for testing the oil pressure and checking the engine compression. Refer to Chapter 2A or 2B for additional engine Specifications.

It's not always easy to determine when, or if, an engine should be completely overhauled, because a number of factors must be considered.

High mileage is not necessarily an indication that an overhaul is needed, while low mileage doesn't preclude the need for an overhaul. Frequency of servicing is probably the most important consideration. An engine that's had regular and frequent oil and filter changes, as well as other required maintenance, will most likely give many thousands of miles of reliable service. Conversely, a neglected engine may require an overhaul very early in its service life.

Excessive oil consumption is an indication that piston rings, valve seals and/or valve guides are in need of attention. Make sure that oil leaks aren't responsible before deciding that the rings and/or guides are bad. Perform a cylinder compression check to determine the extent of the work required (see Section 3). Also check the vacuum readings under various conditions (see Section 4).

Check the oil pressure with a gauge installed in place of the oil pressure sending unit and compare it to this Chapter's Specifications (see Section 2). If it's extremely low, the bearings and/or oil pump are probably worn out.

Loss of power, rough running, knocking or metallic engine noises, excessive valve train noise and high fuel consumption rates may also point to the need for an overhaul, especially if they're all present at the same time. If a complete tune-up doesn't remedy the situation, major mechanical work is the only solution.

An engine overhaul involves restoring the internal parts to the specifications of a new engine. During an overhaul, the piston rings are replaced and the cylinder walls are reconditioned (rebored and/or honed) (see illustrations 1.1 and 1.2). If a rebore is done by an automotive machine shop, new oversize pistons will also be installed. The

1.1 An engine block being bored. An engine rebuilder will use special machinery to recondition the cylinder bores

1.2 If the cylinders are bored, the machine shop will normally hone the engine on a machine like this

1.3 A crankshaft having a main bearing journal ground

trouble free miles.

➡**Note: Critical cooling system components such as the hoses, drivebelts, thermostat and water pump should be replaced with new parts when an engine is overhauled. The radiator should be checked carefully to ensure that it isn't clogged or leaking (see Chapter 3). If you purchase a rebuilt engine or short block, some rebuilders will not warranty their engines unless the radiator has been professionally flushed. Also, we don't recommend overhauling the oil pump - always install a new one when an engine is rebuilt.**

Overhauling the internal components on today's engines is a difficult and time-consuming task which requires a significant amount of specialty tools and is best left to a professional engine rebuilder (see illustrations 1.4, 1.5 and 1.6). A competent engine rebuilder will handle the inspection of your old parts and offer advice concerning the reconditioning or replacement of the original engine, Never purchase parts or have machine work done on other components until the block has been thoroughly inspected by a professional machine shop. As a general rule, time is the primary cost of an overhaul, especially since the vehicle may be tied up for a minimum of two weeks or more. Be aware that some engine builders only have the capability to rebuild the engine you bring them while other rebuilders have a large inventory of rebuilt exchange engines in stock. Also be aware that many machine shops could take as much as two weeks time to completely rebuild your engine depending on shop workload. Sometimes it makes more sense to simply exchange your engine for another engine that's already rebuilt to save time.

main bearings, connecting rod bearings and camshaft bearings are generally replaced with new ones and, if necessary, the crankshaft may be reground to restore the journals (see illustration 1.3). Generally, the valves are serviced as well, since they're usually in less-than-perfect condition at this point. While the engine is being overhauled, other components, such as the starter and alternator, can be rebuilt as well. The end result should be similar to a new engine that will give many

1.4 A machinist checks for a bent connecting rod, using specialized equipment

1.5 A bore gauge being used to check the main bearing bore

1.6 Uneven piston wear like this indicates a bent connecting rod

2 Oil pressure check

▶ **Refer to illustration 2.2**

1   Low engine oil pressure can be a sign of an engine in need of rebuilding. A low oil pressure indicator (often called an idiot light) is not a test of the oiling system. Such indicators only come on when the oil pressure is dangerously low. Even a factory oil pressure gauge in the instrument panel is only a relative indication, although much better for driver information than a warning light. A better test is with a mechanical (not electrical) oil pressure gauge.

2   Locate the oil pressure indicator sending unit on the engine block.

   a) *On 2.4L engines, the oil pressure sending unit is located above the oil filter near the rear of the engine block.*

   b) *On 3.3L and 3.8L engines, the oil pressure sending unit is located on the adapter directly above the oil filter (see illustration).*

3   Unscrew and remove the oil pressure sending unit and then

screw in the hose for your oil pressure gauge. If necessary, install an adapter fitting. Use Teflon tape or thread sealant on the threads of the adapter and/or the fitting on the end of your gauge's hose.

4   Connect an accurate tachometer to the engine, according to the tachometer manufacturer's instructions.

5   Check the oil pressure with the engine running (normal operating temperature) at the specified engine speed, and compare it to this Chapter's Specifications. If it's extremely low, the bearings and/or oil pump are probably worn out.

2.2 Location of the oil pressure sending unit on a V6 engine

3   Cylinder compression check

▶ **Refer to illustration 3.6**

1   A compression check will tell you what mechanical condition the upper end of your engine (pistons, rings, valves, head gaskets) is in. Specifically, it can tell you if the compression is down due to leakage caused by worn piston rings, defective valves and seats or a blown head gasket.

➡ **Note: The engine must be at normal operating temperature and the battery must be fully charged for this check.**

2   Begin by cleaning the area around the spark plugs before you remove them (compressed air should be used, if available). The idea is to prevent dirt from getting into the cylinders as the compression check is being done.

3   Remove all of the spark plugs from the engine (see Chapter 1).

4   Block the throttle wide open.

5   Disable the ignition and fuel systems by unplugging the wiring harness from the ignition coil pack (see Chapter 5) and by removing the fuel pump relay (see Chapter 4).

6   Install a compression gauge in the spark plug hole (see illustration).

7   Crank the engine over at least seven compression strokes and watch the gauge. The compression should build up quickly in a healthy engine. Low compression on the first stroke, followed by gradually increasing pressure on successive strokes, indicates worn piston rings. A low compression reading on the first stroke, which doesn't build up during successive strokes, indicates leaking valves or a blown head gasket (a cracked head could also be the cause). Deposits on the undersides of the valve heads can also cause low compression. Record the highest gauge reading obtained.

8   Repeat the procedure for the remaining cylinders and compare the results to this Chapter's Specifications.

9   Add some engine oil (about three squirts from a plunger-type oil can) to each cylinder, through the spark plug hole, and repeat the test.

10 If the compression increases after the oil is added, the piston rings are definitely worn. If the compression doesn't increase significantly, the leakage is occurring at the valves or head gasket. Leakage

3.6 A compression gauge with a threaded fitting for the spark plug hole is preferred over the type that requires hand pressure to maintain the seal

past the valves may be caused by burned valve seats and/or faces or warped, cracked or bent valves.

11 If two adjacent cylinders have equally low compression, there's a strong possibility that the head gasket between them is blown. The appearance of coolant in the combustion chambers or the crankcase would verify this condition.

12 If one cylinder is slightly lower than the others, and the engine has a slightly rough idle, a worn lobe on the camshaft could be the cause.

13 If the compression is unusually high, the combustion chambers are probably coated with carbon deposits. If that's the case, the cylinder head(s) should be removed and decarbonized.

14 If compression is way down or varies greatly between cylinders, it would be a good idea to have a leak-down test performed by an automotive repair shop. This test will pinpoint exactly where the leakage is occurring and how severe it is.

4   Vacuum gauge diagnostic checks

♦ **Refer to illustrations 4.4 and 4.6**

A vacuum gauge provides inexpensive but valuable information about what is going on in the engine. You can check for worn rings or cylinder walls, leaking head or intake manifold gaskets, restricted

4.4 A simple vacuum gauge can be handy in diagnosing engine condition and performance

exhaust, stuck or burned valves, weak valve springs, improper ignition or valve timing and ignition problems.

Unfortunately, vacuum gauge readings are easy to misinterpret, so they should be used in conjunction with other tests to confirm the diagnosis.

Both the absolute readings and the rate of needle movement are important for accurate interpretation. Most gauges measure vacuum in inches of mercury (in-Hg). The following references to vacuum assume the diagnosis is being performed at sea level. As elevation increases (or atmospheric pressure decreases), the reading will decrease. For every 1,000 foot increase in elevation above approximately 2,000 feet, the gauge readings will decrease about one inch of mercury.

Connect the vacuum gauge directly to the intake manifold vacuum, not to ported (throttle body) vacuum (see illustration). Be sure no hoses are left disconnected during the test or false readings will result.

Before you begin the test, allow the engine to warm up completely. Block the wheels and set the parking brake. With the transaxle in Park, start the engine and allow it to run at normal idle speed.

❋❋ WARNING:

Keep your hands and the vacuum gauge clear of the fans.

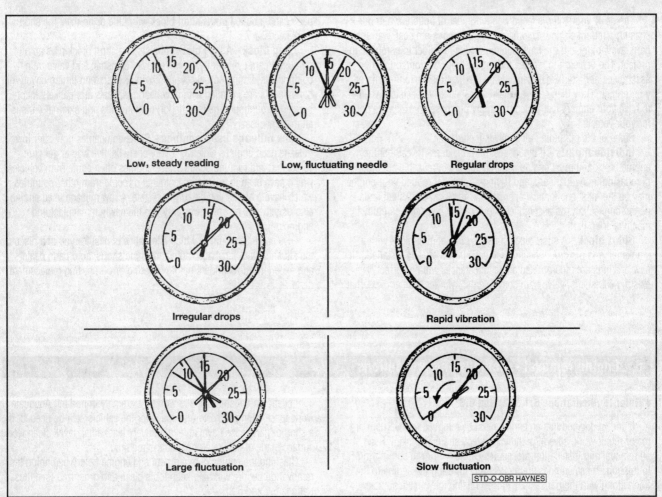

Low, steady reading   Low, fluctuating needle   Regular drops

Irregular drops   Rapid vibration

Large fluctuation   Slow fluctuation

STD-O-OBR HAYNES

4.6 Typical vacuum gauge readings

Read the vacuum gauge; an average, healthy engine should normally produce about 17 to 22 in-Hg with a fairly steady needle (see illustration). Refer to the following vacuum gauge readings and what they indicate about the engine's condition:

1   A low, steady reading usually indicates a leaking gasket between the intake manifold and cylinder head(s) or throttle body, a leaky vacuum hose, late ignition timing or incorrect camshaft timing. Check ignition timing with a timing light and eliminate all other possible causes, utilizing the tests provided in this Chapter before you remove the timing chain cover to check the timing marks.

2   If the reading is three to eight inches below normal and it fluctuates at that low reading, suspect an intake manifold gasket leak at an intake port or a faulty fuel injector.

3   If the needle has regular drops of about two-to-four inches at a steady rate, the valves are probably leaking. Perform a compression check or leak-down test to confirm this.

4   An irregular drop or down-flick of the needle can be caused by a sticking valve or an ignition misfire. Perform a compression check or leak-down test and read the spark plugs.

5   A rapid vibration of about four in-Hg vibration at idle combined with exhaust smoke indicates worn valve guides. Perform a leak-down test to confirm this. If the rapid vibration occurs with an increase in engine speed, check for a leaking intake manifold gasket or head gasket, weak valve springs, burned valves or ignition misfire.

6   A slight fluctuation, say one inch up and down, may mean ignition problems. Check all the usual tune-up items and, if necessary, run the engine on an ignition analyzer.

7   If there is a large fluctuation, perform a compression or leak-down test to look for a weak or dead cylinder or a blown head gasket.

8   If the needle moves slowly through a wide range, check for a clogged PCV system, incorrect idle fuel mixture, throttle body or intake manifold gasket leaks.

9   Check for a slow return after revving the engine by quickly snapping the throttle open until the engine reaches about 2,500 rpm and let it shut. Normally the reading should drop to near zero, rise above normal idle reading (about 5 in-Hg over) and then return to the previous idle reading. If the vacuum returns slowly and doesn't peak when the throttle is snapped shut, the rings may be worn. If there is a long delay, look for a restricted exhaust system (often the muffler or catalytic converter). An easy way to check this is to temporarily disconnect the exhaust ahead of the suspected part and redo the test.

5   Engine rebuilding alternatives

The do-it-yourselfer is faced with a number of options when purchasing a rebuilt engine. The major considerations are cost, warranty, parts availability and the time required for the rebuilder to complete the project. The decision to replace the engine block, piston/connecting rod assemblies and crankshaft depends on the final inspection results of your engine. Only then can you make a cost effective decision whether to have your engine overhauled or simply purchase an exchange engine for your vehicle.

Some of the rebuilding alternatives include:

Individual parts - If the inspection procedures reveal that the engine block and most engine components are in reusable condition, purchasing individual parts and having a rebuilder rebuild your engine may be the most economical alternative. The block, crankshaft and piston/connecting rod assemblies should all be inspected carefully by a machine shop first.

Short block - A short block consists of an engine block with a crankshaft and piston/connecting rod assemblies already installed. All new bearings are incorporated and all clearances will be correct. The existing camshafts, valve train components, cylinder head and external parts can be bolted to the short block with little or no machine shop work necessary.

Long block - A long block consists of a short block plus an oil pump, oil pan, cylinder head, valve cover, camshaft and valve train components, timing sprockets and chain or gears and timing cover. All components are installed with new bearings, seals and gaskets incorporated throughout. The installation of manifolds and external parts is all that's necessary.

Low mileage used engines - Some companies now offer low mileage used engines which is a very cost effective way to get your vehicle up and running again. These engines often come from vehicles which have been in totaled in accidents or come from other countries which have a higher vehicle turn over rate. A low mileage used engine also usually has a similar warranty like the newly remanufactured engines.

Give careful thought to which alternative is best for you and discuss the situation with local automotive machine shops, auto parts dealers and experienced rebuilders before ordering or purchasing replacement parts.

6   Engine removal - methods and precautions

▶ **Refer to illustrations 6.1, 6.2, and 6.3**

If you've decided that an engine must be removed for overhaul or major repair work, several preliminary steps should be taken. Read all removal and installation procedures carefully prior to committing to this job. These engines are removed by lowering the engine to the floor, along with the transaxle, and then raising the vehicle sufficiently to slide the assembly out; this will require a vehicle hoist as well as an engine hoist.

Locating a suitable place to work is extremely important. Adequate work space, along with storage space for the vehicle, will be needed. If a shop or garage isn't available, at the very least a flat, level, clean work surface made of concrete or asphalt is required.

Cleaning the engine compartment and engine before beginning the removal procedure will help keep tools clean and organized (see illustrations 6.1 and 6.2).

An engine hoist will also be necessary. Make sure the hoist is rated in excess of the combined weight of the engine and transaxle. Safety

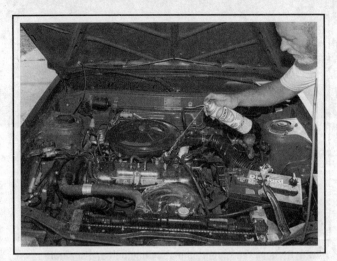

6.1 After tightly wrapping water-vulnerable components, use a spray cleaner on everything, with particular concentration on the greasiest areas, usually around the valve cover and lower edges of the block. If one section dries out, apply more cleaner

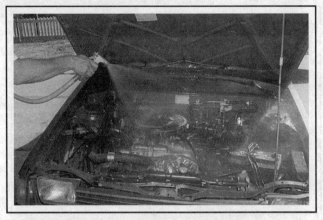

6.2 Depending on how dirty the engine is, let the cleaner soak in according to the directions and then hose off the grime and cleaner. Get the rinse water down into every area you can get at; then dry important components with a hair dryer or paper towels

6.3 Get an engine stand sturdy enough to firmly support the engine while you're working on it. Stay away from three-wheeled models: they have a tendency to tip over more easily, so get a four-wheeled unit.

is of primary importance, considering the potential hazards involved in removing the engine from the vehicle.

If you're a novice at engine removal, get at least one helper. One person cannot easily do all the things you need to do to remove a big heavy engine and transaxle assembly from the engine compartment. Also helpful is to seek advice and assistance from someone who's experienced in engine removal.

Plan the operation ahead of time. Arrange for or obtain all of the tools and equipment you'll need prior to beginning the job (see illustration 6.3). Some of the equipment necessary to perform engine removal and installation safely and with relative ease are (in addition to a vehicle hoist and an engine hoist) a heavy duty floor jack (preferably fitted with a transmission jack head adapter), complete sets of wrenches and sockets as described in the front of this manual, wooden blocks, plenty of rags and cleaning solvent for mopping up spilled oil, coolant and gasoline.

Plan for the vehicle to be out of use for quite a while. A machine shop can do the work that is beyond the scope of the home mechanic. Machine shops often have a busy schedule, so before removing the engine, consult the shop for an estimate of how long it will take to rebuild or repair the components that may need work.

7   Engine - removal and installation

▶ Refer to illustrations 7.9, 7.29, 7.30 and 7.35

❈❈ WARNING 1:

Gasoline is extremely flammable, so take extra precautions when you work on any part of the fuel system. Don't smoke or allow open flames or bare light bulbs near the work area, and don't work in a garage where a gas-type appliance (such as a water heater or clothes dryer) is present. Since gasoline is carcinogenic, wear fuel-resistant gloves when there's a possibility of being exposed to fuel, and, if you spill any fuel on your skin, rinse it off immediately with soap and water. Mop up any spills immediately and do not store fuel-soaked rags where they

could ignite. The fuel system is under constant pressure, so, if any fuel lines are to be disconnected, the fuel pressure in the system must be relieved first (see Chapter 4 for more information). When you perform any kind of work on the fuel system, wear safety glasses and have a Class B type fire extinguisher on hand.

❈❈ WARNING 2:

The engine must be completely cool before beginning this procedure.

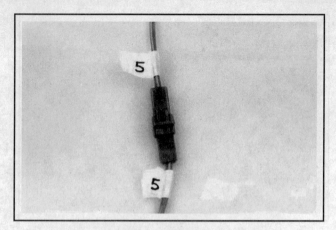

7.9 Label each wire before unplugging the connector

➡Note 1: Engine removal on these models is a difficult job, especially for the do-it-yourself mechanic working at home. Because of the vehicle's design, the manufacturer states that the engine and transaxle have to be removed as a unit from the bottom of the vehicle, not the top. With a floor jack and jackstands, the vehicle can't be raised high enough and supported safely enough for the engine/transaxle assembly to slide out from underneath. The manufacturer recommends that removal of the engine transaxle assembly only be performed on a frame-contact type vehicle hoist.

➡Note 2: Read through the entire Section before beginning this procedure. The engine and transaxle are removed as a unit from below and then separated outside the vehicle.

REMOVAL

1 Have the air conditioning system discharged by an automotive air conditioning technician.

2 Park the vehicle on a frame-contact type vehicle hoist, then engage the arms of the hoist with the jacking points of the vehicle. Raise the hoist arms until they contact the vehicle, but not so much that the wheels come off the ground.

3 Relieve the fuel system pressure (see Chapter 4).

4 Place protective covers on the fenders and cowl and remove the hood (see Chapter 11).

5 Remove the cowl cover (see Chapter 11) and the wiper unit (see Chapter 12).

6 Remove the air filter housing (see Chapter 4).

7 Disconnect the accelerator cable (and cruise control cable, if equipped) and bracket from the engine and position them aside.

8 Remove the battery and the battery tray (see Chapter 5).

9 Clearly label and disconnect all vacuum lines, emissions hoses, wiring harness connectors, ground straps and fuel lines. Masking tape and/or a touch up paint applicator work well for marking items (see illustration). Take instant photos or sketch the locations of components and brackets.

10 Detach the ground cable from the cylinder head (3.3L and 3.8L engines) or at the starter and right engine mount (2.4L engines).

11 Loosen the front wheel lug nuts, then raise the vehicle on the hoist.

➡Note: Keep in mind that during this procedure you'll have to adjust the height of the vehicle to perform certain operations.

12 Drain the cooling system and engine oil and remove the drivebelts (see Chapter 1).

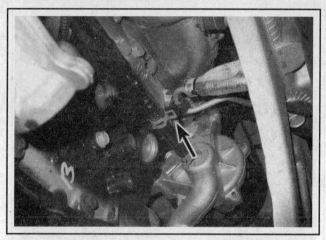

7.29 Remove the support clip attaching bolt and separate the pressure hose from the engine block

13 Remove the alternator and its brackets (see Chapter 5).

14 Remove the power steering fluid reservoir and set it off to the side without disconnecting the fluid lines (see Chapter 10).

15 Detach the lower radiator hose from the engine.

16 Lower the vehicle and detach the heater hoses at the firewall.

17 Detach the upper radiator hose from the thermostat housing.

18 Remove the upper radiator support crossmember (see Chapter 11).

19 Remove the cooling fan(s), shroud(s) and radiator (see Chapter 3).

➡Note: Be sure to install new transmission fluid cooler lines onto the transaxle and the radiator on reassembly (see Chapter 7).

20 Remove the transaxle dipstick tube. Plug the opening with a suitable device.

21 Disconnect the shift cable(s) from the transaxle (see Chapter 7). Also disconnect any wiring harness connectors from the transaxle.

22 Disconnect the upper air conditioning line from the condenser for additional clearance.

23 Disconnect the air conditioning lines at the compressor and the junction inside the engine compartment. Remove the air conditioning compressor (see Chapter 3).

24 Remove the power steering pump and bracket (see Chapter 10).

25 Raise the vehicle on the hoist. Remove the front wheels.

26 Remove the driveaxles (see Chapter 8).

27 Unplug the downstream oxygen sensor electrical connector.

28 Detach the exhaust pipe from the exhaust manifold (see Chapter 4).

29 Remove the power steering pressure hose support clip attaching bolt (see illustration). Separate the power steering hose from the engine block.

30 Remove the power steering fluid cooler and remove the cradle reinforcement plate (see illustration).

31 On 2.4L engines, remove the engine/transaxle structural collar. On 3.3L and 3.8L engines, remove the engine/transaxle brace and the driveplate cover.

32 Mark the position of the driveplate and remove the torque converter bolts (see Chapter 7).

33 Lower the vehicle.

34 Support the engine with a floor jack and block of wood. Remove the right (passenger's) side engine mount, including the portion that bolts to the engine. Using one of the mount-to-engine bolts, attach one

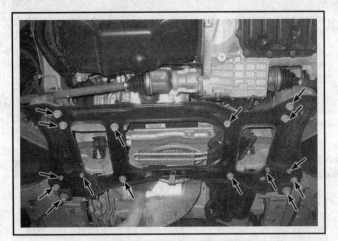

7.30 Cradle reinforcement plate bolt locations

7.35 Remember that the transaxle end of the engine will be heavier, so position the chain on the hoist so it balances the engine and the transaxle level with the vehicle

end of an engine lifting sling or chain to the mount boss. Tighten the bolt securely. Attach the other end of the sling or chain to the other side of the engine, using one of the transaxle-to-engine bolts. Be sure the positioning of the chain or sling will support the engine and transaxle in a balanced attitude.

➡️**Note: The sling or chain must be long enough to allow the engine hoist to lower the engine/transaxle assembly to the ground, without letting the hoist arm contact the vehicle.**

35 Roll the hoist into position and attach the sling or chain to it. Take up the slack until there is slight tension on the hoist, then remove the jack from under the engine. Remember that the transaxle end of the engine will be heavier, so position the chain on the hoist so it balances the engine and the transaxle level with the vehicle (see illustration).

➡️**Note: Depending on the design of the engine hoist, it may be helpful to position the hoist from the side of the vehicle, so that when the engine/transaxle assembly is lowered, it will fit between the legs of the hoist.**

36 Recheck to be sure nothing except the remaining mounts are still connecting the engine to the vehicle or to the transaxle. Disconnect and label anything still remaining.

37 Remove the through-bolt on the driver's side transaxle mount and the upper engine bracket (see Chapter 2A or 2B).

38 Slowly lower the engine/transaxle to the ground.

39 Once the engine/transaxle assembly is on the floor, disconnect the engine lifting hoist and raise the vehicle until it clears the assembly.

40 Reconnect the chain or sling and raise the engine and transaxle. Support the engine with blocks of wood or another floor jack, while leaving the sling or chain attached to the right-side mounting boss. Support the transaxle with another floor jack, preferably one with a transmission jack head adapter. At this point the transaxle can be unbolted and removed from the engine. Be very careful to ensure that the components are supported securely so they won't topple off their supports during disconnection.

41 Reconnect the lifting chain to the engine, then raise the engine and attach it to an engine stand.

INSTALLATION

42 Installation is the reverse of removal, noting the following points:
  a) *Check the engine/transaxle mounts. If they're worn or damaged, replace them.*
  b) *Inspect the torque converter seal and bushing.*
  c) *Attach the transaxle to the engine following the procedure described in Chapter 7.*
  d) *Add coolant, oil, power steering and transmission fluids as needed (see Chapter 1).*
  e) *Run the engine and check for proper operation and leaks. Shut off the engine and recheck fluid levels.*

8 Engine overhaul - disassembly sequence

1 It's much easier to remove the external components if it's mounted on a portable engine stand. A stand can often be rented quite cheaply from an equipment rental yard. Before the engine is mounted on a stand, the flywheel/driveplate should be removed from the engine.

2 If a stand isn't available, it's possible to remove the external engine components with it blocked up on the floor. Be extra careful not to tip or drop the engine when working without a stand.

3 If you're going to obtain a rebuilt engine, all external components must come off first, to be transferred to the replacement engine. These components include:

  Driveplate
  Ignition system components
  Emissions-related components
  Engine mounts and mount brackets
  Engine rear cover (spacer plate between flywheel/driveplate and engine block)
  Intake/exhaust manifolds
  Fuel injection components
  Oil filter
  Spark plug wires and spark plugs
  Thermostat and housing assembly
  Water pump

➡️**Note: When removing the external components from the engine, pay close attention to details that may be helpful or** important during installation. Note the installed position of gaskets, seals, spacers, pins, brackets, washers, bolts and other small items.

4   If you're going to obtain a short block (assembled engine block, crankshaft, pistons and connecting rods), then remove the timing belt/ timing chain, cylinder head, oil pan, oil pump pick-up tube, oil pump and water pump from your engine so that you can turn in your old short block to the rebuilder as a core. See *Engine rebuilding alternatives* for additional information regarding the different possibilities to be considered.

9   Camshaft and bearings (3.3L and 3.8L V6 engines only) - removal, inspection and installation

➡Note: This procedure applies to the 3.3L and 3.8L V6 engines only. Since there isn't enough room to remove the camshaft with the engine in the vehicle, the engine must be out of the vehicle and mounted on a stand to perform this procedure.

REMOVAL

1   Remove the timing chain and sprockets, lifters and pushrods (see Chapter 2B).
2   Remove the bolts and the camshaft thrust plate from the engine block.
3   Use a long bolt in the camshaft sprocket bolt hole as a handle when removing the camshaft from the block.
4   Carefully pull the camshaft out. Support the cam in the block so the lobes don't nick or gouge the bearings as the cam is pulled out.

INSPECTION

▶ Refer to illustration 9.6, 9.7 and 9.8

5   After the camshaft has been removed from the engine, cleaned with solvent and dried, inspect the bearing journals for uneven wear, pitting and evidence of seizure. If the journals are damaged, the bearings in the block are probably damaged as well. Both the camshaft and bearings will have to be replaced.

➡Note: Camshaft bearing replacement requires special tools and expertise that place it beyond the scope of the average home mechanic. The tools for bearing removal and installation are available at stores that carry automotive tools, possibly even found at a tool rental business. It is advisable though, if bearings are bad and the procedure is beyond your ability, remove the engine block and take it to an automotive machine shop to ensure that the job is done correctly.

6   Measure the bearing journals with a micrometer to determine if they are excessively worn or out-of-round (see illustration).
7   Measure the lobe height of each cam lobe on the intake camshaft and record your measurements (see illustration). Compare the measurements for excessive variations. If the lobe heights vary more than 0.005 inch (0.125 mm), replace the camshaft. Compare the lobe height measurements on the exhaust camshaft and follow the same procedure. Do not compare intake camshaft lobe heights with exhaust camshaft lobe heights as they are different. Only compare intake lobes with intake lobes and exhaust lobes with other exhaust lobes.
8   Check the camshaft lobes for heat discoloration, score marks, chipped areas, pitting and uneven wear (see illustration). If the lobes are in good condition and if the lobe lift variation measurements recorded earlier are within the limits, the camshaft can be reused.
9   The inside diameter of each bearing can be determined with a small hole gauge and outside micrometer or an inside micrometer. Subtract the camshaft bearing journal diameters from the corresponding bearing inside diameters to determine the bearing oil clearance. If it's excessive, new bearings will be required regardless of the condition of the originals. Check this Chapter's Specifications.
10 Clean the lifters with solvent and dry them thoroughly without mixing them up.
11 Check each lifter wall, pushrod seat and foot for scuffing, score marks and uneven wear. If the lifter walls are damaged or worn (which is not very likely), inspect the lifter bores in the engine block as well. If

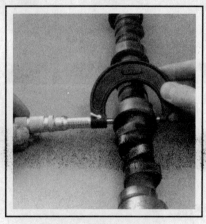

9.6 Check the diameter of each camshaft bearing journal to pinpoint excessive wear and out-of-round conditions

9.7 Measure the camshaft lobe height (greatest dimension) with a micrometer

9.8 Check the cam lobes for pitting, excessive wear and scoring. If scoring is excessive, as shown here, replace the camshaft

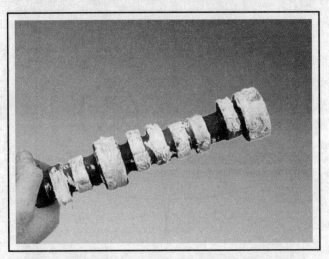

9.14 Be sure to apply camshaft assembly lube to the cam lobes and bearing journals before installing the camshaft

the pushrod seats are worn, check the pushrod ends.

12 If new lifters are being installed, a new camshaft must also be installed. If a new camshaft is installed, then use new lifters as well. Never install used lifters unless the original camshaft is used and the lifters can be installed in their original locations.

13 Check the rollers carefully for wear and damage and make sure they turn freely without excessive play.

INSTALLATION

▶ **Refer to illustration 9.14**

14 Lubricate the camshaft bearing journals and cam lobes with moly-base grease or engine assembly lube (see illustration).

15 Slide the camshaft into the engine. Support the cam near the block and be careful not to scrape or nick the bearings.

16 Install the thrust plate and bolts. Tighten the bolts to the torque in this Chapter's Specifications.

17 See Chapter 2B for the timing chain installation procedure.

---

10 Balance shafts (four-cylinder engine only) - removal, inspection and installation

➡ **Note: This procedure assumes that the engine has been removed from the vehicle and the driveplate, timing belt, oil pan and oil pump have also been removed (see Chapter 2A).**

❊❊ CAUTION:

With the timing belt removed, do not rotate the crankshaft unless the camshafts have first been removed (see Chapter 2A); valve damage may occur.

REMOVAL

1 The balance shafts are installed in a carrier mounted to the main bearing cap/bedplate on the lower part of the engine block. The shafts are connected through two gears which rotate them in opposite directions. These gears are driven by a chain from the crankshaft and are designed to rotate at a 2:1 ratio with the crankshaft (one turn of the crankshaft equals two turns of the balance shafts), which counterbalances reciprocating masses within the engine.

2 Remove the chain cover, guide and tensioner from the engine block.

3 Keep the crankshaft from rotating and remove the balance shaft bolts.

➡ **Note: A block of wood placed tightly between the engine block and the crankshaft counterbalance weight will prevent crankshaft rotation.**

4 Remove the balance shaft chain sprocket, chain, and crankshaft chain sprocket. Use two prybars to work the sprocket back and forth until it is free from the crankshaft.

➡ **Note: The carrier assembly may be removed from the main bearing cap/bedplate at this time, if balance shaft removal is not required.**

5 Remove the special stud (double-ended) from the gear cover. Then remove the gear cover and balance shaft gears.

6 Remove the rear cover from the carrier and pull out the balance shafts.

7 Remove the bolts that hold the carrier to the main bearing cap/bedplate, and separate the carrier from the engine.

CLEANING AND INSPECTION

8 Clean all components with solvent and dry thoroughly. Inspect all components for damage and wear. Pay close attention to the chain, sprocket and gear teeth and the bearing surfaces of the carrier and balance shafts. Replace defective parts as necessary.

INSTALLATION

▶ **Refer to illustrations 10.12 and 10.15**

9 Install the balance shaft carrier on the main bearing cap/bedplate and tighten the bolts to the torque in this Chapter's Specifications.

10 Lubricate the balance shafts with clean engine oil and insert them into the carrier.

11 Install the rear cover and tighten the bolts to the torque in this Chapter's Specifications.

12 Rotate the balance shafts until both shaft keyways are in the 12 o'clock position. Install the short hub drive gear on the sprocket driven shaft and the long hub gear on the gear driven shaft. After installation, the timing marks (dots) must be together (see illustration).

13 Install the gear cover and tighten the double-ended stud to the torque in this Chapter's Specifications.

14 Install the sprocket on the crankshaft with the timing mark facing out, being careful not to cock the sprocket as its being installed.

15 Position the crankshaft so the timing mark on the chain sprocket is lined up with the parting line on the left side of the number 1 main bearing cap (see illustration).

16 Place the chain on the crankshaft sprocket so that the plated link of the chain is located at the timing mark on the crankshaft sprocket (see illustration 10.15).

17 Install the balance shaft sprocket in the chain so that the timing mark on the sprocket (dot) mates with the nickel plated link on the chain (8 links from the upper plated link) (see illustration 10.15).

18 Slide the balance shaft sprocket on the balance shaft. If the sprocket is difficult to install, it may be necessary to loosen the rear cover and push the balance shaft slightly out of the carrier to ease sprocket installation.

➥Note: The timing mark on the balance shaft sprocket and the nickel plated link should align with the notch on the side of the gear cover (see illustration 10.15).

19 Install the balance shaft bolts. Keep the crankshaft from rotating and tighten the balance shaft bolts to the torque in this Chapter's Specifications.

➥Note: A block of wood placed tightly between the engine block and the crankshaft counterbalance will prevent crankshaft rotation.

CHAIN TENSIONING

▶ Refer to illustration 10.20

20 Install the chain tensioner loosely. Place a 0.039 x 2.75 inch shim (a feeler gauge cut to the appropriate size can be used) between the tensioner and the chain (see illustration). Push the tensioner against the chain. Apply force (approximately 5.5 to 6.5 lbs) directly behind the adjustment slot to remove the slack.

21 With pressure applied, tighten the top tensioner bolt first then

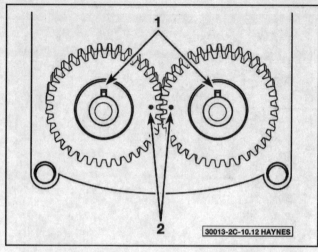

10.12 After gear installation, the balance shaft keyways (1) should be in the 12 o'clock position, and the gear alignment dots (2) should be together as shown

the bottom pivot bolt. Tighten the bolts to the torque in this Chapter's Specifications. Remove the shim.

22 Place the chain guide on the double-ended stud making sure the tab on the guide fits into the slot on the gear cover. Tighten the nut to the torque in this Chapter's Specifications.

23 Install the chain cover and tighten the bolts securely.

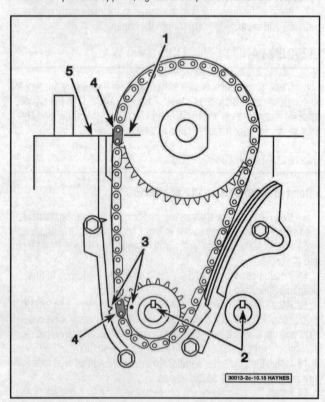

10.15 The timing mark on the crankshaft sprocket, nickel plated links, notch and the yellow dot on the balance shaft sprocket must be aligned for correct timing

1 Mark on crankshaft sprocket	3 Marks in alignment
	4 Plated links
2 Balance shaft keyways	5 Parting line

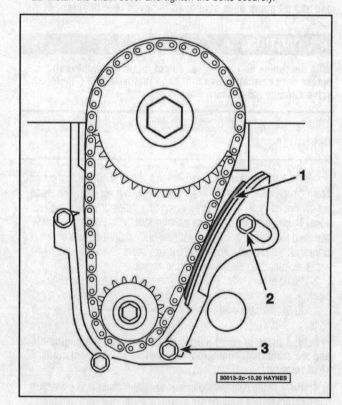

10.20 With the shim in place, apply approximately 5.5 to 6.5 lbs of force to the chain tensioner and tighten the bolt to the torque listed in this Chapter's Specifications

1 Shim
2 Tensioner adjustment bolt
3 Pivot bolt

11 Pistons and connecting rods - removal and installation

REMOVAL

♦ **Refer to illustrations 11.1, 11.3 and 11.4**

➡**Note: Prior to removing the piston/connecting rod assemblies, remove the cylinder head and oil pan (see Chapter 2A or 2B).**

1 Use your fingernail to feel if a ridge has formed at the upper limit of ring travel (about 1/4-inch down from the top of each cylinder). If carbon deposits or cylinder wear have produced ridges, they must be completely removed with a special tool (see illustration). Follow the manufacturer's instructions provided with the tool. Failure to remove the ridges before attempting to remove the piston/connecting rod assemblies may result in piston breakage.

2 After the cylinder ridges have been removed, turn the engine so the crankshaft is facing up.

3 Before the bedplate/main bearing caps and connecting rods are removed, check the connecting rod endplay with feeler gauges. Slide them between the first connecting rod and the crankshaft throw until the play is removed (see illustration). Repeat this procedure for each connecting rod. The endplay is equal to the thickness of the feeler gauge(s). Check with an automotive machine shop for the endplay service limit (a typical end play limit should measure between 0.005 to 0.015 inch [0.127 to 0.369 mm]). If the play exceeds the service limit, new connecting rods will be required. If new rods (or a new crankshaft) are installed, the endplay may fall under the minimum allowable. If it does, the rods will have to be machined to restore it. If necessary, consult an automotive machine shop for advice.

4 Check the connecting rods and caps for identification marks. If they aren't plainly marked, use paint or marker to clearly identify each rod and cap (1, 2, 3, etc., depending on the cylinder they're associated with) (see illustration).

✳✳ CAUTION:

Do not use a punch and hammer to mark the connecting rods or they may be damaged.

5 Loosen each of the connecting rod cap bolts 1/2-turn at a time until they can be removed by hand.

➡**Note: New connecting rod cap bolts must be used when reassembling the engine, but save the old bolts for use when checking the connecting rod bearing oil clearance.**

6 Remove the number one connecting rod cap and bearing insert. Don't drop the bearing insert out of the cap.

7 Remove the bearing insert and push the connecting rod/piston assembly out through the top of the engine. Use a wooden or plastic hammer handle to push on the upper bearing surface in the connecting rod. If resistance is felt, double-check to make sure that all of the ridge was removed from the cylinder.

8 Repeat the procedure for the remaining cylinders.

9 After removal, reassemble the connecting rod caps and bearing inserts in their respective connecting rods and install the cap bolts finger tight. Leaving the old bearing inserts in place until reassembly will help prevent the connecting rod bearing surfaces from being accidentally nicked or gouged.

10 The pistons and connecting rods are now ready for inspection and overhaul at an automotive machine shop.

PISTON RING INSTALLATION

♦ **Refer to illustrations 11.13, 11.14, 11.15, 11.19a, 11.19b and 11.22**

11 Before installing the new piston rings, the ring end gaps must be checked. It's assumed that the piston ring side clearance has been checked and verified correct.

12 Lay out the piston/connecting rod assemblies and the new ring sets so the ring sets will be matched with the same piston and cylinder during the end gap measurement and engine assembly.

13 Insert the top (number one) ring into the first cylinder and square it up with the cylinder walls by pushing it in with the top of the piston (see illustration). The ring should be near the bottom of the cylinder, at the lower limit of ring travel.

11.1 Before you try to remove the pistons, use a ridge reamer to remove the raised material (ridge) from the top of the cylinders

11.3 Checking the connecting rod endplay (side clearance)

11.4 If the connecting rods or caps are not marked, use permanent ink or paint to mark the caps to the rods by cylinder number (for example, this would be number 4 cylinder connecting rod)

11.13 Install the piston ring into the cylinder then push it down into position using a piston so the ring will be square in the cylinder

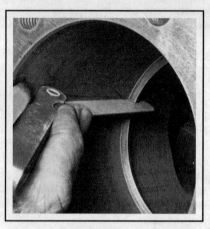

11.14 With the ring square in the cylinder, measure the ring end gap with a feeler gauge

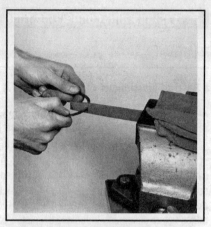

11.15 If the ring end gap is too small, clamp a file in a vise as shown and file the piston ring ends - be sure to remove all raised material

14 To measure the end gap, slip feeler gauges between the ends of the ring until a gauge equal to the gap width is found (see illustration). The feeler gauge should slide between the ring ends with a slight amount of drag. A typical ring gap should fall between 0.010 and 0.020 inch [0.25 to 0.50 mm] for compression rings and up to 0.030 inch [0.76 mm] for the oil ring steel rails. If the gap is larger or smaller than specified, double-check to make sure you have the correct rings before proceeding.

15 If the gap is too small, it must be enlarged or the ring ends may come in contact with each other during engine operation, which can cause serious damage to the engine. If necessary, increase the end gaps by filing the ring ends very carefully with a fine file. Mount the file in a vise equipped with soft jaws, slip the ring over the file with the ends contacting the file face and slowly move the ring to remove material from the ends. When performing this operation, file only by pushing the ring from the outside end of the file towards the vise (see illustration).

16 Excess end gap isn't critical unless it's greater than 0.040 inch (1.01 mm). Again, double-check to make sure you have the correct ring type.

17 Repeat the procedure for each ring that will be installed in the first cylinder and for each ring in the remaining cylinders. Remember to keep rings, pistons and cylinders matched up.

18 Once the ring end gaps have been checked/corrected, the rings can be installed on the pistons.

19 The oil control ring (lowest one on the piston) is usually installed first. It's composed of three separate components. Slip the spacer/expander into the groove (see illustration). If an anti-rotation tang is used, make sure it's inserted into the drilled hole in the ring groove. Next, install the upper side rail in the same manner (see illustration). Don't use a piston ring installation tool on the oil ring side rails, as they may be damaged. Instead, place one end of the side rail into the groove between the spacer/expander and the ring land, hold it firmly in place and slide a finger around the piston while pushing the rail into the groove. Finally, install the lower side rail.

20 After the three oil ring components have been installed, check to make sure that both the upper and lower side rails can be rotated smoothly inside the ring grooves.

21 The number two (middle) ring is installed next. It's usually stamped with a mark which must face up, toward the top of the piston. Do not mix up the top and middle rings, as they have different cross-sections.

11.19a Installing the spacer/expander in the oil ring groove

11.19b DO NOT use a piston ring installation tool when installing the oil control side rails

➡Note: Always follow the instructions printed on the ring package or box - different manufacturers may require different approaches.

22 Use a piston ring installation tool and make sure the identification mark is facing the top of the piston, then slip the ring into the middle groove on the piston (see illustration). Don't expand the ring any more than necessary to slide it over the piston.

23 Install the number one (top) ring in the same manner. Make sure the mark is facing up. Be careful not to confuse the number one and number two rings.

24 Repeat the procedure for the remaining pistons and rings.

INSTALLATION

25 Before installing the piston/connecting rod assemblies, the cylinder walls must be perfectly clean, the top edge of each cylinder bore must be chamfered, and the crankshaft must be in place.

26 Remove the cap from the end of the number one connecting rod (refer to the marks made during removal). Remove the original bearing inserts and wipe the bearing surfaces of the connecting rod and cap with a clean, lint-free cloth. They must be kept spotlessly clean.

Connecting rod bearing oil clearance check

▶ Refer to illustrations 11.30a, 11.30b, 11.35, 11.37 and 11.41

27 Clean the back side of the new upper bearing insert, then lay it in place in the connecting rod.

28 Make sure the tab on the bearing fits into the recess in the rod. Don't hammer the bearing insert into place and be very careful not to nick or gouge the bearing face. Don't lubricate the bearing at this time.

29 Clean the back side of the other bearing insert and install it in the rod cap. Again, make sure the tab on the bearing fits into the recess in the cap, and don't apply any lubricant. It's critically important that the mating surfaces of the bearing and connecting rod are perfectly clean and oil free when they're assembled.

11.22 Use a piston ring installation tool to install the number 2 and the number 1 (top) rings - be sure the directional mark on the piston ring(s) is facing toward the top of the piston

30 Position the piston ring gaps at 90-degree intervals around the piston as shown (see illustrations).

31 Lubricate the piston and rings with clean engine oil and attach a piston ring compressor to the piston. Leave the skirt protruding about 1/4-inch to guide the piston into the cylinder. The rings must be compressed until they're flush with the piston.

32 Rotate the crankshaft until the number one connecting rod journal is at BDC (bottom dead center) and apply a liberal coat of engine oil to the cylinder walls.

33 With the directional stamp (arrow) on top of the piston facing the front (timing belt/timing chain end) of the engine, gently insert the piston/connecting rod assembly into the number one cylinder bore and rest the bottom edge of the ring compressor on the engine block. Install the pistons with the cavity mark(s) facing toward the timing belt.

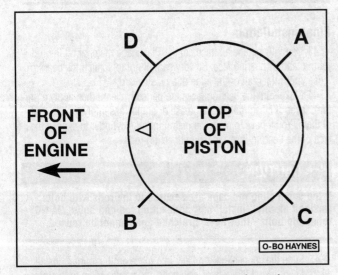

11.30a On 2.4L engines, position the piston ring end gaps as shown here before installing the piston/connecting rod assemblies into the engine

A   Top compression ring gap
B   Second compression ring
    and oil ring spacer gap
C   Upper oil ring gap
D   Lower oil ring gap

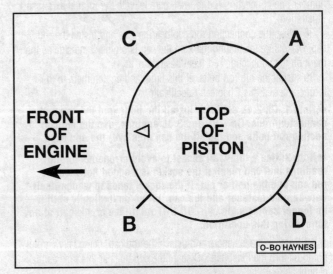

11.30b On 3.3L and 3.8L V6 engines, position the piston ring end gaps as shown here before installing the piston/connecting rod assemblies into the engine

A   Top compression ring gap
B   Second compression ring
    and oil ring spacer gap
C   Upper oil ring gap
D   Lower oil ring gap

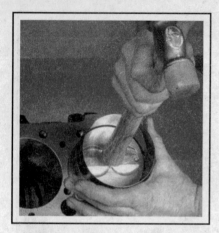

11.35 Use a plastic or wooden hammer handle to push the piston into the cylinder

11.37 Place Plastigage on each connecting rod bearing journal parallel to the crankshaft centerline

11.41 Use the scale on the Plastigage package to determine the bearing oil clearance - be sure to measure the widest part of the Plastigage and use the correct scale; it comes with both standard and metric scales

34 Tap the top edge of the ring compressor to make sure it's contacting the block around its entire circumference.

35 Gently tap on the top of the piston with the end of a wooden or plastic hammer handle (see illustration) while guiding the end of the connecting rod into place on the crankshaft journal. The piston rings may try to pop out of the ring compressor just before entering the cylinder bore, so keep some downward pressure on the ring compressor. Work slowly, and if any resistance is felt as the piston enters the cylinder, stop immediately. Find out what's hanging up and fix it before proceeding. Do not, for any reason, force the piston into the cylinder - you might break a ring and/or the piston.

36 Once the piston/connecting rod assembly is installed, the connecting rod bearing oil clearance must be checked before the rod cap is permanently installed.

37 Cut a piece of the appropriate size Plastigage slightly shorter than the width of the connecting rod bearing and lay it in place on the number one connecting rod journal, parallel with the journal axis (see illustration).

38 Clean the connecting rod cap bearing face and install the rod cap. Make sure the mating mark on the cap is on the same side as the mark on the connecting rod (see illustration 11.4).

39 Install the old rod bolts, at this time, and tighten them to the torque listed in this Chapter's Specifications.

➡**Note 1: On 2.4L engines, install the bolts into the cap and connecting rods. On 3.3L and 3.8L engines, use the old connecting rod bolts and install the cap nuts over the end caps.**

➡**Note 2: Use a thin-wall socket to avoid erroneous torque readings that can result if the socket is wedged between the rod cap and the bolt or nut. If the socket tends to wedge itself between the fastener and the cap, lift up on it slightly until it no longer contacts the cap. DO NOT rotate the crankshaft at any time during this operation.**

40 Remove the fasteners and detach the rod cap, being very careful not to disturb the Plastigage. Discard the cap bolts at this time as they cannot be reused.

➡**Note: You MUST use new connecting rod bolts.**

41 Compare the width of the crushed Plastigage to the scale printed on the Plastigage envelope to obtain the oil clearance (see illustration). The connecting rod oil clearance is usually about 0.001 to 0.002 inch. Consult an automotive machine shop for the clearance specified for the rod bearings on your engine.

42 If the clearance is not as specified, the bearing inserts may be the wrong size (which means different ones will be required). Before deciding that different inserts are needed, make sure that no dirt or oil was between the bearing inserts and the connecting rod or cap when the clearance was measured. Also, recheck the journal diameter. If the Plastigage was wider at one end than the other, the journal may be tapered. If the clearance still exceeds the limit specified, the bearing will have to be replaced with an undersize bearing.

❋❋ CAUTION:

When installing a new crankshaft always use a standard size bearing.

Final installation

43 Carefully scrape all traces of the Plastigage material off the rod journal and/or bearing face. Be very careful not to scratch the bearing - use your fingernail or the edge of a plastic card.

44 Make sure the bearing faces are perfectly clean, then apply a uniform layer of clean moly-base grease or engine assembly lube to both of them. You'll have to push the piston into the cylinder to expose the face of the bearing insert in the connecting rod.

❋❋ CAUTION:

If the connecting rod caps are secured to the rods with bolts (instead of nuts), install new connecting rod cap bolts. Do NOT reuse old bolts - they have stretched and cannot be reused.

45 Slide the connecting rod back into place on the journal, install the rod cap, install the nuts or new bolts and tighten them to the torque listed in this Chapter's Specifications. Again, work up to the torque in three steps.

46 Repeat the entire procedure for the remaining pistons/connecting rods.

47 The important points to remember are:

a) Keep the back sides of the bearing inserts and the insides of the connecting rods and caps perfectly clean when assembling them.

b) *Make sure you have the correct piston/rod assembly for each cylinder.*

c) *The mark on the piston must face the front (timing belt end [2.4L] or timing chain [3.3L/3.8L]) of the engine.*

d) *Lubricate the cylinder walls liberally with clean oil.*

e) *Lubricate the bearing faces when installing the rod caps after the oil clearance has been checked.*

48 After all the piston/connecting rod assemblies have been cor-rectly installed, rotate the crankshaft a number of times by hand to check for any obvious binding.

49 As a final step, check the connecting rod endplay again.

50 Compare the measured endplay to the tolerance listed in this Chapter's Specifications to make sure it's acceptable. If it was correct before disassembly and the original crankshaft and rods were rein-stalled, it should still be correct. If new rods or a new crankshaft were installed, the endplay may be inadequate. If so, the rods will have to be removed and taken to an automotive machine shop for resizing.

12 Crankshaft - removal and installation

REMOVAL

▶ **Refer to illustrations 12.1 and 12.3**

➡**Note: The crankshaft can be removed only after the engine has been removed from the vehicle. It's assumed that the fly-wheel or driveplate, crankshaft pulley, timing belt/timing chain, oil pan, oil pump body, oil filter and piston/connecting rod assemblies have already been removed. The rear main oil seal retainer must be unbolted and separated from the block before proceeding with crankshaft removal.**

1 Before the crankshaft is removed, measure the endplay. Mount a dial indicator with the indicator in line with the crankshaft and just touching the end of the crankshaft as shown (see illustration).

2 Pry the crankshaft all the way to the rear and zero the dial indica-tor. Next, pry the crankshaft to the front as far as possible and check the reading on the dial indicator. The distance traveled is the endplay. A typical crankshaft endplay will fall between 0.003 to 0.010 inch (0.076 to 0.254 mm). If it is greater than that, check the crankshaft thrust sur-faces for wear after it's removed. If no wear is evident, new main bear-ings should correct the endplay.

3 If a dial indicator isn't available, feeler gauges can be used. Gen-tly pry the crankshaft all the way to the front of the engine. Slip feeler gauges between the crankshaft and the front face of the thrust bearing or washer to determine the clearance (see illustration).

4 Loosen the bedplate/main bearing cap bolts 1/4-turn at a time each, until they can be removed by hand.

5 Gently tap the bedplate/main bearing cap with a soft-face hammer around the perimeter of the assembly. Pull the bedplate/main bearing cap straight up and off the cylinder block. Try not to drop the bearing inserts if they come out with the assembly.

6 Carefully lift the crankshaft out of the engine. It may be a good idea to have an assistant available, since the crankshaft is quite heavy and awkward to handle. With the bearing inserts in place inside the engine block and main bearing caps, reinstall the bedplate/main bear-ing caps onto the engine block and tighten the bolts finger tight. Make sure you install the bedplate/main bearing caps with the arrow facing the front end of the engine.

INSTALLATION

7 Crankshaft installation is the first step in engine reassembly. It's assumed at this point that the engine block and crankshaft have been cleaned, inspected and repaired or reconditioned.

8 Position the engine block with the bottom facing up.

9 Remove the mounting bolts and lift off the bedplate (four-cylinder engine) or main bearing caps (V6 engines).

10 If they're still in place, remove the original bearing inserts from the block and from the bedplate (four-cylinder engine) or main bearing caps (V6 engines). Wipe the bearing surfaces of the block and bedplate with a clean, lint-free cloth. They must be kept spotlessly clean. This is critical for determining the correct bearing oil clearance.

12.1 Checking crankshaft endplay with a dial indicator

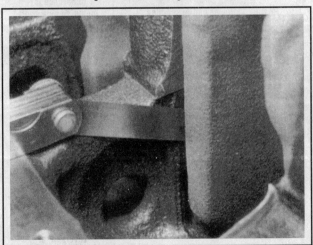

12.3 Checking crankshaft endplay with feeler gauges at the thrust bearing journal

ENGINE BEARING ANALYSIS

Debris

Babbitt bearing embedded with debris from machinings

Microscopic detail of debris

Microscopic detail of gouges

Overplated copper alloy bearing gouged by cast iron debris

Aluminum bearing embedded with glass beads

Damaged lining caused by dirt left on the bearing back

Microscopic detail of glass beads

Misassembly

Result of a lower half assembled as an upper - blocking the oil flow

Excessive oil clearance is indicated by a short contact arc

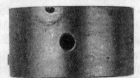 

Polished and oil-stained backs are a result of a poor fit in the housing bore

Result of a wrong, reversed, or shifted cap

Overloading

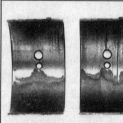

Damage from excessive idling which resulted in an oil film unable to support the load imposed

Damaged upper connecting rod bearings caused by engine lugging; the lower main bearings (not shown) were similarly affected

The damage shown in these upper and lower connecting rod bearings was caused by engine operation at a higher-than-rated speed under load

Misalignment

A warped crankshaft caused this pattern of severe wear in the center, diminishing toward the ends

A poorly finished crankshaft caused the equally spaced scoring shown

A tapered housing bore caused the damage along one edge of this pair

A bent connecting rod led to the damage in the "V" pattern

Lubrication

Result of dry start: The bearings on the left, farthest from the oil pump, show more damage

Result of a low oil supply or oil starvation

Severe wear as a result of inadequate oil clearance

Corrosion

Microscopic detail of corrosion

Corrosion is an acid attack on the bearing lining generally caused by inadequate maintenance, extremely hot or cold operation, or interior oils or fuels

Microscopic detail of cavitation

Example of cavitation - a surface erosion caused by pressure changes in the oil film

Damage from excessive thrust or insufficient axial clearance

Bearing affected by oil dilution caused by excessive blow-by or a rich mixture

© 1986 Federal-Mogul Corporation
Copy and photographs courtesy of Federal Mogul Corporation

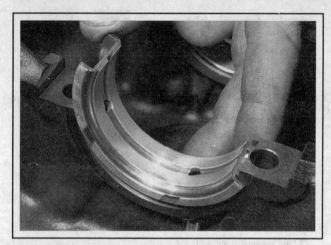

12.11 Installing a crankshaft main bearing onto the engine block main bearing saddle

12.17 Place the Plastigage onto the crankshaft bearing journal as shown

Main bearing oil clearance check

▶ Refer to illustrations 12.11, 12.17 and 12.19

11 Without mixing them up, clean the back sides of the new upper main bearing inserts (with grooves and oil holes) and lay one in each main bearing saddle in the block (see illustration). Each upper bearing has an oil groove and oil hole in it.

❋❋ CAUTION:

The oil holes in the block must line up with the oil holes in the upper bearing inserts.

The thrust washer or thrust bearing insert must be installed in the number 3 crankshaft journal (four-cylinder engine) or the number 2 crankshaft journal (V6 engines). Clean the back sides of the lower main bearing inserts and lay them in the corresponding location in the bedplate or main bearing caps. Make sure the tab on the bearing insert fits into the recess in the block or bedplate or main bearing caps. On V6 engines the upper bearings with the oil holes are installed into the engine block, while the lower bearings without the oil holes are installed in the main bearing caps.

❋❋ CAUTION:

Do not hammer the bearing insert into place and don't nick or gouge the bearing faces. DO NOT apply any lubrication at this time.

12 Clean the faces of the bearing inserts in the block and the crankshaft main bearing journals with a clean, lint-free cloth.

13 Check or clean the oil holes in the crankshaft, as any dirt here can go only one way - straight through the new bearings.

14 Once you're certain the crankshaft is clean, carefully lay it in position in the cylinder block.

15 Before the crankshaft can be permanently installed, the main bearing oil clearance must be checked.

16 Cut several strips of the appropriate size of Plastigage. They must be slightly shorter than the width of the main bearing journal.

17 Place one piece on each crankshaft main bearing journal, parallel with the journal axis as shown (see illustration).

18 Clean the faces of the bearing inserts in the bedplate/main bear-

ing caps. Hold the bearing inserts in place and install the assembly onto the crankshaft and cylinder block. DO NOT disturb the Plastigage. Make sure you install the bedplate or main bearing caps with the arrow facing the front (timing belt/timing chain end) of the engine.

19 Apply clean engine oil to all bolt threads prior to installation, then install all bolts finger-tight. On four-cylinder engines, tighten bedplate bolts (numbers 1 through 10) in the sequence shown (see illustration) progressing in steps, to the torque listed in this Chapter's Specifications. DO NOT rotate the crankshaft at any time during this operation.

➡Note: Be sure the three locating dowels are in place in the engine block. Their locations are indicated by the stars in the diagram. On V6 engines, tighten the main bearing cap bolts to the torque listed in this Chapter's Specifications.

20 Remove the bolts in the reverse order of the tightening sequence and carefully lift the bedplate (four-cylinder engine) or caps (V6 engines) straight up and off the block. Do not disturb the Plastigage or rotate the crankshaft. If the bedplate or cap(s) is difficult to remove, tap

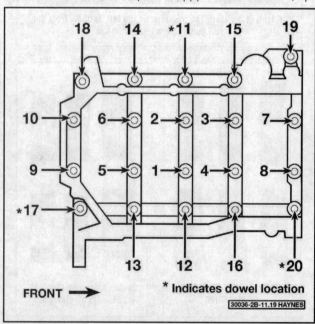

12.19 Main bearing cap bolt and bedplate bolt tightening sequence on the 2.4L engine

12.21 Use the scale on the Plastigage package to determine the bearing oil clearance - be sure to measure the widest part of the Plastigage and use the correct scale; it comes with both standard and metric scales

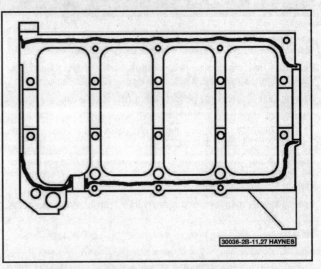

12.27 On 2.4L engines, apply a 1/16-inch bead of special bedplate sealant (or equivalent) to the darkened areas indicated

it gently from side-to-side with a soft-face hammer to loosen it.

21 Compare the width of the crushed Plastigage on each journal to the scale printed on the Plastigage envelope to determine the main bearing oil clearance. Check with an automotive machine shop for the crankshaft main bearing oil clearance limits.

22 If the clearance is not as specified, the bearing inserts may be the wrong size (which means different ones will be required). Before deciding if different inserts are needed, make sure that no dirt or oil was between the bearing inserts and the cap assembly or block when the clearance was measured. If the Plastigage was wider at one end than the other, the crankshaft journal may be tapered. If the clearance still exceeds the limit specified, the bearing insert(s) will have to be replaced with an undersize bearing insert(s).

❊❊ CAUTION:

When installing a new crankshaft always install a standard bearing insert set.

23 Carefully scrape all traces of the Plastigage material off the main bearing journals and/or the bearing insert faces. Be sure to remove all residue from the oil holes. Use your fingernail or the edge of a plastic card - don't nick or scratch the bearing faces.

Final installation

▶ **Refer to illustration 12.27**

24 Carefully lift the crankshaft out of the cylinder block.

25 Clean the bearing insert faces in the cylinder block, then apply a thin, uniform layer of moly-base grease or engine assembly lube to each of the bearing surfaces. Be sure to coat the thrust faces as well as the journal face of the thrust bearing.

26 Make sure the crankshaft journals are clean, then lay the crankshaft back in place in the cylinder block.

27 Clean the bearing insert faces and then apply the same lubricant to them.

➡Note: On four-cylinder engines, make sure the three locating dowels are installed in the engine block (see Step 19). Clean the engine block and the bedplate thoroughly. The surfaces must be free of oil residue. On four-cylinder engines, apply a 1/16-inch bead of anaerobic sealant (Mopar Torque Cure Gasket

Maker or equivalent) to the engine block (see illustration).

28 On four-cylinder engines, hold the bedplate (main bearing assembly) and bearings in place and install it onto the crankshaft and cylinder block. Install the main bearing assembly until the dowels lock together with the assembly. On V6 engines, install the main bearing caps onto the designated journals.

29 Prior to installation, apply clean engine oil to all bolt threads wiping off any excess, then install all bolts finger-tight.

30 On V6 engines, tighten the main bearing cap bolts to the torque listed in this Chapter's Specifications. Start with the center caps and work to the outer caps to allow the crankshaft to be installed level with the block and bearing inserts.

31 On the four-cylinder engine, tighten the bedplate as follows (see illustration 12.19):

a) Tighten bolts 11, 17 and 20 until the assembly contacts the engine block.

b) To ensure correct thrust bearing alignment, rotate the crankshaft until the No. 4 piston is at TDC.

c) Carefully pry the crankshaft all the way towards the rear of the block and then towards the front of the block.

d) Wedge an appropriate tool such as a block of wood, between the engine block and the rearmost crankshaft counterweight to hold the crankshaft in the most forward position. DO NOT drive the wedge between the bedplate and the crankshaft.

e) Tighten bolts 1 through 10 in the sequence shown, to the Step 1 torque listed in this Chapter's Specifications.

f) Remove the wedge, then tighten bolts 1 through 10 to Step 2 then Step 3 (see this Chapter's Specifications).

g) Tighten bolts 11 through 20 in the sequence shown to the torque listed in this Chapter's Specifications.

h) Tighten bolts 11 through 20 in Step 5 to the torque listed in this Chapter's Specifications.

32 Recheck crankshaft endplay with a feeler gauge or a dial indicator. The endplay should be correct if the crankshaft thrust faces aren't worn or damaged and if new bearings have been installed.

33 Rotate the crankshaft a number of times by hand to check for any obvious binding. It should rotate with a running torque of 50 in-lbs or less. If the running torque is too high, correct the problem at this time.

34 Install the new rear main oil seal (see Chapter 2A).

GLOSSARY

B

Backlash - The amount of play between two parts. Usually refers to how much one gear can be moved back and forth without moving gear with which it's meshed.

Bearing Caps - The caps held in place by nuts or bolts which, in turn, hold the bearing surface. This space is for lubricating oil to enter.

Bearing clearance - The amount of space left between shaft and bearing surface. This space is for lubricating oil to enter.

Bearing crush - The additional height which is purposely manufactured into each bearing half to ensure complete contact of the bearing back with the housing bore when the engine is assembled.

Bearing knock - The noise created by movement of a part in a loose or worn bearing.

Blueprinting - Dismantling an engine and reassembling it to EXACT specifications.

Bore - An engine cylinder, or any cylindrical hole; also used to describe the process of enlarging or accurately refinishing a hole with a cutting tool, as to bore an engine cylinder. The bore size is the diameter of the hole.

Boring - Renewing the cylinders by cutting them out to a specified size. A boring bar is used to make the cut.

Bottom end - A term which refers collectively to the engine block, crankshaft, main bearings and the big ends of the connecting rods.

Break-in - The period of operation between installation of new or rebuilt parts and time in which parts are worn to the correct fit. Driving at reduced and varying speed for a specified mileage to permit parts to wear to the correct fit.

Bushing - A one-piece sleeve placed in a bore to serve as a bearing surface for shaft, piston pin, etc. Usually replaceable.

C

Camshaft - The shaft in the engine, on which a series of lobes are located for operating the valve mechanisms. The camshaft is driven by gears or sprockets and a timing chain. Usually referred to simply as the cam.

Carbon - Hard, or soft, black deposits found in combustion chamber, on plugs, under rings, on and under valve heads.

Cast iron - An alloy of iron and more than two percent carbon, used for engine blocks and heads because it's relatively inexpensive and easy to mold into complex shapes.

Chamfer - To bevel across (or a bevel on) the sharp edge of an object.

Chase - To repair damaged threads with a tap or die.

Combustion chamber - The space between the piston and the cylinder head, with the piston at top dead center, in which air-fuel mixture is burned.

Compression ratio - The relationship between cylinder volume (clearance volume) when the piston is at top dead center and cylinder volume when the piston is at bottom dead center.

Connecting rod - The rod that connects the crank on the crankshaft with the piston. Sometimes called a con rod.

Connecting rod cap - The part of the connecting rod assembly that attaches the rod to the crankpin.

Core plug - Soft metal plug used to plug the casting holes for the coolant passages in the block.

Crankcase - The lower part of the engine in which the crankshaft rotates; includes the lower section of the cylinder block and the oil pan.

Crank kit - A reground or reconditioned crankshaft and new main and connecting rod bearings.

Crankpin - The part of a crankshaft to which a connecting rod is attached.

Crankshaft - The main rotating member, or shaft, running the length of the crankcase, with offset throws to which the connecting rods are attached; changes the reciprocating motion of the pistons into rotating motion.

Cylinder sleeve - A replaceable sleeve, or liner, pressed into the cylinder block to form the cylinder bore.

D

Deburring - Removing the burrs (rough edges or areas) from a bearing.

Deglazer - A tool, rotated by an electric motor, used to remove glaze from cylinder walls so a new set of rings will seat.

E

Endplay - The amount of lengthwise movement between two parts. As applied to a crankshaft, the distance that the crankshaft can move forward and back in the cylinder block.

F

Face - A machinist's term that refers to removing metal from the end of a shaft or the face of a larger part, such as a flywheel.

Fatigue - A breakdown of material through a large number of loading and unloading cycles. The first signs are cracks followed shortly by breaks.

Feeler gauge - A thin strip of hardened steel, ground to an exact thickness, used to check clearances between parts.

Free height - The unloaded length or height of a spring.

Freeplay - The looseness in a linkage, or an assembly of parts, between the initial application of force and actual movement. Usually perceived as slop or slight delay.

Freeze plug - See Core plug.

G

Gallery - A large passage in the block that forms a reservoir for engine oil pressure.

Glaze - The very smooth, glassy finish that develops on cylinder walls while an engine is in service.

H

Heli-Coil - A rethreading device used when threads are worn or damaged. The device is installed in a retapped hole to reduce the thread size to the original size.

I

Installed height - The spring's measured length or height, as installed on the cylinder head. Installed height is measured from the spring seat to the underside of the spring retainer.

J

Journal - The surface of a rotating shaft which turns in a bearing.

K

Keeper - The split lock that holds the valve spring retainer in position on the valve stem.

Key - A small piece of metal inserted into matching grooves machined into two parts fitted together - such as a gear pressed onto a shaft - which prevents slippage between the two parts.

Knock - The heavy metallic engine sound, produced in the combustion chamber as a result of abnormal combustion - usually detonation. Knock is usually caused by a loose or worn bearing. Also referred to as detonation, pinging and spark knock. Connecting rod or main bearing knocks are created by too much oil clearance or insufficient lubrication.

L

Lands - The portions of metal between the piston ring grooves.

Lapping the valves - Grinding a valve face and its seat together with lapping compound.

Lash - The amount of free motion in a gear train, between gears, or in a mechanical assembly, that occurs before movement can begin. Usually refers to the lash in a valve train.

Lifter - The part that rides against the cam to transfer motion to the rest of the valve train.

M

Machining - The process of using a machine to remove metal from a metal part.

Main bearings - The plain, or babbitt, bearings that support the crankshaft.

Main bearing caps - The cast iron caps, bolted to the bottom of the block, that support the main bearings.

O

O.D. - Outside diameter.

Oil gallery - A pipe or drilled passageway in the engine used to carry engine oil from one area to another.

Oil ring - The lower ring, or rings, of a piston; designed to prevent excessive amounts of oil from working up the cylinder walls and into the combustion chamber. Also called an oil-control ring.

Oil seal - A seal which keeps oil from leaking out of a compartment. Usually refers to a dynamic seal around a rotating shaft or other moving part.

O-ring - A type of sealing ring made of a special rubberlike material; in use, the O-ring is compressed into a groove to provide the sealing action.

Overhaul - To completely disassemble a unit, clean and inspect all parts, reassemble it with the original or new parts and make all adjustments necessary for proper operation.

P

Pilot bearing - A small bearing installed in the center of the flywheel (or the rear end of the crankshaft) to support the front end of the input shaft of the transmission.

Pip mark - A little dot or indentation which indicates the top side of a compression ring.

Piston - The cylindrical part, attached to the connecting rod, that moves up and down in the cylinder as the crankshaft rotates. When the fuel charge is fired, the piston transfers the force of the explosion to the connecting rod, then to the crankshaft.

Piston pin (or wrist pin) - The cylindrical and usually hollow steel pin that passes through the piston. The piston pin fastens the piston to the upper end of the connecting rod.

Piston ring - The split ring fitted to the groove in a piston. The ring contacts the sides of the ring groove and also rubs against the cylinder wall, thus sealing space between piston and wall. There are two types of rings: Compression rings seal the compression pressure in the combustion chamber; oil rings scrape excessive oil off the cylinder wall.

Piston ring groove - The slots or grooves cut in piston heads to hold piston rings in position.

Piston skirt - The portion of the piston below the rings and the piston pin hole.

Plastigage - A thin strip of plastic thread, available in different sizes, used for measuring clearances. For example, a strip of plastigage is laid across a bearing journal and mashed as parts are assembled. Then parts are disassembled and the width of the strip is measured to determine clearance between journal and bearing. Commonly used to measure crankshaft main-bearing and connecting rod bearing clearances.

Press-fit - A tight fit between two parts that requires pressure to force the parts together. Also referred to as drive, or force, fit.

Prussian blue - A blue pigment; in solution, useful in determining the area of contact between two surfaces. Prussian blue is commonly used to determine the width and location of the contact area between the valve face and the valve seat.

R

Race (bearing) - The inner or outer ring that provides a contact surface for balls or rollers in bearing.

Ream - To size, enlarge or smooth a hole by using a round cutting tool with fluted edges.

Ring job - The process of reconditioning the cylinders and installing new rings.

Runout - Wobble. The amount a shaft rotates out-of-true.

S

Saddle - The upper main bearing seat.

Scored - Scratched or grooved, as a cylinder wall may be scored by abrasive particles moved up and down by the piston rings.

Scuffing - A type of wear in which there's a transfer of material between parts moving against each other; shows up as pits or grooves in the mating surfaces.

Seat - The surface upon which another part rests or seats. For example, the valve seat is the matched surface upon which the valve face rests. Also used to refer to wearing into a good fit; for example, piston rings seat after a few miles of driving.

Short block - An engine block complete with crankshaft and piston and, usually, camshaft assemblies.

Static balance - The balance of an object while it's stationary.

Step - The wear on the lower portion of a ring land caused by excessive side and back-clearance. The height of the step indicates the ring's extra side clearance and the length of the step projecting from the back wall of the groove represents the ring's back clearance.

Stroke - The distance the piston moves when traveling from top dead center to bottom dead center, or from bottom dead center to top dead center.

Stud - A metal rod with threads on both ends.

T

Tang - A lip on the end of a plain bearing used to align the bearing during assembly.

Tap - To cut threads in a hole. Also refers to the fluted tool used to cut threads.

Taper - A gradual reduction in the width of a shaft or hole; in an engine cylinder, taper usually takes the form of uneven wear, more pronounced at the top than at the bottom.

Throws - The offset portions of the crankshaft to which the connecting rods are affixed.

Thrust bearing - The main bearing that has thrust faces to prevent excessive endplay, or forward and backward movement of the crankshaft.

Thrust washer - A bronze or hardened steel washer placed between two moving parts. The washer prevents longitudinal movement and provides a bearing surface for thrust surfaces of parts.

Tolerance - The amount of variation permitted from an exact size of measurement. Actual amount from smallest acceptable dimension to largest acceptable dimension.

U

Umbrella - An oil deflector placed near the valve tip to throw oil from the valve stem area.

Undercut - A machined groove below the normal surface.

Undersize bearings - Smaller diameter bearings used with re-ground crankshaft journals.

V

Valve grinding - Refacing a valve in a valve-refacing machine.

Valve train - The valve-operating mechanism of an engine; includes all components from the camshaft to the valve.

Vibration damper - A cylindrical weight attached to the front of the crankshaft to minimize torsional vibration (the twist-untwist actions of the crankshaft caused by the cylinder firing impulses). Also called a harmonic balancer.

W

Water jacket - The spaces around the cylinders, between the inner and outer shells of the cylinder block or head, through which coolant circulates.

Web - A supporting structure across a cavity.

Woodruff key - A key with a radiused backside (viewed from the side).

13 Engine overhaul - reassembly sequence

1   Before beginning engine reassembly, make sure you have all the necessary new parts, gaskets and seals as well as the following items on hand:

> Common hand tools
> A 1/2-inch drive torque wrench
> New engine oil
> Gasket sealant
> Thread locking compound

2   If you obtained a short block it will be necessary to install the cylinder head, the oil pump and pick-up tube, the oil pan, the water pump, the timing belt/timing chain and timing cover, and the valve cover (see Chapter 2A or 2B). In order to save time and avoid prob-

lems, the external components must be installed in the following general order:

> Thermostat and housing cover
> Water pump
> Intake and exhaust manifolds
> Fuel injection components
> Emission control components
> Spark plug wires and spark plugs
> Ignition coils
> Oil filter
> Engine mounts and mount brackets
> Driveplate (automatic transaxle)

14 Initial start-up and break-in after overhaul

✳✳ WARNING:

Have a fire extinguisher handy when starting the engine for the first time.

1   Once the engine has been installed in the vehicle, double-check the engine oil and coolant levels.

2   With the spark plugs out of the engine and the ignition system and fuel pump disabled, crank the engine until oil pressure registers on the gauge or the light goes out.

3   Install the spark plugs, hook up the plug wires and restore the ignition system and fuel pump functions.

4   Start the engine. It may take a few moments for the fuel system to build up pressure, but the engine should start without a great deal of effort.

5   After the engine starts, it should be allowed to warm up to normal operating temperature. While the engine is warming up, make a thorough check for fuel, oil and coolant leaks.

6   Shut the engine off and recheck the engine oil and coolant levels.

7   Drive the vehicle to an area with minimum traffic, accelerate from 30 to 50 mph, then allow the vehicle to slow to 30 mph with the throttle closed. Repeat the procedure 10 or 12 times. This will load the piston rings and cause them to seat properly against the cylinder walls. Check again for oil and coolant leaks.

8   Drive the vehicle gently for the first 500 miles (no sustained high speeds) and keep a constant check on the oil level. It is not unusual for an engine to use oil during the break-in period.

9   At approximately 500 to 600 miles, change the oil and filter.

10 For the next few hundred miles, drive the vehicle normally. Do not pamper it or abuse it.

11 After 2000 miles, change the oil and filter again and consider the engine broken in.

Specifications

General

Displacement

2.4L	148 cubic inches
3.3L	201 cubic inches
3.8L	231 cubic inches

Bore

2.4L	3.445 inches
3.3L	3.660 inches
3.8L	3.779 inches

Stroke

2.4L	3.976 inches
3.3L	3.188 inches
3.8L	3.425 inches

Compression ratio

2.4L		
	2003	9.4:1
	2004 and later	9.5:1
3.3L		9.35:1
3.8L		9.6:1

Compression pressure

2.4L	170 to 225 psi
3.3L and 3.8L	100 to 220 psi

Oil pressure

2.4L engines		
	At idle speed	4 psi (minimum)
	At 3,000 rpm	25 to 80 psi
3.3L and 3.8L V6		
	At idle speed	5 psi (minimum)
	At 3,000 rpm	30 to 80 psi

Camshaft - 3.3L and 3.8L V6 engines

Camshaft bearing journal diameter

No. 1	1.9970 to 1.9990 inches
No. 2	1.9809 to 1.9828 inches
No. 3	1.9659 to 1.9679 inches
No. 4	1.9499 to 1.9520 inches

Bearing diameter

No. 1	1.9999 to 2.0009 inches
No. 2	1.9839 to 1.9849 inches
No. 3	1.9690 to 1.9699 inches
No. 4	1.9529 to 1.9540 inches

Bearing clearance	0.001 to 0.004 inch
End play	0.010 to 0.020 inch

Torque specifications · Ft-lbs (unless otherwise indicated)

Balance shaft components (2.4L engine)

    Balance shaft chain guide bolt   105 in-lbs

    Balance shaft chain tensioner adjustment bolt   105 in-lbs

    Balance shaft chain tensioner pivot bolt   105 in-lbs

    Balance shaft carrier cover bolts   105 in-lbs

    Balance shaft gear cover (double-ended stud)   105 in-lbs

    Balance shaft sprocket bolts   20

    Balance shaft carrier bolts   40

Camshaft thrust plate bolt (3.3L and 3.8L engines)   105 in-lbs

Driveplate-to-crankshaft bolts   70

Driveplate-to-torque converter bolts   65

Connecting rod bearing cap nuts/bolts*

    2.4L cap bolts

        Step 1   20

        Step 2   Tighten an additional 1/4 turn (90-degrees)

    3.3L and 3.8L cap nuts and bolts

        Step 1   40

        Step 2   Tighten an additional 1/4 turn (90-degrees)

Main bearing assembly - 2.4L engine (see illustration 12.19)

    Main bearing cap bolts (numbers 1 through 10)

        Step 1   30

        Step 2   30

        Step 3   Tighten an additional 1/4 turn (90-degrees)

    Bedplate bolts (numbers 11 through 20)

        Step 1   250 in-lbs

        Step 2   250 in-lbs

Main bearing cap bolts - 3.3L V6 engine

    Step 1   30

    Step 2   Tighten an additional 1/4 turn (90-degrees)

Main bearing cap bolts and cross bolts - 3.8L V6 engine

    Cap bolts

        Step 1   30

        Step 2   Tighten an additional 1/4 turn (90-degrees)

    Cross bolts*   45

*Use new bolts

Section

Reference to other Chapters

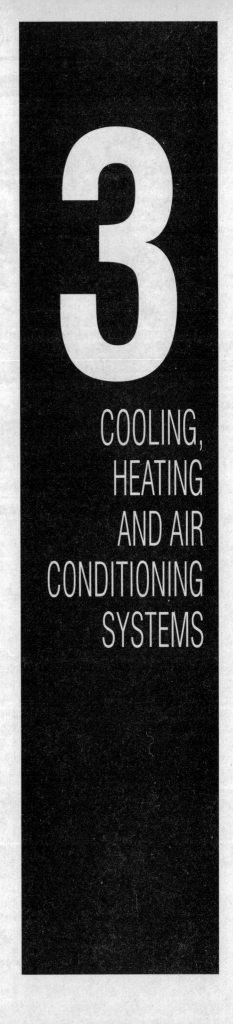

3

COOLING, HEATING AND AIR CONDITIONING SYSTEMS

1   General information

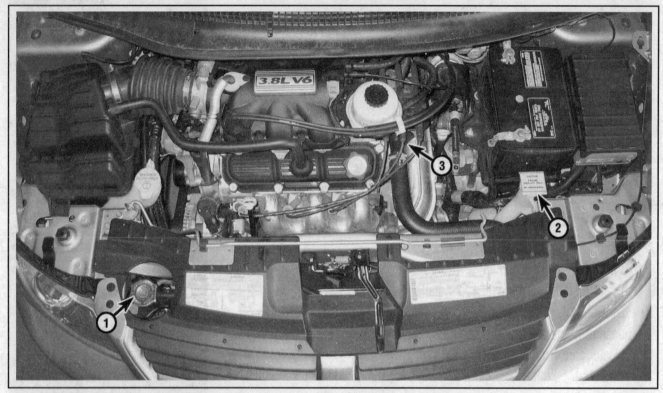

1.1 Basic engine cooling components (V6 shown, others models are similar)

1 Radiator cap (and radiator)	2 Coolant reservoir	3 Thermostat housing

ENGINE COOLING SYSTEM

▶ **Refer to illustrations 1.1 and 1.2**

All vehicles covered by this manual employ a pressurized engine cooling system with thermostatically controlled coolant circulation (see illustration). An impeller-type water pump mounted on the front of the engine pumps coolant through the engine. The pump mounts onto the timing case on the V6 engines, and directly on the engine block on the four-cylinder engines. The coolant flows around the combustion chambers and toward the rear of the engine. Cast-in coolant passages direct coolant near the intake ports, exhaust ports, and spark plug areas.

A wax pellet-type thermostat is located in a housing facing the front of the engine compartment. During warm-up, the closed thermostat prevents coolant from circulating through the radiator. As the engine nears normal operating temperature, the thermostat opens and allows hot coolant to travel through the radiator, where it's cooled before returning to the engine (see illustration).

The cooling system is sealed by a pressure-type cap, which raises the boiling point of the coolant and increases the cooling efficiency of the system. If the system pressure exceeds the cap pressure relief value, the excess pressure in the system forces the spring-loaded valve inside the cap off its seat and allows the coolant to escape through the overflow tube into a coolant reservoir. When the system cools, the excess coolant is automatically drawn from the reservoir back into the radiator.

The coolant reservoir serves as both the point at which fresh cool-

ant is added to the cooling system to maintain the proper fluid level and as a holding tank for overheated coolant. This type of cooling system is known as a closed design because coolant that escapes past the pressure cap is saved and reused.

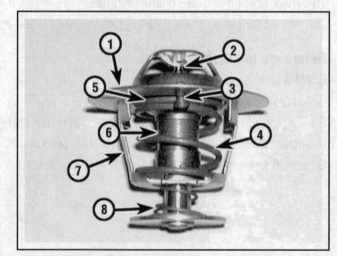

1.2 Typical thermostat

1	Flange	5	Valve seat
2	Piston	6	Valve
3	Jiggle valve	7	Frame
4	Main coil spring	8	Secondary coil spring

ENGINE COOLING FANS

These models are equipped with dual electric cooling fans. A relay and the vehicle's onboard computer or Powertrain Control Module (PCM) controls the fans. The fan relay is located in the engine compartment. The PCM (computer) uses information from various sensors to control the application and speed of the fans.

HEATING SYSTEM

The heating system consists of blower fans and a heater core located in the heater box, with hoses connecting the heater core to the engine cooling system. Hot engine coolant is circulated through the heater core. When the heater mode on the heater/air conditioning control head on the dashboard is activated, a flap door opens to expose the heater box to the passenger compartment. A fan switch on the control head activates the blower motor, which forces air through the core, heating the air. Some models are equipped with a rear heating/air conditioning system mounted in the right rear quarter panel.

AIR CONDITIONING SYSTEM

The air conditioning system consists of a condenser mounted in front of the radiator, an evaporator mounted adjacent to the heater core, a compressor mounted on the engine, a receiver-drier, a pressure transducer (similar to an electronic switch) and the plumbing connecting all of the above components. Some models are equipped with a rear heating/air conditioning system mounted in the right rear quarter panel.

A blower fan forces the warmer air of the passenger compartment through the evaporator core, transferring the heat from the air to the refrigerant (sort of a radiator in reverse). The liquid refrigerant boils off into low-pressure vapor, taking the heat with it when it leaves the evaporator.

2 Antifreeze - general information

▶ **Refer to illustration 2.4**

✺ WARNING:

Do not allow antifreeze to come in contact with your skin or painted surfaces of the vehicle. Rinse off spills immediately with plenty of water. Antifreeze is highly toxic if ingested. Never leave antifreeze lying around in an open container or in puddles on the floor; children and pets are attracted by its sweet smell and may drink it. Check with local authorities about disposing of used antifreeze. Many communities have collection centers which will see that antifreeze is disposed of safely. Never dump used antifreeze on the ground or pour it into drains.

The cooling system should be filled with a water/ethylene glycol based antifreeze solution, which will prevent freezing down to at least -20-degrees F (even lower in cold climates). It also provides protection against corrosion and increases the coolant boiling point. The engines in these vehicles have aluminum cylinder heads. The manufacturer recommends that the correct type of coolant be used and strongly urges that coolant types not be mixed (see the Chapter 1 Specifications).

Drain, flush and refill the cooling system at the service interval listed in the Chapter 1 maintenance schedule. The use of antifreeze solutions for periods of longer than recommended is likely to cause damage and encourage the formation of rust and scale in the system.

2.4 Use an antifreeze hydrometer (available at most auto parts stores) to test the condition of your coolant

Before adding antifreeze to the system, inspect all hose connections. Antifreeze can leak through very minute openings.

Hydrometers are available at most auto parts stores to test the coolant (see illustration). Use antifreeze that meets factory specifications (see Chapter 1).

3 Thermostat - check and replacement

CHECK

1 Before assuming the thermostat is to blame for a cooling system problem, check the coolant level and temperature gauge operation.

2 If the engine seems to be taking a long time to warm up, based on heater output or temperature gauge operation, the thermostat is probably stuck open. Replace the thermostat with a new one.

3 If the engine runs hot, use your hand to check the temperature of the upper radiator hose. If the hose isn't hot, but the engine is, the thermostat is probably stuck closed, preventing the coolant inside the engine from escaping to the radiator. Replace the thermostat.

✺ CAUTION:

Don't drive the vehicle without a thermostat. The computer may stay in open loop and emissions and fuel economy will suffer.

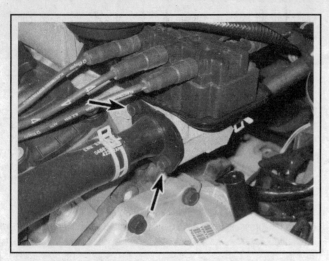

3.9 The thermostat housing cover and mounting bolts (V6 shown, four-cylinder similar)

4   If the upper radiator hose is hot, it means that the coolant is flowing and the thermostat is open. Consult the Troubleshooting Section at the front of this manual for cooling system diagnosis.

REPLACEMENT

▶ **Refer to illustrations 3.9 and 3.10**

✸✸ WARNING:

Do not remove the radiator cap, drain the coolant or replace the thermostat until the engine has cooled completely.

5   Disconnect the cable from the negative battery terminal (see Chapter 5, Section 1).

6   Drain the cooling system (see Chapter 1). If the coolant is relatively new or in good condition, save it and reuse it. Read the **Warning** in Section 2.

7   Follow the upper radiator hose to the engine to locate the thermostat housing cover (see illustration 3.9).

8   Loosen the hose clamp, then detach the hose from the fitting. If it's stuck, grasp it near the end with a pair of adjustable pliers and twist it to break the seal, then pull it off. If the hose is old or deteriorated, cut it off and install a new one.

➥**Note 1: If the outer surface of the large fitting that mates with the hose is deteriorated (corroded, pitted, etc.), it may be damaged further by hose removal. If it is, the thermostat housing cover will have to be replaced.**

➥**Note 2: If the hose has recently been replaced and the fitting is known to be in good condition, the thermostat can be serviced without removing the hose from the housing cover.**

9   Remove the thermostat housing cover fasteners and cover. If the

3.10 On V6 engines, remove the material around the staked areas (A) to remove the original equipment thermostat from the housing cover. Note the keyed areas (B) and the spring direction for reinstallation

cover is stuck, tap it with a soft-face hammer to jar it loose. Be prepared for some coolant to spill as the seal is broken (see illustration).

10   Take note of how the thermostat and gasket are installed. To remove the original equipment thermostat on a V6 engine, remove material from the staked areas of the housing cover that hold the thermostat in place (see illustration).

➥**Note: If the thermostat has been replaced before, unstaking should not be necessary. Also, it is not necessary to stake the replacement thermostat for installation.**

11   Remove all traces of the old gasket from the mating surfaces and clean them thoroughly.

12   Install the new thermostat, with the jiggle pin in the 12 o'clock position, and the spring end directed into the engine.

➥**Note: The thermostat on V6 engines is keyed and will only fit in one position (see illustration 3.10).**

13   Install a new gasket, making sure that it is oriented in the same way as the original.

➥**Note: It is standard practice to use a thin layer of RTV sealant when installing flat replacement gaskets. However, if the gasket is designed with a raised crushable sealing surface (not flat), no RTV sealant is necessary.**

14   Install the thermostat housing cover, tightening the fasteners to the torque listed in this Chapter's Specifications.

15   Reattach the hose and tighten the hose clamp securely, if removed. Install all components that were previously removed.

16   Reconnect the battery (see Chapter 5, Section 1).

17   Refill the cooling system (see Chapter 1).

18   Start the engine and allow it to reach normal operating temperature, then check for leaks and proper thermostat operation (as described in Steps 2 through 4).

4   Engine cooling fans and circuit - check and replacement

※※ WARNING:

To avoid possible injury or damage, DO NOT operate the engine with a damaged fan. Do not attempt to repair the fan blades or shroud assembly - replace the assembly.

→Note: Always check for blown fuses before attempting to diagnose a faulty electrical circuit.

CHECK

▶ Refer to illustration 4.1

1   If the engine is overheating and the cooling fan is not operating,

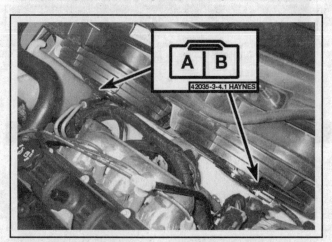

4.1 To test either fan motor, disconnect the electrical connector and use jumper wires to connect the fan motor directly to the battery (B) and ground (A) - if the fan still doesn't work, replace the assembly

unplug the electrical connector at the motor and use fused jumper wires to connect the fan motor directly to the battery (see illustration). If the fan still doesn't work, replace the assembly. Test each motor separately.

※※ CAUTION:

Do not apply battery power to the harness side of the electrical connector.

2   If the motors are OK, but the cooling fan doesn't come on when the engine gets hot, the fault may be in the coolant temperature sensor, the fan relay, the Powertrain Control Module (PCM) or the wiring which connects the components.

3   Carefully check all wiring and connections (wiring diagrams are included at the end of Chapter 12). If no obvious problems are found, further diagnosis should be done by a dealer service department or a qualified repair shop.

REPLACEMENT

▶ Refer to illustrations 4.6 and 4.8

4   Disconnect the cable from the negative battery terminal (see Chapter 5, Section 1) and then disconnect the cooling fan electrical connector(s).

5   Remove the radiator support (see Chapter 11).

6   Remove the cooling fan assembly top fastener(s) (see illustration).

7   Remove either cooling fan assembly by pulling it straight up and out of the engine compartment.

8   Installation is the reverse of removal. Be sure to place the fan assembly back into the retaining clips for the side and bottom (see illustration).

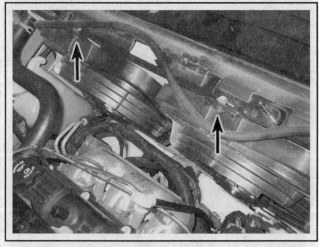

4.6 Fan assembly fasteners

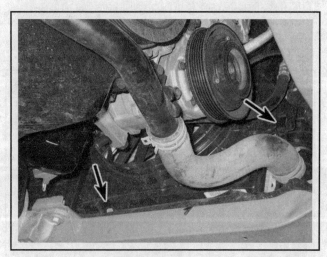

4.8 Fan assembly retaining clips

5 Coolant reservoir - removal and installation

▶ Refer to illustration 5.3

✳✳ WARNING:

Wait until the engine is completely cool before beginning this procedure.

1   Set the parking brake, raise the front of the vehicle and support it securely on jackstands.
2   Place a drain pan under the reservoir and then detach the reservoir hose.
3   Remove the lower mounting bolt from under the vehicle (see illustration).
4   Remove the remaining mounting bolts and lift the reservoir out of the engine compartment.
5   Installation is the reverse of removal. While the tank is off the vehicle, it should be cleaned with soapy water and a brush to remove any deposits inside. Inspect it for damage and replace it if necessary. Fill the reservoir with the proper type and amount of coolant (see Chapter 1).

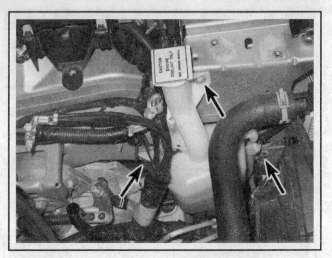

5.3 Coolant reservoir mounting fasteners - the front lower fastener (right arrow) is most easily accessed from underneath

6 Radiator - removal and installation

✳✳ WARNING:

Wait until the engine is completely cool before beginning this procedure.

REMOVAL

▶ Refer to illustrations 6.8a, 6.8b, 6.9 and 6.13

1   Disconnect the cable from the negative battery terminal (see Chapter 5, Section 1).
2   Set the parking brake, raise the front of the vehicle and support it securely on jackstands.

3   Drain the cooling system (see Chapter 1). If the coolant is relatively new and in good condition, save it and reuse it. Read the **Warning** in Section 2.
4   Remove the engine cooling fans (see Section 4).
5   Detach the coolant reservoir hose from the radiator filler neck and retainer and then move it aside.
6   Remove the vapor purge solenoid from it's mounting bracket (see Chapter 6).
7   Remove the lower engine splash shield (see Chapter 2B).
8   Disconnect the upper and lower radiator hoses (see illustrations).
9   Carefully separate the A/C condenser from the radiator by removing the fasteners and then pulling the condenser up to release the lower clips (see illustration 6.13 and the accompanying illustration).

6.8a Use pliers to expand the hose clamp and slide it back on the hose. Detach the upper radiator hose

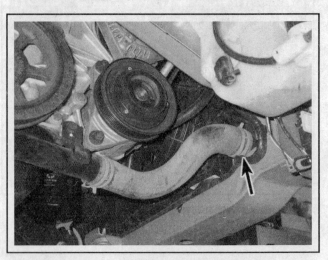

6.8b Remove the hose clamp and detach the lower radiator hose

6.9 Remove the radiator brackets (A) and release the condenser fasteners (B)

6.13 The left-side radiator rubber mount

➡**Note: After separating the condenser, let it rest towards the front of the vehicle, being careful not to damage the cooling fins on it or the radiator.**

10 Note the position of the flexible air seals on each side of the radiator and then carefully lift out the radiator. Don't spill coolant on the vehicle or scratch the paint.

11 Check the radiator for leaks and damage. If it needs repair, have a radiator shop or dealer service department perform the work, as special techniques are required.

12 Bugs and dirt can be removed from the radiator by spraying it with a garden hose nozzle from the back side. The radiator should be flushed out with a garden hose before reinstallation.

13 Check the radiator rubber mounts for deterioration and replace them if necessary (see illustration).

INSTALLATION

14 Installation is the reverse of the removal procedure. Make sure the A/C condenser is properly attached to the radiator before seating the radiator into the lower rubber mounts.

➡**Note: Be sure that the flexible air seals on each side of the radiator are in the correct position while installing the radiator.**

15 After installation, fill the cooling system with the proper mixture of antifreeze and water (see Chapter 1).

16 Start the engine and check for leaks. Allow the engine to reach normal operating temperature, indicated by the upper radiator hose becoming hot. Recheck the coolant level and add more if required.

7 Water pump - check

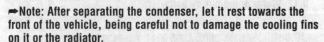

▶ **Refer to illustration 7.2**

1 A failure in the water pump can cause serious engine damage due to overheating.

2 If a failure occurs at the pump seal, coolant will leak from the weep hole(s) on the water pump (see illustration).

➡**Note: The top weep hole is near the pulley shaft on the water pump housing.**

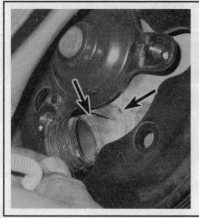

7.2 A water pump weep hole/slot. (The plastic plug and pulley are removed for clarity. It is not necessary to remove them to inspect for leaks - fluid will be seen coming from the slot)

3 Remove the lower engine splash shield (see Chapter 2B).

4 Using a flashlight, look for traces of coolant residue or dried coolant tracks around the weep hole(s). If the seal has leaked, it should be very apparent.

5 If the water pump shaft bearings fail, there may be a howling sound near the water pump while it's running. With the engine off, shaft wear can be felt if the water pump pulley is rocked up-and-down. Don't mistake drivebelt slippage, which causes a squealing sound, for water pump bearing failure.

6 A quick water pump performance check can be done by doing the following:

    a) *Make certain that the coolant level in the system is full.*
    b) *Start the vehicle and warm it up fully.*
    c) *Turn the heater on in the passenger compartment.*
    d) *Check for little or no heat output. If this is the case, the water pump may be failing because coolant flow does not appear to be going through the heater core.*

7 A water pump may still be due for replacement even if it's not leaking or making any noise. The only sure way to tell if replacement is necessary is to remove the pump and examine it closely. A loose or corroded impeller, a leaking shaft seal or a worn shaft bearing are all causes for replacement.

8 Water pump - replacement

⁂ WARNING:

Wait until the engine is completely cool before beginning this procedure.

ALL ENGINES

1   Disconnect the cable from the negative battery terminal (see Chapter 5, Section 1).

2   Set the parking brake, raise the front of the vehicle and support it securely on jackstands.

3   Drain the cooling system (see Chapter 1). If the coolant is relatively new and in good condition, save it and reuse it. Read the **Warning** in Section 2.

4   Remove the engine splash shield (see Chapter 2B).

FOUR-CYLINDER ENGINE

5   Remove the timing belt, the timing belt idler pulley, the camshaft sprockets and the rear timing belt cover (see Chapter 2A).

6   Remove the bolts attaching the water pump to the engine block and remove the pump. If the water pump is stuck, gently tap it with a soft-faced hammer to break the seal.

7   Clean the bolt threads and the threaded holes in the engine to remove the corrosion and sealant. Remove all traces of the old seal from the sealing surfaces.

8   Compare the new pump to the old one to make sure that they're identical.

9   Install a new O-ring seal in the groove that lines the water pump body and then apply a thin film of RTV sealant to hold the seal in place during installation.

⁂ CAUTION:

Make sure that the O-ring seal is correctly seated in the water pump groove to avoid a coolant leak. Carefully mate the pump to the engine.

8.12 Water pump pulley bolts

10 Install the water pump bolts and tighten them to the torque listed in this Chapter's Specifications. Don't overtighten the water pump bolts; doing so will damage the pump.

11 The remainder of installation is the reverse of removal. Refill and bleed the cooling system when you're done (see Chapter 1). Run the engine and check for leaks and proper operation.

V6 ENGINES

▶ **Refer to illustrations 8.12, 8.15 and 8.16**

12 Loosen the water pump pulley bolts (see illustration).

13 Remove the drivebelt (see Chapter 1).

14 Remove the pulley bolts.

15 Position the pulley to allow access to the water pump mounting bolts and then remove them (see illustration).

16 Rotate and move the pulley inward between the pump housing and the hub and then remove the water pump and pulley together (see illustration).

17 Clean the bolt threads and threaded holes in the timing case

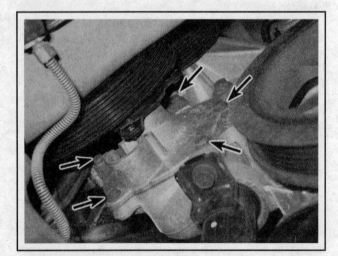

8.15 Water pump mounting bolts

8.16 Placing the water pump pulley towards the pump housing

cover to remove any corrosion and sealant.

18 Remove and discard the old seal and clean the mating surfaces. Be sure not to gouge or scratch the mating surface on the timing case cover.

19 Install a new O-ring seal in the groove that lines the water pump body and then apply a thin film of RTV sealant to hold the seal in place during installation.

※※ **CAUTION:**

Make sure that the O-ring seal is correctly seated in the water pump groove to avoid a coolant leak.

20 Position the water pump pulley loosely between the pump housing and drive hub.

➡**Note: The water pump pulley must be positioned this way to install the water pump and pulley together.**

21 Install the water pump mounting bolts and tighten them to the torque listed in this Chapter's Specifications.

※※ **CAUTION:**

Don't overtighten the mounting bolts; doing so will damage the pump.

22 Position the pulley onto the drive hub and install the mounting bolts finger tight.

23 Install the drivebelt (se Chapter 1).

24 Tighten the pulley bolts to the torque listed in this Chapter's Specifications.

25 The remainder of installation is the reverse of removal. Refill and bleed the cooling system when you're done (see Chapter 1). Run the engine and check for leaks and proper operation.

9 Water inlet tube - removal and installation

▶ **Refer to illustration 9.5**

※※ **WARNING:**

Wait until the engine is completely cool before beginning this procedure.

1 Set the parking brake, raise the front of the vehicle and support it securely on jackstands.

2 Drain the cooling system (see Chapter 1). If the coolant is relatively new and in good condition, save it and reuse it. Read the **Warning** in Section 2.

3 Remove the engine splash shield (see Chapter 2B).

4 Disconnect the lower radiator hose from the water inlet tube.

➡**Note: On four-cylinder models, disconnect the upper radiator hose for access to the inlet tube connections.**

5 Remove the mounting bolts (see illustration).

6 Pull the inlet tube directly out from the timing case cover to remove it.

7 Remove and discard the O-ring seal and inspect the tube for corrosion and pitting.

8 Clean and inspect the inlet tube bore in the timing case cover for corrosion and pitting.

9 Install a new O-ring seal on the inlet tube and coat it with dielectric grease.

9.5 Mounting bolts for the water inlet pipe (V6 shown, four cylinder models are similar)

10 Installation is the reverse of removal. Tighten the mounting bolts to the torque listed in this Chapter's Specifications. Refill and bleed the cooling system when you're done (see Chapter 1). Run the engine and check for leaks.

10 Blower motor resistor/power module and blower motor assembly - replacement

❄❄ WARNING:

The models covered by this manual are equipped with Supplemental Restraint systems (SRS), more commonly known as airbags. Always disable the airbag system before working in the vicinity of any airbag system component to avoid the possibility of accidental deployment of the airbag, which could cause personal injury (see Chapter 12).

1   Disconnect the cable from the negative battery terminal (see Chapter 5, Section 1).

FRONT

2   Remove the glovebox (see Chapter 11).

Blower motor resistor/power module

▶ **Refer to illustration 10.3**

3   Disconnect the electrical connectors for the blower motor resistor or power module (see illustration).

➡**Note: Models equipped with automatic temperature control utilize a power module instead of a blower motor resistor. They are similar in the way they are mounted and connected.**

4   Remove the mounting fasteners and withdraw the unit from the heater/air conditioning housing.

5   Installation is the reverse of removal.

Blower motor assembly

▶ **Refer to illustrations 10.7 and 10.11**

➡**Note: The blower motor and blower wheel are balanced to each other at the factory and replaced as an assembly only.**

6   Disconnect the electrical connector for the blower motor from the resistor or power module (see illustration 10.3).

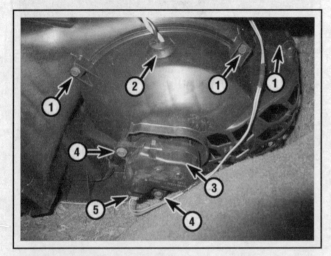

10.7 Air intake housing cover details:

1   *Mounting fasteners (two hidden)*
2   *Blower motor wiring grommet*
3   *Recirculation door actuator*
4   *Actuator mounting fasteners*
5   *Actuator electrical connector*

7   Disconnect the recirculation door actuator electrical connector, remove the mounting fasteners and then remove the actuator (see illustration).

8   Remove the air intake housing cover mounting fasteners (see illustration 10.7).

9   Push the blower motor wiring rubber grommet through the hole in the air intake housing cover. Continue to feed the wires into the hole along with the electrical connector (see illustration 10.7).

10   Carefully remove the air intake housing cover.

11   Carefully move the recirculation air door, as necessary, to remove the three screws securing the blower motor assembly to the housing (see illustration).

12   Gently flex the recirculation air door far enough to remove the blower motor assembly from the lower half of the housing and then remove the assembly.

13   Installation is the reverse of removal.

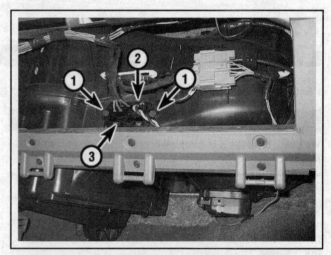

10.3 Blower motor resistor details (the power module is similar):

1   *Mounting fasteners*
2   *Blower motor electrical connector*
3   *Electrical connector*

10.11 Blower motor mounting fasteners

REAR

14 Remove the right rear trim panel (see Chapter 11).

Blower motor resistor/power module

▶ **Refer to illustration 10.15**

15 Disconnect the electrical connector for the blower motor resistor or power module (see illustration).

➡**Note: Models equipped with automatic temperature control utilize a power module instead of a blower motor resistor. They are similar in the way they are mounted and connected.**

16 Remove the mounting fasteners and withdraw the unit from the heater/air conditioning housing.

17 Installation is the reverse of removal.

Blower motor assembly

➡**Note 1: Removal of the rear heater/air conditioning housing is necessary to replace the blower motor assembly.**

➡**Note 2: The blower motor and blower wheel are balanced to each other at the factory and replaced as an assembly only.**

18 Remove the rear heater/air conditioning housing (see Section 18).

19 Remove the three blower motor mounting screws on the rear of

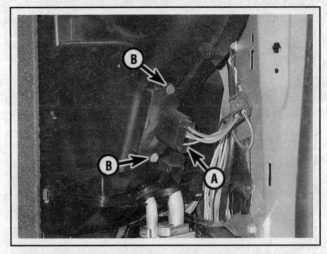

10.15 To remove the rear blower motor resistor, disconnect the electrical connector (A) and remove the mounting fasteners (B) (the power module is similar)

the housing.

20 Remove the blower motor from the housing.

21 Installation is the reverse of removal.

11 Heater core - replacement

❈❈ **WARNING:**

Wait until the engine is completely cool before beginning this procedure.

1 Disconnect the cable from the negative battery terminal (see Chapter 5, Section 1).

FRONT

▶ **Refer to illustrations 11.3, 11.6 and 11.9**

2 Drain the cooling system (see Chapter 1). If the coolant is relatively new or in good condition, save it and reuse it.

3 Remove the mounting fasteners for the intermediate shaft coupler cover/dash seal so that it can be moved aside (see illustration).

➡**Note: This procedure will provide the necessary clearance to remove the heater core without having to remove any part of the steering shaft.**

4 Remove the brake light switch from its bracket and secure it aside (see Chapter 9).

❈❈ **CAUTION:**

Do not move the small lever that is on the brake light switch.

5 Disconnect the power brake booster pushrod from the brake pedal arm (see Chapter 9).

6 Place towels underneath the heater core tube fittings and remove the retaining clips from the fittings (see illustration).

11.3 Pull the carpet out of the way and remove the mounting fasteners for the intermediate shaft coupler cover/dash seal

➡**Note: Remove the clips by pulling them from the opposite side the clip's opening and directly away from the tube fittings.**

7 Pull the tubes from the heater core and carefully rotate them up and out of the way. Plug or cap the openings to minimize contamination and spilled coolant.

8 Remove the heater core retaining bracket fasteners, then remove the bracket (see illustration 11.6).

9 Move the accelerator pedal up and the brake pedal down, and move the intermediate shaft cover/seal to allow enough clearance to remove the core. Carefully pull the heater core out of the heater/air conditioning housing and guide it through the components mentioned above (see illustration).

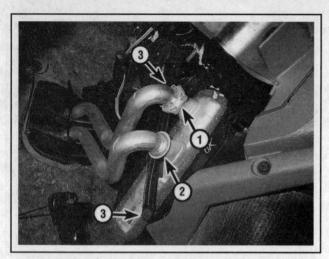

11.6 Front heater core mounting details (2005 model shown, other models similar):

1 Heater core tube fitting with retaining clip installed
2 Heater core tube fitting with retaining clip removed
3 Heater core retaining bracket fasteners (one hidden from view)

10 Installation is the reverse of removal. Use new seals for the heater core fittings and refill the cooling system (see Chapter 1).

➡Note: Use new retaining clips for the heater core fittings if there is any question about the use of the old ones.

REAR

▶ Refer to illustration 11.14

11 Remove the right rear trim panel (see Chapter 11).
12 Remove the upper air duct from the heater/air conditioning housing (see illustration 18.5).
13 Remove the lower air duct from above the rear wheel housing (see illustration 18.6).
14 Pinch off the heater hoses at the heater core with locking pliers, or equivalent, and then detach them from the core (see illustration 18.7 and the accompanying illustration).

➡Note: Be prepared for some coolant to spill when disconnecting the hoses from the heater core and also be careful not to damage the hoses when pinching them off.

15 Remove the heater/air conditioning housing upper mounting fasteners (see illustration 18.7).
16 Carefully release the four plastic retainers while pulling the heater core out of the heater/air conditioning housing (see illustration 11.14).
17 Carefully tilt the heater/air conditioning housing towards the rear of the vehicle; just enough to remove the heater core completely from the housing.

❋❋ CAUTION:

Do not tilt the housing too far because the bottom housing fasteners and A/C refrigerant lines are still attached and tilting the housing too far could break it.

18 Installation is the reverse of removal. Pre-fill the heater core and quickly attach the hoses. Check the cooling system level after reassem-

11.9 Pull the heater core from the heater/air conditioning housing

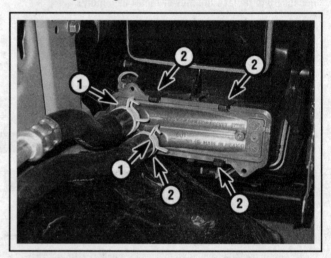

11.14 Rear heater core mounting details (2005 model shown, other models similar):

1 Heater core hose clamps
2 Heater core plastic retainers (one hidden)

bly is complete (see Chapter 1).

➡Note: If the heater core was replaced and not pre-filled, thermal cycle the vehicle TWICE. This procedure ensures that the heater core is filled completely. To thermal cycle the vehicle, it must be operated until the thermostat opens, then turned off and allowed to cool. The coolant level in the reservoir must be maintained during this process. To verify that the rear unit is filled completely, follow this procedure:

a) Begin with the vehicle at room temperature.
b) Start the vehicle and bring the engine to operating temperature.
c) Set the temperature to the full HEAT position in the front A/C control and then turn off the front system.
d) Start the engine and turn the rear A/C system blower on HIGH with the temperature setting in the full HEAT position.
e) The discharge air temperature, measured at the dual register located on the C-pillar base, should be between 135-degrees and 145-degrees F.

12 Heater/air conditioner control assembly - removal and installation

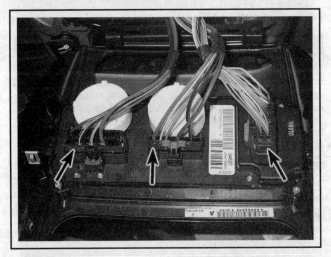

12.3 The front control assembly electrical connectors

✳✳ WARNING:

The models covered by this manual are equipped with Supplemental Restraint systems (SRS), more commonly known as airbags. Always disable the airbag system before working in the vicinity of any airbag system component to avoid the possibility of accidental deployment of the airbag, which could cause personal injury (see Chapter 12).

FRONT

▶ **Refer to illustration 12.3**

1 Disconnect the cable from the negative battery terminal (see Chapter 5, Section 1).

2 Remove the radio and heater/air conditioning control bezel assembly from the instrument panel (see Chapter 11).

3 Disconnect the electrical connectors from the back of the heater/air conditioning control assembly (see illustration).

➡**Note: On models equipped with automatic temperature control, disconnect the additional electrical connector for the infrared sensor located on the back of the center vent of the bezel assembly.**

4 Remove the mounting fasteners at each corner and then remove the control assembly from the bezel.

5 Installation is the reverse of removal. If the heater/air conditioning control assembly is being replaced, calibration/diagnostic tests are necessary for installation (see Section 13).

REAR

▶ **Refer to illustrations 12.7 and 12.8**

6 Disconnect the cable from the negative battery terminal (see Chapter 5, Section 1).

7 Gently pry the rear heater/air conditioning control bezel assembly from the headliner (see illustration).

8 Disconnect the electrical connectors from the back of the control assembly (see illustration).

9 Remove the mounting fasteners (each side and the middle) and then remove the control assembly from the bezel.

10 Installation is the reverse of removal. If the heater/air conditioning control assembly is being replaced, calibration/diagnostic tests are necessary for installation (see Section 13).

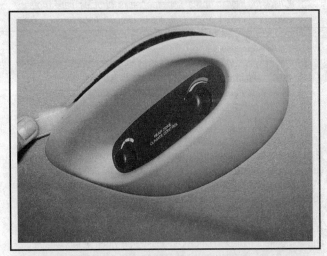

12.7 Use a plastic tool with soft edges to pry the rear control assembly away from the headliner

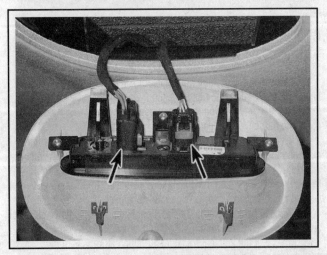

12.8 The rear control assembly electrical connectors

13 Air conditioning and heating system - check and maintenance

♦ Refer to illustration 13.1

❋❋ WARNING:

The air conditioning system is under high pressure. DO NOT loosen any fittings or remove any components until after the system has been discharged. Air conditioning refrigerant must be properly discharged into an EPA-approved container at a dealer service department or an automotive air conditioning repair facility. Always wear eye protection when disconnecting air conditioning system fittings.

1   The following maintenance checks should be performed on a regular basis to ensure the air conditioner continues to operate at peak efficiency.

   a) *Check the compressor drivebelt. If it's worn or deteriorated, replace it (see Chapter 1).*
   b) *Check the drivebelt tension and, if necessary, adjust it (see Chapter 1).*
   c) *Check the system hoses. Look for cracks, bubbles, hard spots and deterioration. Inspect the hoses and all fittings for oil bubbles and seepage. If there's any evidence of wear, damage or leaks, replace the hose(s).*
   d) *Inspect the condenser fins for leaves, bugs and other debris. Use a fin comb or compressed air to clean the condenser.*
   e) *Make sure the system has the correct refrigerant charge.*
   f) *Check the evaporator housing drain tube for blockage (see illustration).*

2   It's a good idea to operate the system for about 10 minutes at least once a month, particularly during the winter. Long term non-use can cause hardening, and subsequent failure, of the seals.

3   Because of the complexity of the air conditioning system and the special equipment necessary to service it, in-depth troubleshooting and repairs are not included in this manual (refer to the *Haynes Automotive Heating and Air Conditioning Repair Manual*). However, simple checks and component replacement procedures are provided in this Chapter.

4   The most common cause of poor cooling is simply a low system refrigerant charge. If a noticeable drop in cool air output occurs, the following quick check will help you determine if the refrigerant level is low.

CHECKING THE REFRIGERANT CHARGE

5   Warm the engine up to normal operating temperature.

6   Place the air conditioning temperature selector at the coldest setting and the blower at the highest setting. Open the vehicle doors (to make sure the air conditioning system doesn't cycle off as soon as it cools the passenger compartment).

7   With the compressor engaged - the clutch will make an audible click and the center of the clutch will rotate - feel the evaporator inlet and outlet lines at the firewall. The inlet (small diameter) line should feel somewhat warm and the outlet (large diameter) line should feel cold. If so, the system charge is probably adequate.

8   Place a thermometer in the dashboard vent nearest the evaporator and operate the system until the indicated temperature is around 40 to 45-degrees F. If the ambient (outside) air temperature is very high, say 110-degrees F, the duct air temperature may be as high as 60-degrees F, but generally the air conditioning is 30 to 40-degrees F cooler than the ambient air.

13.1 The evaporator drain tube location (viewed from underneath the vehicle)

➡Note: Humidity of the ambient air also affects the cooling capacity of the system. Higher ambient humidity lowers the effectiveness of the air conditioning system.

ADDING REFRIGERANT

♦ Refer to illustrations 13.9, 13.12, and 13.15

9   Buy an automotive charging kit at an auto parts store (see illustration). A charging kit includes a can of refrigerant, a tap valve and a short section of hose that can be attached between the tap valve and the system low side service valve.

❋❋ CAUTION 1:

Although the system will hold more than one can of refrigerant, don't add more than one can (you could overfill the system).

❋❋ CAUTION 2:

There are two types of refrigerant used in automotive systems; R-12, which has been widely used on earlier models, and the more environmentally-friendly R-134a used in all models covered by this manual. These two refrigerants (and their appropriate refrigerant oils) are not compatible and must never be mixed or components will be damaged. Use only R-134a refrigerant in the models covered by this manual.

10   Hook up the charging kit by following the manufacturer's instructions.

❋❋ WARNING:

DO NOT hook the charging kit hose to the system high side! The fittings on the charging kit are designed to fit only on the low side of the system.

11   Back off the valve handle on the charging kit and screw the kit onto the refrigerant can, making sure first that the O-ring or rubber seal inside the threaded portion of the kit is in place.

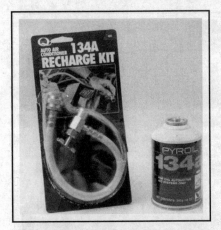

13.9 A basic charging kit for R-134a systems is available at most auto parts stores - it must say R-134a (not R-12) and so should the can of refrigerant

13.12 Attach the kit's quick-connect fitting to the low side service port (A) to administer R-134a into the air conditioning system (V6 model shown, four cylinder models are similar)

13.15 Insert a thermometer in the center vent, turn on the air conditioning system and wait for it to cool down; depending on the humidity, the output air should be 30 to 40-degrees cooler than the ambient air temperature

❉❉ WARNING:

Wear protective eyewear when dealing with pressurized refrigerant cans.

12 Locate the low-side service port in the engine compartment and unscrew the dust cap. Attach the quick-connect fitting to the service port (see illustration).

13 Warm up the engine and turn on the air conditioner. Keep the charging kit hose away from the fan and other moving parts.

➥Note: The charging process requires the compressor to be running. Your compressor may cycle off if the pressure is low due to a low charge. If the clutch cycles off, you can pull the pressure transducer connector (mounted near the receiver-drier) (see illustration 19.1) and attach a jumper wire across two terminals of the electrical connector (on the harness side). This will keep the compressor ON.

14 Turn the valve handle on the kit until the stem pierces the can, then back the handle out to release the refrigerant. You should be able to hear the rush of gas. Add refrigerant to the low side of the system until the temperature of the evaporator inlet and outlet lines is as described in Step 7. Allow stabilization time between each addition.

15 If you have an accurate thermometer, place it in the center air conditioning vent (see illustration) and note the temperature of the air coming out of the vent. A fully charged system which is working correctly should cool down to about 40-degrees F. Generally, an air conditioning system will put out air that is 30 to 40-degrees F cooler than the ambient air. For example, if the ambient (outside) air temperature is very high (over 100-degrees F), the temperature of air coming out of the registers should be 60 to 70-degrees F.

16 When the can is empty, turn the valve handle to the closed position and release the connection from the low-side port. Replace the dust cap.

17 Remove the charging kit from the can and store the kit for future use with the piercing valve in the UP position, to prevent inadvertently piercing the can on the next use.

HEATING SYSTEMS

18 If the carpet under the heater core is damp, or if antifreeze vapor or steam is coming through the vents, the heater core is leaking. Remove it (see Section 11) and install a new unit (most radiator shops will not repair a leaking heater core).

19 If the air coming out of the heater vents isn't hot, the problem could stem from any of the following causes:

a) *The thermostat is stuck open, preventing the engine coolant from warming up enough to carry heat to the heater core. Replace the thermostat (see Section 3).*

b) *There is a blockage in the system, preventing the flow of coolant through the heater core. Feel both heater hoses at the firewall. They should be hot. If one of them is cool, there is an obstruction in one of the hoses or in the heater core. Detach the hoses and back flush the heater core with a water hose. If the heater core is clear but circulation is impeded, remove the two hoses and flush them out with a water hose.*

c) *If flushing fails to remove the blockage from the heater core, the core must be replaced (see Section 11).*

ELIMINATING AIR CONDITIONING ODORS

▶ **Refer to illustration 13.23**

20 Unpleasant odors that often develop in air conditioning systems are caused by the growth of a fungus, usually on the surface of the evaporator core. The warm, humid environment there is a perfect breeding ground for mildew to develop.

21 The evaporator core on most vehicles is difficult to access, and factory dealerships have a lengthy, expensive process for eliminating the fungus by opening up the evaporator case and using a powerful disinfectant and rinse on the core until the fungus is gone. You can service your own system at home, but it takes something much stronger than basic household germ-killers or deodorizers.

22 Aerosol disinfectants for automotive air conditioning systems are available in most auto parts stores, but remember when shopping for them that the most effective treatments are also the most expensive. The basic procedure for using these sprays is to start by running the system in the RECIRC mode for ten minutes with the blower on its highest speed. Use the highest heat mode to dry out the system and keep the compressor from engaging by disconnecting the wiring connector at the compressor (see Section 14).

23 Make sure that the disinfectant can comes with a long spray hose. Guide the hose into the air intake housing just beyond the air recirculation door (see illustration), turn on the A/C and set the blower on high and then spray according to the manufacturer's recommendations. Follow the manufacturer's recommendations for the length of spray and waiting time between applications.

✳✳ WARNING:

Do not place more than two inches of hose into the housing because the blower motor fan blades are just above the air recirculation door and the hose could get caught in the blades.

24 Once the evaporator has been cleaned, the best way to prevent the mildew from coming back again is to make sure your evaporator housing drain tube is clear (see illustration 13.1).

DIAGNOSIS AND TESTING

25 The heater/air conditioning control assembly (module) is capable

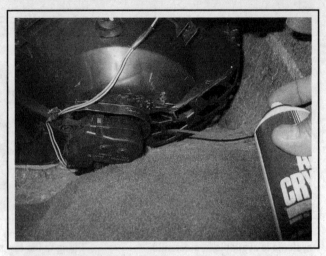

13.23 Insert the disinfectant nozzle into the air intake housing and just a few inches beyond the air recirculation door

of troubleshooting the system during dealer or repair shop servicing. If a problem is detected, an error code is displayed by flashing lights on the module pushbuttons. The error code cannot be erased until diagnostic tests are performed and the condition is repaired. Also, if the heater/air conditioning control module is replaced, calibration and diagnostic tests are absolutely necessary. Because of the complexity of this system, a qualified repair technician should perform these operations.

14 Air conditioning compressor - removal and installation

▶ Refer to illustration 14.4

✳✳ WARNING:

The air conditioning system is under high pressure. DO NOT loosen any fittings or remove any components until after the system has been discharged. Air conditioning refrigerant must be properly discharged into an EPA-approved container at a dealer service department or an automotive air conditioning repair facility. Always wear eye protection when disconnecting air conditioning system fittings.

✳✳ CAUTION:

When replacing entire components, additional refrigerant oil must be added equal to the amount that is removed with the component being replaced. Be sure to read the label on the oil container to verify that it is compatible with the R-134a system before adding any of it to the system.

➡**Note: The receiver-drier should always be replaced when the compressor is replaced.**

1 Have the system discharged and the refrigerant recovered by an air conditioning technician.

2 Disconnect the cable from the negative battery terminal (see Chapter 5, Section 1).

3 Remove the drivebelt (see Chapter 1).

➡**Note: If more access is necessary on V6 models for compressor removal, you can remove the alternator (see Chapter 5).**

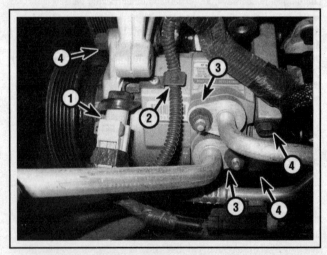

14.4 Air conditioning compressor details (V6 model shown, four-cylinder models similar):

1   *Compressor clutch electrical connector*
2   *Harness bracket (V6 models)*
3   *Line fittings*
4   *Mounting fasteners (two hidden from view in this photo)*

4 On V6 models, disconnect the engine wire harness connector from the compressor clutch coil and remove the bracket on top of the compressor (see illustration). On four-cylinder models, disconnect the compressor clutch electrical connector.

5 Remove the refrigerant lines from the compressor. Plug all open fittings to prevent entry of dirt and moisture.

6 Remove the compressor mounting fasteners and then lift the compressor out of the vehicle.

7 If a new compressor is being installed, pour out the oil from the old compressor into a graduated container and add that amount of new refrigerant oil to the new compressor. Also follow any directions included with the new compressor.

➡Note: The clutch may have to be transferred from the original compressor to the new one.

8 Installation is the reverse of removal. Be sure to install new O-rings onto the line fittings and lightly coat them with the correct refrigerant oil.

➡Note: Only use O-rings that are designed specifically for A/C system applications.

9 Have the system evacuated, recharged and leak tested by the shop that discharged it.

15 Air conditioning receiver-drier - removal and installation

▶ Refer to illustration 15.3

❋❋ **WARNING:**

The air conditioning system is under high pressure. DO NOT loosen any fittings or remove any components until after the system has been discharged. Air conditioning refrigerant must be properly discharged into an EPA-approved container at a dealer service department or an automotive air conditioning repair facility. Always wear eye protection when disconnecting air conditioning system fittings.

❋❋ **CAUTION:**

When replacing entire components, additional refrigerant oil must be added equal to the amount that is removed with the component being replaced. Be sure to read the label on the oil container to verify that it is compatible with the R-134a system before adding any of it to the system.

1 Have the system discharged and the refrigerant recovered by an air conditioning technician.

2 Remove the air filter housing (see Chapter 4).

3 Remove both line fittings from the receiver-drier (see illustration).

➡Note: Plug all openings immediately to prevent contamination.

4 Remove the mounting fasteners retaining the receiver-drier bracket to the shock tower. Note the position of the ground strap (if equipped).

5 Remove the receiver-drier.

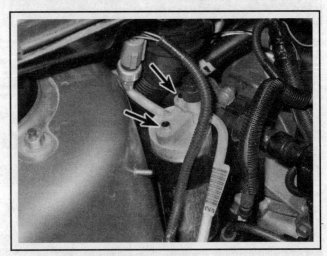

15.3 The receiver-drier line fittings

6 Installation is the reverse of removal. Be sure to install new O-rings onto the line fittings and lightly coat them with the correct refrigerant oil.

➡Note: Only use O-rings that are designed specifically for A/C system applications.

If you are replacing the receiver-drier with a new unit, add 0.8-ounce (25 ml) of refrigerant oil to the replacement.

7 Have the system evacuated, recharged and leak tested by the shop that discharged it.

16 Air conditioning condenser/automatic transaxle fluid cooler - removal and installation

▶ Refer to illustrations 16.5a and 16.5b

❋❋ **WARNING:**

The air conditioning system is under high pressure. DO NOT loosen any fittings or remove any components until after the system has been discharged. Air conditioning refrigerant must be properly discharged into an EPA-approved container at a dealer service department or an automotive air conditioning repair facility. Always wear eye protection when disconnecting air conditioning system fittings.

❋❋ **CAUTION:**

When replacing entire components, additional refrigerant oil must be added equal to the amount that is removed with the component being replaced. Be sure to read the label on the oil container to verify that it is compatible with the R-134a system before adding any of it to the system.

1 Have the system discharged and the refrigerant recovered by an air conditioning technician.

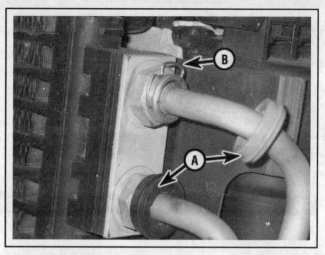

16.5a A/C condenser/ATF cooler details:

1   *Automatic transaxle fluid line fittings (2)*
2   *Refrigerant line fittings*
3   *Mounting retainers*

2   Disconnect the cable from the negative battery terminal (see Chapter 5, Section 1).

3   Remove the front bumper cover and grill assembly (see Chapter 11).

4   Remove the radiator support (see Chapter 11).

5   Disconnect the automatic transaxle fluid cooler lines from the unit (see illustrations).

6   Remove the refrigerant lines from the condenser. Plug all open fittings to prevent entry of dirt and moisture (see illustration 16.5a).

7   Separate the condenser from the plastic clip-type retainers.

16.5b Pull off the secondary plastic clip (A) and then remove the primary spring clip (B) from the fitting and withdraw the line from the A/C condenser/ATF cooler

8   Carefully pull straight up to release the condenser from the lower clips and then remove the condenser from the vehicle.

9   Installation is the reverse of removal. Make certain to fully seat the condenser into the mounting clips and retainers. Install new O-rings onto the line fittings and lightly coat them with refrigerant oil.

➡**Note: Only use O-rings that are designed specifically for A/C system applications.**

If you are replacing the A/C condenser with a new unit, add 1.7-ounce (50 ml) of refrigerant oil to the replacement.

10 Have the system evacuated, recharged and leak tested by the shop that discharged it.

17 Expansion valve - removal and installation

❊❊ **WARNING:**

The air conditioning system is under high pressure. DO NOT loosen any fittings or remove any components until after the system has been discharged. Air conditioning refrigerant must be properly discharged into an EPA-approved container at a dealer service department or an automotive air conditioning repair facility. Always wear eye protection when disconnecting air conditioning system fittings.

1   Have the air conditioning system refrigerant discharged and recovered by an air conditioning technician.

2   Disconnect the cable from the negative battery terminal (see Chapter 5, Section 1).

FRONT

▶ **Refer to illustration 17.5**

3   Remove the air filter housing (see Chapter 4).

4   Remove the right drain tube from the windshield wiper assembly for access to the valve (see Chapter 12).

5   Remove the nut securing both line fittings to the valve and

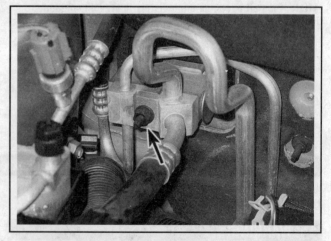

17.5 Refrigerant line fitting nut at the expansion valve

remove the lines while discarding the seals. Plug all openings quickly to minimize contamination (see illustration).

6   Remove the mounting fasteners for the valve and then remove the valve while discarding any other seals. Again, plug all openings.

→Note: On models equipped with a temperature sensor mounted to the expansion valve, remove the electrical connector from it and then remove the sensor fasteners and sensor.

7   Installation is the reverse of removal. Be sure to install new O-rings onto the line fittings and lightly coat them with the correct refrigerant oil.

→Note: Only use O-rings that are designed specifically for A/C system applications.

8   Have the system evacuated, recharged and leak tested by the shop that discharged it.

REAR

▶ **Refer to illustration 17.10**

9   Remove the rear heating and air conditioning housing (see Section 18).

10 Carefully remove the foam insulation from around the expansion valve (see illustration).

11 Remove the nut that holds one line fitting to the valve and remove the line while discarding the seal. Plug all openings quickly to minimize contamination (see illustration 17.10).

12 Remove the fasteners that hold the other line fitting and plate to the valve, separate it from the valve and then remove the valve while discarding any seals. Again, plug all openings (see illustration 17.10).

13 Installation is the reverse of removal. Be sure to install new O-rings onto the line fittings and lightly coat them with the correct refrigerant oil.

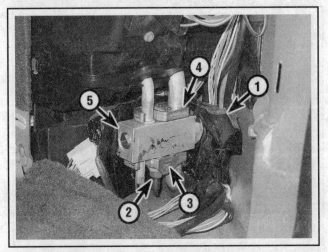

17.10 Rear expansion valve details:

1	Foam insulation	4	Line fitting plate
2	Line fitting nut	5	Expansion valve
3	Line fitting		

→Note: Only use O-rings that are designed specifically for A/C system applications.

14 Have the system evacuated, recharged and leak tested by the shop that discharged it.

18   Rear heating and air conditioning housing - removal and installation

▶ **Refer to illustrations 18.3, 18.5, 18.6 and 18.7**

❋❋ **WARNING 1:**

The air conditioning system is under high pressure. DO NOT loosen any fittings or remove any components until after the system has been discharged. Air conditioning refrigerant must be properly discharged into an EPA-approved container at a dealer service department or an automotive air conditioning repair facility. Always wear eye protection when disconnecting air conditioning system fittings.

❋❋ **WARNING 2:**

Wait until the engine is completely cool before beginning this procedure.

1   Have the air conditioning system refrigerant discharged and recovered by an air conditioning technician.

2   Disconnect the cable from the negative battery terminal (see Chapter 5, Section 1).

3   Remove the refrigerant lines from the heater/air conditioner housing under the vehicle (right-rear corner) and plug or cap all open ends and then remove the housing lower mounting fasteners (see illustration).

→Note: Discard the old refrigerant line seals; new seals will be required when the lines are reconnected.

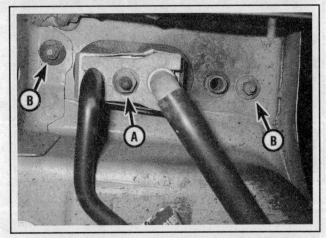

18.3 The rear refrigerant line fitting (A) and the heater/air conditioning housing mounting nuts (B)

4   Remove the right rear trim panels (see Chapter 11).

5   Remove the upper air duct from the heater/air conditioning housing (see illustration).

6   Remove the lower air duct from above the rear wheel housing (see illustration).

7   Pinch off the heater hoses at the rear heater core with locking pliers, or equivalent, and then detach them from the core (see illustration).

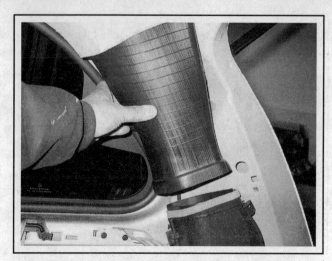

18.5 Pull the duct up from the heater/air conditioning housing and then remove it by pulling it down and away from the housing

※※ **CAUTION:**

Line the jaws of the pliers with a rag to prevent damage to the hose. Plug or cap the hose and core ends to minimize coolant loss.

➡Note: Be prepared for some coolant to spill when disconnecting the hoses from the heater core and also be careful not to damage the hoses when pinching them off.

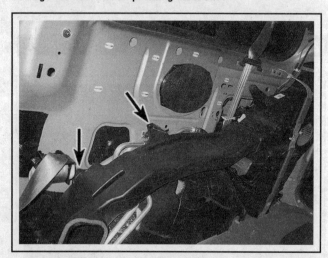

18.6 The lower air duct mounting fasteners

8   Remove the trim panel bracket and disconnect the heater/air conditioning housing wiring harness connector (see illustration 18.7).

9   Remove the housing upper mounting fasteners (see illustration 18.7).

10   Carefully lift the heater/air conditioning housing high enough to clear the floor and then remove it from the vehicle. Be sure that no wires or brackets are still connected to the housing as it is being removed.

11   Installation is the reverse of removal; Install new seals (coated with clean refrigerant oil) at the refrigerant lines. Top off the cooling system and have the air conditioning system evacuated, recharged and leak tested.

➡Note: If the heater core was emptied and not pre-filled, thermal cycle the vehicle TWICE. This procedure ensures that the heater core is filled completely. To thermal cycle the vehicle, it must be operated until the thermostat opens, then turned off and allowed to cool. The coolant level in the reservoir must be maintained during this process. Verify that the rear unit is filled completely by following this procedure:

a)   Begin with the vehicle at room temperature.
b)   Start the vehicle and bring the engine to operating temperature.
c)   Set the temperature to the full HEAT position in the front A/C control and then turn off the front system.
d)   Start the engine and turn the rear A/C system blower on HIGH with the temperature setting in the full HEAT position.
e)   The discharge air temperature, measured at the dual register located on the C-pillar base, should be between 135-degrees and 145-degrees F.

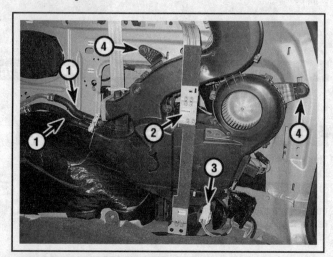

18.7 The rear heater/air conditioning housing mounting details:

1   Heater hoses (pinch off this area)
2   Rear trim bracket
3   Rear housing harness connector
4   Rear housing upper mounting fasteners

19 Air conditioning pressure transducer - removal and installation

▶ Refer to illustration 19.1

➡**Note: The air conditioning pressure transducer detects system pressure and provides feedback (a variable voltage signal) to an electronic control module which controls A/C system operation.**

1 Unplug the electrical connector from the transducer (see illustration).

2 Unscrew the transducer from the A/C line with a wrench.

➡**Note: The transducer can be removed while the A/C system is still under pressure because the A/C line fitting is equipped with a Schrader valve.**

3 Remove the O-ring seal and discard it.

4 Install a new O-ring seal on the transducer fitting and lubricate it with clean refrigerant oil of the correct type.

5 Screw the transducer in place until hand tight, then tighten it securely.

6 Reconnect the electrical connector.

19.1 Location of the air conditioning pressure transducer

Specifications

General

Radiator cap pressure rating	14 to 18 psi
Thermostat rating (opening temperature)	192 degrees F
Cooling system capacity	See Chapter 1
Refrigerant capacity*	
2003 and 2004 models	
Without rear air conditioning	34 ounces
With rear air conditioning	46 ounces
2005 and later models	
Without rear air conditioning	24 ounces
With rear air conditioning	38 ounces

Check the refrigerant capacity listed on the underhood HVAC label; if the charge capacity listed on the label differs from that shown here, assume the label is correct.

Torque specifications

	Ft-lbs (unless otherwise indicated)
Thermostat housing bolts	21
Water inlet tube bolts	
Four-cylinder engine	105 in-lbs
V6 engines	21
Water pump pulley bolts (V6 engines)	105 in-lbs
Water pump mounting bolts	
Four-cylinder engine	105 in-lbs
V6 engines	21

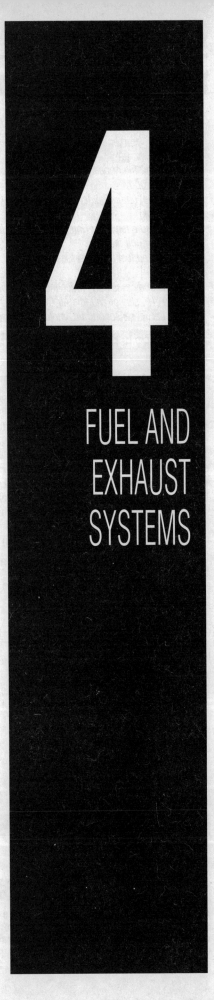

4

FUEL AND EXHAUST SYSTEMS

Section

Reference to other Chapters

1 General information

All models are equipped with a sequential Multi-Port Electronic Fuel Injection (MPI) system. The fuel system consists of the following components:

Air filter, air filter housing and air intake duct between housing and throttle body

Electric fuel pump/fuel level sending unit module (located in the fuel tank)

Fuel pressure regulator (integrated into the fuel pump/fuel level sending unit module)

Fuel rail and fuel injector assembly

Fuel tank

Throttle body assembly, which includes throttle plate, Throttle Position (TP) sensor and Idle Air Control (IAC) motor (for information on the TP sensor and IAC motor, see Chapter 6)

MULTI-PORT ELECTRONIC FUEL INJECTION (MPI) SYSTEM

Intake air is drawn through the air filter housing and air intake duct into the throttle body. Inside the throttle body, the throttle plate controls the amount of air passing into the air intake plenum and then into the cylinders. The intake port for each cylinder is equipped with its own injector. The MPI system injects fuel into the intake ports in the same sequence as the firing order of the engine. The Powertrain Control Module (PCM) controls the injectors. The PCM constantly monitors the operating conditions of the engine - temperature, speed, load, etc. - and then delivers the optimal amount of fuel for these conditions. The amount of fuel delivered by each injector is determined by its pulse width (the period of time during which it's open). The PCM can alter the pulse width so quickly that two successive injectors can deliver a different amount of fuel. In other words, the PCM can alter the pulse width virtually instantaneously in response to changes in engine operating conditions.

FUEL PUMP

The electric fuel pump is located inside the fuel tank. Voltage to the fuel pump circuit is supplied through a 20-amp fuse, then through a fuel pump relay, both of which are located inside the engine compartment fuse and relay box. The Powertrain Control Module (PCM) controls the fuel pump relay. When the ignition key is turned to ON (but not cranked), the PCM energizes the fuel pump relay for one second, which closes the fuel pump circuit long enough to pressurize the fuel system. Then the PCM turns off the fuel pump relay.

When the ignition key is turned to START, current flows from the ignition switch to the starter relay coil and to the PCM, which also receives a signal from the Crankshaft Position (CKP) sensor. When the PCM receives these two signals (from the ignition switch and from the CKP sensor), a transistor inside the PCM that controls the fuel pump relay allows current to flow to the fuel pump relay, which allows current to flow to the fuel pump. As long as the transistor inside the PCM that controls the fuel pump relay continues to receive the CKP sensor signal, it continues to supply current to the fuel pump relay, which continues to supply current to the fuel pump.

When the engine is running, fuel is pumped by the fuel pump inside the fuel tank to the fuel rail and injectors through a metal line running along the underside of the vehicle. There is no fuel return line between the fuel rail and the fuel tank. The fuel pressure regulator, which is an integral part of the fuel pump module, maintains fuel pressure between 53 and 63 psi. If the fuel pressure exceeds this range, the fuel pressure regulator opens and routes excess fuel back to the fuel tank.

FUEL LINE, FUEL HOSES AND QUICK-CONNECT FITTINGS

The metal fuel line underneath the vehicle, which carries pressurized fuel from the fuel tank to the fuel rail, is connected to the fuel pump module and to the fuel rail by hoses that use special quick-connect fittings. For more information on these fittings, refer to Section 4.

EXHAUST SYSTEM

The exhaust system consists of the exhaust manifold, the catalytic converter, the exhaust pipe, the muffler and the tail pipe. For information on servicing the exhaust system, refer to Section 16. The catalytic converter is an emission-control device in the exhaust system that reduces hydrocarbon (HC), carbon monoxide (CO) and oxides of nitrogen (NOx) pollutants. For more information regarding the catalytic converter, refer to Chapter 6.

2 Fuel pressure relief

▶ **Refer to illustration 2.3**

✳✳ WARNING:

Gasoline is extremely flammable, so take extra precautions when you work on any part of the fuel system. Don't smoke or allow open flames or bare light bulbs near the work area, and don't work in a garage where a gas-type appliance (such as a water heater or a clothes dryer) is present. Since gasoline is carcinogenic, wear latex gloves when there's a possibility of being exposed to fuel, and, if you spill any fuel on your skin, rinse it off immediately with soap and water. Mop up any spills immediately and do not store fuel-soaked rags where they could ignite. The fuel system is under constant pressure, so, if any fuel lines are to be disconnected, the fuel pressure in the system must be relieved first. When you perform any kind of work on the fuel system, wear safety glasses and have a Class B type fire extinguisher on hand.

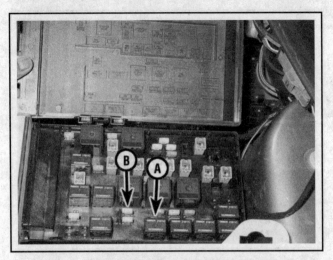

2.3 To relieve the pressure in the fuel system, disable the electric fuel pump by removing the fuel pump relay (A); if you're checking the fuel pump electrical circuit, always check the fuel pump relay and the fuel pump fuse (B)

1   Remove the fuel filler cap to relieve any pressure inside the fuel tank.

2   Start the engine.

3   Remove the fuel pump relay from the engine compartment fuse and relay box (see illustration), which is located on the left side of the engine compartment.

4   The engine will continue to run for a second or two, then it will stall. Crank the engine a couple of more times to make sure it won't start again.

5   Turn the ignition switch to OFF, then disconnect the cable from the negative terminal of the battery (see Chapter 5, Section 1) before working on the fuel system.

6   The fuel system pressure is now relieved. When you're finished working on the fuel system, install the fuel pump relay and reconnect the negative cable to the battery (see Chapter 5, Section 1).

3   Fuel pump/fuel pressure - check

✳✳ WARNING:

Gasoline is extremely flammable, so take extra precautions when you work on any part of the fuel system. See the Warning in Section 2.

GENERAL CHECKS

1   If you suspect insufficient fuel delivery check the following items first:

   a) *Check the battery and make sure that it's fully charged (see Chapter 5).*

   b) *On 2003 models, check the fuel filter (see Section 7) for obstructions (these models have a fuel filter, which is located on top of the fuel tank, but later models are not equipped with this filter).*

   c) *Inspect the fuel line, hoses and quick-connect fittings (see Section 4). Verify that the problem is not simply a leak in a line.*

2   Verify that the fuel pump actually runs. Remove the fuel filler cap and have an assistant crank the engine while you listen carefully for the sound of the fuel pump operating. You should hear a whirring noise as the pump comes on and pressurizes the system. If the fuel pump makes no sound, check the fuel pump electrical circuit (see the wiring diagrams at the end of Chapter 12). If the fuel pump runs, but a fuel system problem persists, proceed to the fuel pump pressure check.

FUEL PUMP PRESSURE CHECK

▸ **Refer to illustrations 3.4, 3.5 and 3.6**

➡**Note: Before proceeding, make sure that you have a fuel pressure gauge capable of measuring fuel pressure up to 70 psi and an adapter suitable for connecting the fuel pressure gauge to the Schrader valve-type test port on the fuel rail.**

3   Relieve the fuel system pressure (see Section 2).

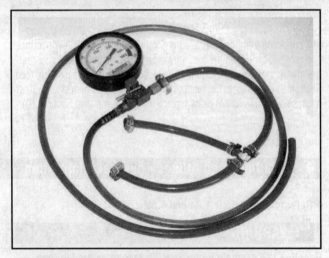

3.4 This typical fuel pressure testing setup includes a fuel pressure gauge capable of measuring the operating pressure range of the fuel injection systems used by the vehicles covered in this manual. It also includes the tee-fitting and hoses that you'll need to tee into the fuel system between the fuel delivery hose and the fuel rail

4   In addition to a fuel pressure gauge capable of reading fuel pressure up to 70 psi, you'll need a hose and an adapter suitable for tee-ing into the fuel system at the quick-connect fitting between the fuel delivery hose and the fuel rail (see illustration).

5   Disconnect the quick-connect fitting (see illustration) at the connection between the fuel delivery hose and the fuel rail (if you're unfamiliar with quick-connect fittings, refer to Section 4).

6   Tee in the fuel pressure gauge between the fuel delivery hose and the fuel rail (see illustration).

7   Turn off all the accessories, then start the engine and let it idle. The fuel pressure should be within the operating range listed in this Chapter's Specifications. If the pressure reading is within the specified

3.5 To tee into the fuel system, disconnect the quick-connect fittings at the fuel rail (shown) and the fuel delivery line (at the other end of this hose) (see Section 4 if you need help disconnecting the fitting)

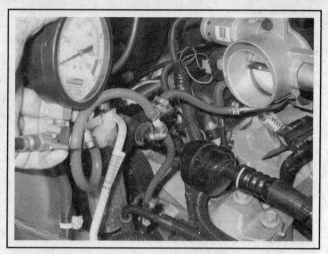

3.6 Hook up the fuel pressure gauge hoses to the fuel delivery hose and to the fuel rail

range, the system is operating correctly.

8   If the fuel pressure is higher than specified, replace the fuel pressure regulator (see Section 9).

9   If the fuel pressure is lower than specified, inspect the fuel delivery lines and hoses for an obstruction or a kink. Also inspect all fuel delivery line and hose quick-connect fittings for leaks. On 2003 models, check the fuel filter (see Section 7). If the lines, hoses, connections and (on 2003 models) the fuel filter are all in good shape, remove the fuel pump/fuel pressure regulator/fuel level sending unit assembly (see Section 8) and inspect the fuel pump inlet strainer for restrictions. If all of these components are okay, replace the fuel pump (see Section 10).

10   After the testing is complete, relieve the fuel pressure (see Section 2), remove the fuel pressure gauge and install the cap on the test port.

FUEL PUMP ELECTRICAL CIRCUIT CHECK

11   If the pump does not turn on, check the fuel pump fuse and the fuel pump relay, both of which are located in the engine compartment fuse and relay box (see illustration 2.3).

12   If the fuse and relay are good, but the fuel pump still doesn't operate, inspect the fuel pump circuit (see the wiring diagrams at the end of Chapter 12).

4   Fuel lines and fittings - general information

▸ **Refer to illustrations 4.3a and 4.3b**

✳✳ WARNING:

Gasoline is extremely flammable, so take extra precautions when you work on any part of the fuel system. See the Warning in Section 2.

1   Always relieve the fuel system pressure before servicing fuel lines or fittings (see Section 2).

2   The fuel supply line extends from the fuel tank to the engine compartment. Anytime you raise the vehicle for underbody service, inspect the lines underneath the vehicle for leaks, kinks and dents.

3   The fuel and EVAP lines are secured to the underbody with plastic clips. To disengage the fuel or EVAP lines from a clip, simply pull the lines straight down (see illustration). To replace a damaged clip, simply disengage the fuel line and EVAP line, then unscrew the clip (see illustration).

4   If you find dirt in the system during disassembly, disconnect the fuel supply line and then blow it out with compressed air. And be sure to inspect the fuel filter on 2003 models (see Section 7) and the fuel pump inlet strainer on all models (see Section 8) for damage and deterioration.

4.3a The fuel supply line and EVAP line are attached to the underside of the vehicle by a series of plastic clips such as this one. To disengage the lines from the clip, simply grasp each line firmly and pull it straight down

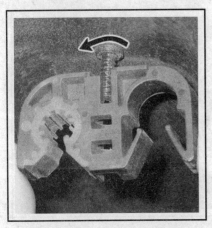

4.3b To replace a plastic fuel line clip, disengage the fuel line and EVAP line, then simply unscrew the clip from its mounting stud

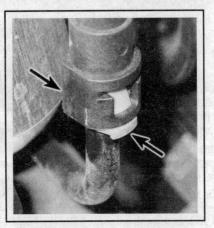

4.17a To disconnect a two-tab type quick-connect fitting, squeeze the two retainer tabs together . . .

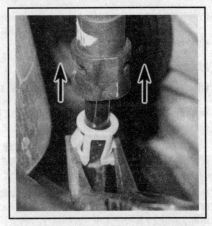

4.17b . . . and pull the fitting off the fuel line

STEEL TUBING

5   If it's necessary to replace a fuel line or EVAP line, use steel tubing that complies with the manufacturer's specifications, or its equivalent.

6   Don't use copper or aluminum tubing to replace steel tubing. These materials cannot withstand normal vehicle vibration.

7   Because steel fuel lines are under high pressure when the engine is running, they require special consideration:

  a) *Inspect all O-rings for cuts, cracks and deterioration. If an O-ring is torn, cracked, hardened or otherwise damaged, replace it.*

  b) *If the lines are replaced, always use original equipment parts, or parts that meet the original equipment standards specified in this Section.*

  c) *Never allow metal lines to chafe against the frame. Maintain a minimum of 1/4-inch clearance around a line to prevent contact with the frame.*

FLEXIBLE HOSES

✳ CAUTION:

Use only original equipment replacement hoses or their equivalent. Unapproved hose material might fail when subjected to the high pressure at which this system operates.

8   Don't route fuel hose within four inches of any part of the exhaust system or within ten inches of the catalytic converter. Never allow rubber hoses to chafe against the frame. Maintain a minimum of 1/4-inch clearance around a hose to prevent contact with the frame.

9   If a hose is equipped with quick-connect fittings at the fuel filter and/or fuel pump, the quick-connect fittings cannot be serviced separately. If the retainer tabs or the hose are damaged, replace the entire fuel hose assembly. Do not attempt to service fuel hoses.

REPLACEMENT

10   If a fuel line or fuel hose is damaged, replace it with factory replacement parts. Do not substitute line or hose of inferior quality; it might not be suitable for, and it might fail from, the operating pressure

of this system.

11   Relieve the fuel system pressure (see Section 2).

12   Disconnect the cable from the negative terminal of the battery (see Chapter 5, Section 1).

13   Remove all clamps and/or clips attaching the line to the vehicle body. Pay close attention to all clips; they not only secure the fuel line and hoses, they also route them correctly. The hoses and line must be reattached to their respective clips when reassembled.

Quick-connect fittings

14   Various types of quick-connect fittings are used on the vehicles covered by this manual. After you locate the fitting, determine which type it is and use whichever of the following procedures that applies to that fitting to disconnect and reconnect it.

15   Relieve the system fuel pressure before servicing fuel lines or fittings (see Section 2).

16   Disconnect the cable from the negative battery terminal (see Chapter 5, Section 1).

Two-tab type

▶ **Refer to illustrations 4.17a, 4.17b, and 4.18**

➡**Note: This type of fitting can be distinguished by the two brightly colored tabs that protrude from the female end. The retainer for a two-tab type quick-connect fitting can be replaced separately, but not the O-rings and spacers. So if this type of fitting is damaged, it cannot be repaired. Instead, you must replace the fitting, and the fuel line to which it's permanently connected, as a single assembly.**

17   Squeeze the plastic retainer tabs into the fitting with your fingers, then pull the fuel line and the fitting apart (see illustrations). The plastic retainer remains on the fuel line. The O-rings and spacer remain inside the quick-connect fitting connector body.

18   Wipe off both halves of the quick-connect fitting with a clean shop rag, then inspect the condition of the fitting body and inspect the condition of the spacer and O-ring inside the fitting (see illustration). If anything is damaged or worn, replace the fitting and the fuel line to which it's attached. Neither the fitting body, the spacer nor the O-ring is available separately.

19   Install a new retainer on the fuel line, lubricate the fuel line with clean engine oil and push the quick-connect fitting onto the fuel line until you hear a click, which indicates that the retainer has seated. Ver-

ify that the two halves are locked together by trying to pull them apart.

20 Reconnect the negative battery cable, then start the engine and check the fitting for leaks.

Plastic retainer ring type

▶ Refer to illustrations 4.21a, 4.21b, 4.22 and 4.23

➡ Note: This type of fitting is distinguished by its one-piece plastic retainer ring, which is usually black in color.

21 Firmly push the fitting toward the fuel line while simultaneously pushing the plastic retainer ring into the fitting and with the plastic ring depressed, pull the fuel line and the fitting apart (see illustrations).

➡ Note: Press the retainer ring squarely into the fitting. If the retainer becomes cocked, disconnecting the fuel line and the fitting will be difficult. If necessary, use a tool such as a small pair of pliers to push the retainer into the fitting. After disconnection, the plastic retainer ring remains with the quick-connect fitting.

22 Wipe off both halves of the quick-connect fitting with a clean shop rag, then inspect the condition of the fitting body and inspect the condition of the O-ring inside the fitting (see illustration). If anything is damaged or worn, replace the fitting and the fuel line to which it's attached. Neither the fitting body nor the O-ring is available separately.

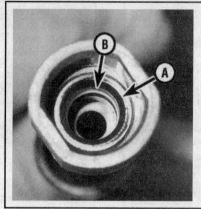

4.18 Inspect the spacer (A) and the O-ring (B). If either of them is damaged or worn, replace the quick-connect fitting (these two parts aren't available separately)

23 Inspect the condition of the plastic retainer. If it's damaged, replace it. Lubricate the fuel line with clean engine oil and push the quick-connect fitting onto the fuel line (see illustration) until you hear a click, which indicates that the raised ridge on the fuel line retainer has been locked into place by the retainer. Verify that the two halves are locked together by trying to pull them apart.

24 Reconnect the negative battery cable, then start the engine and check the fitting for leaks.

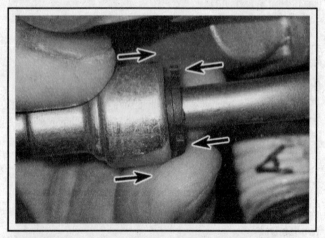

4.21a To disconnect a plastic retainer ring type quick-connect fitting, firmly push the fitting toward the fuel line while simultaneously pushing the plastic retainer ring into the fitting . . .

4.21b . . . and, with the plastic retainer ring still depressed, pull the fuel line and the fitting apart

4.22 Inspect the O-ring. If it's damaged or worn, replace the quick-connect fitting (O-rings aren't available separately)

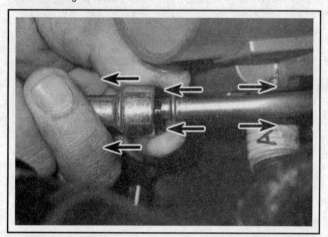

4.23 To connect a plastic retainer type quick connect fitting, push the fitting onto the fuel line until you hear a click, which indicates that the raised ridge (A) on the fuel line has been locked into place by the retainer

5 Fuel tank - removal and installation

▶ Refer to illustrations 5.5, 5.6, 5.7a, 5.7b, 5.7c, 5.8 and 5.10

❊❊ WARNING:

Gasoline is extremely flammable, so take extra precautions when you work on any part of the fuel system. See the Warning in Section 2.

➡Note: The following procedure is much easier to perform if the fuel tank is empty. Some tanks are equipped with a drain plug and some aren't. If the fuel tank doesn't have a drain plug, you can siphon fuel from the tank with a siphon kit, available at most auto parts stores. NEVER start the siphoning action with your mouth!

1   Slowly remove the fuel filler cap to relieve fuel tank pressure.
2   Relieve the system fuel pressure (see Section 2).

3   Disconnect the cable from the negative terminal of the battery (see Chapter 5, Section 1).
4   Loosen the left rear wheel lug nuts. Raise the rear of the vehicle and place it securely on jackstands. Remove the left rear wheel.
5   Locate the fuel tank filler neck vent tube inside the left rear wheel well, disconnect the two-tab type quick-connect fitting (see illustration).
6   Disconnect the fuel tank filler hose from the metal tube at the upper end of the hose, not from the fuel tank (see illustration).
7   Disconnect the fuel line quick-connect fitting and the EVAP line quick-connect fitting, both of which are located at the front of the fuel tank (see illustration). If you're unfamiliar with fuel line quick-connect fittings, refer to Section 4. To disconnect the EVAP fitting, squeeze the two tabs together and pull the EVAP line out of the fitting (see illustration). If the tabs are too difficult to squeeze together with your fingers, use a pair of needle-nose pliers to squeeze them. While the fuel and EVAP fittings are disconnected, be sure to inspect the O-rings inside each fitting (see illustration). If either O-ring is damaged, replace the fitting.

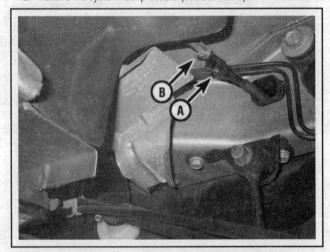

5.5 Disconnect the two-tab type quick-connect fitting (A) from the fuel tank filler neck vent tube (B) (if you're unfamiliar with quick-connect fittings, refer to Section 4)

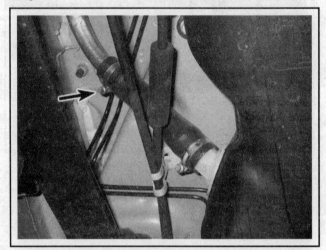

5.6 To disconnect the fuel filler neck hose from the fuel filler neck, loosen this hose clamp screw and pull the hose loose from the metal pipe above it

5.7a At the front of the fuel tank, disconnect the two-tab type fuel line quick-connect fitting (A) and the EVAP line fitting (B). If you're unfamiliar with quick-connect fittings, refer to Section 4. If you're unfamiliar with this type of EVAP line fitting, refer to the next two illustrations

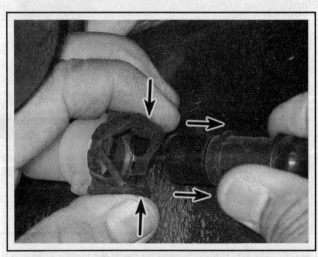

5.7b To disconnect this type of EVAP fitting, squeeze the two tabs together and pull the EVAP line out of the fitting

8 Disconnect the electrical connector from the fuel pump/fuel level sending unit (see illustration).

9 Support the fuel tank with a transmission jack or with a floor jack. If you're using a floor jack, put a piece of plywood between the jack head and the tank to protect the tank.

10 Remove the fuel tank strap bolts (see illustration).

11 Carefully lower the fuel tank from the vehicle.

12 Installation is the reverse of removal. Be sure to tighten the fuel tank strap bolts securely.

13 When you're done, start the engine and check for leaks at any fuel line connectors that you disconnected.

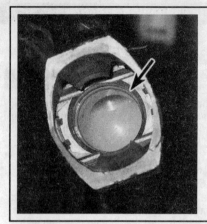

5.7c Inspect the condition of the O-ring inside the EVAP fitting. If it's cracked, torn or otherwise damaged or deteriorated, replace the fitting and the EVAP line

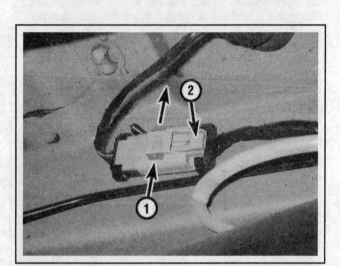

5.8 To disconnect the electrical connector for the fuel pump/ fuel level sending unit harness, slide the lock (1) up, then depress the release button (2) and unplug the connector

5.10 To detach the fuel tank straps, remove the bolts at each end of the straps

6 Fuel tank cleaning and repair - general information

1 The fuel tanks installed in the vehicles covered by this manual are not repairable. If the fuel tank becomes damaged, it must be replaced.

2 Cleaning the fuel tank (due to fuel contamination) should be performed by a professional with the proper training to carry out this critical and potentially dangerous work. Even after cleaning and flush-ing, explosive fumes may remain inside the fuel tank.

3 If the fuel tank is removed from the vehicle, it should not be placed in an area where sparks or open flames could ignite the fumes coming out of the tank. Be especially careful inside a garage where a gas-type appliance is located.

7 Fuel filter (2003 models only) - replacement

✳✳ WARNING:

Gasoline is extremely flammable, so take extra precautions when you work on any part of the fuel system. See the Warning in Section 2.

➡Note: The fuel filter is located on top of the fuel tank, so you'll have to lower the tank slightly to access the fuel filter. The fol-lowing procedure is much easier to perform if the fuel tank is empty. Some tanks are equipped with a drain plug and some aren't. If the fuel tank doesn't have a drain plug, you can siphon fuel from the tank with a siphoning kit, available at most auto parts stores. NEVER start the siphoning action with your mouth!

1 Slowly remove the fuel filler cap to relieve fuel tank pressure.

2 Relieve the system fuel pressure (see Section 2).

3 Disconnect the cable from the negative terminal of the battery (see Chapter 5, Section 1).

4 Raise the rear of the vehicle and place it securely on jackstands.

5 Support the fuel tank with a transmission jack or with a floor jack. If you're using a floor jack, put a piece of plywood between the jack head and the tank to protect the tank.

6 Remove the fuel tank strap bolts (see illustration 5.10).

7 Lower the tank slightly, then disconnect the fuel delivery and return lines from the fuel filter. If you're unfamiliar with quick-connect fittings, refer to Section 4.

8 Remove the fuel filter mounting bolt.

9 Remove the fuel filter.

10 Installation is the reverse of removal.

8 Fuel pump/fuel pressure regulator/fuel level sending unit assembly - removal and installation

▶ **Refer to illustrations 8.4, 8.6, 8.7 and 8.8**

1 Relieve the system fuel pressure (see Section 2).

2 Disconnect the cable from the negative battery terminal (see Chapter 5, Section 1).

3 Remove the fuel tank (see Section 5).

4 Disconnect the fuel delivery line quick-connect fitting from the fuel pump/fuel pressure regulator/fuel level sending unit assembly (see illustration).

5 Disconnect the electrical connector from the fuel pump/fuel pressure regulator/fuel level sending unit assembly.

6 Before removing the fuel pump/fuel pressure regulator/fuel level sending unit assembly, make an alignment mark on the mounting flange for the fuel pump/fuel pressure regulator/fuel level sending unit and on the fuel tank (see illustration). This mark ensures that the assembly will be correctly realigned when it's installed again.

7 Using a brass punch and hammer, loosen the locknut that secures the fuel pump/fuel pressure regulator/fuel level sending unit assembly (see illustration).

8 Carefully lift the fuel pump/fuel pressure regulator/fuel level sending unit assembly from the fuel tank (see illustration). Angle the

8.6 Before removing the fuel pump module, make alignment marks (if none exist) on the mounting flange for the fuel pump/pressure regulator/sending unit assembly and on the fuel tank. These marks will help you reinstall the assembly so it's correctly oriented

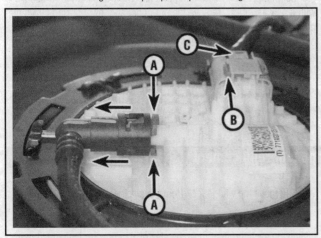

8.4 To disconnect the fuel delivery line from the fuel pump assembly, depress the two tabs (A) and pull off the fitting. To disconnect the electrical connector, slide the lock (B) out then depress the tab (C) and pull off the connector

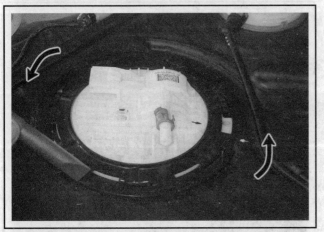

8.7 Using a brass punch and hammer, loosen the locknut that secures the fuel pump/fuel pressure regulator/fuel level sending unit assembly

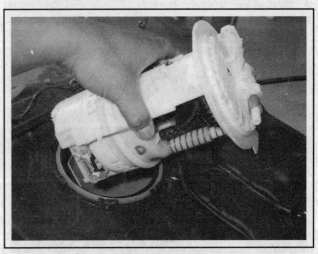

8.8 Carefully remove the fuel pump/fuel pressure regulator/fuel level sending unit from the fuel tank. Angle the assembly so that you don't bend the fuel level sending unit float arm or damage the fuel pump inlet strainer

module so that you don't bend the float arm of the fuel level sending unit or damage the fuel pump inlet strainer.

9 If you want to replace the fuel pressure regulator, see Section 9. If you want to replace the fuel pump or the fuel level sending unit, see Section 10.

10 While the pump is removed, inspect the pump inlet strainer. Make sure that it's not clogged or damaged. If the inlet strainer is dirty, try washing it in clean solvent. If it's still clogged, replace it.

11 Installation is the reverse of removal. Be sure to tighten the fuel pump module locknut securely.

9 Fuel pressure regulator - replacement

✳✳ CAUTION:

The following procedure applies only to earlier style fuel pump/ pressure regulator/sending unit assemblies with a REMOVABLE fuel pressure regulator. If you attempt to remove a non-removable regulator you will damage the fuel pump's plastic housing assembly. Before attempting to remove the regulator, have a dealership parts department verify (through the VIN) that the regulator is removable. If it is, follow the procedure below to replace the regulator. If it isn't, you'll have to replace the fuel pump and fuel pressure regulator as a single assembly. You can, however, purchase the pump/regulator assembly without a new fuel level sending unit, so you can swap your old fuel level sending unit to the new unit (see Section 10). You can also purchase the whole assembly, with a sending unit, if you don't want to use the old sending unit.

1 Relieve the system fuel pressure (see Section 2).
2 Disconnect the cable from the negative battery terminal (see Chapter 5, Section 1).
3 Remove the fuel tank (see Section 5).
4 Remove the fuel pump/fuel pressure regulator/fuel level sending unit assembly (see Section 8).
5 Spread the pressure regulator retaining tabs apart and carefully pry the pressure regulator out of the fuel pump/fuel level sending unit assembly.
6 If you're replacing the fuel pressure regulator, make sure that you use new O-rings when installing it in the fuel pump/fuel level sending unit. If you're simply removing the old fuel pressure regulator from the old fuel pump/fuel level sending unit assembly and plan to re-use it with a new assembly, remove the old upper and lower O-rings from the old regulator and replace them with new ones. Do NOT install a new or used fuel pressure regulator with old O-rings. Coat the new O-rings with a little clean gasoline to install them and coat them again right before installing the new regulator.
7 Installation is otherwise the reverse of removal.

10 Fuel pump/fuel level sending unit assembly - component replacement

♦ **Refer to illustrations 10.2, 10.3, 10.4, 10.5a and 10.5b**

1 Remove the fuel pump/fuel pressure regulator/fuel level sending unit assembly (see Section 8).
2 Depress the release tab (see illustration) and disconnect the electrical connector from the underside of the fuel pump/fuel pressure regulator/fuel level sending unit assembly.

3 Remove the wedge lock from the electrical connector (see illustration).
4 Using a special terminal removal tool or a suitable substitute, disengage each terminal from the electrical connector (see illustration) and pull out the wire and terminal from the backside of the connector.
➡**Note the positions of the wires; they must be returned to their original locations.**

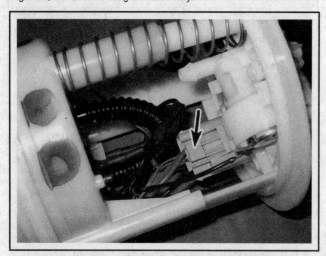

10.2 Depress the release tab and disconnect the fuel pump/fuel level sending unit electrical connector from the underside of the fuel pump mounting flange

10.3 Using a pair of needle-nose pliers, carefully remove the wedge lock from the electrical connector

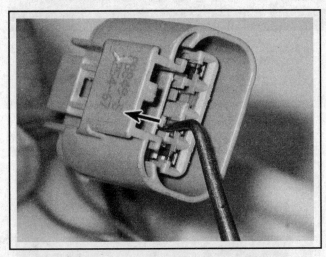

10.4 Insert a special terminal remover tool or a suitable substitute (such as this pick) into the space above each terminal and carefully disengage the terminal from the connector by levering it away from the center of the connector as shown. Then pull the electrical lead and terminal out from the backside of the connector

5   The fuel level sending unit is secured to the fuel pump housing by a pair of mounting rails on the side of the housing. To remove the sending unit from these two rails you must disengage a pair of locking lugs, located on the underside of the sending unit, that can only be disengaged from the mounting rails by aligning them with the cutouts in the rails (see illustration). Using an awl or a small screwdriver, carefully lever the lug on the fuel level sending unit toward the area between the two mounting rails until it disengages from the locking lug on the upper rail (see illustration). Then slide the sending unit to the left until the lugs on the underside of the sending unit are aligned with the cutouts in the mounting rails and lift off the sending unit.

6   Installation is the reverse of removal.

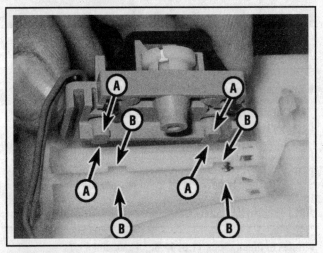

10.5a To remove the sending unit from the mounting rails, disengage the two locking lugs (A) from the mounting rails by aligning them with the cutouts (B) in the rails

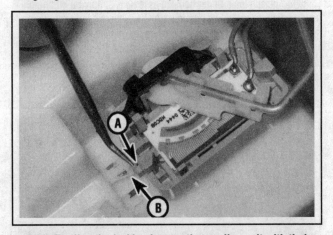

10.5b To align the locking lugs on the sending unit with their corresponding cutouts in the mounting rails, pry this lug (A) toward the area between the two rails until it disengages from the locking lug (B) on the upper rail. Then slide the sending unit to the left, align the lugs on the sending unit with their corresponding cutouts in the mounting rails and lift off the sending unit

11 Air filter housing - removal and installation

AIR INTAKE DUCT

▶ **Refer to illustration 11.1**

1   Disconnect the electrical connector from the Intake Air Temperature (IAT) sensor (see illustration).
2   Loosen the hose clamps that secure the air intake duct to the air filter housing cover and to the throttle body, then remove the air intake duct.
3   Installation is the reverse of removal.

AIR FILTER HOUSING

▶ **Refer to illustrations 11.5, 11.6a, 11.6b and 11.7**

4   Remove the air intake duct (see Steps 1 and 2).
5   Remove the air filter housing mounting bolt (see illustration).
6   To detach the air filter housing assembly, simply pull it straight up and disengage the two grommets on the underside of the housing from their corresponding locator pins on the vehicle (see illustrations).
7   Inspect the rubber mounting grommets on the underside of the air filter housing (see illustration). If the grommets are cracked, dried out, torn or otherwise damaged, replace them.
8   Installation is the reverse of removal.

11.1 To remove the air intake duct, disconnect the electrical connector (1) from the Intake Air Temperature (IAT) sensor, then loosen the two hose clamp screws (2) and detach the air intake duct from the air filter housing and throttle body

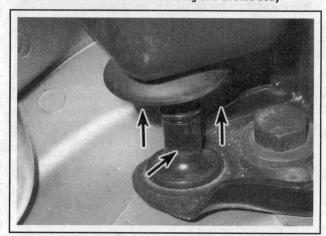

11.6a To detach the air filter housing from the vehicle, simply pull it straight up and disengage the grommets from the lower locator pin . . .

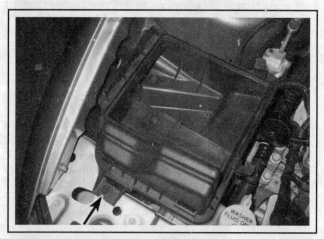

11.5 To detach the air filter housing from the upper radiator crossmember, remove this mounting bolt

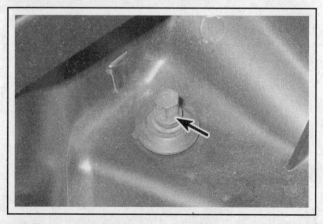

11.6b . . . and from the upper locator pin

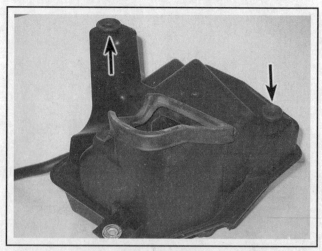

11.7 Inspect the two rubber mounting grommets for the air filter housing. If they're cracked, dried out, torn or otherwise damaged, replace them

12 Accelerator cable - removal and installation

▶ **Refer to illustrations 12.1, 12.2, 12.3 and 12.4**

1   Rotate the throttle linkage cam to the wide-open position and disengage the accelerator cable from the slot in the throttle lever cam (see illustration).

2   Squeeze the retaining ears together (see illustration) and disengage the accelerator cable from the cable bracket.

3   Inside the vehicle, using a flashlight, reach up behind the accelerator pedal, disengage the retainer from the top of the accelerator pedal, then disengage the accelerator cable from the slot in the top of the accelerator pedal assembly (see illustration)

4   Remove the horseshoe-shaped retainer clip that retains the cable grommet to its hole in the firewall (see illustration), work the cable grommet out of the hole, then pull out the cable from the engine compartment side of the firewall.

5   Installation is the reverse of removal.

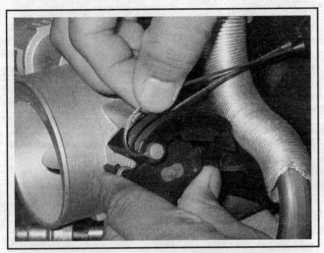

12.1 To disconnect the accelerator cable from the throttle body, rotate the throttle lever cam to the wide-open position and disengage the accelerator cable end plug from its slot in the cam

12.2 To disengage the accelerator cable (A) or the cruise control cable (B) from the cable bracket, squeeze the retaining ears together

12.3 To disengage the accelerator cable from the accelerator pedal, pass the cable out of the retainer (you may need to pry the retainer tangs apart with a small screwdriver), remove the retainer from the cable, then pull the cable through the pedal arm

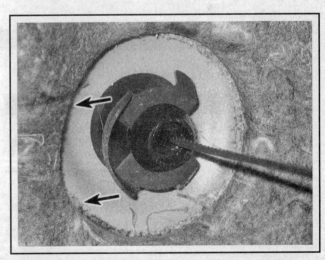

12.4 Remove the horseshoe-shaped retainer clip from the cable grommet, then push the grommet out of its hole into the engine compartment side of the firewall

13 Multi-Port Electronic Fuel Injection (MPI) system - general information

The Multi-Port Electronic Fuel Injection (MPI) system consists of three sub-systems: air intake, electronic control and fuel delivery. The MPI system uses the Powertrain Control Module (PCM) and various information sensors to calculate the correct air/fuel ratio under all operating conditions. The MPI system and the emission control systems are closely linked. For more information on the emission control systems, refer to Chapter 6.

AIR INTAKE SYSTEM

The air intake system consists of the air filter housing, the air intake duct, the throttle body, the idle control system and the intake manifold. All models are equipped with a two-piece intake manifold (see Chapter 2 for the removal and installation procedures for the intake manifold).

The throttle body is a single-barrel, side-draft design. A Throttle Position (TP) sensor is attached to the throttle shaft to monitor changes in the throttle opening.

When the engine is idling, the air/fuel ratio is controlled by the idle air control system, which regulates the amount of airflow bypassing the throttle plate. The idle air control system consists of the PCM, the Idle Air Control (IAC) motor and various sensors such as the Engine Coolant Temperature (ECT) sensor, the Throttle Position (TP) sensor and the Manifold Absolute Pressure (MAP) sensor. The IAC motor is controlled by the PCM in accordance with the running conditions of the engine (air conditioning on, power steering demand, cold or warm temperature, etc.).

ELECTRONIC CONTROL SYSTEM

For information on the electronic control system, the information sensors, the Powertrain Control Module (PCM) and the output actuators, refer to Chapter 6.

FUEL DELIVERY SYSTEM

The fuel delivery system consists of the fuel pump/fuel pressure regulator/fuel level sending unit assembly, the fuel supply line connecting the fuel pump to the fuel rail, the fuel pulsation damper, the fuel rail and the fuel injectors. On 2003 models, an inline fuel filter is located on top of the fuel tank (later models don't have this filter, but all models are equipped with a fuel pump inlet strainer).

The electric fuel pump is located inside the fuel tank. Fuel is drawn through the inlet strainer into the pump, flows through the fuel line and, on 2003 models, the filter, then to the fuel rail, from which it's sprayed by the injectors into the intake ports. The fuel pressure regulator, which is an integral part of the fuel pump/fuel level sending unit module inside the tank, maintains a constant fuel pressure to the fuel rail and injectors.

Each injector consists of a solenoid coil, a pintle valve and the housing. When current is applied to the solenoid by the PCM, the pintle valve raises off its seat and the pressurized fuel inside the housing squirts out the nozzle. The amount of fuel injected is determined by the injector pulse width (the length of time that the pintle valve is open), which is determined by the length of time during which current is supplied to the solenoid. Because the injector pulse width determines the air-fuel mixture ratio, injector timing must be very precise.

14 Fuel injection system - check

▶ **Refer to illustrations 14.7 and 14.9**

✷✷ WARNING:

Gasoline is extremely flammable, so take extra precautions when you work on any part of the fuel system. See the Warning in Section 2.

1   Inspect all system electrical connectors, especially the ground connections. Loose connectors and poor grounds are a common cause of many engine control system problems.

2   Verify that the battery is fully charged. The Powertrain Control Module (PCM) and sensors don't operate correctly without adequate supply voltage.

3   Inspect the air filter element (see Chapter 1). A dirty or partially blocked filter reduces performance and economy.

4   Check fuel pump operation (see Section 3). If the fuel pump fuse is blown, replace it and note whether it blows again. If it does, look for a short in the wiring harness to the fuel pump.

5   Inspect all vacuum hoses connected to the intake manifold for damage, deterioration and leakage.

6   Remove the air intake duct from the throttle body and look for dirt, carbon, varnish, or other residue inside the throttle body bore, particularly around the throttle plate. If it's dirty, refer to Chapter 1 and troubleshoot the PCV system for the cause of the excessive residue

14.7 Use a stethoscope to listen for the clicking sound that indicates that each injector is working correctly; the clicking sound should rise and fall with changes in engine speed

7   With the engine running, place an automotive stethoscope against each injector (see illustration) and listen for a clicking sound, which indicates that the injector is operating. If you don't have a stethoscope, you can place the tip of a long screwdriver against the injector

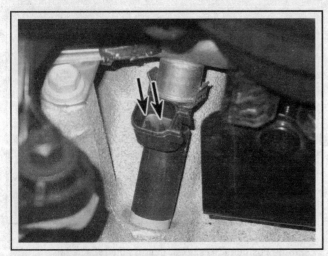

14.9 Using an ohmmeter, measure the resistance across the terminals of each injector

and listen through the handle.

→Note: This step applies only to vehicles with a Single Board Engine Controller type Powertrain Control Module (PCM). There are no injector resistance specifications available for Vehicles with a New Generation Controller type PCM.

8   On 3.3L/3.8L V6 models, remove the upper intake manifold, if necessary, to access all of the fuel injectors (see Chapter 2B).

9   With the engine off and the fuel injector electrical connectors disconnected, measure the resistance of each injector with an ohmmeter (see illustration). Refer to the Specifications at the end of this Chapter for the correct resistance.

→Note: Injector resistance specifications are only available for vehicles with a Single Board Engine Controller (SBEC) type Powertrain Control Module (PCM). There are no injector resistance specifications available for vehicles that use a New Generation Controller (NGC) type PCM, but they can still be checked with an ohmmeter to verify that they aren't short- or open-circuited.

10   Refer to Chapter 6 for other system checks.

15 Throttle body - inspection, removal and installation

❊❊ WARNING:

Gasoline is extremely flammable, so take extra precautions when you work on any part of the fuel system. See the Warning in Section 2.

INSPECTION

♦ Refer to illustration 15.2

1   Verify that the accelerator pedal operates smoothly. If it doesn't, inspect the routing of the accelerator cable. Make sure that it's not

kinked or pinched somewhere. If the cable appears to be correctly routed, with no kinks anywhere, remove the cable (see Section 12) and see if the cable is binding. If it is, replace it. If the cable is okay, inspect the throttle shaft (see the next Step).

2   Remove the air intake duct (see Section 11), then inspect the area around and behind the throttle plate for residue build-up. If it's dirty, clean it with carburetor cleaner and a tooth brush. Make sure that the can specifically states that it is safe with oxygen sensor systems and catalytic converters (see illustration).

❊❊ CAUTION:

Do not clean the Throttle Position (TP) sensor or the Idle Air Control (IAC) valve with solvent. Doing so will ruin them.

REMOVAL AND INSTALLATION

♦ Refer to illustrations 15.6a, 15.6b, 15.7 and 15.8

❊❊ WARNING:

Wait until the engine is completely cool before beginning this procedure.

3   Disconnect the cable from the negative terminal of the battery (see Chapter 5, Section 1).

4   Remove the air intake duct (see Section 11).

5   Disconnect the accelerator cable and cruise control cable (if equipped) from the throttle body (see Section 12).

6   Disconnect the electrical connectors from the Idle Air Control (IAC) motor (see illustration) and from the Throttle Position (TP) sensor (see illustration).

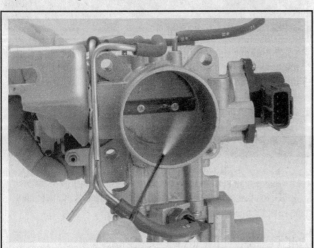

15.2 With the engine off, use aerosol carburetor cleaner (make sure it's approved for use with catalytic converters and oxygen sensors), a toothbrush and a rag to clean the throttle body; be sure to open the throttle plate and clean behind it

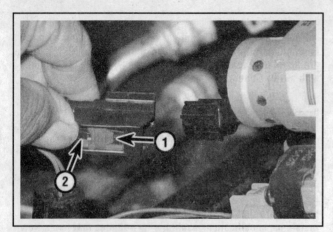

15.6a To disconnect the electrical connector from the Idle Air Control (IAC) motor, slide the lock (1) out (away from the IAC motor, toward the harness), then depress the release tab (2) and pull off the connector

15.6b To disconnect the electrical connector from the Throttle Position (TP) sensor, depress the release tab and pull off the connector

7   Unscrew the throttle body mounting bolts (see illustration) and remove the throttle body.

8   Remove the throttle body gasket (see illustration) and inspect it for cracks, tears and deterioration. If it isn't in perfect condition, replace it.

9   Make sure that the gasket mating surfaces of the throttle body and the intake manifold are clean.

10 Installation is the reverse of removal. Be sure to tighten the throttle body bolts to the torque listed in this Chapter's Specifications.

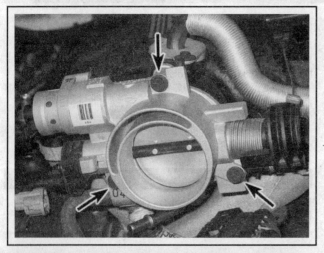

15.7 To detach the throttle body from the intake manifold, remove the mounting bolts (V6 engine shown - the throttle body on the 2.4L four-cylinder engine is secured by two bolts)

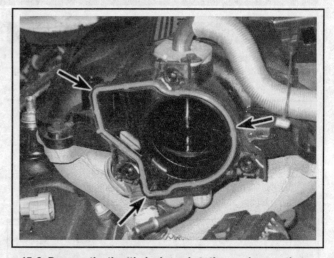

15.8 Remove the throttle body gasket, then make sure that the gasket mating surfaces of the throttle body and the intake manifold are perfectly clean

16 Fuel rail and injectors - removal and installation

✳✳ WARNING 1:

Gasoline is extremely flammable, so take extra precautions when you work on any part of the fuel system. See the Warning in Section 2.

✳✳ WARNING 2:

Wait until the engine is completely cool before beginning this procedure.

1   Relieve the system fuel pressure (see Section 2).

2   Disconnect the cable from the negative terminal of the battery (see Chapter 5, Section 1).

2.4L FOUR-CYLINDER MODELS

♦ **Refer to illustrations 16.3a, 16.3b, 16.5 and 16.7**

3   Disconnect the fuel injector electrical connectors (see illustra-

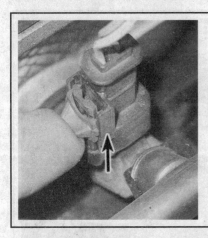

16.3a To disconnect the electrical connector from each fuel injector, push up on the lock . . .

16.3b . . . then squeeze the tab and pull up (2.4L four-cylinder models)

tions), detach the injector wiring harness from its mounting clips and set the harness aside, or disconnect the main harness electrical connector and remove the harness.

4   Disconnect the fuel delivery line quick-connect fitting and disconnect the fuel supply line from the fuel rail (if you're unfamiliar with quick-connect fittings, see Section 4).

5   Remove the fuel rail mounting bolts (see illustration).

16.5 To detach the fuel rail from the intake manifold, remove these two bolts (2.4L four-cylinder models)

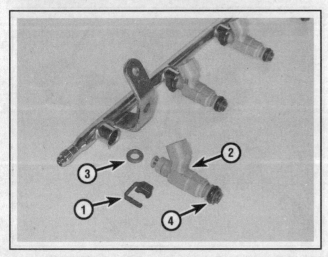

16.7 To disassemble the fuel rail assembly, pull off each retaining clip (1), pull out the injector (2) and remove the O-rings (3 and 4) (2.4L four-cylinder models)

6   Carefully pull up on the fuel rail to disengage the injectors from their respective bores in the intake manifold, then remove the fuel rail and injectors as a single assembly. The injectors might initially stick in their bores, but they'll pull free when sufficient force is applied.

7   Remove the injector retaining clips and detach the injectors from the fuel rail (see illustration). Again, the injectors might initially stick to their bores, but if you pull and wiggle them, they will come out.

8   Remove the O-rings from each injector. Discard these pieces and replace them with new O-rings and a new grommet.

9   Installation is the reverse of removal. Be sure to tighten the fuel rail retaining bolts to the torque listed in this Chapter's Specifications.

10   When you're done, start the engine and check for leaks at the quick-connect fitting that connects the fuel supply hose to the fuel rail. Also look for leaks at the upper end of each injector, where it's installed into the fuel rail.

3.3L/3.8L V6 MODELS

▶ **Refer to illustrations 16.12, 16.13a, 16.13b, 16.13c, 16.15, 16.16, 16.17, 16.18a and 16.18b**

11   Remove the upper intake manifold (see Chapter 2B).

12   Disconnect the fuel delivery line quick-connect fitting (see illustration) and disconnect the fuel delivery line from the fuel rail (if you're unfamiliar with quick-connect fittings, see Section 4).

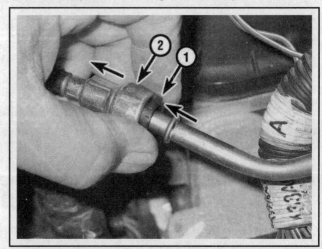

16.12 To disconnect the fuel delivery line quick-connect fitting from the fuel rail delivery pipe, push the retainer (1) into the fitting body (2) and, holding the retainer in this depressed position, pull off the fitting

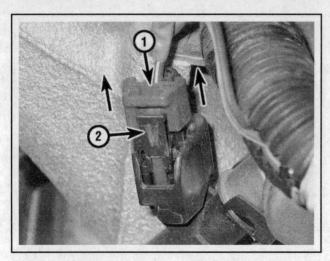

16.13a To disconnect each fuel injector electrical connector, slide the lock (1) up (away from the injector), then depress the release tab (2) and pull off the connector

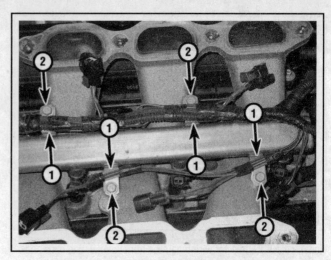

16.13b Detach the fuel injector harness clips (1) from the fuel rail, then remove the fuel rail mounting bolts (2)

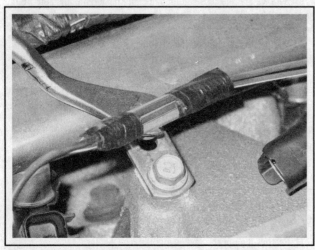

16.13c Use a trim panel removal tool or a similar suitable tool to pry the injector harness clips out of their mounting holes in the fuel rail mounting brackets

16.15 Carefully pull up on the fuel rail to disengage the injectors from their respective bores in the intake manifold, then remove the fuel rail and injectors as a single assembly

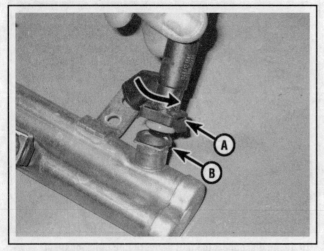

16.16 Rotate each injector to disengage the retainer (A) from the flange (B) on the injector mounting pipe and pull it out of the fuel rail (the retaining clip stays on the injector)

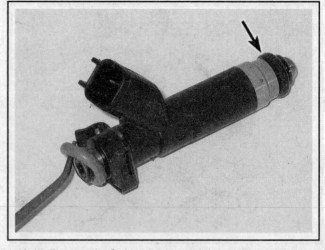

16.17 Remove the O-rings from each injector. Discard them and install new O-rings

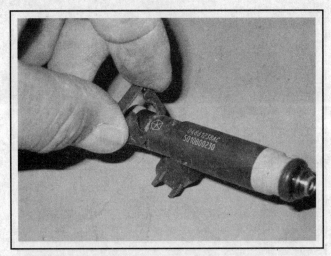

16.18a Before installing each injector into the fuel rail, be sure to install the injector clip by sliding the open end into the top slot of the injector

16.18b Make sure that the flat side (A) of the retainer clip is aligned with the flat side (B) of the flange on the injector mounting pipe and that the slots (C) in each side of the retainer clip are aligned with the curved parts (D) of the flange. Then, with the injector square to the bore of the mounting pipe, push it into the pipe until it seats

13 Disconnect the fuel injector electrical connectors (see illustration), then detach the injector wiring harness mounting clips from the fuel rail (see illustrations) and set the harness aside.

14 Remove the fuel rail mounting bolts (see illustration 16.13b).

15 Carefully pull up on the fuel rail to disengage the injectors from their respective bores in the intake manifold, then remove the fuel rail and injectors as a single assembly (see illustration). The injectors might initially stick in their bores, but they'll pull free when sufficient force is applied.

16 Rotate each injector to disengage the retainer clip from the flange on the injector mounting pipe and pull it out of the fuel rail (see illustration) (the retainer clip stays on the injector).

17 Remove the O-rings from each injector (see illustration) and discard them. Install new O-rings and coat them with some clean engine oil to facilitate installation of the injectors.

18 Before installing each injector into the fuel rail install the injector retainer clip by sliding the open end into its slot in the injector

(see illustration). When installing each injector, make sure that the flat side of the retainer clip is aligned with the flat side of the flange on the injector mounting pipe, and that the slots in the other two sides of the retainer clip are aligned with the curved parts of the flange (see illustration). Then make sure that the injector is square to the bore of the mounting pipe and push it down into the mounting pipe until it's fully seated.

19 Installation is otherwise the reverse of removal. Be sure to tighten the fuel rail retaining bolts to the torque listed in this Chapter's Specifications.

20 When you're done, start the engine and check for leaks at the quick-connect fitting that connects the fuel supply hose to the fuel rail. Also look for leaks at the upper end of each injector, where it's installed into the fuel rail.

17 Exhaust system servicing - general information

▶ Refer to illustrations 17.1a, 17.1b and 17.4

❊❊ WARNING:

Inspect and repair exhaust system components only after the system components are completely cooled off.

1 The exhaust system consists of the exhaust manifolds, the catalytic converter(s), the muffler, the tailpipe and all connecting pipes, brackets, hangers and clamps. The exhaust system is attached to the body with mounting brackets and rubber hangers (see illustrations). If any of these parts are damaged or deteriorated, excessive noise and vibration will be transmitted to the body.

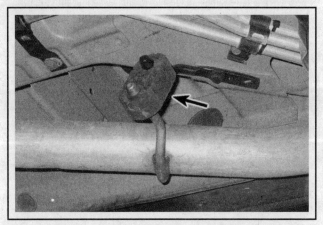

17.1a A typical rubber exhaust pipe hanger. Inspect all rubber hangers regularly, and anytime that you have to raise the vehicle to service an under-vehicle component

17.1b A pair of rubber exhaust hangers also suspends the muffler

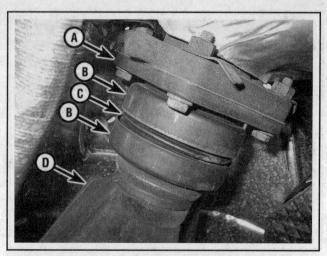

17.4 This flex joint is welded to the catalytic converter and bolted to the exhaust manifold flange. Make sure that you don't damage, bend or dent this joint when disassembling or reassembling the exhaust system

A   *Forward flange (bolted to the exhaust manifold flange with four bolts and four flag nuts)*
B   *End caps*
C   *Flexible bellows*
D   *Catalytic converter (welded to the end cap)*

2   Conducting regular inspections of the exhaust system will keep it safe and quiet. Look for any damaged or bent parts, open seams, holes, loose connections, excessive corrosion or other defects which could allow exhaust fumes to enter the vehicle. Pay particular attention to rubber exhaust hangers.

3   If the exhaust system components are extremely corroded or rusted together, they will probably have to be cut from the exhaust system. The convenient way to accomplish this is to have a muffler repair shop remove the corroded sections with a cutting torch. If, however, you want to save money by doing it yourself and you don't have an oxy/acetylene welding outfit with a cutting torch, simply cut off the old components with a hack-saw. If you have compressed air, special pneumatic cutting chisels can also be used. If you do decide to tackle the job at home, be sure to wear eye protection to protect your eyes from metal chips and work gloves to protect your hands.

4   The flex-joint coupling between the exhaust manifold and the catalytic converter has a flexible bellows between the two end caps (see illustration). The flex-joint consists of four bolts, four flag nuts and a gasket, and the flex-joint itself, which is welded to the front end of the catalyst. When servicing the flex-joint, make SURE that you don't bend or dent the joint. If you do, the flex-joint will quickly fail. And if the flex-joint fails, you will have to replace the catalytic converter.

5   Here are some simple guidelines to apply when repairing the exhaust system:

   a) *Work from the back to the front when removing exhaust system components.*

   b) *Apply penetrating oil to the exhaust system component fasteners to make them easier to remove.*
   c) *Use new gaskets, hangers and clamps when installing exhaust system components.*
   d) *Apply anti-seize compound to the threads of all exhaust system fasteners during reassembly. Be sure to allow sufficient clearance between newly installed parts and all points on the underbody to avoid overheating the floor pan and possibly damaging the interior carpet and insulation. Pay particularly close attention to the catalytic converter and its heat shield.*

❊❊ WARNING:

The catalytic converter operates at very high temperatures and takes a long time to cool. Wait until it's completely cool before attempting to remove the converter. Failure to do so could result in serious burns.

Specifications

Fuel system

Fuel system pressure (all models)	53 to 63 psi
Injector resistance	
SBEC-equipped vehicles	10 to 16 ohms
NGC-equipped vehicles	N/A

Torque specifications   Ft-lbs (unless otherwise indicated)

Fuel rail bolts (all engines)	200 in-lbs
Throttle body mounting bolts	
2.4L four-cylinder	200 to 300 in-lbs
3.3L/3.8L V6	85 to 125 in-lbs

Notes

Section

Reference to other Chapters

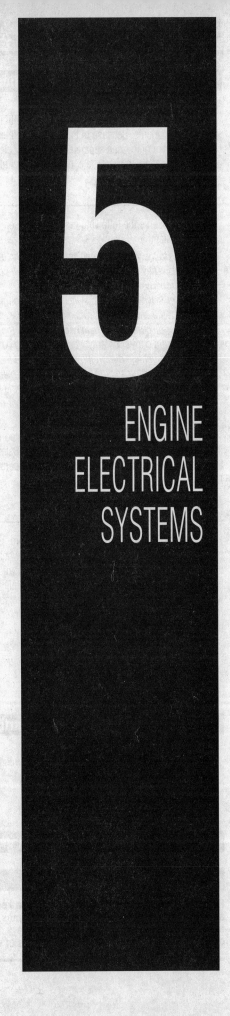

5

ENGINE ELECTRICAL SYSTEMS

1 General information, precautions and battery disconnection

The engine electrical systems include all ignition, charging and starting components. Because of their engine-related functions, these components are discussed separately from body electrical devices such as the lights, the instruments, etc. (which are included in Chapter 12).

PRECAUTIONS

Always observe the following precautions when working on the electrical system:

a) *Be extremely careful when servicing engine electrical components. They are easily damaged if checked, connected or handled improperly.*

b) *Never leave the ignition switched on for long periods of time when the engine is not running.*

c) *Never disconnect the battery cables while the engine is running.*

d) *Maintain correct polarity when connecting battery cables from another vehicle during jump starting - see the Booster battery (jump) starting section at the front of this manual.*

e) *Always disconnect the negative battery cable from the battery before working on the electrical system, but read the following battery disconnection procedure first.*

It's also a good idea to review the safety-related information regarding the engine electrical systems located in the Safety first! section at the front of this manual, before beginning any operation included in this Chapter.

BATTERY DISCONNECTION

Some electrical systems - radio, alarm system, power door locks, power windows, etc. - need battery power even when the engine is turned off. And some modules - Powertrain Control Module (PCM), body control module, etc. - need power to maintain volatile memory, which would be lost if the battery were disconnected. So when you must disconnect the battery, note the following to ensure that there are no unforeseen consequences of this action:

a) *The PCM might lose some information stored in its memory when the battery is disconnected. This includes idling and operat-*

ing values and any stored Diagnostic Trouble Codes (DTCs). So be aware that whenever you disconnect the battery, the computer might require some time to relearn the operating values.

b) *On any vehicle with power door locks, it is a wise precaution to remove the key from the ignition and to keep it with you, so that it does not get locked inside if the power door locks should engage accidentally when the battery is reconnected!*

Devices known as memory-savers can be used to avoid some of the above problems. The typical memory-saver is plugged into the cigarette lighter and connected to a spare battery. The vehicle battery is then disconnected from the electrical system, and the memory-saver provides enough current to keep the clock running, maintain audio unit presets and PCM memory values, etc.

✳✳ WARNING 1:

Some of these devices allow a considerable amount of current to pass, which can mean that many of the vehicle's systems are still operational when the main battery is disconnected. If a memory-saver is used, ensure that the circuit concerned is actually dead before carrying out any work on it!

✳✳ WARNING 2:

If work is to be performed around any of the airbag system components, the battery must be disconnected and no memory-saver device may be used. If a memory-saver device is used, power will be supplied to the airbag and personal injury may result if the airbag is accidentally deployed.

The battery on all vehicles is located in the front left corner of the engine compartment. To disconnect the battery for service procedures requiring power to be cut from the vehicle, remove the cover from the air filter housing (see Chapter 1, Section 13), then loosen the negative cable clamp nut and detach the negative cable from the negative battery post (see Section 3). Isolate the cable end to prevent it from accidentally coming into contact with the battery post.

2 Battery - emergency jump starting

Refer to the *Booster battery (jump) starting* procedure at the front of this manual.

3 Battery - check, removal and installation

✳✳ WARNING:

Hydrogen gas is produced by the battery, so keep open flames and lighted cigarettes away from it at all times. Always wear eye protection when working around a battery. Rinse off spilled electrolyte immediately with large amounts of water.

CHECK

▶ **Refer to illustrations 3.1a and 3.1b**

1 A battery cannot be accurately tested until it is at or near a fully charged state. Disconnect the negative battery cable from the battery

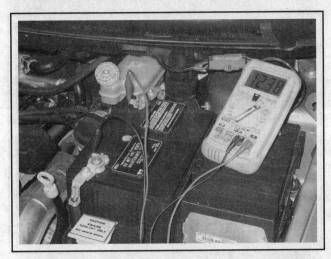

3.1a To test the open circuit voltage of the battery, connect the black probe of the voltmeter to the negative terminal and the red probe to the positive terminal of the battery. A fully charged battery should indicate about 12.5 volts, depending on the outside air temperature

and perform the following tests:

a) **Battery state of charge test** - *Visually inspect the indicator eye (if equipped) on the top of the battery. If the indicator eye is dark in color, charge the battery as described in Chapter 1. If the battery is equipped with removable caps, check the battery electrolyte. The electrolyte level should be above the upper edge of the plates. If the level is low, add distilled water. DO NOT OVERFILL. The excess electrolyte may spill over during periods of heavy charging. Test the specific gravity of the electrolyte using a hydrometer. Remove the caps and extract a sample of the electrolyte and observe the float inside the barrel of the hydrometer. Follow the instructions from the tool manufacturer and determine the specific gravity of the electrolyte for each cell. A fully charged battery will indicate approximately 1.270 (green zone) at 68-degrees F (20-degrees C). If the specific gravity of the electrolyte is low (red zone), charge the battery as described in Chapter 1.*

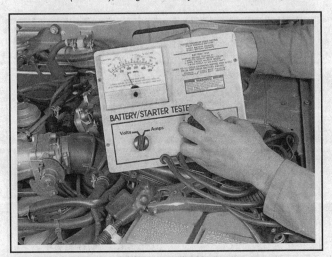

3.1b Some battery load testers are equipped with an ammeter which enables the battery load to be precisely dialed in, as shown - less expensive testers have a load switch and a voltmeter only

b) **Open circuit voltage test** - *Using a digital voltmeter, perform an open circuit voltage test (see illustration). Connect the negative probe of the voltmeter to the negative battery post and the positive probe to the positive battery post. The battery voltage should be greater than 12.5 volts. If the battery is less than the specified voltage, charge the battery before proceeding to the next test. Do not proceed with the battery load test until the battery is fully charged.*

c) **Battery load test** - *An accurate check of the battery condition can only be performed with a load tester (available at most auto parts stores). This test evaluates the ability of the battery to operate the starter and other accessories during periods of heavy amperage draw (load). Install a special battery load-testing tool onto the battery terminals (see illustration). Load test the battery according to the tool manufacturer's instructions. This tool utilizes a carbon pile to increase the load demand (amperage draw) on the battery. Maintain the load on the battery for 15 seconds and observe that the battery voltage does not drop below 9.6 volts. If the battery condition is weak or defective, the tool will indicate this condition immediately.*

➡Note: Cold temperatures will cause the minimum voltage requirements to drop slightly. Follow the chart given in the tool manufacturer's instructions to compensate for cold climates. Minimum load voltage for freezing temperatures (32 degrees F/0-degrees C) should be approximately 9.1 volts.

d) **Battery drain test** - *This test will indicate whether there's a constant drain on the vehicle's electrical system that can cause the battery to discharge. Make sure all accessories are turned off. If the vehicle has an underhood light, verify it's working properly, then disconnect it. Connect one lead of a digital ammeter to the disconnected negative battery cable clamp and the other lead to the negative battery post. A drain of approximately 100 milliamps or less is considered normal (due to the Powertrain Control Module, digital clocks, digital radios and other components that normally cause a key-off battery drain). An excessive drain (approximately 500 milliamps or more) will cause the battery to discharge. To locate the problem circuit or component, remove the fuses, one at a time, until the excessive current drain ceases and the meter indicates normal drain.*

REPLACEMENT

Battery

▶ Refer to illustrations 3.2 and 3.4

✳✳ CAUTION:

Always disconnect the negative cable first and hook it up last or you might accidentally short the battery with the tool you're using to loosen the cable clamps.

2   Loosen the cable clamp nut and remove the negative battery cable from the negative battery post. Isolate the cable end to prevent it from accidentally coming into contact with the battery post (see illustration).

3   Loosen the cable clamp nut and remove the positive battery cable from the positive battery post.

4   Remove the battery thermo-wrap (see illustration).

5   Remove the battery hold-down clamp nut and the hold-down clamp.

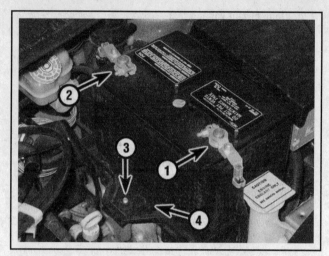

3.2 When disconnecting the cables from the battery terminals, disconnect the negative cable (1) FIRST, then the positive cable (2). To remove the battery, remove the hold-down clamp nut (3) and the hold-down clamp (4)

3.4 Remove the thermo-wrap from the battery

6   Lift out the battery. Be careful - it's heavy.

➡**Note: Battery straps and handlers are available at most auto parts stores for a reasonable price. They make it easier to remove and carry the battery.**

7   If you are replacing the battery, make sure you replace it with a battery with the identical dimensions, amperage rating, cold cranking rating, etc.

8   Installation is the reverse of removal. Be sure to tighten the hold-down clamp bolt securely, but don't overtighten it, or you will crack the plastic tray.

Battery tray

▶ **Refer to illustrations 3.10 and 3.12**

9   Remove the battery.
10   Disconnect the hose from the vacuum reservoir (see illustration).
11   Remove the battery tray mounting bolt and nuts (see illustration 3.10).
12   Lift up the battery tray and disconnect the electrical connector from the battery temperature sensor (see illustration).
13   If you're removing the battery tray to replace the battery temperature sensor, refer to *Battery temperature sensor - replacement* in Chapter 6.
14   Thoroughly wash the battery tray in clean water, then dry it with compressed air.
15   Installation is the reverse of removal.

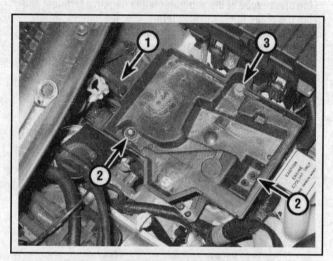

3.10 Before detaching the battery tray, disconnect the vacuum hose (1) from the vacuum reservoir, then remove the two nuts (2) and bolt (3)

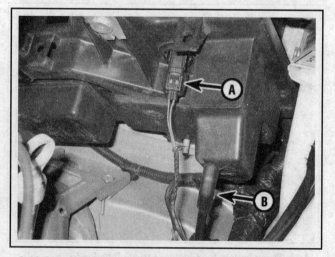

3.12 Lift up the battery tray and disconnect the electrical connector (A) from the battery temperature sensor. It's NOT necessary to disconnect the drain hose (B) from the battery tray to remove the tray, but you should inspect this hose and make sure that it's unobstructed and in good shape

4   Battery cables - replacement

ALL CABLES

1   Periodically inspect the entire length of each battery cable for damage, cracked or burned insulation and corrosion. Poor battery cable connections can cause starting problems and decreased engine performance.

2   Check the cable-to-terminal connections at the ends of the cables for cracks, loose wire strands and corrosion. The presence of white, fluffy deposits under the insulation at the cable terminal connection is a sign that the cable is corroded and should be replaced. Check the terminals for distortion, missing mounting bolts and corrosion.

3   When removing the cables always disconnect the negative cable from the negative battery post first and hook it up last, or the tool used to loosen the cable clamps could accidentally short the battery. Even if you're only replacing the positive cable, be sure to disconnect the negative cable first (see Chapter 1 for further information regarding battery cable maintenance).

BATTERY GROUND CABLES

▶ **Refer to illustrations 4.5 and 4.6**

4   Disconnect the battery ground cable from the negative battery terminal (see illustration 3.2).

5   A transaxle-to-engine mounting bolt serves as the ground bolt for one battery ground cable (see illustration). Remove the nut from the stud on the bolt head, disconnect the battery ground cable, then install the nut again so that you don't lose it.

6   The other ground bolt (see illustration) is located on the lower left side of the engine compartment. You'll have to remove the battery and the battery tray to access this ground bolt (see Section 3). Then remove this nut and disconnect the ground cable.

7   Using a pair of diagonal cutters, snip off any cable ties that secure the harness carrying the ground cables. Then carefully cut off the electrical tape wrapped around the harness. This harness also includes wiring for other engine electrical components like the alternator and the starter motor, so when you're cutting off the tape, be extremely careful not to cut any wires. After removing the electrical tape, carefully disengage the battery ground cables from the harness.

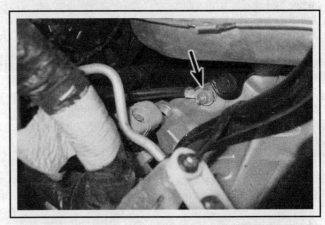

4.5 One battery ground cable is grounded to the engine/ driveaxle assembly by this transaxle-to-engine mounting bolt

8   The ground path is extremely important to the correct operation of engine management systems in modern vehicles. If you're replacing the ground cables, make sure that you obtain cables of the exact same length and gauge (diameter). It's a good idea to take the old cables with you to ensure that you purchase the correct cables.

9   After you have installed the new ground cables, carefully re-wrap the harness with new electrical tape.

10 Installation is otherwise the reverse of removal.

BATTERY POSITIVE CABLE

▶ **Refer to illustrations 4.13a, 4.13b and 4.15**

11 Disconnect the negative cable from the battery negative terminal, then disconnect the battery positive cable from the battery positive terminal (see illustration 3.2).

12 Remove the engine compartment fuse and relay box (see Chapter 12).

13 Flip the fuse and relay box upside down and disconnect the battery positive cable from the fuse box (see illustrations).

14 Raise the vehicle and place it securely on jackstands.

15 Remove the nut on the starter solenoid terminal (see illustration),

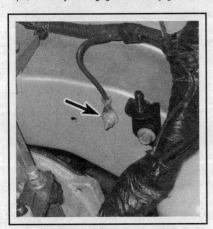

4.6 The other battery ground cable is grounded to the vehicle body below the battery tray (which you'll have to remove to access the bolt)

4.13a To disconnect the battery positive cable from the fuse and relay box, slide out this red lock . . .

4.13b . . . then depress this release tab and unplug the connector

then disconnect the positive battery cable from the starter solenoid.

16 Using a pair of diagonal cutters, snip off any cable ties that secure the harness carrying the battery positive cables. Then carefully cut off the electrical tape wrapped around the harness. This harness also includes wiring for other engine electrical components like the alternator and the starter motor, so when you're cutting off the tape, be extremely careful not to cut any wires. After removing the electrical tape, carefully disengage the battery positive cables from the harness.

17 If you're replacing the battery positive cable, make sure that you obtain a cable of the exact same length and gauge (diameter). It's a good idea to take the old cable with you to ensure that you purchase the correct cables.

18 Clean the threads of the starter solenoid terminal or ground connection with a wire brush to remove rust and corrosion. Apply a light coat of battery terminal corrosion inhibitor or petroleum jelly to the threads to prevent future corrosion.

19 After you have installed the new battery positive cables, carefully re-wrap the harness with new electrical tape.

20 Before connecting the new cable(s) to the battery make sure that the cable reaches the battery post without having to be stretched. Installation is otherwise the reverse of removal.

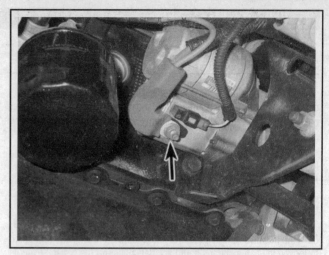

4.15 Remove the nut on the solenoid terminal, then disconnect the positive battery cable from the starter solenoid

5   Ignition system - general information and precautions

1   All models are equipped with a distributorless ignition system, which is referred to as a Direct Ignition System (DIS). As the name implies, there is no distributor. The DIS system includes the Powertrain Control Module (PCM), the Camshaft Position (CMP) sensor, the Crankshaft Position (CKP) sensor, the knock sensor, the ignition coil pack, the spark plug wires and the spark plugs. For more information on the spark plug wires and the spark plugs, refer to Chapter 1. For more information on the CMP sensor, the CKP sensor, the knock sensor and the PCM, refer to Chapter 6.

2   The coil pack on 2.4L four-cylinder models consists of two ignition coils in one unit and is mounted on top of the valve cover. The coil pack on 3.3L/3.8L V6 models consists of three ignition coils in one unit and is mounted at the left end of the cylinder head. The Auto Shutdown Relay (ASD) controls battery voltage to the coil. A pair of drivers inside the PCM control the ground circuit for each coil. The ignition system is a waste spark design. Each time the PCM fires an ignition coil (each time a driver opens the ground circuit of a coil), the coil fires two spark plugs. One of these plugs is at the cylinder under compression, in which the piston is about to begin its power stroke. The other plug is at the cylinder in which the piston is on its exhaust stroke.

3   On four-cylinder models, which have a firing order of 1-3-4-2, the rear coil fires cylinder numbers 1 and 4; the front coil fires cylinder

numbers 2 and 3. So, for example, when the ignition coil for the No. 1 cylinder fires the No. 1 spark plug, it also fires the spark plug for the No. 4 cylinder, which is also at Top Dead Center (TDC), but which is on its exhaust stroke, not its power stroke. Hence the spark is "wasted."

4   On V6 models, which have a firing order of 1-2-3-4-5-6, the center coil fires cylinder numbers 1 and 4; the right coil fires cylinder numbers 2 and 5; and the left coil fires cylinder numbers 3 and 6. So, for example, when the ignition coil fires cylinder number 1, it also fires cylinder number 4, which is also at Top Dead Center (TDC) but is on its exhaust stroke. Hence the spark is "wasted."

5   When working on the ignition system take the following precautions:

a) *Do not keep the ignition switch on for more than 10 seconds if the engine will not start.*

b) *Always connect a tachometer in accordance with the manufacturer's instructions. Some tachometers may be incompatible with this ignition system. Consult an auto parts counterperson before buying a tachometer for use with this vehicle.*

c) *Never allow the ignition coil terminals to touch ground. Grounding the coil could result in damage to the igniter and/or the ignition coil.*

d) *Do not disconnect the battery when the engine is running.*

6   Ignition system - check

▶ **Refer to illustrations 6.2 and 6.3**

❋❋ WARNING:

Because of the high voltage generated by the ignition system, be extremely careful when performing a procedure involving ignition components. This includes the ignition coil and spark plug wires, and related components such as plug connectors and even test equipment such as a spark tester.

1   If the engine turns over but won't start, disconnect the spark plug wire from the number one spark plug and attach it to a calibrated ignition tester, which is available at most auto parts stores.

2   If you're using an old-style spark tester, connect the clip on the tester to a bolt or metal bracket on the engine (see illustration).

3   If you're using a new-style spark tester, connect one end (the end with its own spark plug boot) to the spark plug and insert the other end into the spark plug boot (see illustration).

6.2 To use a conventional calibrated ignition tester, connect it to a spark plug wire boot, clip the tester to a convenient ground and, with the fuel system pressure relieved and the fuel system disabled, crank the engine. If there's enough power to fire the plug, sparks will be visible between the electrode tip and the tester body

4   Relieve the fuel system pressure (see Chapter 4). Keep the fuel system disabled while testing the ignition system.

5   Crank the engine and watch the tester to see if bright blue, well-defined sparks occur (old-style tester), or if the tester body flashes (new style tester).

6   If the tester sparks or flashes, sufficient voltage is reaching the two companion spark plugs (Nos. 1 and 4) to fire them.

7   If there is no spark or flash, or only an intermittent spark or flash, verify that there is battery voltage to the ignition coils.

6.3 To use a new-style calibrated ignition tester, connect one end to the spark plug wire boot and the other end to the spark plug boot

8   If there is battery voltage to the coils, inspect the plug wires (see Chapter 1).

9   If the spark plug wires are okay, remove and check the spark plugs for fouling (see Chapter 1). If necessary, install new plugs.

10 If the spark plugs are good, check the coil resistance (see Section 7).

11 If the ignition system checks out, the CMP sensor, the CKP sensor or the PCM might be defective (see Chapter 6).

12 When you're done, remove the spark tester and reconnect the spark plug wire.

7   Ignition coil pack - replacement

2.4L FOUR-CYLINDER MODELS

▸ **Refer to illustration 7.3**

1   Disconnect the cable from the negative terminal of the battery (see Section 1).

2   Label the spark plug wires, then disconnect them from the ignition coil (see Chapter 1). Pay close attention to the routing of the spark plug wires to ensure that they're correctly routed when reinstalled.

3   Disconnect the ignition coil electrical connector (see illustration).

4   Remove the ignition coil mounting bolts and remove the coil pack from the valve cover.

5   Installation is the reverse of removal.

3.3L/3.8L V6 MODELS

▸ **Refer to illustrations 7.7a, 7.7b, 7.8, 7.10 and 7.11**

6   Disconnect the cable from the negative terminal of the battery (see Section 1).

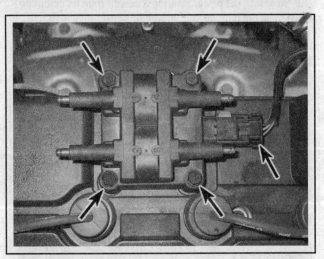

7.3 To detach the ignition coil pack from the valve cover on a 2.4L four-cylinder model, disconnect the electrical connector and remove the coil mounting bolts

7.7a To access the ignition coil on 3.3L/3.8L V6 models, disengage the accelerator and cruise control cables from this clip (1), then remove the two power steering fluid reservoir mounting bracket bolts (2)

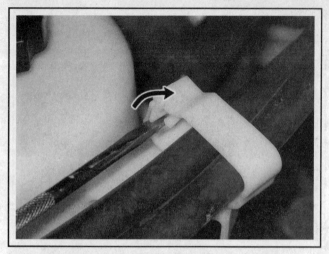

7.7b To disengage the accelerator and cruise control cables from this clip, carefully insert a screwdriver as shown and twist it to disengage the two ends of the clip (3.3L/3.8L V6 models)

7   Disengage the accelerator and cruise control cables from the clip on the power steering fluid reservoir (see illustrations).

8   Remove the two power steering reservoir mounting bolts (see illustration 7.7a), loosen the lower power steering reservoir mounting nut from the stud on the ignition coil mounting bracket (see illustration), then lift up the power steering reservoir and set it aside.

9   Disconnect the spark plug wires from the ignition coil pack (see Chapter 1).

10 Remove the two ignition coil mounting nuts (see illustration).

11 Remove the ignition coil pack and disconnect the electrical connector from the coil (see illustration).

12 Installation is the reverse of removal.

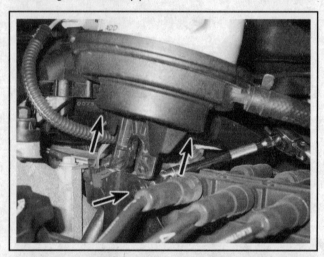

7.8 To detach the power steering reservoir from its mounting bracket on the ignition coil, loosen this lower mounting nut, lift up the reservoir and set it aside (3.3L/3.8L V6 models)

7.10 To detach the ignition coil pack from its mounting bracket on 3.3L/3.8L V6 models, remove these two nuts

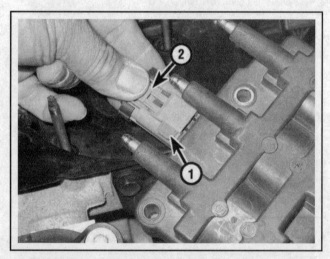

7.11 To disconnect the electrical connector from the ignition coil pack on 3.3L/3.8L V6 models, slide the lock out (1), then depress the release tab (2) and pull off the connector

8   Charging system - general information and precautions

The charging system includes the battery, the battery temperature sensor, the Powertrain Control Module (PCM), the alternator, the Electronic Voltage Regulator (EVR) (which is located inside the PCM), the voltage light (on the instrument cluster) and the wiring between all the components. The charging system supplies electrical power for the ignition system, the lights, the radio, etc. The alternator is driven by a drivebelt at the right end of the engine. The voltage regulator limits the alternator's voltage to 14.7 volts to prevent power surges, circuit overloads, etc. during peak voltage output.

The PCM maintains the system charging voltage within a range of 13.5 to 14.7 volts. It controls the charging voltage in response to both the monitored output voltage of the alternator and the temperature of the battery. The voltage regulator is located inside the PCM, so if it must be replaced you must replace the PCM.

The charging system doesn't ordinarily require periodic maintenance. However, the drivebelt, battery and wires and connections should be inspected at the intervals outlined in Chapter 1.

The voltage light should come on when the ignition key is turned to START, then should go off immediately. If it remains on, there is a malfunction in the charging system.

Be very careful when making electrical circuit connections to a vehicle equipped with an alternator and note the following:

a) *When reconnecting wires to the alternator from the battery, be sure to note the polarity.*

b) *Before using arc welding equipment to repair any part of the vehicle, disconnect the wires from the alternator and the battery terminals.*

c) *Never start the engine with a battery charger connected.*

d) *Always disconnect both battery leads before using a battery charger.*

e) *The alternator is driven by an engine drivebelt, which could cause serious injury if your hand, hair or clothes become entangled in it with the engine running.*

f) *Because the alternator is connected directly to the battery, it could arc or cause a fire if overloaded or shorted out.*

9   Charging system - check

♦ **Refer to illustration 9.3**

1   If a malfunction occurs in the charging circuit, do not immediately assume that the alternator is causing the problem. First, check the following items:

a) *Make sure the battery cable clamps, where they connect to the battery, are clean and tight.*

b) *Test the condition of the battery (see Section 3). If it does not pass all the tests, replace it with a new battery.*

c) *Check the external alternator wiring and connections.*

d) *Check the drivebelt condition and tension (see Chapter 1).*

e) *Check the alternator mounting bolts for tightness.*

f) *Run the engine and check the alternator for abnormal noise. If the alternator is making excessive or abnormal noises, check the alternator mounting bolts first. Make sure that they're fully installed and tight. If the bolts are tight, inspect the drivebelt (see Chapter 1). Make sure that it's not worn, damaged or incorrectly adjusted. Also make sure that it's the right belt! If the belt is okay, inspect the pulley. Make sure that the pulley is correctly mounted. If the pulley is okay, the problem is internal. It could be a worn, loose or defective bearing, a bad diode or stator, or the internal fins might be damaged. If the problem is caused by anything besides the mounting bolts, the belt or the pulley, remove the alternator and replace it with a new or rebuilt unit. The alternator cannot be serviced at home.*

g) *Check the voltage light on the dash. It should illuminate when the ignition key is turned ON (engine not running). If it does not, check the circuit from the alternator to the charge light on the dash.*

h) *Check all the fuses that are in series with the charging system circuit. The location of these fuses may vary from year and model but the designations are generally the same. Refer to the wiring schematics at the end of Chapter 12 for additional information.*

2   With the ignition key off and all accessories turned off, check the

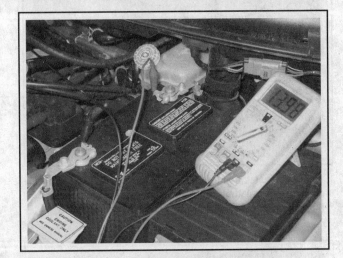

9.3 To test the battery voltage with the engine running, connect the black probe of the voltmeter to the negative terminal and the red probe to the positive terminal of the battery, then start the engine and note the reading. The battery voltage should be higher than it was before you turned on the engine, but not more than 14.7 volts

battery open circuit voltage (see illustration 3.1a). It should be about 12.5 volts. (It might be slightly higher if the engine has been operating within the last hour, or slightly lower if the vehicle has not been operated for awhile.)

3   Start the engine and check the battery voltage again (see illustration). It should now be greater than the voltage recorded in Step 2, but not more than 14.7 volts. Turn on all the vehicle accessories (air conditioning, rear window defogger, blower motor, etc.) and increase the engine speed to 2,000 rpm - the voltage should not drop much below 13.5 volts.

4 If the indicated voltage is greater than the specified charging voltage, the Electronic Voltage Regulator (EVR) is malfunctioning. The EVR isn't a conventional voltage regulator unit inside the alternator; it's actually a voltage regulating circuit located inside the Powertrain Control Module (PCM). So if the EVR is defective, replace the PCM.

5 If the indicated voltage reading is less than the specified charging

voltage, the alternator is probably defective. Have the charging system checked at a dealer service department or other properly equipped repair facility.

➡Note: Many auto parts stores will bench test an alternator off the vehicle. Refer to your local auto parts store regarding their policy; many will perform this service free of charge.

10 Alternator - removal and installation

2.4L FOUR-CYLINDER MODELS

1 Disconnect the cable from the negative terminal of the battery (see Section 1).

2 Remove the air intake duct (see Air filter housing - removal and installation in Chapter 4).

3 Remove the Evaporative Emissions Control (EVAP) system purge solenoid from its mounting bracket (see Chapter 6) and set it aside.

4 Disconnect the field wire electrical connector from the alternator.

5 Remove the nut that secures the B+ wire terminal to the stud on the back of the alternator and disconnect the field wire from the stud.

6 Remove the alternator drivebelt (see Chapter 1).

7 Remove the alternator adjustment bolt and pivot bolt and remove the alternator.

8 Installation is the reverse of removal. Be sure to tighten the alternator bolts securely.

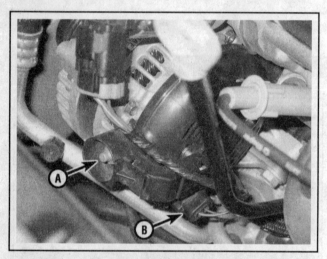

10.10 Remove the nut from the B+ stud terminal (A) and disconnect the battery cable from the stud, then disconnect the field wire electrical connector (B) from the alternator

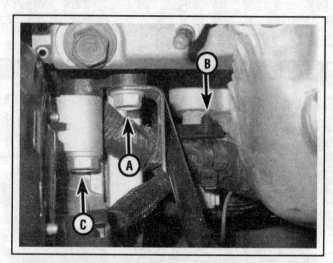

10.15 Remove the lower oil dipstick tube retaining bolt (A), detach the wiring harness clip (B) from its bracket on the dipstick tube and remove the lower alternator mounting bolt (C)

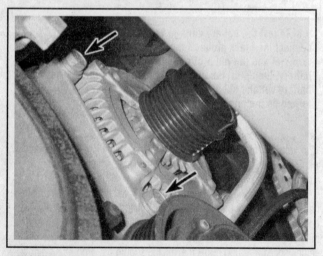

10.17 To detach the alternator, remove these two bolts

10.20 Carefully remove the alternator from the top

3.3L/3.8L V6 MODELS

▶ **Refer to illustrations 10.10, 10.15, 10.17 and 10.20**

9 Disconnect the cable from the negative terminal of the battery (see Section 1).

10 Remove the nut that secures the B+ wire terminal to the stud on the back of the alternator and disconnect the field wire from the stud (see illustration).

11 Disconnect the field wire electrical connector from the alternator.

12 Raise the front of the vehicle and place it securely on jackstands.

13 Remove the right front lower splash shield (see Chapter 11).

14 Remove the alternator drivebelt (see Chapter 1).

15 Remove the lower oil dipstick tube retaining bolt (see illustration).

16 Detach the wiring harness from the oil dipstick tube.

17 Remove the lower alternator mounting bolt and remove the two mounting bolts from the drivebelt side of the alternator (see illustration).

18 Lower the vehicle.

19 Remove the dipstick tube.

20 Remove the alternator (see illustration).

21 Installation is the reverse of removal. Be sure to tighten the alternator bolts securely.

11 Starting system - general information and precautions

The starting system consists of the battery, the ignition switch and key lock cylinder, the starter relay, the starter motor, the starter solenoid and the electrical circuit connecting these components. The starting system includes a Transmission Range (TR) switch, which is located on the transaxle (see Chapter 7). The starter motor/solenoid assembly is installed on the front of the engine block, next to the transaxle bellhousing, on all engines. The solenoid is an integral part of the starter motor.

When the ignition key is turned to the START position, battery voltage energizes the starter relay, which sends current to the starter solenoid. The starter solenoid then connects the battery to the starter. The battery supplies the electrical energy to the starter motor, which does the actual work of cranking the engine.

The starter motor on a vehicle equipped with a manual transaxle can be operated only when the clutch pedal is depressed. The starter on a vehicle equipped with an automatic transaxle can be operated only when the transaxle shift lever is in the PARK or NEUTRAL position.

Always observe the following precautions when working on the starting system:

a) *Excessive cranking of the starter motor can overheat it and cause serious damage. Never operate the starter motor for more than 15 seconds at a time without pausing to allow it to cool for at least two minutes.*

b) *The starter is connected directly to the battery and could arc or cause a fire if mishandled, overloaded or short-circuited.*

c) *Always detach the cable from the negative terminal of the battery before working on the starting system.*

12 Starter motor and circuit - check

▶ **Refer to illustration 12.3**

1 If a malfunction occurs in the starting circuit, do not immediately assume that the starter is causing the problem. First, check the following items:

a) *Make sure the battery cable clamps, where they connect to the battery, are clean and tight.*

b) *Check the condition of the battery cables (see Section 4). Replace any defective battery cables with new parts.*

c) *Test the condition of the battery (see Section 3). If it does not pass all the tests, replace it with a new battery.*

d) *Check the starter solenoid wiring and connections. Refer to the wiring diagrams at the end of Chapter 12.*

e) *Check the starter mounting bolts for tightness.*

f) *Check the ignition switch circuit for correct operation.*

g) *Check the operation of the Transmission Range switch (automatic transaxle) or clutch start switch (manual transaxle). Make sure the shift lever is in PARK or NEUTRAL (automatic transaxle) or the clutch pedal is depressed (manual transaxle). Refer to Chapter 7 for the Transmission Range switch adjustment procedure. Refer to*

the wiring diagrams at the end of Chapter 12, if necessary, when performing circuit checks. These systems must operate correctly to provide battery voltage to the ignition solenoid.

h) *Check the operation of the starter relay. The starter relay is located in the fuse/relay box inside the engine compartment. Refer to Chapter 12 for the relay testing procedure.*

2 If the starter does not actuate when the ignition switch is turned to the start position, check for battery voltage to the solenoid. This will determine if the solenoid is receiving the correct voltage signal from the ignition switch. Connect a test light or voltmeter to the starter solenoid positive terminal and while an assistant turns the ignition switch to the start position. If voltage is not available, refer to the wiring diagrams in Chapter 12 and check all the fuses and relays in series with the starting system. If voltage is available but the starter motor does not operate, remove the starter (see Section 13) and bench test it (see Step 4).

3 If the starter turns over slowly, check the starter cranking voltage and the current draw from the battery. This test must be performed with the starter assembly on the engine. Crank the engine over (for 10 seconds or less) and observe the battery voltage. It should not drop

below 8.0 volts on manual transaxle models or 8.5 volts on automatic transaxle models. Also, observe the current draw using an ammeter (see illustration). It should not exceed 400 amps or drop below 250 amps.

❈❈ CAUTION:

The battery cables can become overheated because of the high level of current being drawn from the battery. Discontinue the testing until the starting system has cooled down. If the starter motor cranking amp values are not within the correct range, replace it with a new unit. There are several conditions that may affect the starter cranking potential. The battery must be in good condition and the battery cold-cranking rating must not be under-rated for the particular application. Be sure to check the battery specifications carefully. The battery terminals and cables must be clean and not corroded. Also, in cases of extreme cold temperatures, make sure the battery and/or engine block is warmed before performing the tests.

4   If the starter is receiving voltage but does not activate, remove and check the starter/solenoid assembly on the bench. Most likely the solenoid is defective. In some rare cases, the engine may be seized so be sure to try and rotate the crankshaft pulley (see Chapter 2) before proceeding. With the starter/solenoid assembly mounted in a vise on the bench, connect one jumper cable from the negative battery terminal to the body of the starter. Connect the other jumper cable from the positive battery terminal to the B+ terminal on the starter. Connect a starter switch and apply battery voltage to the solenoid S terminal (for 10

12.3 To use an inductive ammeter, simply hold the ammeter over the positive or negative cable (whichever is easier to access in terms of clearance)

seconds or less) and see if the solenoid plunger, shift lever and over-running clutch extends and rotates the pinion drive. If the pinion drive extends but does not rotate, the solenoid is operating but the starter motor is defective. If there is no movement but the solenoid clicks, the solenoid and/or the starter motor is defective. If the solenoid plunger extends and rotates the pinion drive, the starter/solenoid assembly is working properly.

13 Starter motor - removal and installation

1   Disconnect the cable from the negative terminal of the battery (see Section 1).

2.4L FOUR-CYLINDER MODELS

▶ **Refer to illustrations 13.4a and 13.4b**

2   Disconnect the solenoid electrical connector from the solenoid terminal.

3   Remove the nut that secures the battery (B+) cable and disconnect the cable from the starter terminal.

4   Remove the starter mounting bolts (see illustrations), then remove the starter assembly. If any ground wires are secured by the mounting bolt on the bellhousing side, don't forget to reattach them when installing the starter.

5   Installation is the reverse of removal. Be sure to tighten the starter mounting bolts to the torque listed in this Chapter's Specifications.

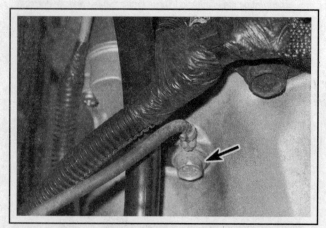

13.4a To detach the starter motor and solenoid from a 2.4L four-cylinder engine, remove this bolt from the bellhousing side (don't forget to reattach the ground wire when installing this bolt again) . . .

13.4b . . . then remove this bolt from the starter side

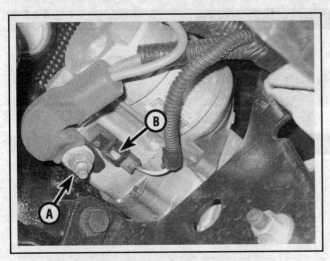

13.7 Remove the nut that secures the battery cable to the stud terminal on the solenoid (A), disconnect the B+ cable, then depress this release tab (B) and disconnect the electrical connector from the solenoid

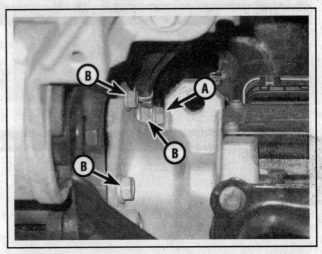

13.8 To detach the starter motor from the transaxle, remove the nut (A) and disconnect the ground wire from the stud, then remove the starter motor mounting bolts (B)

3.3L/3.8L V6 MODELS

▶ **Refer to illustrations 13.7, 13.8, 13.9 and 13.10**

6   Raise the front of the vehicle and place it securely on jackstands.

7   Remove the nut that secures the battery (B+) cable to the stud terminal on the solenoid, disconnect the B+ cable, then disconnect the solenoid electrical connector from the solenoid (see illustration).

8   Remove the starter motor mounting bolts (see illustration), then

remove the starter assembly.

9   Remove the starter spacer (see illustration).

10 When installing the starter, don't forget to install the spacer. Make sure that the word UP on the spacer is facing toward the starter motor (see illustration) and that the lip on the spacer is inserted between the block and the transaxle bellhousing (see illustration 13.9).

11 Installation is otherwise the reverse of removal. Don't forget to install the spacer, and be sure to tighten the starter mounting bolts securely.

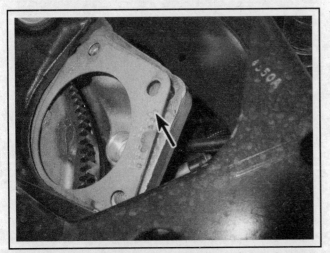

13.9 Remove the starter spacer and put it someplace safe so that you don't lose it. The spacer MUST be installed along with the starter

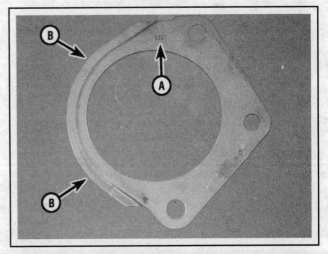

13.10 When installing the spacer, make sure that the words UP (A) are at the top and facing toward the starter motor. Also make sure that the lip (B) on the left side of the spacer is inserted between the engine block and the transaxle bellhousing

Specifications

Charging system

Charging voltage	13.5 to 14.5 volts

Torque specifications	Ft-lbs
Starter mounting bolts (all engines)	35

Section

6

EMISSIONS AND ENGINE CONTROL SYSTEMS

1 General information

♦ **Refer to illustration 1.6**

To prevent pollution of the atmosphere from incompletely burned and evaporating gases, and to maintain good driveability and fuel economy, a number of emission control systems are incorporated. They include the:

On-Board Diagnostic II (OBD-II) system
Multi-Port Electronic Fuel Injection (MPI) system
Exhaust Gas Recirculation (EGR) system
Evaporative Emissions Control (EVAP) system
Positive Crankcase Ventilation (PCV) system
Catalytic converter

The Sections in this Chapter include general descriptions, checking procedures within the scope of the home mechanic and component replacement procedures (when possible) for each of the systems listed above.

Before assuming that an emissions control system is malfunctioning, check the fuel and ignition systems carefully. The diagnosis of some emission control devices requires specialized tools, equipment and training. If checking and servicing become too difficult or if a procedure is beyond your ability, consult a dealer service department or other repair shop. Remember, the most frequent cause of emissions problems is simply a loose or broken wire or vacuum hose, so always check the hose and wiring connections first.

This doesn't mean, however, that emissions control systems are particularly difficult to maintain and repair. You can quickly and easily perform many checks and do most of the regular maintenance at home with common tune-up and hand tools.

➡**Note: Because of a Federally mandated warranty which covers the emissions control system components, check with your dealer about warranty coverage before working on any emissions-related systems. Once the warranty has expired, you can save money by replacing components yourself.**

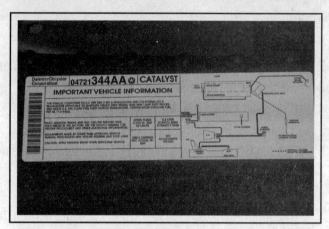

1.6 The Vehicle Emission Control Information (VECI) label contains such essential information as the types of emission control systems installed on the engine and the spark plug type and gap; a vacuum hose routing diagram is also included

Pay close attention to any special precautions outlined in this Chapter. It should be noted that the illustrations of the various systems may not exactly match the system installed on your vehicle because of changes made by the manufacturer during production or from year-to-year.

A Vehicle Emissions Control Information (VECI) label is attached to the underside of the hood (see illustration). Part of this label, the Vacuum Hose Routing Diagram, provides a vacuum hose schematic with emissions components identified. When servicing the engine or emissions systems, the VECI label and the vacuum hose routing diagram in your particular vehicle should always be checked for up-to-date information.

2 On-Board Diagnostic (OBD) system and trouble codes

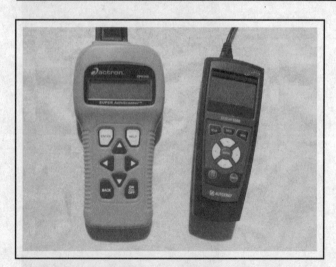

2.2 Scanners like these from Actron and AutoXray are powerful and (compared to professional-level scanners) relatively inexpensive

SCAN TOOL INFORMATION

♦ **Refer to illustration 2.2**

1   Hand-held scanners are the most powerful and versatile tools for analyzing engine management systems used on later model vehicles.

➡**Note: An aftermarket generic scanner should work with any model covered by this manual. Before purchasing a generic scan tool, verify that it will work properly with the OBD-II system you want to scan. If necessary, of course, you can always have the codes extracted by a dealer service department or an independent repair shop with a professional scan tool.**

2   With the arrival of the Federally mandated emission control system (OBD-II), specially designed aftermarket scanners have been developed. Several tool manufacturers have released OBD-II scan tools for the home mechanic (see illustration).

OBD SYSTEM GENERAL DESCRIPTION

3   All models are equipped with the second-generation on-board diagnostic (OBD-II) system. This system consists of an on-board computer known as the Powertrain Control Module (PCM), and information sensors, which monitor various functions of the engine and send data to the PCM. This system incorporates a series of diagnostic monitors that detect and identify fuel injection and emissions control systems faults and store the information in the computer memory. This updated system also tests sensors and output actuators, diagnoses drive cycles, freezes data and clears codes.

4   This powerful diagnostic computer must be accessed using an OBD-II scan tool and the 16 pin Data Link Connector (DLC) located under the driver's dash area. The PCM is the brain of the electronically controlled fuel and emissions system. It receives data from a number of sensors and other electronic components (switches, relays, etc.). Based on the information it receives, the PCM generates output signals to control various relays, solenoids (i.e. fuel injectors) and other actuators. The PCM is specifically calibrated to optimize the emissions, fuel economy and driveability of the vehicle.

5   It isn't a good idea to attempt diagnosis or replacement of the PCM or emission control components at home while the vehicle is under warranty. Because of a Federally mandated warranty which covers the emissions system components and because any owner-induced damage to the PCM, the sensors and/or the control devices may void this warranty, take the vehicle to a dealer service department if the PCM or a system component malfunctions.

INFORMATION SENSORS

➡**Note: The following list provides a brief description of the function and location of each of the important information sensors.**

6   **Battery temperature sensor** - The PCM uses the battery temperature sensor, along with data from monitored line voltage, to control charging system voltage. The battery temperature sensor is mounted in the battery tray.

7   **Camshaft Position (CMP) sensor** - The CMP sensor is one of two sensors that the PCM uses for cylinder identification (the CKP sensor is the other sensor), which enables it to synchronize the ignition and fuel injection systems. The CMP sensor is a Hall Effect sensor that generates square-wave pulses as groups of notches on the camshaft sprocket pass underneath it. The PCM keeps track of crankshaft rotation and identifies each cylinder by the pulses generated by the notches on the cam sprocket. Four crankshaft pulses follow each group of camshaft pulses.

When metal passes by the CMP sensor, voltage goes low (less than 0.3 volt). When a notch passes by the sensor, voltage goes high (5.0 volts). As a group of notches pass by the sensor, the voltage switches from low (metal) to high (notch), then back to low, and so on. The number of notches determines the number of pulses. Top Dead Center (TDC) doesn't occur when the notches on the cam sprocket pass by the sensor. Instead, it occurs after the camshaft pulse (or pulses) and after the four crankshaft pulses associated with that particular cylinder.

On 2.4L four-cylinder models, the CMP sensor is located on the left end of the cylinder head. On 3.3L/3.8L V6 models, the CMP sensor is located in the timing chain cover.

8   **Crankshaft Position (CKP) sensor** - The CKP sensor is used by the PCM, with help from the CMP sensor, to determine crankshaft position (which piston will be at TDC next). The CKP sensor detects slots cut into a tone wheel on the crankshaft (2.4L four-cylinder models) or slots cut into the transmission driveplate (3.3L/3.8L V6 models). On 2.4L four-cylinder models, the CKP sensor is located on the rear side of the engine block, near the timing belt cover. On 3.3L/3.8L V6, the CKP sensor is located on the backside of the transaxle housing, above the differential housing.

9   **Engine Coolant Temperature (ECT) sensor** - The ECT sensor monitors engine coolant temperature and sends the PCM a voltage signal that affects PCM control of the fuel mixture, ignition timing and EGR operation. The ECT sensor is a Negative Temperature Coefficient (NTC) type thermistor, whose resistance decreases as the temperature increases. On 2.4L four-cylinder models, the ECT sensor is located on the thermostat housing. On 3.3L/3.8L V6 models, the ECT sensor is located on the lower intake manifold, near the thermostat.

10   **Intake Air Temperature (IAT) sensor** - The IAT sensor is used by the PCM to calculate air density, which is one of the variables it must know in order to calculate injector pulse width and adjust ignition timing (to prevent spark knock when air intake temperature is high). Like the ECT sensor, the IAT sensor is a Negative Temperature Coefficient (NTC) type thermistor, whose resistance decreases as the temperature increases. The IAT sensor is located on the air intake duct on all models.

11   **Knock sensor** - The knock sensor monitors engine vibration caused by detonation. When the knock sensor detects a knock in one of the cylinders, it signals the PCM so that the PCM can retard ignition timing accordingly. The knock sensor contains a piezoelectric material, a certain type of piezoresistive crystal, that has the ability to produce a voltage when subjected to a mechanical stress. The piezoelectric crystal in the knock sensor vibrates constantly and produces an output signal that's proportional to the intensity of the vibration. As the intensity of the vibration increases, so does the voltage of the output signal. When the intensity of the crystal's vibration reaches a specified threshold, the PCM stores that value in its memory and retards ignition timing in all cylinders (the PCM does not selectively retard timing only at the affected cylinder). The PCM doesn't respond to the knock sensor's input when the engine is idling; it only responds when the engine reaches a specified speed. The knock sensor is located on the front side of the engine block, below the intake manifold. On 2.4L four-cylinder models, the knock sensor is located on the front side of the engine block, near the starter motor. On 3.3L/3.8L V6 models, the knock sensor is located on the rear side of the block.

12   **Manifold Absolute Pressure (MAP) sensor** - The MAP sensor measures the intake manifold vacuum that draws the air/fuel mixture into the combustion chambers. The PCM uses this information to help it calculate injector pulse width and spark advance. Like the knock sensor, the MAP sensor contains a piezoresistive crystal (see Knock sensor). The PCM provides a "5-volt" (4.8 to 5.1 volts) reference to the MAP sensor and the MAP sensor returns a voltage signal that represents manifold pressure. A 0.5-volt output equals zero pressure; a 4.5-volt output equals ambient air pressure (14.7 psi at sea level, lower at altitude). The MAP sensor is also grounded through the PCM.

The MAP sensor is the single most important information sensor for determining the pulse width (on time) of the fuel injectors because it is, in effect, a barometer. The PCM needs to know the barometric pressure because air density changes with altitude. As the altitude increases the barometric pressure decreases, i.e. the amount of oxygen in the air decreases. Besides pulse-width and barometric pressure, the PCM also uses the MAP sensor to help it calculate engine load, manifold pressure, spark advance, shift point strategies (on some automatic transaxles), idle speed and deceleration fuel shut-off.

When you start the engine, the first thing that the PCM does after powering up is to look at the MAP sensor's output signal so that it knows the barometric pressure. (At sea level on a nice day - no stormy weather - barometric pressure equals 29.92 in-Hg. It drops 0.10 in-Hg for every 100 feet of altitude.) After the engine has been started the PCM looks at the MAP sensor signal every 12 milliseconds and compares each reading to the level of voltage right before the engine was started. The difference equals intake manifold vacuum. The MAP sensor is located on the intake manifold on all models.

13 **Oxygen sensors** - Oxygen sensors generate a voltage signal that varies in accordance with the amount of oxygen in the exhaust stream. The PCM uses the data from the upstream oxygen sensor to calculate the injector pulse width. The downstream oxygen sensor monitors the oxygen content of the exhaust gases as they exit the catalytic converter. This information is used by the PCM to predict catalyst deterioration and/or failure. One job of the catalytic converter is to store excess oxygen. As long as the catalyst is functioning correctly, the downstream sensor should show little activity because there should be little oxygen exiting the catalyst. But as the catalyst deteriorates its ability to store oxygen is compromised. When the output signal from the downstream sensor starts to look like the output signal from the upstream sensor, the PCM stores a DTC and turns on the MIL to let you know that it's time to replace the catalyst.

On 2.4L four-cylinder models, the upstream oxygen sensor is located on the exhaust manifold. On 3.3L/3.8L V6 models, the upstream oxygen sensor is located on the rear exhaust manifold. The downstream sensors on all models are located on the side of the catalytic converter housing.

14 **Throttle Position (TP) Sensor** - The TP sensor, which is located on the throttle body, is a variable resistor that produces a variable voltage signal in proportion to the opening angle of the throttle plate. The PCM sends 5 volts to the TP sensor. As the plate opens and closes, the resistance of the TP sensor changes with it, altering the signal back to the PCM. The output voltage of the TP sensor is about 0.6 volt at idle (closed throttle plate) to 4.5 volts at wide-open throttle. This variable signal enables the PCM to calculate the position (opening angle) of the throttle plate. The PCM uses the TP sensor input, along with other sensor inputs, to adjust fuel injector pulse-width and ignition timing.

15 **Transmission Range (TR) sensor** - Like the Park/Neutral Position (PNP) switch that it replaces, the TR sensor prevents you from starting the engine unless the automatic transaxle is in Park or Neutral, and it activates the back-up lights when you put the shift lever in Reverse. Unlike the PNP switch, however, the TR sensor also tells the PCM and/or the Transmission Control Module (TCM) what gear the transaxle is in. The PCM uses this information to determine what gear the transaxle should be in and to determine when to upshift and downshift. If the TR sensor fails, the PCM uses pressure switch data to calculate the correct shift lever position. The TR sensor is mounted on top of the valve body inside the transaxle, so it can be replaced only by removing the valve body, which is beyond the scope of most home mechanics. So if the TR sensor is defective, we recommend having it serviced by a dealership or a transmission repair shop.

16 **Transmission temperature sensor** - The transmission temperature sensor is a thermistor (see *Engine Coolant Temperature* sensor) that is used by the PCM to monitor the sump temperature of the transaxle. Fluid temperature affects transaxle shift quality and converter lock-up, so the PCM and/or TCM needs to know the temperature of the transaxle to determine which shift schedule to use. The PCM also uses the transmission temperature sensor to alert it to an overheating condition, at which point it turns on the engine cooling fans (which also cool the transmission oil cooler). The transmission temperature sensor is an integral component of the TR sensor (see *Transmission Range* sensor), which is located inside the transaxle. If the transmission temperature sensor is defective, have it serviced at a dealership or at a transmission repair shop.

17 **Vehicle Speed Sensor (VSS)** - The VSS provides information to the PCM to indicate vehicle speed. The PCM uses this information to determine when a deceleration occurs. On 2.4L models with a manual transaxle, the VSS is located on the transaxle case, above the differential. On 3.3L/3.8L V6 models with a manual transaxle, the VSS function is handled by the Anti-Lock Brake (ABS) system. (Manual transaxles are not covered in this manual because they are only available on delivery and commercial vehicles.) On models with an automatic transaxle (all vehicles covered by this manual), the Transmission Control Module (TCM) handles the VSS function. If the VSS function is lost, replace the TCM.

OUTPUT ACTUATORS

➡**Note: Based on the information it receives from the information sensors described above, the PCM adjusts fuel injector pulse width, idle speed, ignition spark advance, ignition coil dwell and EVAP canister purge operation. It does so by controlling the output actuators. The following list provides a brief description of the function and location of each of the important output actuators.**

18 **Auto Shutdown (ASD) relay** - When energized by the PCM, the ASD relay provides battery voltage to the fuel injectors, the ignition coil, the alternator field, the oxygen sensor heaters (upstream and downstream), the Evaporative Emissions Control (EVAP) purge solenoid, the Exhaust Gas Recirculation (EGR) solenoid and the Natural Vacuum Leak Detection (NVLD) system. The ASD relay is located inside the engine compartment fuse and relay box in the engine compartment. For information about testing relays, refer to Chapter 12.

19 **Exhaust Gas Recirculation (EGR) valve** - When you pull a trailer, pass another vehicle or go up a steep hill, the temperature inside the combustion chambers heats up. When the temperature inside the combustion chambers reaches 2500 degrees F., the engine begins to produce oxides of nitrogen (NOx), which is an odorless, colorless and toxic gas. The EGR system reduces NOx by introducing a controlled amount of spent exhaust gases into the intake manifold, which dilutes the air/fuel mixture, lowers combustion chamber temperatures and reduces the creation of NOx.

The EGR system consists of the EGR valve, the EGR tube, the electronic EGR transducer and the connecting hoses. On 2.4L four-cylinder models, the EGR valve/transducer assembly is located at the left rear corner of the cylinder head. On 3.3L/3.8L V6 models, the EGR valve/transducer assembly is located at the right front corner of the engine, where it's bolted to the right end of the front cylinder head. For more information about the EGR system, see Section 18.

20 **Fuel injectors** - The PCM opens the fuel injectors sequentially (in firing order sequence). The PCM also controls the pulse width, the interval of time during which each injector is open. The pulse width of an injector (measured in milliseconds) determines the amount of fuel delivered. For more information on the fuel delivery system and the fuel injectors, including injector replacement, refer to Chapter 4.

21 **Fuel pump relay** - When energized by the PCM, the fuel pump relay connects battery voltage to the fuel pump. The fuel pump relay provides battery voltage to the fuel pump. The fuel pump relay is located inside the fuse and relay box in the engine compartment.

22 **Idle Air Control (IAC) motor** - The PCM-controlled IAC motor, which is mounted on the throttle body, allows a certain amount of air to bypass the throttle plate when the throttle plate is at its (nearly closed) idle position. At idle, the IAC motor is adjusted by the PCM in response to inputs from the TP, CKP, ECT and MAP sensors, the VSS and various switches such as the brake, Park/Neutral and air conditioning switches. When the engine speed is above idle, the IAC motor functions as an off-idle dashpot. And it's also used by the PCM for controlling airflow during deceleration and for controlling air conditioning compressor loads.

23 **Ignition coils** - The ignition coils are triggered by the PCM. Refer to Chapter 5 for more information on the ignition coils.

24 **Leak Detection Pump (LDP)** - OBD-II vehicles must have some way of checking the integrity of the Evaporative Emissions Control (EVAP) system. On vehicles equipped with a Single Board Engine Controller (SBEC) type PCM, this job is handled by the PCM-controlled LDP. When commanded to do so by the PCM, the LDP pumps up the EVAP system, then notes whether the system can hold the pressure for a specified period of time. If it detects a leak, the PCM stores a DTC and turns on the MIL. The LDP is located underneath the vehicle, near the EVAP canister. For more information about the EVAP system, see Section 17.

25 **Natural Vacuum Leak Detection (NVLD) assembly** - OBD-II vehicles must have some way of checking the integrity of the Evaporative Emissions Control (EVAP) system. When commanded to do so by the PCM, the NVLD assembly measures (relative) vacuum to determine whether the EVAP system is leaking. If it detects a leak, the PCM stores a DTC and turns on the MIL. The NVLD is located underneath the rear part of the engine compartment, to the left of the power steering cooler. For more information about the EVAP system, see Section 17.

26 **Proportional purge solenoid** - When the engine is cold or still warming up, no captive fuel vapors are allowed to escape from the EVAP canister. After the engine is warmed up, the PCM energizes the proportional purge solenoid, which regulates the flow of these vapors from the canister to the intake manifold. The rate of the flow of vapors is regulated by the proportional purge solenoid in accordance with the current level, which is controlled by the PCM. The proportional purge solenoid is located in the front of the engine compartment, on a bracket near the right end of the radiator. For more information about the EVAP system, see Section 17.

OBD-II DIAGNOSTIC TROUBLE CODES (DTCS) AND THE MALFUNCTION INDICATOR LIGHT (MIL)

27 To test the critical emission control components, circuit and systems on an OBD-II vehicle, the PCM runs a series of *monitors* during each vehicle *trip*. The monitors are a series of testing protocols used by the PCM to determine whether each monitored component, circuit or system is functioning satisfactorily. The monitors must be run in a certain order. For example, the oxygen sensor monitor cannot run until the engine, the catalytic converter and the oxygen sensors are all warmed up. Another example, the misfire monitor cannot run until the engine is in closed-loop operation. An OBD-II *trip* consists of operating the vehicle (after an engine-off period) and driving it in such a manner that all of the monitored components, circuits and systems are monitored at least once by the PCM's monitors.

28 If the PCM recognizes a fault in some component, circuit or system while it's running the monitors, it stores a Diagnostic Trouble Code (DTC) and turns on the Malfunction Indicator Light (MIL) on the instrument cluster. A DTC can self-erase, but only after the MIL has been extinguished. For example, the MIL might be extinguished for a misfire or fuel system malfunction if the fault doesn't recur when monitored during the next three subsequent sequential driving cycles in which the conditions are similar to those under which the malfunction was first identified. (For other types of malfunctions, the criteria for extinguishing the MIL can vary.)

29 Once the MIL has been extinguished, the PCM must pass the diagnostic test for the most recent DTC for 40 warm-up cycles (80 warm-up cycles for the fuel system monitor and the misfire monitor). A warm-up cycle consists of the following components:

   a) *The engine has been started and is running*
   b) *The engine temperature rises by at least 40-degrees above its temperature when it was started*
   c) *The engine coolant temperature crosses the 160-degree F mark*
   d) *The engine is turned off after meeting the above criteria*

OBTAINING DTCS

▶ **Refer to illustration 2.30**

30 Of course, if the MIL does NOT go out after several driving cycles, it's probably an indication that something must be repaired or replaced before the DTC can be erased and the MIL extinguished. This means that you will need to extract the DTC(s) from the PCM, make the necessary repair or replace a component, then erase the DTC yourself. You can extract the DTCs from the PCM by plugging a generic OBD-II scan tool (see illustration 2.2) into the PCM's data link connector (see illustration), which is located under the left side of the dash. Plug the scan tool into the 16-pin data link connector (DLC), then follow the instructions included with the scan tool to extract all the diagnostic codes.

ERASE THE DTC(S), TURN OFF THE MIL AND VERIFY THE REPAIR

31 Once you've completed the repair or replaced the component, use your code reader or scan tool to erase the DTC(s) and turn off the MIL. On most tools, you simply press a button to erase DTCs and turn off the MIL, but on some tools you'll have to locate this function by using the menu on the tool's display. If it isn't obvious, follow the instructions that come with your tool.

2.30 The 16-pin Data Link Connector (DLC) is located under the left side of the dash

DIAGNOSTIC TROUBLE CODES

➡ **Note: Not all trouble codes apply to all models**

Trouble code	Code identification
P0016	Crankshaft/camshaft timing misalignment
P0031	Upstream oxygen sensor (cylinder bank no. 1), heater circuit low voltage
P0032	Upstream oxygen sensor heater (cylinder bank no. 1), heater circuit high voltage
P0037	Downstream oxygen sensor (cylinder bank no. 1), heater circuit low voltage
P0038	Downstream oxygen sensor (cylinder bank no. 1), heater circuit high voltage
P0068	Manifold pressure/throttle position correlation - high-flow/vacuum leak
P0070	Ambient temperature sensor stuck
P0071	Ambient temperature sensor performance
P0072	Ambient temperature sensor, low voltage
P0073	Ambient temperature sensor, high voltage
P0106	Manifold Absolute Pressure (MAP) sensor performance
P0106	Barometric pressure out of range
P0107	Manifold Absolute Pressure (MAP) sensor, low voltage
P0108	Manifold Absolute Pressure (MAP) sensor, high voltage
P0110	Intake Air Temperature (IAT) sensor, stuck
P0111	Intake Air Temperature (IAT) sensor performance
P0112	Intake Air Temperature (IAT) sensor, low voltage
P0113	Intake Air Temperature (IAT) sensor, high voltage
P0116	Engine Coolant Temperature (ECT) sensor performance
P0117	Engine Coolant Temperature (ECT) sensor, low voltage
P0118	Engine Coolant Temperature (ECT) sensor, high voltage
P0121	Throttle Position (TP) sensor performance
P0121	TP sensor voltage doesn't agree with Manifold Absolute Pressure (MAP) sensor
P0122	Throttle Position (TP) sensor, low voltage
P0123	Throttle Position (TP) sensor, high voltage
P0125	Insufficient coolant temperature for closed-loop control; closed-loop temperature not reached
P0128	Thermostat rationality
P0129	Barometric pressure out-of-range (low)
P0131	Upstream oxygen sensor (cylinder bank no. 1), low voltage or shorted to ground
P0132	Upstream oxygen sensor (cylinder bank no. 1), high voltage or shorted to voltage

Trouble code	Code identification
P0133	Upstream oxygen sensor (cylinder bank no. 1), slow response
P0134	Upstream oxygen sensor (cylinder bank no. 1), sensor remains at center (not switching)
P0135	Upstream oxygen sensor (cylinder bank no. 1), heater failure
P0137	Downstream oxygen sensor (cylinder bank no. 1), low voltage or shorted to ground
P0138	Downstream oxygen sensor (cylinder bank no. 1), high voltage or shorted to voltage
P0139	Downstream oxygen sensor (cylinder bank no. 1), slow response
P0140	Downstream oxygen sensor (cylinder bank no. 1), sensor remains at center (not switching)
P0141	Downstream oxygen sensor (cylinder bank no. 1), heater failure
P0171	Fuel control system too lean (cylinder bank no. 1)
P0172	Fuel control system too rich (cylinder bank no. 1)
P0201	Injector circuit malfunction - cylinder no. 1
P0202	Injector circuit malfunction - cylinder no. 2
P0203	Injector circuit malfunction - cylinder no. 3
P0204	Injector circuit malfunction - cylinder no. 4
P0205	Injector circuit malfunction - cylinder no. 5
P0206	Injector circuit malfunction - cylinder no. 6
P0300	Multiple cylinder misfire detected
P0301	Cylinder no. 1 misfire detected
P0302	Cylinder no. 2 misfire detected
P0303	Cylinder no. 3 misfire detected
P0304	Cylinder no. 4 misfire detected
P0305	Cylinder no. 5 misfire detected
P0306	Cylinder no. 6 misfire detected
P0315	No crank sensor learned
P0320	No crankshaft reference signal at Powertrain Control Module (PCM)
P0325	Knock sensor circuit malfunction
P0335	Crankshaft Position (CKP) sensor circuit
P0339	Crankshaft Position (CKP) sensor intermittent
P0340	Camshaft Position (CMP) sensor circuit
P0340	No camshaft signal at Powertrain Control Module (PCM)
P0344	Camshaft Position (CMP) sensor intermittent
P0351	Ignition coil no. 1, primary circuit
P0352	Ignition coil no. 2, primary circuit

DIAGNOSTIC TROUBLE CODES (CONTINUED)

→Note: Not all trouble codes apply to all models

Trouble code	Code identification
P0353	Ignition coil no. 3, primary circuit
P0401	Exhaust Gas Recirculation (EGR) system failure
P0403	Exhaust Gas Recirculation (EGR) solenoid circuit
P0420	Catalytic converter efficiency below threshold (upstream catalyst, cylinder bank no. 1)
P0432	Catalyst system efficiency below threshold (cylinder bank no. 2)
P0440	General Evaporative Emission Control (EVAP) system failure
P0441	Evaporative Emission Control (EVAP) system, incorrect purge flow
P0442	Evaporative Emission Control (EVAP) system, medium leak (0.040-inch) detected
P0443	Evaporative Emission Control (EVAP) system, purge solenoid circuit malfunction
P0452	Natural Vacuum Leak Detector (NVLD) pressure sensor circuit, low voltage
P0453	Natural Vacuum Leak Detector (NVLD) pressure sensor circuit, high input
P0455	Evaporative Emission Control (EVAP) system, large leak detected
P0456	Evaporative Emission Control (EVAP) system, small leak (0.020-inch) detected
P0460	Fuel level sending unit, no change as vehicle is operated
P0461	Fuel level sensor circuit, range or performance problem
P0462	Fuel level sending unit or sensor circuit, low voltage
P0463	Fuel level sending unit or sensor circuit, high voltage
P0480	Low-speed fan control relay circuit malfunction
P0498	Natural Vacuum Leak Detector (NVLD) canister vent valve solenoid circuit, low voltage
P0499	Natural Vacuum Leak Detector (NVLD) canister vent valve solenoid circuit, high voltage
P0500	No vehicle speed signal (four-speed automatic transaxles)
P0501	Vehicle speed sensor, range or performance problem
P0506	Idle speed control system, rpm lower than expected
P0507	Idle speed control system, rpm higher than expected
P0508	Idle Air Control (IAC) valve circuit, low voltage
P0509	Idle Air Control (IAC) valve circuit, high voltage
P0513	Invalid SKIM key (engine immobilizer problem)
P0516	Battery temperature sensor, low voltage
P0517	Battery temperature sensor, high voltage
P0519	Idle speed performance

Trouble code	Code identification
P0522	Engine oil pressure sensor/switch circuit, low voltage
P0532	Air conditioning refrigerant pressure sensor, low voltage
P0533	Air conditioning refrigerant pressure sensor, high voltage
P0551	Power Steering Pressure (PSP) switch circuit, range or performance problem
P0562	Battery voltage low
P0563	Battery voltage high
P0579	Speed control switch circuit, range or performance problem
P0580	Speed control switch circuit, low voltage
P0581	Speed control switch circuit, high voltage
P0582	Speed control vacuum solenoid circuit
P0586	Speed control vent solenoid circuit
P0594	Speed control servo power circuit
P0600	Serial communication link malfunction
P0601	Powertrain Control Module (PCM), internal memory checksum invalid
P0601	Powertrain Control Module (PCM), internal controller failure
P0622	Alternator field control circuit malfunction or field not switching correctly
P0627	Fuel pump relay circuit
P0630	Vehicle Identification Number (VIN) not programmed in Powertrain Control Module (PCM)
P0632	Odometer not programmed in Powertrain Control Module (PCM)
P0633	SKIM key not programmed in Powertrain Control Module (PCM)
P0645	Air conditioning clutch relay circuit
P0685	Automatic Shutdown (ASD) relay control circuit
P0688	Automatic Shutdown (ASD) relay sense circuit, low voltage
P0700	Electronic Automatic Transaxle (EATX) control system malfunction or DTC present
P0703	Brake switch circuit malfunction
P0833	Clutch released switch circuit
P0850	Park/Neutral switch malfunction

3   Battery temperature sensor - replacement

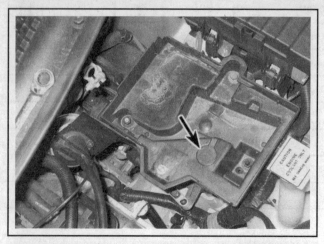

3.2 The battery temperature sensor is located under this flap

♦ Refer to illustrations 3.2, 3.3a and 3.3b

➥Note: The battery temperature sensor is located on the battery tray. Once the battery has been removed, the battery tempera-. ture sensor can be accessed by lifting up a flap in the floor of the battery tray.

1   Remove the battery (see Chapter 5).

2   The battery temperature sensor is located underneath a flap in the floor of the battery tray (see illustration). A pair of locking tabs secures it to the floor of the tray.

3   Reach under the battery tray and squeeze the two locking tabs together (see illustration), lift up the flap, pull the battery temperature sensor up through the hole in the tray (see illustration) and disconnect the electrical connector.

4   Installation is the reverse of removal. Don't forget to install the wave washer before installing the battery temperature sensor.

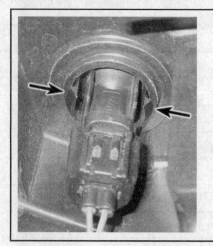

3.3a To detach the battery temperature sensor from the battery tray, squeeze these two locking tabs together . . .

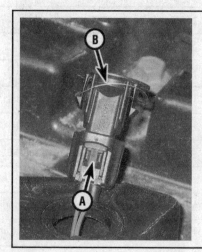

3.3b . . . pull the battery temperature sensor up through the hole in the battery tray, depress the lock (A) and disconnect the electrical connector from the sensor. Make sure that the wave washer (B) is in place before you install the battery temperature sensor

4   Camshaft Position (CMP) sensor - replacement

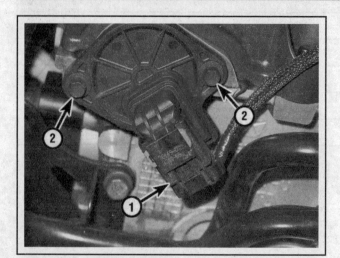

4.2 To detach the CMP sensor from the cylinder head of a 2.4L four-cylinder engine, disconnect the electrical connector (1) and remove the sensor mounting bolts (2)

2.4L FOUR-CYLINDER MODELS

♦ Refer to illustrations 4.2, 4.4 and 4.5

➥Note: The CMP sensor is located on the left end of the cylinder head.

1   Disconnect the cable from the negative terminal of the battery (see Chapter 5, Section 1).

2   Disconnect the CMP sensor electrical connector (see illustration).

4.4 To detach the CMP sensor target magnet from the end of the camshaft, remove this screw

4.5 When installing the CMP sensor target magnet, make sure that the locating dowels on the back of the magnet are aligned with the locating holes in the end of the camshaft

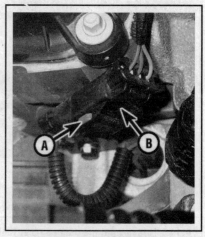

4.9 To disconnect the electrical connector from the CMP sensor on a 3.3L/3.8L V6, slide the red lock (A) to the left, then depress the release tab (B) and pull off the connector

3   Remove the CMP sensor retaining bolts and remove the CMP sensor.

4   Remove the screw that attaches the target magnet to the camshaft (see illustration) and then remove the target magnet.

5   When installing the target magnet, make sure that the locating dowels on the back of the magnet are aligned with the locating holes in the end of the camshaft (see illustration). Tighten the target magnet retaining screw to the torque listed in this Chapter's Specifications.

6   Installation is otherwise the reverse of removal. Be sure to tighten the CMP sensor retaining bolts to the torque listed in this Chapter's Specifications.

3.3L/3.8L V6 MODELS

▶ Refer to illustrations 4.9, 4.10, 4.11, 4.13, 4.14a, 4.14b and 4.14c

➡ Note: The CMP sensor is located at the right end of the engine, on the timing chain cover.

7   Disconnect the cable from the negative terminal of the battery (see Chapter 5, Section 1).

8   Remove the air intake duct and the air filter housing (see *Air filter housing - removal and installation* in Chapter 4).

9   Disconnect the CMP sensor electrical connector (see illustration).

10 Remove the CMP sensor mounting bolt (see illustration).

11 Rotate the CMP sensor away from the block (see illustration), then pull it up and out of the timing chain cover. The O-ring on the sensor might make removal somewhat difficult. If it does, do NOT pull on the wiring harness. Instead, lightly tap the top of the sensor and try again.

12 If you're going to reinstall the same sensor, remove the paper spacer from the end of the sensor, if it's still there (there probably won't be a spacer on the end of the sensor because the tone wheel has already knocked it off).

13 Remove the old O-ring from the CMP sensor (see illustration).

14 If you're installing the old CMP sensor, thoroughly clean off the

4.10 To detach the CMP sensor from the timing chain cover on a 3.3L/3.8L V6, remove the sensor mounting bolt

4.11 Before pulling the CMP sensor out of the timing chain cover on a 3.3L/3.8L V6, rotate the sensor away from the engine as shown

4.13 Remove the old O-ring from the CMP sensor

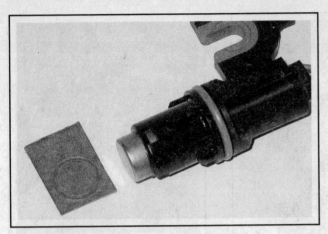

4.14a This is what the paper spacer looks like when you buy it at the parts department. Pop the pre-cut spacer out, peel off the adhesive backing . . .

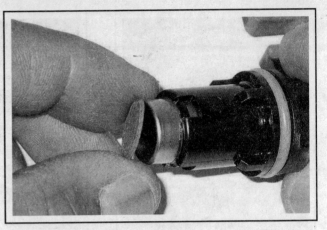

4.14b . . . and install the spacer on the end of the CMP sensor

4.14c Here's what the installed spacer should look like

sensor face and install a new paper spacer on the face before installing the sensor (see illustrations). (If you're installing a new CMP sensor the paper spacer should already be installed. If not, make sure that you install one before installing the sensor.)

15 If you're installing the old CMP sensor, inspect the old O-ring for cracks, tears and deterioration. If the old O-ring is damaged or worn, replace it.

16 Apply a few drops of clean engine oil to the O-ring, then carefully install the CMP sensor in the timing chain cover and rotate it into position.

17 Installation is otherwise the reverse of removal. Be sure to tighten the CMP sensor mounting bolt to the torque listed in this Chapter's Specifications.

5   Crankshaft Position (CKP) sensor - replacement

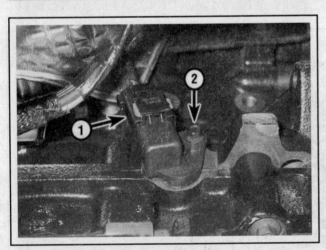

5.3 To detach the CKP sensor from the engine block on a 2.4L four-cylinder model, disconnect the electrical connector (1) and remove the sensor mounting bolt (2)

2.4L FOUR-CYLINDER MODELS

▶ **Refer to illustration 5.3**

➡**Note: The CKP sensor is located on the backside of the engine block, above the rear engine mount.**

1   Disconnect the cable from the negative terminal of the battery (see Chapter 5, Section 1).

2   Raise the front of the vehicle and place it securely on jackstands.

3   Disconnect the CKP sensor electrical connector (see illustration).

4   Remove the CKP sensor mounting bolt.

5   Installation is the reverse of removal.

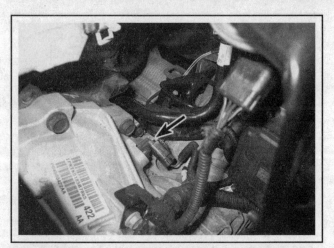

5.8a On 3.3L/3.8L V6 models, the CKP sensor is located on the upper backside of the transaxle bellhousing

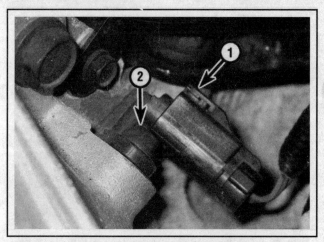

5.8b To detach the CKP sensor from the transaxle bellhousing on a 3.3L/3.8L V6, depress this release tab (1) and disconnect the sensor electrical connector, then remove the CKP sensor mounting bolt (2) and remove the sensor

3.3L/3.8L V6 MODELS

♦ Refer to illustrations 5.8a and 5.8b

➡Note: The CKP sensor is located on the upper part of the transaxle bellhousing, above the differential.

6   Disconnect the cable from the negative terminal of the battery (see Chapter 5, Section 1).

7   Raise the vehicle and place it securely on jackstands.
8   Disconnect the electrical connector from the CKP sensor (see illustrations).
9   Remove the CKP sensor mounting bolt (see illustration 5.8b) and remove the CKP sensor.
10 Installation is the reverse of removal.

---

6   Engine Coolant Temperature (ECT) sensor - replacement

✳✳ WARNING:

Wait until the engine has cooled completely before beginning this procedure.

✳✳ CAUTION:

Handle the Engine Coolant Temperature (ECT) sensor with care. Damage to the ECT sensor will affect the operation of the entire fuel injection system.

2.4L FOUR-CYLINDER MODELS

♦ Refer to illustration 6.5

➡Note: The ECT sensor is located on the thermostat housing.

1   Disconnect the cable from the negative terminal of the battery (see Chapter 5, Section 1).
2   Drain the engine coolant below the level of the thermostat housing (see Chapter 1).
3   Disconnect the electrical connector from the ECT sensor.
4   To remove the ECT sensor, unscrew it with a deep socket.
5   Before installing the new ECT sensor, wrap the threads of the sensor with Teflon tape to prevent coolant leakage (see illustration).
6   Installation is otherwise the reverse of removal. Be sure to tighten

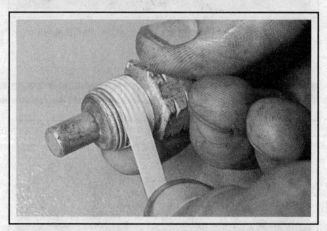

6.5 Wrap the threads of the ECT sensor with Teflon tape to prevent coolant from leaking past the threads

the ECT sensor to the torque listed in this Chapter's Specifications.
7   When you're done, refill the cooling system (see Chapter 1).

3.3L/3.8L V6 MODELS

♦ Refer to illustrations 6.11, 6.12 and 6.13

➡Note: The ECT sensor is located at the left end of the engine, on the lower intake manifold.

6.11 To detach the ignition coil mounting bracket, simply lift it off the coil mounting studs

6.12 To disconnect the electrical connector from the ECT sensor on a 3.3L/3.8L V6, push the red lock (1) away from the sensor (toward the harness), then depress the release tab (2) and pull off the connector

8 Disconnect the cable from the negative terminal of the battery (see Chapter 5, Section 1).
9 Drain the engine coolant (see Chapter 1).
10 Detach the power steering fluid reservoir (see Chapter 10) and set it aside (don't disconnect the power steering fluid hoses).
11 Remove the ignition coil (see Chapter 5), then remove the ignition coil mounting bracket (see illustration).
12 Disconnect the electrical connector from the ECT sensor (see illustration).
13 Unscrew the ECT sensor from the lower intake manifold (see illustration).
14 Before installing the new ECT sensor, wrap the threads of the sensor with Teflon tape to prevent coolant leakage (see illustration 6.5).
15 Installation is otherwise the reverse of removal. Be sure to tighten the ECT sensor to the torque listed in this Chapter's Specifications.
16 When you're done, refill the cooling system (see Chapter 1).

6.13 Unscrew the ECT from the lower intake manifold with a wrench

7 Intake Air Temperature (IAT) sensor - replacement

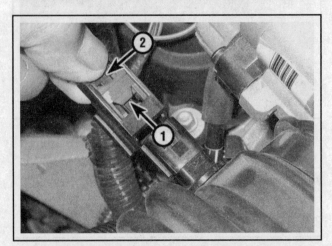

7.2 To disconnect the electrical connector from the IAT sensor, push the red lock (1) away from the sensor (toward the harness), then depress the release tab (2) and pull off the connector

▶ Refer to illustrations 7.2 and 7.3

➡Note: The IAT sensor is located on the air intake duct on all models. The IAT sensor depicted in the accompanying photos is on a 3.8L V6, but the IAT sensors used on 3.3L V6 and on 2.4L four-cylinder models are virtually identical to the one shown here.

1 Disconnect the cable from the negative terminal of the battery (see Chapter 5, Section 1).
2 Disconnect the electrical connector from the IAT sensor (see illustration).

3   Remove the IAT sensor by pulling it out of the air intake duct (see illustration).

4   Inspect the condition of the IAT sensor mounting hole. If the bore of the hole is cracked, torn or otherwise deteriorated, replace the air intake duct. If the IAT sensor is not a tight fit in this mounting hole, an air leak could occur.

5   Installation is the reverse of removal.

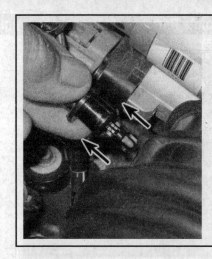

7.3 To remove the IAT sensor from the air intake duct, carefully pull it out

8   Knock sensor - replacement

✳✳ WARNING:

Wait for the engine to cool completely before performing this procedure.

2.4L FOUR-CYLINDER MODELS

▶ **Refer to illustration 8.2**

➡**Note: The knock sensor is located on the front side of the engine block, near the starter motor.**

1   Disconnect the cable from the negative terminal of the battery (see Chapter 5, Section 1).

2   Disconnect the electrical connector from the knock sensor (see illustration).

3   Unscrew the knock sensor.

4   Installation is the reverse of removal. Be sure to tighten the knock sensor to the torque listed in this Chapter's Specifications.

3.3L/3.8L V6 MODELS

▶ **Refer to illustration 8.7**

➡**Note: The knock sensor is located on the rear side of the engine block.**

5   Disconnect the cable from the negative terminal of the battery (see Chapter 5, Section 1).

6   Raise the front of the vehicle and place it securely on jackstands.

7   Disconnect the electrical connector from the knock sensor (see illustration).

8   Unscrew the knock sensor with a crowfoot socket.

9   Installation is the reverse of removal. Be sure to tighten the knock sensor to the torque listed in this Chapter's Specifications.

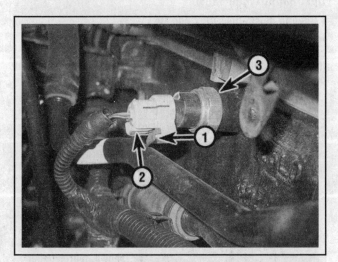

8.2 To disconnect the electrical connector from the knock sensor on 2.4L four-cylinder engine, push the red tab (1) away from the sensor, then depress the locking tab (2) and pull off the connector. To remove the knock sensor (3), unscrew it with a crowfoot socket

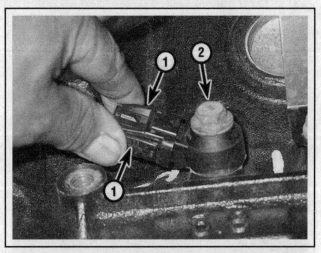

8.7 To disconnect the electrical connector from the knock sensor on a 3.3L/3.8L V6 engine, depress the two release tabs (1) on the side of the connector and pull off the connector, then remove the sensor mounting bolt (2)

9 Manifold Absolute Pressure (MAP) sensor - replacement

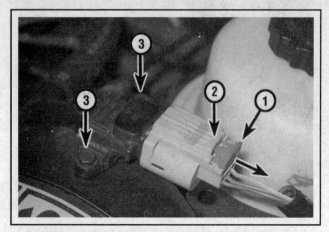

9.2 To detach the MAP sensor from the intake manifold, slide the red lock (1) to the right, depress the release tabs (2) and disconnect the electrical connector, then remove the sensor retaining screws (3) (3.3L/3.8L V6 model shown, 2.4L four-cylinder model similar)

▶ Refer to illustration 9.2

➥Note: The MAP sensor is located on the intake manifold on all engines. The MAP sensor shown in the accompanying illustration is on a 3.8L V6 engine. However, the MAP sensors used on 3.3L V6 and 2.4L four-cylinder engines are very similar to this unit.

1   Disconnect the cable from the negative terminal of the battery (see Chapter 5, Section 1).
2   Disconnect the electrical connector from the MAF sensor (see illustration).
3   Remove the MAF sensor retaining screws and remove the sensor.
4   Installation is the reverse of removal.

10 Oxygen sensors - general information and replacement

GENERAL INFORMATION

1   Use special care when servicing an oxygen sensor:
a) *Oxygen sensors have a permanently attached pigtail and electrical connector that cannot be removed from the sensor. Damage or removal of the pigtail or electrical connector will ruin the sensor.*
b) *Grease, dirt and other contaminants should be kept away from the electrical connector and the louvered end of the sensor.*
c) *Do not use cleaning solvents of any kind on an oxygen sensor or air/fuel ratio sensor.*
d) *Do not drop or roughly handle an oxygen sensor or air/fuel ratio sensor.*
e) *Be sure to install the silicone boot in the correct position to prevent the boot from melting and to allow the sensor to operate properly.*

10.4 To disconnect the electrical connector for the upstream oxygen sensor, depress the release tab and pull off the connector (3.3L/3.8L V6 shown)

REPLACEMENT

➥Note: Because it is installed in the exhaust manifold or catalytic converter, both of which contract when cool, an oxygen sensor might be very difficult to loosen when the engine is cold. Rather than risk damage to the sensor, start and run the engine for a minute or two, then shut it off. Be careful not to burn yourself during the following procedure.

2   Disconnect the cable from the negative terminal of the battery (see Chapter 5, Section 1).
3   Raise the vehicle and place it securely on jackstands.

Upstream oxygen sensor

▶ Refer to illustrations 10.4 and 10.5

➥Note: On 2.4L four-cylinder engines, the upstream oxygen sensor is located on top of the exhaust manifold, above the flange. On 3.3L/3.8L V6 engines, the upstream sensor is located on top of the rear exhaust manifold, above the flange.

4   Trace the electrical lead from the upstream oxygen sensor to the

10.5 Unscrew the upstream oxygen sensor with a special oxygen sensor socket (3.3L/3.8L V6 shown, four-cylinder models similar)

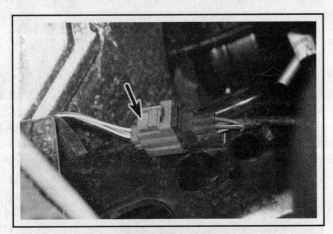

10.11 Disconnect the electrical connector for the downstream oxygen sensor (3.3L/3.8L V6 shown)

10.12 Unscrew the downstream oxygen sensor. An oxygen sensor socket is being used to unscrew the downstream sensor, but there's plenty of room to work here so you could also use a wrench on this sensor (3.3L/3.8L V6 shown, 2.4L four-cylinder models similar)

electrical connector (see illustration) and disconnect it.

5 Using a special oxygen sensor socket, unscrew the sensor (see illustration).

6 After removing the old upstream oxygen sensor, clean the threads of the sensor bore in the exhaust manifold.

7 If you're going to install the old sensor, apply anti-seize compound to the threads of the sensor to facilitate future removal. If you're going to install a new oxygen sensor, it's not necessary to apply anti-seize compound to the threads. The threads on new sensors already have anti-seize compound on them.

8 Install the upstream oxygen sensor and tighten it securely.

9 Installation is otherwise the reverse of removal.

Downstream oxygen sensor

♦ **Refer to illustrations 10.11 and 10.12**

➡**Note: The downstream oxygen sensor is located on the side of the catalytic converter on all models.**

10 Raise the vehicle and place it securely on jackstands.

11 Trace the electrical lead from the downstream oxygen sensor to the electrical connector and disconnect it (see illustration).

12 Unscrew and remove the downstream oxygen sensor (see illustration).

13 After removing the old downstream oxygen sensor, clean the threads of the sensor bore in the catalytic converter.

14 If you're going to install the old sensor, apply anti-seize compound to the threads of the sensor to facilitate future removal.

15 If you're going to install a new oxygen sensor, it's not necessary to apply anti-seize compound to the threads. The threads on new sensors already have anti-seize compound on them.

16 Install the upstream oxygen sensor and tighten it securely.

17 Installation is otherwise the reverse of removal.

11 Throttle Position (TP) sensor - replacement

♦ **Refer to illustrations 11.3, 11.5a and 11.5b**

1 Disconnect the cable from the negative terminal of the battery (see Chapter 5, Section 1).

2 Remove the throttle body (see Chapter 4).

3 Remove the two TP sensor mounting screws (see illustration) and remove the TP sensor.

4 Remove and inspect the old TP sensor O-ring. If it's cracked, dried out, torn or otherwise deteriorated or damaged, replace it. (To preclude the possibility of an air leak, it's always a good idea to simply install a new O-ring on the sensor regardless of the apparent condition of the old O-ring.)

11.3 To detach the TP sensor from the throttle body, remove these two screws (3.3L/3.8L V6 model shown, 2.4L four-cylinder models similar)

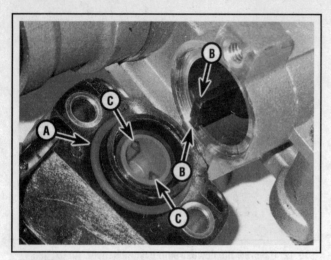

11.5a When installing the TP sensor, make sure that the O-ring (A) is installed and make sure that the blade (B) on the end of the throttle shaft fits between the two lugs (C) on the backside of the sensor

11.5b Once the blade on the throttle shaft is centered between the TP sensor lugs, rotate the TP sensor as necessary to align the mounting holes in the sensor with the mounting holes in the throttle body

5   When installing the TP sensor, make sure that the new O-ring is in place, then align the lugs on the backside of the sensor with the blade on the end of the throttle shaft (see illustration). The blade MUST fit between these two lugs or the TP sensor will not operate correctly. Once the blade on the throttle shaft is centered between the TP sensor

lugs, rotate the TP sensor as necessary to align the mounting holes in the sensor with the mounting holes in the throttle body (see illustration).

6   Installation is otherwise the reverse of removal.

12 Transmission Range (TR) and transmission temperature sensors - replacement

The TR sensor and transmission temperature sensor (which is an integral part of the TR sensor) are located on the automatic transaxle valve body. In order to replace the TR sensor/transmission temperature

sensor you must remove the valve body, which is beyond the scope of the home mechanic.

13 Transaxle speed sensors - replacement

13.3 Location of the transaxle input speed sensor

➡Note: The transaxle speed sensors are located on the top of the transaxle. The sensor closest to the engine is the input speed sensor and the sensor on the far right end (driver's side) is the output speed sensor.

1   Disconnect the cable from the negative battery terminal (see Chapter 5, Section 1).

2   Raise the vehicle and place it securely on jackstands.

INPUT SPEED SENSOR

▶ **Refer to illustration 13.3**

3   Disconnect the electrical connector from the TSS sensor (see illustration).

4   Unscrew the sensor from the case.

5   If you're going to install the same sensor, remove the old O-ring from the sensor and install a new one.

6   Installation is the reverse of removal. Be sure to tighten the sensor to the torque listed in this Chapter's Specifications.

OUTPUT SPEED SENSOR

▶ Refer to illustration 13.7

7 Disconnect the electrical connector from the sensor (see illustration).

8 Unscrew the sensor from the case.

9 If you're going to install the same sensor, remove the old O-ring from the sensor and install a new one.

10 Installation is the reverse of removal. Be sure to tighten the sensor to the torque listed in this Chapter's Specifications.

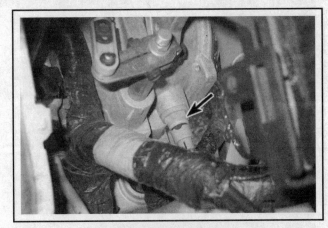

13.7 Location of the transaxle output speed sensor

14 Powertrain Control Module (PCM) - replacement

✳✳ **CAUTION:**

To avoid electrostatic discharge damage to the PCM, handle the PCM only by its case. Do not touch the electrical terminals during removal and installation. If available, ground yourself to the vehicle with an anti-static ground strap, available at computer supply stores.

➡Note: 2003 through 2005 models use either a Single Board Engine Controller (SBEC) type PCM or a New Generation Controller (NGC) type PCM. If you don't know which type of PCM your vehicle uses, note the PCM's location to make this distinction, because the two types of PCMs are installed in different locations. On SBEC-equipped vehicles the PCM is located in the left front corner of the engine compartment, between the battery and the headlight housing. On NGC-equipped vehicles the PCM is located in the void at the front lower left corner of the vehicle, behind the left end of the bumper cover and ahead of the wheel well splash shield. On all 2006 models the PCM is located in the same place - and is similar in appearance to - an SBEC unit.

2003 THROUGH 2005 MODELS WITH SINGLE-BOARD ENGINE CONTROLLER (SBEC)-TYPE PCM AND ALL 2006 MODELS

➡Note: The PCM is located in the left front corner of the engine compartment, between the battery and the headlight housing.

1 Disconnect the cable from the negative terminal of the battery (see Chapter 5, Section 1).

2 Remove the battery shield.

3 Remove the two upper PCM mounting bracket bolts.

4 Disconnect the electrical connectors from the PCM.

5 Remove the headlight housing (see Chapter 12).

6 Remove the lower PCM mounting bolt and remove the PCM.

✳✳ **CAUTION:**

Avoid any static electricity damage to the computer by grounding yourself to the body before touching the PCM and using a special anti-static pad to store the PCM on once it is removed.

7 Installation is the reverse of removal.

2003 THROUGH 2005 MODELS WITH NEW GENERATION CONTROLLER (NGC)-TYPE PCM

▶ Refer to illustrations 14.11 and 14.12

➡Note 1: The PCM is located in the void at the front lower left corner of the vehicle, behind the left end of the bumper cover and ahead of the wheel well splash shield.

➡Note 2: If you're replacing the PCM on a vehicle with over 200 miles on it you must update the mileage and the Vehicle Identification Number (VIN) in the new PCM, or a Diagnostic Trouble Code (DTC) might be set. If this situation occurs, drive the vehicle to a dealer after installing the new PCM and have a dealer program these two values into the unit.

8 Disconnect the cable from the negative terminal of the battery (see Chapter 5, Section 1).

9 Loosen the left front wheel lug nuts. Raise the front of the vehicle and place it securely on jackstands. Remove the left front wheel.

10 Remove the left front inner fender splash shield (see Chapter 11).

11 Unlock the electrical connectors (see illustration) and disconnect them from the PCM.

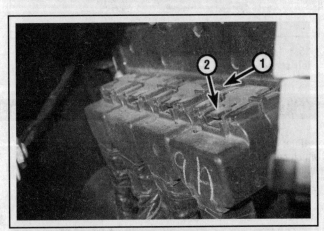

14.11 To unlock each of the four electrical connectors on an NGC type PCM, slide the red lock (1) away from the PCM, then depress the release tab (2) and disconnect the connector

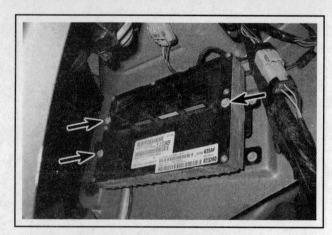

14.12 To detach an NGC type PCM from the vehicle, remove these three bolts

12 Remove the PCM mounting bolts (see illustration) and remove the PCM.

✳✳ CAUTION:

Avoid any static electricity damage to the computer by grounding yourself to the body before touching the PCM and using a special anti-static pad to store the PCM on once it is removed.

---

13 Installation is the reverse of removal.

15 Idle Air Control (IAC) motor - replacement

▶ **Refer to illustrations 15.3 and 15.4**

➡**Note: The Idle Air Control motor is located on the throttle body.**

1 Disconnect the cable from the negative terminal of the battery (see Chapter 5, Section 1).
2 Remove the throttle body (see Chapter 4).

3 Remove the IAC motor mounting screw (see illustration) and detach the IAC motor from the throttle body.
4 If you're going to re-use the same IAC motor, remove and discard the old O-rings from the IAC motor (see illustration).
5 Install new O-rings on the IAC motor.
6 Install the IAC motor and tighten the mounting screw securely.
7 Installation is otherwise the reverse of removal.

15.3 To detach the IAC motor from the throttle body, remove this screw

15.4 Remove the old O-rings from the IAC motor and replace them with new O-rings

16 Catalytic converter - general information, check and replacement

➡**Note: Because of the Federally mandated extended warranty which covers emissions-related components such as the catalytic converter, check with a dealer service department before replacing the converter at your own expense.**

GENERAL DESCRIPTION

1 The catalytic converter is an emission control device installed in the exhaust system that reduces pollutants from the exhaust gas stream. There are two types of converters: The oxidation catalyst reduces the levels of hydrocarbon (HC) and carbon monoxide (CO) by adding oxygen to the exhaust stream to produce water vapor (H_2O) and carbon dioxide (CO_2). The reduction catalyst lowers the levels of oxides of nitrogen (NOx) by removing oxygen from the exhaust gases to produce nitrogen (N) and oxygen. These two types of catalysts are combined into a three-way catalyst that reduces all three pollutants.

2 The amount of oxygen entering the catalyst is critical to its operation because without oxygen it cannot convert harmful pollutants into harmless compounds. The catalyst is most efficient at capturing and storing oxygen when it converts the exhaust gases of an intake charge

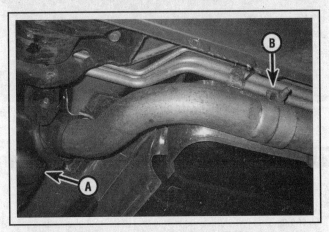

16.10a To disconnect the rear end of the catalytic converter (A) from the exhaust pipe, loosen this clamp bolt (B)

16.10b To disconnect the forward end of the catalytic converter from the exhaust manifold, remove these four bolts (upper right bolt not visible in this photo) . . .

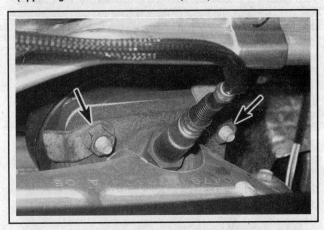

16.10c . . . and the flag nuts at the exhaust manifold flange. If you have to replace these flag nuts, make sure that you use original equipment flag nuts or a suitable substitute

that's mixed at the ideal (stoichiometric) air/fuel ratio of 14.7:1. If the air/fuel ratio is leaner than stoichiometric for an extended period of time, the catalyst will store even more oxygen. But if the air/fuel ratio is richer than stoichiometric for any length of time, the oxygen content in the catalyst can become totally depleted. If this condition occurs, the catalyst will not convert anything!

3   Because the catalyst's ability to store oxygen is such an important factor in its operation, it can also be considered a factor in the catalyst's eventual inability to do its job. Catalysts do wear out. And one of the reasons that they do so is that they can no longer store oxygen. So the PCM monitors the oxygen content going into and coming out of the catalyst by comparing the voltage signals from the upstream and downstream oxygen sensors. When the catalyst is functioning correctly, there is very little oxygen to monitor at the outlet end of the catalyst because it's capturing, storing and releasing oxygen as needed to convert HC, CO and NOx into more benign substances. But as the catalyst ages, it slowly loses its ability to store oxygen, and the downstream oxygen sensor tells the PCM that the oxygen content in the catalyzed exhaust gases is going up. When the amount of oxygen exiting the catalyst reaches a specified threshold, the PCM stores a Diagnostic Trouble Code (DTC) and turns on the Malfunction Indicator Light (MIL).

CHECK

4   The equipment for testing a catalytic converter is expensive. If you suspect that the converter on your vehicle is malfunctioning, take it to a dealer or authorized emissions inspection facility for diagnosis and repair.

5   Whenever the vehicle is raised for servicing underbody components, inspect the converter for leaks, corrosion, dents and other damage. Inspect the welds/flange bolts that attach the front and rear ends of the converter to the exhaust system. If damage is discovered, the converter should be replaced.

6   Although catalytic converters don't break too often, they can become plugged. The easiest way to check for a restricted converter is to use a vacuum gauge to diagnose the effect of a blocked exhaust on intake vacuum.

   a) *Connect a vacuum gauge to an intake manifold vacuum source (see Chapter 2).*
   b) *Warm the engine to operating temperature, place the transaxle in Park (automatic) or Neutral (manual) and apply the parking brake.*
   c) *Note and record the vacuum reading at idle.*

   d) *Quickly open the throttle to near full throttle and release it. Note and record the vacuum reading.*
   e) *Perform the test three more times, recording the reading after each test.*
   f) *If the reading after the fourth test is more than one in-Hg lower than the reading recorded at idle, the exhaust system may be restricted (the catalytic converter could be plugged or an exhaust pipe or muffler could be restricted).*

REPLACEMENT

▶ **Refer to illustrations 16.10a, 16.10b and 16.10c**

7   Raise the vehicle and place it securely on jackstands.

8   Remove the downstream oxygen sensor (see Section 10).

9   Before trying to loosen the nuts and bolts at the exhaust manifold flange and the clamp bolt and nut behind the catalyst, spray them with penetrating oil and wait the specified amount of time (see the instructions on the can) for the penetrant to loosen things up.

10 Loosen the clamp behind the catalytic converter and slide it back, then remove the nuts and bolts that attach the catalyst to the exhaust manifold (see illustrations). Notice the odd nuts used with the bolts that secure the catalyst mounting flange to the exhaust manifold flange (see illustration). They're referred to as "flag nuts" because the small "flags"

attached to the nuts mean that you can loosen or tighten the bolts without having to hold the nuts. If you have to replace these flag nuts, use original equipment flag nuts, or you might have a hard time tightening the new bolts. And you will most certainly have a hard time loosening the same bolts the next time that you have to separate the catalyst from the exhaust manifold.

11 Separate the catalytic converter from the exhaust system.

12 If you're replacing the old catalytic converter, take it with you when you purchase a new unit. Make sure that the new unit is identical to the old unit.

13 Before installing the catalyst, coat the threads of the exhaust manifold flange nuts and bolts and the clamp bolt with anti-seize compound. Be sure to tighten the fasteners securely.

14 Installation is otherwise the reverse of removal.

17 Evaporative emissions control (EVAP) system - general description and component replacement

GENERAL DESCRIPTION

1 The Evaporative Emissions Control (EVAP) system absorbs fuel vapors (unburned hydrocarbons) and, during engine operation, releases them into the intake manifold from which they're drawn into the intake ports where they mix with the incoming air-fuel mixture. The EVAP canister and Leak Detection Pump (LDP) or Natural Vacuum Leak Detection (NVLD) assemble are located underneath the vehicle, right behind the lower left corner of the engine compartment. The EVAP canister purge solenoid is located on the right side of the engine compartment, near the right end of the radiator.

2 When the engine is not operating, fuel vapors migrate through a system of hoses from the fuel tank and intake manifold to the EVAP canister, where they are stored until the next time the vehicle is operated. Vapors are routed through the control valve and then through the liquid separator on their way to the EVAP canister. The liquid separator prevents fuel from contaminating the EVAP canister. The liquid separator is replaceable, but the control valve is not. If the control valve malfunctions, the fuel tank must be replaced. A rollover valve, which is located in the top of the fuel tank, prevents the flow of fuel through the vapor hoses if the vehicle rolls over. The rollover valve is also not serviceable. If it malfunctions, replace the fuel tank.

3 The Powertrain Control Module (PCM) purges the EVAP canister through the proportional purge solenoid. The solenoid regulates the rate of flow of vapors from the canister to the throttle body. The solenoid is not energized during cold starts and during warm-up. After the engine has been started and warmed up to its normal operating temperature, the PCM energizes the solenoid, which controls the rate of flow in proportion to the current level, which is controlled by the PCM.

4 On vehicles with a Single Board Engine Controller (SBEC) type PCM, the EVAP system is equipped with a Leak Detection Pump (LDP), which is mounted under the vehicle, near the EVAP canister. The LDP, which is controlled by the PCM, tests for, and can detect, leaks in the system. When commanded to do so by the PCM, the LDP pressurizes the EVAP system and then monitors the system to verify whether it can hold the pressure for a specified period of time. If it detects a leak, the PCM stores a Diagnostic Trouble Code and turns on the Malfunction Indicator Light (see Section 2).

5 On vehicles with a New Generation Controller (NGC) type PCM, the EVAP system is equipped with a Natural Vacuum Leak Detection (NVLD) assembly. Instead of pressurizing the EVAP system, then monitoring it for leaks, the NVLD monitors the system's ability to hold a (relative) vacuum. If the PCM determines that the system cannot hold a vacuum, it stores a Diagnostic Trouble Code and turns on the Malfunction Indicator Light (see Section 2).

REPLACEMENT

WARNING:

Gasoline is extremely flammable, so take extra precautions when you work on any part of the fuel system. Don't smoke or allow open flames or bare light bulbs near the work area, and don't work in a garage where a gas-type appliance (such as a water heater or a clothes dryer) is present. Since gasoline is carcinogenic, wear latex gloves when there's a possibility of being exposed to fuel, and, if you spill any fuel on your skin, rinse it off immediately with soap and water. Mop up any spills immediately and do not store fuel-soaked rags where they could ignite. The fuel system is under constant pressure, so, if any fuel lines are to be disconnected, relieve the system fuel pressure first (see Chapter 4). When you perform any kind of work on the fuel system, wear safety glasses and have a Class B type fire extinguisher on hand.

EVAP canister purge solenoid

▶ Refer to illustrations 17.6 and 17.8

➡Note: The EVAP canister purge solenoid is located in the right front corner of the engine compartment, near the right end of the radiator.

6 Clearly label the EVAP hoses to ensure correct reassembly (see illustration), then disconnect them from the solenoid.

17.6 Clearly label the EVAP hoses (1, from the EVAP canister; 2, to the intake manifold), then disconnect them from the EVAP canister purge solenoid. To disconnect the electrical connector from the EVAP canister purge solenoid, push the red lock (3) to the right (away from the radiator, toward the right front fender), then depress the release tab (4) and pull off the connector

17.8 To disengage the EVAP canister purge solenoid from its mounting bracket (A), depress the release tab (B) and slide the solenoid off the bracket

7   Disconnect the electrical connector from the EVAP canister purge solenoid.

8   Detach the EVAP canister purge solenoid from its mounting bracket (see illustration).

9   Installation is the reverse of removal.

Leak Detection Pump (LDP)

➡Note: The LDP is located under the vehicle, near the EVAP canister (the LDP is in the same location as, and looks quite similar to, the NVLD, which is shown in illustration 17.16).

10   Raise the vehicle and place it securely on jackstands.

11   Disconnect the electrical connector from the LDP.

12   Clearly label the EVAP hoses to ensure correct reassembly, then disconnect them from the LDP.

13   Remove the three LDP mounting bolts and remove the LDP.

14   Installation is the reverse of removal.

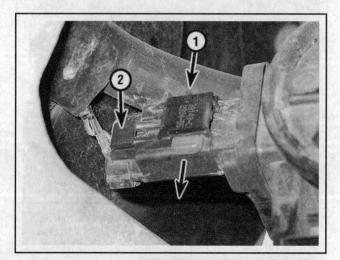

17.17 To disconnect the electrical connector from the NVLD, slide the red lock (1) to its UNLOCKED position, then depress the release tab (2) and pull off the connector

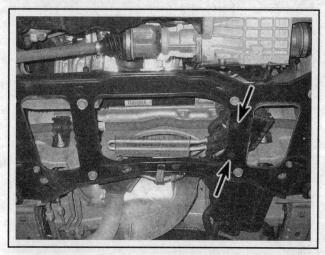

17.16 To detach the NVLD mounting bracket from the subframe/cradle reinforcement plate, remove these two bolts, then pull down the NVLD and its bracket so that you can access the electrical connector and the EVAP hoses connected to the NVLD

Natural Vacuum Leak Detection (NVLD) assembly

▶ Refer to illustrations 17.16, 17.17, 17.18 and 17.19

➡Note: The NVLD is located under the vehicle, near the EVAP canister.

15   Raise the vehicle and place it securely on jackstands.

16   Remove the NVLD mounting bracket bolts (see illustration) and pull down the NVLD and its mounting bracket so that you can access the electrical connector and the EVAP hoses connected to the NVLD.

17   Unlock and disconnect the electrical connector from the NVLD (see illustration).

18   Clearly label the EVAP hoses to ensure correct reassembly (see illustration), then disconnect them from the NVLD.

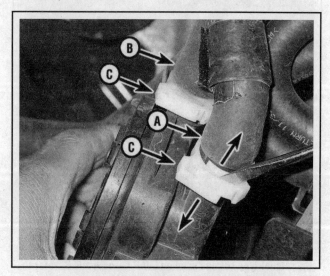

17.18 Clearly label these two EVAP hoses (A, from the EVAP canister; B, to the breather element). Then insert a screwdriver into each ratcheting clamp (C), twist the tip to disengage the ratcheting teeth on the ends of each clamp, disconnect the clamps and disconnect the EVAP hoses from the NVLD

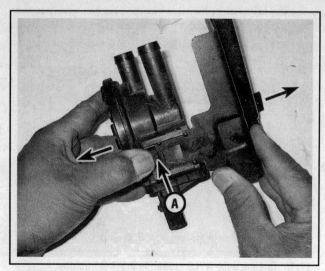

17.19 To disengage the NVLD from its mounting bracket, depress the release tab (A) and slide the NVLD and the mounting bracket apart

19 Detach the NVLD from its mounting bracket (see illustration).
20 Installation is the reverse of removal.

EVAP canister

▶ Refer to illustrations 17.22, 17.23 and 17.24

➡Note: The EVAP canister is located under the vehicle, right behind the left rear corner of the engine compartment.

21 Raise the vehicle and place it securely on jackstands.
22 Loosen the EVAP canister mounting bracket bolts (see illustration) and lower the EVAP canister and mounting bracket assembly slightly to access the EVAP hoses connected to the canister.

17.22 To access the EVAP hoses, loosen the rear canister mounting bracket bolt (A) and the two left front bolts (B, bolts not visible), then lower the bracket and canister assembly slightly. To detach the EVAP canister from its mounting bracket, remove the single mounting bolt (C)

23 Clearly label the EVAP hoses (see illustration) to ensure correct reassembly, then disconnect them from the canister (for help with disconnecting the ratcheting-type clamps used on two of the hoses, see illustration 17.18).
24 To detach the rear end of the EVAP canister from its mounting bracket, remove the mounting bolt from the underside of the bracket (see illustration 17.22). Then pull the EVAP canister to the rear to disengage the locator pins at the front from the mounting bracket (see illustration).
25 Installation is the reverse of removal.

17.23 Clearly label the EVAP hoses connected to the EVAP canister, then disconnect them (for help with disconnecting the ratchet-type clamps used on EVAP hoses A and B, refer to illustration 17.18)

A   EVAP hose, from fuel tank
B   EVAP hose, to canister purge solenoid in engine compartment
C   EVAP hose, to Leak Detection Pump (LDP) or to Natural Vacuum Leak Detector (NVLD)

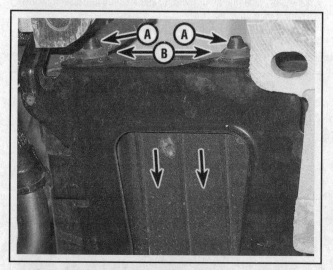

17.24 To detach the rear end of the EVAP canister from its mounting bracket, remove the canister mounting bolt, then pull the canister to the rear and disengage the two locator pins (A) from their respective grommets (B)

18 Exhaust Gas Recirculation (EGR) system - general description and component replacement

GENERAL DESCRIPTION

1 When you pull a trailer, pass another vehicle or go up a steep hill, the temperature inside the combustion chambers heats up. When the temperature inside the combustion chambers reaches 2500-degrees F, the engine begins to produce oxides of nitrogen (NOx), which is an odorless, colorless and toxic gas that causes health problems. The EGR system reduces NOx by introducing a controlled amount of spent exhaust gases into the intake manifold, which dilutes the air/fuel mixture, lowers combustion chamber temperatures and reduces the creation of NOx.

2 The EGR system consists of the EGR valve, the EGR tube, the electronic EGR transducer and the connecting hoses. On 2.4L four-cylinder models, the EGR valve/transducer assembly is located at the left rear corner of the cylinder head. On 3.3L/3.8L V6 models, the EGR valve/transducer assembly is located at the right front corner of the engine, where it's bolted to the right end of the front cylinder head.

3 The EGR transducer consists of a PCM-controlled solenoid and a backpressure transducer. When the PCM energizes the solenoid, no vacuum reaches the transducer; when the PCM de-energizes the solenoid, vacuum flows to the transducer. When exhaust backpressure reaches a specified threshold, it closes a bleed valve inside the transducer. When the bleed valve is closed by backpressure and the solenoid is de-energized by the PCM, vacuum flows through the transducer to operate the EGR valve. When exhaust backpressure has not fully closed the bleed valve and the PCM has de-energized the solenoid, a partial vacuum flows to the EGR valve, which reduces the amount of exhaust gases allowed to enter the engine.

COMPONENT REPLACEMENT

> ❊❊ **WARNING:**
>
> **Make sure that the engine is cool before removing any EGR component.**

2.4L four-cylinder models

EGR valve control assembly (solenoid and transducer)

➡**Note: The EGR valve control assembly is located at the left rear corner of the cylinder head, right above the EGR valve.**

4 Disconnect the electrical connector from the EGR valve solenoid.

5 Disconnect the vacuum hose that connects the EGR valve solenoid to the EGR valve diaphragm.

6 Disconnect the backpressure hose that connects the transducer (the flat circular part on the underside of the EGR valve solenoid) to the EGR valve base.

7 Remove the EGR valve solenoid/transducer assembly.

8 Installation is the reverse of removal.

EGR valve tube

➡**Note: The EGR tube, which connects the EGR valve to the intake manifold, is routed across the front of the cylinder head.**

9 Remove the bolts that attach the EGR tube to the intake manifold.

10 Remove the bolts that attach the EGR tube to the EGR valve.

11 Remove the EGR tube.

12 Installation is the reverse of removal. Be sure to tighten the EGR tube bolts to the torque listed in this Chapter's Specifications.

EGR valve

➡**Note: The EGR valve is located at the left rear corner of the cylinder head, right below the EGR valve control assembly.**

13 Remove the EGR valve control assembly (see Steps 4 through 7).

14 Disconnect the EGR tube from the EGR valve.

15 Remove the EGR valve mounting bolts.

16 Remove the EGR valve.

17 Installation is the reverse of removal. Be sure to tighten the EGR valve mounting bolts to the torque listed in this Chapter's Specifications.

3.3L/3.8L V6 models

EGR tube

▶ **Refer to illustration 18.18**

➡**Note: The EGR tube connects the EGR valve (which is located at the right front corner of the front cylinder head) to the top of the intake manifold.**

18 Remove the bolts that attach the EGR tube to the intake manifold (see illustration).

19 Remove the bolts that attach the EGR tube to the EGR valve (see illustration 18.18).

20 Remove the EGR tube.

21 Installation is the reverse of removal. Be sure to use new gaskets and tighten the EGR tube bolts to the torque listed in this Chapter's Specifications.

EGR valve/transducer assembly

▶ **Refer to illustrations 18.22, 18.24 and 18.25**

➡**Note: The EGR valve/transducer assembly is located at the right front corner of the front cylinder head.**

18.18 To detach the EGR tube from the EGR valve and from the intake manifold, remove these four bolts

18.22 To disconnect the electrical connector from the EGR valve transducer, slide the red lock (1) up, then depress the release tab (2) and pull off the connector

18.24 To detach the EGR valve from the cylinder head, remove these two bolts

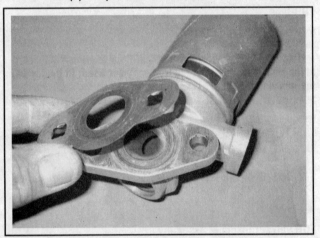

18.25 Remove and discard the old EGR valve gasket

22 Disconnect the electrical connector from the transducer (see illustration).

23 Remove the bolts that attach the EGR tube to the EGR valve (see illustration 18.18).

24 Remove the two EGR valve mounting bolts (see illustration) and remove the EGR valve and transducer assembly.

25 Remove the old EGR valve gasket (see illustration) and discard it. Be sure to clean off all old gasket material from the gasket mating surfaces of the EGR valve and the cylinder head.

26 Installation is the reverse of removal. Be sure to use a new gasket and tighten the EGR valve bolts and the EGR tube bolts to the torque listed in this Chapter's Specifications.

19 Positive Crankcase Ventilation (PCV) system

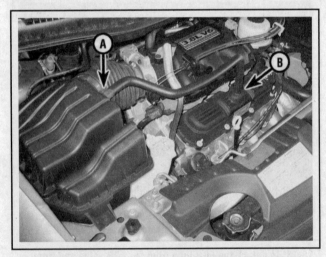

19.2a The fresh air inlet hose connects the air filter housing (A) to the valve cover (2.4L four-cylinder models) or the front valve cover (B) (3.3L/3.9L V6 models, shown)

▶ **Refer to illustrations 19.2a and 19.2b**

1 The Positive Crankcase Ventilation (PCV) system reduces hydrocarbon emissions by scavenging crankcase vapors. It does this by circulating fresh air from the air filter housing through the crankcase, where it mixes with blow-by gases, before being drawn through a PCV valve into the intake manifold.

2 The PCV system consists of the PCV valve and two hoses. The fresh air inlet hose connects the air filter housing to the valve cover (2.4L four) or to the front valve cover (3.3L/3.8L V6) (see illustration). The crankcase ventilation hose (or PCV hose) connects the valve cover (2.4L four) or the rear valve cover (3.3L/3.8L V6) to the intake manifold (see illustration). The PCV valve is located at the valve cover end of the crankcase ventilation hose that connects to the intake manifold.

3   To maintain idle quality, the PCV valve restricts the flow when the intake manifold vacuum is high. If abnormal operating conditions (such as piston ring problems) arise, the system is designed to allow excessive amounts of blow-by gases to flow back through the crankcase vent tube into the air cleaner to be consumed by normal combustion.

4   Checking and replacement of the PCV valve is covered in Chapter 1.

19.2b The crankcase ventilation hose (or PCV hose) connects the valve cover (2.4L four-cylinder models) or the rear valve cover (A) (3.3L/3.8L V6 models, shown) to the intake manifold (B). The PCV valve is located at the valve cover end of this hose on all models

Specifications

Torque specifications

Camshaft Position (CMP) sensor mounting bolt	
2.4L four cylinder engine	
CMP sensor target magnet retaining screw	30 in-lbs
CMP sensor mounting bolts	115 in-lbs
3.3L/3.8L V6 engines	125 in-lbs
Engine Coolant Temperature (ECT) sensor	
2.4L four cylinder engine	60 in-lbs
3.3L/3.8L V6 engines	150 in-lbs
Exhaust Gas Recirculation (EGR) valve	
2.4L four cylinder engine	
EGR tube flange-to-EGR valve bolts	85 to125 in-lbs
EGR tube flange-to-intake manifold bolts	85 to 125 in-lbs
EGR valve-to-cylinder head mounting bolts	175 to 225 in-lbs
3.3L/3.8L V6 engines	
EGR tube flange-to-EGR valve bolts	85 to 125 in-lbs
EGR tube flange-to-intake manifold bolts	
3.3L	40 to 60 in-lbs
3.8L	85 to 125 in-lbs
EGR valve-to-adapter mounting bolts	175 to 225 in-lbs
Knock sensor	84 in-lbs
Oxygen sensors (all sensors, all models)	20 ft-lbs
Transmission speed sensors (input and output)	20 ft-lbs

Notes

Section

Reference to other Chapters

7

AUTOMATIC
TRANSAXLE

1 General information

These models are equipped with the 41TE or the 40TE automatic transaxle. The automatic transaxle and the differential are housed in a compact, lightweight, two-piece aluminum alloy housing.

These models are equipped with a Transmission Control Module (TCM) which is the "brain" of the transaxle. The TCM monitors engine and transaxle operating parameters through numerous sensors and then generates output signals to various relays and solenoids to regulate hydraulic pressures, optimize driveability, provide efficient torque management and maintain maximum fuel economy. The TCM is a separate component on 2003 through 2005 four-cylinder models and is mounted behind the left front fender splash shield. All V6 models and 2006 models incorporate the TCM into the PCM. The TCM is part of the On-Board Diagnostic system OBD-II. For more information, see Chapter 6.

Because of the complexity of the automatic transaxles and the specialized equipment necessary to perform most service operations, this Chapter contains only those procedures related to general diagnosis, adjustment and removal and installation procedures.

If the transaxle requires major repair work, it should be left to a dealer service department or an automotive or transmission repair shop. Once properly diagnosed you can, however, remove and install the transaxle yourself and save the expense, even if the repair work is done by a transmission shop.

2 Diagnosis - general

1 Automatic transaxle malfunctions may be caused by five general conditions:

   a) *Poor engine performance*
   b) *Improper adjustments*
   c) *Hydraulic malfunctions*
   d) *Mechanical malfunctions*
   e) *Malfunctions in the computer or its signal network*

2 Diagnosis of these problems should always begin with a check of the easily repaired items: fluid level and condition (see Chapter 1), shift cable adjustment and shift lever installation. Next, perform a road test to determine if the problem has been corrected or if more diagnosis is necessary. If the problem persists after the preliminary tests and corrections are completed, additional diagnosis should be performed by a dealer service department or other qualified transmission repair shop. Refer to the *Troubleshooting Section* at the front of this manual for information on symptoms of transaxle problems.

PRELIMINARY CHECKS

3 Drive the vehicle to warm the transaxle to normal operating temperature.

4 Check the fluid level as described in Chapter 1:

   a) *If the fluid level is unusually low, add enough fluid to bring the level within the designated area of the dipstick, then check for external leaks (see following).*
   b) *If the fluid level is abnormally high, drain off the excess, then check the drained fluid for contamination by coolant. The presence of engine coolant in the automatic transaxle fluid indicates that a failure has occurred in the internal radiator oil cooler walls that separate the coolant from the transaxle fluid (see Chapter 3).*
   c) *If the fluid is foaming, drain it and refill the transaxle, then check for coolant in the fluid, or a high fluid level.*

5 Check the engine idle speed.

➡**Note: If the engine is malfunctioning, do not proceed with the preliminary checks until it has been repaired and runs normally.**

6 Check and adjust the shift cable, if necessary (see Section 4).

7 If hard shifting is experienced, inspect the shift cable under the center console and at the manual lever on the transaxle (see Section 4).

FLUID LEAK DIAGNOSIS

8 Most fluid leaks are easy to locate visually. Repair usually consists of replacing a seal or gasket. If a leak is difficult to find, the following procedure may help.

9 Identify the fluid. Make sure it's transaxle fluid and not engine oil or brake fluid (automatic transaxle fluid is a deep red color).

10 Try to pinpoint the source of the leak. Drive the vehicle several miles, then park it over a large sheet of cardboard. After a minute or two, you should be able to locate the leak by determining the source of the fluid dripping onto the cardboard.

11 Make a careful visual inspection of the suspected component and the area immediately around it. Pay particular attention to gasket mating surfaces. A mirror is often helpful for finding leaks in areas that are hard to see.

12 If the leak still cannot be found, clean the suspected area thoroughly with a degreaser or solvent, then dry it thoroughly.

13 Drive the vehicle for several miles at normal operating temperature and varying speeds. After driving the vehicle, visually inspect the suspected component again.

14 Once the leak has been located, the cause must be determined before it can be properly repaired. If a gasket is replaced but the sealing flange is bent, the new gasket will not stop the leak. The bent flange must be straightened.

15 Before attempting to repair a leak, check to make sure that the following conditions are corrected or they may cause another leak.

➡**Note: Some of the following conditions cannot be fixed without highly specialized tools and expertise. Such problems must be referred to a qualified transmission shop or a dealer service department.**

Gasket leaks

16 Check the pan periodically. Make sure the bolts are tight, no bolts are missing, the gasket is in good condition and the pan is flat (dents in the pan may indicate damage to the valve body inside).

17 If the pan gasket is leaking, the fluid level or the fluid pressure may be too high, the vent may be plugged, the pan bolts may be too tight, the pan sealing flange may be warped, the sealing surface of the transaxle housing may be damaged, the gasket may be damaged or the

transaxle casting may be cracked or porous. If sealant instead of gasket material has been used to form a seal between the pan and the transaxle housing, it may be the wrong type of sealant.

Seal leaks

18 If a transaxle seal is leaking, the fluid level may be too high, the vent may be plugged, the seal bore may be damaged, the seal itself may be damaged or improperly installed, the surface of the shaft protruding through the seal may be damaged or a loose bearing may be causing excessive shaft movement.

19 Make sure the dipstick tube seal is in good condition and the tube is properly seated. Periodically check the area around the sensors for leakage. If transaxle fluid is evident, check the seals for damage.

Case leaks

20 If the case itself appears to be leaking, the casting is porous and will have to be repaired or replaced.

21 Make sure the oil cooler hose fittings are tight and in good condition.

Fluid comes out vent pipe or fill tube

22 If this condition occurs, the possible causes are: the transaxle is overfilled; there is coolant in the fluid; the dipstick is incorrect; the vent is plugged or the drain-back holes are plugged.

---

3 Driveaxle oil seals - replacement

▶ **Refer to illustrations 3.3 and 3.5**

1 The driveaxle oil seals are located on the sides of the transaxle, where the inner ends of the driveaxles are splined into the differential side gears. If you suspect that a driveaxle oil seal is leaking, raise the vehicle and support it securely on jackstands. If the seal is leaking, you'll see lubricant on the side of the transaxle, below the seal.

2 Remove the driveaxle (see Chapter 8).

3 Using a screwdriver or prybar, carefully pry the oil seal out of the transaxle bore (see illustration).

4 If the oil seal cannot be removed with a screwdriver or prybar, a special oil seal removal tool (available at auto parts stores) will be required.

5 Using a seal installer, install the new oil seal. Drive it into the bore squarely until it bottoms (see illustration).

6 Install the driveaxle (see Chapter 8).

3.3 Using a large screwdriver or prybar, carefully pry the oil seal out of the transaxle (if you can't remove the oil seal with a screwdriver or prybar, you may need to obtain a special seal removal tool - available at most auto parts stores - to do the job)

3.5 Using a seal installer, large section of pipe or a large deep socket as a drift, drive the new seal squarely into the bore and make sure that it's completely seated; lubricate the lip of the new seal with multi-purpose grease

4   Shift cable - removal, installation and adjustment

❊❊ **WARNING 1:**

The models covered by this manual are equipped with Supplemental Restraint systems (SRS), more commonly known as airbags. Always disarm the airbag system before working in the vicinity of any airbag system component to avoid the possibility of accidental deployment of the airbag, which could cause personal injury (see Chapter 12). Do not use a memory saving device to preserve the PCM's memory when working on or near airbag system components.

❊❊ **WARNING 2:**

Do not attempt this procedure until the vehicle has cooled completely. The exhaust system components must be cold to avoid physical harm.

REMOVAL

▸ **Refer to illustrations 4.4, 4.5, 4.7, 4.8 and 4.9**

1   Raise the hood and place a blanket over the left (driver's) fender to protect it.

2   Remove the cruise control actuator and position it off to the side without disconnecting the cables.

3   Remove the battery and battery tray (see Chapter 5).

4   Working in the engine compartment, disconnect the shift cable from the shift lever (see illustration).

5   Working in the engine compartment, disconnect the shift cable from the bracket (see illustration).

6   Working inside the vehicle, remove the lower trim panel and knee bolster (see Chapter 11).

7   Working under the steering column, disconnect the shift cable from the gear shift lever stud (see illustration).

8   Disconnect the shift cable from the steering column bracket (see illustration).

9   Remove the grommet from the panel opening between the engine compartment and the passenger compartment (see illustration), pull out and remove the cable from the passenger side.

INSTALLATION

10 Working under the steering column, install the shift cable through the panel opening into the engine compartment.

4.4 Pry the shift cable from the lever using a trim panel tool or flat-bladed screwdriver

4.5 Squeeze the plastic tabs and slide the shift cable through the bracket on the transaxle

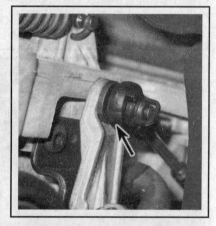

4.7 Carefully pry the shift cable from the stud on the shift lever arm

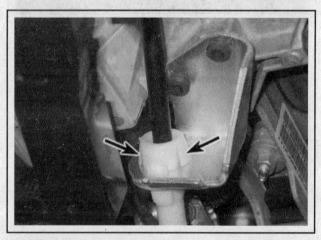

4.8 Push the tabs on the shift cable housing and slide the cable through the steering column bracket

4.9 Remove the grommet from the panel opening

4.18 Shift cable adjustment screw

11 Connect the shift cable onto the shift lever stud. Make sure it snaps into place.

12 Connect the shift cable to the cable bracket.

13 Working in the engine compartment, connect the shift cable to the shift lever.

14 The remainder of installation is the reverse of removal.

15 Adjust the shift cable as described in the following steps.

ADJUSTMENT

▶ **Refer to illustration 4.18**

16 Park the vehicle on flat surface and set the parking brake.

17 Place the shift lever in the Park position. Remove the key from the ignition.

18 Loosen the shift cable adjustment screw at the transaxle shift lever (see illustration).

19 Make sure the shift lever at the transaxle is in the Park position by pushing it forward all the way. The parking pawl must be engaged when adjusting the cable. Rock the vehicle back and forth to ensure that the parking pawl is fully engaged.

20 Tighten the shift cable adjustment screw.

21 Check the shift lever for proper operation. It should operate smoothly without binding. The engine should start only in the Park or Neutral positions.

22 Shift the transaxle into all gear positions to make sure the cable is functioning properly. Readjust if necessary.

---

5 Brake Transmission Shift Interlock (BTSI) system - description, check and replacement

DESCRIPTION

1 The Brake Transmission Shift Interlock (BTSI) system prevents the shift lever from being moved out of PARK unless the brake pedal is depressed. The BTSI system also prevents the ignition key from being turned to the LOCK or ACCESSORY position unless the shift lever is fully locked into the PARK position.

CHECK

2 Verify that the ignition key can be removed only when the shift lever is in the PARK position.

3 When the shift lever is in the PARK position, you should be able to rotate the ignition key from OFF to LOCK. But when the shift lever is in any gear position other than PARK (including NEUTRAL), you should not be able to rotate the ignition key to the LOCK position.

4 You should be able to move the shift lever out of the PARK position when the ignition key is turned to the OFF position.

5 You should not be able to move the shift lever out of the PARK position when the ignition key is turned to the RUN or START position until you depress the brake pedal.

6 With the shifter in any gear selection other than Park, you should not be able to turn the key back to the ACC or LOCK position.

7 Once in gear, with the ignition key in the RUN position, you should be able to move the shift lever between gears, or put it into NEUTRAL or PARK, without depressing the brake pedal.

8 If the BTSI system doesn't operate as described, have the system diagnosed by a dealer service department or other qualified auto repair facility.

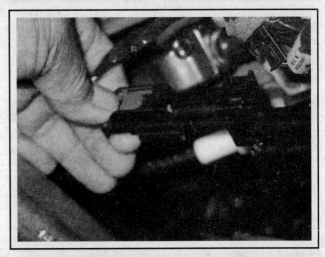

5.12 Press down the tab and slide the BTSI electrical connector off the solenoid

REPLACEMENT

▶ **Refer to illustrations 5.12, 5.14 and 5.15**

9 Disconnect the cable from the negative terminal of the battery (see Chapter 5, Section 1).

10 Remove the lower trim panel and the knee bolster (see Chapter 11).

11 Remove the steering column covers (see Chapter 11).

12 Release the BTSI connector (see illustration).

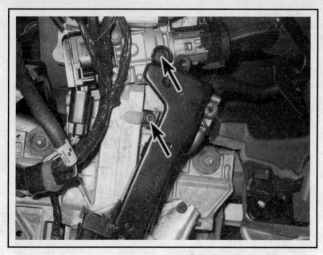

5.14 Location of the BTSI solenoid mounting screws

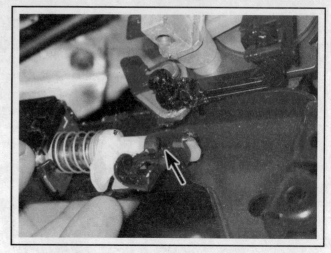

5.15 Be sure to align the BTSI plunger with the lever on the steering column

13 Make sure that the shift lever is in the PARK position.
14 Remove the BTSI solenoid retaining screws (see illustration) and separate the solenoid from the steering column.

15 Installation is the reverse of the removal. Be sure to align the plunger with the lever (see illustration).

6 Transmission Control Module (TCM) (2003 through 2005 four-cylinder models) - removal and installation

❋❋ CAUTION 1:

The Transmission Control Module (TCM) is an Electro-Static Discharge (ESD) sensitive electronic device, meaning a static electricity discharge from your body could possibly damage electrical components. Be sure to properly ground yourself and the TCM before handling it. Avoid touching the electrical terminals of the TCM.

❋❋ CAUTION 2:

If the Transmission Control Module (TCM) is replaced with a new unit, the module must be reprogrammed utilizing the pinion calibration and quick-learn software. Have the TCM reprogrammed by a dealer service department or other qualified auto repair facility.

1 Disconnect the cable from the negative battery terminal (see Chapter 5, Section 1).
2 Loosen the left front wheel lug nuts, then raise the vehicle and support it securely on jackstands.
3 Remove the left front wheel.
4 Remove the left fenderwell splash shield (see Chapter 11).
5 Detach the electrical connector from the TCM.
6 Remove the TCM bracket mounting screws and withdraw the TCM from the vehicle.
7 Installation is the reverse of removal.

7 Transaxle oil cooler - removal and installation

▶ **Refer to illustration 7.5**

➡**Note: On later models the transaxle oil cooler and air conditioning condenser are serviced as an assembly. See Chapter 3 for the condenser removal procedure.**

1 Disconnect the cable from the negative battery terminal (see Chapter 5, Section 1).
2 Raise the front of the vehicle and place it securely on jackstands.

3 Remove the radiator (see Chapter 3).
4 Put a drain pan underneath the oil cooler line fittings to catch any spilled transaxle fluid.
5 Disconnect the transaxle oil cooler line fittings (see illustrations). Plug the lines to prevent fluid spills.

➡**Note: To prevent potential leaks, the manufacturer recommends replacing the oil cooler lines whenever they are disconnected from the cooler.**

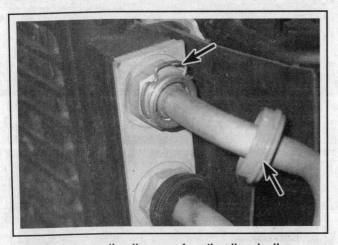

7.5 First remove the clip covers from the oil cooler line connectors and remove the circlip from the slots in the flange by lifting up

6   Remove the transaxle oil cooler mounting bolts and remove the transaxle oil cooler.

7   If you removed the cooler in order to flush it after a transaxle failure, have it flushed by a dealer service department or by a transaxle shop. A number of special tools are needed to flush the cooler correctly.

8   Installation is the reverse of removal. Be sure to install new transaxle fluid lines.

9   When you're done, check the transaxle fluid level and add some if necessary (see Chapter 1).

8   Automatic transaxle - removal and installation

REMOVAL

▶ **Refer to illustrations 8.5, 8.17, 8.18 and 8.19**

1   Remove the battery and the battery tray (see Chapter 5).

2   Loosen the front wheel lug nuts and the driveaxle/hub nuts (see Chapter 8).

➡ **Note: Depending on the type of wheels installed on the vehicle and the thickness of the socket you are using, you may have to loosen the driveaxle/hub nuts after the wheels have been removed (see Chapter 8).**

3   Remove the air filter housing and air intake duct assembly (see Chapter 4).

4   Remove the coolant reservoir (see Chapter 3).

5   Detach the transaxle oil cooler lines and plug them to prevent fluid from spilling (see illustration).

6   Clearly label, then unplug, all electrical connectors from the transaxle.

7   Disconnect the shift cable from the manual lever and bracket (see Section 4).

8   Remove the transaxle dipstick.

9   Disconnect the Leak Detection Pump (LDP) or Natural Vacuum Leak Detection (NVLD) system lines from the retaining straps and reposition them off to the side (see Chapter 6).

10 Raise the vehicle and support it securely on jackstands. Remove the wheels.

11 Drain the transaxle fluid (see Chapter 1).

12 Remove both driveaxles (see Chapter 8).

13 Remove the bolts securing the power steering cooler to the crossmember (see Chapter 10). Position the power steering cooler off to the side without disconnecting the fluid lines.

14 Remove the starter motor (see Chapter 5).

15 Support the engine from above with a hoist or engine support fixture, or place a jack and a block of wood under the oil pan.

16 Remove the structural collar on 2.4L engines (see Chapter 2A) or the transaxle brace on 3.3L/3.8L engines (see Chapter 2B).

17 Remove the torque converter cover (see illustration).

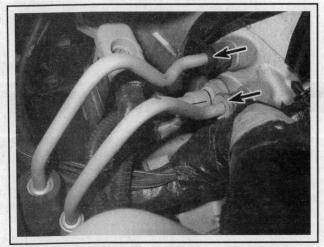

8.5 Location of the clip covers on the transaxle oil cooler lines at the transaxle

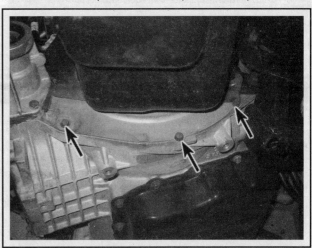

8.17 Location of the torque converter cover bolts

18 Mark the relationship of the torque converter to the driveplate so they can be installed in the same position (see illustration).

19 Remove the torque converter-to-driveplate bolts (see illustration). After all the bolts are removed, push the torque converter into the bellhousing so it doesn't stay with the engine when the transaxle is removed.

20 Support the transaxle with a transmission jack, if available, or use a floor jack. Secure the transaxle to the jack using straps or chains so it doesn't fall off during removal.

21 Remove the transaxle upper mount-to-bracket bolts (see Chapter 2A or 2B) Remove the upper transaxle-to-engine bolts.

22 Remove the front transaxle/engine bracket and the rear engine mount and bracket (see Chapter 2A or 2B).

23 Remove the lower transaxle-to-engine bolts.

24 Make a final check that all wires and hoses have been disconnected from the transaxle, then move the transaxle jack toward the side of the vehicle until the transaxle is clear of the engine locating dowels. Make sure you keep the transaxle level as you do this.

INSTALLATION

25 Installation of the transaxle is a reversal of the removal procedure, but note the following points:

a) As the torque converter is reinstalled, ensure that the drive tangs at the center of the torque converter hub engage with the recesses in the automatic transaxle fluid pump inner gear. This can be confirmed by turning the torque converter while pushing it towards the transaxle. If it isn't fully engaged, it will "clunk" into place.

b) When installing the transaxle, make sure the matchmarks you made on the torque converter and driveplate line up.

c) Install all of the driveplate-to-torque converter bolts before tightening any of them.

d) Tighten the driveplate-to-torque converter bolts to the torque listed in this Chapter's Specifications.

e) Tighten the transaxle mounting bolts to the torque listed in this Chapter's Specifications.

f) Tighten the driveaxle/hub nuts to the torque value listed in the Chapter 8 Specifications.

g) Tighten the wheel lug nuts to the torque listed in the Chapter 1 Specifications.

h) Fill the transaxle with the correct type and amount of automatic transaxle fluid as described in Chapter 1.

i) On completion, adjust the shift cable (see Section 4).

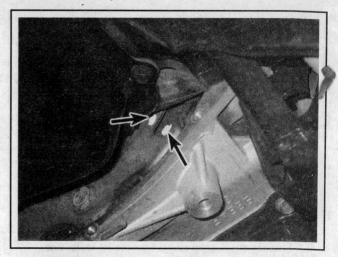

8.18 Mark the relationship of the torque converter to the driveplate

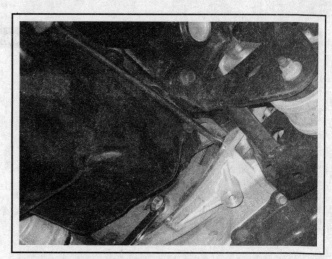

8.19 Wedge a screwdriver between the teeth on the driveplate and the engine block at the transaxle to prevent the engine from turning while loosening the torque converter bolts

9   Automatic transaxle overhaul - general information

In the event of a problem occurring, it will be necessary to establish whether the fault is electrical, mechanical or hydraulic in nature, before repair work can be contemplated. Diagnosis requires detailed knowledge of the transaxle's operation and construction, as well as access to specialized test equipment, and so is deemed to be beyond the scope of this manual. It is therefore essential that problems with the automatic transaxle are referred to a dealer service department or other qualified repair facility for assessment.

Note that a faulty transaxle should not be removed before the vehicle has been diagnosed by a knowledgeable technician equipped with the proper tools, as troubleshooting must be performed with the transaxle installed in the vehicle.

Specifications

General

Lubricant type and capacity	See Chapter 1

Torque specifications	Ft-lbs
Torque converter-to-driveplate bolts	65
Transaxle-to-engine bolts	70
Transaxle brace	See Chapter 2B
Structural collar	See Chapter 2A

Notes

Section

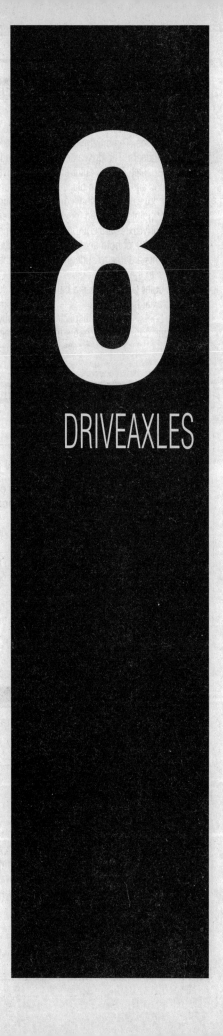

8

DRIVEAXLES

1 Driveaxles - general information and inspection

1   Power is transmitted from the transaxle to the wheels through a pair of driveaxles. The inner end of each driveaxle is splined to the differential side gears. The driveaxles can be pulled out to replace the oil seals (see Chapter 7). The outer ends of the driveaxles are splined to the front hubs and locked in place by a large nut.

2   Each driveaxle assembly consists of an inner and outer constant velocity (CV) joint connected together by a driveaxle shaft. The inner ends of the driveaxles are equipped with a "tri-pot" type joint. The design is capable of both angular and axial motion. In other words, the inner CV joints are free to slide in-and-out as the driveaxle moves up-and-down with the wheel.

3   The outer CV joints use a ball-and-cage design, capable of angular but not axial movement.

4   The boots should be inspected periodically for damage and leaking lubricant. Torn CV joint boots must be replaced immediately or the joints can be damaged. Boot replacement involves removal of the driveaxle (see Section 2).

→**Note: Some auto parts stores carry "split" type replacement boots, which can be installed without removing the driveaxle from the vehicle. This is a convenient alternative; however, the driveaxle should be removed and the CV joint disassembled and cleaned to ensure the joint is free from contaminants such as moisture and dirt which will accelerate CV joint wear.**

The most common symptom of worn or damaged CV joints, besides lubricant leaks, is a clicking noise in turns, a clunk when accelerating after coasting and vibration at highway speeds. To check for wear in the CV joints and driveaxle shafts, grasp each axle (one at a time) and rotate it in both directions while holding the CV joint housings, feeling for play indicating worn splines or sloppy CV joints. Also check the axleshafts for cracks, dents and distortion.

2 Driveaxle - removal and installation

REMOVAL

▶ **Refer to illustrations 2.2a, 2.2b, 2.3, 2.9 and 2.10**

1   Set the parking brake. Remove the wheel cover or hubcap.

2   Remove the cotter pin, lock nut, and spring washer from the stub axle (see illustrations).

3   Loosen, but do not remove, the driveaxle/hub nut (see illustration).

4   Loosen, but do not remove, the wheel lug nuts.

5   Raise the vehicle and support it securely on jackstands, then remove the front wheel lug nuts and the wheel.

6   Remove the brake caliper and disc (see Chapter 9).

7   If equipped with antilock brakes, remove the speed sensor cable routing bracket from the steering knuckle (see Chapter 9).

8   Remove the two steering knuckle-to-strut bracket bolts (see Chapter 10).

❊❊ **CAUTION:**

The steering knuckle-to-strut bolts are serrated and must not be turned during removal.

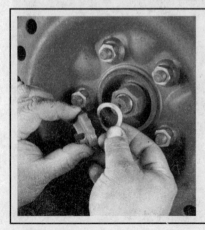

2.2b . . . the lock nut, and the spring washer

2.2a Remove the cotter pin . . .

2.3 Loosen the front hub nut before you raise the vehicle and remove the wheel

➡ Note: If the strut assembly is attached to the steering knuckle using a cam bolt in the lower slotted hole, mark the relationship of the cam bolt to the strut to preserve the wheel alignment setting on reassembly. **Separate the strut from the steering knuckle.**

9 Remove the driveaxle/hub nut and pull the steering knuckle out and away from the outer CV joint of the driveaxle (see illustration). Strike the end of the stub shaft with a soft-faced hammer to separate the splines from the hub and bearing assembly, if necessary.

10 Support the outer end of the driveaxle and insert a prybar between the inner CV joint and the transaxle case (see illustration). Pry out sharply to disengage the inner CV joint from the transaxle. Make sure you have a drain pan under the transaxle, as some oil will leak out.

11 Carefully withdraw the inner CV joint from the transaxle. Do not let the spline or the snap-ring drag across the sealing lip of the driveaxle oil seal.

INSTALLATION

12 Installation is the reverse of the removal procedure, noting the following additional points:

a) Thoroughly clean the splines and bearing shield on the outer CV joint. This is very important, as the bearing shield protects the wheel bearings from water and contamination. Also clean the wheel bearing area of the steering knuckle.

b) Thoroughly clean the splines and oil seal sealing surface on the inner CV joint. Apply an even bead of multi-purpose grease around the oil seal sealing surface of the inner CV joint.

c) When installing the driveaxle, push it sharply in to seat the snap-ring on the inner CV joint stub shaft into its groove in the differential gears inside the transaxle. Pull out on the inner CV joint housing to ensure it's seated. *

d) Tighten the steering knuckle-to-strut bolts to the torque listed in Chapter 10.

e) The steering knuckle-to-balljoint stud clamping bolt and nut should not be reused. A new clamping bolt and nut should always be used. Be sure to tighten it to the torque listed in the Chapter 10 Specifications.

f) Tighten the driveaxle/hub nut to the torque listed in this Chapter's Specifications.

g) Tighten the lug nuts to the torque listed in the Chapter 1 Specifications.

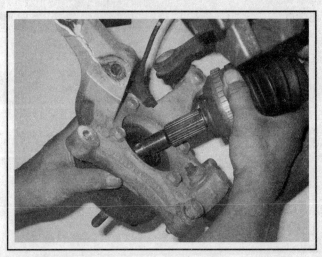

2.9 Pull the steering knuckle away from the outer CV joint

2.10 Using a large pry bar, pry the inner CV joint out sharply to disengage the snap-ring from the differential gears inside the transaxle

3   Driveaxle boot replacement

➡ Note: If the CV joints or boots must be replaced, explore all options before beginning the job. Complete, rebuilt driveaxles are available on an exchange basis, eliminating much time and work. Whichever route you choose to take, check on the cost and availability of parts before disassembling the vehicle.

1 Remove the driveaxle (see Section 2).

2 Mount the driveaxle in a vise with wood-lined jaws, to prevent damage to the axleshaft. Check the CV joints for excessive play in the radial direction, which indicates worn parts. Check for smooth operation throughout the full range of motion for each CV joint. If a boot is torn, the recommended procedure is to disassemble the joint, clean the components and inspect for damage due to loss of lubrication and possible contamination by foreign matter. If the CV joint is in good condition, lubricate it with CV joint grease and install a new boot.

INNER CV JOINT

Disassembly

▸ Refer to illustrations 3.5, 3.6 and 3.7

3 Cut the boot clamps with side-cutters, then remove and discard them.

4 Using a screwdriver, pry up on the edge of the boot, pull it off the CV joint housing and slide it down the axleshaft, exposing the tri-pot spider assembly. Pull the CV joint housing straight off.

➡ Note: When removing the housing, hold the rollers in place on the spider trunnion to prevent the rollers and the needle bearings from falling free.

3.5 Remove the snap-ring with a pair of snap-ring pliers

3.6 Mark the relationship of the tri-pot bearing assembly to the axleshaft

3.7 Drive the tri-pot joint off the axleshaft with a brass punch and hammer; be careful not to damage the bearing surfaces or the splines on the shaft

3.10a Wrap the axleshaft splines with electrical tape to prevent damaging the boot as it's slid onto the shaft

3.10b Install the tri-pot spider on the axleshaft (make sure your match mark is facing out and aligned with the mark on the axleshaft)

3.10c Place grease at the bottom of the CV joint housing

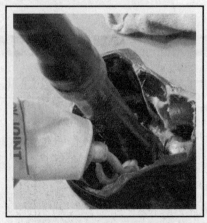

3.10d Install the boot and clamps onto the axleshaft, then insert the tri-pot into the housing, followed by the rest of the grease

3.11 Make sure that the thinnest groove on the axleshaft is the only one showing

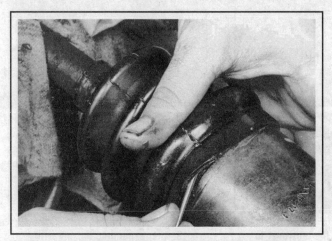

3.12 Equalize the pressure inside the boot by inserting a screwdriver between the boot and the CV joint housing

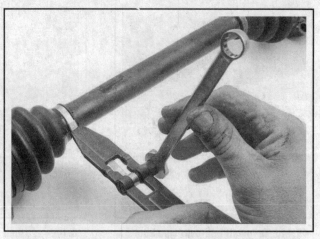

3.14a You'll need a special tightening tool to install "band" type boot clamps: Install the band with its end pointing in the direction of axle rotation and tighten it securely . . .

5   Remove the spider assembly snap-ring with a pair of snap-ring pliers (see illustration).

6   Mark the tri-pot to the axleshaft to ensure that they are reassembled properly (see illustration).

7   Use a hammer and a brass drift to drive the spider assembly from the axleshaft (see illustration).

8   Slide the boot off the shaft.

Inspection

9   Thoroughly clean all components with solvent until the old CV joint grease is completely removed. Inspect the bearing surfaces of the inner tri-pots and housings for cracks, pitting, scoring and other signs of wear. If any part of the inner CV joint is worn, you must replace the entire driveaxle assembly (inner tri-pot joint, axleshaft and outer CV joint). The only components that can be purchased separately are the boots themselves and the boot clamps.

Reassembly

▶ Refer to illustrations 3.10a, 3.10b, 3.10c, 3.10d, 3.11, 3.12 3.14a, 3.14b, 3.14c, 3.14d and 3.14e

10   Wrap the splines on the inner end of the axleshaft with electrical or duct tape to protect the boots from the sharp edges of the splines, then slide the clamps and boot onto the axleshaft (see illustration).

Remove the tape and place the tri-pot spider on the axleshaft with the chamfer toward the shaft (see illustration). Tap the spider onto the shaft (aligning the marks made in Step 6) with a brass drift until it's seated, then install the snap-ring. Apply grease to the tri-pot assembly and inside the housing (see illustration). Insert the tri-pot into the housing and pack the remainder of the grease around the tri-pot (see illustration).

11   Slide the boot into place, making sure the raised bead on the inside of the seal boot is positioned in the groove on the interconnecting shaft. If the driveaxle has multiple locating grooves on the shaft, position the boot so only one of the grooves (the thinnest) is exposed (see illustration). Position the sealing boot into the groove on the tri-pot housing retaining groove.

12   Position the CV joint mid-way through its travel, then equalize the pressure in the boot (see illustration).

13   Make sure each end of the boot is seated properly, and the boot is not distorted.

14   Install the boot clamps. There are three types of clamps you're likely to encounter: the band type, which requires a special tightening tool, the crimp type (which also requires a special tool), or the fold-over type (see illustrations).

15   Install the driveaxle as outlined in Section 2.

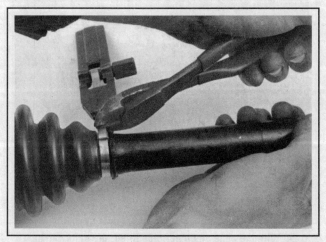

3.14b . . . then bend down the end of the clamp back and cut off the excess

3.14c If you're installing crimp-type boot clamps, you'll need a pair of special crimping pliers (available at most auto parts stores)

3.14d To install fold-over type boot clamps, bend the tang down . . .

3.14e . . . then tap the tabs over to hold it in place

3.19 After expanding the snap-ring, the outer joint assembly can be removed

OUTER CV JOINT

Removal

▶ **Refer to illustrations 3.19, 3.23, 3.24, 3.26, 3.27, 3.30a and 3.30b**

16 Cut the boot clamps with side-cutters, then remove and discard them.

17 Using a screwdriver, pry up on the edge of the boot, pull it off the CV joint housing and slide it down the axleshaft.

18 Wipe the grease from the joint.

19 Using a pair of snap-ring pliers, expand the snap-ring retaining the outer joint to the shaft, then remove the joint (see illustration).

20 Slide the boot off the driveaxle.

21 Clean the axle spline area and inspect for wear, damage, corrosion and broken splines.

22 Clean the outer CV joint bearing assembly with a clean cloth to remove excess grease.

23 Mark the relative position of the bearing cage, inner race and housing (see illustration).

24 Mount the CV joint in the vise with wood blocks to protect the stub shaft. Push down one side of the cage and remove the ball bearing from the opposite side (see illustration). The balls may have to be pried out.

25 Repeat this procedure until all of the balls are removed. If the joint is tight, tap on the inner race (not the cage) with a hammer and brass drift.

26 Remove the bearing assembly from the housing by tilting it vertically and aligning two opposing cage windows in the area between the ball grooves (see illustration).

27 Turn the inner race 90-degrees to the cage and align one of the spherical lands with an elongated cage window. Raise the land into the window and swivel the inner race out of the cage (see illustration).

28 Clean all of the parts with solvent and dry them with compressed air (if available).

29 Inspect the housing, splines, balls and races for damage, corrosion, wear and cracks.

30 Check the inner race for wear and scoring. If any of the components are not serviceable, the entire CV joint assembly must be replaced with a new one (see illustrations).

3.23 Mark the bearing cage, inner race and housing relationship after removing the grease

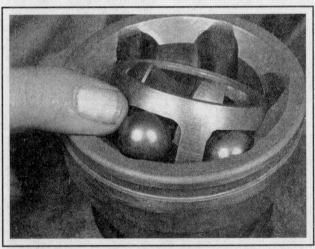

3.24 With the cage and inner race tilted, the balls can be removed one at a time

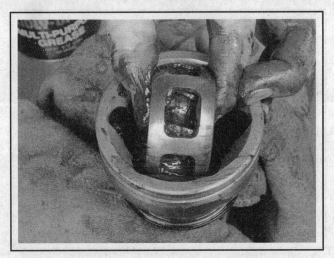

3.26 Align one of the elongated windows in the cage with one of the lands on the housing (outer race), then rock the cage and inner race out of the housing

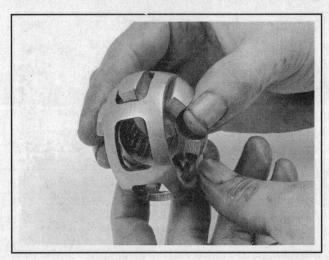

3.27 Tilt the inner race 90-degrees, align the race lands with the windows in the cage, then separate the two components

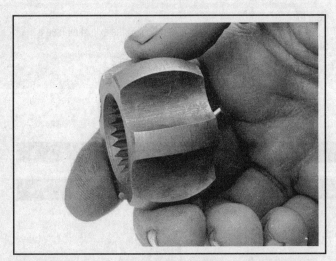

3.30a Check the inner race lands and grooves for pitting and score marks

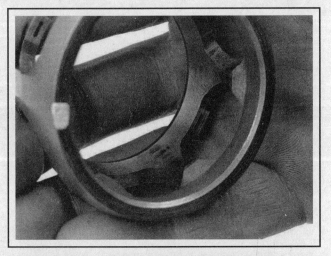

3.30b Check the cage for cracks, pitting and score marks (shiny spots are normal and don't affect operation)

Assembly

▶ **Refer to illustrations 3.36a, 3.36b and 3.37**

31 Apply a thin film of oil to all CV joint components before beginning reassembly.

32 Align the marks and install the inner race in the cage so one of the race lands fits into the elongated window (see illustration 3.27).

33 Rotate the inner race into position in the cage and install the assembly in the CV joint housing, again using the elongated window for clearance (see illustration 3.26).

34 Rotate the inner race into position in the housing. Be sure the large counterbore of the inner race faces out. The marks made during disassembly should face out and be aligned.

35 Pack the lubricant from the kit into the ball races and grooves.

36 Install the balls into the holes, one at a time, until they are all in position. Using needle-nose pliers, place the retaining ring into the groove on the outer CV joint housing (see illustrations).

37 Fill the joint with grease through the splined hole, then insert a wooden dowel into the splined hole to force the grease into the joint (see illustration).

3.36a Use needle-nose pliers to lower the snap-ring into the groove . . .

3.36b . . . then seat it into the groove with snap-ring pliers

3.37 Apply grease through the splined hole, then insert a wooden dowel into the hole and push down - the dowel will force the grease into the joint

38 Place the driveaxle in the vise and slide the inner clamp and boot over it (wrap the shaft splines with tape to prevent damaging the boot) (see illustration 3.10a).

39 Place the CV joint housing in position on the axle, align the splines and push it into place. If necessary, tap it on with a soft-face hammer. Make sure it is seated on the snap-ring by attempting to pull it

from the shaft.

40 Install the outer CV joint sealing boot to the axle shaft (see Steps 11 to 14).

41 Install the driveaxle as outlined in Section 2.

Specifications

Torque specifications	Ft-lbs
Driveaxle/hub nut	180
Wheel lug nuts	See Chapter 1

Section

Reference to other Chapters

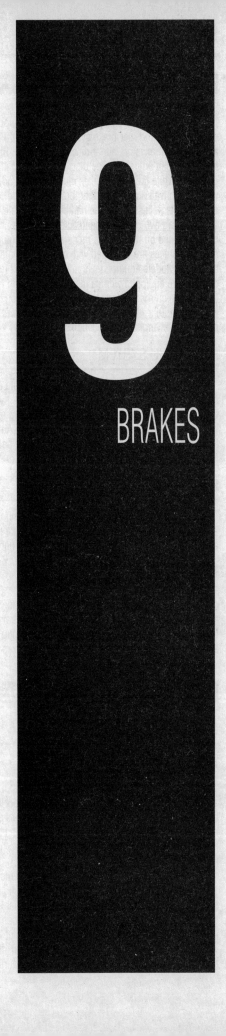

9

BRAKES

1 General information

The vehicles covered by this manual are equipped with hydraulically operated front and rear brake systems. The front brakes are disc type and the rear brakes are either disc or drum type. Both the front and rear brakes are self adjusting. The disc brakes automatically compensate for pad wear, while the drum brakes incorporate an adjustment mechanism which is activated as the parking brake is applied. Also, there are no adjustments necessary for the parking brake cable.

There are two different manufacturers for the brake caliper assemblies installed on the various models. Models equipped with front and rear disc brakes are equipped with calipers manufactured by Continental Teves. Models equipped with a front disc and rear drum brake combination are equipped with calipers manufactured by TRW. It's important to know which manufacturer made the calipers on the vehicle you're working on; this will help avoid confusion when obtaining replacement parts or following repair procedures.

HYDRAULIC SYSTEM

The hydraulic system consists of two separate circuits. The master cylinder has separate reservoir chambers for the two circuits, and, in the event of a leak or failure in one hydraulic circuit, the other circuit will remain operative. For models without ABS (Anti-lock Braking System), a dual proportioning valve provides brake balance between the front and rear brakes.

POWER BRAKE BOOSTER

The power brake booster utilizes engine manifold vacuum and atmospheric pressure to provide assistance to the hydraulically operated brakes. It is mounted on the firewall in the engine compartment.

PARKING BRAKE

The parking brake operates the rear brakes only, through cable actuation. On drum brake models, the parking brake cables pull on a lever attached to the brake shoe assembly, causing the shoes to expand against the drum. On models with rear disc brakes, the cables pull on actuators that expand the parking brake shoes in the center portion of the rear brake disc that resembles a brake drum.

SERVICE

After completing any operation involving disassembly of any part of the brake system, always test drive the vehicle to check for proper braking performance before resuming normal driving. When testing the brakes, perform the tests on a clean, dry, flat surface. Conditions other than these can lead to inaccurate test results.

Test the brakes at various speeds with both light and heavy pedal pressure. The vehicle should stop evenly without pulling to one side or the other. Avoid locking the brakes, because this slides the tires and diminishes braking efficiency and control of the vehicle.

Tires, vehicle load and wheel alignment are factors which also affect braking performance.

PRECAUTIONS

There are some general cautions and warnings involving the brake system on this vehicle:

a) *Use only brake fluid conforming to DOT 3 specifications.*
b) *The brake pads and linings contain fibers which are hazardous to your health if inhaled. Whenever you work on brake system components, clean all parts with brake system cleaner. Do not allow the fine dust to become airborne. Also, wear an approved filtering mask.*
c) *Safety should be paramount whenever any servicing of the brake components is performed. Do not use parts or fasteners which are not in perfect condition, and be sure that all clearances and torque specifications are adhered to. If you are at all unsure about a certain procedure, seek professional advice. Upon completion of any brake system work, test the brakes carefully in a controlled area before putting the vehicle into normal service. If a problem is suspected in the brake system, don't drive the vehicle until it's fixed.*

2 Anti-lock Brake System (ABS) - general information

GENERAL INFORMATION

♦ **Refer to illustration 2.2**

1   The Anti-lock Brake System is designed to maintain vehicle steerability, directional stability and optimum deceleration under severe braking conditions on most road surfaces. It does so by monitoring the rotational speed of each wheel and controlling the brake line pressure to each wheel during braking. This prevents the wheels from locking up.

2   The ABS system has three main components - the wheel speed sensors, an electronic control unit and a hydraulic unit. Four wheel speed sensors - one at each wheel - send a variable voltage signal to the control unit, which monitors these signals, compares them to its program and determines whether a wheel is about to lock up. When a wheel is about to lock up, the control unit signals the hydraulic unit to reduce hydraulic pressure (or not increase it further) at that wheel's

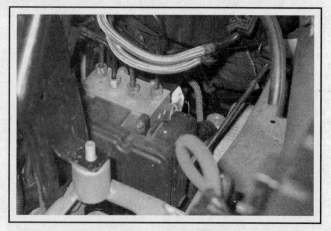

2.2 An integrated electronic and hydraulic control unit (located below the brake master cylinder)

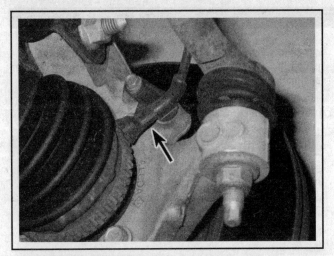

2.9 The front wheel speed sensor is mounted to the steering knuckle

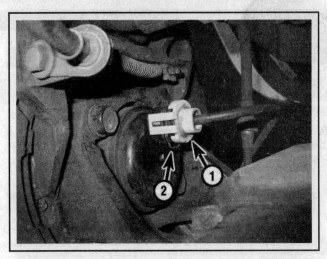

2.10 The rear wheel speed sensor location and details

   1 Outer plastic clip   *2 Metal retaining clip*

brake caliper. Pressure modulation is handled by electrically-operated solenoid valves within the hydraulic control unit (see illustration).

3 If a problem develops within the system, an "ABS" warning light will glow on the dashboard. Sometimes, a visual inspection of the ABS system can help you locate the problem. Carefully inspect the ABS wiring harness. Pay particularly close attention to the harness and connections near each wheel. Look for signs of chafing and other damage caused by incorrectly routed wires. If a wheel sensor harness is damaged, it must be replaced along with the sensor (if they are assembled together).

✳✳ WARNING:

Do NOT try to repair an ABS wiring harness. The ABS system is sensitive to even the smallest changes in resistance. Repairing the harness could alter resistance values and cause the system to malfunction. If the ABS wiring harness is damaged in any way, it must be replaced.

✳✳ CAUTION:

Make sure the ignition is turned off before unplugging or reattaching any electrical connections.

DIAGNOSIS AND REPAIR

4 If the ABS warning light comes on and stays on while the vehicle is in operation, the ABS system requires attention. Although special electronic ABS diagnostic testing tools are necessary to properly diagnose the system, you can perform a few preliminary checks before taking the vehicle to a dealer service department.

a) *Check the brake fluid level in the reservoir.*
b) *Verify that the computer electrical connectors are securely connected.*
c) *Check the electrical connectors at the hydraulic control unit.*
d) *Check the fuses.*
e) *Follow the wiring harness to each wheel and verify that all connections are secure and that the wiring is undamaged.*

5 If the above preliminary checks do not solve the problem, the vehicle should be diagnosed by a dealer service department or other qualified repair shop. Due to the complex nature of the ABS system, all actual repair work must be done by a qualified automotive technician.

WHEEL SPEED SENSOR - REMOVAL AND INSTALLATION

▶ **Refer to illustrations 2.9 and 2.10**

6 Loosen the wheel lug nuts, raise the vehicle and support it securely on jackstands. Remove the wheel.

7 Make sure the ignition key is turned to the Off position.

8 Trace the wiring back from the sensor, detaching all brackets and clips while noting its correct routing, then disconnect the electrical connector.

9 For the front wheel sensor, remove the mounting fastener and carefully detach the sensor from the knuckle (see illustration).

10 For the rear wheel sensor, remove the two clips that secure the sensor to the rear of the hub/wheel bearing assembly (see illustration).

11 Installation is the reverse of the removal procedure.

12 Install the wheel and lug nuts, lower the vehicle and tighten the lug nuts to the torque specified in Chapter 1.

3 Disc brake pads - replacement

❋❋ WARNING:

Disc brake pads must be replaced on both front or both rear wheels at the same time; never replace the pads on only one side. Also, the dust created by the brake system is harmful to your health. Never blow it out with compressed air and don't inhale any of it. An approved filtering mask should be worn when working on the brakes. Do not, under any circumstances, use petroleum-based solvents to clean brake parts. Use brake system cleaner only!

❋❋ CAUTION:

Don't depress the brake pedal with the caliper removed.

➡Note: There are two different brake caliper assemblies used on the various models. Models equipped with front and rear disc brakes are equipped with calipers manufactured by Continental Teves. Models equipped with a front disc and rear drum brake combination are equipped with calipers manufactured by TRW. These two caliper assemblies are different and parts can-

not be interchanged. Be certain to compare the replacement pads with the worn pads to confirm that they are correct for your application.

1   Using a syringe or equivalent, remove approximately two-thirds of the fluid from the master cylinder reservoir and discard it.

❋❋ CAUTION:

Brake fluid will damage paint. If any fluid is spilled, wash it off immediately with plenty of clean, cold water.

2   Loosen the wheel lug nuts, raise the end of the vehicle you will be working on and support it securely on jackstands. Block the wheels that remain on the ground.

3   Remove the wheels. Work on one brake assembly at a time, using the assembled brake for reference if necessary.

FRONT

▶ Refer to illustrations 3.4, 3.5 and 3.6a through 3.6o

4   Position a drain pan under the brake assembly and clean the caliper and surrounding area with brake system cleaner (see illustration).

3.4 Spray the disc and brake pads with brake cleaner to remove brake dust; DO NOT blow brake dust off with compressed air - collect the contaminated fluid in a suitable container and dispose of it properly!

3.5 Use a C-clamp to press the caliper piston into its bore

3.6a Remove the anti-rattle spring (Teves only)

3.6b On Teves calipers, to remove the brake caliper, remove the guide pins

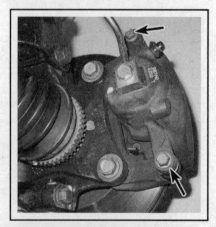

3.6c On TRW calipers, to remove the brake caliper, remove the guide pin bolts

3.6d Lift the caliper off its bracket

3.6e Remove the outer brake pad from the caliper mounting bracket

3.6f On Teves calipers, remove the inner brake pad from the caliper. On TRW calipers, remove the inner pad from the caliper mounting bracket

5   Push the piston back into its bore using a C-clamp (see illustration). As the piston is depressed to the bottom of the caliper bore, the fluid in the master cylinder will rise as the brake fluid is displaced. Make sure it doesn't overflow. If necessary, remove more of the fluid.

6   To replace the brake pads, follow the accompanying photos, beginning with illustration 3.6a. Be sure to stay in order and read the caption under each illustration.

7   While the pads are removed, inspect the caliper for brake fluid

3.6g Hang the caliper from the spring with a piece of wire - don't let it hang by the brake hose

3.6h On TRW calipers, remove the anti-rattle clips. Clean, inspect and reinstall them. Replace them if they are severely worn

3.6i On Teves calipers, remove, clean and inspect the guide pins. Lubricate them with high-temperature grease before installing the caliper

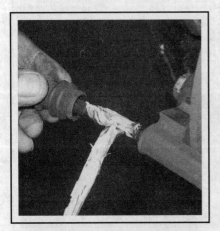

3.6j On TRW calipers, remove, clean and inspect the guide pins. Lubricate them with high-temperature grease before installing the caliper

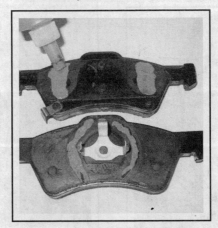

3.6k Apply an anti-squeal compound to the back of the pads where they mate with the caliper and piston

3.6l On the Teves caliper, install the inner brake pad - make sure the retaining spring is fully seated into the piston bore

3.6m On the Teves caliper, install the outer brake pad into the caliper bracket. On the TRW caliper, install both brake pads onto the caliper bracket seated within the anti-rattle clips

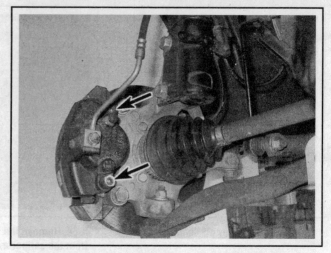

3.6n Place the caliper onto the disc and match it to the caliper bracket, install the guide pins or guide pin bolts and tighten them to the torque listed in this Chapter's Specifications

leaks and ruptures of the piston dust boot. Replace the caliper if necessary (see Section 4). Also inspect the brake disc carefully (see Section 5). If machining is necessary, follow the information in that Section to remove the disc. Inspect the brake hoses for damage and replace if necessary (see Section 10).

8 Before installing the caliper, clean and inspect the guide pins for corrosion and damage. If they're significantly corroded or damaged, replace them. Also check the guide pin rubber bushings (or boots on TRW calipers) for wear. When installing the caliper, be sure to tighten the guide pins (or guide pin bolts on TRW calipers) to the torque listed in this Chapter's Specifications.

9 Repeat the procedure on the opposite wheel, then install the wheels and lug nuts, lower the vehicle and tighten the lug nuts to the torque specified in the Chapter 1.

10 Add the specified type of brake fluid to the reservoir until it's full (see Chapter 1).

11 Pump the brake pedal a few times to bring the pads into contact with the disc. Check the level of the brake fluid, adding some if necessary.

12 Check the operation of the brakes carefully before placing the

vehicle into normal service. Try to avoid heavy brake application until the brakes have been applied lightly several times to seat the pads.

REAR

▶ **Refer to illustrations 3.14 and 3.15a through 3.15h**

13 Position a drain pan under the brake assembly and clean the caliper and surrounding area with brake system cleaner (see illustration 3.4).

14 If necessary, use a C-clamp to push the caliper piston slightly into its bore and just enough to loosen the pads from the brake disc (see illustration).

➥Note: The anti-rattle spring on the outboard pad prevents the caliper from moving enough to push the piston completely into the bore. The worn inboard brake pad can be used with the C-clamp to push the piston completely to the bottom of the caliper bore after the caliper is removed. The fluid in the master cylinder will rise as the brake fluid is displaced. Make sure it doesn't overflow. If necessary, remove more of the fluid.

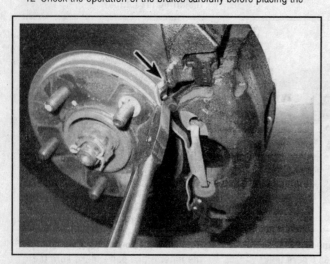

3.6o On the Teves caliper, install the anti-rattle spring and hook the end over the caliper bracket tab

3.14 Use a C-clamp to press the caliper piston slightly into its bore - just enough to loosen the brake pads from the brake disc

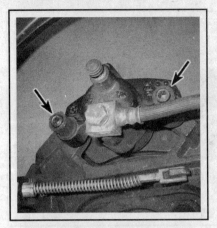

3.15a Remove the two guide pins from the rear brake caliper

3.15b Lift the caliper from its mounting bracket at an angle to relieve tension on the anti-rattle spring

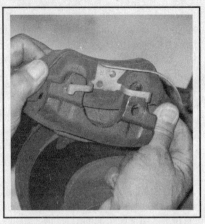

3.15c Remove the outer brake pad from the caliper

3.15d Remove the inner brake pad from the caliper

3.15e With the caliper resting on the leaf spring (and not hanging by the brake hose), remove, clean and inspect the guide pins. Lubricate them with high-temperature grease before installing the caliper

15 To replace the brake pads, follow the accompanying photos, beginning with illustration 3.15a. Be sure to stay in order and read the caption under each illustration.

16 While the pads are removed, inspect the caliper for brake fluid leaks and ruptures of the piston dust boot. Replace the caliper if necessary (see Section 4). Also inspect the brake disc carefully (see Sec-

tion 5). If machining is necessary, follow the information in that Section to remove the disc. Inspect the brake hoses for damage and replace if necessary (see Section 10).

3.15f Install the inner brake pad - make sure the retaining spring is fully seated into the piston bore

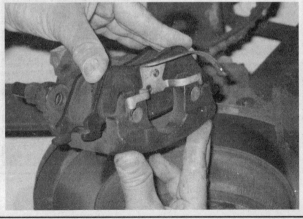

3.15g Install the outer brake pad, making sure the retaining spring is properly engaged with the caliper body

17 Before installing the caliper guide pins, clean and inspect them for corrosion and damage. If they're significantly corroded or damaged, replace them. Also check the guide pin rubber bushings for wear. Be sure to tighten them to the torque listed in this Chapter's Specifications

18 Repeat the procedure on the opposite wheel, then install the wheels and lug nuts, lower the vehicle and tighten the lug nuts to the torque specified in Chapter 1.

19 Add the specified type of brake fluid to the reservoir until it's full (see Chapter 1).

20 Pump the brake pedal a few times to bring the pads into contact with the disc. Check the level of the brake fluid, adding some if necessary.

21 Check the operation of the brakes carefully before placing the vehicle into normal service. Try to avoid heavy brake application until the brakes have been applied lightly several times to seat the pads.

3.15h Place the caliper on the caliper bracket making sure that the anti-rattle spring is seated under the rear abutment on the bracket. Install the caliper guide pins and tighten them to the torque listed in this Chapter's Specifications

4   Disc brake caliper - removal and installation

✶✶ WARNING:

Dust created by the brake system is harmful to your health. Never blow it out with compressed air and don't inhale any of it. An approved filtering mask should be worn when working on the brakes. Do not, under any circumstances, use petroleum-based solvents to clean brake parts. Use brake system cleaner only.

→Note: If replacement is indicated (usually because of fluid leakage), it is recommended that the calipers be replaced, not overhauled. New and factory rebuilt units are available on an exchange basis. Always replace the calipers in pairs - never replace just one of them.

REMOVAL

◆ Refer to illustration 4.2

1 Loosen the wheel lug nuts, raise the vehicle and support it securely on jackstands. Remove the wheel.

2 Remove the banjo bolt and disconnect the brake hose from the caliper (see illustration). Plug the brake hose to keep contaminants out of the brake system and to prevent losing any more brake fluid than is necessary. Discard the sealing washers - new ones should be used during installation.

→Note: If the caliper is being removed for access to other components, don't disconnect the hose.

3 Remove the caliper guide pins or pin bolts (see illustration 4.2 [front] or 3.15a [rear]).

INSTALLATION

4 Install the caliper by reversing the removal procedure. Remember to replace the sealing washers at the brake hose-to-caliper connection. Tighten the caliper guide pins or pin bolts to the torque listed in this Chapter's Specifications.

5 Bleed the brake circuit according to the procedure in Section 11 (only if the brake hose was disconnected). Make sure there are no leaks from the hose connections. If you didn't disconnect the hose, be sure to pump the brake pedal several times to bring the pads into contact with the disc.

6 Test the brakes carefully before returning the vehicle to normal service.

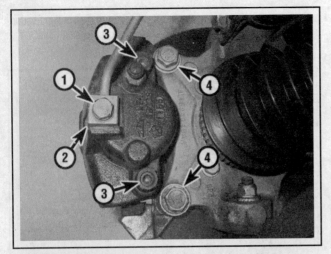

4.2 Front caliper details:

1 Banjo bolt	3 Guide pins
2 Brake line fitting	4 Mounting bracket bolts

5 Brake disc - inspection, removal and installation

✳✳ WARNING:

Dust created by the brake system is harmful to your health. Never blow it out with compressed air and don't inhale any of it. An approved filtering mask should be worn when working on the brakes. Do not, under any circumstances, use petroleum-based solvents to clean brake parts. Use brake system cleaner only.

➡Note: This procedure applies to both front and rear brake discs.

INSPECTION

◆ Refer to illustrations 5.3, 5.4a, 5.4b, 5.5a and 5.5b

1   Loosen the wheel lug nuts, raise the vehicle and support it securely on jackstands. Remove the wheel and reinstall the lug nuts to hold the disc in place (washers may be required). If the rear brake disc is being worked on, release the parking brake.

2   Remove the brake caliper and pads (see Section 3). Don't disconnect the brake hose from the caliper, or you'll have to bleed the brakes when everything is reassembled. After removing the caliper, suspend it out of the way with a piece of wire.

3   Visually inspect the disc surface for score marks and other damage. Light scratches and shallow grooves are normal after use and may not always be detrimental to brake operation, but deep scoring requires disc removal and refinishing by an automotive machine shop. Be sure to check both sides of the disc (see illustration). If pulsating has been noticed during application of the brakes, suspect excessive disc runout.

4   To check disc runout, place a dial indicator at a point about 1/2-inch from the outer edge of the disc (see illustration). Set the indicator to zero and turn the disc. The indicator reading should not exceed the specified allowable runout limit. If it does, the disc should be refinished by an automotive machine shop.

➡Note: The discs should be resurfaced regardless of the dial indicator reading, as this will impart a smooth finish and ensure a perfectly flat surface, eliminating any brake pedal pulsation or other undesirable symptoms related to questionable discs. At the very least, if you elect not to have the discs resurfaced, remove the glaze from the surface with emery cloth using a swirling motion (see illustration).

5   It's absolutely critical that the disc not be machined to a thickness under the specified minimum allowable thickness. The minimum thick-

5.3 The brake pads on this vehicle were obviously neglected - they wore down completely and cut deep grooves into the disc (wear this severe means the disc must be replaced)

5.4a Use a dial indicator to measure disc runout - if the reading exceeds the maximum allowable runout limit, the disc will have to be machined or replaced

5.4b Using a swirling motion, remove the glaze from the disc surface with sandpaper or emery cloth

5.5a The minimum wear dimension is cast into the back side of the disc (typical)

5.5b Use a micrometer to measure disc thickness

ness is cast into the inside of the front disc (see illustration). The disc thickness can be checked with a micrometer (see illustration).

➡Note: The rear disc has the minimum thickness specification cast into it as well, although the location may vary.

REMOVAL

6   If you're removing a front disc, remove the caliper mounting bracket (see illustration 4.2). Remove the lug nuts which were put on to hold the disc in place and remove the disc from the hub.

➡Note: Remove and discard any retaining clips on the wheel studs that hold the disc to the hub. These clips are not necessary for reinstallation of the brake disc.

INSTALLATION

7   Place the disc in position over the wheel studs. Install the mounting bracket (if you're installing a front disc), tightening the bolts to the torque listed in this Chapter's Specifications.

8   Install the brake pads and caliper (see Section 3). Tighten the caliper guide pins or pin bolts to the torque listed in this Chapter's Specifications.

9   Install the wheel, lower the vehicle and tighten the lug nuts to the torque listed in the Chapter 1 Specifications.

10 Pump the brake pedal a few times to bring the brake pads into contact with the disc. Bleeding won't be necessary unless the brake hose was disconnected from the caliper. Check the operation of the brakes carefully before driving the vehicle.

6   Drum brake shoes - replacement

♦ Refer to illustrations 6.2, 6.3, 6.4a through 6.4x and 6.5

✳✳ WARNING:

Drum brake shoes must be replaced on both wheels at the same time - never replace the shoes on only one wheel. Also, the dust created by the brake system is harmful to your health. Never blow it out with compressed air and don't inhale any of it. An approved filtering mask should be worn when working on the brakes. Do not, under any circumstances, use petroleum-based solvents to clean brake parts. Use brake system cleaner only!

✳✳ CAUTION:

Whenever the brake shoes are replaced, the return and hold-down springs should also be replaced. Due to the continuous heating/cooling cycle that the springs are subjected to, they lose their tension over a period of time and may allow the shoes to drag on the drum and wear at a much faster rate than normal.

1   Loosen the wheel lug nuts, raise the rear of the vehicle and support it securely on jackstands. Block the front wheels to keep the vehicle from rolling. Release the parking brake. Remove the wheel.

➡Note: To avoid mixing up parts, work on only one brake assembly at a time.

2   Remove the brake drum. If the drum will not come off, retract the brake shoes by using the adjuster port in the brake backing plate (see illustration).

➡Note: Refer to illustration 6.4d and note the gear on the adjuster. Use a screwdriver to reach the gear (through the port) and turn it. If the gear stops turning and the brake drum will not move, turn the gear in the other direction until the brake drum becomes loose and can be removed from the hub.

3   Clean the brake shoe assembly with brake system cleaner before beginning work (see illustration).

4   Follow the accompanying illustrations for the brake shoe replace-

6.2 The adjuster port (rubber plug removed) allows access to the adjuster - reach the adjuster inside with a screwdriver and turn the gear on the adjuster to retract the brake shoes

6.3 Before disassembling the brake shoe assembly, spray it with brake cleaner to remove brake dust; DO NOT blow brake dust off with compressed air - collect the contaminated fluid in a suitable container and dispose of it properly!

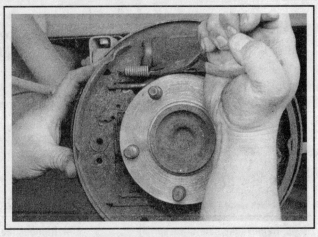

6.4a Remove the hold-down spring and pin from the leading brake shoe by depressing the retainer and turning it 90-degrees - the tool shown here is available at most auto parts stores and greatly simplifies this task

ment procedure (see illustrations 6.4a through 6.4x). Be sure to stay in order and read the caption under each illustration.

5   Before reinstalling the drum, carefully examine it for cracks,

6.4b Disconnect the upper return spring from the brake shoe

score marks, deep scratches and hard spots, which will appear as small discolored areas. If the hard spots cannot be removed with fine emery cloth or if any of the other conditions listed above exist, the drum must be taken to an automotive machine shop to have it resurfaced.

➡**Note: Professionals recommend resurfacing the drums whenever a brake job is performed. Resurfacing will eliminate the**

6.4c Disconnect the adjustment lever spring from the brake shoe

6.4d Remove the upper return spring (A), the tension clip (B), and the automatic adjuster (C)

6.4e Remove the adjustment lever and the spring

6.4f Disconnect the two return springs from the leading brake shoe and remove the shoe

6.4g Remove the parking brake actuating strut

6.4h Remove the hold-down spring and pin from the trailing brake shoe

6.4i Remove the trailing brake shoe and the parking brake actuating lever

6.4j Clean, then lubricate the automatic adjuster screw threads with high-temperature grease

possibility of out-of-round drums. If the drums are worn so much that they can't be resurfaced without exceeding the maximum allowable diameter (see illustration), then new ones will be required. At the very least, if you elect not to have the drums resurfaced, remove the glazing from the surface with emery cloth or sandpaper using a swirling motion.

6 Install the brake drum onto the hub flange. Remove the rubber plug covering the adjuster port (see illustration 6.2). Insert a screwdriver into the adjusting port in the brake backing plate and turn the gear on the adjuster until the brake shoes drag on the drum as it's

6.4k Lubricate the contact surfaces of the backing plate with hightemperature grease

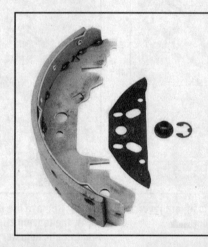

6.4l Remove the parking brake actuator plate from the old leading brake shoe and install it on the new leading shoe. Be sure the retaining clip seats properly

6.4m Connect the parking brake actuating lever to the parking brake cable

6.4n Install the trailing brake shoe

6.4o Install the hold-down pin and spring

6.4p Install the parking brake actuating strut

6.4q Install the automatic adjuster, the tension clip and the upper return spring

6.4r Install the leading brake shoe

rotated. Back off the adjustment enough so that the shoes don't drag when the drum is turned. Reinstall the rubber plug into the backing plate.

7 Mount the wheel and install the lug nuts. Lower the vehicle and tighten the lug nuts to the torque listed in the Chapter 1 Specifications.

8 Make a number of forward and reverse stops and operate the parking brake to adjust the brakes until satisfactory pedal action is obtained.

9 Check the operation of the brakes carefully before driving the vehicle.

6.4s Install the hold-down pin and spring

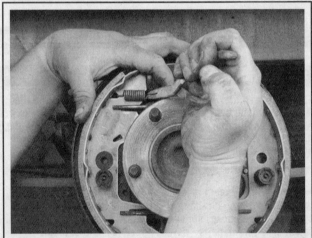

6.4t Connect the upper return spring to the leading brake shoe

6.4u Attach the automatic adjustment lever . . .

6.4v . . . and the actuating spring

6.4w Connect the top lower return spring

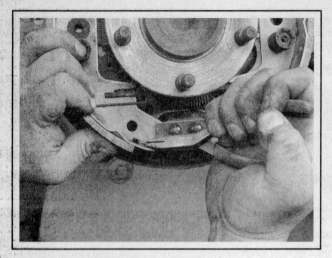

6.4x Connect the bottom lower return spring

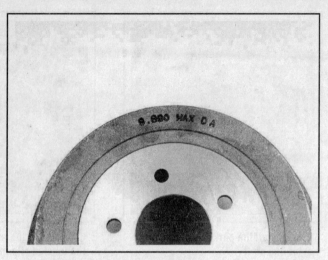

6.5 The maximum allowable diameter is cast into the drum (typical)

7   Wheel cylinder - removal and installation

✳✳ WARNING:

The dust created by the brake system is harmful to your health. Never blow it out with compressed air and don't inhale any of it. An approved filtering mask should be worn when working on the brakes. Do not, under any circumstances, use petroleum-based solvents to clean brake parts. Use brake system cleaner only!

➡**Note: If replacement is indicated (usually because of fluid leakage or sticky operation), it is recommended that the wheel cylinders be replaced, not overhauled. Always replace the wheel cylinders in pairs - never replace just one of them.**

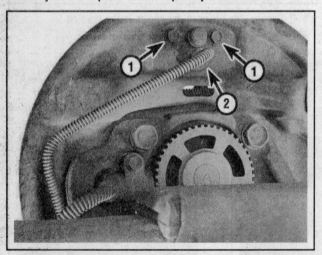

7.4 Wheel cylinder mounting details:

1   Mounting bolt   *2   Brake line fitting*

REMOVAL

▶ **Refer to illustration 7.4**

1   Raise the rear of the vehicle and support it securely on jackstands. Block the front wheels to keep the vehicle from rolling.

2   Remove the brake shoe assembly (see Section 6).

3   Remove all dirt and foreign material from around the wheel cylinder.

4   Disconnect the brake line (see illustration). Don't pull the brake line away from the wheel cylinder.

5   Remove the wheel cylinder mounting bolts.

6   Detach the wheel cylinder from the brake backing plate and immediately plug the brake line to prevent fluid loss and contamination.

INSTALLATION

7   Apply a small amount of RTV sealant between the backing plate and wheel cylinder, then place the wheel cylinder in position and install the bolts finger tight. Connect the brake line to the cylinder, being careful not to cross thread the fitting. Tighten the wheel cylinder mounting bolts to the torque listed in this Chapter's Specifications. Now tighten the brake line fitting securely.

8   Install the brake shoe assembly (see Section 6).

9   Bleed the brakes (see Section 11).

10 Check the operation of the brakes carefully before driving the vehicle.

8 Master cylinder - removal and installation

❋❋ CAUTION:

Brake fluid will quickly damage paint. Cover all body parts and be careful not to spill fluid during any of the following procedures. Wipe up any spilled fluid immediately and then flush the area thoroughly with water.

REMOVAL

▶ **Refer to illustration 8.6**

1 The master cylinder is located in the engine compartment, mounted to the power brake booster.

2 With the engine off, pump the brake pedal several times to relieve the vacuum reserve inside the power brake booster.

➡**Note: This step will prevent contaminants from being sucked into the power brake booster when the cylinder is removed.**

3 Remove the battery (see Chapter 5).

4 Using a syringe or equivalent, siphon the brake fluid from the master cylinder reservoir and dispose of it properly.

5 Place rags under the fluid fittings and prepare caps or plastic bags to cover the ends of the lines once they are disconnected.

6 Loosen the fittings at the ends of the brake lines where they enter the master cylinder (see illustration). To prevent rounding off the corners on these nuts, the use of a flare-nut wrench, which wraps around the nut, is preferred. Pull the brake lines slightly away from the master cylinder and quickly plug the ends to prevent contamination.

7 Thoroughly clean the area where the master cylinder mounts to the power booster. Remove the nuts attaching the master cylinder to the power booster (see illustration 8.6). Pull the master cylinder off the studs and out of the engine compartment. Again, be careful not to spill any fluid as this is done.

8 If necessary, remove the roll pins from the old reservoir and transfer it to the new master cylinder (see illustration 8.6).

➡**Note: Be sure to install new seals between the master cylinder and reservoir.**

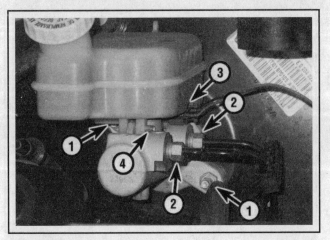

8.6 Master cylinder details:

1	*Mounting nut*	*4*	*Reservoir roll-pin fastener*
2	*Brake line fitting*		*(one hidden in this photo)*
3	*Level sensor connector*		

INSTALLATION

▶ **Refer to illustration 8.10**

9 Bench bleed the new master cylinder before installing it. Mount the master cylinder in a vise, with the jaws of the vise clamping on the mounting flange.

10 Attach a pair of master cylinder bleeder tubes to the outlet ports of the master cylinder (see illustration).

11 Fill the reservoir with brake fluid of the recommended type (see Chapter 1).

12 Slowly push the pistons into the master cylinder (a large Phillips screwdriver can be used for this) - air will be expelled from the pressure chambers and into the reservoir. Because the tubes are submerged in fluid, air can't be drawn back into the master cylinder when you release the pistons.

13 Repeat the procedure until no more air bubbles are present.

14 Remove the bleed tubes, one at a time, and install plugs in the open ports to prevent fluid leakage and air from entering. Install the reservoir cap.

15 Install a new vacuum seal onto the master cylinder where it mates with the power booster.

❋❋ WARNING:

Do not skip this step or a vacuum leak could occur and render the power booster ineffective; this results in greatly increased pedal effort and longer stopping distances.

16 Install the master cylinder over the studs on the power brake booster and tighten the attaching nuts only finger tight at this time.

17 Carefully thread the brake line fittings into the master cylinder. Since the master cylinder is still a bit loose, it can be moved slightly in order for the fittings to thread in easily. Do not strip the threads as the fittings are tightened.

18 Fully tighten the mounting nuts, and then the brake line fittings. Tighten the nuts to the torque listed in this Chapter's Specifications.

19 Fill the master cylinder reservoir with fluid, then bleed the master cylinder and the brake system as described in Section 11. To bleed the

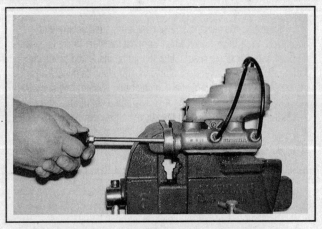

8.10 The best way to bleed air from the master cylinder before installing it on the vehicle is with a pair of bleeder tubes that direct brake fluid into the reservoir during bleeding

cylinder on the vehicle, have an assistant depress the brake pedal and hold the pedal to the floor. Loosen the fitting to allow air and fluid to escape. Repeat this procedure on both fittings until the fluid is clear of air bubbles.

✳✳ CAUTION:

Have plenty of rags on hand to catch the fluid - brake fluid will ruin painted surfaces. After the bleeding procedure is completed, rinse the area under the master cylinder thoroughly with clean water.

20 Test the operation of the brake system carefully before placing the vehicle into normal service.

✳✳ WARNING:

Do not operate the vehicle if you are in doubt about the effectiveness of the brake system. It is possible for air to become trapped in the anti-lock brake system hydraulic control unit, so, if the pedal continues to feel spongy after repeated bleedings or the BRAKE or ANTI-LOCK light stays on, have the vehicle towed to a dealer service department or other qualified shop to be bled with the aid of a scan tool.

9 Proportioning valves - check and replacement

➡Note: Models that are equipped with anti-lock brakes (ABS) do not have proportioning valves.

DESCRIPTION

1 There are two proportioning valves (in a single assembly) that balance front-to-rear braking by controlling the increase in rear system hydraulic pressure above a preset level. Under light pedal pressure, the valve allows full hydraulic pressure to the front and rear brakes. But above a certain pressure - known as the "split point" - the proportioning valve reduces the amount of pressure increase to the rear brakes in accordance with a predetermined ratio. This reduces the chance of rear wheel lock-up and skidding.

CHECK

2 If either rear wheel skids prematurely under hard braking, it could indicate a defective proportioning valve. If this occurs, have the system checked out by your local dealer service department or other qualified repair shop. A pair of special pressure gauges and adapter fittings are required for proper diagnosis of the proportioning valves. While diagnosis is beyond the scope of the home mechanic, you may still save money by replacing the valves yourself.

REPLACEMENT

3 Raise the rear of the vehicle and support it securely on jackstands.
4 Block the front wheels to prevent the vehicle from rolling.
5 Locate the valve assembly above the rear axle attached to the left side of the frame rail.

➡Note: There is a long rod attached to a bracket mounted to the axle that is part of the valve assembly.

6 Loosen the brake lines from the proportioning valve with a flare-nut wrench to prevent rounding off the corners of the fittings. Plug the ends of the lines to prevent loss of brake fluid and the entry of dirt.
7 Remove the mounting bolts and detach the valve and bracket.
8 Installation is the reverse of removal.
9 Bleed the brakes (see Section 11). Carefully test brake operation before resuming normal operation.

10 Brake hoses and lines - inspection and replacement

BRAKE HOSE INSPECTION

1 Whenever the vehicle is raised and supported securely on jackstands, the rubber hoses which connect the steel brake lines with the front and rear brake assemblies should be inspected for cracks, chafing of the outer cover, leaks, blisters and other damage. These are important and vulnerable parts of the brake system and inspection should be thorough. A light and mirror will be helpful for a complete check. If a hose exhibits any of the above conditions, replace it immediately.

FLEXIBLE HOSE REPLACEMENT

▸ Refer to illustration 10.3

2 Clean all dirt away from the hose and line fittings.
3 Using a flare-nut wrench, disconnect the metal brake line from the hose fitting and immediately plug the metal line to prevent excessive leakage and contamination (see illustration). Be careful not to bend the metal line. If the threaded fitting is corroded, spray it with a pen-

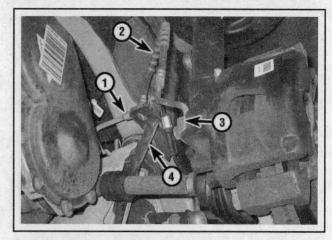

10.3 Front brake hose/line details:

1 Brake line fitting	4 Brake hose bracket
2 Flexible brake hose	(integral with flexible
3 Brake line fitting at caliper	brake hose)

etrating oil and allow it to soak in for about 10 minutes, then try again. If you try to break loose a brake tube nut that's stuck, you will kink the metal line, which will then have to be replaced.

4   Remove the brake hose bracket/fitting assembly by removing the bracket's mounting bolt.

5   On the front brake hose(s), unscrew the banjo bolt at the caliper and remove the hose, discarding the sealing washers on either side of the fitting.

6   Attach the new brake hose to the caliper.

➡Note: **When replacing the brake hoses, always use new sealing washers.**

7   Tighten the banjo bolt to the torque listed this Chapter's Specifications.

8   Attach the brake hose bracket/fitting assembly to the vehicle making sure the hose isn't kinked or twisted. Then connect the metal line to the hose fitting, tightening the hose bracket and brake line fitting securely.

9   Carefully check to make sure the suspension or steering components don't make contact with the hose. Have an assistant push down on the vehicle while you watch to see whether the hose interferes with suspension operation. If you're replacing a front hose, have your assis-

tant turn the steering wheel lock-to-lock while you make sure the hose doesn't interfere with the steering linkage or the steering knuckle.

10   After installation, check the master cylinder fluid level and add fluid as necessary. Bleed the brakes (see Section 11). Carefully test brake operation before resuming normal operation.

METAL BRAKE LINE REPLACEMENT

11   When replacing brake lines, be sure to use the correct parts. Do not use copper tubing for any brake system components. Purchase steel brake lines from a dealer parts department or auto parts store.

12   Prefabricated brake lines, with the tube ends already flared and fittings installed, are available at auto parts stores and dealer parts departments. These lines can be bent to the proper shapes using a tubing bender.

13   When installing the new line make sure it's well supported in the brackets and has plenty of clearance between moving or hot components. Make sure you tighten the fittings securely.

14   After installation, check the master cylinder fluid level and add fluid as necessary. Bleed the brakes (see Section 11). Carefully test brake operation before resuming normal operation.

---

11   Brake system - bleeding

▶ **Refer to illustration 11.8**

※※ WARNING 1:

The following procedure is a manual bleeding procedure. This is the only bleeding procedure which can be performed at home without special tools. However, if air has found its way into the hydraulic control unit, the entire system must be bled manually, then with a DRB scan tool (or equivalent), then manually a second time. If the brake pedal feels "spongy" even after bleeding the brakes, or the ABS light on the instrument panel does not go off, or if you have any doubts whatsoever about the effectiveness of the brake system, have the vehicle towed to a dealer service department or other repair shop equipped with the necessary tools for bleeding the system.

※※ WARNING 2:

Wear eye protection when bleeding the brake system. If the fluid comes in contact with your eyes, immediately rinse them with water and seek medical attention.

➡Note: **Bleeding the hydraulic system is necessary to remove any air that manages to find its way into the system when it's been opened during removal and installation of a hydraulic component.**

1   It will be necessary to bleed the complete system if air has entered the system due to low fluid level, or if the brake lines have been disconnected at the master cylinder.

2   If a brake line was disconnected only at a wheel, then only that caliper or wheel cylinder must be bled.

3   If a brake line is disconnected at a fitting located between the master cylinder and any of the brakes, that part of the system served by the disconnected line must be bled. The following procedure describes bleeding the entire system, however.

4   Remove any residual vacuum from the brake power booster by applying the brake several times with the engine off.

5   Remove the cap from the master cylinder reservoir and fill the reservoir with brake fluid. Reinstall the cap.

➡Note: **Check the fluid level often during the bleeding operation and add fluid as necessary to prevent the fluid level from falling low enough to allow air bubbles into the master cylinder.**

6   Have an assistant on hand, as well as a supply of new brake fluid, a clear container partially filled with clean brake fluid, a length of clear tubing to fit over the bleeder valve and a wrench to open and close the bleeder valve.

7   Begin the bleeding process by bleeding the first wheel in the bleeding sequence, loosen the bleeder valve slightly, then tighten it to a point where it is snug but can still be loosened quickly and easily. The bleeding sequence is as follows:

> *Left rear*
> *Right front*
> *Right rear*
> *Left front*

8   Place one end of the hose over the bleeder valve and submerge the other end in brake fluid in the container (see illustration).

9   Have the assistant push the brake pedal slowly to the floor, then hold the pedal firmly depressed.

10   While the pedal is held depressed, open the bleeder valve just enough to allow a flow of fluid to leave the valve. Watch for air bubbles

to exit the submerged end of the tube. When the fluid flow slows after a couple of seconds, close the valve and have your assistant release the pedal.

11 Repeat Steps 9 and 10 until no more air is seen leaving the tube, then tighten the bleeder valve and proceed to bleed the other calipers/ wheel cylinders, in the proper sequence, using the same procedure. Be sure to check the fluid in the master cylinder reservoir frequently.

➡**Note: Be careful not to over-tighten the bleeder valve.**

12 Never use old brake fluid. It contains moisture which can boil, rendering the brakes inoperative.

13 Refill the master cylinder with fluid at the end of the operation.

14 Check the operation of the brakes. The pedal should feel solid when depressed, with no sponginess. If necessary, repeat the entire process.

❋❋❋ **WARNING:**

If, after bleeding the system you do not have a firm brake pedal, or if the ABS light on the instrument panel does not go off, or if you have any doubts whatsoever about the effectiveness of the brake system, have it towed to a dealer service department or other repair shop to have the system bled.

11.8 When bleeding the brakes, a hose is connected to the bleed screw at the caliper or wheel cylinder and then submerged in clean brake fluid - air will be seen as bubbles exiting the tube (all air must be expelled before moving to the next wheel)

12 Power brake booster - check, removal and installation

OPERATING CHECK

1 Depress the pedal and start the engine. If the pedal goes down slightly, operation is normal.

2 Depress the brake pedal several times with the engine running and make sure that there is no change in the pedal reserve distance.

AIRTIGHTNESS CHECK

3 Start the engine and turn it off after one or two minutes. Depress the brake pedal several times slowly. If the pedal goes down farther the first time but gradually rises after the second or third depression, the booster is airtight.

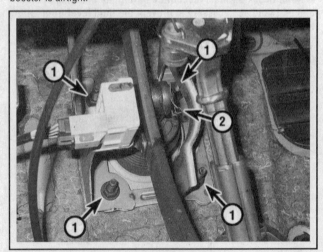

12.13 Power brake booster mounting details:

1   Mounting nuts
2   Pushrod-to-brake pedal retaining clip (DO NOT reuse)

4 Depress the brake pedal while the engine is running, then stop the engine with the pedal depressed. If there is no change in the pedal reserve travel after holding the pedal for 30 seconds, the booster is airtight.

REMOVAL

▸ **Refer to illustration 12.13**

5 The power brake booster unit requires no special maintenance apart from periodic inspection of the vacuum hoses and the case. The booster should never be disassembled. If a problem develops, it must be replaced with a new one.

6 Remove any vacuum from the booster by pumping the pedal several times with the engine off, until the pedal feels hard to push.

7 Remove the battery and battery tray (see Chapter 5). If equipped, detach the bracket for the cruse control servo unit from the left motor mount bracket and move it aside (disconnect the electrical connector and vacuum hose to the servo if necessary).

8 Remove the wiper motor and linkage assembly (see Chapter 12).

9 Clean the area where the master cylinder attaches to the power brake booster.

10 Detach the master cylinder from the brake booster and carefully move it aside while keeping it supported (see Section 8).

➡**Note: It is not necessary to disconnect the brake lines from the master cylinder when detaching it from the brake booster. Be careful not to kink or damage the brake lines when placing it aside.**

11 Disconnect the vacuum hose from the check valve that's located on the outside of the brake booster.

❋❋❋ **WARNING:**

Do not remove the check valve from the booster.

12 Remove the knee bolster from the instrument panel on the drivers side (see Chapter 11).

13 Working under the dash, disconnect the brake pedal pushrod from the top of the brake pedal by prying off the retaining clip (see illustration). For safety reasons, discard the old pushrod retaining clip and buy a new clip for reassembly.

14 Remove the nuts attaching the booster to the firewall (see illustration 12.13).

15 Working inside the engine compartment, carefully withdraw the brake booster unit from the firewall and out of the engine compartment.

INSTALLATION

16 To install the booster, place it into position on the firewall and then tighten the retaining nuts to the torque listed in this Chapter's Specifications. Connect the brake pedal to the brake booster pushrod using a new retainer clip.

❋❋ WARNING:

DO NOT reuse the old booster pushrod retaining clip.

17 The remaining installation steps are the reverse of removal. Be sure to install a new vacuum seal on the master cylinder before reinstalling it to the power brake booster.

18 Carefully test the operation of the brakes before placing the vehicle in normal operation.

13 Parking brake shoes (models with rear disc brakes) - replacement

▶ Refer to illustrations 13.5a through 13.5s

❋❋ WARNING:

Parking brake shoes must be replaced on both wheels at the same time - never replace the shoes on only one wheel. Also, the dust created by the brake system is harmful to your health. Never blow it out with compressed air and don't inhale any of it. An approved filtering mask should be worn when working on the brakes. Do not, under any circumstances, use petroleum-based solvents to clean brake parts. Use brake system cleaner only!

1 Loosen the rear wheel lug nuts, raise the rear of the vehicle and support it securely on jackstands. Block the front wheels and remove the rear wheels. Release the parking brake.

2 Remove the rear calipers (see Section 4). Support the caliper assemblies with a coat hanger or heavy wire and don't disconnect the brake line from the caliper.

3 Remove the rear discs (see Section 5). Remove the rear hub and bearing assemblies (see Chapter 10).

4 Clean the parking brake assembly with brake system cleaner.

5 Follow the accompanying sequence of photos to replace the parking brake shoes (see illustrations). Be sure to stay in order and read the caption under each illustration.

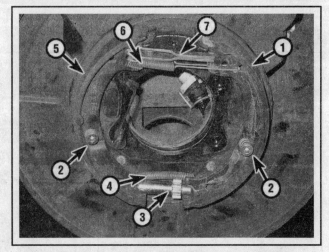

13.5a Parking brake details (right side)

1	Leading shoe	5	Trailing shoe
2	Hold-down spring and pin	6	Upper return spring
3	Adjuster screw assembly	7	Parking brake actuator
4	Lower return spring		lever

13.5b Use a cable tie (or equivalent) to hold the brake backing plate in place

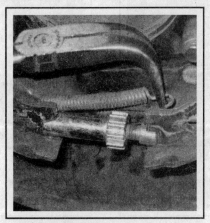

13.5c Remove the lower return spring

13.5d Remove the hold-down spring and pin from the leading shoe

13.5e Pull the leading shoe back and remove the adjuster screw assembly (note how it's installed; it must be reinstalled the same way)

13.5f Unhook the outboard upper return spring . . .

6   Inspect the drum surface inside the disc for score marks, deep grooves, hard spots (which appear as small, discolored areas) and

cracks. If the disc/drum is worn, scored or out of round, it will have to be resurfaced by an automotive machine shop, or replaced.
7   Install the hub and bearing assemblies (see Chapter 10).
8   Install the disc/drum over the shoes. Using a screwdriver, turn

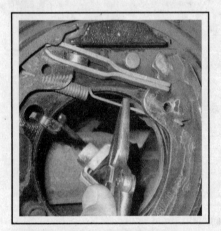

13.5g . . . then unhook the inboard upper return spring and remove the leading shoe

13.5h Remove the hold-down spring and pin from the trailing shoe . . .

13.5i . . . and remove the trailing shoe

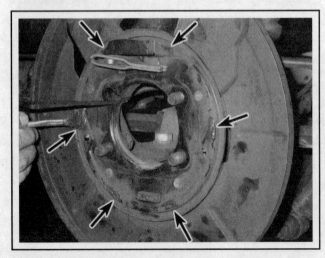

13.5j Clean the backing plate, then apply a thin coat of high-temperature grease to the shoe contact points on the backing plate

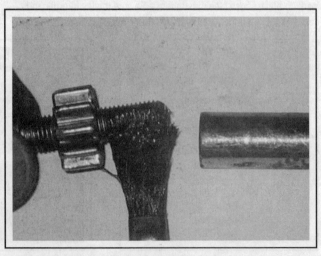

13.5k Clean and lubricate the threads of the adjuster screw assembly

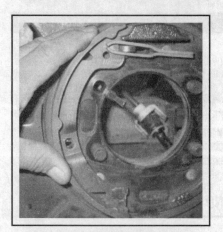

13.5l Mount the trailing shoe on the backing plate, making sure the notch in the shoe engages with the actuator lever . . .

13.5m . . . and secure the shoe with the hold-down spring and pin

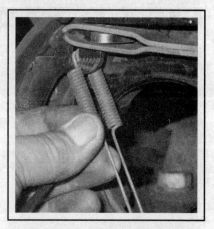

13.5n Connect the upper return springs to the top of the trailing shoe . . .

the star wheel on the parking brake shoe adjuster until the shoes slightly drag as the disc is turned, then back-off the adjuster until the shoes don't drag.

➡**Note: Access to the star wheel is through a plugged port on the brake backing plate. Remove the rubber plug near the bottom and backside of the backing plate.**

9   Install the caliper (see Section 4).

10   Repeat this sequence on the parking brake shoes for the other rear wheel.

13.5o . . . and to the top of the leading shoe

13.5p Place the leading shoe in position . . .

13.5q . . . and secure the shoe with the hold-down spring and pin

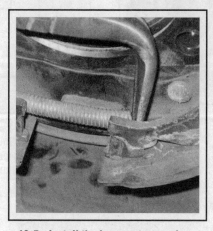

13.5r Install the lower return spring

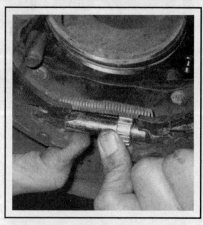

13.5s Spread the shoes apart and install the adjuster screw assembly

14 Brake light switch - check, replacement and adjustment

▶ Refer to illustration 14.1

1   The brake light switch is located along the arm of the brake pedal and is attached to a bracket near the brake power booster mount (see illustration). When the brake pedal is applied, the pedal arm moves away from the switch and a spring-loaded plunger closes the circuit to the brake lights.

2   Models equipped with cruise control use a dual-purpose brake light switch that also deactivates the cruise control system when the brake pedal is depressed.

CHECK

▶ Refer to illustration 14.5

❄❄ CAUTION:

This switch can only be adjusted once and this occurs when the switch is installed. Do not move the small lever on the switch or remove the switch unless you intend on replacing it. Once the switch is removed, it cannot be reused.

3   Check the brake light fuse (see Chapter 12). If the fuse has blown, replace it. If it blows again, look for a short in the brake light circuit.

4   If the fuse is okay, use a test light or voltmeter to verify that there's voltage to the switch. If there's no voltage to the switch, look for an open or short in the power wire to the switch. Repair as necessary.

5   If the brake lights still don't come on when the brake pedal is applied, unplug the electrical connector from the brake light switch and, using an ohmmeter, verify that there is continuity between the switch terminals when the brake pedal is applied, i.e. when the switch is closed. If continuity is not detected, replace the switch (see illustration).

6   If there is continuity between the switch terminals when the brake is applied (it closes the circuit), but the brake lights don't come on when the brake pedal is applied, check for power to the brake light bulb sockets when the pedal is depressed. If voltage is present, replace the bulbs (it isn't very likely that all of them would fail simultaneously, but it is possible that they could be burned out). If voltage is not available, check the wiring between the switch and the brake lights for an open circuit and repair as necessary.

REPLACEMENT AND ADJUSTMENT

7   Disconnect the cable from the negative battery terminal (see Chapter 5, Section 1).

8   Depress and hold the brake pedal, then rotate the brake light switch about 30-degrees in a counterclockwise direction and remove it from the mounting bracket.

9   Unplug the electrical connector from the switch, remove the switch from the vehicle and discard it.

10   Pull the plunger out on the new switch, depress the brake pedal and install the switch into the bracket by aligning the slots, inserting the switch and rotating it about 30-degrees clockwise.

❄❄ CAUTION:

Do not move the small lever on the switch before it is fully installed.

11   Release the brake pedal and gently pull it back to make certain that it is seated against the pedal striker. The switch plunger will ratchet backward to the correct position.

12   Plug the electrical connector into the switch.

13   Move the small lever on the switch to the horizontal position (see illustration 14.1).

14   Reconnect the battery and then test the brake lights for proper operation.

14.1 Brake light switch details:

1   *Electrical connector*
2   *Locking tab for electrical connector*
3   *Brake light switch*
4   *Adjustment lever (used only once during installation)*

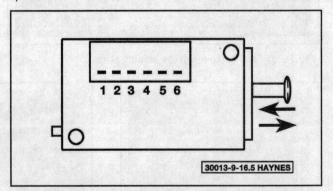

30013-9-16.5 HAYNES

14.5 With the switch closed (plunger extended fully), there should be continuity between terminals 1 and 2 and no continuity between terminals 3 and 4 or 5 and 6. With the switch open (plunger compressed), the opposite should occur

Specifications

General

Brake fluid type	See Chapter 1

Disc brakes

Brake pad minimum thickness	See Chapter 1
Disc lateral runout limit	0.005 inch
Disc minimum thickness	Cast into disc
Thickness variation (parallelism)	0.0005 inch

Drum brakes

Minimum brake lining thickness	See Chapter 1
Maximum drum diameter	Cast into drum

Torque specifications   Ft-lbs (unless otherwise indicated)

Brake booster mounting nuts	250 in-lbs
Brake hose banjo bolt-to-caliper	35
Caliper guide pins or guide pin bolts	26
Caliper mounting bracket bolts	125
Master cylinder-to-brake booster mounting nuts	225 in-lbs
Wheel cylinder-to-backing plate mounting nuts	75 in-lbs
Wheel speed sensor bolt	115 in-lbs
Wheel lug nuts	See Chapter 1

Notes

Section

Reference to other Chapters

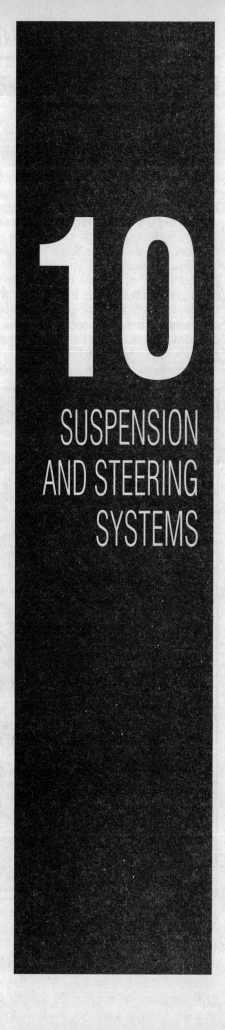

10

SUSPENSION AND STEERING SYSTEMS

1 General information

♦ **Refer to illustrations 1.1 and 1.2**

The front suspension (see illustration) on these vehicles is a MacPherson strut design. The upper end of each strut is attached to the vehicle's body strut support. The lower end of the strut is connected to the upper end of the steering knuckle. The steering knuckle is attached by a balljoint mounted to the outer end of the suspension control arm. The control arm is held longitudinally by the front suspension subframe/cradle. A stabilizer bar, mounted to the subframe/cradle and connected to the strut, reduces body roll while cornering.

The rear suspension (see illustration) on these vehicles is composed of leaf springs and a tube axle housing mounted in isolator bushings on axle mount brackets. The leaf springs are a mono-leaf design. Side-to-side axle movement is controlled by a rear track bar attached to the top of the axle housing and the frame. Further stability is provided by the rear stabilizer bar attached to the rear axle tube, and the rear frame rails through rubber bushings.

The power-assisted rack-and-pinion steering gear is attached to the front suspension subframe/cradle. The steering gear actuates the tie-rods, which are attached to the steering knuckles. The steering column is designed to collapse in the event of an accident.

Frequently, when working on the suspension or steering system components, you may come across fasteners that seem impossible to loosen. These fasteners on the underside of the vehicle are continually subjected to water, road grime, mud, etc., and can become rusted or "frozen," making them extremely difficult to remove. In order to unscrew these stubborn fasteners without damaging them (or other components), be sure to use lots of penetrating oil and allow it to soak in for a while. Using a wire brush to clean exposed threads will also ease removal of the nut or bolt and prevent damage to the threads. Sometimes a sharp blow with a hammer and punch will break the bond between a nut and bolt threads, but care must be taken to prevent the punch from slipping off the fastener and ruining the threads. Heating the stuck fastener and surrounding area with a torch sometimes helps too, but isn't recommended because of the obvious dangers associated with fire. Long breaker bars and extension, or "cheater," pipes will

1.1 Front suspension and steering components

1	*Balljoint*	*4*	*Control arm*	*7*	*Subframe/cradle reinforcement plate*
2	*Steering knuckle*	*5*	*Stabilizer bar and bushing retainer*	*8*	*Strut/coil spring assembly*
3	*Tie-rod end*	*6*	*Steering gear*	*9*	*Brake caliper*

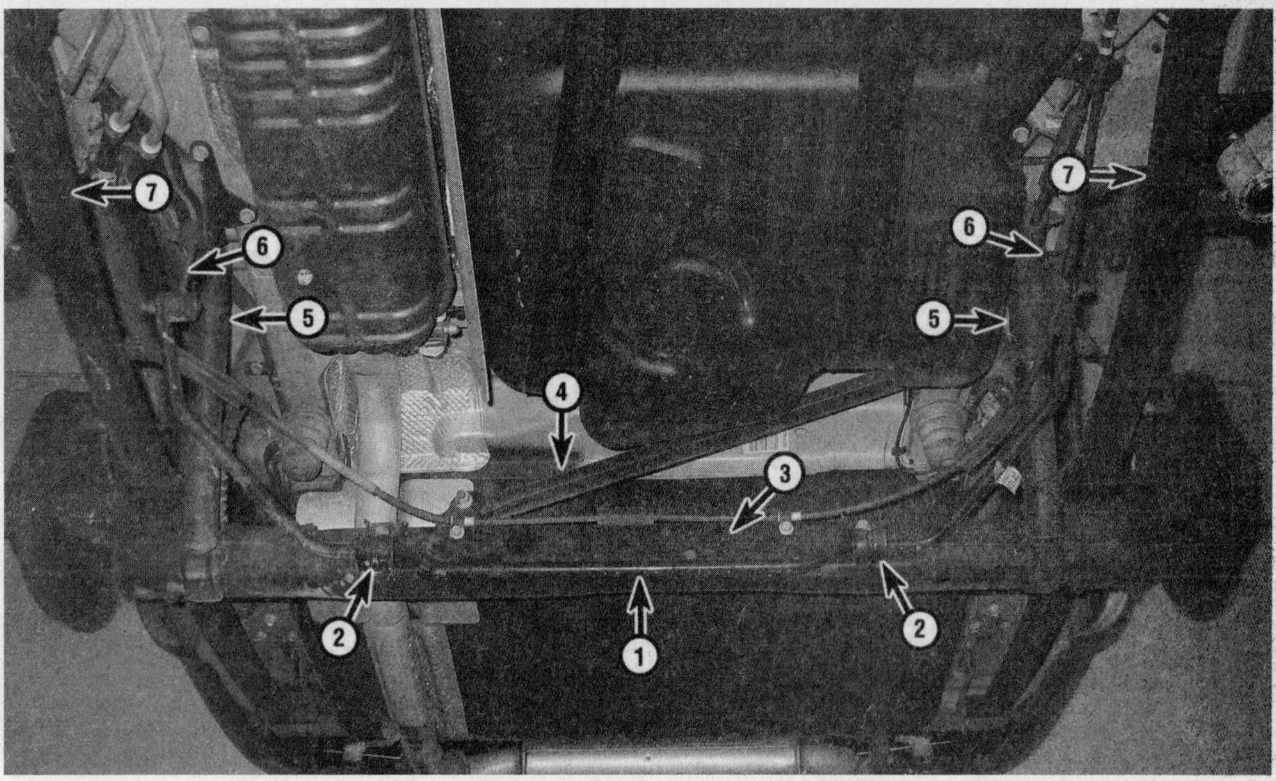

1.2 Rear suspension components

1	Stabilizer bar	4	Track bar	6	Stabilizer bar link
2	Stabilizer bar bushing retainer	5	Shock absorber	7	Leaf spring
3	Axle assembly				

increase leverage, but never use an extension pipe on a ratchet - the ratcheting mechanism could be damaged. Sometimes tightening the nut or bolt first will help to break it loose. Fasteners that require drastic measures to remove should always be replaced with new ones.

Since most of the procedures dealt with in this Chapter involve jacking up the vehicle and working underneath it, a good pair of jackstands will be needed. A hydraulic floor jack is the preferred type of jack to lift the vehicle, and it can also be used to support certain components during various operations.

❈❈ WARNING:

Never, under any circumstances, rely on a jack to support the vehicle while working on it. Whenever any of the suspension or steering fasteners are loosened or removed they must be inspected and, if necessary, replaced with new ones of the same part number or of original equipment quality and design. Torque specifications must be followed for proper reassembly and component retention. Never attempt to heat or straighten any suspension or steering components. Instead, replace any bent or damaged part with a new one.

2 Stabilizer bar and bushings (front) - removal and installation

REMOVAL

▶ **Refer to illustrations 2.3 and 2.4**

1   Loosen the front wheel lug nuts, raise the front of the vehicle and support it securely on jackstands. Apply the parking brake and block the rear wheels to keep the vehicle from rolling off the stands. Remove the front wheels.

2   Remove the subframe/cradle reinforcement plate (see Section 16).

➡**Note: There is no need to remove the subframe/cradle if you are just replacing the stabilizer bar bushings or links.**

3   Remove the stabilizer bar link nuts to detach the link from the stabilizer bar (see illustration).

➡**Note: Hold the stud on the link with a Torx bit so that it does not rotate when removing the nut. The link can be detached from the stabilizer bar and the strut assembly entirely if replacement is necessary.**

4   Remove the stabilizer bar bushing retainers from the subframe/cradle (see illustration).

➡**Note: Be sure to note how the bushing sits in the retainer and where the bushing is slit for removal and installation.**

5   Remove the stabilizer bar and bushings from the vehicle.

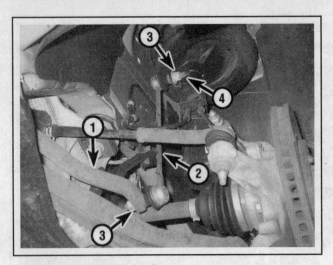

2.3 Stabilizer bar link details

1	Stabilizer bar	3	Link nut
2	Stabilizer bar link	4	Link stud

2.4 Stabilizer bar bushing and retainer

INSTALLATION

6 Install the stabilizer bar, bushings and bushing retainers onto the subframe/cradle but do not tighten them yet.

7 Center the stabilizer bar on the subframe/cradle. Attach the bar

links to the stabilizer bar and tighten the link nuts to the torque listed in this Chapter's Specifications.

8 Tighten the bushing retainer nuts to the torque listed in this Chapter's Specifications.

9 Install the subframe/cradle reinforcement plate (see Section 16).

10 Install the wheels and lug nuts. Lower the vehicle and tighten the wheel lug nuts to the torque listed in the Chapter 1 Specifications.

3 Strut assembly (front) - removal, inspection and installation

REMOVAL

▸ **Refer to illustrations 3.4 and 3.6**

✳✳ WARNING:

Always replace the struts and/or coil springs in pairs - never replace just one strut or one coil spring; this could cause dangerous handling peculiarities.

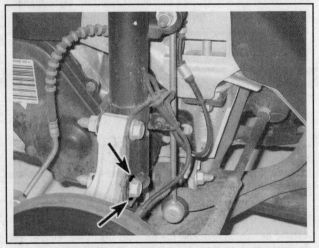

3.4 The lower mounting bolt and strut bracket marked before removing the bolts

➡**Note: If both strut assemblies are going to be removed, mark the assemblies Right and Left so they will be reinstalled on the correct side.**

1 Loosen the wheel lug nuts, raise the vehicle and support it securely on jackstands. Remove the wheels.

2 On models equipped with ABS, detach the speed sensor wiring harness from the strut (see Chapter 9).

3 Disconnect the stabilizer bar link from the strut assembly (see Section 2).

4 Mark the position of the strut to the steering knuckle (see illustration).

➡**Note: This is only necessary if special camber adjusting bolts have been installed in place of the regular strut-to-knuckle bolts.**

✳✳ CAUTION:

The bolts are serrated and must not be turned. Hold the bolts with a wrench and then remove the strut-to-knuckle nuts. Knock the bolts out with a hammer and punch, but note their direction because they are installed differently for each side of the vehicle.

5 Separate the strut from the steering knuckle. Be careful not to overextend the inner CV joint. Also, don't let the steering knuckle fall outward and strain the brake hose.

6 Secure the steering knuckle safely aside, have an assistant support the strut and spring assembly, then remove the three strut-to-body nuts (see illustration). Remove the assembly from the fenderwell.

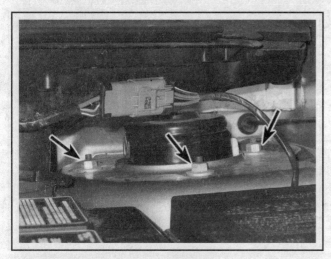

3.6 Strut assembly upper mounting nuts

INSPECTION

7   Check the strut body for leaking fluid, dents, cracks and other obvious damage which would warrant repair or replacement.

8   Check the coil spring for chips or cracks in the spring coating (this will cause premature spring failure due to corrosion). Inspect the spring seat for cuts, hardness and general deterioration.

9   If any undesirable conditions exist, proceed to the strut disassembly procedure (see Section 4).

INSTALLATION

10   Guide the strut assembly up into the fenderwell and insert the upper mounting studs through the holes in the body. Once the studs protrude, install the nuts so the strut won't fall back through. This is most easily accomplished with the help of an assistant, as the strut is quite heavy and awkward.

11   Tighten the upper mounting nuts to the torque listed in this Chapter's Specifications.

12   Slide the steering knuckle into the strut flange and insert the two bolts. Install the nuts, align the previously made matchmarks (if applicable) and tighten them to the torque listed in this Chapter's Specifications.

➥**Note: Make certain that the bolts are installed in their original direction; the direction is different for each side of the vehicle.**

13   If the vehicle is equipped with ABS, install the speed sensor wiring harness bracket.

14   Connect the stabilizer bar link to the strut. Tighten the nut to the torque listed in this Chapter's Specifications.

15   Install the wheel and lug nuts, then lower the vehicle and tighten the lug nuts to the torque listed in the Chapter 1 Specifications.

16   Drive the vehicle to an alignment shop to have the front end alignment checked, and if necessary, adjusted.

4   Strut/coil spring - replacement

❊❊ **WARNING:**

Struts and/or coil springs must be replaced in pairs - never replace just one of them.

➥**Note: You'll need a spring compressor for this procedure. Spring compressors are available on a daily rental basis at most auto parts stores or equipment rental yards.**

1   If the struts or coil springs exhibit the telltale signs of wear

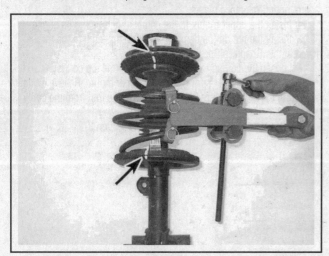

4.3 The strut assembly is carefully clamped in a vise with necessary components marked for disassembly and with a spring compressor installed

(leaking fluid, loss of damping capability, chipped, sagging or cracked coil springs) explore all options before beginning any work. The strut body is not serviceable and must be replaced if a problem develops. However, complete strut assemblies (with springs) may be available on an exchange basis; which eliminates much time and work. Whichever route you choose to take, check on the cost and availability of parts before disassembling your vehicle.

❊❊ **WARNING:**

Disassembling a strut assembly is potentially dangerous and utmost attention must be directed to the job, or serious injury may result. Use only a high-quality spring compressor and carefully follow the manufacturer's instructions furnished with the tool. After removing the coil spring from the strut, set it aside in a safe, isolated area.

DISASSEMBLY

▶ **Refer to illustrations 4.3, 4.5 and 4.6**

2   Remove the strut and spring assembly (see Section 3).

3   Mount the strut clevis bracket portion of the strut assembly in a vise and mark the components for reassembly (see illustration).

❊❊ **CAUTION:**

Do not clamp any other portion of the strut assembly in the vise; it will be damaged. Line the vise jaws with wood or rags to prevent damage to the unit and don't tighten the vise excessively.

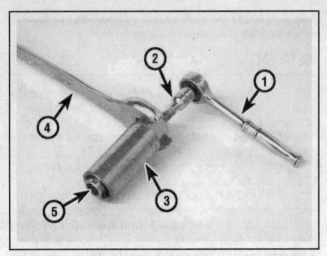

4.5 Here's the setup that can be used to unscrew the damper shaft nut

1	1/4-inch drive ratchet	4	Wrench to turn socket
2	Extension	5	10 mm socket (to hold
3	13/16-inch spark plug		damper shaft)
	socket		

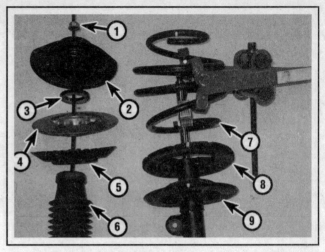

4.6 Front strut/coil assembly details

1	Nut	6	Dust boot (rubber bumper
2	Upper mount		underneath - hidden by
3	Pivot bearing		dust boot)
4	Upper spring seat	7	Coil spring (with spring
5	Upper spring isolator		compressor)
		8	Lower spring isolator
		9	Damper unit

4 Following the tool manufacturer's instructions, install the spring compressor on the spring and compress it sufficiently to relieve all pressure from the upper mount (see illustration 4.3). This can be verified by wiggling the spring.

5 While holding the damper shaft from turning, loosen the shaft nut with a socket. A special tool is available to do this, but a substitute can be made from a 13/16-inch spark plug socket (with a hex surface at the top), a ratchet, a 1/4-inch drive extension inserted through the hole in the spark plug socket, and a 10 mm socket attached to the extension (see illustration).

6 Remove the nut and upper mount (see illustration). Inspect the pivot bearing for smooth operation. If it doesn't turn smoothly, replace it. Remove the upper spring seat and check the upper spring isolator for cracking and general deterioration. Replace any parts that are damaged or worn.

7 Carefully lift the compressed spring from the assembly.

✳✳ WARNING:

When removing the compressed spring, lift it off very carefully and set it in a safe place. Keep the ends of the spring away from your body.

8 Remove the dust boot from the damper shaft.

9 Slide the rubber bumper off the damper shaft. Check the lower spring isolator for cracking and hardness; replace it if necessary (see illustration 4.6).

REASSEMBLY

10 Extend the damper rod to its full length and install the rubber bumper.

11 Install the dust boot onto the damper.

12 Carefully place the coil spring onto the damper. Align the coil spring on the damper using the reference marks made during disassembly. If a new spring or strut damper unit is being installed, use the marks on the old component to help you orient the spring properly.

13 Install the upper spring isolator and seat onto the damper shaft, again, noting reference marks.

14 Install the upper mount to the damper shaft noting its alignment.

15 Install the nut on the damper shaft and tighten it to the torque listed in this Chapter's Specifications.

16 Loosen the coil spring compressor until the top coil is properly seated against the upper spring seat and upper mount. Relieve all tension from the spring compressor and remove the tool from the coil spring.

17 Install the strut/spring assembly (see Section 3).

5 Control arm - removal, inspection, and installation

REMOVAL

♦ **Refer to illustrations 5.4 and 5.5**

➡**Note: New lower control arm pivot bolts will be required for installation.**

1 Loosen the wheel lug nuts, raise the front of the vehicle and support it securely on jackstands. Remove the wheel.

2 Remove the steering knuckle (see Section 8).

3 Remove the subframe/cradle reinforcement plate (see Section 16).

4 If you're removing the right control arm, remove the control arm pivot bolt and discard it and then remove the control arm (see illustration).

5 If you're removing the left control arm, support the left side of the subframe/cradle with a floor jack and loosen (but do not remove) the left subframe/cradle bolt (see illustration). Mark the relationship between the subframe/cradle and chassis and then carefully lower the subframe/cradle enough to remove the left pivot bolt.

➡**Note: The pivot bolt cannot clear the transmission without lowering the subframe/cradle.**

6 Remove the pivot bolt and discard it, then remove the control arm.

INSPECTION

7 Make sure the control arm is straight. If it is bent, replace it. Do not attempt to straighten a bent control arm.

8 Inspect all bushings for cracks, distortion, and tears. If a bushing is torn or worn, take the assembly to an automotive machine shop and have it replaced.

➡**Note: Rear bushings designed with a slit can be removed and replaced easily without having to take the control arm to a machine shop.**

INSTALLATION

9 Position the control arm in the subframe/cradle and install a new pivot bolt but do not tighten the bolt yet.

➡**Note: Make certain that the rear bushing is positioned correctly in the subframe/cradle.**

10 If you're installing the left control arm, raise the subframe/cradle back into position and tighten the bolt to the torque listed in this Chapter's Specifications.

11 Reinstall the subframe/cradle reinforcement plate (see Section 16). Make certain that the rear control arm bushings are seated correctly as the plate is installed.

12 Reinstall the steering knuckle (see Section 16).

13 Place a floor jack under the control arm (as close to the balljoints as possible). Raise the control arm to simulate normal ride height.

14 Tighten the control arm pivot bolt to the torque listed in this Chapter's Specifications.

15 Install the wheel and lug nuts, lower the vehicle and tighten the lug nuts to the torque listed in the Chapter 1 Specifications.

16 Have the front wheel alignment checked and, if necessary, adjusted.

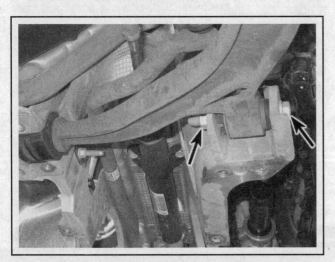

5.4 Remove the pivot bolt and nut that attaches the control arm to the subframe/cradle

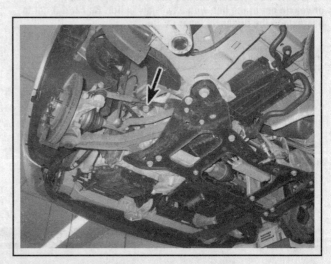

5.5 Location of the left subframe/cradle bolt

6   Balljoints - replacement

The balljoints on these vehicles are not serviceable. If the balljoint is defective, the control arm must be replaced (see Section 5). The balljoint seal can be replaced by prying it off and pressing on a new one using a large deep socket or appropriately sized piece of pipe.

7   Hub and bearing assembly (front) - removal and installation

REMOVAL

▶ **Refer to illustration 7.6**

➡**Note: If the hub/bearing assembly cannot be removed easily and appears frozen in the steering knuckle, it will have to be pressed out of the steering knuckle. If this is the case, remove the steering knuckle (see Section 8) and take it to an automotive machine shop or other repair facility for service.**

1   Loosen the driveaxle/hub nut (see Chapter 8).
2   Loosen the wheel lug nuts, raise the vehicle and support it securely on jackstands and remove the wheel.
3   Remove the brake caliper, the caliper mounting bracket and the brake disc from the hub (see Chapter 9).

➡**Note: Be sure to support the brake caliper as described in Chapter 9.**

4   Remove the driveaxle/hub nut.
5   Remove the hub/bearing assembly mounting bolts from the rear of the steering knuckle (see illustration).
6   Remove the hub/bearing assembly from the steering knuckle.

➡**Note: If the driveaxle splines stick in the hub, push the driveaxle out of the hub with a two-jaw puller. Be careful not to overextend the driveaxle inner CV joint.**

INSTALLATION

7   Make sure that the mounting surface inside the steering knuckle and on the driveaxle splines is smooth and free of burrs and nicks prior to installing the hub/bearing assembly.
8   Lubricate the driveaxle splines with multi-purpose grease. Install the hub/bearing assembly onto the driveaxle and into the steering knuckle until it is seated on the steering knuckle.
9   Install the hub/bearing assembly-to-steering knuckle bolts.

7.6 Remove the hub/bearing mounting bolts (two of the bolts are not visible in this photo)

Tighten the bolts equally in a criss-cross pattern until the hub/bearing assembly is seated securely against the steering knuckle. Tighten the bolts to the torque listed in this Chapter's Specifications.
10   Install the driveaxle/hub nut. Do not tighten the nut yet.
11   Install the brake disc, the caliper mounting bracket and the caliper; tighten the fasteners to the torque values listed in the Chapter 9 Specifications.
12   Install the wheel and lug nuts, remove the jackstands, and lower the vehicle.
13   Tighten the driveaxle/hub nut to the torque listed in the Chapter 8 Specifications.
14   Tighten the lug nuts to the torque listed in the Chapter 1 Specifications.

8   Steering knuckle - removal and installation

➡**Note: The steering knuckle is not a repairable component. It must be replaced if it is bent, broken, or damaged in any way.**

REMOVAL

▶ **Refer to illustration 8.8**

1   Loosen the wheel lug nuts and the driveaxle/hub nut (see Chapter 8), raise the vehicle and support it securely on jackstands.
2   Remove the wheel.
3   Remove the driveaxle/hub nut.

4   Remove the brake disc and, if equipped, the ABS front wheel speed sensor (see Chapter 9).
5   Detach the tie-rod end from the steering knuckle (see Section 18).
6   Remove the two steering knuckle-to-strut bolts - noting their direction (see Section 3).

❋❋ **CAUTION:**

The steering knuckle-to-strut assembly bolts are serrated and must not be turned during removal - turn the nuts only.

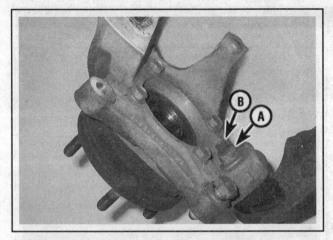

8.8 Remove the balljoint nut (A) from the ballstud (B)

➡**Note: If the strut assembly is attached to the steering knuckle using a cam bolt in the lower slotted hole, mark the relationship of the cam bolt to the strut to preserve the wheel alignment setting on reassembly (see Section 3).**

7 Separate the driveaxle from the steering knuckle and suspend it safely aside (see Chapter 8).

➡**Note: By tilting the steering knuckle, with the balljoint still attached, the driveaxle can be removed.**

✲✲✲ CAUTION:

Do not separate the inner CV joint during this operation. Do not allow the driveshaft to hang by the inner CV joint. If the driveaxle splines stick in the hub, push the driveaxle out with a two-jaw puller.

8 Support the steering knuckle, then remove the nut holding the balljoint to the knuckle (see illustration).
9 Separate the knuckle from the balljoint and then remove it.

➡**Note: The procedure used in Section 18 for separating the tie-rod end from the steering knuckle can be used for separating the balljoint from the steering knuckle (see illustration 18.4b).**

INSTALLATION

10 Installation is the reverse of removal. When connecting the balljoint with the steering knuckle, insert a tool in the end of the ballstud to keep it from turning while tightening the balljoint nut. Be sure to tighten all suspension fasteners to the torque listed in this Chapter's Specifications.
11 Install the wheel, lower the vehicle and tighten the lug nuts to the torque listed in the Chapter 1 Specifications.
12 Have the front end alignment checked and, if necessary, adjusted.

9   Stabilizer bar (rear) - removal and installation

REMOVAL

▸ **Refer to illustrations 9.2 and 9.3**

1 Raise the rear of the vehicle and place it securely on jackstands. Block the front wheels to prevent the vehicle from rolling.
2 Detach the stabilizer bar links from the bar (see illustration).
3 Unbolt the stabilizer bar bushing retainers from the rear axle and remove the stabilizer bar (see illustration).
4 Open the retainers enough to remove them from the bar.
5 Check the bushings for wear, hardness, distortion, cracking and other signs of deterioration, replacing them if necessary. Check the link

bushings for wear also.
6 Clean the areas of the bar where the bushings ride.

INSTALLATION

7 Connect the links to the frame brackets. Do not tighten them yet.
8 Place the bushings and retainers onto the stabilizer bar.
9 Place the bar on the axle and move the bushings and retainers with the slit facing toward the front of the vehicle. Install the retainer bolts but do not tighten them yet.
10 Lower the vehicle so the weight of the vehicle is on the tires. Tighten all bolts to the torque listed in this Chapter's Specifications.

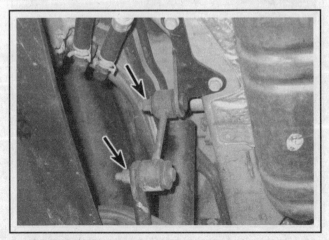

9.2 Stabilizer bar link fasteners

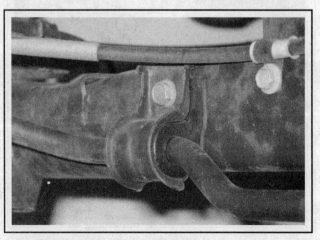

9.3 Stabilizer bar retainer and bushing

10 Track bar - removal and installation

REMOVAL

♦ **Refer to illustration 10.2**

1   Raise the vehicle and support it securely on jackstands. Block the front wheels to keep the vehicle from moving.

2   Remove the track bar lower bolt and nut at the axle (see illustration).

➡**Note: The mounting bolts are inserted from the rear to the front.**

3   Remove the track bar upper bolt and nut and then remove the track bar.

4   To remove the mount, remove the bolts retaining the mount to the body.

➡**Note: It is not necessary to remove the mount unless it is being replaced.**

INSTALLATION

5   Install the track bar mount, if removed. Tighten the bolts to the torque listed in this Chapter's Specifications.

6   Install the track bar.

10.2 Track bar fasteners

7   Install the track bar bolts with the bolt heads facing towards the rear. Do not tighten the bolts yet.

8   Lower the vehicle so the weight of the vehicle is on the tires. Tighten the track bar bolts to the torque listed in this Chapter's Specifications.

11 Leaf spring mounts - removal and installation

REMOVAL

♦ **Refer to illustrations 11.2 and 11.7**

1   Raise the vehicle and support it securely on jackstands. Block the front tires to keep the vehicle from moving.

Rear mount

2   Remove the shackle bracket nuts (see illustration).

3   Place a floor jack under the axle and raise it until the weight is off the leaf spring.

4   Remove the lower shock absorber mounting bolt.

5   Remove the rear spring mount bolts (see illustration 11.2).

6   Lower the floor jack and the rear of the leaf spring. Remove the shackle and leaf spring mount.

Front mount

7   Loosen the leaf spring front pivot bolt (see illustration).

8   Place a floor jack under the axle and raise it until the weight is off the leaf spring.

9   Remove the lower shock absorber mounting bolt.

10   Remove the leaf spring front pivot bolt.

11   Lower the leaf spring and remove the front spring mount bolts.

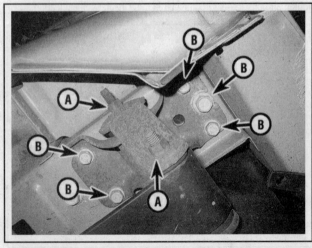

11.2 Remove the leaf spring shackle nuts (A) and the rear spring mount bolts (B)

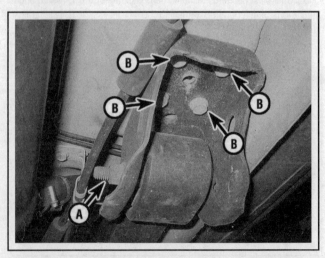

11.7 Leaf spring front pivot bolt (A) and front spring mount bolts (B)

INSTALLATION

12 Installation is the reverse of removal. Tighten the front spring mount bolts to the torque listed in this Chapter's Specifications.

13 Do not tighten the rear spring shackle nuts or the front pivot bolt nut until the vehicle is lowered and the full weight of the vehicle is on the rear wheels.

14 Tighten the nuts and bolts to the torque listed in this Chapter's Specifications.

12 Leaf spring - removal and installation

REMOVAL

▶ **Refer to illustration 12.5**

1 Raise the vehicle and support it securely on jackstands.
2 Support the axle with a floor jack.
3 Remove the lower shock absorber bolt (see illustration 13.3).
4 Raise the axle assembly just enough to relieve the weight on the rear springs.
5 Remove the axle plate bolts on the leaf springs (see illustration).
6 Lower the rear axle assembly, letting the springs hang free.
7 Loosen and remove the bolts for the front spring mount (see illustration 11.7).
8 Loosen and remove the rear spring shackle nuts and plate, remove the spring from the shackle (see illustration 11.2).
9 Remove the leaf spring from the vehicle.
10 Remove the pivot bolt from the front spring mount.

INSTALLATION

11 Assemble the front spring mount to the front of the spring eye and install the pivot bolt and nut. Do not tighten the nut.
12 Raise the front of the spring and install the spring mount bolts. Tighten the bolts to the torque listed in this Chapter's Specifications.
13 Install the rear of the spring onto the rear spring shackle. Install the shackle plate, but do not tighten the nuts yet.
14 Position the lower leaf spring isolator.

12.5 Remove the axle plate bolts

15 Raise the axle assembly into position with the axle centered under the spring locator post.
16 Install the axle plate bolts and tighten them to the torque listed in this Chapter's Specifications.
17 Install the shock absorber bolts. Do not tighten them yet.
18 Lower the vehicle to the floor with the full weight of the vehicle on the wheels. Tighten all components to the torque values listed in this Chapter's Specifications.

13 Shock absorbers (rear) - removal and installation

REMOVAL

▶ **Refer to illustration 13.3**

1 Raise the vehicle and support it securely on jackstands. Block the front wheels to keep the vehicle from moving.
2 Support the axle with a floor jack. Raise the jack just enough to support the weight of the axle.
3 Remove the lower shock absorber bolt (see illustration).
4 Remove the upper mounting bolt (see illustration 13.3).

INSTALLATION

5 Install the upper shock absorber bolt finger tight.
6 Swing the shock absorber into position, and tighten the lower shock absorber bolt finger-tight.
7 Lower the vehicle to the ground and tighten the bolts to the torque listed in this Chapter's Specifications.

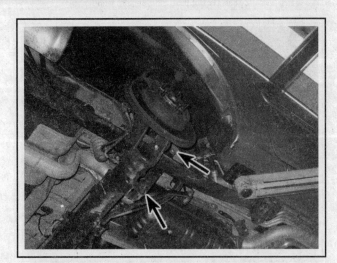

13.3 Shock absorber mounting bolts

14 Rear axle assembly - removal and installation

REMOVAL

1   Loosen the rear wheel lug nuts, raise the vehicle and support it securely on jackstands. Block the front wheels to keep the vehicle from moving.

2   Remove the rear wheels, brake drums or discs, ABS sensors (see Chapter 9) and the rear hub/bearing assembly (see Section 15). Suspend the rear brake backing plates.

3   Remove any brake line and parking brake cable fasteners attached to the axle.

➡Note: On models with rear disc brakes, the rear brake lines and parking brake cables do not have to be disconnected because the brake components they are connected to can be suspended out of the way. On models with rear drum brakes, brake lines that are disconnected need to be capped to avoid contamination of the brake system. Note how the lines and cables are routed for reinstallation of the axle.

4   On models without ABS, disconnect the rod that is attached to the bracket on the axle for the proportioning valve.

5   Support the axle with a floor jack.

6   Remove the shock absorber lower bolts.

7   Remove the track bar-to-axle bolt and nut.

8   Remove the stabilizer bar retainers from the axle (see illustration 9.3).

9   Remove the axle plate bolts (see illustration 12.5).

➡Note: Carefully suspend any brake line brackets held in place by the axle plate bolts.

10   Carefully lower the axle assembly.

INSTALLATION

11   Place the lower leaf spring isolator in the correct position on the axle.

12   Raise the axle assembly while aligning the isolators and mounting brackets on the axle with the locator post on each leaf spring.

13   Install the axle plate and bolts. Tighten the bolts to the torque listed in this Chapter's Specifications.

➡Note: Reinstall any brake line brackets that are held by the axle plate bolts.

14   Install the stabilizer bar retainers. Tighten the bolts to the torque listed in this Chapter's Specifications.

15   Install the lower shock absorber bolts but do not tighten them yet.

16   Install the track bar bolt and nut but do not tighten them yet.

17   Reattach any brake line or parking brake cable fasteners removed from the axle.

18   Install the hub/bearing assemblies and all brake components while utilizing proper torque values listed in the Chapter 9 Specifications.

19   Install the wheel and lug nuts. Lower the vehicle and tighten the lug nuts to the torque listed in the Chapter 1 Specifications.

20   With the vehicle on the ground, tighten the track bar and the lower shock absorber fasteners to the torque values listed in this Chapter's Specifications.

21   If any brake lines were disconnected, bleed the rear brakes before placing the vehicle back in service (see Chapter 9).

15 Hub and bearing assembly (rear) - removal and installation

▶ **Refer to illustrations 15.4 and 15.5**

1   Loosen the rear wheel lug nuts, raise the rear of the vehicle, support it securely on jackstands and remove the wheels.

2   Remove the brake drum or disc (see Chapter 9).

3   Remove the rear wheel speed sensor (see Chapter 9).

4   Remove the bolts retaining the hub/bearing assembly to the rear axle (see illustration).

5   Remove the hub/bearing assembly from the axle (see illustration).

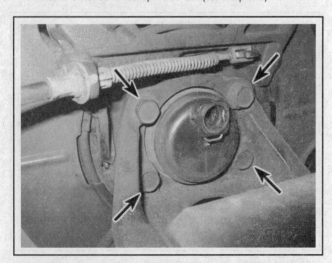

15.4   The hub and bearing assembly mounting bolts

15.5   The hub and bearing assembly should come off easily. If it is stuck, a special factory tool will be needed because a slide hammer will damage the bearing

✳✳ CAUTION:

If the hub/bearing assembly sticks in the axle, DO NOT remove it with a slide hammer unless you intend to replace it. The manufacturer recommends the use of a special press tool to remove the hub/bearing assembly without damaging it.

6   Installation is the reverse of removal. Tighten the hub/bearing mounting bolts to the torque listed in this Chapter's Specifications. On models with rear disc brakes, tighten the caliper guide pins to the torque listed in the Chapter 9 Specifications.

7   Install the wheel and lug nuts. Lower the vehicle and tighten the lug nuts to the torque listed in the Chapter 1 Specifications.

16 Subframe/cradle reinforcement plate - removal and installation

▶ Refer to illustration 16.3

1   Apply the parking brake, then raise the front of the vehicle and support it securely on jackstands. Block the rear wheels.

2   Remove the power steering fluid cooler and suspend it carefully aside (see Section 22).

3   Remove the EVAP emission control component and suspend it carefully aside (see illustration).

4   Remove the mounting bolts and lower the reinforcement plate.

5   Installation is the reverse of removal. Tighten all reinforcement plate mounting bolts to the torque listed in this Chapter's Specifications.

➡Note: Be sure to use the correct torque value for the various sized mounting bolts used to fasten the reinforcement plate to the subframe/cradle and body.

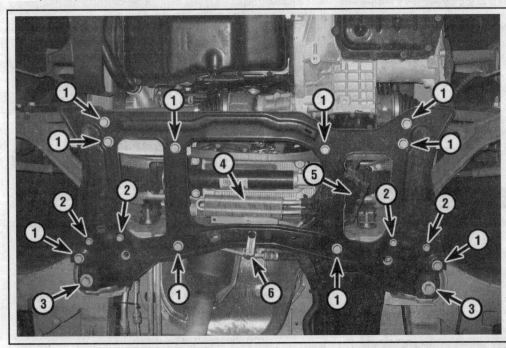

16.3 Subframe/cradle reinforcement plate mounting details (2005 shown, other models similar)

1   Mounting bolts
2   Mounting bolts near control arm bushings (smaller)
3   Reinforcement plate-to-frame mounting bolts (larger)
4   Power steering fluid cooler
5   EVAP system leak detection pump
6   Power steering hose bracket

17 Steering wheel - removal and installation

✳✳ WARNING 1:

These models have airbags. Always disarm the airbag system before working in the vicinity of the impact sensors, steering column, or instrument panel to avoid accidental deployment of the airbag, which could cause personal injury (see Chapter 12).

✳✳ WARNING 2:

Do not use a memory saving device to preserve the ECM's memory when working on or near airbag system components.

REMOVAL

▶ Refer to illustrations 17.2, 17.3, 17.4 and 17.8

1   Park the vehicle with the wheels pointing straight ahead and the steering wheel centered. Disconnect the cable from the negative terminal of the battery (see Chapter 5, Section 1).

✳✳ WARNING:

Wait at least two minutes before proceeding with the following steps.

17.2 Remove the fasteners that retain the airbag module to the steering wheel

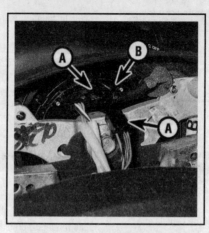

17.3 Disconnect the horn and cruise control connector (A) and the radio control switch connector (B)

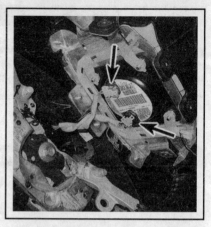

17.4 Disconnect the airbag module connectors from the module (steering wheel turned for clarity)

2   Remove the fasteners holding the airbag module to the steering wheel (see illustration).

3   Pull the top of the airbag module away from the steering wheel and then disconnect the horn and cruise control electrical connector. Also, disconnect the radio control switch electrical connector, if equipped (see illustration).

4   Remove the airbag module from the steering wheel and then disconnect the electrical connectors (see illustration).

→Note: Squeeze the small tabs on the sides of the connectors to release them from the module. Note that they are color-coded.

5   Set the module aside in a safe, isolated area, with the airbag side of the module facing UP.

✳✳ WARNING:

When carrying the airbag module, keep the driver's (trim) side facing away from you.

6   Remove the steering wheel retaining bolt and mark the position of the steering wheel to the shaft, if marks don't already exist or don't line up.

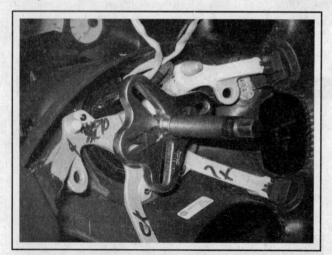

17.8 Use a steering wheel puller to remove the steering wheel from the steering shaft

7   Partially reinstall the bolt leaving a 1/2-inch of thread between the bolt head and the steering wheel.

8   Remove the steering wheel using a steering wheel puller (see illustration). The puller screw must contact the steering wheel bolt.

✳✳ CAUTION 1:

Don't thread the bolts of the puller into the steering wheel more than five turns, as they could contact the airbag clockspring and damage it.

✳✳ CAUTION 2:

While the steering wheel is removed, DO NOT turn the steering shaft. If you do so, the airbag clockspring could be damaged when the vehicle is put back in service.

INSTALLATION

→Note: If necessary, the clockspring can be replaced by removing the steering column covers (see Chapter 11) and then removing the mounting fasteners.

9   If the clockspring needs to be centered because the steering shaft was moved, do the following:

   a)   *Turn the clockspring rotor clockwise until it stops (don't apply too much force).*

   b)   *Rotate the clockspring rotor counterclockwise two full turns; the wires will now be in the 12 o'clock position.*

   c)   *The clockspring is now in the centered position and the steering wheel can be installed.*

10   Install the wheel on the steering shaft making sure to align the shaft splines correctly. Also, engage the slot in the bottom portion of the steering wheel with the pin on the clockspring.

→Note: Make sure the clockspring wires are routed correctly through the steering wheel.

11   Install the steering wheel retaining bolt and tighten it to the torque listed in this Chapter's Specifications.

12   Reconnect the radio control switch electrical connector, if equipped.

13 Reconnect the airbag module and the horn and cruise control electrical connectors and place the airbag module on the steering wheel.

14 Install the airbag module fasteners and tighten them to the torque listed in this Chapter's Specifications.

15 Connect the cable to the negative battery terminal (see Chapter 5, Section 1).

16 Turn the ignition key On and verify that the airbag system is oper- ating properly by watching the airbag warning light in the instrument cluster (see Chapter 12).

❋❋ WARNING:

If the airbag system is not operating DO NOT drive the vehicle, have the airbag system repaired at a dealership service depart- ment or other qualified repair shop.

18 Tie-rod ends - removal and installation

REMOVAL

▶ **Refer to illustrations 18.2, 18.3, 18.4a and 18.4b**

1 Loosen the wheel lug nuts, raise the front of the vehicle and sup- port it securely on jackstands. Apply the parking brake and block the rear wheels to keep the vehicle from rolling off the jackstands. Remove the wheel.

2 Loosen the tie-rod end jam nut (see illustration).

3 Mark the relationship of the tie-rod end to the threaded portion of the tie-rod. This will ensure the toe-in setting is restored when reas- sembled (see illustration).

4 Loosen the nut from the tie-rod end ballstud a few turns (see illustration). Disconnect the tie-rod end ballstud from the steering knuckle arm with a puller (see illustration).

5 Remove the nut from the ballstud, separate the tie-rod end from the steering knuckle, then unscrew the tie-rod end from the tie-rod.

INSTALLATION

6 Thread the tie-rod end onto the tie-rod to the marked position and connect the tie-rod end to the steering arm. Install the nut on the ballstud and tighten it to the torque listed in this Chapter's Specifica- tions.

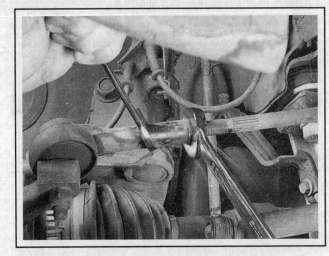

18.2 Hold the tie-rod end while breaking loose the jam nut

7 Tighten the jam nut securely and install the wheel. Lower the vehicle and tighten the lug nuts to the torque listed in the Chapter 1 Specifications.

8 Have the front end alignment checked and, if necessary, adjusted.

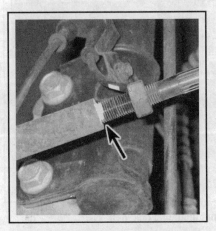

18.3 Back-off the jam nut and mark the exposed threads

18.4a If the tie-rod end stud spins when loosening the nut, hold the stud with a wrench or socket

18.4b Use a two-jaw puller to push the tie-rod end out of the steering knuckle

19 Steering column - removal and installation

✸✸ WARNING 1:

These models have airbags. Always disarm the airbag system before working in the vicinity of the impact sensors, steering column, or instrument panel to avoid accidental deployment of the airbag, which could cause personal injury (see Chapter 12).

✸✸ WARNING 2:

Do not use a memory saving device to preserve the PCM's memory when working on or near airbag system components.

REMOVAL

▸ **Refer to illustrations 19.5, 19.7 and 19.8**

1 Park the vehicle with the wheels pointing straight ahead. Disconnect the cable from the negative terminal of the battery (see Chapter 5, Section 1).
2 Remove the steering wheel (see Section 17).

✸✸ CAUTION:

Do not move the steering shaft after the steering wheel has been removed or damage to the clockspring could occur when the vehicle is put back into service.

3 Remove the steering column covers and the lower knee bolster (see Chapter 11).
4 Remove the knee blocker panel (see Chapter 11) and the reinforcement behind it, or, on models so equipped, the knee blocker airbag and reinforcement (see Chapter 12).
5 Disconnect all electrical connectors coming from the large harness on the side of the steering column and any ground wires that may be attached to the steering column from the other side (see illustration).
6 Remove the shift cable from the steering column (see Chapter 7).

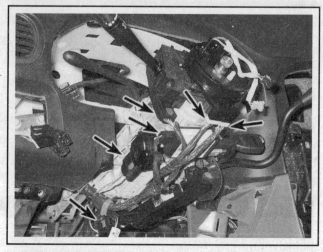

19.5 Disconnect all electrical connectors from the steering column components

7 Mark the relationship of the intermediate shaft to the steering column coupler and then remove the pinch bolt and separate the intermediate shaft from the coupler by compressing the shaft (see illustration).
8 Remove the steering column mounting fasteners; carefully lower the column, making sure nothing is still connected, and remove it (see illustration).

INSTALLATION

9 Guide the steering column into position, then install the steering column mounting fasteners and tighten them to the torque listed in this Chapter's Specifications.
10 Connect the steering column coupler to the intermediate shaft and install the pinch bolt and nut, tightening it to the torque listed in this Chapter's Specifications.
11 The remainder of installation is the reverse of removal. Reconnect the negative battery cable (see Chapter 5, Section 1).

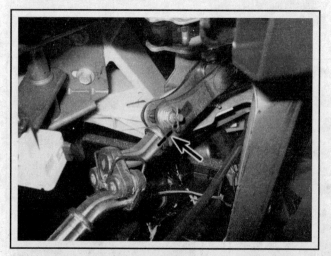

19.7 The steering column coupler and intermediate shaft marked before separation

19.8 Steering column mounting fasteners

20 Steering gear - removal and installation

※※ WARNING:

Lock the steering wheel to keep it from moving while the steering shaft is disconnected or damage to the airbag system could occur when the vehicle is placed back in service. With the ignition key in the LOCK position, turn the steering wheel just enough to lock it or secure it with the seatbelt.

REMOVAL

▶ Refer to illustrations 20.3, 20.4, 20.10, and 20.11

1 Park the vehicle with the wheels pointing directly forward.

2 Remove as much fluid as possible from the power steering pump reservoir.

3 Remove the intermediate shaft coupler cover/dash seal fasteners so the cover can be slid up the intermediate shaft (see illustration).

4 Mark the relationship of the intermediate shaft coupler to the steering gear, then disconnect it by removing the roll pin (see illustration).

➡**Note: Compress the intermediate shaft to separate the coupler from the steering gear and then suspend it aside.**

5 Loosen the wheel lug, raise the vehicle, support it securely on jackstands, and remove the wheels.

6 Remove the emissions vapor canister (see Chapter 6).

7 Disconnect one hose from the power steering cooler to drain the fluid from the system and then remove the cooler (see Section 22)

8 Remove both tie-rod ends from the steering knuckles (see Section 18).

9 Remove the subframe/cradle reinforcement plate (see Section 16).

10 Detach the power steering fluid pressure and return lines from the power steering gear using a flare nut wrench (see illustration). Cap or plug all openings to prevent contamination from entering the power steering system.

➡**Note: Mark the lines so they can be installed in the same position when they are reconnected.**

11 Remove the steering gear mounting bolts and carefully guide the steering gear out of the subframe/cradle (see illustration).

20.3 The intermediate shaft coupler cover/dash seal mounting fasteners

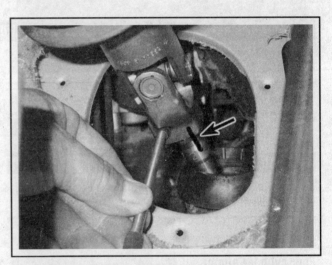

20.4 The intermediate shaft coupler and steering gear marked before the roll pin is driven out with a punch

20.10 The power steering fluid pressure and return lines at the steering gear

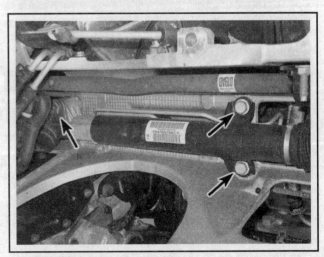

20.11 Steering gear mounting bolts

INSTALLATION

> **⁂ WARNING:**
>
> If a new steering gear is being installed, the clockspring must be removed and re-centered after the steering gear is installed (see Section 17).

12 Installation is the reverse of removal, noting the following points:

a) If a new steering gear is being installed, center the gear by turning the input shaft clockwise until it stops. Turn the input shaft counterclockwise and count the number of rotations until it stops. Divide that number by two and turn the input shaft clockwise that amount.

b) If a new steering gear is being installed, remove the steering wheel and clockspring (see Section 17).

c) Install the mounting bolts and tighten them to the torque listed in this Chapter's Specifications.

d) Be sure to align the index marks on the steering gear shaft and intermediate shaft coupler before installing the roll pin in the coupler.

e) Be sure to install the fluid lines to the steering gear in the correct position and tighten them securely.

f) Install the subframe/cradle reinforcement bolts to the torque listed in this Chapter's Specifications.

g) Install the wheels and lug nuts. Lower the vehicle, then tighten the lug nuts to the torque listed in the Chapter 1 Specifications.

h) If a new steering gear is being installed, temporarily reinstall the steering wheel and set the front wheels in the straight-ahead position. Then remove the steering wheel, center the clockspring, and reinstall the steering wheel (see Section 17).

i) Fill the power steering pump reservoir with the recommended fluid (see Chapter 1) and then bleed the power steering system (see Section 23).

j) Have the front wheel alignment checked and, if necessary, adjusted.

---

21 Power steering pump - removal and installation

REMOVAL

1 Disconnect the cable from the negative terminal of the battery (see Chapter 5, Section 1).

2 Remove the fluid from the reservoir using a siphon or equivalent.

> **⁂ CAUTION:**
>
> Be careful not to tear any mesh filter that may be present just under the surface of the fluid.

3 Remove the accessory drivebelt (see Chapter 1).

Four-cylinder engine

4 Raise the vehicle and support it securely on jackstands.

5 Disconnect the oxygen sensor wiring harness from the vehicle wiring harness near the rear motor mount bracket.

6 Remove the catalytic converter from the exhaust manifold (see Chapter 4).

> **⁂ WARNING:**
>
> Wait until the engine is completely cool before beginning this procedure.

7 Remove the exhaust system hangers/isolators from the brackets on the exhaust system and remove the exhaust system (see Chapter 4).

8 Detach the fluid supply hose coming from the reservoir to the fitting on the power steering pump. Plug the hose to prevent excess fluid loss.

9 Remove the power steering fluid pressure line and return hose from the power steering pump. Plug them to avoid fluid loss.

10 Remove the nut attaching the rear of the power steering pump to the mounting bracket.

11 Loosen the three bolts attaching the power steering pump to the front mounting bracket.

12 Remove the power steering pump and the front bracket as an assembly through the exhaust tunnel under the vehicle.

13 Remove the three bolts from Step 12 and separate the power steering pump from the front bracket.

V6 engines

▶ **Refer to illustration 21.18**

14 Remove the windshield wiper motor/module assembly (see Chapter 12).

15 Raise the vehicle and support it securely on jackstands.

16 Remove the accessory drivebelt splash shield (see Chapter 2B).

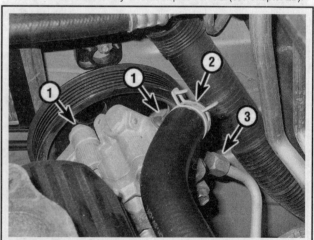

21.18 Power steering pump details (V6 shown)

1 Mounting bolt location (one hidden from view - proximity shown)
2 Feed hose and clamp
3 Pressure line

17 Remove the bracket that secures the pressure line to the engine.

➡ **Note: Follow the pressure line from the pump towards the engine; the bracket is mounted nearby.**

18 Remove the power steering fluid pressure line and return hose from the power steering pump. Plug them to avoid fluid loss (see illustration).

19 Remove the power steering pump from the mounting bracket (see illustration 21.18).

INSTALLATION

20 Installation is the reverse of removal.

21 Tighten all power steering mounting hardware to the torque listed in this Chapter's Specifications.

22 Tighten the pressure line-to-pump fitting securely.

23 Make sure the hoses are properly routed and all hose clamps are tightened securely.

24 Fill the power steering fluid reservoir with the recommended fluid (see Chapter 1).

25 Connect the negative battery cable to the battery (see Chapter 5, Section 1).

26 Bleed the power system (see Section 23). Stop the engine, check the fluid level, and inspect the system for leaks.

22 Power steering fluid cooler - removal and installation

▶ **Refer to illustration 22.4**

The power steering fluid cooler is designed to keep the power steering fluid temperature within a specific temperature level to maintain the maximum performance from the power steering system.

1 Use a shop syringe and remove as much of the power steering fluid from the fluid reservoir as possible.

2 Raise the vehicle and support it securely on jackstands.

3 Place a drip pan under the fluid cooler. Remove the hose clamps and disconnect both hoses from the fluid cooler.

4 Remove the two mounting bolts and remove the fluid cooler (see illustration).

5 Installation is the reverse of removal. Bleed the power system (see Section 23). Start the engine and check the system for leaks.

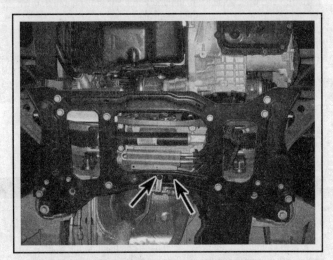

22.4 Power steering fluid cooler mounting bolts

23 Power steering system - bleeding

1 Following any operation in which the power steering fluid lines have been disconnected, the power steering system must be bled to remove all air and obtain proper steering performance.

2 With the front wheels in the straight ahead position, check the power steering fluid level (see Chapter 1).

3 Start the engine and allow it to run at fast idle. Recheck the fluid level and add fluid if necessary.

4 Bleed the system by turning the wheels from side to side, without hitting the stops. This will work the air out of the system. Maintain the proper fluid level as this is done.

5 When the air is worked out of the system, return the wheels to the straight ahead position and leave the vehicle running for several more minutes before shutting it off.

6 Road test the vehicle to be sure the steering system is functioning normally and noise free.

7 Recheck the fluid level to be sure it is correct. Add fluid if necessary

24 Wheels and tires - general information

▶ **Refer to illustration 24.1**

1   All vehicles covered by this manual are equipped with metric-sized fiberglass or steel belted radial tires (see illustration). Use of other size or type of tires may affect the ride and handling of the vehicle. Don't mix different types of tires, such as radials and bias belted, on the same vehicle as handling may be seriously affected. It's recommended that tires be replaced in pairs on the same axle, but if only one tire is being replaced, be sure it's the same size, structure and tread design as the other.

2   Because tire pressure has a substantial effect on handling and wear, the pressure on all tires should be checked at least once a month or before any extended trips (see Chapter 1).

3   Wheels must be replaced if they are bent, dented, leak air, have elongated bolt holes, are heavily rusted, out of vertical symmetry or if the lug nuts won't stay tight. Wheel repairs that use welding or peening are not recommended.

4   Tire and wheel balance is important in the overall handling, braking and performance of the vehicle. Unbalanced wheels can adversely affect handling and ride characteristics as well as tire life. Whenever a tire is installed on a wheel, the tire and wheel should be balanced by a shop with the proper equipment.

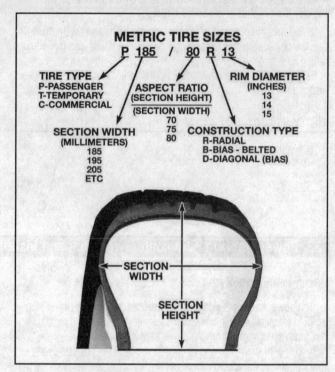

24.1 Metric tire size code

25 Wheel alignment - general information

▶ **Refer to illustration 25.1**

A wheel alignment refers to the adjustments made to the wheels so they are in proper angular relationship to the suspension and the ground. Wheels that are out of proper alignment not only affect vehicle control, but also increase tire wear. The front end angles normally measured are camber, caster and toe-in (see illustration). Toe-in is the only routine adjustment made; camber is adjustable, but only after installing special strut-to-knuckle bolts. If the caster is not correct, check for bent components. There are no adjustments possible to the rear wheels.

Getting the proper wheel alignment is a very exacting process, one in which complicated and expensive machines are necessary to perform the job properly. Because of this, you should have a technician with the proper equipment perform these tasks. We will, however, use this space to give you a basic idea of what is involved with a wheel alignment so you can better understand the process and deal intelligently with the shop that does the work.

Toe-in is the turning in of the wheels. The purpose of a toe specification is to ensure parallel rolling of the wheels. In a vehicle with zero toe-in, the distance between the front edges of the wheels will be the same as the distance between the rear edges of the wheels. The actual amount of toe-in is normally only a fraction of an inch. Toe-in is controlled by the tie-rod end position on the tie-rod. Incorrect toe-in will cause the tires to wear improperly by making them scrub against the road surface.

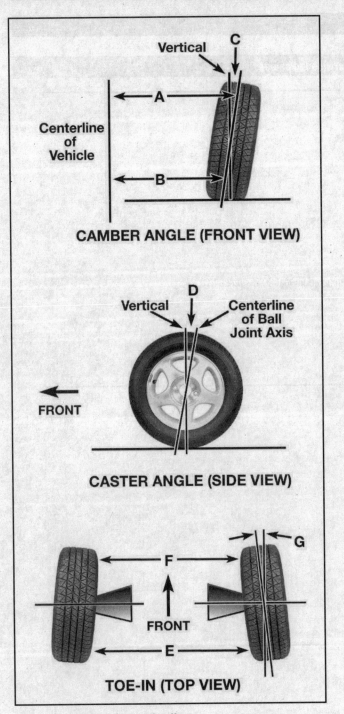

CAMBER ANGLE (FRONT VIEW)

CASTER ANGLE (SIDE VIEW)

TOE-IN (TOP VIEW)

25.1 Front end alignment details

Camber is the tilting of the wheels from vertical when viewed from one end of the vehicle. When the wheels tilt out at the top, the camber is said to be positive (+). When the wheels tilt in at the top the camber is negative (-). The amount of tilt is measured in degrees from vertical and this measurement is called the camber angle. This angle affects the amount of tire tread which contacts the road and compensates for changes in the suspension geometry when the vehicle is cornering or traveling over an undulating surface. On the front end it is adjusted using special camber adjusting bolts, which alter the relationship between the strut and the steering knuckle.

Caster is the tilting of the front steering axis from the vertical. A tilt toward the rear is positive caster and a tilt toward the front is negative caster.

Specifications

Torque specifications   Ft-lbs (unless otherwise indicated)

Front suspension

Control arm pivot bolt	135
Hub and bearing-to-steering knuckle bolts	45
Stabilizer bar link nuts	65
Stabilizer bar bushing retainer bolts	50
Steering knuckle-to-balljoint stud nut	80
Strut upper mounting nuts	21
Strut damper shaft nut	75
Strut-to-steering knuckle nuts	
Step 1	60
Step 2	Tighten an additional 90-degrees
Subframe/cradle reinforcement plate bolts	
M14 bolts	113
M12 bolts	78
M10 bolts	45
Subframe/cradle-to-body bolts	120

Rear suspension

Hub and bearing-to-axle mounting bolts	95
Leaf spring rear mount bolts	45
Leaf spring front mount bolts	45
Leaf spring front through-bolt	115
Leaf spring axle plate bolts	70
Shackle nuts	45
Shock absorber bolts	65
Stabilizer bar-to-link arm	45
Stabilizer bar bushing retainer bolts	45
Stabilizer link arm-to-frame rail bracket	45
Stub axle nut	180
Track bar bolts	70
Track bar mounting bolts	45

Steering system

Airbag module mounting screws	90 in-lbs
Power steering pump mounting bolts	40
Power steering fluid cooler mounting bolts	100 in-lbs
Steering column coupler pinch bolt	21
Steering column mounting nuts	105 in-lbs
Steering gear-to-subframe/cradle mounting bolts	
M14	135
M12	70
Steering wheel retaining bolt	45
Tie-rod end-to-steering knuckle nut	55
Wheel lug nuts	See Chapter 1

Section

11

BODY

1 General information

These models feature a "unibody" layout, using a floorpan with front and rear frame side rails which support the body components, front and rear suspension systems and other mechanical components. Certain components are particularly vulnerable to accident damage and can be unbolted and repaired or replaced. Among these parts are the body

moldings, bumpers, front fenders, doors, the hood and liftgate and all glass. Only general body maintenance practices and body panel repair procedures within the scope of the do-it-yourselfer are included in this Chapter.

2 Body - maintenance

1   The condition of your vehicle's body is very important, because the resale value depends a great deal on it. It's much more difficult to repair a neglected or damaged body than it is to repair mechanical components. The hidden areas of the body, such as the wheel wells, the frame and the engine compartment, are equally important, although they don't require as frequent attention as the rest of the body.

2   Once a year, or every 12,000 miles, it's a good idea to have the underside of the body steam-cleaned. All traces of dirt and oil will be removed and the area can then be inspected carefully for rust, damaged brake lines, frayed electrical wires, damaged cables and other problems.

3   At the same time, clean the engine and the engine compartment with a steam cleaner or water-soluble degreaser.

4   The wheel wells should be given close attention, since under-coating can peel away and stones and dirt thrown up by the tires can

cause the paint to chip and flake, allowing rust to set in. If rust is found, clean down to the bare metal and apply an anti-rust paint.

5   The body should be washed about once a week. Wet the vehicle thoroughly to soften the dirt, then wash it down with a soft sponge and plenty of clean soapy water. If the surplus dirt is not washed off very carefully, it can wear down the paint.

6   Spots of tar or asphalt thrown up from the road should be removed with a cloth soaked in kerosene. Scented lamp oil is available in most hardware stores and the smell is easier to work with than straight kerosene.

7   Once every six months, wax the body and chrome trim. If a chrome cleaner is used to remove rust from any of the vehicle's plated parts, remember that the cleaner also removes part of the chrome, so use it sparingly. On any plated parts where chrome cleaner is used, use a good paste wax over the plating for extra protection.

3 Vinyl trim - maintenance

Don't clean vinyl trim with detergents, caustic soap or petroleum-based cleaners. Plain soap and water works just fine, with a soft brush to clean dirt that may be ingrained. Wash the vinyl as frequently as the rest of the vehicle.

After cleaning, application of a high quality rubber and vinyl protectant will help prevent oxidation and cracks. The protectant can also be applied to weather stripping, vacuum lines and rubber hoses, which often fail as a result of chemical degradation, and to the tires.

4 Upholstery and carpets - maintenance

1   Every three months remove the floormats and clean the interior of the vehicle (more frequently if necessary). Use a stiff whisk broom to brush the carpeting and loosen dirt and dust, then vacuum the upholstery and carpets thoroughly, especially along seams and crevices.

2   Dirt and stains can be removed from carpeting with basic household or automotive carpet shampoos available in spray cans. Follow the directions and vacuum again, then use a stiff brush to bring back the "nap" of the carpet.

3   Most interiors have cloth or vinyl upholstery, either of which can be cleaned and maintained with a number of material-specific cleaners or shampoos available in auto supply stores. Follow the directions on the product for usage, and always spot-test any upholstery cleaner on an inconspicuous area (bottom edge of a backseat cushion) to ensure that it doesn't cause a color shift in the material.

4   After cleaning, vinyl upholstery should be treated with a protectant.

➡Note: Make sure the protectant container indicates the prod-

uct can be used on seats - some products may make a seat too slippery.

❊❊ CAUTION:

Do not use protectant on steering wheels.

5   Leather upholstery requires special care. It should be cleaned regularly with saddlesoap or leather cleaner. Never use alcohol, gasoline, nail polish remover or thinner to clean leather upholstery.

6   After cleaning, regularly treat leather upholstery with a leather conditioner, rubbed in with a soft cotton cloth. Never use car wax on leather upholstery.

7   In areas where the interior of the vehicle is subject to bright sunlight, cover leather seating areas of the seats with a sheet if the vehicle is to be left out for any length of time.

FLEXIBLE PLASTIC BODY PANELS (FRONT AND REAR BUMPER FASCIA)

The following repair procedures are for minor scratches and gouges. Repair of more serious damage should be left to a dealer service department or qualified auto body shop. Below is a list of the equipment and materials necessary to perform the following repair procedures on plastic body panels. Although a specific brand of material may be mentioned, it should be noted that equivalent products from other manufacturers may be used instead.

Wax, grease and silicone removing solvent
Cloth-backed body tape
Sanding discs
Drill motor with three-inch disc holder
Hand sanding block
Rubber squeegees
Sandpaper
Non-porous mixing palette
Wood paddle or putty knife
Curved-tooth body file
Flexible parts repair material

1   Remove the damaged panel, if necessary or desirable. In most cases, repairs can be carried out with the panel installed.

2   Clean the area(s) to be repaired with a wax, grease and silicone removing solvent applied with a water-dampened cloth.

3   If the damage is structural, that is, if it extends through the panel, clean the backside of the panel area to be repaired as well. Wipe dry.

4   Sand the rear surface about 1-1/2 inches beyond the break.

5   Cut two pieces of fiberglass cloth large enough to overlap the break by about 1-1/2 inches. Cut only to the required length.

6   Mix the adhesive from the repair kit according to the instructions included with the kit, and apply a layer of the mixture approximately 1/8-inch thick on the backside of the panel. Overlap the break by at least 1-1/2 inches.

7   Apply one piece of fiberglass cloth to the adhesive and cover the cloth with additional adhesive. Apply a second piece of fiberglass cloth to the adhesive and immediately cover the cloth with additional adhesive in sufficient quantity to fill the weave.

8   Allow the repair to cure for 20 to 30 minutes at 60-degrees to 80-degrees F.

9   If necessary, trim the excess repair material at the edge.

10 Remove all of the paint film over and around the area(s) to be repaired. The repair material should not overlap the painted surface.

11 With a drill motor and a sanding disc (or a rotary file), cut a "V" along the break line approximately 1/2-inch wide. Remove all dust and loose particles from the repair area.

12 Mix and apply the repair material. Apply a light coat first over the damaged area; then continue applying material until it reaches a level slightly higher than the surrounding finish.

13 Cure the mixture for 20 to 30 minutes at 60-degrees to 80-degrees F.

14 Roughly establish the contour of the area being repaired with a body file. If low areas or pits remain, mix and apply additional adhesive.

15 Block sand the damaged area with sandpaper to establish the actual contour of the surrounding surface.

16 If desired, the repaired area can be temporarily protected with several light coats of primer. Because of the special paints and techniques required for flexible body panels, it is recommended that the vehicle be taken to a paint shop for completion of the body repair.

STEEL BODY PANELS

See photo sequence

Repair of minor scratches

17 If the scratch is superficial and does not penetrate to the metal of the body, repair is very simple. Lightly rub the scratched area with a fine rubbing compound to remove loose paint and built up wax. Rinse the area with clean water.

18 Apply touch-up paint to the scratch, using a small brush. Continue to apply thin layers of paint until the surface of the paint in the scratch is level with the surrounding paint. Allow the new paint at least two weeks to harden, then blend it into the surrounding paint by rubbing with a very fine rubbing compound. Finally, apply a coat of wax to the scratch area.

19 If the scratch has penetrated the paint and exposed the metal of the body, causing the metal to rust, a different repair technique is required. Remove all loose rust from the bottom of the scratch with a pocket knife, then apply rust inhibiting paint to prevent the formation of rust in the future. Using a rubber or nylon applicator, coat the scratched area with glaze-type filler. If required, the filler can be mixed with thinner to provide a very thin paste, which is ideal for filling narrow scratches. Before the glaze filler in the scratch hardens, wrap a piece of smooth cotton cloth around the tip of a finger. Dip the cloth in thinner and then quickly wipe it along the surface of the scratch. This will ensure that the surface of the filler is slightly hollow. The scratch can now be painted over as described earlier in this Section.

REPAIR OF DENTS

20 When repairing dents, the first job is to pull the dent out until the affected area is as close as possible to its original shape. There is no point in trying to restore the original shape completely as the metal in the damaged area will have stretched on impact and cannot be restored to its original contours. It is better to bring the level of the dent up to a point which is about 1/8-inch below the level of the surrounding metal. In cases where the dent is very shallow, it is not worth trying to pull it out at all.

21 If the back side of the dent is accessible, it can be hammered out gently from behind using a soft-face hammer. While doing this, hold a block of wood firmly against the opposite side of the metal to absorb the hammer blows and prevent the metal from being stretched.

22 If the dent is in a section of the body which has double layers, or some other factor makes it inaccessible from behind, a different technique is required. Drill several small holes through the metal inside the damaged area, particularly in the deeper sections. Screw long, self tapping screws into the holes just enough for them to get a good grip in the metal. Now the dent can be pulled out by pulling on the protruding heads of the screws with locking pliers.

23 The next stage of repair is the removal of paint from the damaged area and from an inch or so of the surrounding metal. This is easily done with a wire brush or sanding disk in a drill motor, although it can be done just as effectively by hand with sandpaper. To complete the

These photos illustrate a method of repairing simple dents. They are intended to supplement Body repair - minor damage in this Chapter and should not be used as the sole instructions for body repair on these vehicles.

1   If you can't access the backside of the body panel to hammer out the dent, pull it out with a slide-hammer-type dent puller. In the deepest portion of the dent or along the crease line, drill or punch hole(s) at least one inch apart . . .

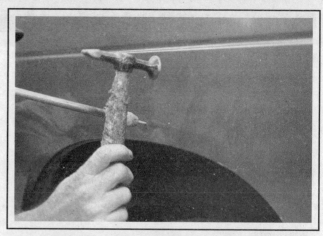

2   . . . then screw the slide-hammer into the hole and operate it. Tap with a hammer near the edge of the dent to help 'pop' the metal back to its original shape. When you're finished, the dent area should be close to its original contour and about 1/8-inch below the surface of the surrounding metal

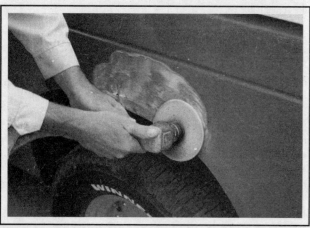

3   Using coarse-grit sandpaper, remove the paint down to the bare metal. Hand sanding works fine, but the disc sander shown here makes the job faster. Use finer (about 320-grit) sandpaper to feather-edge the paint at least one inch around the dent area

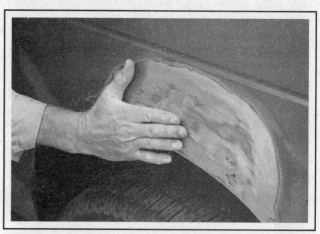

4   When the paint is removed, touch will probably be more helpful than sight for telling if the metal is straight. Hammer down the high spots or raise the low spots as necessary. Clean the repair area with wax/silicone remover

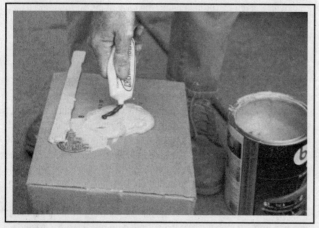

5   Following label instructions, mix up a batch of plastic filler and hardener. The ratio of filler to hardener is critical, and, if you mix it incorrectly, it will either not cure properly or cure too quickly (you won't have time to file and sand it into shape)

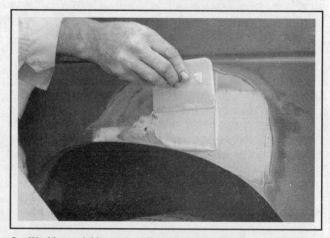

6   Working quickly so the filler doesn't harden, use a plastic applicator to press the body filler firmly into the metal, assuring it bonds completely. Work the filler until it matches the original contour and is slightly above the surrounding metal

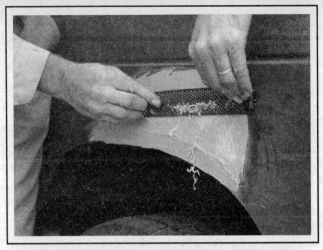

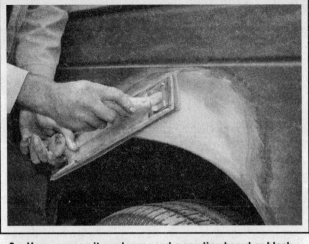

7 Let the filler harden until you can just dent it with your fingernail. Use a body file or Surform tool (shown here) to rough-shape the filler

8 Use coarse-grit sandpaper and a sanding board or block to work the filler down until it's smooth and even. Work down to finer grits of sandpaper - always using a board or block - ending up with 360 or 400 grit

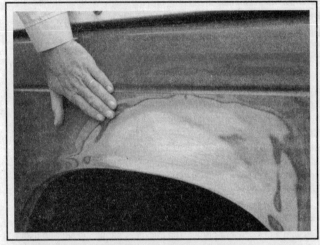

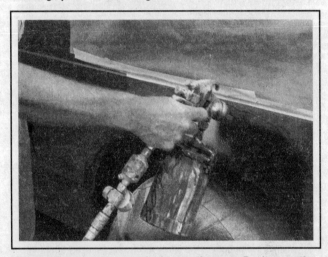

9 You shouldn't be able to feel any ridge at the transition from the filler to the bare metal or from the bare metal to the old paint. As soon as the repair is flat and uniform, remove the dust and mask off the adjacent panels or trim pieces

10 Apply several layers of primer to the area. Don't spray the primer on too heavy, so it sags or runs, and make sure each coat is dry before you spray on the next one. A professional-type spray gun is being used here, but aerosol spray primer is available inexpensively from auto parts stores

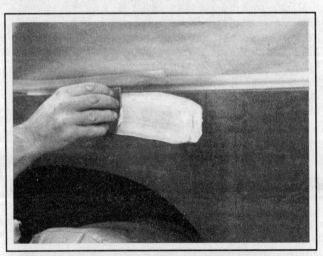

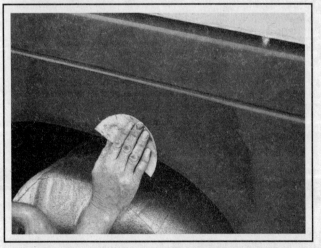

11 The primer will help reveal imperfections or scratches. Fill these with glazing compound. Follow the label instructions and sand it with 360 or 400-grit sandpaper until it's smooth. Repeat the glazing, sanding and respraying until the primer reveals a perfectly smooth surface

12 Finish sand the primer with very fine sandpaper (400 or 600-grit) to remove the primer overspray. Clean the area with water and allow it to dry. Use a tack rag to remove any dust, then apply the finish coat. Don't attempt to rub out or wax the repair area until the paint has dried completely (at least two weeks)

preparation for filling, score the surface of the bare metal with a screwdriver or the tang of a file or drill small holes in the affected area. This will provide a good grip for the filler material. To complete the repair, see the Section on filling and painting.

REPAIR OF RUST HOLES OR GASHES

24 Remove all paint from the affected area and from an inch or so of the surrounding metal using a sanding disk or wire brush mounted in a drill motor. If these are not available, a few sheets of sandpaper will do the job just as effectively.

25 With the paint removed, you will be able to determine the severity of the corrosion and decide whether to replace the whole panel, if possible, or repair the affected area. New body panels are not as expensive as most people think and it is often quicker to install a new panel than to repair large areas of rust.

26 Remove all trim pieces from the affected area except those which will act as a guide to the original shape of the damaged body, such as headlight shells, etc. Using metal snips or a hacksaw blade, remove all loose metal and any other metal that is badly affected by rust. Hammer the edges of the hole in to create a slight depression for the filler material.

27 Wire brush the affected area to remove the powdery rust from the surface of the metal. If the back of the rusted area is accessible, treat it with rust inhibiting paint.

28 Before filling is done, block the hole in some way. This can be done with sheet metal riveted or screwed into place, or by stuffing the hole with wire mesh.

29 Once the hole is blocked off, the affected area can be filled and painted. See the following subsection on filling and painting.

FILLING AND PAINTING

30 Many types of body fillers are available, but generally speaking, body repair kits which contain filler paste and a tube of resin hardener are best for this type of repair work. A wide, flexible plastic or nylon applicator will be necessary for imparting a smooth and contoured finish to the surface of the filler material. Mix up a small amount of filler on a clean piece of wood or cardboard (use the hardener sparingly). Follow the manufacturer's instructions on the package, otherwise the filler will set incorrectly.

31 Using the applicator, apply the filler paste to the prepared area. Draw the applicator across the surface of the filler to achieve the desired contour and to level the filler surface. As soon as a contour that approximates the original one is achieved, stop working the paste. If you continue, the paste will begin to stick to the applicator. Continue to add thin layers of paste at 20-minute intervals until the level of the filler

is just above the surrounding metal.

32 Once the filler has hardened, the excess can be removed with a body file. From then on, progressively finer grades of sandpaper should be used, starting with a 180-grit paper and finishing with 600-grit wet-or-dry paper. Always wrap the sandpaper around a flat rubber or wooden block, otherwise the surface of the filler will not be completely flat. During the sanding of the filler surface, the wet-or-dry paper should be periodically rinsed in water. This will ensure that a very smooth finish is produced in the final stage.

33 At this point, the repair area should be surrounded by a ring of bare metal, which in turn should be encircled by the finely feathered edge of good paint. Rinse the repair area with clean water until all of the dust produced by the sanding operation is gone.

34 Spray the entire area with a light coat of primer. This will reveal any imperfections in the surface of the filler. Repair the imperfections with fresh filler paste or glaze filler and once more smooth the surface with sandpaper. Repeat this spray-and-repair procedure until you are satisfied that the surface of the filler and the feathered edge of the paint are perfect. Rinse the area with clean water and allow it to dry completely.

35 The repair area is now ready for painting. Spray painting must be carried out in a warm, dry, windless and dust free atmosphere. These conditions can be created if you have access to a large indoor work area, but if you are forced to work in the open, you will have to pick the day very carefully. If you are working indoors, dousing the floor in the work area with water will help settle the dust which would otherwise be in the air. If the repair area is confined to one body panel, mask off the surrounding panels. This will help minimize the effects of a slight mismatch in paint color. Trim pieces such as chrome strips, door handles, etc., will also need to be masked off or removed. Use masking tape and several thickness of newspaper for the masking operations.

36 Before spraying, shake the paint can thoroughly, then spray a test area until the spray painting technique is mastered. Cover the repair area with a thick coat of primer. The thickness should be built up using several thin layers of primer rather than one thick one. Using 600-grit wet-or-dry sandpaper, rub down the surface of the primer until it is very smooth. While doing this, the work area should be thoroughly rinsed with water and the wet-or-dry sandpaper periodically rinsed as well. Allow the primer to dry before spraying additional coats.

37 Spray on the top coat, again building up the thickness by using several thin layers of paint. Begin spraying in the center of the repair area and then, using a circular motion, work out until the whole repair area and about two inches of the surrounding original paint is covered. Remove all masking material 10 to 15 minutes after spraying on the final coat of paint. Allow the new paint at least two weeks to harden, then use a very fine rubbing compound to blend the edges of the new paint into the existing paint. Finally, apply a coat of wax.

6   Body repair - major damage

1   Major damage must be repaired by an auto body shop specifically equipped to perform unibody repairs. These shops have the specialized equipment required to do the job properly.

2   If the damage is extensive, the body must be checked for proper alignment or the vehicle's handling characteristics may be adversely affected and other components may wear at an accelerated rate.

3   Due to the fact that some of the major body components (hood, fenders, doors, etc.) are separate and replaceable units, any seriously damaged components should be replaced rather than repaired. Sometimes the components can be found in a wrecking yard that specializes in used vehicle components, often at considerable savings over the cost of new parts.

7 Hinges and locks - maintenance

Once every 3,000 miles, or every three months, the hinges and latch assemblies on the doors, hood and trunk (or liftgate) should be given a few drops of light oil or lock lubricant. The door latch strikers should also be lubricated with a thin coat of grease to reduce wear and ensure free movement. Lubricate the door and trunk (or liftgate) locks with spray-on graphite lubricant.

8 Windshield and fixed glass - replacement

Replacement of the windshield and fixed glass requires the use of special fast-setting adhesive/caulk materials and some specialized tools and techniques. These operations should be left to a dealer service department or a shop specializing in glass work.

9 Hood - removal, installation and adjustment

➡ **Note: The hood is heavy and somewhat awkward to remove and install - at least two people should perform this procedure.**

REMOVAL AND INSTALLATION

▶ **Refer to illustrations 9.2 and 9.4**

1   Use blankets or pads to cover the cowl area of the body and the fenders. This will protect the body and paint as the hood is lifted off.
2   Scribe alignment marks around the bolt heads and hinge attachment locations to insure proper alignment during installation - a permanent-type felt-tip marker also will work for this (see illustration).
3   Remove the top bolts holding the hood to the hinge and loosen the bottom bolts until they can be removed by hand.
4   Have an assistant on the opposite side of the vehicle support the weight of the hood. Simultaneously remove the bottom bolts holding the hood to the hinge and lift off the hood (see illustration).
5   Installation is the reverse of removal.

ADJUSTMENT

▶ **Refer to illustrations 9.9 and 9.10**

6   Front-and-back and side-to-side adjustment of the hood is done by moving the hood in relation to the hinge plate after loosening the bolts.

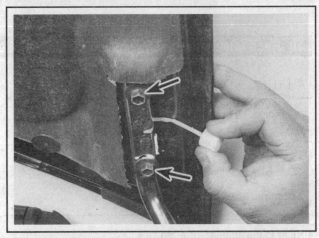

9.2 Mark the hinge plate and bolt head locations and loosen the bolts (arrows) for latch adjustment or removal

7   Scribe or trace a line around the entire hinge plate so you can judge the amount of movement.
8   Loosen the bolts or nuts and move the hood into correct alignment. Move it only a little at a time. Tighten the hinge bolts or nuts and carefully lower the hood to check the alignment.
9   Adjust the hood bumpers on the radiator support so the hood is flush with the fenders when closed (see illustration).

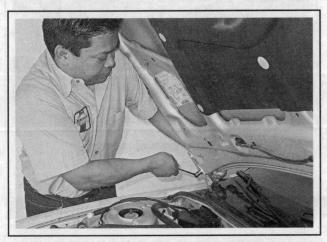

9.4 Support the hood with your shoulder while removing the hood bolts

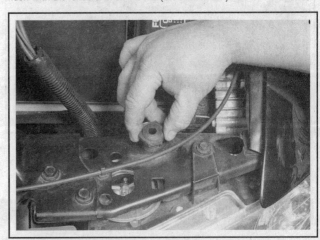

9.9 Adjust the hood height by screwing the hood bumpers in or out

10 Mark the hood latch as a guide for adjustment (or removal and replacement). The hood latch assembly can also be adjusted up-and-down and side-to-side after loosening the bolts (see illustration).

11 The hood latch assembly, as well as the hinges, should be periodically lubricated with white lithium-base grease to prevent sticking and wear.

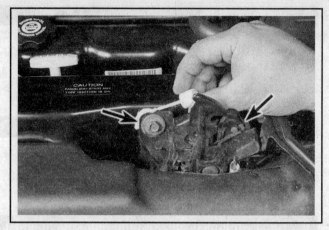

9.10 Mark the position of the hood latch, loosen the bolts and move the latch to adjust the hood in the closed position

10 Hood latch and cable - removal and installation

LATCH

1 Remove the bolts holding the hood latch to the radiator support and detach the latch assembly.

2 Referring to Step 4, detach the hood release cable, then remove the latch from the radiator support.

3 Installation is the reverse of removal.

CABLE

▶ **Refer to illustrations 10.4 and 10.6**

4 Release the cable end, then slide the cable case end sideways in the keyhole slot of the hood latch while pinching the barb on the cable case closed (see illustration).

5 Remove the cable from the latch.

6 In the passenger compartment, remove the screws and detach the hood release cable and handle assembly (see illustration).

7 Under the dash remove the rubber cable insulator from the hole in the dash panel.

8 Connect a string or piece of wire to the engine compartment end of the cable, then detach the cable and pull it through the firewall into the passenger compartment.

9 Connect the string or wire to the new cable and pull it through the firewall into the engine compartment.

10 The remainder of installation is the reverse of removal.

10.4 Detach the cable end from the latch lever

10.6 Hood release handle mounting fasteners

11 Radiator grille - removal and installation

1 Remove the front bumper cover (see Section 12).

2 Detach the clips securing the grille to the front bumper cover.

3 Carefully lift the grille away from the bumper cover.

4 Installation is the reverse of removal.

12 Bumper covers - removal and installation

FRONT BUMPER COVER

▶ **Refer to illustrations 12.1 and 12.7**

1   Release the hood latch and open the hood. Remove the fasteners attaching the grille to the radiator support (see illustration).

2   Remove the headlight housings (see Chapter 12).

3   Remove the bolts holding the bumper cover to the headlight mounting panel at each side of the grille.

4   Raise the vehicle and support it securely on jackstands.

5   Remove the front wheels.

6   Remove the front inner fender splash shield fasteners as necessary to gain access to the bolts holding the front cover to the fender (see Section 13).

7   Remove the fasteners securing the bottom of the bumper cover (see illustration).

8   Disconnect the fog light/parking and turn signal light electrical connector, if necessary.

9   Remove the bumper cover from the vehicle.

10 Installation is the reverse of removal.

REAR BUMPER COVER

▶ **Refer to illustrations 12.13 and 12.14**

11 Open the liftgate.

12 Raise the vehicle and support it securely on jackstands.

13 Remove the upper mounting fasteners (see illustration).

14 Remove the fasteners securing the bottom of the bumper cover (see illustration).

15 Disconnect the parking assist electrical connector, if equipped.

16 Release the hooks on the sides of the bumper cover from the tabs in the rear cover brackets.

17 Remove the rear bumper cover from the vehicle.

18 Installation is the reverse of removal.

12.1 Remove the front bumper cover upper mounting fasteners

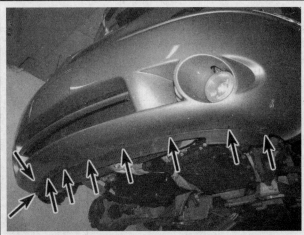

12.7 Remove the front bumper cover lower mounting fasteners

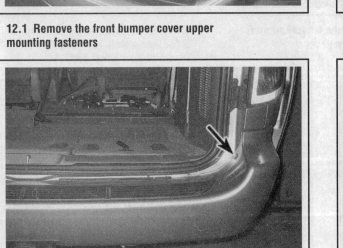

12.13 Remove the rear bumper cover upper mounting fasteners (one per side)

12.14 Remove the rear bumper cover lower mounting fasteners (not all fasteners visible in photo)

13 Front fender - removal and installation

▶ **Refer to illustrations 13.2, 13.4, 13.5a, 13.5b, 13.6 and 13.7**

1   Loosen the wheel lug nuts. Raise the vehicle and support it securely on jackstands, then remove the front wheel.

2   Remove the fasteners retaining the fender inner splash shield (see illustration).

3   Remove the front bumper cover (see Section 12). If you're removing the right-side fender, remove the antenna mast (see Chapter 12, if necessary).

4   Remove the side view mirror (see Section 22), then remove the fender bolt behind the mirror (see illustration).

5   Remove the fender-to-rocker panel bolt and the fender-to-door pillar bolt (see illustrations).

6   Remove the bolts retaining the fender to the headlight housing opening (see illustration).

7   Remove the remaining fender mounting bolts (see illustration).

8   Detach the fender. It's a good idea to have an assistant support the fender while it's being moved away from the vehicle to prevent damage to the surrounding body panels. If you're removing the right-side fender, disconnect the antenna cable (see Chapter 12).

9   Installation is the reverse of removal.

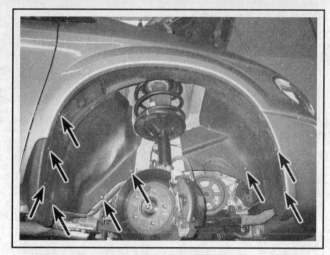

13.2 Remove the fender inner splash shield mounting fasteners

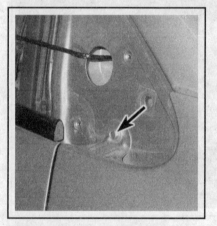

13.4 With the side view mirror removed, remove this fastener

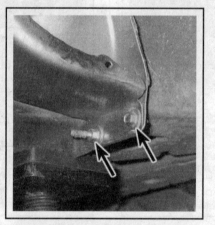

13.5a Remove the fender-to-rocker panel bolt and nut . . .

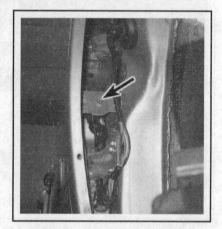

13.5b . . . then working inside the inner fender well, remove the fender-to-door panel bolt

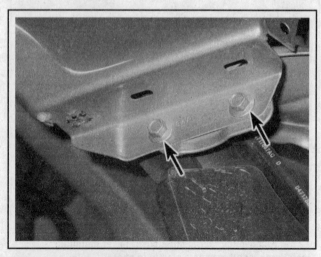

13.6 Remove the bolts near the front of the fender, at the headlight housing opening

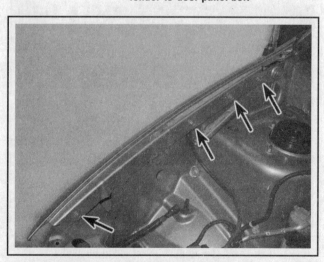

13.7 Remove the fender upper mounting bolts and lift off the fender

14 Cowl cover - removal and installation

▶ **Refer to illustrations 14.1 and 14.3**

1   Remove the windshield wiper arms (see Chapter 12), then remove the screws that hold the lower area of the cowl cover to the wiper module (see illustration).

2   Disengage the quarter-turn fasteners that hold the outer ends of

the cowl cover to the wiper module.

3   Open the hood and lift the cowl cover up enough to get to the washer hose. Disconnect the washer hose from the washer in line connector (see illustration).

4   Lift the cowl cover toward the windshield and off the vehicle.

5   Installation is the reverse of removal.

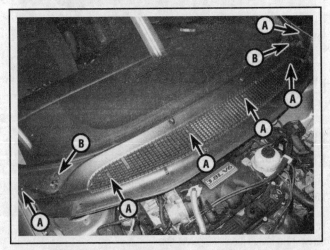

14.1 Cowl cover mounting details

    A   Mounting screws   *B   Quarter-turn fasteners*

14.3 Disconnect the washer hose

15 Door trim panels - removal and installation

REMOVAL

Front door trim panel

▶ **Refer to illustrations 15.1a, 15.1b, 15.1c, 15.2a, 15.2b, 15.3, 15.4 and 15.5**

1   On manual window models, remove the window crank (see

illustration). On power window models, use a small flat-bladed pry tool to remove the door switch panel and the control switch assembly (see illustrations).

2   Remove all door trim panel retaining screws and door pull/arm-rest assemblies (see illustrations).

3   Remove the door trim panel using a door panel removal tool (see illustration). Start from the bottom of the trim panel and work around the perimeter until all the fasteners have been released from the door.

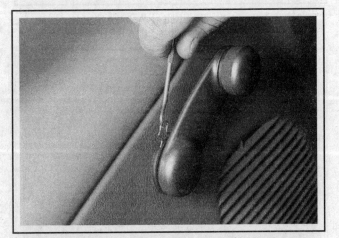

15.1a Remove the retaining clip, then detach the window crank handle. A hooked tool like this one can be used, but special window crank clip removal tools are available at most auto parts stores, and make this step much easier

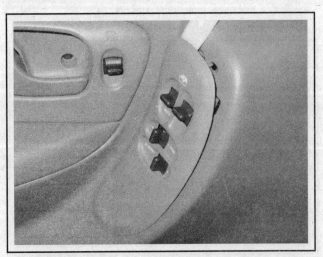

15.1b Using a trim stick, carefully pry the door switch panel from the door . . .

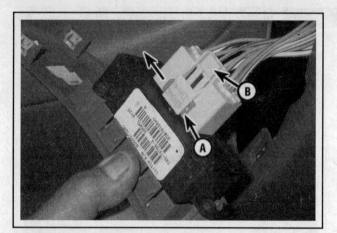

15.1c ... then disconnect the electrical connector; slide the lock out in the direction of the arrow, then depress the tab and pull the connector off

4   Disconnect the inner door handle lock rod from the handle (see illustration). Unplug any electrical connectors remaining and remove the door panel.

5   For access to the door outside handle or door window regulator inside the door, raise the window fully, then carefully peel back the plastic watershield (see illustration).

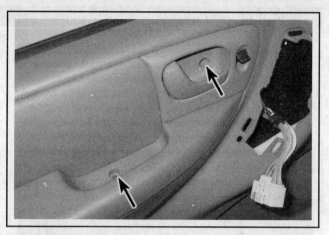

15.2a Remove the upper ...

Sliding door trim panel

▶ **Refer to illustrations 15.6 and 15.8**

6   Close the door and remove the upper frame molding (see illustration).

7   Remove any screws holding the trim panel to the inner door panel. If you're removing the left sliding door trim panel, remove the screw from inside the ash receiver bezel.

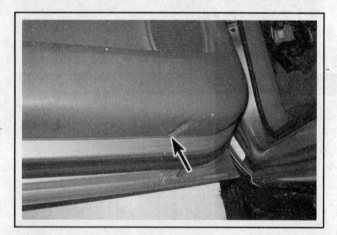

15.2b ... and lower mounting fasteners

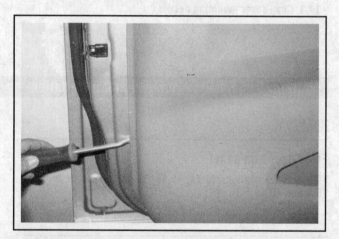

15.3 Carefully pry the clips free so the door trim panel can be removed

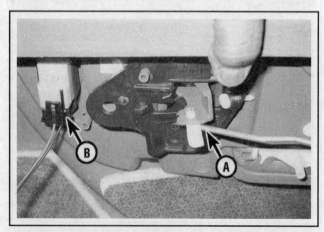

15.4 Disconnect the inner door handle lock rod (A) and unplug any electrical connectors (B)

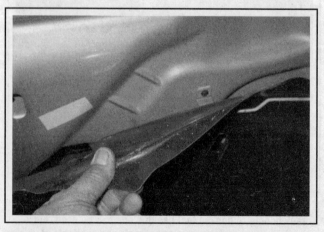

15.5 Carefully peel back the plastic watershield

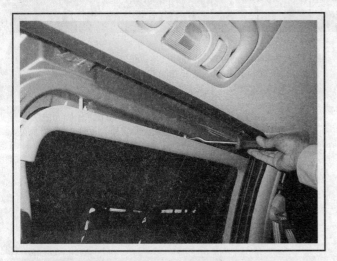

15.6 Using a trim removal tool, remove the upper frame molding

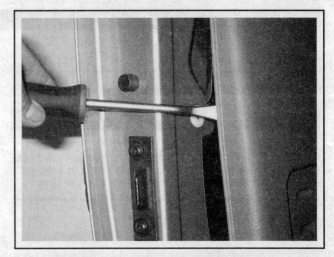

15.8 Carefully pry the clips free so the door trim panel can be removed

8   Remove the door trim panel using a door panel removal tool (see illustration). Start from the bottom of the trim panel and work around the perimeter until all the fasteners have been released from the door.

Liftgate trim panel

▶ **Refer to illustrations 15.9, 15.10 and 15.11**

9   Remove the liftgate upper frame molding and the side moldings (see illustration).

10   Remove the screws holding the pull handle (see illustration).

11   Remove the door trim panel using a door panel removal tool (see illustration). Start from the bottom of the trim panel and work around the perimeter until all the fasteners have been released from the door.

12   Disconnect the wire connector from the courtesy lamps and remove the trim panel.

INSTALLATION

13   Prior to installation of the door trim panels and/or the tailgate trim panel, be sure to reinstall any clips in the panel which may have come out when you removed the panel.

14   Position the wire harness connectors for the power door lock

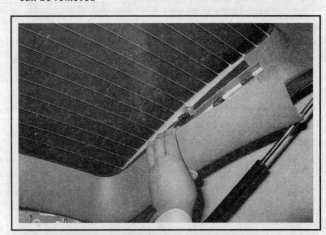

15.9 Using a trim removal tool, remove the upper frame molding

switch and the power window switch (if equipped) on the back of the panel, then place the panel in position in the door. Press the door panel into place until the clips are seated.

15   The remainder of the installation is the reverse of removal.

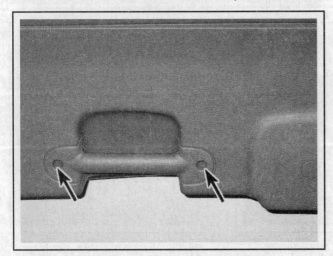

15.10 Remove the fasteners securing the pull handle

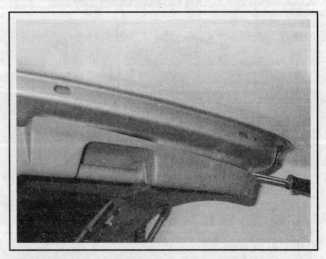

15.11 Carefully pry the clips free so the door trim panel can be removed

16 Door - removal and installation

FRONT DOOR

▶ Refer to illustrations 16.2 and 16.4

✳✳ CAUTION:

If the hinge pin must be removed from the hinge, do not reuse the original pin. If you plan to remove the pin be sure you have a new one before starting the job. The retaining clips used on the door hinge pins should also be replaced with new ones.

1 Remove the fender inner splash shield (see illustration 13.2).
2 Disconnect the door harness connector from the body harness (see illustration).
3 Depress the lock tab holding the wire connector halves together and disconnect the door harness from the body wiring harness.
4 Remove the bolts holding the door check strap to the A-pillar (see illustration). Place a jack under the door or have an assistant on hand to support it when the hinge bolts are removed.
➡Note: If a jack is used, place a rag between it and the door to protect the door's painted surfaces.
5 Scribe around the hinge bolt heads with a marking pen. Remove

16.2 Disconnect the door harness wire connector

the bolts holding the lower hinge to the door end frame. Keeping the door steady, remove the bolts holding the upper hinge to the door end frame and carefully lift off the door.
6 Installation is the reverse of removal, making sure to align the hinge with the marks made during removal before tightening the bolts.
7 Following installation of the door, check the alignment and adjust it if necessary as follows:
   a) *Up-and-down and in-and-out adjustments are made by loosening the hinge-to-door bolts and moving the door as necessary.*
   b) *Forward-and-backward adjustments are made by loosening the hinge-to-body bolts and moving the door as necessary.*
   c) *The door lock striker can also be adjusted both up-and-down and sideways to provide positive engagement with the lock mechanism. This is done by loosening the mounting screws and moving the striker as necessary.*

SLIDING DOOR

▶ Refer to illustrations 16.11, 16.12a, 16.12b, 16.13, 16.14, 16.15 and 16.17

✳✳ CAUTION:

Apply several layers of masking tape to the body around the rear end of the upper roller channel and the forward edge of the quarter glass to avoid damaging the paint.

➡Note: This procedure applies to both the manual and electrically operated sliding door removal and installation and applies to both right and left side sliding doors. It does not apply to the electrically operated mechanism for the door.

8 Apply masking tape to the outside surface of the quarter panel below the center roller channel, rearward of the door opening.
9 Release the sliding door latch and open the door.
10 Apply masking tape to the door jamb area, rearward of the upper roller channel.
11 Remove the screw holding the upper roller arm stop bumper to the upper roller arm (see illustration).
12 Remove the trim cover and center stop bumper from the door (see illustrations).

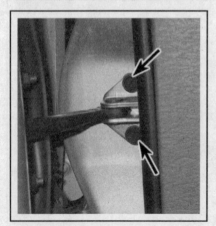

16.4 Remove the door check strap mounting bolts

16.11 Remove this screw holding the upper roller arm stop bumper to the upper roller arm

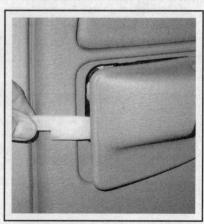

16.12a Using a trim stick, carefully remove the center stop bumper trim cover . . .

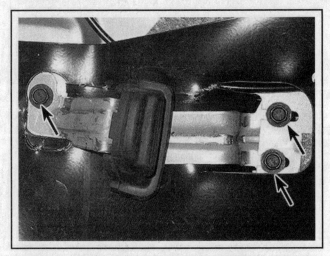

16.12b . . . then remove the center stop bumper mounting fasteners

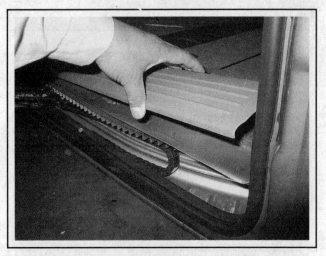

16.13 Carefully remove the door sill trim from the body by lifting along the inner edge to release the clips

13 Remove the sliding door sill trim (see illustration).
14 Remove the hold open striker (see illustration).
15 On power sliding door models, disconnect the electrical connector for the motor mechanism (see illustration).
16 Open quarter glass.
17 Remove the center roller channel end cover (see illustration). Support the sliding door on a suitable lifting device that has a padded upper surface. The door must be moveable while on the lifting device.

❈ CAUTION:

Do not allow the center hinge roller to contact the quarter glass. This could break the glass.

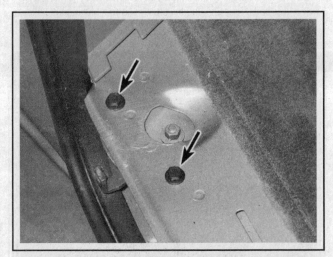

16.14 Remove the fasteners securing the hold open striker, then remove the striker

18 Roll the door rearward until the lower rollers disengage from the lower channel.
19 Roll the door rearward until the upper and center hinge rollers exit the upper and center channels.
20 Remove the sliding door from the vehicle.
21 Installation is the reverse of removal. Be aware of **Cautions** above about the hinge roller and quarter glass.

16.15 Disconnect the electrical connector for the motor mechanism

16.17 With the quarter glass open, remove the fastener securing the center roller channel end cover, then remove the cover

LIFTGATE

▶ **Refer to illustration 16.27**

22 Have an assistant support the liftgate in its fully open position.

23 Disconnect all cables and wire harness connectors that would interfere with removal of the liftgate.

24 Remove the liftgate upper frame molding and disconnect the rear window washer hose from the spray nozzle.

25 On power liftgate models, disconnect the lift mechanism actuator rod from the liftgate.

26 While an assistant supports the liftgate, detach the support struts (see Section 17).

27 Mark or scribe around the hinges, then remove the hinge bolts and detach the liftgate from the vehicle (see illustration).

28 Installation is the reverse of removal.

29 After installation, close the liftgate and make sure it is in proper alignment with the surrounding body panels. Adjustments are made by changing the position of the hinge bolts in the slots. To adjust it, loosen the hinge bolts and reposition the hinges either side-to-side or front and back the desired amount and retighten the bolts.

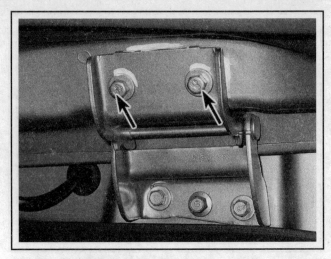

16.27 Liftgate hinge-to-liftgate bolts

30 The engagement of the liftgate can be adjusted by loosening the lock striker bolts, repositioning the striker and retightening the bolts.

17 Liftgate struts - replacement

▶ **Refer to illustration 17.3**

1 Have an assistant support the liftgate in its fully open position.

2 Pull away the weatherstrip from the D-pillar flange next to the strut assembly end pivot.

3 Remove the mounting bolt where the strut attaches to the body (see illustration).

4 Remove the bolt holding the strut to the liftgate, and remove the strut from the vehicle.

5 Installation is the reverse of removal.

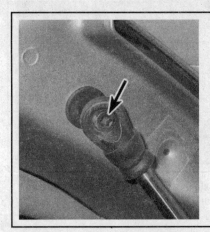

17.3 Remove the strut-to-body mounting bolt

18 Door latch, lock and handle - removal and installation

FRONT DOOR LATCH

▶ **Refer to illustrations 18.3 and 18.4**

1 Close the window completely and remove the front door trim panel (see Section 15). Carefully peel back the plastic water shield as needed to access the inner door components.

2 If equipped with power door locks, remove the wire connector from the power door lock motor.

3 Release the clips holding the linkage to door latch, and remove the linkages from the door latch (see illustration).

4 Remove the screws holding the door latch to the door end frame (see illustration) and remove the latch from the door.

5 Installation is the reverse of removal.

➡**Note: The manufacturer recommends that new screws be used if the latch has been removed.**

6 After installing the door latch with new screws, insert the linkage into the latch, engage clips to hold the linkage to the door latch and connect the electrical connector to the power door lock motor, if equipped. Insert a hex wrench through the oval hole located in the door shut face above the latch and loosen the Allen head screw.

7 Pull outward on the outside door handle and release, then tighten the Allen head screw.

8 Check that the door latch and power door lock operate, then install the plastic shield and front door trim panel.

FRONT DOOR OUTSIDE HANDLE

▶ **Refer to illustrations 18.10 and 18.12**

9 Close the window completely and remove the front door trim panel (see Section 15). Carefully peel back the plastic water shield

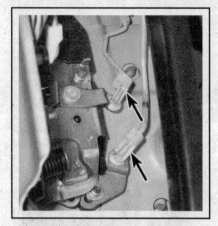

18.3 Release the clips holding the linkage to the door latch

18.4 Remove the latch mounting fasteners

18.10 Release the clips holding the door latch linkage and the lock linkage to the door handle

18.12 Remove the door handle mounting nuts

18.18 Remove the foam insulation block

18.19a Remove the inside handle mounting fasteners . . .

as needed to access the inner door components. If equipped with the Vehicle Theft Security System (VTSS), use the access hole at the rear of the inner door panel and disconnect the switch connector from the door harness. Release the push-in fasteners holding the VTSS switch harness to the inner door reinforcement.

10 Release the clips holding the door latch linkage and the lock link-

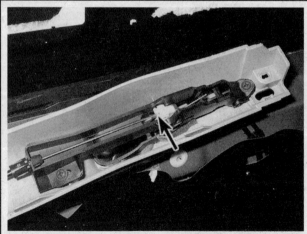

18.19b . . . then disengage the cable from the inside handle

age to the door handle (see illustration).
11 Remove the latch linkage and the lock linkage from the handle.
12 Remove the nuts holding the outside door handle to the door outer panel and remove the handle from the vehicle (see illustration).
13 Installation is the reverse of removal.

FRONT DOOR LOCK CYLINDER

14 Proceed as above to remove the front door outside handle. Release the clip holding the lock cylinder into the outside handle and pull the lock from the door handle.
15 Install the lock cylinder retaining clip into the door handle. Position the link arm toward the rear of vehicle, push the lock cylinder into the door handle until the lock cylinder snaps into place. The remainder of installation is the reverse of removal.

SLIDING DOOR LATCH/LOCK CONTROL

▶ **Refer to illustrations 18.18, 18.19a and 18.19b**

16 Remove the sliding door trim panel (see Section 15), the door stop bumper, and the plastic water shield.
17 Disconnect the external cable from the latch/lock control.
18 Remove the foam insulation block (see illustration).
19 Remove the inside latch handle (see illustrations).

20 Release the clip holding the inside door handle bellcrank link to the control above and separate the inside door handle bellcrank link from the latch/lock control.

21 Remove the bolts holding the latch/lock control to the sliding door (see illustration 18.4), (if equipped with power door locks, disconnect the wire connector from the power door lock motor).

22 Remove the latch lock from the vehicle.

23 Installation is the reverse of removal.

SLIDING DOOR OUTSIDE HANDLE

▶ **Refer to illustration 18.26**

24 Remove the sliding door trim panel (see Section 15), the door stop bumper, and the plastic water shield.

25 Release the clip holding the outside door handle linkage to the door handle, then separate the linkage from the outside door handle.

26 Remove the nuts holding the outside door handle to the outer door panel (see illustration) and remove the door handle from the vehicle.

27 Installation is the reverse of removal.

LIFTGATE LATCH

▶ **Refer to illustrations 18.29 and 18.30**

28 Remove the trim panel and watershield from the inside of liftgate (see Section 15).

29 Remove the outside lock cylinder link from the clip on the latch, then disconnect the wire connector from the liftgate latch (see illustration).

30 Remove the screws holding the latch to the liftgate and remove it from the vehicle (see illustration).

31 Installation is the reverse of removal.

LIFTGATE OUTSIDE HANDLE

32 Remove the trim panel and watershield from the inside of liftgate (see Section 15).

33 Disconnect the electrical connectors for the liftgate outside handle.

34 Remove the two outside and two inside handle mounting screws.

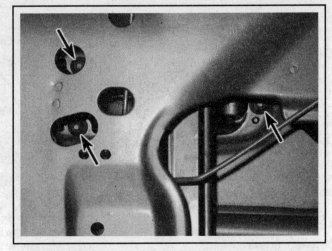

18.26 Remove the door handle mounting nuts

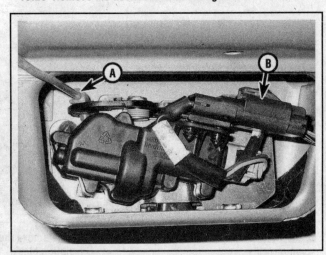

18.29 Disconnect the outside lock cylinder link from the clip on the latch (A), then disconnect the wire connector from the liftgate latch (B)

35 Remove the outside handle from the vehicle.
36 Installation is the reverse of removal.

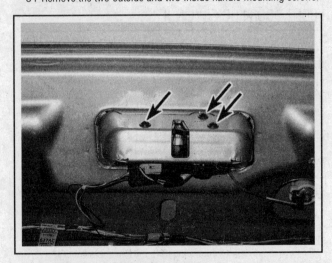

18.30 Liftgate latch mounting screws

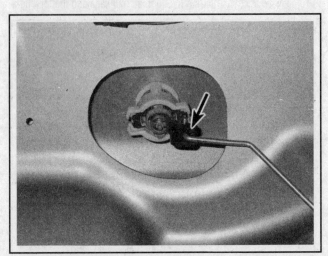

18.38 Release this clip to disconnect the latch link from the lock cylinder

LIFTGATE LOCK CYLINDER

▶ **Refer to illustration 18.38**

37 Remove the trim panel and watershield from the inside of the liftgate (see Section 15).

38 Release the clip holding the latch link to the lock cylinder (see illustration).

39 Disconnect the electrical connector, if equipped.

40 Rotate the plastic nut on the lock cylinder one quarter turn and remove the lock cylinder.

41 Installation is the reverse of removal.

19 Front door window glass - removal and installation

▶ **Refer to illustration 19.4**

1 Remove the door trim panel and plastic shield (see Section 15).

2 Remove the inner belt molding.

3 Lower the glass so that you can get to the front and rear regulator lift plates through the front and rear access holes in the door panel.

4 Loosen the two screws that hold the door glass to the regulator lift plates (see illustration), and remove the glass from the lift plates.

5 Remove the weatherstrip from the glass and then insert the front of the glass between the glass run channel and the outer door panel.

6 Carefully lift the glass upward and out of the exterior opening at the top of the door.

7 Installation is the reverse of removal.

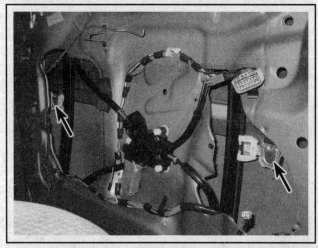

19.4 With the window in this position, loosen the two screws that hold the door glass to the regulator lift plates

20 Quarter window glass - removal and installation

▶ **Refer to illustration 20.3**

1 Remove the interior trim that is around the window to be removed (see Section 26), then open the window to the vent position.

2 Disconnect the vent motor arm from the quarter window retainer (see Section 21).

3 Remove the nuts that hold the glass to the pillar (see illustration) and remove the glass from the vehicle.

4 Installation is the reverse of removal.

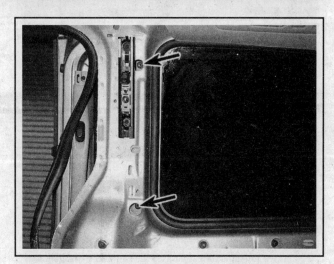

20.3 Remove the two nuts that secure the glass to the pillar

---

21 Window glass regulators - removal and installation

FRONT DOOR

▶ **Refer to illustration 21.4**

1 Remove the door trim panel and watershield (see Section 15).
2 Remove the door glass (see Section 19).
3 On power window models, unplug the electrical connector.
4 Loosen the screws holding the front and rear guide rails to the door panel (see illustration).
5 Remove the screw heads on the guide rails from the key hole slots in the door panel, lift up to detach the regulator, then slide it rearward and remove it through the access hole in the door. Remove the front guide rail through the front access hole and the rear guide rail through the rear access hole.
6 Installation is the reverse of removal.

QUARTER WINDOW

▶ **Refer to illustrations 21.8 and 21.9**

7 Remove the rear trim panel (see Section 26).
8 Disconnect the electrical connector from the vent motor (see illustration).
9 Remove the circular actuator link tab, then remove the arm from

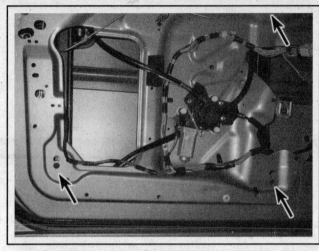

21.4 Front door window regulator mounting fasteners (upper left fastener not visible in photo)

the window ball socket (see illustration).
10 Remove the vent motor mounting fasteners and remove the vent motor.
11 Installation is the reverse of removal.

21.8 Vent motor electrical connector

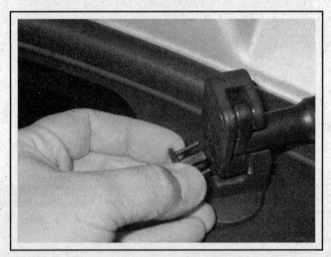

21.9 Remove the circular actuator link tab

---

22 Mirrors - removal and installation

OUTSIDE MIRRORS

▶ **Refer to illustrations 22.1, 22.2 and 22.3**

1 On models equipped with power mirrors, lift up the instrument panel top pad enough to gain access to the electrical connector for the mirror (see Section 25). Then disconnect the electrical connector (see illustration).
2 Remove the upper trim cover from the mirror (see illustration).
3 Remove the mirror mounting screws and detach the mirror (see illustration).
4 Installation is the reverse of removal.

INSIDE MIRROR

▶ **Refer to illustration 22.5**

5 Use a Phillips head screwdriver to remove the set screw, then slide the mirror up off the button on the windshield (see illustration).
➡**Note: If the mount plate itself has come off the windshield, adhesive kits are available at auto parts stores to re-secure it. Follow the instructions included with the kit.**

6 Installation is the reverse of removal.

22.1 Disconnect the power mirror electrical connector

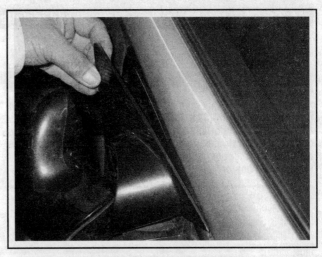

22.2 Remove the outside mirror upper trim cover

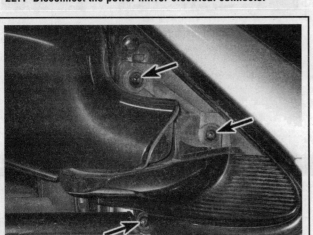

22.3 Remove the outside mirror mounting fasteners

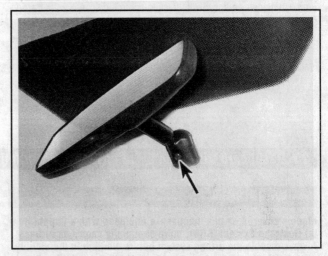

22.5 Remove the mirror set screw

23 Overhead console - removal and installation

▶ **Refer to illustration 23.2**

1 Open the eyeglass bin door and remove the screw holding the console to the headliner.

2 Grasp the sides of the overhead console (see illustration), pull straight down evenly, and disengage the two snap clips at the rear.

3 Lower the overhead console sufficiently to gain access to the electrical connectors. Disconnect the electrical connectors and remove the overhead console.

4 Installation is the reverse of removal.

23.2 Grasp the sides of the overhead console and pull straight down

24 Steering column covers - removal and installation

♦ Refer to illustration 24.2

❋❋❋ WARNING:

Models covered by this manual are equipped with a Supplemental Restraint System (SRS), more commonly known as airbags. Always disable the airbag system before working in the vicinity of any airbag system component to avoid the possibility of accidental deployment of the airbag, which could cause personal injury (see Chapter 12).

1   Disconnect the cable from the negative battery terminal (see Chapter 5, Section 1).

2   Remove the screws from the lower steering column cover (see illustration).

3   Separate the cover halves and detach them from the steering column. On models equipped with traction control, disconnect the traction control disable switch.

4   Installation is the reverse of removal.

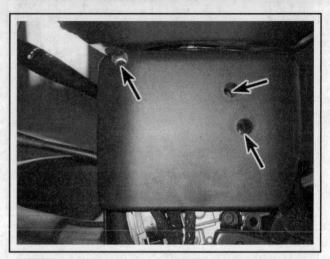

24.2 Remove the three screws from the lower steering column cover

25 Dashboard trim panels - removal and installation

❋❋❋ WARNING:

Models covered by this manual are equipped with a Supplemental Restraint System (SRS), more commonly known as airbags. Always disable the airbag system before working in the vicinity of any airbag system component to avoid the possibility of accidental deployment of the airbag, which could cause personal injury (see Chapter 12).

1   Disconnect the cable from the negative battery terminal (see Chapter 5, Section 1).

INSTRUMENT PANEL END CAPS

♦ Refer to illustration 25.2

2   If you're working on the left end cap, remove the attaching screws (see illustration), then detach it from the dashboard.

3   If you're working on the right side end cap, grasp the cover securely and pull sharply to remove it.

4   Installation is the reverse of removal.

25.2 The instrument panel end cap on the left side is secured by three screws

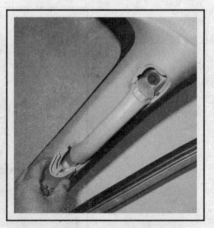

25.5a Remove the end caps from the pull handle, remove the handle mounting fasteners and remove the pull handle . . .

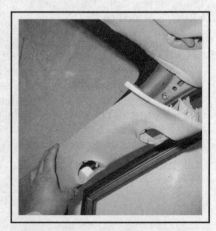

25.5b . . . then carefully release the clips securing the A-pillar trim

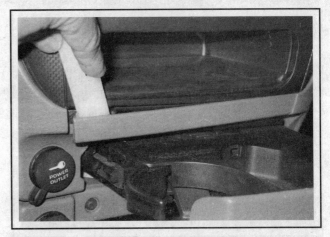

25.6 Using a trim stick, carefully remove the instrument panel top cover

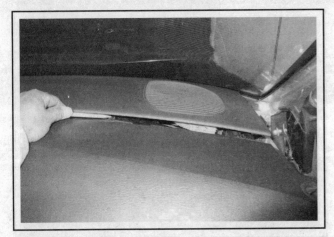

25.8 With the cupholder open, carefully pry loose the access cover

INSTRUMENT PANEL TOP COVER

▶ Refer to illustrations 25.5a, 25.5b and 25.6

5   Remove the A-pillar trim (see illustrations).

6   Using a trim stick, start from the bottom of the trim panel and work around the perimeter until all the fasteners have been released,

then remove the cover (see illustration).

7   Installation is the reverse of removal.

RADIO AND HEATER/AIR CONDITIONING CONTROL PANEL BEZEL

▶ Refer to illustrations 25.8, 25.9 and 25.10

8   Open the cupholder, then, using a trim stick, remove the access cover (see illustration).

9   Remove the mounting screws from the bottom of the control panel bezel (see illustration).

10 Using a trim stick, carefully pry around the bezel to release the mounting clips (see illustration), then disconnect any electrical connectors and remove the bezel from the instrument panel.

11 Installation is the reverse of removal.

INSTRUMENT CLUSTER BEZEL

▶ Refer to illustrations 25.12 and 25.13

12 Remove the steering column bezel (see illustration).

13 Remove the instrument cluster bezel mounting screws (see illustration).

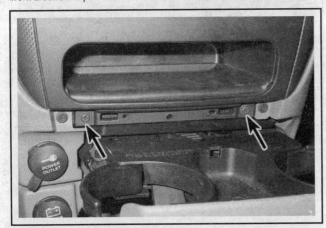

25.9 Remove the control panel bezel mounting fasteners

25.10 Using a trim stick, carefully pry around the bezel

25.12 With a firm pull straight up, lift the steering column bezel off the steering column

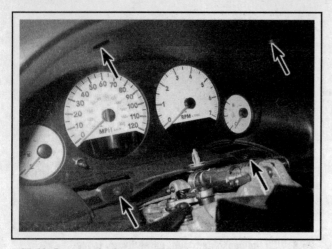

25.13 Remove the fasteners securing the instrument cluster bezel

14 Tilt the steering column down.

15 Grasp the bezel with both hands and pull straight out to disengage the bezel from the instrument panel.

16 Installation is the reverse of removal.

KNEE BOLSTER

▶ **Refer to illustration 25.17**

17 Remove the bolster mounting screws (see illustration).

18 Grasp the cover with both hands and pull straight out to disengage the bezel from the instrument panel.

19 Installation is the reverse of removal.

GLOVE BOX

▶ **Refer to illustration 25.20**

20 Open the glove box, grasp the sides of the glove box with both hands and push on the sides, then lower the door (see illustration).

21 Pivot the glove box in a downward position and disengage the

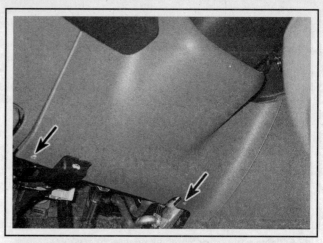

25.17 Knee bolster mounting fasteners

25.20 Push on the sides of the glove box then lower the door

hinge hooks from the instrument panel.

22 Installation is the reverse of removal.

26 Rear trim panels - removal and installation

▶ **Refer to illustrations 26.4a, 26.4b, 26.4c, 26.4d and 26.4e**

1 Disconnect the cable from the negative battery terminal (see Chapter 5, Section 1).

2 Remove the first and, if equipped, the second rear seat.

3 Remove the plastic plugs from the trim panel that is being removed. Use a flat bladed screwdriver.

4 Separate the trim panels from the body. Remove all mounting screws with a screwdriver and release the mounting clips (see illustrations). Disconnect any wire connectors from accessory power outlets, if so equipped.

5 Installation is the reverse of removal. Tighten the seat belt mounting bolt to the torque listed in this Chapter's Specifications.

26.4a Remove the rear header trim . . .

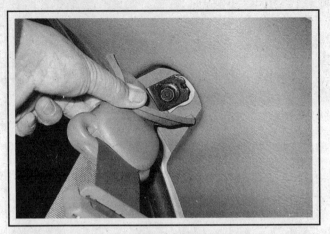

26.4b ... remove the third row seat upper seat belt anchor ...

26.4c ... using a trim panel removal tool, carefully pry loose the D-pillar trim panel ...

26.4d ... and the speaker cover trim panel ...

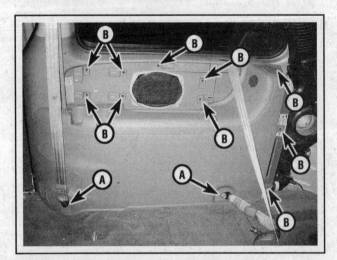

26.4e ... remove the lower second and third row seat belt mounting bolts (A) and the quarter trim panel mounting screws (B)

27 Seats - removal and installation

✳✳ WARNING:

Models covered by this manual are equipped with a Supplemental Restraint System (SRS), more commonly known as airbags. Always disable the airbag system before working in the vicinity of any airbag system component to avoid the possibility of accidental deployment of the airbag, which could cause personal injury (see Chapter 12).

1   Disconnect the cable from the negative battery terminal (see Chapter 5, Section 1).

FRONT SEATS

▶ **Refer to illustrations 27.3a and 27.3b**

2   Raise the vehicle and support it securely on jackstands. On 2005 and later models, lower the spare tire.

3   Working under the vehicle, remove the seat mounting fasteners (see illustrations).

27.3a On 2005 and later models, remove the spare tire heat shield by removing the push pin fasteners

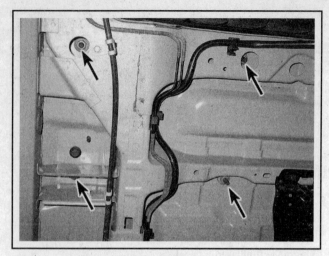

27.3b Front seat mounting fasteners

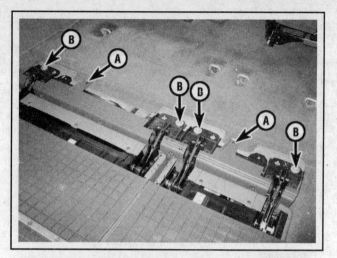

27.12 Remove the two fasteners securing the lower trim (A) and the seat mounting fasteners (B)

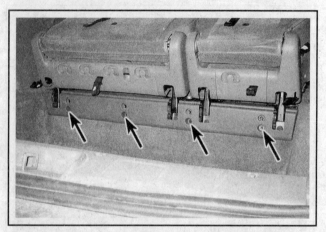

27.13 Remove the remaining fasteners securing the lower trim

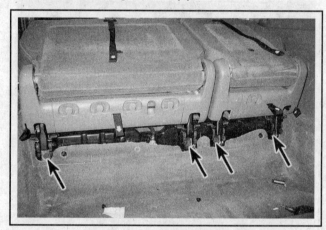

27.14 Remove the remaining fasteners securing the seat

4   Working inside the vehicle, tilt the seat forward and disconnect any electrical connectors, then remove the seat from the vehicle.
5   Installation is the reverse of removal.

SECOND ROW SEATS

Stow-n-go seat

Prop rod

6   With the seat in the upright position, remove the lower front shield.
7   Remove the upper and lower mounting fasteners for the prop rod. Remove the prop rod.
8   Installation is the reverse of removal.

Non stow-n-go seat

9   Lift the release handle on the lower side of the seat and lift the rear of the seat.
10 Pull the release bar at the bottom of the seat and release the seat from its attachments. Remove the seat from the vehicle.
11 Installation is the reverse of removal.

THIRD ROW SEATS

Stow-n-go seat

▶ **Refer to illustrations 27.12, 27.13 and 27.14**

12 With the seats in the downward position, remove the lower trim and seat mounting fasteners (see illustration).
13 Raise the seats to the upright position, then remove the remaining fasteners securing the lower trim and remove the trim (see illustration).
14 Remove the remaining seat mounting fasteners (see illustration).
15 Installation is the reverse of removal.

Specifications

Torque specifications	Ft-lbs
Seat belt mounting bolts	29

Notes

Section

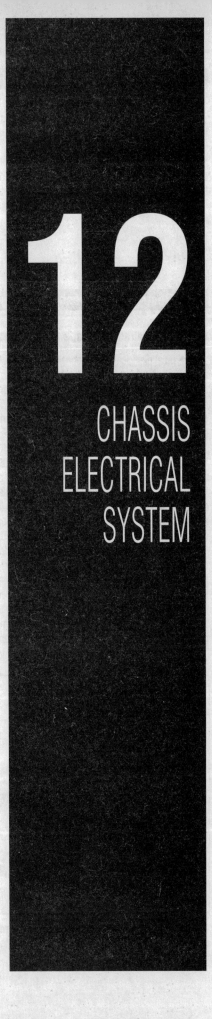

12

CHASSIS ELECTRICAL SYSTEM

1 General information

The electrical system is a 12-volt, negative ground type. Power for the lights and all electrical accessories is supplied by a lead/acid-type battery, which is charged by the alternator.

This Chapter covers repair and service procedures for the various electrical components not associated with the engine. Information on the battery, alternator, distributor and starter motor can be found in Chapter 5.

It should be noted that when portions of the electrical system are serviced, the cable should be disconnected from the negative battery terminal (see Chapter 5, Section 1) to prevent electrical shorts and/or fires.

2 Electrical troubleshooting - general information

♦ **Refer to illustrations 2.5a, 2.5b, 2.6 and 2.9**

A typical electrical circuit consists of an electrical component, any switches, relays, motors, fuses, fusible links or circuit breakers related to that component and the wiring and connectors that link the component to both the battery and the chassis. To help you pinpoint an electrical circuit problem, wiring diagrams are included at the end of this Chapter.

Before tackling any troublesome electrical circuit, first study the appropriate wiring diagrams to get a complete understanding of what makes up that individual circuit. Noting if other components related to the circuit are operating properly, for instance, can often narrow down trouble spots. If several components or circuits fail at one time, chances are the problem is in a fuse or ground connection, because several circuits are often routed through the same fuse and ground connections.

Electrical problems usually stem from simple causes, such as loose or corroded connections, a blown fuse, a melted fusible link or a failed relay. Visually inspect the condition of all fuses, wires and connections in a problem circuit before troubleshooting the circuit.

If test equipment and instruments are going to be utilized, use the diagrams to plan ahead of time where you will make the necessary connections in order to accurately pinpoint the trouble spot.

For electrical troubleshooting, you'll need a voltmeter, a circuit tester or a 12-volt bulb with a set of test leads; a continuity tester, which includes a bulb, battery and set of test leads; and a jumper wire, with a circuit breaker, which can be used to bypass electrical components (see illustrations). Before attempting to locate a problem with test instruments, use the wiring diagram(s) to decide where to make the connections.

VOLTAGE CHECKS

Voltage checks should be performed if a circuit is not functioning properly. Connect one lead of a circuit tester to either the negative battery terminal or a known good ground. Connect the other lead to a connector in the circuit being tested, preferably nearest to the battery or fuse (see illustration). If the bulb of the tester lights, voltage is present, which means that the part of the circuit between the connector and the battery is problem free. Continue checking the rest of the circuit in the same fashion. When you reach a point at which no voltage is present, the problem lies between that point and the last test point with voltage. Most of the time the problem can be traced to a loose connection.

➡**Note: Keep in mind that some circuits receive voltage only when the ignition key is in the ACC (accessory) or ON/RUN position.**

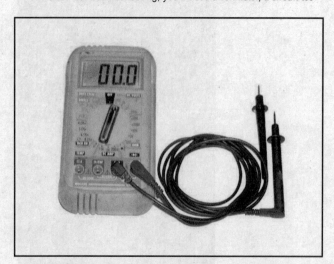

2.5a The most useful tool for electrical troubleshooting is a digital multimeter that can check volts, amps, and test continuity

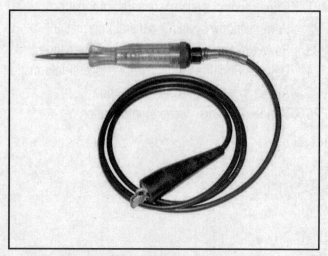

2.5b A simple test light is a very handy tool for testing voltage

2.6 In use, a basic test light's lead is clipped to a known good ground, then the pointed probe can test connectors, wires or electrical sockets - if the bulb lights, the circuit being tested has battery voltage

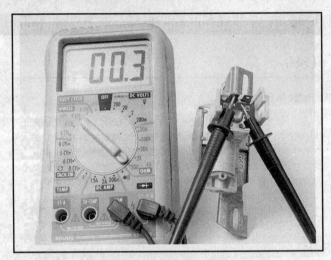

2.9 With a multimeter set to the ohm scale, resistance can be checked across two terminals - when checking for continuity, a low reading indicates continuity, a high reading or infinity indicates lack of continuity

FINDING A SHORT

One method of finding shorts in a live circuit is to remove the fuse and connect a test light in place of the fuse terminals (fabricate two jumper wires with small spade terminals, plug the jumper wires into the fuse box and connect the test light). There should be voltage present in the circuit. Move the suspected wiring harness from side-to-side while watching the test light. If the bulb goes off, there is a short to ground somewhere in that area, probably where the insulation has rubbed through.

GROUND CHECK

Perform a ground test to check whether a component is properly grounded. Disconnect the battery and connect one lead of a continuity tester or multimeter (set to the ohm scale), to a known good ground. Connect the other lead to the wire or ground connection being tested. If the resistance is low (less than 5 ohms), the ground is good. If the bulb on a self-powered test light does not go on, the ground is not good.

CONTINUITY CHECK

A continuity check is done to determine if there are any breaks in a circuit - if it is passing electricity properly. With the circuit off (no power in the circuit), a self-powered continuity tester or multimeter can be used to check the circuit. Connect the test leads to both ends of the circuit (or to the power end and a good ground), and if the test light comes on the circuit is passing current properly (see illustration). If the resistance is low (less than 5 ohms), there is continuity; if the reading is 10,000 ohms or higher, there is a break somewhere in the circuit. The same procedure can be used to test a switch, by connecting the continuity tester to the switch terminals. With the switch turned On, the test light should come on (or low resistance should be indicated on a meter).

FINDING AN OPEN CIRCUIT

When diagnosing for possible open circuits, it is often difficult to locate them by sight because the connectors hide oxidation or terminal misalignment. Merely wiggling a connector on a sensor or in the wiring harness may correct the open circuit condition. Remember this when an open circuit is indicated when troubleshooting a circuit. Intermittent problems may also be caused by oxidized or loose connections.

Electrical troubleshooting is simple if you keep in mind that all electrical circuits are basically electricity running from the battery, through the wires, switches, relays, fuses and fusible links to each electrical component (light bulb, motor, etc.) and to ground, from which it is passed back to the battery. Any electrical problem is an interruption in the flow of electricity to and from the battery.

CONNECTORS

Most electrical connections on these vehicles are made with multiwire plastic connectors. The mating halves of many connectors are secured with locking clips molded into the plastic connector shells. The mating halves of large connectors, such as some of those under the instrument panel, are held together by a bolt through the center of the connector.

To separate a connector with locking clips, use a small screwdriver to pry the clips apart carefully, then separate the connector halves. Pull only on the shell, never pull on the wiring harness as you may damage the individual wires and terminals inside the connectors. Look at the connector closely before trying to separate the halves. Often the locking clips are engaged in a way that is not immediately clear. Additionally, many connectors have more than one set of clips.

Each pair of connector terminals has a male half and a female half. When you look at the end view of a connector in a diagram, be sure to understand whether the view shows the harness side or the component side of the connector. Connector halves are mirror images of each other, i.e. a terminal shown on the right side end-view of one half will be on the left side end view of the other half.

3 Fuses and fusible links - general information

FUSES

♦ **Refer to illustrations 3.1 and 3.3**

The electrical circuits of the vehicle are protected by a combination of fuses, circuit breakers and fusible links. The fuse and relay box is located on the left side of the engine compartment (see illustration). Each of the fuses is designed to protect a specific circuit, and the various circuits are identified on the fuse panel cover. You'll also find a guide to these fuses and relays in your owner's manual.

There is no fuse and relay box inside the passenger compartment. However, there are a number of fuses, relays and circuit breakers in various locations under the dash. The heated mirror circuits and the circuit for the lower instrument panel power outlet (in the floor console) are fused with self-resetting fuses that are only serviceable by an authorized dealer. The power seat circuits are protected by a 30-amp circuit breaker located under the driver's seat. The power windows are fused by a 25-amp circuit breaker, which is located under the instrument panel, near the steering column.

Miniaturized fuses are employed in the fuse blocks. These compact

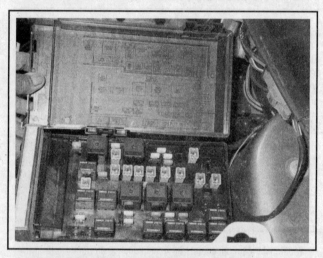

3.1 The engine compartment fuse and relay box is located on the left side of the engine compartment. After removing the fuse box lid, refer to the fuse and relay guide embossed on the underside of the lid for help with locating the fuse or relay you want to check (you'll also find a guide inside your owner's manual)

fuses, which use blade-type terminals, can be removed and installed without any special tools. If an electrical component fails, always check the fuse first. The best way to check a fuse is with a test light. Check for power at the exposed terminal tips of each fuse. If power is present on one side of the fuse but not the other, the fuse is blown. A blown fuse can also be confirmed by visually inspecting it (see illustration).

Be sure to replace blown fuses with the correct type. Fuses of different ratings are physically interchangeable, but only fuses of the proper rating should be used. Replacing a fuse with one of a higher or lower value than specified is not recommended. Each electrical circuit needs a specific amount of protection. The amperage value of each fuse is molded into the fuse body.

If the replacement fuse immediately fails, don't replace it again until the cause of the problem is isolated and corrected. In most cases, this will be a short circuit in the wiring caused by a broken or deteriorated wire.

FUSIBLE LINKS

Some circuits, such as the part of the starter circuit that connects the starter motor to the alternator, are protected by fusible links. Fusible links are used in circuits that carry high current or are not ordinarily fused. Cartridge type fusible links (also referred to as "maxi-fuses") are located in the engine compartment fuse and relay box and are similar to a large fuse. After disconnecting the negative battery cable, simply unplug and replace a fusible link with a new unit of the same amperage.

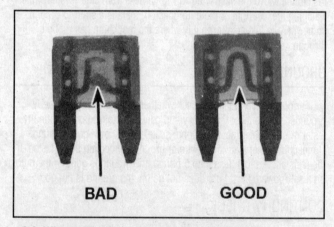

BAD   **GOOD**

3.3 When a fuse blows, the element between the terminals melts

4 Circuit breakers - general information

Circuit breakers protect certain circuits, such as the power windows or heated seats. Depending on the vehicle's accessories, there might be one or two circuit breakers, and they're usually located inside the vehicle, where they're scattered throughout the area under the instrument panel.

Because circuit breakers reset automatically, an electrical overload in a circuit-breaker-protected system will cause the circuit to fail momentarily, then come back on. If the circuit does not come back on, check it immediately.

For a basic check, pull the circuit breaker up out of its socket on the fuse panel, but just far enough to probe with a voltmeter. The breaker should still contact the sockets.

With the voltmeter negative lead on a good chassis ground, touch each end prong of the circuit breaker with the positive meter probe. There should be battery voltage at each end. If there is battery voltage only at one end, the circuit breaker must be replaced.

Some circuit breakers must be reset manually.

5 Relays - general information and testing

GENERAL INFORMATION

1   Several electrical accessories in the vehicle, such as the fuel injection system, horns, starter, and fog lamps use relays to transmit the electrical signal to the component. Relays use a low-current circuit (the control circuit) to open and close a high-current circuit (the power circuit). If the relay is defective, that component will not operate properly. Most relays are mounted in the engine compartment fuse and relay box (see illustration 3.1). If you suspect a faulty relay, simply remove it and test it using the procedure below. Or have it tested by a dealer service department. Defective relays cannot be repaired; they must be replaced with a new unit.

TESTING

▶ **Refer to illustrations 5.2a and 5.2b**

2   Most of the relays used in these vehicles are of a type often called ISO relays, which refers to the International Standards Organization. The terminals of ISO relays are numbered to indicate their usual circuit connections and functions. There are two basic layouts of terminals on the relays used in the covered vehicles (see illustrations).

3   Refer to the wiring diagram for the circuit to determine the proper connections for the relay you're testing. If you can't determine the correct connection from the wiring diagrams, however, you may be able to determine the test connections from the information that follows.

4   Two of the terminals are the relay control circuit and connect to the relay coil. The other relay terminals are the power circuit. When the relay is energized, the coil creates a magnetic field that closes the larger contacts of the power circuit to provide power to the circuit loads.

5   Terminals 85 and 86 are normally the control circuit. If the relay contains a diode, terminal 86 must be connected to battery positive

(B+) voltage and terminal 85 to ground. If the relay contains a resistor, terminals 85 and 86 can be connected in either direction with respect to B+ and ground.

6   Terminal 30 is normally connected to the battery voltage (B+) source for the circuit loads. Terminal 87 is connected to the ground side of the circuit, either directly or through a load. If the relay has several alternate terminals for load or ground connections, they usually are numbered 87A, 87B, 87C, and so on.

7   Use an ohmmeter to check continuity through the relay control coil.

   a) Connect the meter according to the polarity shown in the illustration for one check; then reverse the ohmmeter leads and check continuity in the other direction.

   b) If the relay contains a resistor, resistance will be indicated on the meter, and should be the same value with the ohmmeter in either direction.

   c) If the relay contains a diode, resistance should be higher with the ohmmeter in the forward polarity direction than with the meter leads reversed.

   d) If the ohmmeter shows infinite resistance in both directions, replace the relay.

8   Remove the relay from the vehicle and use the ohmmeter to check for continuity between the relay power circuit terminals. There should be no continuity between terminal 30 and 87 with the relay de-energized.

9   Connect a fused jumper wire to terminal 86 and the positive battery terminal. Connect another jumper wire between terminal 85 and ground. When the connections are made, the relay should click.

10 With the jumper wires connected, check for continuity between the power circuit terminals. Now, there should be continuity between terminals 30 and 87.

11 If the relay fails any of the above tests, replace it.

5.2a Most of the relays on these vehicles have a schematic printed on them . . .

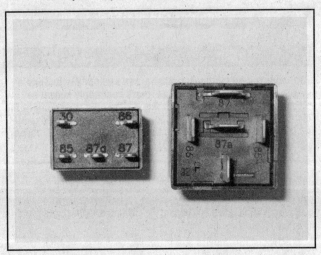

5.2b . . . and, on the underside, the terminals are numbered

6 Multi-function switch - replacement

▶ Refer to illustrations 6.3a, 6.3b and 6.4

✳✳ WARNING:

The models covered by this manual are equipped with Supplemental Restraint Systems (SRS), more commonly known as airbags. Always disable the airbag system before working in the vicinity of any airbag system components to avoid the possibility of accidental deployment of the airbags, which could cause personal injury (see Section 25).

➡Note: The multi-function switch is located on the steering column. It includes the turn signal switch, the headlight dimmer switch and the windshield wiper/washer switch.

1   Disconnect the cable from the negative terminal of the battery (see Chapter 5, Section 1).
2   Remove the upper and lower steering column covers (see Chapter 11).
3   Disconnect the electrical connector from the multi-function switch (see illustrations).
4   Remove the multi-function switch retaining screws (see illustration), then remove the switch from the steering column.
5   Installation is the reverse of removal.

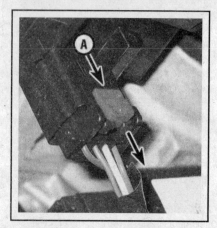

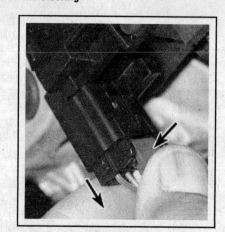

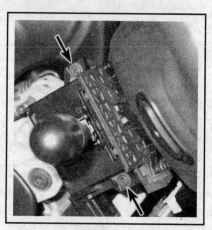

6.3a To disconnect the electrical connector from the multi-function switch, slide the lock down (toward the harness) . . .

6.3b . . . then depress the lock and pull off the connector

6.4 To detach the multi-function switch from the steering column, remove these two mounting screws

7 Key lock cylinder and ignition switch - replacement

✳✳ WARNING:

The models covered by this manual are equipped with Supplemental Restraint Systems (SRS), more commonly known as airbags. Always disable the airbag system before working in the vicinity of any airbag system components to avoid the possibility of accidental deployment of the airbags, which could cause personal injury (see Section 25).

1   Disconnect the cable from the negative terminal of the battery (see Chapter 5, Section 1).
2   Remove the knee bolster and the steering column covers (see Chapter 11).

KEY LOCK CYLINDER

▶ Refer to illustration 7.3

3   Put the key lock cylinder in the ON position, depress the key lock cylinder retaining tab and remove the key lock cylinder (see illustration).
4   Install the upper and lower steering column covers (see Chapter 11).

7.3 To remove the key lock cylinder, put the ignition key in the RUN position, depress the key lock cylinder retaining tab (A) and pull out the key lock cylinder

5   Put the ignition key in the ON position, then install the key lock cylinder.
6   Connect the cable to the negative battery terminal (see Chapter 5, Section 1).

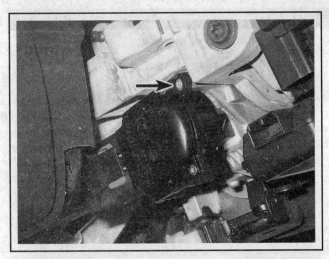

7.7 To detach the ignition switch from the steering column, remove this Torx head mounting screw with a No. 10 Torx bit

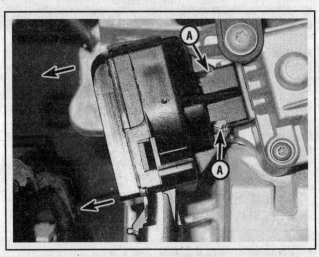

7.8 To release the ignition switch from the steering column, depress these two retaining tabs (A) and pull off the switch

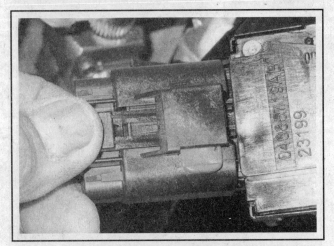

7.9 To disconnect the electrical connector from the ignition switch, depress this release tab and pull off the connector

IGNITION SWITCH

▶ **Refer to illustrations 7.7, 7.8, 7.9, 7.10a, 7.10b and 7.10c**

7 Remove the ignition switch Torx head mounting screw (see illustration).

8 Depress the ignition switch retaining tabs (see illustration), then detach the switch from the steering column.

9 Disconnect the electrical connector from the ignition switch (see illustration).

10 Before installing the ignition switch, make sure that the ignition key is in the ON position and that the actuator shaft in the key lock cylinder housing is in the ON position (see illustration). Also make sure that the square receptacle in the ignition switch is in the ON position (see illustration). Then install the ignition switch (see illustration). Make sure that the retaining tabs snap into place.

11 Install the upper and lower steering column covers (see Chapter 11).

12 Connect the cable to the negative battery terminal (see Chapter 5, Section 1).

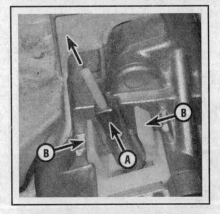

7.10a Before installing the ignition switch, make sure that the ignition key is in the ON position and that the actuator shaft (A) in the key lock cylinder housing is in the ON position. When you install the ignition switch onto the actuator shaft, it will snap over these two retaining tabs (B)

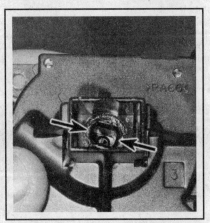

7.10b Also make sure that the square receptacle in the ignition switch is in the ON position

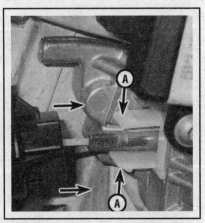

7.10c To install the ignition switch, align the receptacle in the switch with the actuator shaft, then push the switch onto the key lock cylinder housing until the two retaining tabs (A) snap into place

8   Instrument panel switches - replacement

※※ **WARNING:**

The models covered by this manual are equipped with Supplemental Restraint Systems (SRS), more commonly known as airbags. Always disable the airbag system before working in the vicinity of any airbag system components to avoid the possibility of accidental deployment of the airbag(s), which could cause personal injury (see Section 25).

HEADLIGHT SWITCH AND RHEOSTAT/POWER MIRROR CONTROL SWITCH

▶ **Refer to illustrations 8.2, 8.3a, 8.3b and 8.4**

1   Disconnect the cable from the negative battery terminal (see Chapter 5, Section 1).

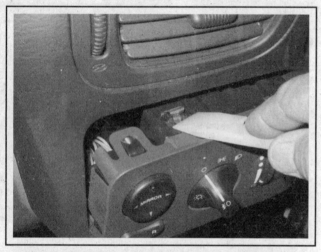

8.2 Using a trim removal tool, carefully pry the trim panel for the power mirror switch and headlight switch/rheostat from the instrument panel

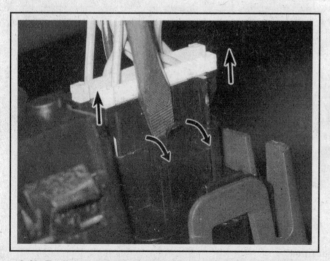

8.3b To disconnect the electrical connector from the power mirror switch, pry this release tab away from the connector with a screwdriver and pull off the connector

2   Carefully pry the headlight switch/rheostat panel from the instrument panel (see illustration).
3   Disconnect the electrical connectors from the power mirror switch, headlight switch and rheostat (see illustrations).
4   If you're going to replace either the headlight switch and rheostat, or the power mirror control switch, release the locking tabs that secure the power mirror switch to the panel (see illustration) and detach the power mirror switch from the panel.
5   Installation is the reverse of removal.

HAZARD FLASHER SWITCH

▶ **Refer to illustrations 8.7 and 8.8**

6   Disconnect the cable from the negative battery terminal (see Chapter 5, Section 1).

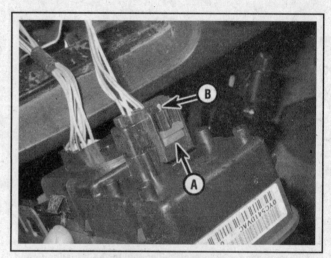

8.3a To disconnect the electrical connector from the headlight switch and rheostat, push the lock (A) toward the harness, then depress the release tab (B) and pull off the connector

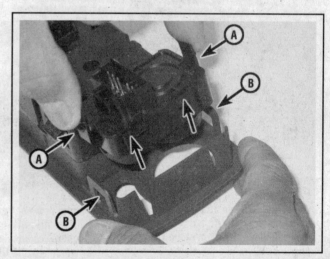

8.4 To detach the power mirror control switch from the panel, depress the release tabs (A) to disengage them from their locks (B) and pull off the switch

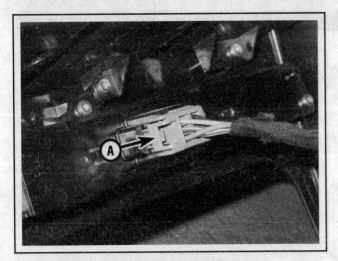

8.7 To disconnect the electrical connector from the hazard flasher switch, depress the release tab (A) and pull off the connector

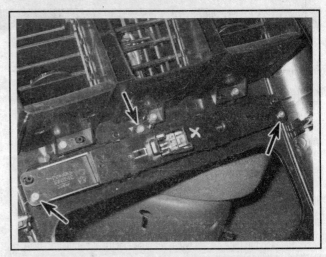

8.8 To detach the hazard flasher switch from the center instrument panel bezel, remove these three screws

7   Remove the center instrument panel bezel (see Chapter 11).

8   Disconnect the electrical connector from the hazard flasher switch (see illustration).

9   Remove the hazard flasher switch from the center instrument panel bezel (see illustration).

10   Installation is the reverse of removal.

9   Instrument cluster - removal and installation

▶ Refer to illustrations 9.3 and 9.4

❖❖ WARNING:

The models covered by this manual are equipped with Supplemental Restraint Systems (SRS), more commonly known as airbags. Always disable the airbag system before working in the vicinity of any airbag system components to avoid the possibility of accidental deployment of the airbag(s), which could cause personal injury (see Section 25).

1   Disconnect the cable from the negative terminal of the battery (see Chapter 5, Section 1).

2   Remove the over-steering-column cover and the instrument cluster bezel (see Chapter 11).

3   Remove the instrument cluster mounting screws (see illustration) and pull the instrument cluster out of the instrument panel just far enough to access the electrical connector on the backside of the cluster.

4   Disconnect the electrical connector from the backside of the cluster (see illustration).

5   Installation is the reverse of removal.

9.3 To detach the instrument cluster from the instrument panel, remove these mounting screws

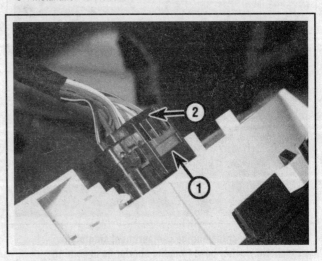

9.4 To disconnect the electrical connector from the instrument cluster, slide the lock (1) away from the cluster (toward the harness), then depress the release tab (2) and pull off the connector

10 Wiper motor - replacement

FRONT WIPER MOTOR ASSEMBLY

▶ Refer to illustrations 10.1, 10.2, 10.3, 10.5, 10.6, 10.7a, 10.7b, 10.11, 10.12 and 10.13

1 Pry off the protective caps over the wiper arm nuts (see illustration).

2 Remove the nuts that attach the wiper arms to their splined shafts (see illustration).

3 Mark the position of each wiper arm in relation to its shaft (see illustration), then remove the wiper arms. If the arm is difficult to remove from the shaft, use a small two-jaw puller.

4 Remove the cowl cover (see Chapter 11).

5 Release the lock on the wiper module electrical connector, then disconnect the connector from the wiper motor (see illustration).

6 Disconnect the windshield washer hose from the coupling out-

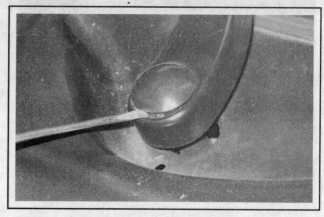

10.1 To access each front wiper arm retaining nut, carefully pry off the protective cap that covers up the nut

10.2 To detach each front wiper arm from the wiper motor shaft, remove this nut

10.3 Mark the position of the wiper arm in relation to its shaft, then remove the arm. If the arm is difficult to remove from the shaft, use a small two-jaw puller

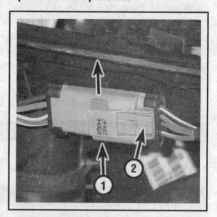

10.5 To disconnect the front wiper motor electrical connector, push the lock (1) up, then depress the release tab (2) and pull off the connector

10.6 Disconnect the engine compartment side of the windshield washer hose from the shorter hose coming out of the wiper assembly. Be sure to inspect the condition of both hoses and the condition of the plastic coupling that joins the two hoses. If either hose or the coupling is damaged, replace it

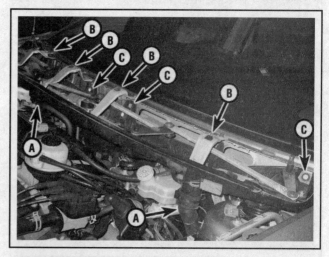

10.7a Windshield wiper assembly details:

A   Drain tubes
B   Wiper assembly support brackets
C   Bolts that secure the wiper assembly to the firewall (far right bolt not visible)

10.7b To disconnect the drain tubes from the pipes on the bottom of the wiper assembly, insert a screwdriver between the ratcheting teeth, twist the screwdriver to spread the two ends of the clamp apart, then pull off the hose (left drain tube shown, right drain tube identical)

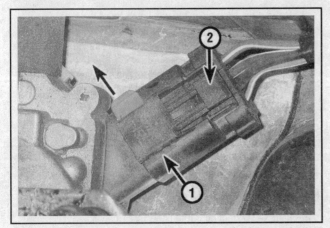

10.12 To disconnect the electrical connector from the wiper motor, push the lock (1) up, press the release tab (2) and pull off the connector

10.11 Pry off the two link arms from the wiper motor crank arm (do NOT remove the crank arm from the motor)

side the wiper assembly (see illustration).

7   Disconnect the drain tubes from the pipes on the bottom of the wiper assembly (see illustrations).

8   Remove the nuts that attach the wiper assembly support brackets to the welded studs on the upper edge of the firewall (see illustration 10.7a).

9   Remove the bolts that attach the wiper assembly to the firewall (see illustration 10.7a).

10 Lift the wiper assembly off the welded studs on the upper edge of the firewall and place the assembly on a clean workbench.

11 Detach the wiper links from the wiper motor crank arm (see illustration). Do NOT remove the crank arm from the motor.

12 Disconnect the electrical connector from the wiper motor (see illustration).

13 Remove the nuts that attach the two middle support brackets to the front edge of the windshield wiper motor assembly (see illustration), then remove the windshield wiper motor mounting bolts and remove the motor.

14 Installation is the reverse of removal.

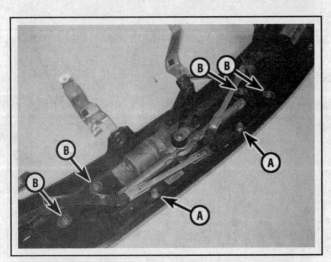

10.13 To remove the windshield wiper motor, remove the two nuts (A) that secure the two middle support brackets, swing the support brackets back out of the way, then remove the motor mounting bolts (B) and remove the motor

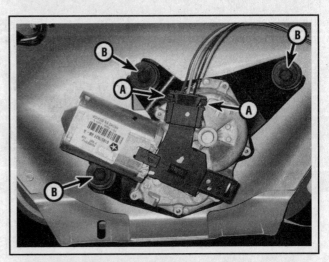

10.19 To disconnect the electrical connector from the rear wiper motor, depress the two release tabs (A) and pull off the connector. To detach the rear wiper motor, remove these three mounting bolts (B)

REAR WIPER MOTOR

♦ **Refer to illustration 10.19**

15 Remove the cap that covers up the wiper arm retaining nut (see illustration 10.1).

16 Remove the wiper arm retaining nut.

17 Mark the position of the wiper arm in relation to the wiper motor shaft (see illustration 10.3), then remove the arm from the shaft. If the

wiper arm is difficult to remove from the shaft splines, use a small two-jaw puller to detach the arm.

18 Remove the liftgate trim panel (see Chapter 11).

19 Disconnect the electrical connector from the rear wiper motor (see illustration).

20 Remove the rear wiper motor mounting bolts (see illustration 10.19) and remove the motor.

21 Installation is the reverse of removal.

11 Radio and speakers - removal and installation

※※ WARNING:

The models covered by this manual are equipped with Supplemental Restraint Systems (SRS), more commonly known as airbags. Always disable the airbag system before working in the vicinity of any airbag system components to avoid the possibility of accidental deployment of the airbag(s), which could cause personal injury (see Section 25).

1 Disconnect the cable from the negative terminal of the battery (see Chapter 5, Section 1).

RADIO

♦ **Refer to illustration 11.3, 11.4a and 11.4b**

2 Remove the cup holder, the trim panel above the cup holder and the center instrument panel bezel (see Chapter 11).

3 Remove the radio retaining screws (see illustration), then pull the radio out of the instrument panel.

4 Disconnect the electrical connectors and the antenna lead from the backside of the radio (see illustrations) and remove the radio.

5 Installation is the reverse of removal.

SPEAKERS

Front door speakers

♦ **Refer to illustrations 11.7 and 11.8**

6 Remove the front door trim panel (see Chapter 11).

7 Remove the speaker mounting screws (see illustration).

8 Pull out the speaker, disconnect the electrical connector from the speaker (see illustration) and remove the speaker.

9 Installation is the reverse of removal.

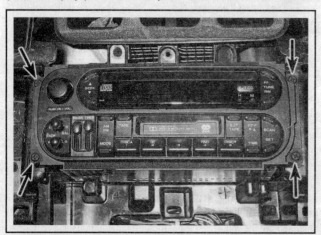

11.3 To detach the radio from the instrument panel, remove these four mounting screws

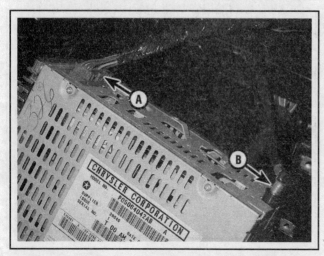

11.4a After pulling the radio out of the instrument panel, depress the release tab (A) and disconnect the electrical connector, then disconnect the antenna lead (B) from the backside of the radio . . .

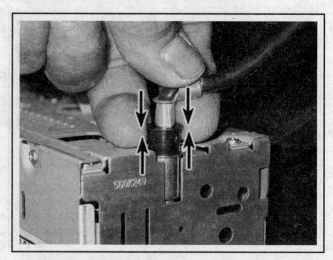

11.4b . . . by pushing down on the cable while simultaneously pulling up on the locking connector, then pulling the cable from the radio

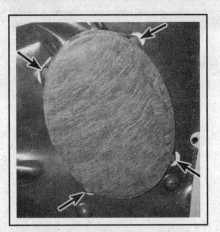

11.7 To detach a front door speaker from the door, remove these four screws . . .

11.8 . . . then pull the speaker out of the door, depress the release tab on the electrical connector and disconnect the connector

11.11 To detach a speaker from the instrument panel, remove these two screws . . .

Instrument panel speakers

▶ **Refer to illustration 11.11 and 11.12**

10 Remove the A-pillar trim and the instrument panel top pad (see Chapter 11).

11 Remove the speaker mounting screws (see illustration).

12 Pull out the speaker, disconnect the electrical connector (see illustration) and remove the speaker.

13 Installation is the reverse of removal.

Quarter-panel speakers

▶ **Refer to illustration 11.14 and 11.15**

14 Remove the speaker grille from the trim panel (see illustration).

15 Remove the four speaker retaining screws (see illustration).

16 Pull out the speaker, disconnect the electrical connector (see illustration 11.8) and remove the speaker.

17 Installation is the reverse of removal.

D-pillar speakers

18 If you're removing the left D-pillar speaker, remove the jack cover.

19 If you're removing the right D-pillar speaker, remove the rear header trim (see Chapter 11).

20 Slide the speaker out of its retainer, then disconnect the electrical connector from the speaker and remove the speaker.

11.12 . . . pull the speaker out of the instrument panel, depress the release tab (A) on the electrical connector and pull off the connector

11.14 Carefully pry the speaker grille from the quarter-panel speaker

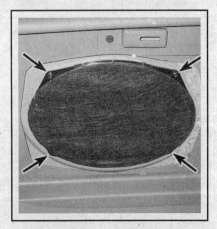

11.15 To detach the quarter-panel speaker from the trim panel, remove these screws

12 Antenna and cables - replacement

❋❋ **WARNING:**

The models covered by this manual are equipped with Supplemental Restraint Systems (SRS), more commonly known as airbags. Always disable the airbag system before working in the vicinity of any airbag system components to avoid the possibility of accidental deployment of the airbag(s), which could cause personal injury (see Section 25).

ANTENNA MAST, ANTENNA BASE AND ANTENNA CABLE

Antenna mast

1   Use an antenna wrench or a small open end wrench to unscrew the antenna mast from the body (see illustration).
2   Installation is the reverse of removal.

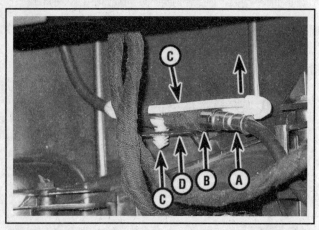

12.5 Lift up the clip, then disconnect the antenna cable from the extension cable

A   *Antenna cable (from the antenna)*
B   *Extension cable (to the radio)*
C   *Cable clip*
D   *Cable clip bracket*

Antenna base and antenna cable

▶ Refer to illustration 12.5, 12.8, 12.9 and 12.10

3   Remove the antenna mast.
4   Remove the glove box (see Chapter 11).
5   Disconnect the antenna cable connector from the extension cable (see illustration).
6   Remove the right kick panel.
7   Loosen the right front wheel lug nuts, raise the vehicle, remove the right front wheel and remove the splash shield from the right front wheelwell (see Chapter 11).
8   From inside the wheelwell, locate the rubber grommet insulator, in the upper left corner of the wheelwell, that insulates the hole where the antenna cable goes through into the cabin (see illustration). Remove the antenna cable grommet, then pull the cable through the grommet hole into the wheelwell.
9   Using an antenna wrench or a special "cap nut" socket, unscrew the cap nut that secures the antenna base to the front fender (see illustration). A pair of needle-nose or snap-ring pliers will

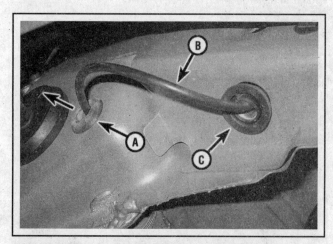

12.8 Working inside the wheelwell, remove the rubber grommet insulator (A) then pull the antenna cable (B) through the grommet hole into the wheelwell. Do NOT attempt to pull down the antenna assembly (C) until you have completed the next step

12.9 Using an antenna wrench (shown) or a special "cap nut" socket, unscrew the cap nut that secures the antenna base to the front fender

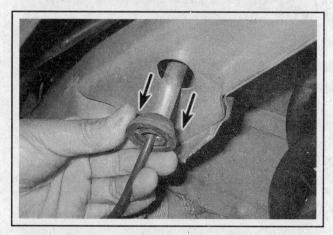

12.10 Remove the antenna base from the underside of the front fender

also work, but be very careful not to let the pliers slip off the nut and scratch the paint.

10 Pull the antenna assembly down into the wheelwell (see illustration) and remove it.

11 Installation is the reverse of removal.

EXTENSION CABLE

→**Note: The extension cable connects the antenna cable to the radio.**

12 Remove the glove box (see Chapter 11).

13 Disconnect the extension cable from the antenna cable (see illustration 12.5).

14 Detach the antenna cable clip from the small bracket on the heating/air conditioning assembly (see illustration 12.5).

15 Remove the radio (see Section 11) and disconnect the extension cable from the backside of the radio (see illustration 11.4b).

16 Installation is the reverse of removal.

13 Rear window defogger - check and repair

1 The rear window defogger consists of a number of horizontal elements baked onto the glass surface.

2 Small breaks in the element can be repaired without removing the rear window.

CHECK

▶ **Refer to illustrations 13.4, 13.5 and 13.7**

3 Turn the ignition switch and defogger system switches to the ON position. Using a voltmeter, place the positive probe against the defogger grid positive terminal and the negative probe against the ground terminal. If battery voltage is not indicated, check the fuse, defogger switch and related wiring. If voltage is indicated, but all or part of the defogger doesn't heat, proceed with the following tests.

4 When measuring voltage during these tests, wrap a piece of aluminum foil around the tip of the voltmeter positive probe and press the foil against the heating element with your finger (see illustration). Place the negative probe on the defogger grid ground terminal.

5 Check the voltage at the center of each heating element (see illustration). If the voltage is 5 or 6-volts, the element is okay (there is no break). If there is not voltage, the element is broken between the center of the element and the positive end. If the voltage is 10 to 12 volts the element is broken between the center of the element and ground. Check each heating element.

6 Connect the negative lead to a good body ground. The reading should stay the same. If it doesn't, the ground connection is bad.

7 To find the break, place the voltmeter negative probe against the defogger ground terminal. Place the voltmeter positive probe with the foil strip against the heating element at the positive terminal end and slide it toward the negative terminal end. The point at which the voltmeter deflects from several volts to zero is the point at which the heating element is broken (see illustration).

13.4 When measuring the voltage at the rear window defogger grid, wrap a piece of aluminum foil around the positive probe of the voltmeter and press the foil against the wire with your finger

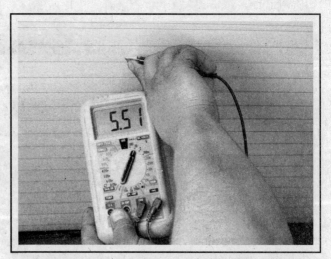

13.5 To determine if a heating element has broken, check the voltage at the center of each element. If the voltage is 5 or 6-volts, the element is unbroken; if the voltage is 10 or 12-volts, the element is broken between the center and the ground side; if there is no voltage, the element is broken between the center and the positive side

13.7 To find the break, touch the voltmeter negative lead to the defogger ground terminal, place the voltmeter positive lead with the foil strip against the heating element at the positive terminal end and slide it toward the negative terminal end. The point at which the voltmeter reading changes abruptly is the point at which the element is broken

REPAIR

▶ Refer to illustration 13.13

8   Repair the break in the element using a repair kit specifically recommended for this purpose, available at most auto parts stores. Included in this kit is plastic conductive epoxy.

9   Prior to repairing a break, turn off the system and allow it to cool

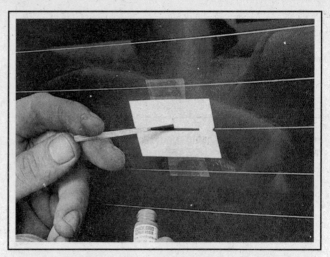

13.13 To use a defogger repair kit, apply masking tape to the inside of the window at the damaged area, then brush on the special conductive coating

off for a few minutes.

10 Lightly buff the element area with fine steel wool, then clean it thoroughly with rubbing alcohol.

11 Use masking tape to mask off the area being repaired.

12 Thoroughly mix the epoxy, following the instructions provided with the repair kit.

13 Apply the epoxy material to the slit in the masking tape, overlapping the undamaged area about 3/4-inch on either end (see illustration).

14 Allow the repair to cure for 24 hours before removing the tape and using the system.

14 Headlight housing - replacement

▶ Refer to illustrations 14.2, 14.3a and 14.3b

✳✳ WARNING:

These vehicles are equipped with halogen gas-filled headlight bulbs, which are under pressure and may shatter if the surface is damaged or the bulb is dropped. Wear eye protection and handle the bulbs carefully, grasping only the base whenever possible. Do not touch the surface of the bulb with your fingers because the oil from your skin could cause it to overheat and fail prematurely. If you do touch the bulb surface, clean it with rubbing alcohol.

1   Disconnect the cable from the negative battery terminal (see Chapter 5, Section 1).

2   Remove the headlight housing retaining bolts (see illustration).

3   Pull out the headlight housing assembly and disconnect the electrical connectors from the front park and turn signal bulb and from the headlight bulb (see illustrations). (The accompanying illustrations depict the headlight housing on a 2005 Dodge Caravan. To disconnect

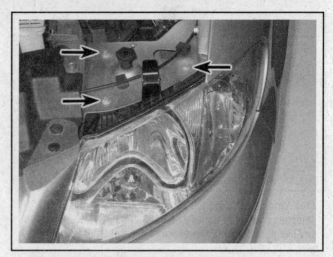

14.2 To detach the headlight housing from the radiator crossmember, remove these bolts

14.3a Pull out the headlight housing assembly, depress this release tab and disconnect the electrical connector from the front park and turn signal bulb . . .

14.3b . . . then disconnect the electrical connector from the headlight bulb (Dodge Caravan shown; for Chrysler models, see text)

the headlight bulb connector on Chrysler models, slide the red latch lock to the rear, depress the release tab, then disconnect the connector.)

4   If you want to replace the headlight bulb, refer to Section 15. If

you want to replace the front park and turn signal bulb, see Section 17.

5   Installation is the reverse of removal. When you're finished, be sure to adjust the headlights (see Section 16).

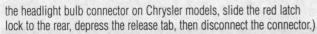

15   Headlight bulb - replacement

▶ Refer to illustrations 15.3a, 15.3b and 15.4

✻✻ WARNING:

Halogen gas filled bulbs are under pressure and may shatter if the surface is scratched or the bulb is dropped. Wear eye protection and handle the bulbs carefully, grasping only the base whenever possible. Do not touch the surface of the bulb with

your fingers because the oil from your skin could cause it to overheat and fail prematurely. If you do touch the bulb surface, clean it with rubbing alcohol.

1   Disconnect the cable from the negative battery terminal (see Chapter 5, Section 1).

2   Remove the headlight housing (see Section 14).

3   Rotate the headlight bulb retaining ring counterclockwise and pull out the bulb socket (see illustrations).

4   Replace the headlight bulb and socket as a unit. When installing the new bulb, align the three slots on the circumference of the bulb

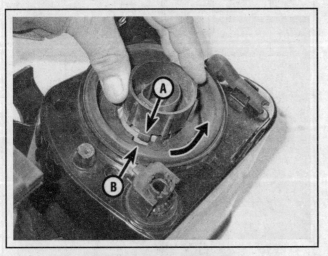

15.3a Rotate the headlight bulb retaining ring counterclockwise and remove it. When installing the retaining ring, make sure that each of the three tabs (A) on the ring is aligned with its corresponding cutout (B) in the mounting flange

15.3b To remove the bulb socket, pull it straight out

socket's mounting flange with the three bosses on the inside edge of the mounting hole in the headlight assembly (see illustration). When installing the retaining ring, align the retaining ring's three metal tabs with their corresponding grooves in the plastic headlight housing (see illustration 15.3a).

✳✳ CAUTION:

Don't touch the surface of the bulb with your fingers because the oil from your skin could cause it to overheat and fail prematurely. If you accidentally touch the bulb surface, clean it with rubbing alcohol.

5   Installation is otherwise the reverse of removal.

15.4 When installing a new headlight bulb, align the three metal tabs with their corresponding grooves in the plastic headlight housing

16 Headlights - adjustment

▶ **Refer to illustrations 16.1 and 16.4**

➡**Note: The headlights must be aimed correctly. If adjusted incorrectly they could blind the driver of an oncoming vehicle and cause a serious accident or seriously reduce your ability to see the road. The headlights should be checked for proper aim every 12 months and any time a new headlight housing is installed or front-end bodywork is performed. It should be emphasized that the following procedure is only an interim step, which will provide temporary adjustment until a properly equipped shop can adjust the headlights.**

1   These vehicles have a vertical adjustment screw located on the backside of the headlight housing. You can access the Torx-head adjustment screw through a hole in the radiator crossmember (see illustration).

2   Adjustment should be made with the vehicle on a level surface,

with a full gas tank and a normal load in the vehicle.

3   There are several methods of adjusting the headlights. The simplest method requires masking tape, a blank wall and a level floor.

4   Position masking tape vertically on the wall to indicate the vehicle centerline and the centerline of each headlight bulb (see illustration).

16.1 You can access the headlight's vertical adjustment screw through this hole (right headlight shown, left headlight adjustment hole in same spot)

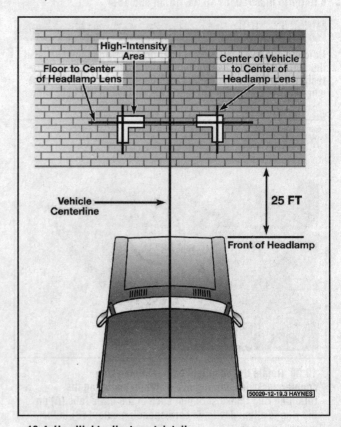

16.4 Headlight adjustment details

5   Position a horizontal tape line in reference to the centerline of all the headlights.

➡**Note: It may be easier to position the tape on the wall with the vehicle parked only a few inches away.**

6   Adjustment should be made with the vehicle parked 25 feet (7.6 meters) from the wall, sitting level, the gas tank half-full and no unusually heavy load in the vehicle.

7   Position the high intensity zone so it is two inches below the horizontal line and two inches to the side of the headlight vertical line, away from oncoming traffic. Adjustment is made by turning the horizontal adjusting screw to move the beam left or right. The high beams on these aero type headlights are automatically adjusted along with the low beam.

8   Have the headlights adjusted by a dealer service department or service station at the earliest opportunity.

17 Bulb replacement

EXTERIOR LIGHT BULBS

Front park and turn signal bulbs

▶ **Refer to illustrations 17.2 and 17.3**

1   Unbolt the headlight housing (see illustration 14.2), pull it out and disconnect the electrical connectors from the headlight and from the front park and turn signal bulb (see illustrations 14.3a and 14.3b).

2   Turn the park and turn signal bulb socket counterclockwise and

remove it from the headlight housing (see illustration).

3   Remove the front park and turn signal bulb from the socket (see illustration).

4   Install the new bulb in the socket.

5   Installation is the reverse of removal.

Front fog light bulbs

▶ **Refer to illustrations 17.7 and 17.8**

6   Raise the front of the vehicle and place it securely on jackstands.

7   Disconnect the bulb electrical connector (see illustration).

8   Rotate the bulb socket counterclockwise and pull it out of the fog light housing (see illustration).

9   Replace the bulb and socket as a unit.

❈❈ CAUTION:

Do not touch the surface of the bulb with your fingers, because the oil from your skin could cause it to overheat and fail prematurely. If you accidentally touch the bulb surface, clean it with rubbing alcohol.

10 Installation is the reverse of removal.

Center high-mounted brake light bulb

▶ **Refer to illustrations 17.11a, 17.11b and 17.12**

11 Remove the two high-mount brake light retaining screws and pull out the center high-mount brake light assembly (see illustrations).

17.2 To remove a front park and turn signal bulb socket from the headlight housing, turn it counterclockwise and pull it out

17.3 To remove the bulb from the front park and turn signal bulb socket, pull it straight out

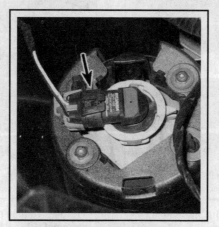

17.7 Disconnect the electrical connector from the front fog light bulb socket

17.8 To remove a fog light bulb socket, rotate it counterclockwise and pull it out

17.11a Remove these two retaining screws . . .

17.11b . . . and pull out the center high-mount brake light assembly

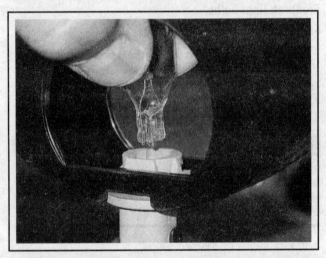

17.12 To remove the center high-mount brake light bulb from its socket, pull it straight out

17.14 Using a trim removal tool or a screwdriver, carefully pry out the two taillight housing pop fasteners

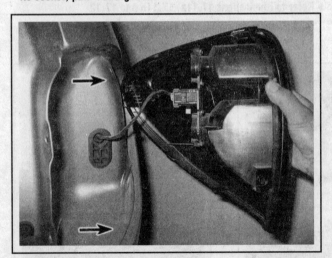

17.15a To remove the taillight assembly from the vehicle, rotate the taillight away from the vehicle body . . .

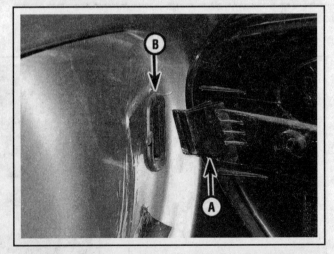

17.15b . . . then disengage the hook (A) from the rubber grommet (B) in the quarter-panel opening. Be sure to inspect the condition of the grommet. If it's cracked, torn or otherwise damaged, replace it

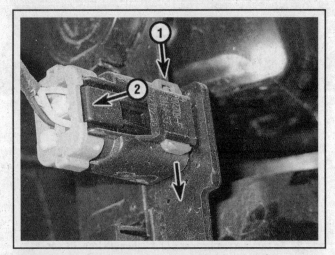

17.16 To disconnect the electrical connector from the taillight housing, slide the lock (1) down, then depress the release tab (2) and pull off the connector

17.18 To remove a bulb socket from the taillight housing, squeeze the tabs on the bulb socket and pull out the socket

12 Remove the center high-mount brake light bulb from its socket (see illustration).
13 Installation is the reverse of removal.

17.19 To remove a bulb from a taillight housing socket, pull it straight out

17.17 Typical 2005 and later taillight housing with two bulbs; 2004 and earlier models use three bulbs

A   Back-up light bulb socket (2005 and later)
B   Brake, taillight and turn signal bulb socket (2005 and later)

Tail light bulbs

▶ **Refer to illustrations 17.14, 17.15a, 17.15b, 17.16, 17.17, 17.18 and 17.19**

14 Remove the two taillight housing retaining screws (see illustration).
15 To remove the taillight assembly from the vehicle, rotate the taillight away from the vehicle body to disengage the hook from the rubber grommet in the quarter-panel opening (see illustrations).
16 Disconnect the electrical connector from the taillight housing (see illustration) and remove the housing.
17 There are two or three bulbs in the taillight housing (see illustration).
18 Remove the bulb socket from the taillight housing (see illustration).
19 Remove the bulb from the socket (see illustration).
20 Installation is the reverse of removal.

License plate light bulbs

▶ **Refer to illustrations 17.21, 17.22 and 17.24**

21 Remove the license plate light screws (see illustration).

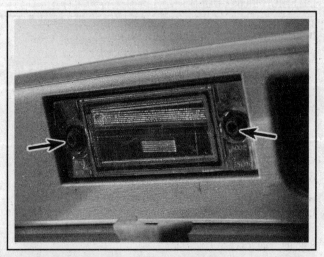

17.21 To detach the license plate light, remove these two screws

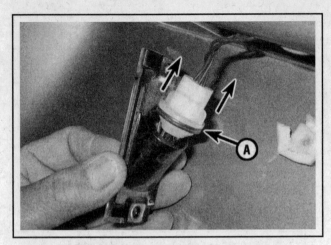

17.22 Pull down the license plate light assembly and remove the socket (A) from the assembly

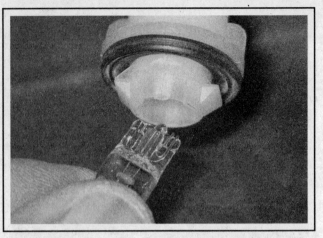

17.24 To remove the license plate light bulb from its socket, pull it straight out

17.27a Instrument cluster light bulbs

22 Pull down the license plate light assembly (see illustration).
23 Pull the bulb socket out of the license plate light assembly.
24 Remove the bulb from the socket (see illustration).
25 Installation is the reverse of removal.

INTERIOR LIGHT BULBS

Instrument cluster illumination bulbs

▶ **Refer to illustrations 17.27a and 17.27b**

26 Remove the instrument cluster (see Section 9).
27 To remove an instrument cluster light bulb socket, turn it counterclockwise and pull it out of the cluster (see illustrations).
28 To install an instrument cluster light bulb socket, insert it into the cluster and turn it clockwise.
29 Install the instrument cluster (see Section 9).

Courtesy light bulbs

➡ **Note: The (optional) courtesy lights, if equipped, are located in the front doors.**

30 Using a trim stick or panel removal tool, pry the courtesy light from the door trim panel (see illustration).
31 Disconnect the electrical connector from the courtesy light.
32 Remove the lens from the courtesy light assembly.

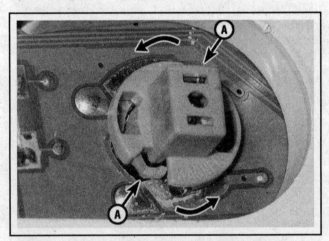

17.27b To remove an instrument cluster light bulb socket, carefully pry up both of the two locking arms (A) so that they clear the backside of the cluster, then turn the socket counterclockwise and pull it out of the cluster

33 Remove the bulb from the courtesy light assembly.
34 Installation is the reverse of removal.

Dome/cargo light

▶ **Refer to illustrations 17.35 and 17.36**

➡ **Note: The dome/cargo lights are located above the sliding doors and above the rear side windows.**

35 Using a trim panel removal tool or a screwdriver, pry off the dome/cargo light lens (see illustration).
36 Remove the bulb from the dome/cargo light assembly (see illustration).
37 Installation is the reverse of removal.

Glove box light

➡ **Note: The (optional) glove box light, if equipped, is located in the upper part of the glove box.**

38 Open the glove box door and push the switch through from behind.
39 Disconnect the electrical connector from the switch.
40 Pull the bulb from the switch.
41 Installation is the reverse of removal.

17.35 Using a trim panel removal tool or a screwdriver, pry off the dome/cargo light lens

17.36 To disengage a dome/cargo light bulb from its retaining clip/conductors, carefully pry it loose (only pry on the metal ends)

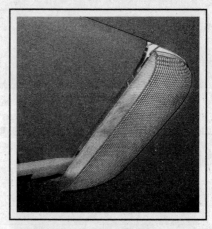

17.42 Using a flat-bladed tool, pry the liftgate light lens from the liftgate trim panel

Liftgate light bulb

▶ Refer to illustrations 17.42 and 17.43

➡Note: The liftgate light bulb is located in the lower left corner of the liftgate trim panel.

42 Using a flat-bladed tool, pry the liftgate light lens from the liftgate trim panel (see illustration).

43 Remove the liftgate light bulb (see illustration).

44 Installation is the reverse of removal.

Reading light

▶ Refer to illustrations 17.45 and 17.46

➡Note: The reading lights are located in the overhead console.

45 Using a flat-bladed tool, pry off the reading light lens (see illustration).

46 Remove the bulb from the reading light assembly (see illustration).

47 Installation is the reverse of removal.

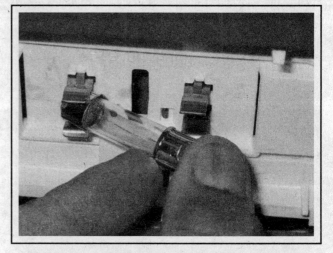

17.43 To disengage the liftgate light bulb from its retaining clip/conductors, carefully pull it out (if necessary, pry on the metal ends, not the glass)

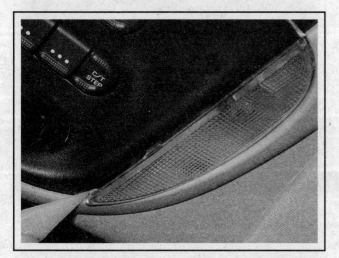

17.45 Using a flat-bladed tool, pry off the reading light lens

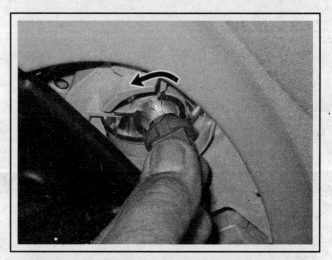

17.46 To remove the bulb from the reading light assembly, turn it counterclockwise until the lugs on the bulb socket are aligned with the cutouts in the reading light assembly, then pull it down

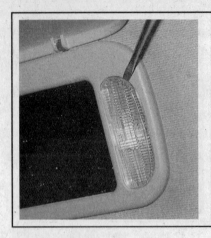

17.48 Pry off the vanity light lens with a trim panel removal tool or with a screwdriver

Vanity light

▶ Refer to illustrations 17.48 and 17.49

➡Note: The vanity lights are located in the sun visors.

48 Pry off the vanity light lens (see illustration).
49 Remove the light bulb from the vanity light housing (see illustration).
50 Installation is the reverse of removal.

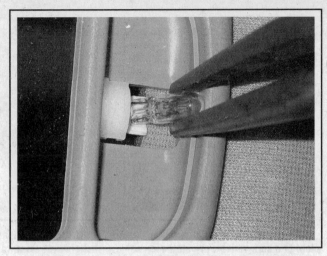

17.49 Removing a light bulb from the vanity light housing is tricky because the bulb is small, it's deeply recessed and it's very tough to pull out, so pulling it out with your fingers is almost impossible. Instead, use a small pair of needle-nose pliers to pull it out (just be careful not to squeeze the bulb too tightly! To be safe, wear eye protection)

18 Horn - replacement

▶ Refer to illustration 18.3

➡Note: The horn is located inside the void behind the left end of the bumper cover and ahead of the left front wheelwell.

1 Loosen the left front wheel lug nuts. Raise the vehicle, support it on jackstands and remove the left front wheel.
2 Remove the inner fender splash shield (see Chapter 11).
3 Disconnect the electrical connector from the horn (see illustration).
4 Remove the horn mounting bracket nut from the bottom of the radiator closure panel (see illustration).
5 Installation is the reverse of removal.

18.3 To remove the horn assembly, disconnect the electrical connector (1) and remove the horn mounting bracket bolt

19 Sliding door motor - removal and installation

▶ Refer to illustrations 19.2, 19.3, 19.4 and 19.5

➡Note: The sliding door motors are located inside the sliding doors.

1 Remove the sliding door trim panel (see Chapter 11).
2 Remove the retaining clip that secures the flex drive assembly to the sliding door motor (see illustration).

3 Disconnect the flex drive cable from the sliding door motor (see illustration).
4 Disconnect the electrical connector from the sliding door motor (see illustration).
5 Carefully pry out the push-pin fasteners that secure the door motor (see illustration).
6 Installation is the reverse of removal.

19.2 Use a screwdriver or a pair of needle-nose pliers to remove the retaining clip that secures the flex drive assembly to the motor

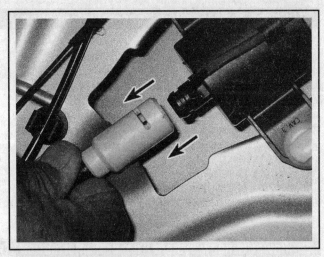

19.3 To disconnect the flex drive cable from the sliding door motor, pull it straight off

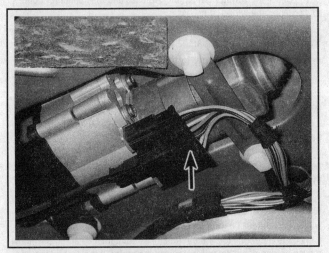

19.4 To disconnect the electrical connector from the sliding door motor, depress this release tab and pull off the connector

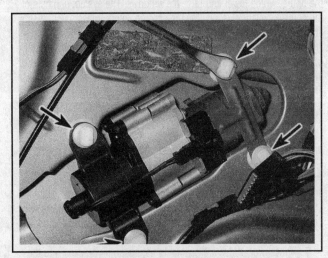

19.5 To detach the motor assembly from the sliding door, carefully pry out these four push-pin fasteners with a trim panel removal tool (shown) or with a screwdriver

20 Electric side view mirrors - general information

1   Most electric rear view mirrors use two motors to move the glass; one for up and down adjustments and one for left-right adjustments.

2   The control switch has a selector portion that sends voltage to the left or right side mirror. With the ignition ON but the engine OFF, roll down the windows and operate the mirror control switch through all functions (left-right and up-down) for both the left and right side mirrors.

3   Listen carefully for the sound of the electric motors running in the mirrors.

4   If the motors can be heard but the mirror glass doesn't move, there's a problem with the drive mechanism inside the mirror.

5   If the mirrors do not operate and no sound comes from the mir-

ror motors, check the fuse (see Section 3).

6   If the fuse is OK, remove the mirror control switch. Have the switch continuity checked by a dealership service department or other qualified automobile repair facility.

7   Test the ground connections.

8   If the mirror still doesn't work, remove the mirror and check the wires at the mirror for voltage.

9   If there's not voltage in each switch position, check the circuit between the mirror and control switch for opens and shorts.

10   If there's voltage, remove the mirror and test it off the vehicle with jumper wires. Replace the mirror if it fails this test.

21 Cruise control system - general information

1   The cruise control system maintains vehicle speed with an electronically controlled, vacuum operated servo located in the engine compartment, which is connected to the throttle body by a cable. The system consists of the PCM, vacuum servo, brake switch, control switches and vehicle speed sensor. Some features of the system require special testers and diagnostic procedures, which are beyond the scope of this manual. Listed below are some general procedures that may be used to locate common problems.

2   Check the fuses (see Section 3).

3   Have an assistant operate the brake pedal while you check the brake lights (voltage from the brake light switch deactivates the cruise control).

4   If the brake lights don't come on or stay on all the time, correct the problem and retest the cruise control.

5   Visually inspect the control cable between the cruise control servo and the throttle linkage for free movement. Replace it if necessary.

6   The cruise control system uses inputs from the Vehicle Speed Sensor (VSS). Refer to Chapter 6 for more information on the VSS.

7   Test drive the vehicle to determine if the cruise control is now working. If it isn't, take it to a dealer service department or an automotive electrical specialist for further diagnosis.

22 Power window system - general information

1   The power window system operates electric motors, mounted in the doors, which lower and raise the windows. The system consists of the control switches, relays, the motors, regulators, glass mechanisms and associated wiring.

2   The power windows can be lowered and raised from the master control switches by the driver or by remote switches located at the individual windows. Each window has a separate motor that is reversible. The position of the control switch determines the polarity and therefore the direction of operation.

3   The circuit is protected by a fuse and a circuit breaker. Each motor is also equipped with an internal circuit breaker; this prevents one stuck window from disabling the whole system.

4   The power window system will only operate when the ignition switch is ON. In addition, many models have a window lockout switch at the master control switch that, when activated, disables the switches at the rear windows and, sometimes, the switch at the passenger's window also. Always check these items before troubleshooting a window problem.

5   These procedures are general in nature, so if you can't find the problem using them, take the vehicle to a dealer service department or other properly equipped repair facility.

6   If the power windows won't operate, always check the fuse and circuit breaker first.

7   If only the rear windows are inoperative, or if the windows only operate from the master control switch, check the rear window lockout switch for continuity in the unlocked position. Replace it if it doesn't have continuity.

8   Check the wiring between the switches and fuse panel for continuity. Repair the wiring, if necessary.

9   If only one window is inoperative from the master control switch, try the other control switch at the window.

➡ **Note: This doesn't apply to the driver's door window.**

10 If the same window works from one switch, but not the other, check the switch for continuity. Have the switch checked at a dealer service department or other qualified automobile repair facility.

11 If the switch tests OK, check for a short or open in the circuit between the affected switch and the window motor.

12 If one window is inoperative from both switches, remove the trim panel from the affected door and check for voltage at the switch and at the motor while the switch is operated.

13 If voltage is reaching the motor, disconnect the glass from the regulator (see Chapter 11). Move the window up and down by hand while checking for binding and damage. Also check for binding and damage to the regulator. If the regulator is not damaged and the window moves up and down smoothly, replace the motor. If there's binding or damage, lubricate, repair or replace parts, as necessary.

14 If voltage isn't reaching the motor, check the wiring in the circuit for continuity between the switches and motors. You'll need to consult the wiring diagram for the vehicle. If the circuit is equipped with a relay, check that the relay is grounded properly and receiving voltage.

15 Test the windows after you are done to confirm proper repairs.

23 Power door lock system - general information

1   A power door lock system operates the door lock actuators mounted in each door. The system consists of the switches, actuators, a control unit and associated wiring. Diagnosis can usually be limited to simple checks of the wiring connections and actuators for minor faults that can be easily repaired.

2   Power door lock systems are operated by bi-directional solenoids located in the doors. The lock switches have two operating positions: Lock and Unlock. When activated, the switch sends a ground signal to the door lock control unit to lock or unlock the doors. Depending on which way the switch is activated, the control unit reverses polarity to the solenoids, allowing the two sides of the circuit to be used alternately as the feed (positive) and ground side.

3   Some vehicles may have an anti-theft system incorporated into the power locks. If you are unable to locate the trouble using the following general Steps, consult a dealer service department or other qualified repair shop.

4   Always check the circuit protection first. Some vehicles use a combination of circuit breakers and fuses.

5   Operate the door lock switches in both directions (LOCK and UNLOCK) with the engine off. Listen for the click of the solenoids operating.

6   Test the switches for continuity. Remove the switches and have them checked by a dealer service department or other qualified automobile repair facility.

7   Check the wiring between the switches, control unit and solenoids for continuity. Repair the wiring if there's no continuity.

8   Check for a bad ground at the switches or the control unit.

9   If all but one of the lock solenoids operates, remove the trim panel from the door with the non-operational solenoid (see Chapter 11), then check for voltage to the solenoid while operating the lock switch. One of the wires should have voltage in the LOCK position; the other should have voltage in the UNLOCK position.

10   If the inoperative solenoid is receiving voltage, replace the solenoid.

11   If the inoperative solenoid isn't receiving voltage, check the relay for an open or short in the wire between the lock solenoid and the control unit.

➡**Note: It's common for wires to break in the portion of the harness between the body and door (opening and closing the door fatigues and eventually breaks the wires).**

24 Daytime Running Lights (DRL) - general information

The Daytime Running Lights (DRL) system, which is required on new Canadian models, illuminates the headlights when the engine is running. The DRL system supplies reduced power to the headlights so they won't be too bright for daytime use, which also prolongs headlight life.

25 Airbag system - general information and precautions

GENERAL INFORMATION

1   All models are equipped with a frontal-impact airbag system, which is referred to as the Supplemental Restraint System (SRS). The SRS is designed to protect the driver and the front seat passenger from serious injury in the event of a head-on or frontal collision. The SRS is controlled by the Occupant Restraint Controller (ORC), also referred to as the Airbag Control Module (ACM), which is mounted in the center of the vehicle, on the floor transmission tunnel, right below the center of the instrument panel. The SRS uses an array of airbags to protect the front-seat occupants (and on models equipped with side curtain airbags, the rear seat passengers, too): the driver's airbag in the steering wheel; the knee blocker airbag (2005 and later models), which is located below the steering column; the passenger airbag, which is located in the right end of the instrument panel, beneath the instrument panel top pad and above the glove box; and, on models so equipped, the side curtain airbags, which are located above the side windows, in the outer edges of the headliner, between the A- and D-pillars. The SRS is activated by a pair of front impact sensors located on the front of the frame, just behind the bumper attachments. Other important components in the SRS include the clockspring, a wind-up coil that delivers battery voltage to the steering wheel airbag, and the AIRBAG readiness light on the instrument cluster.

In addition to the airbags, seat belt pre-tensioners are incorporated into the front seat belt retractor mechanisms. These are pyrotechnic (explosive) devices which retract the seat belts up to four inches when the airbag system is activated.

Driver airbag

2   The airbag inflator module contains a housing incorporating the cushion (airbag) and inflator unit, mounted in the center of the steering wheel. The inflator assembly is mounted on the back of the housing over a hole through which gas is expelled, inflating the bag almost instantaneously when an electrical signal is sent from the system. The clockspring assembly on the steering column under the steering wheel carries this signal to the module. The clockspring assembly can transmit an electrical signal regardless of steering wheel position. The igniter in the airbag converts the electrical signal to heat and ignites the powder, which inflates the bag.

3   In the event of a frontal collision serious enough to trigger SRS deployment, the knee blocker airbag inflates toward the driver's knees to help protect them and to help put the driver in the optimal position for deployment of the driver's airbag. The knee blocker airbag deploys in about 50 milliseconds.

Passenger airbag

4   The airbag is mounted in the right end of the instrument panel, beneath the instrument panel top pad and above the glove box. It consists of an inflator containing an igniter, a bag assembly, a reaction housing and a trim cover. The passenger airbag is considerably larger than the steering wheel-mounted unit and is supported by the steel reaction housing. The trim cover is textured and painted to match the instrument panel and has a molded seam that splits when the bag inflates.

5   Unlike the inflatable airbag knee blocker on the driver's side, the passenger knee blocker is simply a structural reinforcement that's an integral part of the glove box. But it does the same thing as the driver's inflatable knee blocker: it offers a degree of protection for the passenger's knees in a frontal impact and it positions the passenger for deployment of the passenger airbag.

Side-impact window airbags

6   Optional side-impact window airbags protect vehicle occupants in the event of a side impact. The side-impact window airbags are located above the windows, between the A- and D-pillars. If you're not sure whether your vehicle is equipped with side-impact window airbags, look for the words "SRS AIRBAG" imprinted on a small identification trim button located above the B-and C-pillars.

7   Vehicles equipped with side-impact window airbags use six side-impact sensors, three on the left side of the vehicle and three more on the right side. The front row side-impact sensors are located inside the B-pillars, right above the front seatbelt retractors. The second-row side-impact sensors are located in the sliding door track openings, just ahead of the C-pillars. The third-row sensors are located behind the quarter-trim panels, between the C- and D-pillars, above the rear wheelwells.

Occupant Restraint Controller (ORC) or Airbag Control Module (ACM)

8   The ORC or ACM supplies current to the SRS in the event of a collision, even if battery power is cut off. The ORC/ACM checks the SRS every time the vehicle is started, and indicates that it is doing so by turning on the AIRBAG readiness light. If the SRS is operating properly, the ORC/ACM turns off the AIRBAG readiness light. If it detects a fault in the system, the AIRBAG readiness light will remain on. If this condition occurs, take the vehicle to your dealer immediately for service.

DISARMING THE SYSTEM AND OTHER PRECAUTIONS

✳✳ WARNING:

Failure to follow these precautions could result in accidental deployment of the airbag and personal injury.

9   Whenever you are working in the vicinity of the driver airbag in the steering wheel or any of the other airbags on your vehicle, DISARM THE SYSTEM. To disarm the system:
  a) *Point the wheels straight ahead and turn the ignition key to the LOCK position.*
  b) *Disconnect the cable from the negative battery terminal. Isolate the cable terminal so it won't accidentally contact the battery post.*
  c) *Wait at least two minutes for the back-up power supply to be depleted. (Back-up power is supplied by a capacitor that takes about two minutes to fully discharge. During this two-minute interval the SRS is still capable of deploying.)*

10   Whenever handling an airbag, always keep the airbag opening (the trim side) pointed away from your body. Never place the airbag on a bench or other surface with the airbag opening facing the surface. Always place the airbag module in a safe location with the airbag opening facing up.

11   Never measure the resistance of any SRS component. An ohmmeter has a built-in battery supply that could accidentally deploy the airbag.

12   Never dispose of a "live" airbag. Return it to a dealer service department or other qualified repair shop for safe deployment and disposal.

COMPONENT REMOVAL AND INSTALLATION

Driver airbag and clockspring

13   Refer to Chapter 10, *Steering wheel - removal and installation*, for the driver's side airbag module and clockspring removal and installation procedures.

Driver knee blocker airbag
Refer to illustrations 25.16 and 25.17

14   Disarm the airbag system (see Step 9).

15   Remove the knee bolster and the instrument panel left end cover (see Chapter 11).

16   Disconnect the knee blocker airbag electrical connector (see illustration).

17   Remove the five knee blocker airbag mounting bolts (see illustration) and remove the knee blocker airbag. Be sure to heed the precautions outlined previously in this Section.

18   Installation is the reverse of removal procedure.

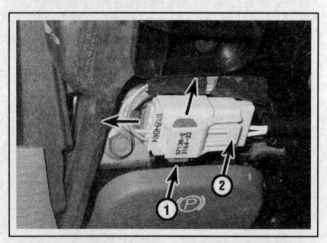

25.16 To disconnect the electrical connector for the driver's knee blocker airbag, push the lock (1) up, then depress the release tab (2) and pull out the connector to the left

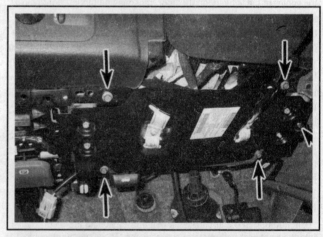

25.17 To detach the driver knee blocker airbag, remove these five bolts

26 Wiring diagrams - general information

Since it isn't possible to include all wiring diagrams for every year covered by this manual, the following diagrams are those that are typical and most commonly needed.

Prior to troubleshooting any circuits, check the fuse and circuit breakers (if equipped) to make sure they're in good condition. Make sure the battery is properly charged and check the cable connections (see Chapters 1 and 5).

When checking a circuit, make sure that all connectors are clean, with no broken or loose terminals. When unplugging a connector, do not pull on the wires. Pull only on the connector housings.

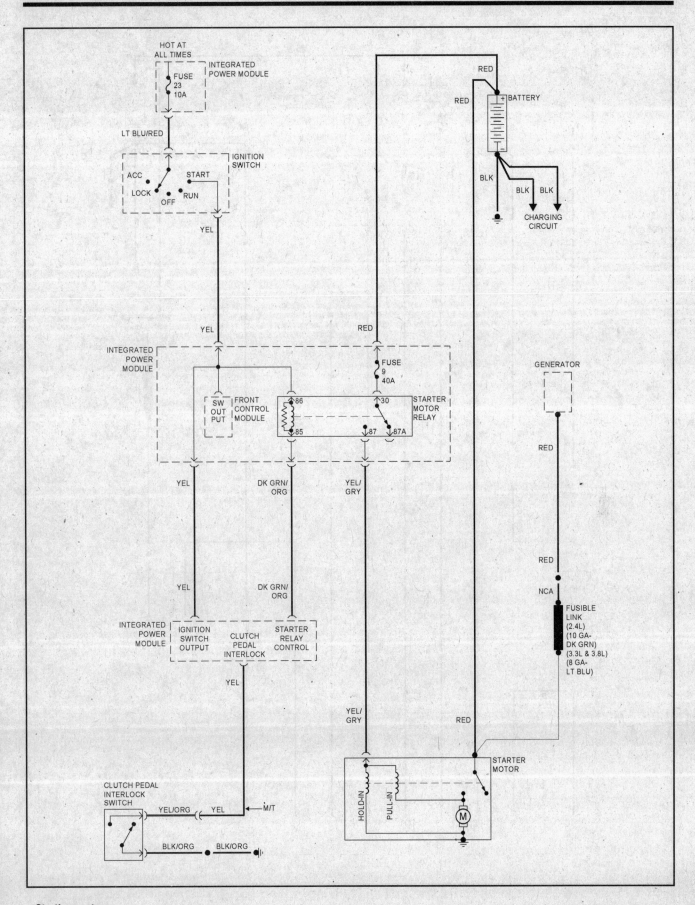

Starting system

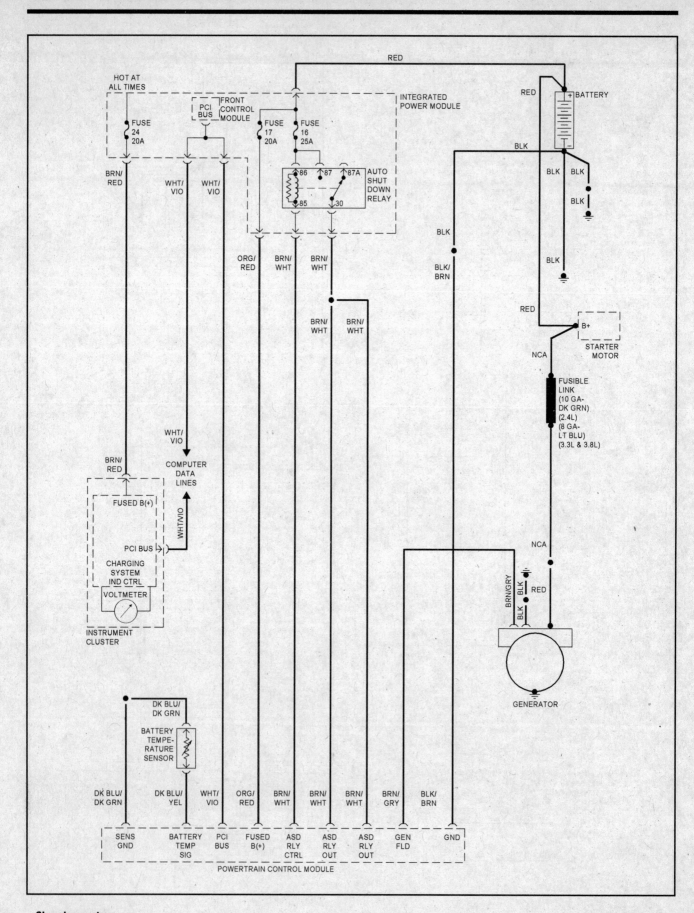

Charging system

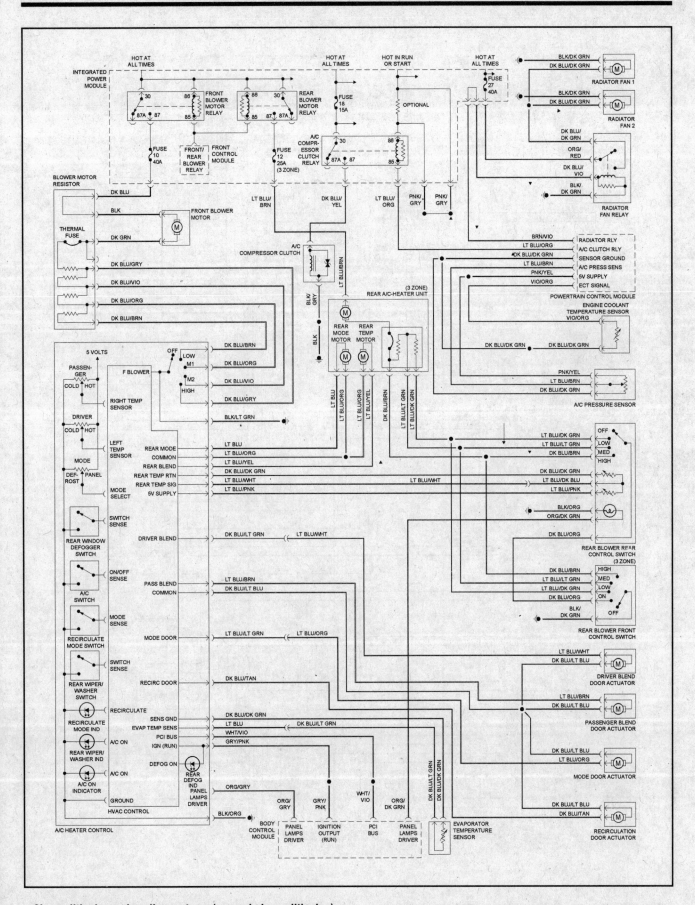

Air conditioning and cooling systems (manual air conditioning)

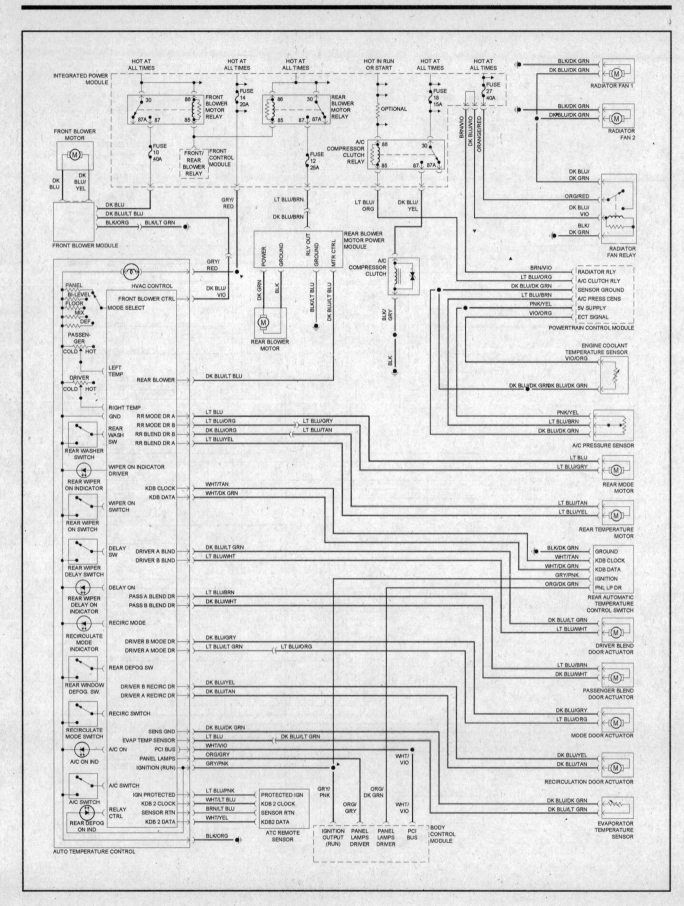

Air conditioning and cooling systems (automatic air conditioning)

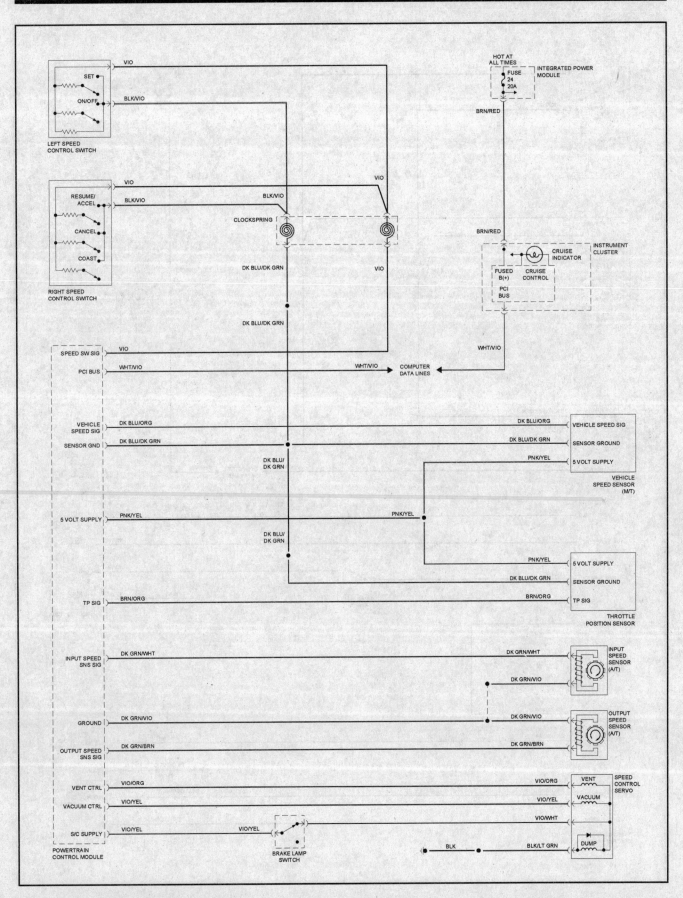

Cruise control system (four-cylinder models)

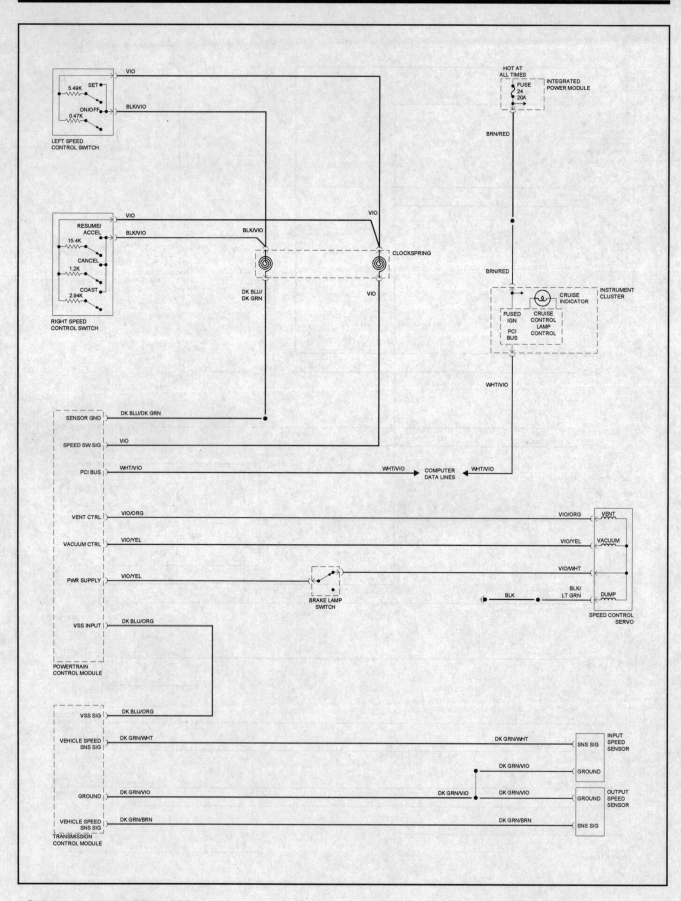

Cruise control system (V6 models)

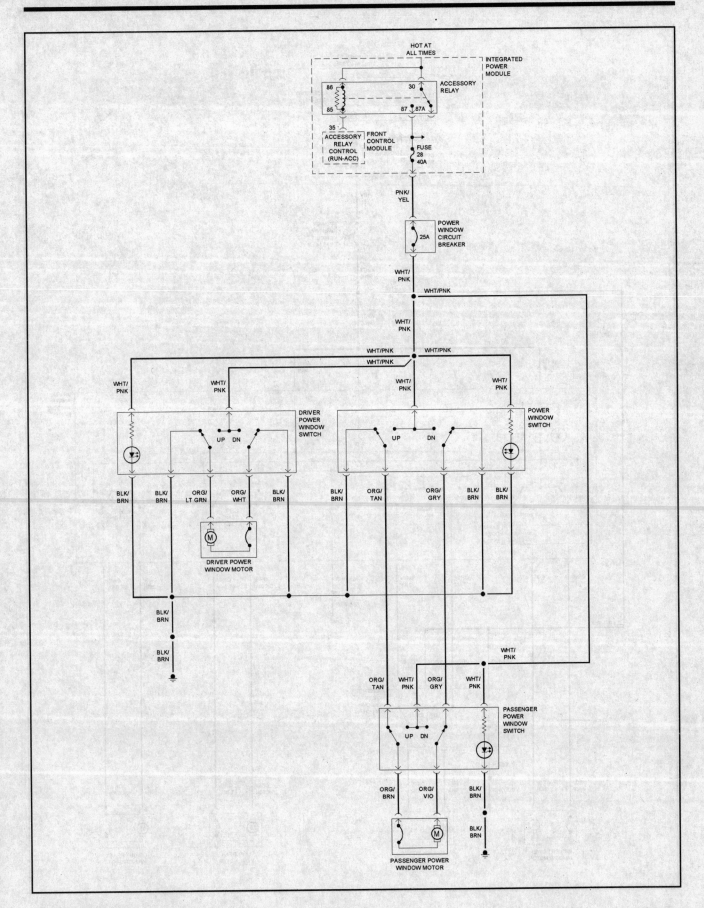

Power windows (base models)

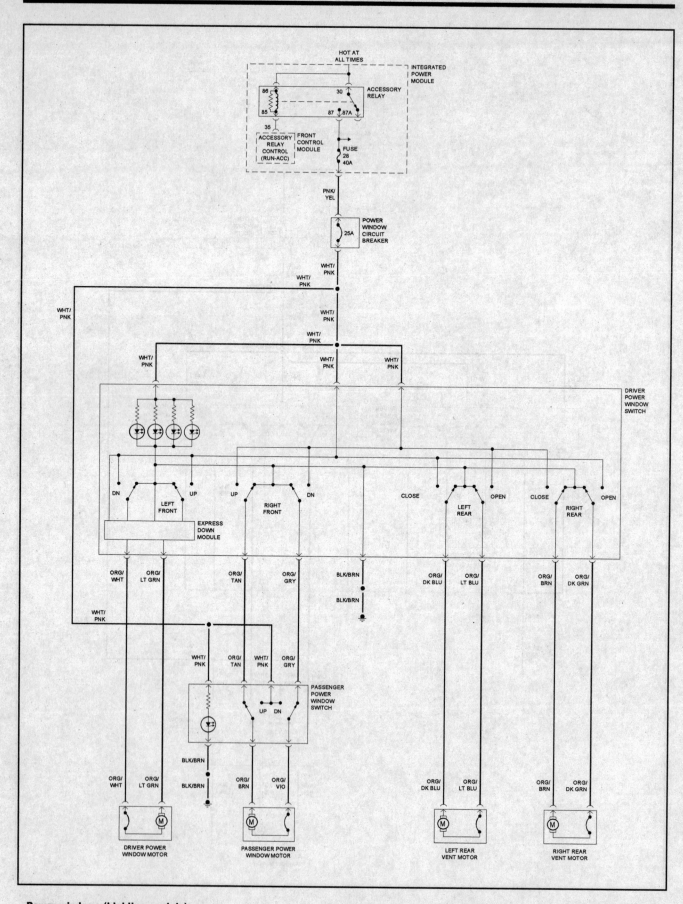

Power windows (highline models)

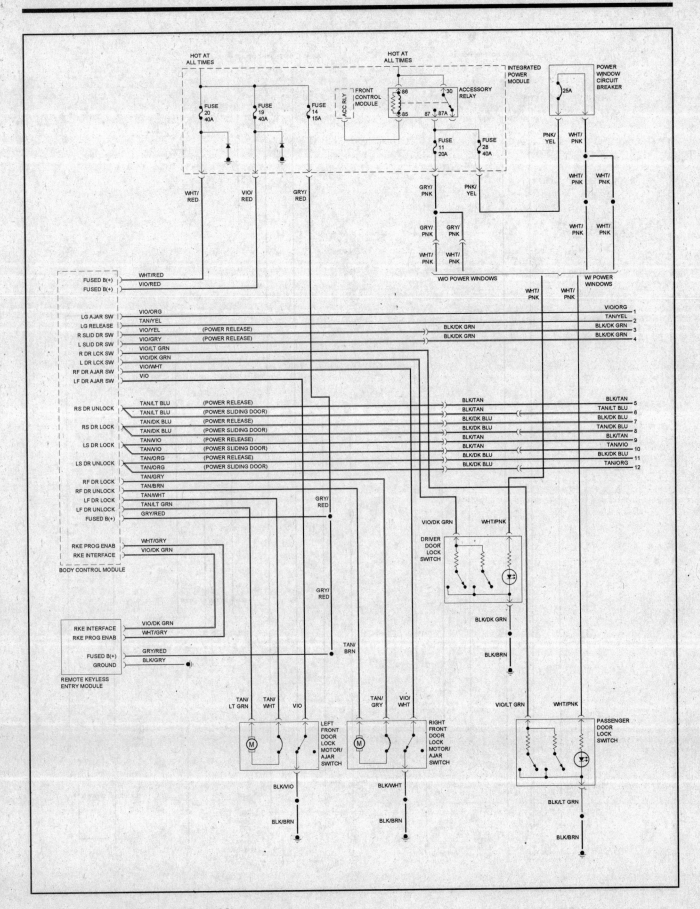

Power door locks (2003 models) - 1 of 2

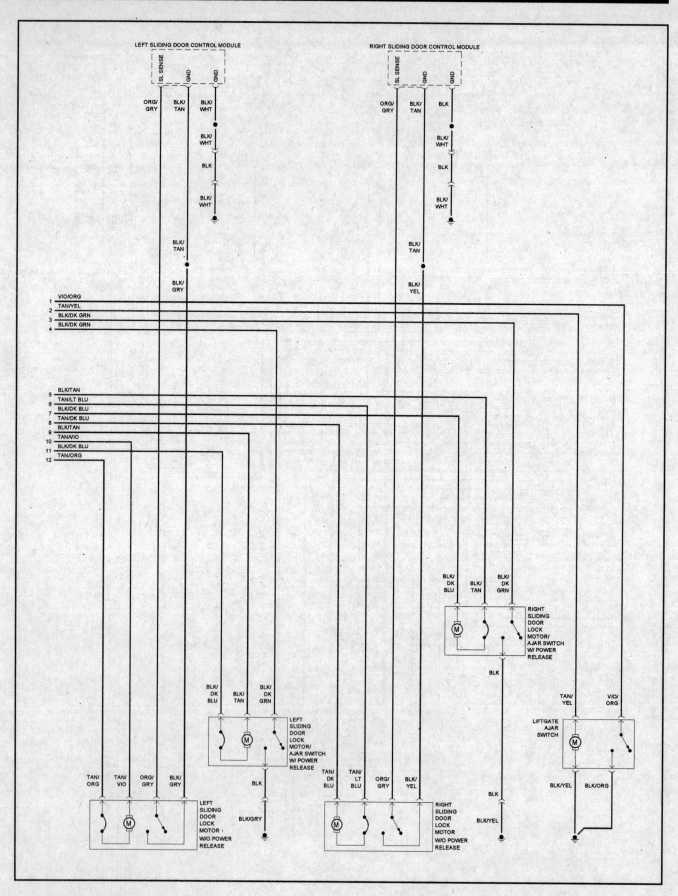

Power door locks (2003 models) - 2 of 2

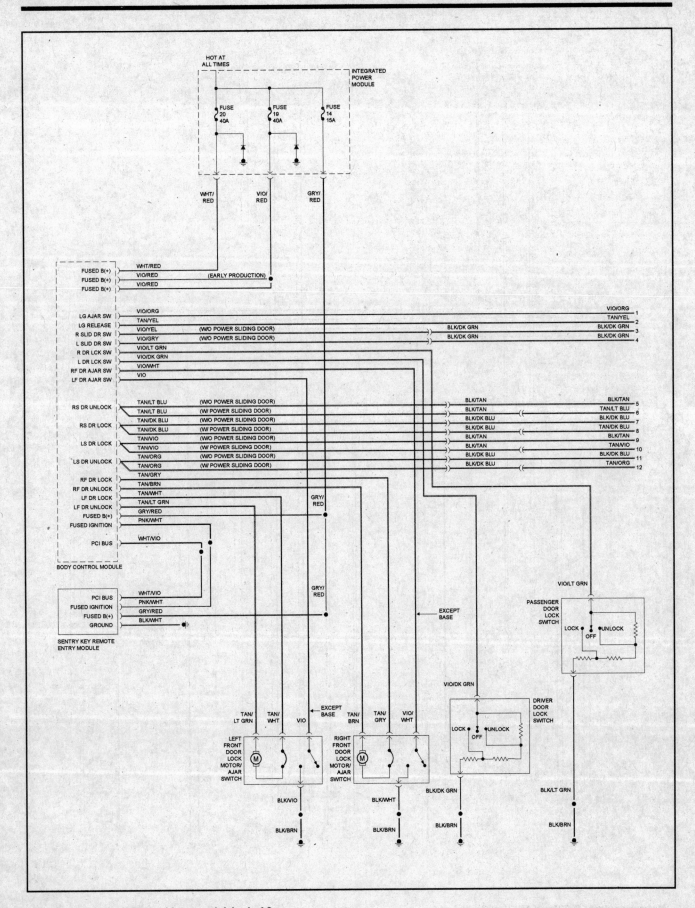

Power door locks (2004 and later models) - 1 of 2

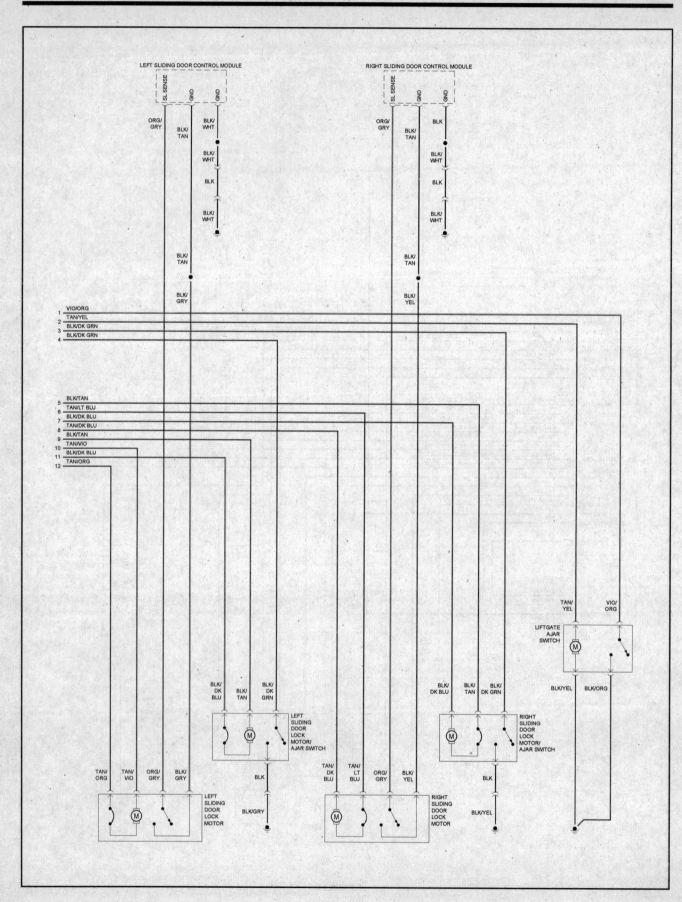

Power door locks (2004 and later models) - 2 of 2

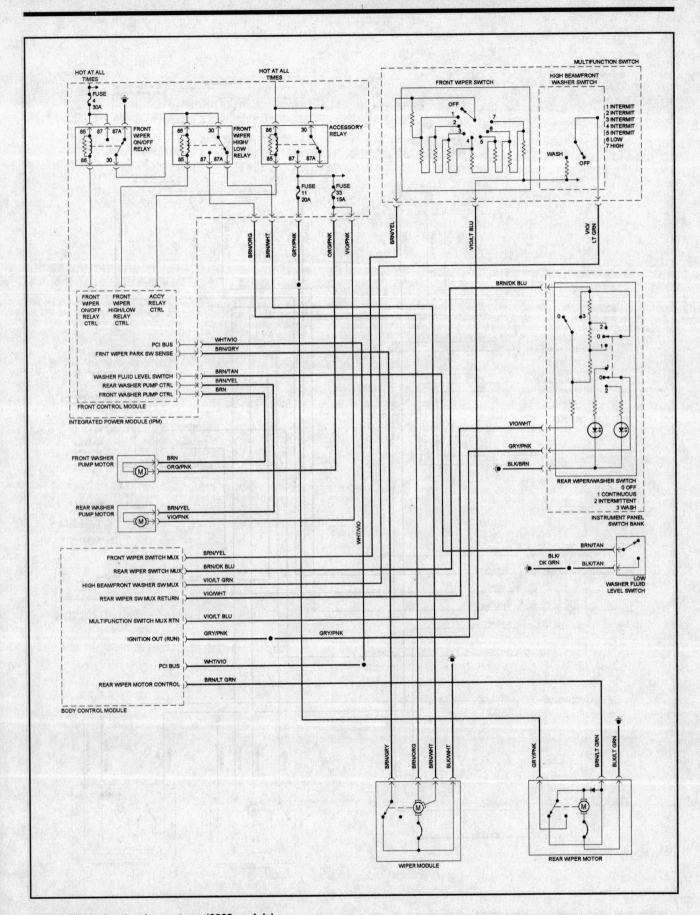

Windshield wiper/washer systems (2003 models)

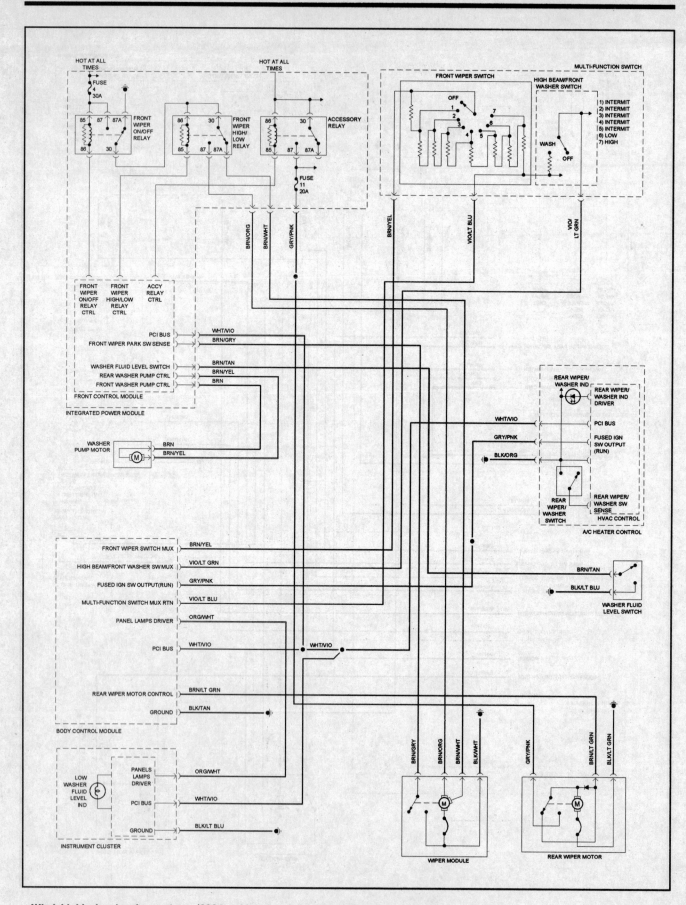

Windshield wiper/washer systems (2004 and later models with manual air conditioning)

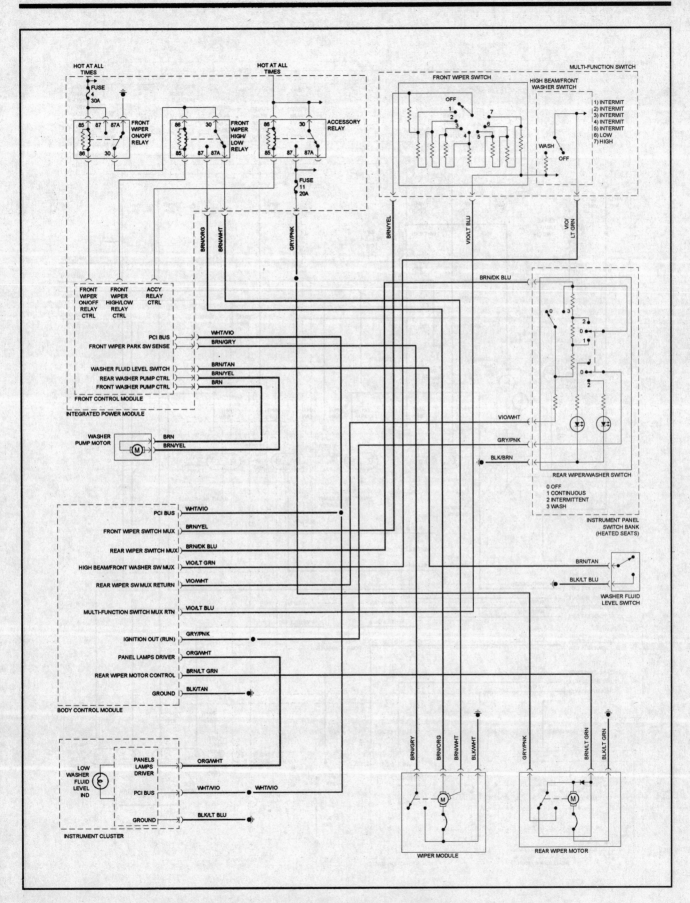

Windshield wiper/washer systems (2004 and later models with automatic air conditioning)

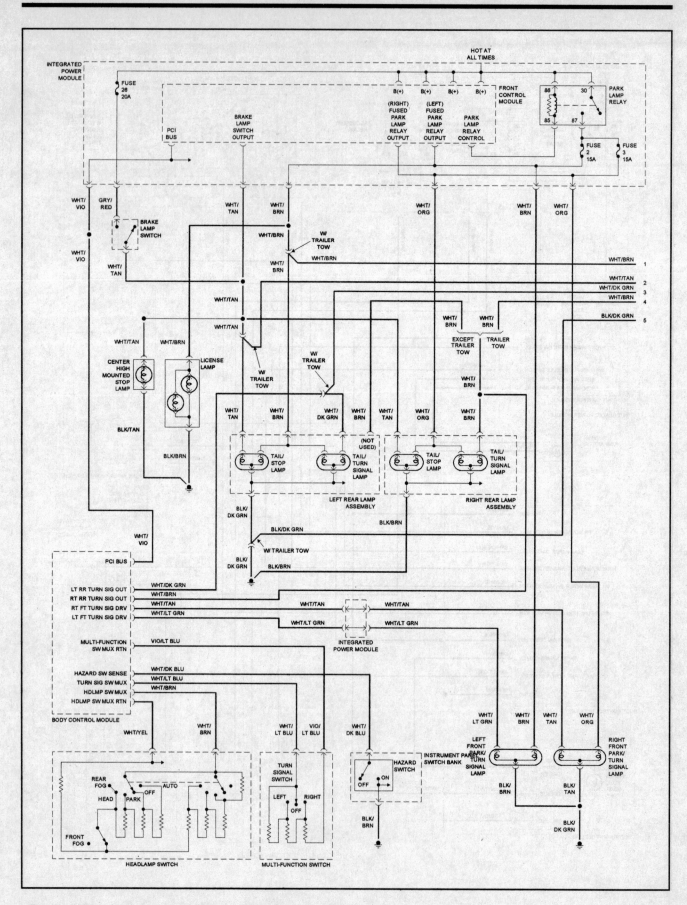

Exterior lighting systems, except headlights (2003 models) - 1 of 2

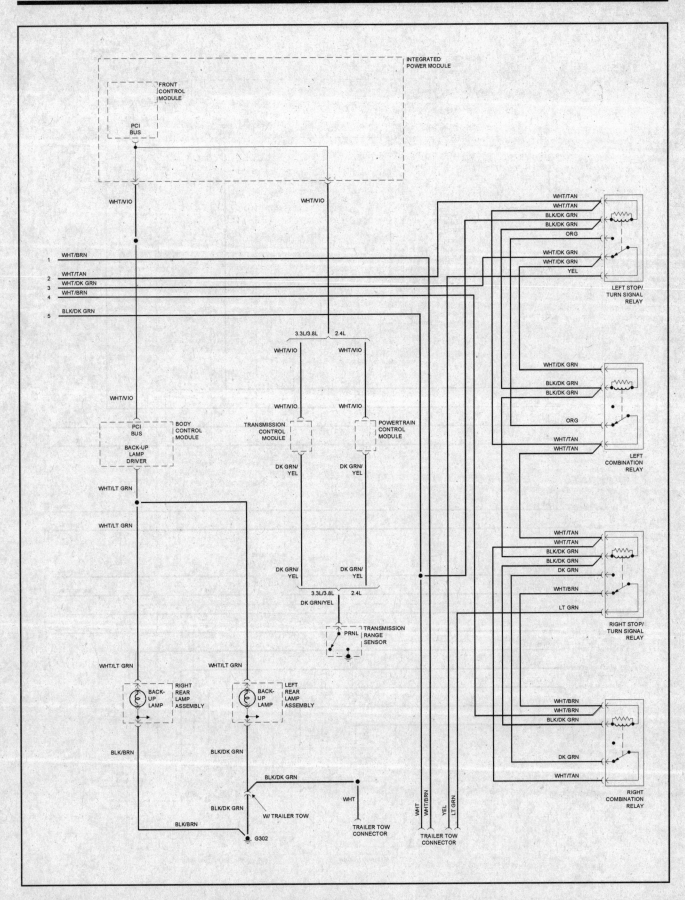

Exterior lighting systems, except headlights (2003 models) - 2 of 2

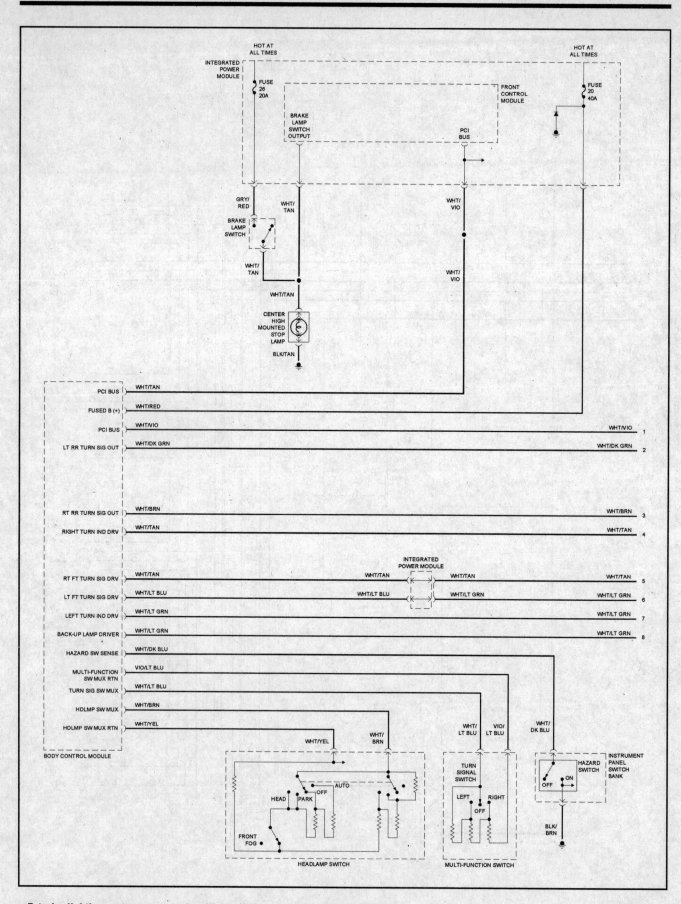

Exterior lighting systems, except headlights (2004 and later models) - 1 of 2

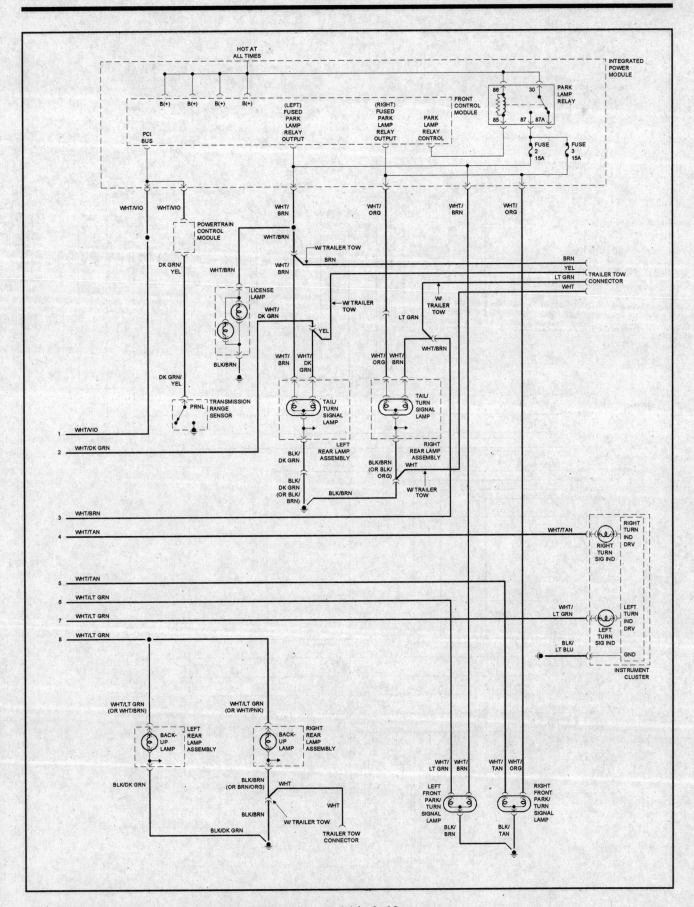

Exterior lighting systems, except headlights (2004 and later models) - 2 of 2

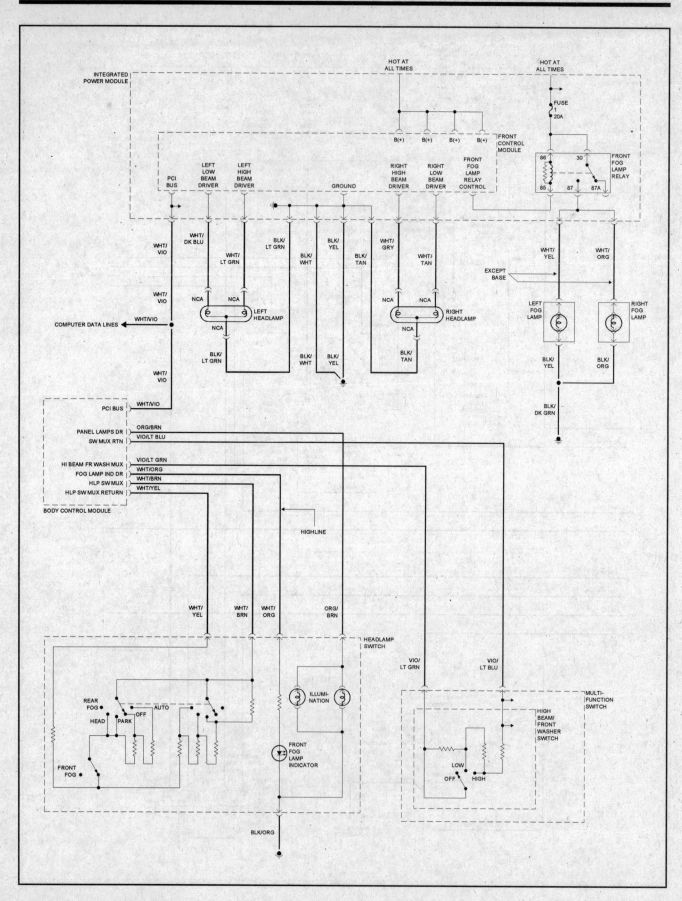

Headlight system (2003 models)

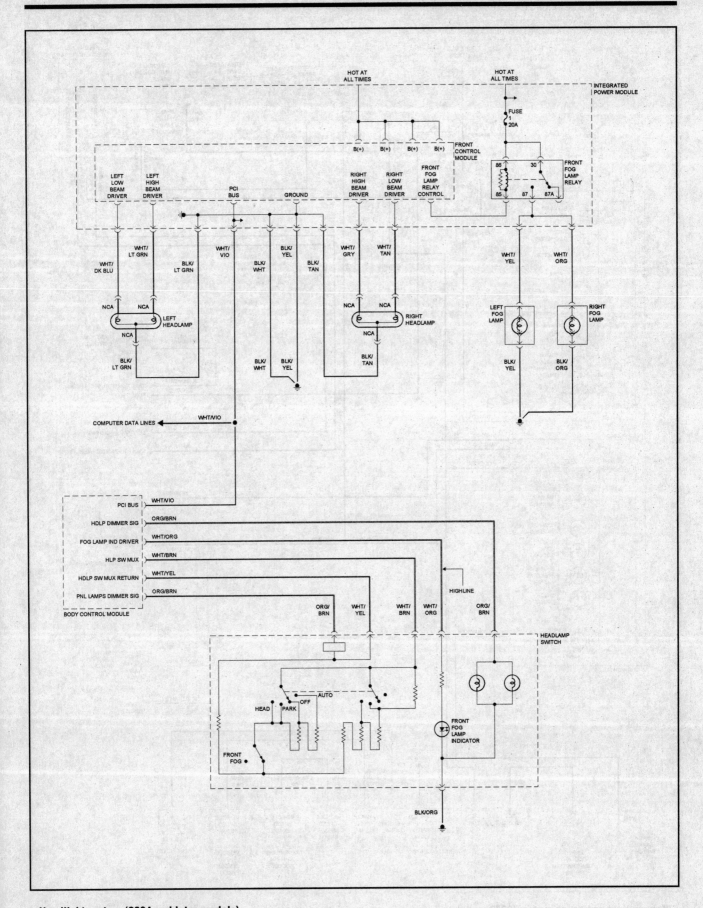

Headlight system (2004 and later models)

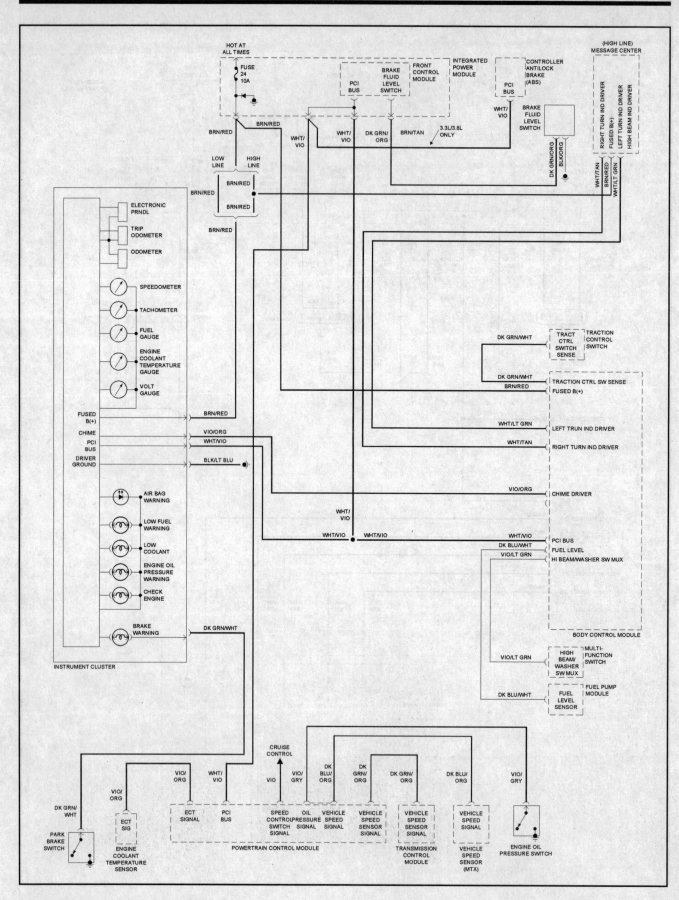

Warning light and gauge system (2003 models)

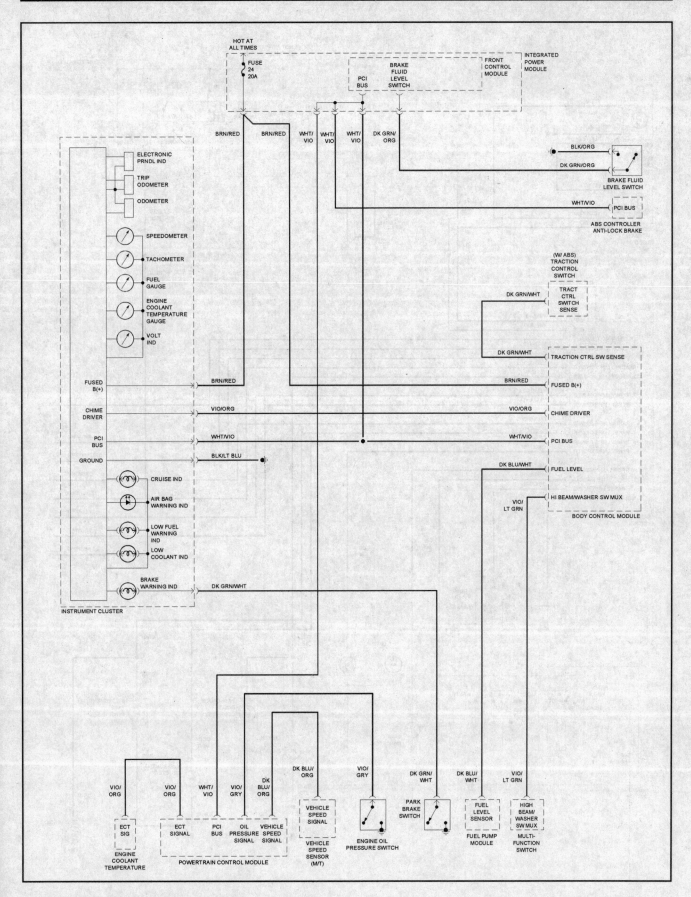

Warning light and gauge system (2004 and later models)

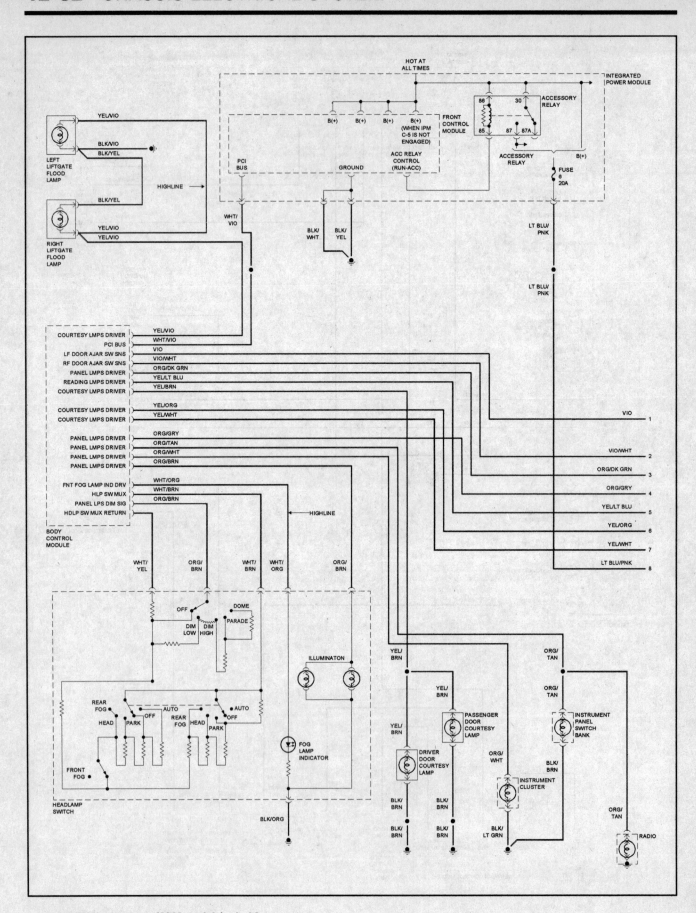

Interior lighting systems (2003 models) - 1 of 2

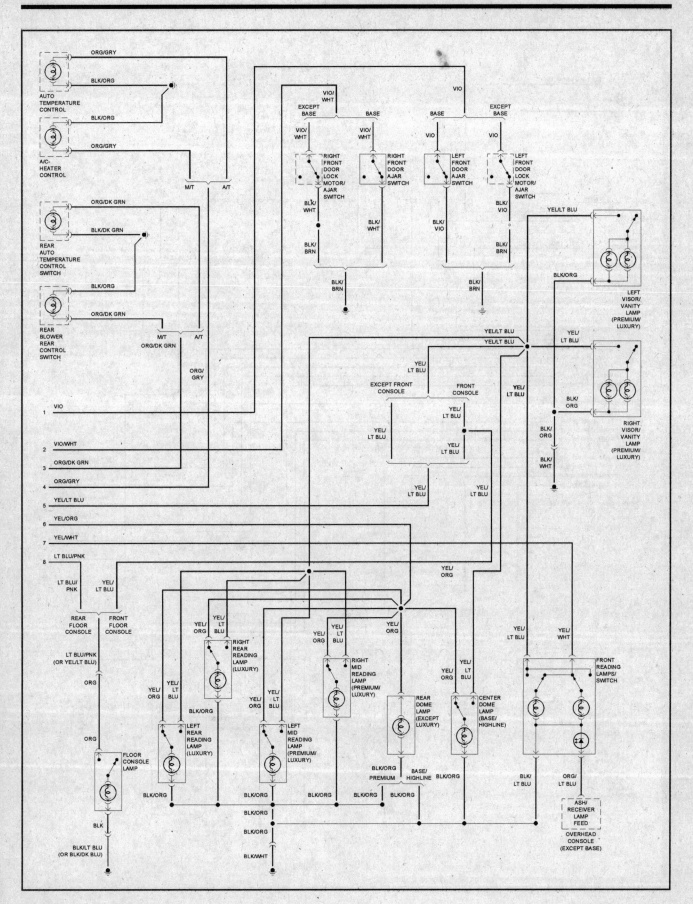

Interior lighting systems (2003 models) - 2 of 2

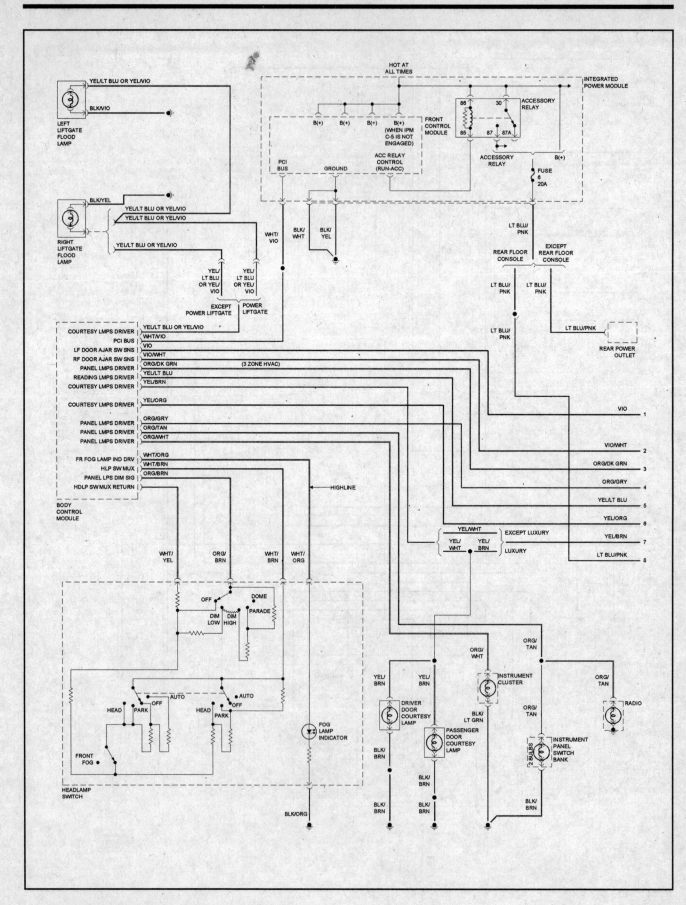

Interior lighting systems (2004 and later models) - 1 of 2

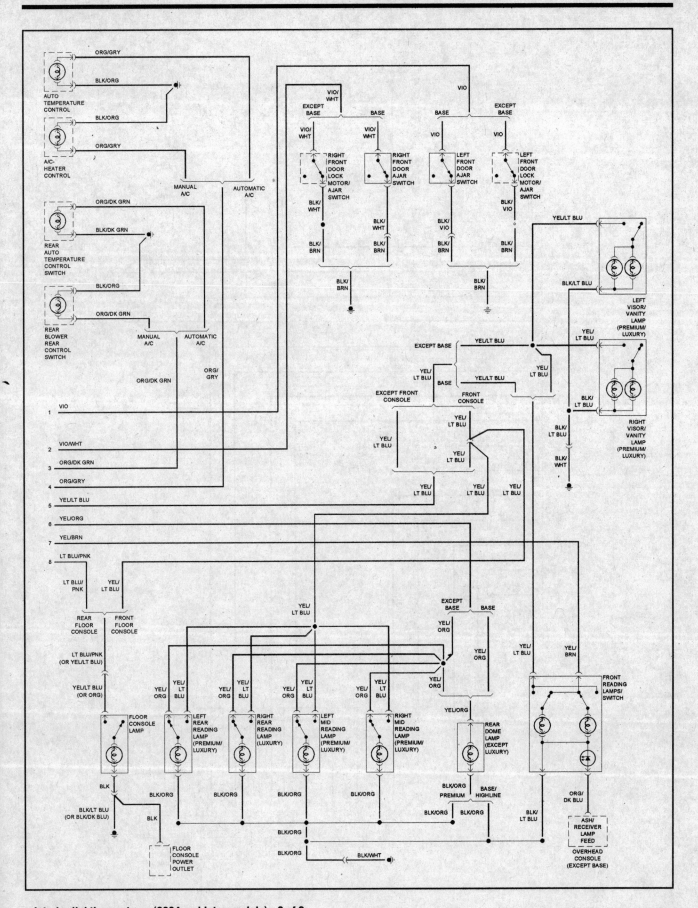

Interior lighting systems (2004 and later models) - 2 of 2

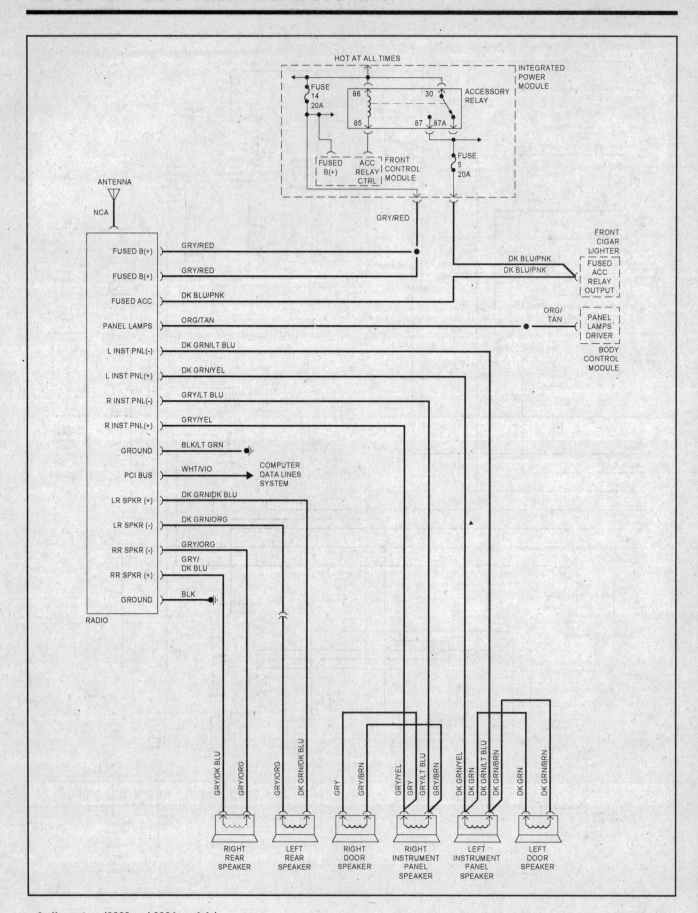

Audio system (2003 and 2004 models)

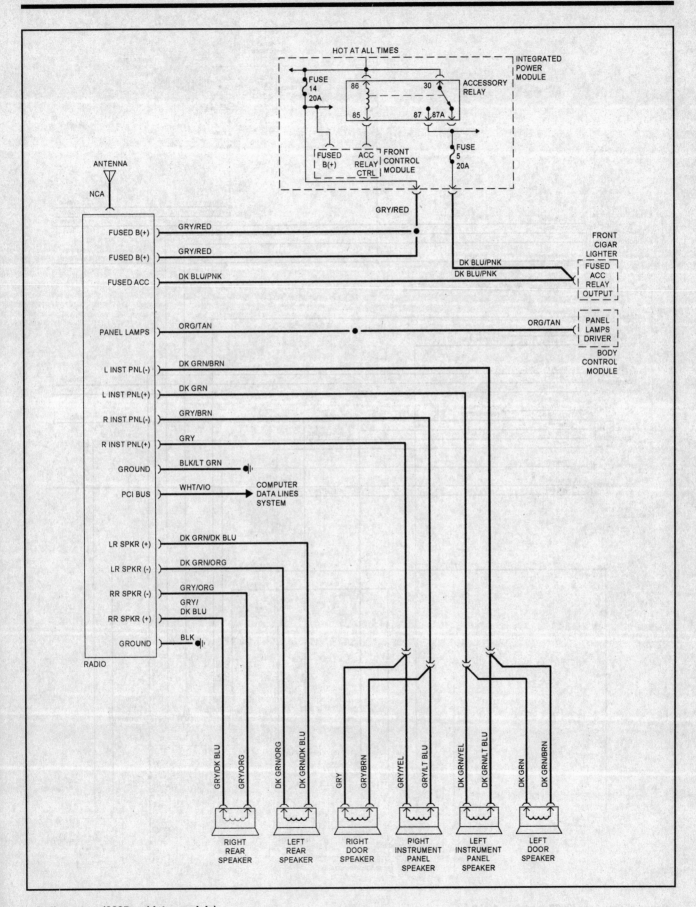

Audio system (2005 and later models)

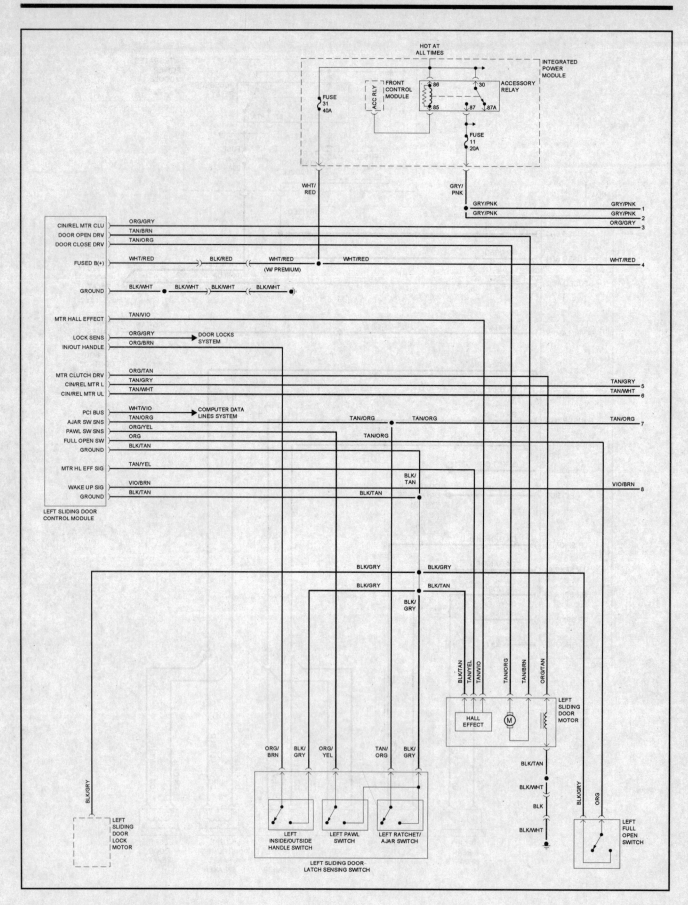

Power sliding door (2003 models) - 1 of 3

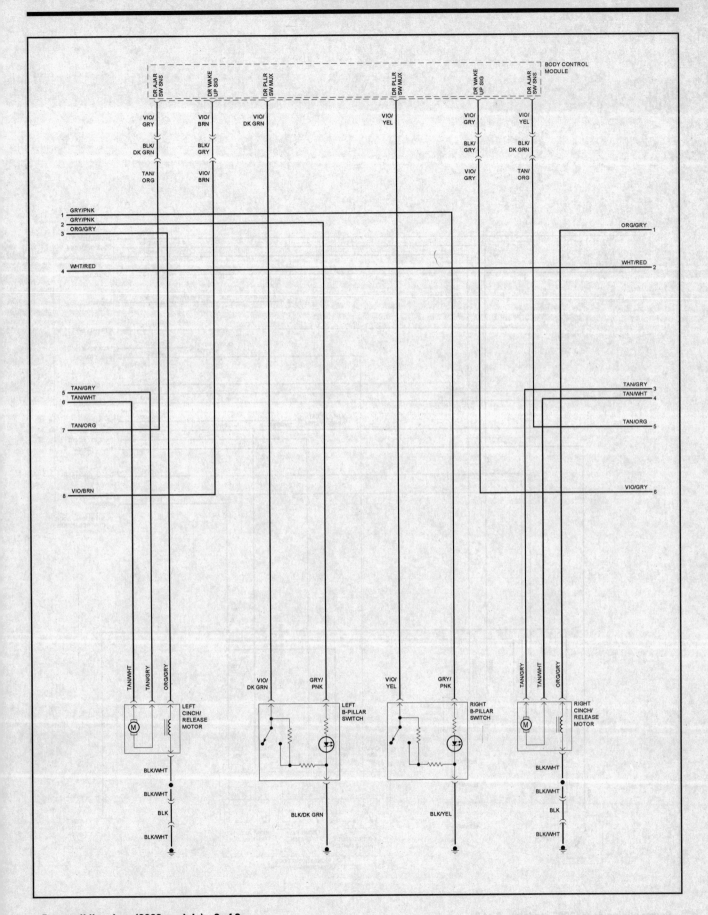

Power sliding door (2003 models) - 2 of 3

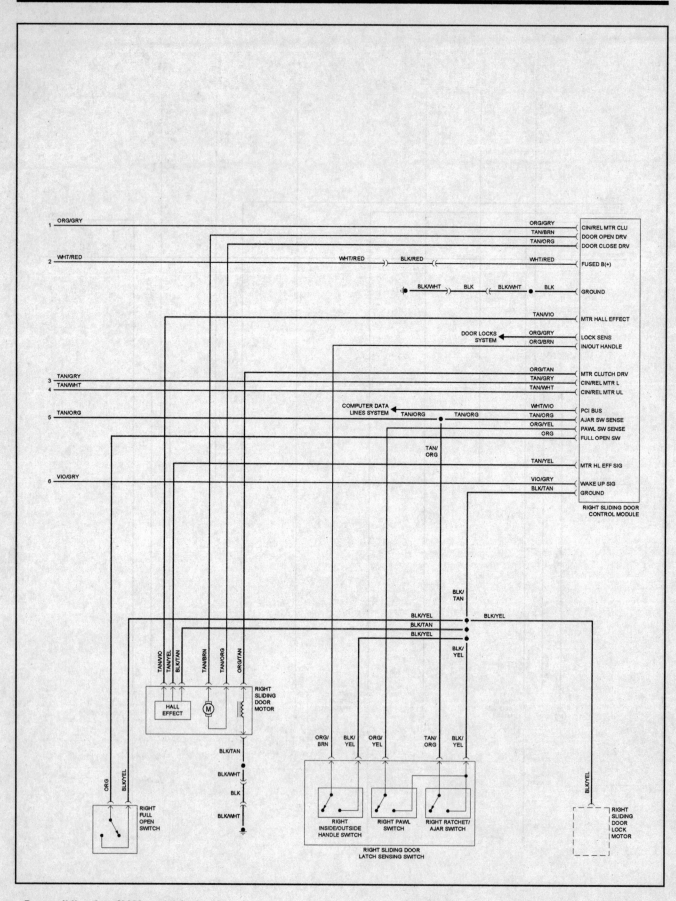

Power sliding door (2003 models) - 3 of 3

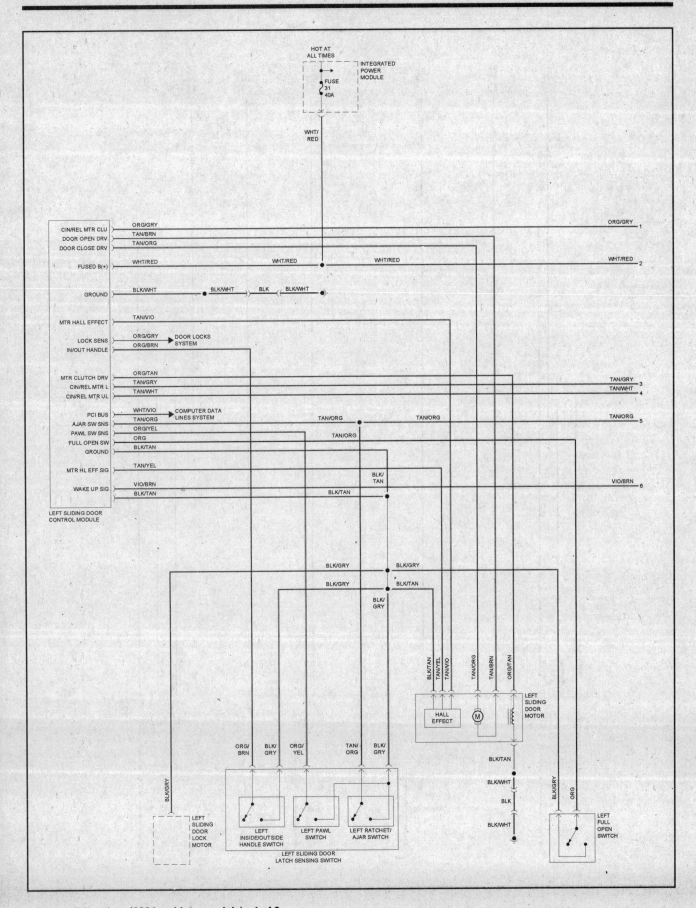

Power sliding door (2004 and later models) - 1 of 3

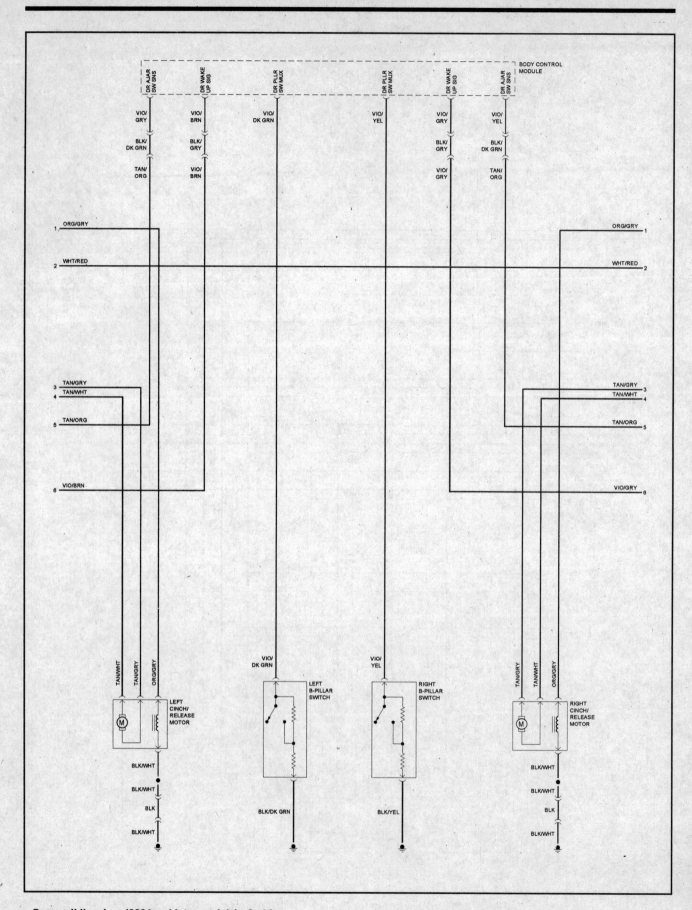

Power sliding door (2004 and later models) - 2 of 3

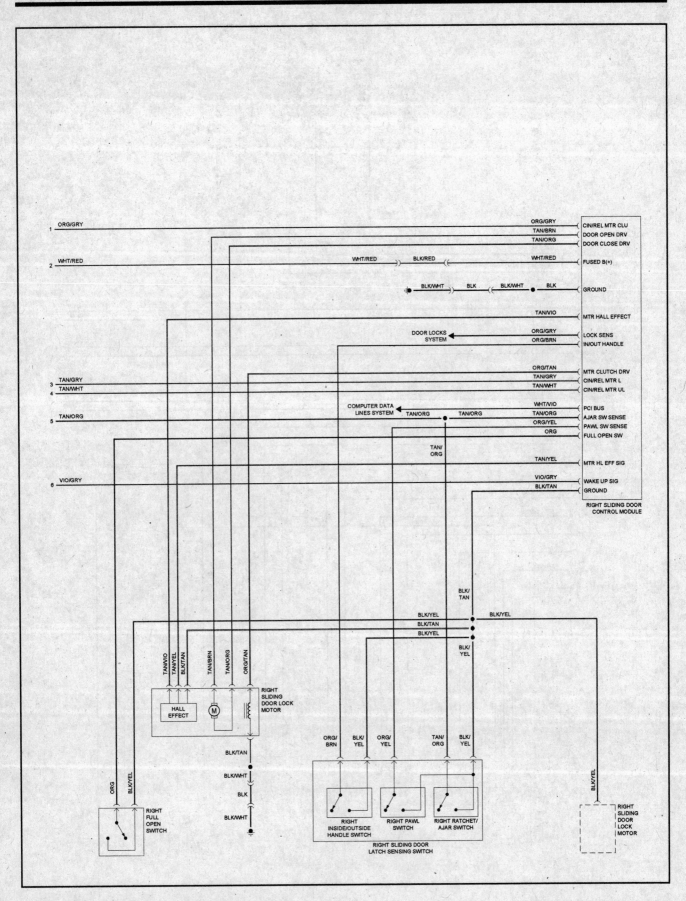

Power sliding door (2004 and later models) - 3 of 3

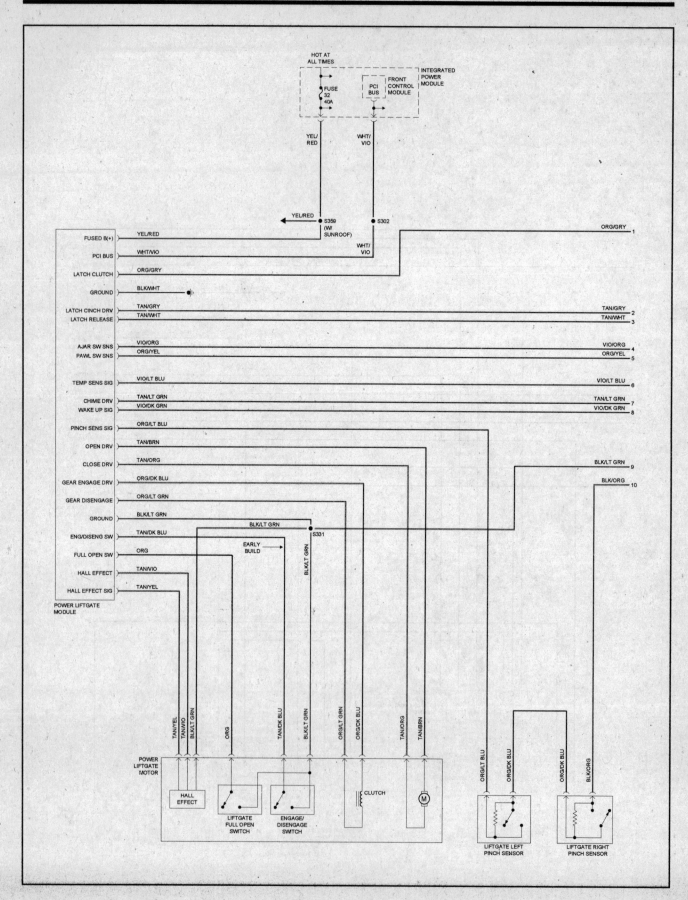

Power rear tailgate - 1 of 2

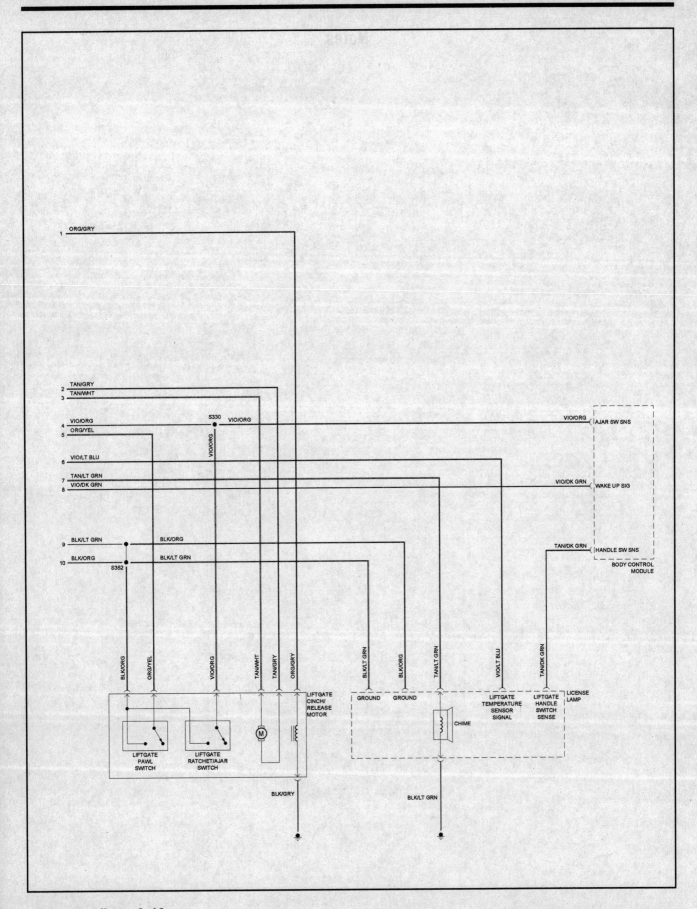

Power rear tailgate - 2 of 2

Notes

GLOSSARY

AIR/FUEL RATIO: The ratio of air-to-gasoline by weight in the fuel mixture drawn into the engine.

AIR INJECTION: One method of reducing harmful exhaust emissions by injecting air into each of the exhaust ports of an engine. The fresh air entering the hot exhaust manifold causes any remaining fuel to be burned before it can exit the tailpipe.

ALTERNATOR: A device used for converting mechanical energy into electrical energy.

AMMETER: An instrument, calibrated in amperes, used to measure the flow of an electrical current in a circuit. Ammeters are always connected in series with the circuit being tested.

AMPERE: The rate of flow of electrical current present when one volt of electrical pressure is applied against one ohm of electrical resistance.

ANALOG COMPUTER: Any microprocessor that uses similar (analogous) electrical signals to make its calculations.

ARMATURE: A laminated, soft iron core wrapped by a wire that converts electrical energy to mechanical energy as in a motor or relay. When rotated in a magnetic field, it changes mechanical energy into electrical energy as in a generator.

ATMOSPHERIC PRESSURE: The pressure on the Earth's surface caused by the weight of the air in the atmosphere. At sea level, this pressure is 14.7 psi at 32°F (101 kPa at 0°C).

ATOMIZATION: The breaking down of a liquid into a fine mist that can be suspended in air.

AXIAL PLAY: Movement parallel to a shaft or bearing bore.

BACKFIRE: The sudden combustion of gases in the intake or exhaust system that results in a loud explosion.

BACKLASH: The clearance or play between two parts, such as meshed gears.

BACKPRESSURE: Restrictions in the exhaust system that slow the exit of exhaust gases from the combustion chamber.

BAKELITE: A heat resistant, plastic insulator material commonly used in printed circuit boards and transistorized components.

BALL BEARING: A bearing made up of hardened inner and outer races between which hardened steel balls roll.

BALLAST RESISTOR: A resistor in the primary ignition circuit that lowers voltage after the engine is started to reduce wear on ignition components.

BEARING: A friction reducing, supportive device usually located between a stationary part and a moving part.

BIMETAL TEMPERATURE SENSOR: Any sensor or switch made of two dissimilar types of metal that bend when heated or cooled due to the different expansion rates of the alloys. These types of sensors usually function as an on/off switch.

BLOWBY: Combustion gases, composed of water vapor and unburned fuel, that leak past the piston rings into the crankcase during normal engine operation. These gases are removed by the PCV system to prevent the buildup of harmful acids in the crankcase.

BRAKE PAD: A brake shoe and lining assembly used with disc brakes.

BRAKE SHOE: The backing for the brake lining. The term is, however, usually applied to the assembly of the brake backing and lining.

BUSHING: A liner, usually removable, for a bearing; an anti-friction liner used in place of a bearing.

CALIPER: A hydraulically activated device in a disc brake system, which is mounted straddling the brake rotor (disc). The caliper contains at least one piston and two brake pads. Hydraulic pressure on the piston(s) forces the pads against the rotor.

CAMSHAFT: A shaft in the engine on which are the lobes (cams) which operate the valves. The camshaft is driven by the crankshaft, via a belt, chain or gears, at one half the crankshaft speed.

CAPACITOR: A device which stores an electrical charge.

CARBON MONOXIDE (CO): A colorless, odorless gas given off as a normal byproduct of combustion. It is poisonous and extremely dangerous in confined areas, building up slowly to toxic levels without warning if adequate ventilation is not available.

CARBURETOR: A device, usually mounted on the intake manifold of an engine, which mixes the air and fuel in the proper proportion to allow even combustion.

CATALYTIC CONVERTER: A device installed in the exhaust system, like a muffler, that converts harmful byproducts of combustion into carbon dioxide and water vapor by means of a heat-producing chemical reaction.

CENTRIFUGAL ADVANCE: A mechanical method of advancing the spark timing by using flyweights in the distributor that react to centrifugal force generated by the distributor shaft rotation.

CHECK VALVE: Any one-way valve installed to permit the flow of air, fuel or vacuum in one direction only.

CHOKE: A device, usually a moveable valve, placed in the intake path of a carburetor to restrict the flow of air.

CIRCUIT: Any unbroken path through which an electrical current can flow. Also used to describe fuel flow in some instances.

CIRCUIT BREAKER: A switch which protects an electrical circuit from overload by opening the circuit when the current flow exceeds a predetermined level. Some circuit breakers must be reset manually, while most reset automatically.

COIL (IGNITION): A transformer in the ignition circuit which steps up the voltage provided to the spark plugs.

COMBINATION MANIFOLD: An assembly which includes both the intake and exhaust manifolds in one casting.

COMBINATION VALVE: A device used in some fuel systems that routes fuel vapors to a charcoal storage canister instead of venting them into the atmosphere. The valve relieves fuel tank pressure and allows fresh air into the tank as the fuel level drops to prevent a vapor lock situation.

COMPRESSION RATIO: The comparison of the total volume of the cylinder and combustion chamber with the piston at BDC and the piston at TDC.

CONDENSER: 1. An electrical device which acts to store an electrical charge, preventing voltage surges. 2. A radiator-like device in the air conditioning system in which refrigerant gas condenses into a liquid, giving off heat.

CONDUCTOR: Any material through which an electrical current can be transmitted easily.

CONTINUITY: Continuous or complete circuit. Can be checked with an ohmmeter.

COUNTERSHAFT: An intermediate shaft which is rotated by a mainshaft and transmits, in turn, that rotation to a working part.

CRANKCASE: The lower part of an engine in which the crankshaft and related parts operate.

CRANKSHAFT: The main driving shaft of an engine which receives reciprocating motion from the pistons and converts it to rotary motion.

CYLINDER: In an engine, the round hole in the engine block in which the piston(s) ride.

CYLINDER BLOCK: The main structural member of an engine in which is found the cylinders, crankshaft and other principal parts.

CYLINDER HEAD: The detachable portion of the engine, usually fastened to the top of the cylinder block and containing all or most of the combustion chambers. On overhead valve engines, it contains the valves and their operating parts. On overhead cam engines, it contains the camshaft as well.

DEAD CENTER: The extreme top or bottom of the piston stroke.

DETONATION: An unwanted explosion of the air/fuel mixture in the combustion chamber caused by excess heat and compression, advanced timing, or an overly lean mixture. Also referred to as "ping".

DIAPHRAGM: A thin, flexible wall separating two cavities, such as in a vacuum advance unit.

DIESELING: A condition in which hot spots in the combustion chamber cause the engine to run on after the key is turned off.

DIFFERENTIAL: A geared assembly which allows the transmission of motion between drive axles, giving one axle the ability to turn faster than the other.

DIODE: An electrical device that will allow current to flow in one direction only.

DISC BRAKE: A hydraulic braking assembly consisting of a brake disc, or rotor, mounted on an axle, and a caliper assembly containing, usually two brake pads which are activated by hydraulic pressure. The pads are forced against the sides of the disc, creating friction which slows the vehicle.

DISTRIBUTOR: A mechanically driven device on an engine which is responsible for electrically firing the spark plug at a predetermined point of the piston stroke.

DOWEL PIN: A pin, inserted in mating holes in two different parts allowing those parts to maintain a fixed relationship.

DRUM BRAKE: A braking system which consists of two brake shoes and one or two wheel cylinders, mounted on a fixed backing plate, and a brake drum, mounted on an axle, which revolves around the assembly.

DWELL: The rate, measured in degrees of shaft rotation, at which an electrical circuit cycles on and off.

ELECTRONIC CONTROL UNIT (ECU): Ignition module, module, amplifier or igniter. See Module for definition.

ELECTRONIC IGNITION: A system in which the timing and firing of the spark plugs is controlled by an electronic control unit, usually called a module. These systems have no points or condenser.

END-PLAY: The measured amount of axial movement in a shaft.

ENGINE: A device that converts heat into mechanical energy.

EXHAUST MANIFOLD: A set of cast passages or pipes which conduct exhaust gases from the engine.

FEELER GAUGE: A blade, usually metal, or precisely predetermined thickness, used to measure the clearance between two parts.

FIRING ORDER: The order in which combustion occurs in the cylinders of an engine. Also the order in which spark is distributed to the plugs by the distributor.

FLOODING: The presence of too much fuel in the intake manifold and combustion chamber which prevents the air/fuel mixture from firing, thereby causing a no-start situation.

FLYWHEEL: A disc shaped part bolted to the rear end of the crankshaft. Around the outer perimeter is affixed the ring gear. The starter drive engages the ring gear, turning the flywheel, which rotates the crankshaft, imparting the initial starting motion to the engine.

FOOT POUND (ft. lbs. or sometimes, ft.lb.): The amount of energy or work needed to raise an item weighing one pound, a distance of one foot.

FUSE: A protective device in a circuit which prevents circuit overload by breaking the circuit when a specific amperage is present. The device is constructed around a strip or wire of a lower amperage rating than the circuit it is designed to protect. When an amperage higher than that stamped on the fuse is present in the circuit, the strip or wire melts, opening the circuit.

GEAR RATIO: The ratio between the number of teeth on meshing gears.

GENERATOR: A device which converts mechanical energy into electrical energy.

HEAT RANGE: The measure of a spark plug's ability to dissipate heat from its firing end. The higher the heat range, the hotter the plug fires.

HUB: The center part of a wheel or gear.

HYDROCARBON (HC): Any chemical compound made up of hydrogen and carbon. A major pollutant formed by the engine as a byproduct of combustion.

HYDROMETER: An instrument used to measure the specific gravity of a solution.

INCH POUND (inch lbs.; sometimes in.lb. or in. lbs.): One twelfth of a foot pound.

INDUCTION: A means of transferring electrical energy in the form of a magnetic field. Principle used in the ignition coil to increase voltage.

INJECTOR: A device which receives metered fuel under relatively low pressure and is activated to inject the fuel into the engine under relatively high pressure at a predetermined time.

INPUT SHAFT: The shaft to which torque is applied, usually carrying the driving gear or gears.

INTAKE MANIFOLD: A casting of passages or pipes used to conduct air or a fuel/air mixture to the cylinders.

JOURNAL: The bearing surface within which a shaft operates.

KEY: A small block usually fitted in a notch between a shaft and a hub to prevent slippage of the two parts.

MANIFOLD: A casting of passages or set of pipes which connect the cylinders to an inlet or outlet source.

MANIFOLD VACUUM: Low pressure in an engine intake manifold formed just below the throttle plates. Manifold vacuum is highest at idle and drops under acceleration.

MASTER CYLINDER: The primary fluid pressurizing device in a hydraulic system. In automotive use, it is found in brake and hydraulic clutch systems and is pedal activated, either directly or, in a power brake system, through the power booster.

MODULE: Electronic control unit, amplifier or igniter of solid state or integrated design which controls the current flow in the ignition primary circuit based on input from the pick-up coil. When the module opens the primary circuit, high secondary voltage is induced in the coil.

NEEDLE BEARING: A bearing which consists of a number (usually a large number) of long, thin rollers.

OHM: (Ω) The unit used to measure the resistance of conductor-to-electrical flow. One ohm is the amount of resistance that limits current flow to one ampere in a circuit with one volt of pressure.

OHMMETER: An instrument used for measuring the resistance, in ohms, in an electrical circuit.

OUTPUT SHAFT: The shaft which transmits torque from a device, such as a transmission.

OVERDRIVE: A gear assembly which produces more shaft revolutions than that transmitted to it.

OVERHEAD CAMSHAFT (OHC): An engine configuration in which the camshaft is mounted on top of the cylinder head and operates the valve either directly or by means of rocker arms.

OVERHEAD VALVE (OHV): An engine configuration in which all of the valves are located in the cylinder head and the camshaft is located in the cylinder block. The camshaft operates the valves via lifters and pushrods.

OXIDES OF NITROGEN (NOx): Chemical compounds of nitrogen produced as a byproduct of combustion. They combine with hydrocarbons to produce smog.

OXYGEN SENSOR: Use with the feedback system to sense the presence of oxygen in the exhaust gas and signal the computer which can reference the voltage signal to an air/fuel ratio.

PINION: The smaller of two meshing gears.

PISTON RING: An open-ended ring with fits into a groove on the outer diameter of the piston. Its chief function is to form a seal between the piston and cylinder wall. Most automotive pistons have three rings: two for compression sealing; one for oil sealing.

PRELOAD: A predetermined load placed on a bearing during assembly or by adjustment.

PRIMARY CIRCUIT: the low voltage side of the ignition system which consists of the ignition switch, ballast resistor or resistance wire, bypass, coil, electronic control unit and pick-up coil as well as the connecting wires and harnesses.

PRESS FIT: The mating of two parts under pressure, due to the inner diameter of one being smaller than the outer diameter of the other, or vice versa; an interference fit.

RACE: The surface on the inner or outer ring of a bearing on which the balls, needles or rollers move.

REGULATOR: A device which maintains the amperage and/or voltage levels of a circuit at predetermined values.

RELAY: A switch which automatically opens and/or closes a circuit.

RESISTANCE: The opposition to the flow of current through a circuit or electrical device, and is measured in ohms. Resistance is equal to the voltage divided by the amperage.

RESISTOR: A device, usually made of wire, which offers a preset amount of resistance in an electrical circuit.

RING GEAR: The name given to a ring-shaped gear attached to a differential case, or affixed to a flywheel or as part of a planetary gear set.

ROLLER BEARING: A bearing made up of hardened inner and outer races between which hardened steel rollers move.

ROTOR: 1. The disc-shaped part of a disc brake assembly, upon which the brake pads bear; also called, brake disc. 2. The device mounted atop the distributor shaft, which passes current to the distributor cap tower contacts.

SECONDARY CIRCUIT: The high voltage side of the ignition system, usually above 20,000 volts. The secondary includes the ignition coil, coil wire, distributor cap and rotor, spark plug wires and spark plugs.

SENDING UNIT: A mechanical, electrical, hydraulic or electromagnetic device which transmits information to a gauge.

SENSOR: Any device designed to measure engine operating conditions or ambient pressures and temperatures. Usually electronic in nature and designed to send a voltage signal to an on-board computer, some sensors may operate as a simple on/off switch or they may provide a variable voltage signal (like a potentiometer) as conditions or measured parameters change.

SHIM: Spacers of precise, predetermined thickness used between parts to establish a proper working relationship.

SLAVE CYLINDER: In automotive use, a device in the hydraulic clutch system which is activated by hydraulic force, disengaging the clutch.

SOLENOID: A coil used to produce a magnetic field, the effect of which is to produce work.

SPARK PLUG: A device screwed into the combustion chamber of a spark ignition engine. The basic construction is a conductive core inside of a ceramic insulator, mounted in an outer conductive base. An electrical charge from the spark plug wire travels along the conductive core and jumps a preset air gap to a grounding point or points at the end of the conductive base. The resultant spark ignites the fuel/air mixture in the combustion chamber.

SPLINES: Ridges machined or cast onto the outer diameter of a shaft or inner diameter of a bore to enable parts to mate without rotation.

TACHOMETER: A device used to measure the rotary speed of an engine, shaft, gear, etc., usually in rotations per minute.

THERMOSTAT: A valve, located in the cooling system of an engine, which is closed when cold and opens gradually in response to engine heating, controlling the temperature of the coolant and rate of coolant flow.

TOP DEAD CENTER (TDC): The point at which the piston reaches the top of its travel on the compression stroke.

TORQUE: The twisting force applied to an object.

TORQUE CONVERTER: A turbine used to transmit power from a driving member to a driven member via hydraulic action, providing changes in drive ratio and torque. In automotive use, it links the driveplate at the rear of the engine to the automatic transmission.

TRANSDUCER: A device used to change a force into an electrical signal.

TRANSISTOR: A semi-conductor component which can be actuated by a small voltage to perform an electrical switching function.

TUNE-UP: A regular maintenance function, usually associated with the replacement and adjustment of parts and components in the electrical and fuel systems of a vehicle for the purpose of attaining optimum performance.

TURBOCHARGER: An exhaust driven pump which compresses intake air and forces it into the combustion chambers at higher than atmospheric pressures. The increased air pressure allows more fuel to be burned and results in increased horsepower being produced.

VACUUM ADVANCE: A device which advances the ignition timing in response to increased engine vacuum.

VACUUM GAUGE: An instrument used to measure the presence of vacuum in a chamber.

VALVE: A device which control the pressure, direction of flow or rate of flow of a liquid or gas.

VALVE CLEARANCE: The measured gap between the end of the valve stem and the rocker arm, cam lobe or follower that activates the valve.

VISCOSITY: The rating of a liquid's internal resistance to flow.

VOLTMETER: An instrument used for measuring electrical force in units called volts. Voltmeters are always connected parallel with the circuit being tested.

WHEEL CYLINDER: Found in the automotive drum brake assembly, it is a device, actuated by hydraulic pressure, which, through internal pistons, pushes the brake shoes outward against the drums.

NOTES

MASTER INDEX

A